SUPPORTED EMPLOYMENT

MODELS, METHODS, AND ISSUES

FRANK R. RUSCH
Editor

Dedicated to Alexia and Emily Rusch
who continuously show me new ways to view people

Library of Congress Cataloging in Publication Data

Supported employment: models, methods, and issues/Frank R. Rusch
(editor).
p. cm.
Includes bibilographical references.
ISBN 0-9625233-0-5
1. Vocational rehabilitation–United States. 2. Handicapped-
-Employment–United States. I. Rusch, Frank R.
HD7256.U5S875 1990 89-26286
362.4'084–dc20 CIP

Sycamore Publishing Company
P.O. Box 133
Sycamore, IL 60178

Sycamore Publishing Company is dedicated to publishing effective approaches to educating persons with diverse abilities.

Marc Gold

Robert A. Henderson*
University of Illinois at Urbana-Champaign

Marc Gold was an achiever: in his short lifetime he managed to obtain bachelor and master degrees while working part time in his father's bicycle repair shop, taught students with moderate mental retardation in the Los Angeles Public Schools, spent three years as a full-time graduate student at the University of Illinois where he was awarded a Ph.D. in special education in 1969, remained there as a researcher in the Institute of Child Behavior and Development, and, when he had perfected his "Try Another Way" system, formed his own company to disseminate it throughout this country and abroad. Just as he was reaching his peak of productivity, he died from cancer.

Marc was a very caring person. Long before it became popular to do so, Marc was expounding the rights of individuals with severe disabilities to become productive citizens instead of objects of pity and charity. This is best illustrated by the philosophical principles that he posited as the basis for the "Try Another Way" system:

1. One can best serve persons with handicaps by teaching them to do marketable tasks.
2. Persons labeled retarded respond best to a learning situation based on respect of their human worth and capabilities.
3. Those labeled handicapped have the breadth and depth of capabilities to demonstrate competence, given training appropriate to their needs.
4. A lack of learning in any particular situation should first be interpreted as a result of inappropriate or insufficient use of teaching strategy, rather than inability on the part of the learner.
5. To this point in its development, testing is at best limiting to the person labeled mentally retarded.
6. Labeling is both unfair and counterproductive. (Gold, 1980, p. 3).

Marc's work with adults with severe disabilities gained praise from rehabilitation workers in some twenty states that utilized his system, and employers nationally were made aware of his work through an article entitled, "Real Jobs for the Retarded" in the November 6, 1978, issue of *Business Week*.

Despite his entrepreneurial skills and heavy business demands, Marc always had time to assist a graduate student or to serve professional organizations. He was President of the Workshop Division of the Illinois Rehabilitation Association, a member of the Executive Board of the American Association for the Education of the Severely/Profoundly Handicapped (now The Association for Persons with Severe Handicaps), Vice-President of the Vocational Rehabilitation Division of the American Association on Mental Deficiency (now the American Association on Mental Retardation), and consulting editor of *Mental Retardation, Education and Treatment of Children,* and the *American Journal of Mental Deficiency*.

Although his life was cut short, his application of the basic principles of learning to the teaching of individuals with severe handicapping conditions will serve as a lasting memorial.

REFERENCE

Gold, M. (1980) *Did I Say That?*, Champaign, IL: Research Press.

---

*Professor Henderson served as Marc Gold's advisor during his doctoral studies at the University of Illinois.

Contents

Contributors

Paul E. Bates, Ph.D.
Department of Special Education
Southern Illinois University
Carbondale, IL 62901

Wendy K. Berg, Ph.D.
Division of Developmental Disabilities
251 Hospital School
University of Iowa
Iowa City, IA 52242

Jay Buckley, Ph.D.
Specialized Training Program
135 Education Building
University of Oregon
Eugene, OR 97403

Janis Chadsey-Rusch, Ph.D.
Department of Special Education
288 Education Building
College of Education
1310 S. Sixth Street
University of Illinois
Champaign, IL 61820

Ronald W. Conley, Ph.D.
Administration on Developmental Disabilities
Room 374D
200 Independence Avenue, SW
Washington, DC 20201

Rita Curl, Ph.D.
Developmental Center for Handicapped Persons
Outreach Development and Dissemination Division
Utah State University
Logan, UT 84322-6805

Lizanne DeStefano, Ph.D.
Department of Educational Psychology
210 Education Building
College of Education
1310 S. Sixth Street
University of Illinois
Champaign, IL 61820

Denetta L. Dowler
Rehabilitation Research and Training Center
806 Allen Hall
West Virginia University
Morgantown, WV 26506-6122

Warren K. Ellis
Transition Institute at Illinois
110 Education Building
College of Education
1310 S. Sixth Street
University of Illinois
Champaign, IL 61820

Jane M. Everson, Ph.D.
Technical Assistance Center
Helen Keller National Center
Sands Point, NY 11050

Thomas H. Flynn
Division of Developmental Disabilities
251 Hospital School
University of Iowa
Iowa City, IA 52242

Cynthia C. Flynn
Office of Programs for the Handicapped
South Carolina Department of Education
Koger Executive Center
Santee Building, Suite 21
Columbia, SC 29210

Steven L. Fullmer
Rehabilitation Research and Training Center
West Virginia University
806 Allen Hall
Morgantown, WV 26506-6122

Robert Gaylord-Ross, Ph.D.
Department of Special Education
1600 Holloway Ave.
San Francisco State University
San Francisco, CA 94132

Cheryl Hanley-Maxwell, Ph.D.
Rehabilitation Institute
Southern Illinois University
Carbondale, IL 62901

Mark Hill
Director
Office of Supported Employment
DMHMRSAS
P.O. Box 1797
Richmond, VA 23214

Robert H. Horner, Ph.D.
Specialized Training Program
135 Education Building
University of Oregon
Eugene, OR 97403

Carolyn Hughes, Ph.D.
Transition Institute at Illinois
110 Education Building
College of Education
1310 S. Sixth Street
University of Illinois
Champaign, IL 61820

Margaret P. Hutchins, Ph.D.
Department of Special Education
288 Education Building
College of Education
1310 S. Sixth Street
University of Illinois
Champaign, IL 61820

John R. Johnson
Transition Institute at Illinois
110 Education Building
College of Education
1310 S. Sixth Street
University of Illinois
Champaign, IL 61820

William E. Kiernan, Ph.D.
Training and Research Institute for People with Disabilities
Gardner 4, 300 Longwood Avenue
Children's Hospital
Boston, MA 02115

John Kregel, Ph.D.
Rehabilitation Research and Training Center
Box 2011
College of Education
Virginia Commonwealth University
Richmond, VA 23284-0001

Thomas R. Lagomarcino, Ph.D.
Transition Institute at Illinois
110 Education Building
College of Education
1310 S. Sixth Street
University of Illinois
Champaign, IL 61820

David Mank, Ph.D
The Employment Network
135 Education Building
University of Oregon
Eugene, OR 97403

James E. Martin, Ph.D.
School of Education
Austin Bluffs Parkway
University of Colorado
Colorado Springs, CO 80907

Wendy McCaughrin, Ph.D.
Illinois Supported Employment Project
110 Education Building
College of Education
1310 S. Sixth Street
University of Illinois
Champaign, IL 61820

Richard P. Melia, Ph.D.
National Institute of Disability and Rehabilitation Research
Room 3428
330 C Street, SW
Washington, DC 20202

Bruce M. Menchetti, Ph.D.
Department of Special Education
Florida State University
Tallahassee, FL 32306-3030

Dennis E. Mithaug, Ph.D.
School of Education
Austin Bluffs Parkway
University of Colorado
Colorado Springs, CO 80907

M. Sherril Moon, Ph.D.
Training and Research Institute for People with Disabilities
Gardner 4, 300 Longwood Avenue
Children's Hospital
Boston, MA 02115

Jack H. Noble, Jr., Ph.D.
Rehabilitation Research and Training Center
SUNY at Buffalo
197 Farber Hall
3435 Main Street
Buffalo, NY 14214

Wendy S. Parent
Rehabilitation Research and Training Center
Box 2011
College of Education
Virginia Commonwealth University
Richmond, VA 23284-0001

Randall M. Parker, Ph.D.
Rehabilitation Counselor Education Program
Special Education Department
EDB 306
The University of Texas at Austin
Austin, TX 78712

Adelle M. Renzaglia, Ph.D.
Department of Special Education
288 Education Building
College of Education
1310 S. Sixth Street
University of Illinois
Champaign, IL 61820

W. Grant Revell, Ph.D.
Rehabilitation Research and Training Center
Box 2011
College of Education
Virginia Commonwealth University
Richmond, VA 23284-0001

Larry E. Rhodes, Ph.D.
The Employment Network
135 Education Building
University of Oregon
Eugene, OR 97403

Frank R. Rusch, Ph.D.
Transition Institute at Illinois
110 Education Building
College of Education
1310 S. Sixth Street
University of Illinois
Champaign, IL 61820

Dennis Sandow
The Employment Network
135 Education Building
University of Oregon
Eugene, OR 97403

Robert L. Schalock, Ph.D.
Department of Psychology
7th & Turner
Hastings College
Hastings, NE 68901

Dale T. Snauwaert
Transition Institute at Illinois
College of Education
110 Education Building
1310 S. Sixth Street
University of Illinois
Champaign, IL 61820

Susan S. Suter, Director
Illinois Department of Public Aid
Harris 2 Building, Third Floor
100 S. Grand
Springfield, IL 62762

Edna Szymanski, Ph.D.
Deptartment of Rehabilitation, Psychology, and Special Education
University of Wisconsin
432 N. Murray St.
Madison, WI 53706

John S. Trach, Ph.D.
Supported Employment Long-Term Training Program
Department of Special Education
110 Education Building
College of Education
1310 S. Sixth Street
University of Illinois
Champaign, IL 61820

Jho-Ju-Tu, Ph.D.
Transition Institute of Illinois
College of Education
110 Education Building
1310 S. Sixth Street
University of Illinois
Champaign, IL 61820

R. Timm Vogelsberg, Ph.D.
Developmental Disabilities Center
13th & Columbia
Temple University
Philadelphia, PA 19122

David P. Wacker, Ph.D.
Division of Developmental Disabilities
251 Hospital School
University of Iowa
Iowa City, IA 52242

Richard T. Walls, Ph.D.
Rehabilitation, Research, and Training Center
806 Allen Hall
West Virginia University
Morgantown, WV 26506-6122

Paul Wehman, Ph.D.
Rehabilitation Research and Training Center
Box 2011
College of Education
Virginia Commonwealth University
Richmond, VA 23284-0001

Claude W. Whitehead
Employment Related Associates
12327 Golden Oak Circle
Hudson, FL 34669

Foreword

Perhaps more than any other program developed for people with severe disabilities that has surfaced during the past decade, supported employment embodies the essence of integration.

I predict that the initial debates over its effectiveness and concerns for long-term funding will fade as data on supported employment continue to accumulate in its favor. No other program yet developed holds the promise of reducing the staggering unemployment among our nation's citizens with severe disabilities the way that supported employment does. For too long, these Americans have had to rely on the public welfare system or family assistance to meet their basic needs and their needs for income, housing, and job training. Now comes the concept of supported employment with its potential to change all that. Real work performed for real pay with on-the-job supports, job coaches, accommodations to the work place, and flexible work schedules in *integrated* job settings represent important developments for people with disabilities.

Supported employment is the result of a major change in the way our society accepts its members with disabilities. Fading are the stereotypes of what disabled people are supposed to be, or what they're supposed to be able to do. Today's citizens with disabilities desperately want to be contributors and true participants at work, at home, and in their communities.

Supported employment, besides the opportunities it provides both on and off the job, also offers the chance for friendships and a life that extends beyond the barriers of an institution or a group home. It provides after-hours links to the neighborhood that, until now, have often been lacking in the lives of people with disabilities.

Development of a program of this magnitude has called on social service agencies to work together to create blends of funding and staffing that will help to ensure the continued success of supported employment. It has required leadership that has dared to take the risk and extend the concept of work for people with severe disabilities into employment settings never before dreamed possible. This leadership has extended all the way from local service agencies to Washington.

Supported employment has my wholehearted endorsement. Opportunities for integration and the paychecks supported employment provides are the keys to equal opportunities and full participation for a substantial number of Americans who, until now, have been mistakenly considered "too severely disabled" to hold a job.

Susan S. Suter, Director
Illinois Department of Public Aid

Preface

In 1985, we were on the threshold of one of the most significant pieces of rehabilitation legislation for persons with severe disabilities since the passage of the Rehabilitation Act of 1973. The Rehabilitation Act Amendments of 1986 (P.L. 99-506) introduced "supported employment" as an eligible service option for persons with severe handicaps. This legislation has had an enormous impact on (a) the lives of persons with handicaps, (b) the expectations and values we hold as service providers, and (c) the knowledge base that has emerged as we better understand integrated employment.

Public Law 99-506 defined supported employment as "competitive work in an integrated work setting for individuals who, because of their handicaps, need ongoing support service to perform that work" (p. 30546). The rules and regulations clarify this definition by identifying three critical elements of supported employment: (1) competitive work in (2) an integrated work setting with (3) ongoing support services.

As you read this text in light of 99-506, however, you should continue to be concerned about our present and future efforts to deliver supported employment-related services. These concerns should relate to our interpretation of each of the three defining characteristics of supported employment (i.e., wages, integration, and support) and to the impact that our interpretation of what constitutes supported employment has on the lives of people with disabilities. Earning a wage per se is not a unique characteristic of supported employment, nor is support. Indeed, traditional vocational alternatives (e.g., sheltered workshops, work activity centers, and adult day care programs) have been "transitioning adults into competitive employment for years." These same programs have also provided a net of "supportive" services to employees, which has taken many forms. For example, some employees who lose their jobs are re-admitted to sheltered workshops.

Integration is the defining characteristic of supported employment. Although this text introduces supported employment issues, and new and improved strategies for program implementation, let us all remember that *integration is what all the fuss is about.* Integrated employment is achieved when persons with disabilities are afforded an equal opportunity to participate in the workplace. An integrated workplace is formed only when individual differences are accepted and individual competence is maximized.

We are not very advanced in our understanding of what defines integration, its goals, and its standards. Many of our goals for integration focus on how *we* define "quality of life." These goals have followed fairly narrow conceptual paradigms. Typically, we merely focus on physical integration without regard to the texture of participation and the richness of opportunity to become an equal participant in the workplace. We focus, for example, on the ratio of persons with and without severe disabilities who are working in one setting as opposed to what the supported employee personally gains as a result of participation (e.g., new friends, job satisfaction, increased competence).

This text is yet another milestone in defining our attempt to integrate persons with severe disabilities into the employment mainstream. The chapters contained in this text are unique, and they represent enormous gains in our understanding of employment. Clearly, the knowledge base supporting integrated employment is expanding at an enormous rate. However, this text underscores Herb Prehm's premonition "that, while significant gains have been made, there is much more ground to cover, and many, many promises to keep" (Rusch, 1986, p. xii). We are just beginning to understand the full scope of our efforts to provide integrated employment opportunities to persons with severe disabilities.

We have witnessed an incredible groundswell of interest in integration and competitive employment resulting in new expectations in relation to individual competence. I hope that we continue to realize that we have much to learn about the incredibly complex individuals for whom we are advocates.

ACKNOWLEDGEMENTS

Over the past fifteen years there have been a number of individuals who have influenced my thinking. In particular, the writing and advocacy of Marc Gold, Dennis Mithaug, Paul Wehman, David Wacker, Lou Brown, and Tom Bellamy continue to shape my ideas.

Also, I have worked with a number of talented persons who have spent short periods of their professional lives with me at Illinois. Among them are Timm Vogelsberg, Richard Schutz, Bruce Menchetti, Jim Martin, Martin Agran, Cheryl Hanley-Maxwell, Jeff Tines, Jeff McNair, Tom Lagomarcino, John Trach, Carolyn Hughes, John Johnson, Warren Ellis, and Phil Wilson.

The authors of this text also represent persons who clearly are at the forefront of supported employment. They will continue to formulate important questions about how we study supported employment.

Special thanks are extended to Phil Wilson and Mark O'Reilly for preparing the questions that appear after each chapter. Also, we thank Marian Heal, production coordinator, and Lori Martinsek who made all the important decisons. Our logo was created by James Van Winkle.

Finally, Janis Chadsey-Rusch deserves special acknowledgement. She is my closest friend and colleague.

FRANK R. RUSCH

PART

I

Introduction to Supported Employment

Richard P. Melia
National Institute of Disability and Rehabilitation Research
Washington DC

Before the introduction of supported employment, we assumed that people with severe disabilities could not function in regular work settings. Rusch and Hughes document the emergence of supported employment and events that influenced our beliefs. Over the past twenty years, changes described by Rusch and Hughes have been substantial—including placing persons into integrated job sites.

These changes were based, in part, on research that asked new questions. When a person had difficulty learning a task in one setting and transferring his or her learning, researchers asked how to restructure community-based work training programs; they did not simply allow this person to remain in a sheltered workshop setting. They applied behavioral interventions to mobility, communication, attention to task, self-management, and community living, viewing supported employment as the ultimate outcome to be measured by wages, hours, and social contact with nondisabled co-workers.

In Virginia, Paul Wehman and his colleagues introduced organizational change through widespread implementation. They identified a product–the outcomes possible for people with severe disabilities through supported employment–and found support for marketing demonstrations.

Two key problems were faced in Virginia. First, supported employment required direct service staff skilled in the behavioral methods described in Chapter 1. Second, a new understanding of the importance of support had to be developed. Wehman and his colleagues addressed the first problem through on-going inservice program development and the professionalization of the "employment specialists" (Wehman & Melia, 1985). They confronted the second issue by developing "fee for service" and vendor arrangements that allowed the state rehabilitation system to purchase "employment specialist" services just as they had purchased blocks of evaluation time for persons with severe disabilities for many years from traditional rehabilitation facilities.

Virginia now is addressing continuing issues in program development and implementation. It serves as a reminder that ever-changing environmental conditions, social and policy contexts, new technologies, and concern for moral dimensions and values must be part of supported employment's growth. Chapter 2 identifies many of these same issues, such as incorporation of new disability groups into the model, use of supervisors and co-workers in support at the worksite, and interpretation of data to make corrections and improvements in program implementation.

It was Jeffrey Manditch Prottas of Harvard University who told us that bureaucracies cannot stand people; rather, they need "clients" to process and forms to standardize procedures for each client (Prottas, 1979). But supported employment faces a dilemma when faced with bureaucracy. To succeed, supported employment needs to free itself from the bureaucratic mold—to break the bonds of assessment, evaluation, documentation, simulation, readiness, and "flow-through." These concepts have all too often been used to characterize people with severe disabilities as in need of separate environments where, excluded from the tasks of everyday life, they had little hope of learning or demonstrating competence. In short, complex rules, eligibility standards, and other bureaucratic measures have often transformed people with severe disabilities into clients that bureaucracies have been able to handle with uniform solutions. Yet, even in supported employment, our ever-present bureaucracy requires categories that determine whether an individual will be served, descriptors of who is being served, and operating procedures for the people in direct service roles whom Prottas calls "street-level" bureaucrats.

In Chapter 3, Frank Rusch and his colleagues have, with increasing sophistication over the past ten years, researched and solved these potential tensions in supported employment. Rusch and his colleagues identify "low expectations" about people with severe disabilities as a major factor contributing to employment practices. In Illinois, program development and evaluation research activities have identified key components of supported employment. Their approach to accountability differs fundamentally from the informal or reactionary bureaucratic mechanisms that so often characterize service systems. Illinois has defined outcome measures for individual accomplishments that represent important supported employment values.

Significantly greater state direction and management is described in Chapter 4, by Vogelsberg, Richard, and Nicoll. The primary message these authors deliver is that supported employment must be outcome-oriented, with its impact assessed by the evaluation of demographic, financial, training, follow-up, and job-specific data. The authors warn the reader that their data are descriptive and that, even with substantial state and local management, planning, and budgeting, it is difficult to assess the full impact of supported employment upon persons with severe disabilities.

Readers will note a sense of frustration in the rapid-fire listing of problems and concerns facing Pennsylvania's supported employment management teams. These teams are attempting to build a consensus, address major issues of choice for individuals with severe disabilities, confront rigidity in bureaucracy and policy, and recognize what does and does not work in new service patterns. And they are doing so in a rapidly changing administrative, educational, and legal environment. Also, while they are facing these obstacles, they are facing "second-generation" issues such as multiple consumer groups, conversion, and quality of life. This chapter alerts us to the difficult challenges facing supported employment.

John Trach presents a cogent summary of "supported employment program characteristics" in Chapter 5. Trach's overview suggests that much has indeed been accomplished and that early program models have evolved enormously.

Trach explains what factors are most important in planning and operating supported employment programs in today's social and educational environment by providing a benchmark for measuring the progress of the past decade. Yet he also recognizes that, all too often, we face major gaps in the attempt to implement and maintain what is essential in supported employment.

Supported employment began with model programs organized by early pioneers. We now have federal legislation driving the emergence of "second generation" issues of maintaining program quality, challenging personal values, and identifying new outcomes. Supported employment is maintaining the enthusiasm of the "models" described by Rusch, Wehman, and others while gaining the recognition and resources associated with popularly demanded programs. The five chapters in Section One provide an excellent introduction to supported employment and its goals. These chapters also challenge us to consider implementing new and improved services based upon new values and data related to program effectiveness while shaping new responses to emerging challenges.

NOTE: The author wishes to note that the views expressed in this paper do not necessarily reflect the views taken by the U.S. Department of Education.

REFERENCES

Prottas, J. M. (1979). *People-processing: The street-level bureaucrat in public service bureaucracies.* Lexington, MA: Lexington Books.

Wehman P. & Melia, R. (1985). The job coach: Function in transitional and supported employment. *American Rehabilitation, 11*(2), 4-7.

CHAPTER

1

Historical Overview of Supported Employment

Frank R. Rusch
Carolyn Hughes
University of Illinois at Urbana-Champaign

Sufficient empirical evidence was accumulated in the 1970s to challenge the prevailing theory that mental retardation is a long-term debilitating condition with poor prognosis for remediation. Early studies conducted primarily in segregated, sheltered workshop and educational settings demonstrated that individuals with mental retardation could acquire specific job skills (Brown & Pearce, 1970; Brown, Van Deventer, Perlmutter, Jones, & Sontag, 1972; Cohen & Close, 1975; Evans & Spradlin, 1966; Gold, 1973; Gold & Barclay, 1973; Huddle, 1967; Hunter & Bellamy, 1976; Jens & Shores, 1969; Mithaug, 1979; Schroeder, 1972; Wehman, Schutz, Renzaglia, & Karan, 1977; Zimmerman, Overpeck, Eisenberg, & Garlick, 1969). In particular, Crosson (1969), Gold (1972), and Bellamy, Peterson, and Close (1975) provided "illustrations of competence" among persons with mental retardation who learned complex vocational skills. Bellamy, Horner, and Inman (1979) proceeded to develop instructional strategies for individuals with severe mental retardation working in sheltered workshop settings. These illustrations of competence among persons with mental retardation were revolutionary in that they ultimately challenged previously accepted paradigms of service delivery.

EARLY RESEARCH IN NONSHELTERED SETTINGS

Toward the end of the 1970s research began to appear that demonstrated that individuals with mental retardation could be placed in nonsheltered, competitive employment. Rusch, Connis, and Sowers (1978) reported on an employee who learned to increase her working time in a restaurant; Schutz, Rusch, and Lamson (1979) evaluated the effectiveness of verbal reprimands in reducing verbally abusive statements made by three dishwashers; and Rusch (1979) demonstrated the relationship between attending to task and completing work assignments (production). Wehman, Hill, and Koehler (1979a) also reported case studies of three food service employees who learned to spend more time in the performance of their assigned work duties. These studies were important because they suggested that individuals who typically were placed in sheltered workshops could also work in nonsheltered, integrated work environments. The stage was set for future researchers to identify new goals and to test an emerging behavioral technology in the context of integrated work environments.

DISSATISFACTION WITH PREVAILING ADULT SERVICES

At the same time that "illustrations of competence" were being conducted in segregated settings and reported in mainstream journals (including the *American Journal on Mental Deficiency*, *Journal of Applied Behavior Analysis*, *Mental Retardation*, *Education and Training of the Mentally Retarded*), there was growing recognition that our human service delivery system was "broken." Whitehead (1979) indicated that more than 200,000 adults with severe disabilities were being served by our sheltered workshops, while more than 6,000,000 others were not receiving services, even though work activity centers grew by over 600% during the period between 1968 and 1977. Whitehead pointed out that the only individuals who attained competitive employment once they entered sheltered workshops were those who did not require skill training.

Gold (1975) pointed out that transition to competitive employment among persons with severe disabilities was "unusual"; he maintained that the typical sheltered workshop staff lacked knowledge of what skills should be taught, how best to teach these skills, and how best to structure their programs to facilitate movement toward nonsheltered, competitive employment. Sheltered workshops traditionally rely upon staff who have little knowledge about the instructional technology or industrial design necessary to develop an individual's potential for employment (Pomerantz & Marholin, 1977). In their review of social and work behavior research before 1980, Gifford, Rusch, Martin, and White (1984) concluded that the primary method of training in sheltered workshops was "supervision with vague instructions and occasional prompts to stay on task" (p. 287).

Almost a decade earlier, a major philosophical milestone had marked the beginning of reform in the human service delivery system—normalization (Nirje, 1969; Wolfensberger, 1972). The normalization principle has as its rudimentary tenet the delivery of services in environs and under contingencies that are as culturally normal as possible. In the 1970s, interpretation of normalization led to widespread disapproval of services, activities, and events that appeared to be available only to persons with handicaps.

The emergence of supported employment appeared to be fueled by our dissatisfaction with a mental retardation service system that prepared people endlessly for jobs that never materialized (Whitehead, 1979). Existing vocational options (e.g., sheltered workshops, day activities centers, adult day care centers) purportedly were transitional, but were clearly holding people back (Bellamy, Rhodes, Bourbeau, & Mank, 1986). Also, there was growing dissatisfaction with service options that resulted in institutionalization of persons with handicaps.

The concept of supported employment reflected a reversal in our thinking about mental retardation in two ways. First, supported employment held that the issue was not whether people with severe disabilities can perform real work, but what support systems were needed to achieve that goal (Rhodes & Valenta, 1985). Second, the concept proposed that the unsuccessful "place and pray" orientation, commonplace in education and rehabilitation, should be replaced by the more pragmatic approach of finding a job for the person with disabilities and then providing the training necessary for successful integration (Revell, Wehman, & Arnold, 1984).

EMERGENCE OF SUPPORTED EMPLOYMENT PROGRAMS

The success of supported employment can be attributed to the early identification of relevant characteristics that continue to be addressed systematically and consistently as the field progresses (refer to Chapter 5). The rationale that underlies supported employment is the awareness that some individuals can remain successfully employed if we can provide continuing long-term support. The rationale for "supported" employment was an obvious solution to the challenge presented by persons who were defined by their inability to learn complex discriminations (e.g., responding correctly to requests to change from one work activity to another) and by a community of employers who did not possess the knowledge or resources to train a new workforce (Wool, 1976).

Rather than using a "place and pray" approach, early supported employment model program developers adopted a "place-train-maintain" approach that expected continued support to be available to employees in the workplace (Rusch & Mithaug, 1980). As early as the mid-1970s, supported employment programs began to surface across the country. In 1975, the University of Washington began placing and training persons with moderate and severe mental retardation into competitive food-service jobs in the greater Seattle area (cf. Rusch & Schutz, 1979). Shortly thereafter, Wehman (see Chapter 2), Rusch (see Chapter 3), Vogelsberg (see Chapter 4), and others began similar programs in other areas of the United States (cf. Wehman, 1981). Wehman's Project Employability (Wehman, Hill, & Koehler, 1979b), begun in 1977, achieved national recognition after Virginia Commonwealth University was awarded a rehabilitation research and training grant in 1980 that focused on "employment for mentally retarded individuals."

These early programs contributed enormously to the development of the supported employment paradigm. Most importantly, these model program innovators applied basic behavioral concepts to vocational training and competitive employment. Rusch and Mithaug (1980) and Wehman (1981), in particular, focused applied behavior analysis techniques on the problems associated with their emerging model programs. These problems were new to vocational "habilitation" because prior research had been conducted in sheltered or simulated workshop settings and the outcome of this research was not directly applicable to nonsheltered employment. Although a behavioral technology was developing, this technology did not address the varying expectations and demands of co-workers, supervisors, and the supported employees themselves, let alone travel, housing, and income maintenance concerns. These were new target behaviors involving more complicated interactions between the employee and his or her environment.

Nonsheltered, competitive employment is not insulated from the expectations of significant others in the mainstream of integrated work. Supported employees are expected to become contributing members of the work force by learning and performing their jobs, often to the changing expectations of employers (cf. Chadsey-Rusch & Rusch, 1988). Before the emergence of competitive employment research, adults with varying levels of mental retardation had been taught how to pull plungers (Evans & Spradlin, 1966), fold boxes (Loos & Tizard, 1955), drop marbles (Tramontana, 1972), stuff envelopes (Brown & Pearce, 1970), and thread labels (Teasdale & Joynt, 1967). Although not without merit, this research contributed very little to our understanding of how to teach generalized problem solving, independence, and other skills needed for competitive employment (see Chapter 9).

Social validation had significant implications for integrated employment (see Chapter 11). Indeed, the perceived value of nonsheltered employment could be established by asking significant others (e.g., employers) to set employment goals, identify procedures to meet those goals, and evaluate the outcomes achieved by implementing the procedures. Social criteria, based on the expectations and opinions of significant others, ensured that applied interventions were both important to the consumer and valued by society. "Social validation [ensured] that intervention priorities regarding focus, procedures, and results [were] not arbitrarily or stipulatively prescribed, but [were] preferred and consensually agreed upon by community members" (White, 1986, p. 109). Supported employment adopted an ecological perspective that has remained critical to evaluating vocational behavior (see Chapter 7) and potential jobs in the community (see Chapter 6).

During the mid-1970s, for example, Zifferblatt and Hendricks (1974) recommended that behavioral intervention be designed to fit target environments, including an analysis of behaviors and contingencies that formed the "culture" of the target environment. Rogers-Warren (1977) recommended an "ecobehavioral" assessment. This approach, applied to supported employment, includes analyzing future settings to identify behavioral expectations; placing the individual in the target setting; adjusting the performance of supported employees; achieving concordance in the expectations of employers, co-workers, and the supported employee; and developing strategies for long-term behavioral adjustment.

MODEL PROGRAM EVALUATION

A defining characteristic of supported employment has been its consistent emphasis on employment outcomes. Historically, the success of supported employment has been measured in terms of job retention, increased earnings, and a favorable social cost-benefit ratio (Rusch, Chadsey-Rusch, & Johnson, in press). Wehman and his colleagues have reported consistent and positive outcomes related to job retention, wages, and benefits versus costs (Hill & Wehman, 1983; Hill, Wehman, Kregel, Banks, & Metzler, 1987; Wehman, Hill, & Koehler, 1979a; Wehman & Kregel, 1985). Clearly, supported employees earn more than their counterparts in sheltered employment (Tines, Rusch, McCaughrin, & Conley, in press). Additionally, Noble and Conley (1987) found all supported employment programs are more productive in terms of earnings and less costly than adult day care, work activity centers, and sheltered workshop alternatives. In another study, Rhodes (1982) compared vocational services for individuals with handicaps from the perspective of the direct service recipient. Rhodes (1982) concluded that the highest marginal net benefit for the direct service recipient (the supported employee) was provided by supported employment. Hill et al. (1987) provided one of the most detailed analyses of the financial impact of supported employment on consumers. A similar analysis was presented by Hill and Wehman (1983) and Tines et al. (in press). The results of these studies suggest that supported employment programs yield positive benefits for persons with handicaps as well as for the taxpayer.

LEGISLATIVE HISTORY OF SUPPORTED EMPLOYMENT

The emergence of supported employment is reflected in legislation that cumulatively has promoted the employment of individuals with handicaps. Work-study programs for youth with handicaps first emerged in the 1950s and later became the leading strategy in the public schools for preparing these youth for postschool employment (Brolin, 1976; Clark, 1976). In the proposed work-study models, youth were provided with controlled, in-school work, followed by placement in specialized job situations in the community (Miller, Ewing, & Phelps, 1980).

The Kennedy era marked the beginning of a period of considerable federal interest and growth in special education, vocational education, vocational rehabilitation, and other programs designed to assist unemployed youth and adults with handicaps. The Rehabilitation Act of 1973 placed a major emphasis on services for individuals with severe disabilities. State vocational rehabilitation agencies were mandated to improve services by ensuring client involvement in the design and delivery of vocational rehabilitation services, to expand program and service capacities, and to organize services around the multiple problems associated with a disability (e.g., transportation, housing, employment).

The job training and employment programs enacted under the Comprehensive Employment and Training Act (CETA) and presently continuing under the Job Training Partnership Act (JTPA) are also focused on serving individuals with special needs. Additionally, Congress enacted the Targeted Jobs Tax Credit program in the 1970s to provide tax incentives for employers who hire individuals referred through state vocational rehabilitation programs.

In 1984, Congress passed two key pieces of legislation: the 1984 Amendments to the Education of the Handicapped Act (P.L. 98-199), which cited a lack of transitional services for special education students, and the Developmental Disabilities Assistance and Bill of Rights Act of 1984 (P.L. 98-527), which provided a mandate for addressing employment-related activities as a major priority. Supported employment was one of the "employment-related" activities specifically defined in P.L. 98-527. According to the Developmental Disabilities Act of 1984, supported employment is:

> Paid employment which (i) is for persons with developmental disabilities for whom competitive employment at or above the minimum wage is unlikely and who, because of their disabilities, need ongoing support to perform in a work setting; (ii) is conducted in a variety of settings, particularly work sites in which persons without disabilities are employed; and (iii) is supported by any activity needed to sustain paid work by persons with disabilities, including supervision, training, and transportation. ("Developmental Disabilities Act of 1984," p. 2665)

The Developmental Disabilities Act of 1984 is important because it stipulates that the focus of supported employment is *integration* ("competitive employment (at) worksites in which persons without disabilities are employed") with *wages* ("paid work by persons with disabilities") and *support* ("including supervision, training, and transportation"). These outcomes have been expanded upon since 1984. For example, subsequent to the Developmental Disabilities Act, the Rehabilitation Act Amendments of 1986 (PL 99–506) set forth regulations to guide standards for supported employment services and the population to be served. The amendments defined supported employment as competitive work in an integrated work setting for individuals with severe handicaps for whom competitive employment has not occurred or for whom competitive employment has been interrupted or intermittent. Accordingly, individuals considered eligible for supported employment services are those who cannot function independently in employment without intensive on-going support services and require these on-going support services for the duration of their employment. These regulations also set at twenty the minimum number of hours a supported employee may work.

Integrated work settings are defined as settings where (a) most workers are not handicapped and (b) individuals with handicaps are not part of a work group consisting only of others with handicaps, or are part of a small work group of not more than eight individuals with handicaps. Additionally, if there are no co-workers or the only co-workers are members of a small group of not more than eight individuals with handicaps, individuals with handicaps must have regular contact with nonhandicapped individuals, other than personnel who provide support services. Finally, these regulations require that supported employees be provided follow-up services at least twice monthly at the job site, except in the case of individuals with chronic mental illness. Table 1.1 displays the primary outcomes of supported employment and the criteria that regulate their acceptance in the rehabilitation community.

Although neither of these laws actually created an entitlement for employment, they clearly recognized the importance of work to the independence and community integration of all persons with disabilities. In 1985, Congress appropriated $3.7 million for "supported work," and under the leadership of Madeleine Will, the Office of Special Education and Rehabilitative Services and the Administration on Developmental Disabilities (part of the Office of Human Development Services in HHS) jointly funded Sup-

Table 1.1 Supported Employment Outcomes and Criteria for Minimal Compliance among Persons with Severe Handicaps for Whom Employment Has Not Occurred or Employment Has Been Intermittent or Interrupted

Outcome	Criteria
Competitive work	Averages at least 20 hours per week for each pay period
Integrated work setting	Workgroup of not more than eight individuals with handicaps; regular contact with nonhandicapped co-workers
Ongoing support services	Continuous or periodic job skill training services provided at least twice monthly at the job site (except for individuals with chronic mental illness)

ported Employment Demonstration Projects in 10 states (Alaska, Arizona, California, Kentucky, Maryland, Michigan, Minnesota, Utah, Virginia, and Washington). In 1986, this initiative was expanded to include an additional 17 states (see Chapter 8 for a review of this federal program).

TYPES OF PLACEMENT MODELS

Four different placement approaches have been developed in relation to employing persons with handicaps in competitive employment. They include: (1) the individual placement model, (2) the clustered placement model, (3) the mobile crew model, and (4) the entrepreneurial model. Typically, group models (i.e., clustered placement, mobile crew, and entrepreneurial models) are considered appropriate only for individuals with the most severe disabilities who require more intensive support than is provided by the individual placement model. Although hours worked per week are typically somewhat greater for employees of clustered placements or mobile work crews, mean hourly wages and level of integration are greater for workers who are individually placed (Kregel, Wehman, & Banks, 1989).

When implementing the *individual placement* model, an "employment specialist" locates a job in a conventional private sector company, and then places the individual with a disability into the job (Bellamy, Rhodes, Mank, & Albin, 1988). Continuous on-site training is provided until the supported employee performs the job within acceptable standards. Over time, the type and level of assistance provided by the employment specialist typically is decreased, although at least two contacts per month are provided for the duration of the employment (Wehman & Moon, 1988).

The *clustered placement* model (also referred to as the enclave model) differs from the individual placement model in that a group of individuals, typically less than eight, works in close proximity, often performing the same work. Typically, follow-up staff provide continuous training and support for the duration of the employment period, not just during the initial training period (Bellamy et al., 1988). Clustered placements are located within a community-based business referred to as the "host company," and on-site support is provided through the ongoing presence of an employment specialist who serves as a work supervisor.

Mobile crews typically consist of less than eight supported employees who provide specialized contract services throughout a community (Wehman & Moon, 1988). Services often are provided from a van (thus the reference to "mobile" work crew) and include janitorial or groundskeeping work. Training and continuous supervision are provided by an on-site work supervisor.

Finally, the *entrepreneurial approach* is similar to the clustered placement model; however, rather than providing janitorial or groundskeeping services, eight or fewer supported employees typically are hired by a manufacturing company to provide a specific product or service (Mithaug, Martin, Husch, Rusch, & Agran 1988). For example, the "benchwork model" developed by the Specialized Training Program at the University of Oregon includes a network of small electronics assembly businesses supported through subcontracts to the sponsoring agency while the sponsoring agency (typically a local adult rehabilitation agency) supplies the manpower to complete job assignments, typically only persons with handicaps (Mank, Rhodes, & Bellamy, 1986). The entrepreneurial model serves individuals with the most severe disabilities who require intensive, continuous supervision.

CONCLUSION

Supported employment has changed many of our expectations about the employment of persons with severe disabilities. It cannot be disputed that a large number of individuals with disabilities have been employed competitively over the past ten years. Unlike initiatives that preceded supported employment, this vocational alternative has proven to be more cost effective than its predecessors. As an intervention, supported employment also has proven to be a catalyst for the development of behavioral principles that focus upon generalization and autonomy in the workplace.

The continuing challenge to those who implement supported employment is implied in Skinner's (1974) statement that "to understand the principles involved in solving a problem is not to have the solution" (p. 250). The complexities of our everyday lives are not very well understood, and indeed, supported employment's influence upon the lives of others is not at all clear.

As supported employment continues to gain in popularity, it will face enormous challenges. At this stage in its development, one clear challenge may be our failure to implement the characteristics of supported employment that have resulted in its growing popularity. Clearly, integration, wages, and support are defining characteristics of supported employment outcomes. These employment outcomes, however, are influenced by the degree to which the intervention is implemented (Trach & Rusch, 1989).

As an intervention, supported employment consists of multiple components. These components include behavioral strategies directed toward target employees, strategies focused upon small groups of co-workers, and strategies that are directed toward interagency cooperation. This text introduces supported employment methods that have proven successful in promoting employment integration.

As we begin to better understand the work world, we will improve the outcomes associated with supported employment, including better integration, higher wages, and appropriate support systems. Of these three characteristics, the third, support, must be taken as the hallmark of supported employment. Integration, however, may be its most defining contribution. Employment is represented by a number of different individuals working toward mutually agreed-upon goals. As rehabilitation and special educators begin to understand these goals, our understanding of how to design and implement human service systems that make a positive impact will grow. Once we focus upon what integration is, our professional, personal, and social perspectives will develop in fundamentally important "personal and social values. Indeed, one of our best values is to recognize that We and They are the sample people" (Baer, 1988, p. x).

QUESTIONS (For answers see p. 427)

1. Research demonstrating persons with mental retardation are capable of performing work tasks began approximately when?

2. Studies of individuals with mental retardation placed in nonsheltered employment settings began approximately when?

3. Name two ways that the concept of supported employment reflected a reversal in traditional ways of thinking about mental retardation.

4. How does the "place-train-maintain" approach of supported employment differ from the traditional "place and pray" approach to competitive employment?

5. Identify the function of social validation in the supported employment model.

6. What is the major challenge that supported employment faces today?

7. Why is a multiple intervention strategy needed to promote supported employment?

8. What are three outcomes associated with supported employment?

9. What do the authors propose may be the most defining contribution of supported employment?

REFERENCES

Baer, D. (1988). Forward. In F. R. Rusch, T. Rose, & C. R. Greenwood, *Behavior analysis in special education* (pp. xiii–xv). Englewood Cliffs, NJ: Prentice-Hall.

Bellamy, G. T., Horner, R. H., & Inman, D. P. (1979). *Vocational rehabilitation of severely retarded adults: A direct service technology.* Baltimore: University Park Press.

Bellamy, G. T., Peterson, L., & Close, D. (1975). Habilitation of the severely and profoundly retarded: Illustrations of competence. *Education and Training of the Mentally Retarded, 10,* 174–186.

Bellamy, G. T., Rhodes, L. E., Bourbeau, P. E., & Mank, D. M. (1986). Mental retardation services in sheltered workshops and day activity programs: Consumer benefits and policy alternatives. In

F. R. Rusch (Ed.), *Competitive employment issues and strategies* (pp. 257–271). Baltimore: Paul H. Brookes.

Bellamy, G. T., Rhodes, L. E., Mank, D. M., & Albin, J. M. (1988). *Supported employment: A community implementation guide*. Baltimore: Paul H. Brookes.

Brolin, D. (1976). *Vocational preparation of retarded citizens* . Columbus, OH: Charles E. Merrill.

Brown, L. & Pearce, E. (1970). Increasing the production of rate of trainable retarded students in a public school simulated workshop. *Education and Training of the Mentally Retarded*, *5*, 15–22.

Brown, L., VanDeventer, P., Perlmutter, L., Jones, S., & Sontag, E. (1972). Effects of the consequences on production rates of trainable retarded and severely emotionally disturbed students in a public school workshop. *Education and Training of the Mentally Retarded*, *7*, 74–81.

Chadsey-Rusch, J. & Rusch, F. (1988). Social ecology of the workplace. In R. Gaylord-Ross (Ed.), *Vocational education for persons with special needs* (pp. 234–256). Palo Alto, CA: Mayfield.

Clark, G. M. (1976). The state of the art in secondary programs for the handicapped. *Thresholds in Secondary Education*, 2(3), 10–11, 22–23.

Cohen, M. E. & Close, D. W. (1975). Retarded adults' discrete work performance in a sheltered workshop as a function of overall productivity and motivation. *American Journal of Mental Deficiency*, *60*, 733–743.

Crosson, J. A. (1969). A technique for programming sheltered workshop environments for training severely retarded workers. *American Journal of Mental Deficiency*, *73*, 814–818.

"Developmental Disabilities Act of 1984" (PL 98-527, 19 Oct. 1984), *United States Statutes at Large* 98, pp. 2662-2685.

Evans, G. & Spradlin, J. (1966). Incentives and instructions as controlling variables in productivity. *American Journal of Mental Deficiency*, *71*, 129–132.

Gifford, J. L., Rusch, F. R., Martin, D. E., & White, D. M. (1984). Autonomy and adaptability in work behavior of retarded clients. In N. W. Ellis & N. R. Bray (Eds.), *International review of research in mental retardation* (Vol. 12, pp. 285–318). New York: Academic Press.

Gold, M. (1972). Stimulus factors in skill training of the retarded on a complex assembly task: Acquisition, transfer, and retention. *American Journal of Mental Deficiency*, *76*, 517–526.

Gold, M. (1973). Factors affecting production by the retarded: Base rates. *Mental Retardation*, *11*, 9–11.

Gold, M. W. (1975). Vocational training. In J. Wortis (Ed.), *Mental retardation and developmental disabilities : An annual review* (Vol. 7, pp. 254–264). New York: Brunner/Mazel.

Gold, M. & Barclay, C. R. (1973). *The effects of verbal labels on the acquisition and retention of a complex assembly task* . Urbana: Childrens Research Center, University of Illinois.

Hill, M. & Wehman, P. (1983). Cost benefit analysis of placing moderately and severely handicapped individuals into competitive employment. *Journal of the Association for the Severely Handicapped*, *8*, 30–39.

Hill, M., Wehman, P., Kregel, J., Banks, P. D., & Metzler, H. M. D. (1987). Employment outcomes for people with moderate and severe disabilities: An eight-year longitudinal analysis of supported competitive employment. *Journal of the Association for Persons with Severe Handicaps*, *12*, 182–189.

Huddle, D. (1967). Work performance of trainable adults as influenced by competition, cooperation, and monetary reward. *American Journal of Mental Deficiency*, *72*, 198–211.

Hunter, J. & Bellamy, T. (1976). Cable harness construction for severely retarded adults: A demonstration of a training technique. *AAESPH Review*, *1*, 2–13.

Jens, K. & Shores, R. (1969). Behavioral graphs as reinforcers for work behavior of mentally retarded adolescents. *Education and Training of the Mentally Retarded*, *4*, 21–26.

Kregel, J., Wehman, P., & Banks, P. D. (1989). *The effects of consumer characteristics and type of employment model on individual outcomes in supported employment*. Manuscript submitted for publication.

Loos, F. & Tizard, J. (1955). The employment of adult imbeciles in a hospital workshop. *American Journal of Mental Deficiency*, *59*, 394–403.

Mank, D. M., Rhodes, L. E., & Bellamy, G. T. (1986). Four supported employment alternatives. In W. E.

Kiernan & J. A. Stark (Eds.) *Pathways to employment for adults with developmental disabilities*. Baltimore: Paul H. Brookes.

Miller, S., Ewing, N., & Phelps, L. (1980). Career and vocational education for the handicapped: A historical perspective. In L. Mann & D. Sabatino (Eds.), *The fourth review of special education* (pp. 215–243). New York: Grune & Stratton.

Mithaug, D. E. (1979). The relation between programmed instruction and task analysis in the prevocational training of severely and profoundly handicapped persons. *AAESPH Review, 4*, 162–178.

Mithaug, D. E., Martin, J. E., Husch, J. V., Rusch, F. R., & Agran, M. (1988). *When will persons in supported employment need less support?* Colorado Springs, CO: Ascent Publications.

Nirje, B. (1969). The normalization principle and its human management implications. In R. Jugel & W. Wolfensberger (Eds.), *Changing patterns of residential services for the mentally retarded*. Washington, DC: President's Committee on Mental Retardation.

Noble, J. H. & Conley, R. W. (1987). Accumulating evidence on the benefits and costs of supported and transitional employment for persons with severe disabilities. *Journal of the Association for Persons with Severe Handicaps, 12*, 163–174.

Pomerantz, D. & Marholin, D. (1977). Vocational habilitation: A time for change. In E. Sontag (Ed.), *Educational programming for the severely and profoundly handicapped*. Reston, VA: Council for Exceptional Children, Division on Mental Retardation.

Revell, G., Wehman, P., & Arnold, S. (1984). Supported work model of competitive employment for persons with mental retardation: Implications for rehabilitation services. *Journal of Rehabilitation, 50*, 33–38.

Rhodes, L. (1982). *Alternative investment analysis of services for severely handicapped people*. Unpublished doctoral dissertation, University of Oregon, Eugene.

Rhodes, L. E. & Valenta, L. (1985). Industry-based supported employment: An enclave approach. *Journal of the Association for Persons with Severe Handicaps, 10*, 12–20.

Rogers-Warren, A. (1977). Planned change: Ecobehaviorally based interventions. In A. Rogers-Warren & S. R. Warren (Eds.), *Ecological perspectives in behavior analysis*. Baltimore: University Park Press.

Rusch, F. R. (1979). A functional analysis of the relationship between attending and producing in a vocational training program. *The Journal of Special Education, 13*(4), 399–411.

Rusch, F. R., Chadsey-Rusch, J., & Johnson, J. R. (in press). Emerging opportunities for employment integration. In L. Meyer, C. Peck, & L. Brown (Eds.), *Critical issues in the lives of people with severe disabilities*. Baltimore: Paul H. Brookes.

Rusch, F. R., Connis, R. T., & Sowers, J. (1978). The modification and maintenance of time spent attending to task using social reinforcement, token reinforcement and response cost in an applied restaurant setting. *Journal of Special Education Technology, 2*, 18–26.

Rusch, F. R. & Mithaug, D. E. (1980). *Vocational training for mentally retarded adults: A behavioral analytic approach*. Champaign, IL: Research Press.

Rusch, F. R. & Schutz, R. P. (1979). Nonsheltered employment of the mentally retarded adult: Research to reality? *Journal of Contemporary Business, 8* (4), 85–98.

Schroeder, S. R. (1972). Parametric effects of reinforcement frequency, amount of reinforcement, and required response force on sheltered workshop behavior. *Journal of Applied Behavior Analysis, 5*, 431–441.

Schutz, R. P., Rusch, F. R., & Lamson, D. S. (1979). Evaluation of an employer's procedure to eliminate unacceptable behavior on the job. *Community Services Forum, 1*, 4–5.

Skinner, B. F. (1974). *About behaviorism*. New York: Alfred A. Knopf.

Tines, J., Rusch, F. R., McCaughrin, W., & Conley, J. (in press). Benefit-cost analysis of supported employment in Illinois: A statewide evaluation. *American Journal on Mental Retardation*.

Teasdale, R. & Joynt, D. (1967). Some effects of incentives on the behavior of adolescent retardates. *American Journal of Mental Deficiency, 71*, 925–930.

Trach, J. S. & Rusch, F. R. (1989). Evaluating supported employment programs: The degree of implementation. *American Journal of Mental Retardation, 94*, 134–139.

Tramontana, J. (1972). Social versus edible rewards as a function of intellectual level and socio-economic class. *American Journal of Mental Deficiency, 77,* 33–38.

Wehman, P. (1981). *Competitive employment: New horizons for severely disabled individuals.* Baltimore: Paul H. Brookes.

Wehman, P., Hill, J. W., & Koehler, F. (1979a). Placement of developmentally disabled individuals into competitive employment: Three case studies. *Education and Training of the Mentally Retarded, 14,* 269–276.

Wehman, P., Hill, J. W., & Koehler, F. (1979b). Helping severely handicapped persons enter competitive employment. *AAESPH Review, 4*(3), 274–290.

Wehman, P. & Kregel, J. (1985). A supported work approach to competitive employment of individuals with moderate and severe handicaps. *The Journal of the Association for Persons with Severe Handicaps, 10,* 3–11.

Wehman, P. & Moon, M. S. (1988). *Vocational rehabilitation and supported employment.* Baltimore: Paul H. Brookes.

Wehman, P., Schutz, R., Renzaglia, A., & Karan, O. (1977). The use of positive practice training in work adjustment with two profoundly retarded adolescents. *Vocational Evaluation and Work Adjustment Bulletin, 14,* 14–22.

White, D. M. (1986). Social validation. In F. R. Rusch (Ed.), *Competitive employment issues and strategies* (pp. 199–213). Baltimore: Paul H. Brookes.

Whitehead, C. W. (1979). Sheltered workshops in the decade ahead: Work and wages, or welfare. In G. T. Bellamy, G. O'Connor, & O. C. Karan (Eds.), *Vocational rehabilitation of severely handicapped persons* (pp. 71–84). Baltimore: University Park Press.

Wolfensberger, W. (1972). *Normalization: The principle of normalization in human services.* Toronto: National Institute on Mental Retardation.

Wool, H. (1976). *The labor supply for low level occupations.* Research and Development Monograph (42). Washington, DC: U.S. Department of Labor, Employment and Training Administration.

Zifferblatt, S. M. & Hendricks, C. G. (1974). Applied behavioral analysis of societal problems: Population change, a case in point. *American Psychologist, 29,* 750–761.

Zimmerman, J., Overpeck, C., Eisenberg, H., & Garlick, B. (1969). Operant conditioning in a sheltered workshop. *Rehabilitation Literature, 30,* 323–334.

CHAPTER

2

Supported Employment in Virginia

John Kregel
Paul Wehman
W. Grant Revell
Virginia Commonwealth University
Mark Hill
Office of Supported Employment
Richmond, Virginia

The purpose of this chapter is to examine empirically supported employment implementation in Virginia in order to evaluate the success of this program. Specifically, we address the following questions:

• Who is participating in supported employment programs?

• What is the level of severity (i.e., functioning capability) of those participating in supported employment?

• What impact is supported employment having on the state vocational rehabilitation program?

• How many hours per week are supported employment participants working?

• What effect is supported employment having on government benefits received by participants?

• What type of supported employment models are being used?

• What kinds of wages and fringe benefits are people receiving?

• What types of employment positions are people taking?

• What is the nature of target employee job retention?

In order to answer these questions, we undertook an in-depth analysis of ongoing data submitted by local service providers to the Virginia Commonwealth University Rehabilitation Research and Training Center. This chapter describes the major outcome measures that have been reported. However, before describing the data management system and program results, it will be helpful to review briefly the historical basis under which Virginia built supported employment into the present state system. What follows is a description of supported employment development in Virginia and a presentation of the outcome data associated with this implementation.

SUPPORTED EMPLOYMENT IN VIRGINIA: A BRIEF HISTORICAL REVIEW

Virginia's efforts to redirect center-based day support and work-oriented services for persons who are mentally retarded toward support in the competitive labor market formally began in 1978. The Department of Rehabilitative Services, the state's general vocational rehabilitation agency, granted Innovation and Expansion (I&E) funds to Virginia Commonwealth University to research and demonstrate the feasibility of placing and maintaining in competitive employment persons traditionally served in work activity and sheltered work programs. Project Employability operated in Richmond, Virginia, for three years through the I&E grant and provided the foundation for the job placement, job site training, and ongoing follow-along service model, now called the supported competitive employment outcome. From 1978 through 1981, Project Employability also focused on the importance and viability of full participation of the state vocational rehabilitation (VR) system and the local VR counselor in generating and supporting nonsegregated employment opportunities for persons with severe disabilities (Wehman & Hill, 1979, 1980).

In 1981, Virginia Commonwealth University received a three-year Special Projects grant from the Federal Rehabilitation Services Administration to replicate in other communities in Virginia the services demonstrated through Project Employability in Richmond. Replication took place in Norfolk in cooperation with the Eggleston Center, a private nonprofit sheltered workshop, and in Virginia Beach through the city's mental retardation adult services program. In addition to the replication sites coordinated through VCU, localities such as the city of Alexandria and the county of Fairfax/Falls Church in northern Virginia initiated efforts similar to Project Employability during the time period from 1981 to 1984. Facility grant funds from the Department of Rehabilitative Services, CETA manpower service awards, and redirection of state and local day support service funds supported these local efforts. By 1984, persons with severe disabilities were being supported in competitive employment in the five communities previously referenced plus Roanoke and Marion in southwest Virginia (Revell, Wehman, & Arnold, 1984).

The progress achieved in Virginia through 1984 relied heavily on federal and state discretionary grants, through short-term manpower funding and through local efforts to pool scarce service funds not specifically targeted for supporting persons with disabilities in the competitive labor market. It therefore became critically important to move from grant funding to a permanent interagency funding system based on the service needs of specific individuals. In Virginia, the State Department of Mental Health, Mental Retardation and Substance Abuse Services is designated as the state authority for alcoholism, drug abuse, mental health, and mental retardation services. The delivery of these services is administered at the local level through a system of approximately 40 Community Service Boards (CSBs). In 1984 a fee-based approach to funding was initiated for both time-limited employment services through the vocational rehabilitation system and ongoing support service funding through the CSB system. This change required state level interagency agreement regarding the concept of shared funding, followed by negotiations at the local level to ensure services through specific providers for individual clients (Hill, Wehman, Kregel, Banks, & Metzler, 1987).

Fee-based participation by the Department of Rehabilitative Services (DRS) in a supported employment service program began in 1984 with the approval of VCU as a provider of services for which the VR counselor could give authorization. The actual shared funding arrangement began in 1985 with the approval of DRS of five provider agencies that utilized both time-limited VR funds and long-term support funds provided through individual CSBs. As of the end of 1988, this provider system had expanded to 45 supported employment service agencies with fee-for-service agreements with DRS and commitments for long-term support funding from CSBs. Approximately 15 of these providers are private nonprofit sheltered workshops; approximately 19 are operated by CSBs; and the remainder are specialized nonprofit or publicly operated programs involved in supported employment. In addition to the 45 fee-based agencies, seven agencies are developing supported employment programs through start-up grants and will be entering into fee-for-service agreements with DRS early in 1989.

The impact of this growth in service capacity on the vocational system in Virginia has been significant. From July 1, 1986 through June 30, 1987, 210 state VR clients received time-limited services through the supported employment program; from July 1, 1987 through June 30, 1988, 492 VR clients received these services. Growth in sponsorship of clients in supported employment by the Department of Rehabilitative Services has paralleled participation by the CSB system. As of the end of 1988, approximately 80% of the Boards are actively engaged in funding or directly providing ongoing support services in supported employment. Through state appropriated funds, in the fall of 1988 DRS initiated a program to serve persons with physical disabilities in need of supported employment services who were not eligible for services through the CSB system.

In September, 1985, Virginia received one of the original 10 state change grants awarded by the Federal Office of Special Education and Rehabilitative Services to develop a state system of supported employment over a five-year period. Virginia's state system began in 1978 as a demonstration effort but has since become a truly statewide initiative that is focused on making community integrated employment the predominant nature of day and work services for persons with severe disabilities. The Virginia Supported Employment Information System discussed in this chapter was piloted for one year with 12 start-up grant recipients funded through the state change grant in September, 1986. Effective October 1, 1987, participation in the Information System became mandatory for provider agencies receiving fees from DRS for clients in supported employment service programs. Data submission continues during the provision of ongoing support services after the termination of VR funded time-limited services.

VIRGINIA SUPPORTED EMPLOYMENT INFORMATION SYSTEM

A comprehensive management information system has been developed to monitor the employment outcomes of target employees participating in the Virginia supported employment initiative and to serve as a management and program evaluation tool. First developed as a research data base to evaluate the results of demonstration programs operated by Virginia Commonwealth University (Wehman & Kregel, 1989a, 1989b), the Virginia Supported Employment Information System (VSEIS) has expanded to track the progress of the large number of local community-based employment programs begun between 1985 and 1988 as a result of the state's supported employment initiative.

As noted earlier, the present system represents a cooperative effort of the DRS, the Office of Supported Employment in the Department of Mental Health, Mental Retardation, and Substance Abuse Services (DMHMRSAS), the VCU-RRTC, and 45 local programs vendored by DRS to provide supported employment services. The Department of Rehabilitative Services provides administrative leadership in the design and implementation of the system. Vendor agreements with local service providers require the submission of data to the system as a condition for receiving reimbursement for services. The VCU-RRTC, through a contract with DRS, is responsible for system maintenance, data analysis, and the preparation and dissemination of monthly and quarterly reports. Regional consultants from the Office for Supported Employment serve as liaisons between local providers and the RRTC, training local providers in the use of the system, assisting in the collection of data, and interpreting technical reports for local agencies and employment specialists.

Purposes of the VSEIS

The VSEIS has been designed to achieve several distinct purposes. At the state level, aggregate information is used by DRS and DMHMRSAS to document the scope and effectiveness of supported employment, communicate the results of the supported employment initiative to state agencies and legislators, provide an empirical basis for policy formulation and program management, and detect trends and emerging issues to be addressed as the supported employment initiative evolves over time.

At the local program level, the system allows program administrators to track the growth and progress of their program on a quarter-to-quarter basis and to compare the outcomes of their efforts to state and regional averages. Specialized reports, such as the Monthly Intervention Report, are designed as management tools that allow administrators to monitor specific aspects of programs. The Regional Consultants from the Office of Supported Employment make extensive use of the system when providing feedback to local agencies and designing technical assistance activities.

Because extensive data are continuously collected on each target employee, as opposed to aggregated program data, the VSEIS is also used to evaluate the effect of supported employment participation on individual target employees. The system is sensitive to subtle changes in an individual's employment situation. Each target employee can be monitored on a monthly and quarterly basis to guarantee that the individual receives maximum benefits from the services received from the supported employment program.

Overview of the Data Management Process

The VSEIS consists of over 200 data elements organized into nine data collection forms. The system provides detailed information on target employee demographic and functional characteristics, consumer assessment information, the results of job analyses, comprehensive data on the type of job performed by the employee, the amount and types of services provided by the supported employment program, supervisors' evaluations of target employees' work performance, and complete information regarding employment retention and reasons for job separation. Some data elements are collected one time only, others are collected on regular three- or six-month intervals, and still others are collected on a daily basis.

Regional consultants train local employment specialists in the use of the system. Individual employment specialists are responsible for the completion of all data forms for each employee in their caseload. The data collection forms have been designed to serve as clinical tools for the employment specialists. For example, consumer assessment, job analysis, supervisor evaluation, and other forms are designed to assist directly in the job placement, training, and follow-along process.

Data forms are submitted on a prescribed schedule to the RRTC. The schedule for data completion is based on a consumer's date of placement rather than on a specific calendar month, enabling data collection to be dispersed over a longer period of time rather than at the end of each fiscal quarter. Instead of forcing employment specialists to collect and sort large amounts of data several times a year, data collection becomes a component of the employment specialists' daily routine.

Once data are received by the RRTC, a data management specialist reviews each form for completeness, accuracy, and consistency with previously submitted data. The data management specialist contacts local programs to clarify and obtain missing data, then codes each form for data entry and analysis.

Summary reports are returned to state agencies and local programs on a quarterly and monthly basis. All VSEIS participants receive aggregated statewide reports that contain both numerical tables and graphic depictions of data. Regional consultants receive both statewide and regional aggregate reports to allow the comparison of local programs within their specific region. Each of the 45 local providers receives a quarterly report that details the outcomes of his own agency. All quarterly reports contain complete information on the immediate quarter as well as cumulative information to allow all participants to monitor the results and growth of an individual program over time.

Each individual program also receives a quarterly report summarizing the key employment outcomes for every target employee currently receiving services. This report lists type of job, wages earned, hours worked per week, changes in employment or benefit status, hours of service provided, and other key variables for each target employee. Another feature of the reporting system is the monthly intervention report. Every provider receives a monthly report on each employment specialist and target employee. The report details the type of intervention provided, the amount (number of hours) of intervention delivered to each employee by the employment specialists, and the days on which intervention was provided. The report is intended to be a management tool for program administrators, to enable them to review the activities of employment specialists and monitor the scope and quality of services provided to individual target employees.

IMPACT OF SUPPORTED EMPLOYMENT

This section first overviews previous research on the impact of supported employment on target workers, employers, and service providers. Second, information is presented that summarizes the current status of supported employment in the state. Third, ongoing efforts to investigate major implementation issues such as employment retention, reasons for separation, and the amount and type of services provided by employment specialists are discussed.

Previous Research on Supported Employment in Virginia

The VCU-RRTC has engaged in an ongoing research effort to document the monetary and non-monetary outcomes associated with participation in supported employment. In addition to the general outcome studies of all supported employment participants cited above, specialized analyses have been completed that focused on the impact of supported employment on specific groups of individuals, such as persons with severe mental retardation (Wehman, Hill, Wood, & Parent, 1987), transition-aged individuals (Wehman, Parent, Wood, Michaud, Ford, Miller, Marchant, & Walker, in press), and persons with traumatic brain injury (Wehman, Kreutzer, Stonnington, Wood, Sherron, Diambra, Fry, & Groah, 1988).

Numerous other studies have examined more specific issues central to the success of supported employment programs. The relative success of individuals with moderate and severe mental retardation, as opposed to those with mild mental retardation, was investigated through a study of demographic and functional characteristics that correlated with long-term employment retention (Hill, Hill, Wehman, Banks, Pendleton, & Britt, 1985). The satisfaction of employers has been studied through an employer attitude survey (Shafer, Hill, Seyfarth, & Wehman, 1987) and an analysis of supervisors' evaluations of the work performance of target employees (Shafer, Kregel, Banks, & Hill, 1988). Other research has included an investigation of the effects of supported employment on target employees' quality of life (Inge, Banks, Wehman, Hill, & Shafer, 1988) and an examination of the attitudes of target employees' co-workers (Shafer, Rice, Metzler, & Haring, 1989). Finally, a series of investigations has examined the economic benefits and costs of supported employment from the perspectives of the target employees, taxpayers, and society at large (Hill, Banks, Handrich, Wehman, Hill & Shafer, 1987; Hill, Wehman, Kregel, Banks, & Metzler, 1987; Wehman, Kregel, Banks, Hill, & Moon, 1987).

Current Status of Supported Employment

Between 1978 and 1988, Virginia's supported employment program grew from a single university-based demonstration program to a statewide system serving 944 individuals. Early placement efforts focused on individuals with mental retardation. As of September 30, 1988, target employees with mental retardation accounted for 83.1 percent of all persons participating in supported employment. Over 40 percent of all individuals were reported to have a secondary disability, such as cerebral palsy, convulsive disorders, or hearing, language, or visual impairments. The primary disability of all individuals placed into supported employment is delineated in Table 2.1.

Although the overwhelming number of target employees participating in supported employment are individuals with mental retardation, there has been a definite trend since 1987 toward placing individuals with other primary disabilities. In 1988, for example, approximately 20 percent of all new placements involved individuals with long-term mental illness, and approximately 10 percent involved individuals with traumatic brain injury. In view of recent policy statements and financial appropriations by various state agencies, it is likely that, in the future, Virginia's supported employment initia-

Table 2.1 Primary Disability of Target Employees ($N = 944$)

Primary Disability	Percentage of All Target Employees
Mental retardation	83.1
Long-term mental illness	8.8
Traumatic brain injury	2.3
Other physical disabilities	1.5
Learning disability	0.8
Other neurological disabilities	0.7
Cerebral palsy	0.6
Hearing impairment	0.5
Visual impairment	0.5
Autism	0.4
Convulsive disorder	0.3
Other	0.3

tive will serve individuals with a variety of disabilities.

Another trend that emerged in 1987 and 1988 was the increasing number of individuals with mild mental retardation who have been placed into competitive employment. As indicated in Table 2.2, in 1988 individuals with *mild* mental retardation accounted for 43 percent of all persons with mental retardation, while persons with *moderate* mental retardation represented 38.2 percent of the persons served. In contrast, 1987 data (Wehman & Kregel, 1989a and 1989b) indicated that 51 percent of all persons served were individuals with moderate mental retardation, whereas only 33 percent of all individuals were diagnosed as individuals with mild mental retardation. The data in Table 2.2 represent all individuals in the VSEIS with mental retardation as an identified primary or secondary disability.

Table 2.2 Diagnosed Functioning Level of Employees Labeled Mentally Retarded

Functioning Level	Percentage
Borderline	8.6
Mild	43.0
Moderate	38.2
Severe	9.6
Profound	0.6

Table 2.3 Percentage of Target Employees Working in Major Employment Models

Type of Employment Program	Percentage of Target Employees
Individual placement	83.9
Enclave	8.3
Work crew	6.6
Entrepreneurial	1.2

Type of Employment Program. Since the inception of supported employment in 1978, providers in Virginia have been philosophically committed to the use of the individual placement, or supported work model of competitive employment (Wehman & Kregel, 1985). The prevailing belief is that the individual placement model: (a) allows the target employee maximum choice in selecting a job that meets his or her individual preference; (b) offers the greatest opportunity for target employees to be optimally integrated in the workplace; and (c) allows the individual to earn competitive wages. Although in recent years there has been a trend toward developing group employment options (e.g., enclaves, work crews) to accommodate individuals unable to succeed in an individual placement, the individual placement approach remains the dominant model in use in the state. In 1988, 83.9 percent of all target employees were served in the individual placement model. Table 2.3 describes the percentage of all target employees working in each of the major supported employment models in the state.

Wages Earned And Hours Worked Per Week. The average hourly wage for all positions held by target employees in Virginia from 1978 to 1988 was $3.64 per hour, a figure that has remained remarkably consistent over time. For example, Wehman and Kregel (1989a and 1989b), relying on 1986 data, reported an average hourly wage of $3.56 per hour. It should be noted that some individual placements were made before 1981, when the minimum wage was less than the current level of $3.35 per hour, a factor that somewhat deflates the overall average.

The mean and range of hourly wages for all

Table 2.4 Hourly Wages for Target Employees in Various Employment Models

Employment Program	Average Hourly Wage	Range
Individual placement	$3.79	$2.65–$13.80
Enclave	$2.64	$0.77– $5.00
Work crew	$2.63	$0.58– $4.91
Entrepreneurial	$1.57	$0.50– $3.35

employment models is listed in Table 2.4. Wages range from an average of $1.57 per individual in the entrepreneurial model to $3.79 in the individual placement model. Wages vary considerably within specific models. For example, wages range from less than $1.00 per hour to $5.00 per hour in the enclave model. This variability indicates that sophisticated job development in group employment options can allow some target employees to earn significant wages.

The cumulative wages earned by all target employees since the initiation of supported employment in 1978 is $6,339,090. Presently, the total earned by all individuals working each quarter averages about $750,000.

Target employees work an average of twenty-eight hours per week. Approximately half of all individuals (49 percent) work thirty to forty hours per week, with 42 percent working twenty to thirty hours per week. A small number of individuals (8.3 percent) work less than ten hours per week. This figure should be viewed cautiously, because some individuals held two or more jobs simultaneously that totaled more than twenty hours per week in combination. Table 2.5 provides a categorical breakdown of the hours worked per week across all employment models.

LEVEL OF INTEGRATION. An important concern for Virginia supported employment providers is the level of vocational and social integration in the workplace experienced by target employees. In addition to the opportunity to earn significant wages, integration is the primary motivating principle underlying the supported employment movement (Wehman & Moon, 1986). The VSEIS requires employment specialists to gauge the level of integration in the workplace for each target employee on a five-point scale that ranges from complete segregation to frequent work related interaction. Table 2.6 summarizes the percentage of all target employees at each level of integration.

The data in Table 2.6 suggest that the overwhelming majority of target employees are experiencing a significant amount of integration through their participation in the supported employment program. A moderate or frequent level of work-related interaction is reported for 84 percent of all individuals. Although these results are quite encouraging, relatively little is known about the *quality* of this integration. In-depth investigations are currently underway to examine more specifically the nature and quality of integration experienced by target employees in various supported employment models.

FRINGE BENEFITS RECEIVED BY TARGET EMPLOYEES. An important consideration in the identification of appropriate jobs for persons with severe disabilities is the availability of fringe benefits. Health insurance, paid vacations, sick leave, and other fringe benefits not only have the effect of enhancing the quality or value of a position, but also provide a significant economic benefit, particularly to individuals who experience a decrease in disability benefits because of their participation in supported employment. All fringe benefits received by target employees are summarized in Table 2.7.

As is evident from Table 2.7, between one-third and one-half of all individuals receive the key fringe benefits of sick leave, paid vacations, and medical insurance. No fringe benefits were reported for 30.1 percent of all positions. The percentage of positions not providing any fringe benefits has decreased dramatically over time. As recently as 1987, nearly half of all positions reported no fringe benefits. This trend can be directly attributed to the job development skills of employment specialists in the state. Although entry level service occupations—the primary types of positions held by target employees—frequently do not provide fringe benefits, employment specialists have been dedicated to identifying the best possible job for each target employee.

Table 2.5 Hours Worked Per Week by Target Employees in Various Supported Employment Models (*N* = 678)

Hours Per Week	Individual (*N* = 515)	Enclave (*N* = 84)	Work Crew (*N* = 67)	Entrepreneurial (*N* = 12)
Less than 20	9.3	2.4	8.9	0.0
20–30	40.4	39.3	50.8	83.3
30–40	49.7	58.3	40.3	0.0
More than 40	0.6	0.0	0.0	16.7

Note: Percentages contained in each column represent the percentage of individuals working in that *particular* employment model. Data represent all positions held by target employees who worked at any time during FY 88.

MAJOR IMPLEMENTATION ISSUES

An emerging issue of considerable significance to the Virginia supported employment initiative is that of employment retention. The ability of target employees to retain employment for an extended period of time has tremendous implications for employees, their families, and program managers. For individuals who have little or no previous experience in community-based employment settings, employment retention may be conceptualized in a number of different ways. Table 2.8 illustrates one approach to analyzing the degree to which target employees retain their jobs.

Table 2.8 describes the employment status of all employees in the VSEIS at several points in time after their initial placement. The number of individuals represented at each time period (e.g., three months, six months) declines over time because many individuals have only recently been placed into employment and have not yet had the opportunity to work the entire twenty-four month period represented in the table. Three categories of employment retention are identified for each of the time periods: the percentage of individuals remaining employed in their original jobs, the percentage of individuals no longer employed in their original jobs but employed in subsequent jobs, and the percentage of individuals no longer employed in any supported employment option.

Several trends are readily apparent from an examination of the data in Table 2.8. First, the number of individuals who remain employed in their initial jobs declines significantly over time. While approximately two-thirds (66.3 percent) of all target employees remain in their initial jobs at six months after placement, this percentage decreases to approximately one-half (50.4 percent) after twelve months and one-third (33.2 percent) after twenty-four months.

Second, the fact that a target employee is no longer employed in his or her original position does not mean that the individual has failed in a supported employment position and is no longer working at all. Many individuals obtain a different job or succeed in an alternative supported employment model. As the table indicates, from twelve months to twenty-four months after initial placement, between 15 and 20 percent of all individuals are employed in subsequent employment situations. Placement into supported employment appears to indicate a relatively fluid situa-

Table 2.6 Level of Integration with Nonhandicapped Co-workers in the Workplace

Level of Integration	Percentage of Total Placements
Frequent work-related interaction	42.9
Moderate level of work-related interaction	41.1
No work-related interaction	9.9
General physical separation	4.8
Complete segregation	1.4

Table 2.7 Fringe Benefits Received by Target Employees

Fringe Benefits	Percentage of Total Positions
Sick leave	33.9
Paid vacation	45.1
Medical insurance	33.6
Dental insurance	7.9
Employee discount	16.3
Free/reduced meals	30.1
Other benefits	13.7
No fringe benefits	32.7

Table 2.8 Employment Status of Target Employees at 3 to 24 Months after Initial Placement (%)

	3 Months (*N* = 842)	6 Months (*N* = 727)	9 Months (*N* = 642)	12 Months (*N* = 562)	18 Months (*N* = 398)	24 Months (*N* = 293)
Still employed in first job	78.6	66.3	57.0	50.4	37.8	33.2
Employed in subsequent job(s)	4.7	8.0	11.0	16.3	19.6	18.3
No longer employed	16.7	25.7	32.0	33.3	42.8	48.5

Note: The declining *N*s over time reflect the fact that a large number of individuals have been placed into employment quite recently and have therefore not yet had the opportunity to work an entire 24 months.

tion in which target employees frequently change jobs. These job changes may represent individuals who were unsuccessful in their original placement and were subsequently placed in a different job, individuals who resigned their positions to obtain a better employment situation, or individuals who moved from one type of supported employment alternative to another.

Third, it is apparent that a year or two after initial placement a sizeable number of target employees are no longer employed in any supported employment alternative. This information can be interpreted in two different ways. From one perspective, the fact that 74.3 percent of target employees are employed six months after placement and 66.7 percent are employed after one year is admirable, given that the vast majority of the target employees have had no community-based employment experience before their placement in supported employment. At the same time, however, the fact that 48.5 percent are no longer employed twenty-four months after placement clearly indicates that a large number of individuals placed into supported employment will not remain employed indefinitely.

Virginia has demonstrated unequivocally that a large number of individuals with no previous work experience can successfully enter competitive employment. However, it is also clear that not all individuals are able to maintain employment indefinitely. Program managers as well as target employees and their families are responding to the fact that a sizeable number of target employees will not be employed in any supported employment alternative at some time after placement. Employment specialists throughout the state are working diligently to provide the type and amount of ongoing support services required to maximize each target employee's job retention. Program managers recognize the need to develop policies and options to provide alternatives for individuals unable to succeed in supported employment. These options may include the development of additional supported employment alternatives within a given program to provide a needed service for individuals unsuccessful in presently available alternatives, or procedures to ensure that a target employee who loses his or her job will not be forced to wait an extensive amount of time before again receiving services.

Target employees and their families are also weighing this information carefully when deciding whether or not to participate in supported employment programs operated by the local agency in their community. Employment specialists must openly and accurately explain the alternatives available should the individual be unsuccessful in supported employment. Target employees and their families are also becoming aware of the potential consequences of unsuccessful supported employment placements. In some communities in the state, for example, individuals who remain employed for over sixty days, then lose their jobs, are returned to a waiting list for services. These individuals may face a wait of a year or more before they are again eligible for services. Individuals and their families are considering this situation, as well as other potential risks and benefits of supported employment placement, when making the decision to participate in supported employment.

Separation from Employment

Target employees working in supported employment situations may be separated from their jobs for any of a number of reasons. Resignations, layoffs, terminations, or leaves of absence for medical or other reasons account for all separations of individuals represented in the VSEIS. The relative percentage of these types of separations are delineated in Table 2.9.

The most frequently occurring type of separation from employment results from employee resignation (43.3 percent). Target employees may resign because they simply no longer wish to work in a particular job. Frequently, resignations occur because the individual has located a better job. In a few instances, the resignation is initiated by the individual's parents or guardians. Finally, a resignation may be the result of a mutual agreement among the target employee, the employment specialist, and the employer indicating that the current placement may not be appropriate or feasible for the individual.

The second most frequently cited type of separation is termination from employment initiated by the employer (38.0 percent). Previous research on supported employment programs in Virginia (Hill, Wehman, Hill, & Goodall, 1986) has indicated that individuals with mild mental retardation are significantly more likely to be terminated from employment than individuals with moderate or severe mental retardation. Individuals with moderate or severe mental retardation are more likely to be forced to resign from supported employment positions due to factors outside their control, such as transportation problems or resignations initiated by their parents or guardians.

A significant number of individuals (16.8 percent) were separated from employment because of layoffs. This has significant implications for the job development activities of employment specialists. While employment specialists in the state make every effort to identify positions for target employees that are not seasonal in nature or susceptible to changes in the economic situation, it appears inevitable that in some instances business closings or workforce cutbacks will leave individuals temporarily unemployed. The effects of layoff on disability benefits and service interruptions must be carefully considered by employment specialists.

Table 2.9 Type of Separation from Employment (*N* = 600)

Type of Separation	Percentage
Resigned	43.3
Terminated	38.0
Laid off	16.8
Leave of absence	1.9

Reasons for Separation

A major issue within the national supported employment movement that has received considerable study concerns the *reasons* for which target employees are separated from employment. Previous analyses of the reasons for separation from employment in Virginia have been provided by Hill, Wehman, Hill, & Goodall (1986) and Wehman, Hill, Goodall, Cleveland, Brooke & Pentecost (1982) and the issue has been extensively studied by other researchers (Brickey, Browning, & Campbell, 1982; Ford, Dineen, & Hall, 1984; Greenspan & Shoultz, 1981; Schalock & Harper, 1978). In the VSEIS, when an individual is separated from employment, the employment specialist is asked to identify the main factor contributing to the separation. A wide variety of different causes of separation are frequently identified, generally consistent with the results of previous studies. Table 2.10 presents a complete list of reasons for separation for all target employees.

The most frequently cited reason for separation is the economic situation (13.8 percent), a factor very likely to contribute to layoffs of target employees. Another major reason as reported by employment specialists is that clients no longer wish to work (11.1 percent). Although this is unfortunate, it must be viewed in the context of a large number of individuals who are entering community-based employment settings for the first time. For individuals with no previous work experience, it should perhaps be anticipated that a small number of individuals will express dissatisfaction when facing the challenges of competitive employment for the first time.

A significant number of individuals (10.3 percent) resigned their positions in order to take better jobs, reinforcing the concept of movement and advancement in competitive employment discussed above. Other reasons for separation frequently cited include a number of factors related to vocational competence—including slow work, low-quality work, the need for continual prompting—and a large number of factors related to social competence and ability to interact with supervisors and co-workers—such as poor social skills, employer discomfort, insubordinate behavior, and aberrant behavior.

It is interesting to note that a number of factors hypothesized to be very important in the long-term job maintenance of target employees are rarely cited as primary reasons for job separation. Parental interference and interference with disability benefits such as SSI and SSDI were both reported less than 1 percent of the time as the reason for separation. Transportation problems were cited in only 2 percent of the cases.

Amount and Type of Intervention Time Provided to Target Employees

The overriding philosophy of the Virginia supported employment initiative is to evaluate its success based on the key employment outcomes achieved by the individuals participating in the program. At the same time, however, program managers and employment specialists are constantly striving to make local community-based employment programs as efficient as possible. To achieve this goal, the Virginia supported employment initiative has completed a series of investigations into the amount and type of services provided to individuals placed into competitive employment.

Table 2.10 Reason for Separation from Employment

Reason for Separation	Percentage
Economic situation	13.8
Does not want to work	11.1
Resigned to take better job	10.3
Poor work attitude	6.5
Poor attendance/tardiness	5.7
Employer uncomfortable with situation	5.2
Slow work	4.8
Poor job match	4.8
Parent/guardian initiated resignation	4.7
Low quality work	4.3
Insubordinate behavior	4.3
Medical/health problem	4.0
Aberrant behavior	3.3
Continual prompting required	3.2
Seasonal layoff	3.0
Transportation problem	2.0
Parental interference	0.8
SSI-SSDI interference	0.2
Other reasons	8.0

The unit of measure for these analyses has been the amount of intervention time provided to specific target employees (Kregel, Hill, & Banks, 1988). Intervention time refers to all activities conducted by an employment specialist that are designed to enable a specific target employee to obtain, learn, perform, or maintain a job. As such, intervention time may be used to gauge the intensity of services provided to a specific individual.

Analyzing the amount and type of intervention provided to target employees is useful for many reasons. Employment specialists may use this information to plan the process of fading their presence from the worksite, analyzing the types of services most frequently required by specific individuals, and managing their own time. Program managers can use intervention time to monitor the activities of their staff, estimate the number of individuals who can be served by their program at any one time, determine the number of job coaches needed to achieve program goals, and project the costs of serving a specified number of consumers.

Previous research has focused on the amount of employment specialist intervention time provided to consumers in demonstration placement programs operated by the VCU-RRTC. In an analysis of fifty-one representative consumers, Kregel et al. (1988) reported that the average number of hours of intervention provided to individuals during their first year of employment was 161. Further, results of the study indicated that individuals with moderate or severe mental retardation did not require a significantly greater amount of intervention time than individuals with mild or borderline mental retardation.

Present analyses of all individuals presented in the VSEIS who have worked a minimum of twelve months indicate that an average of

174.5 hours of intervention time is provided to each individual during his or her first year of employment. As is expected in the individual placement model, the vast majority of intervention time is provided during the initial stages of employment. Approximately one-half of all intervention is provided during the first four weeks of employment, two-thirds during the first twelve weeks of employment, and 90 percent in the first six months of employment. Figure 2.1 illustrates this decline over time.

The figure of 174.5 hours per individual during the first year of employment should be interpreted cautiously. First, it must be recognized that this average resulted from a group of individuals with a mean IQ score of fifty-three who worked an average of twenty-eight hours per week in a state whose economy was generally growing during the time period in question. Programs involving individuals with different characteristics who are working at jobs under significantly different economic conditions may achieve results substantially different from those obtained in Virginia. Second, it is important to note that this figure represents an *average* for all individuals. Considerable variability exists among the target employees represented in the VSEIS, and in fact many target employees who require even several times the number of hours of intervention during the first year are able to maintain employment successfully with minimal intervention for many years thereafter.

In addition to investigating the amount of intervention provided to target employees, an issue of considerable importance in Virginia is the *type* of service provided to the individual. An analysis of the type of activities engaged in by employment specialists will help to define the major duties of these individuals as well as the kinds of services most needed by target employees.

In the VSEIS, employment specialists report all intervention on behalf of specific target employees in eight different categories. Two categories relate to job-site training activities (time active and time inactive) and six categories represent activities that in many instances occur away from the job site (travel/transportation

FIGURE 2.1 Total Intervention Time as a Percentage of Total Hours Worked Per Week Reported by Virginia Providers.

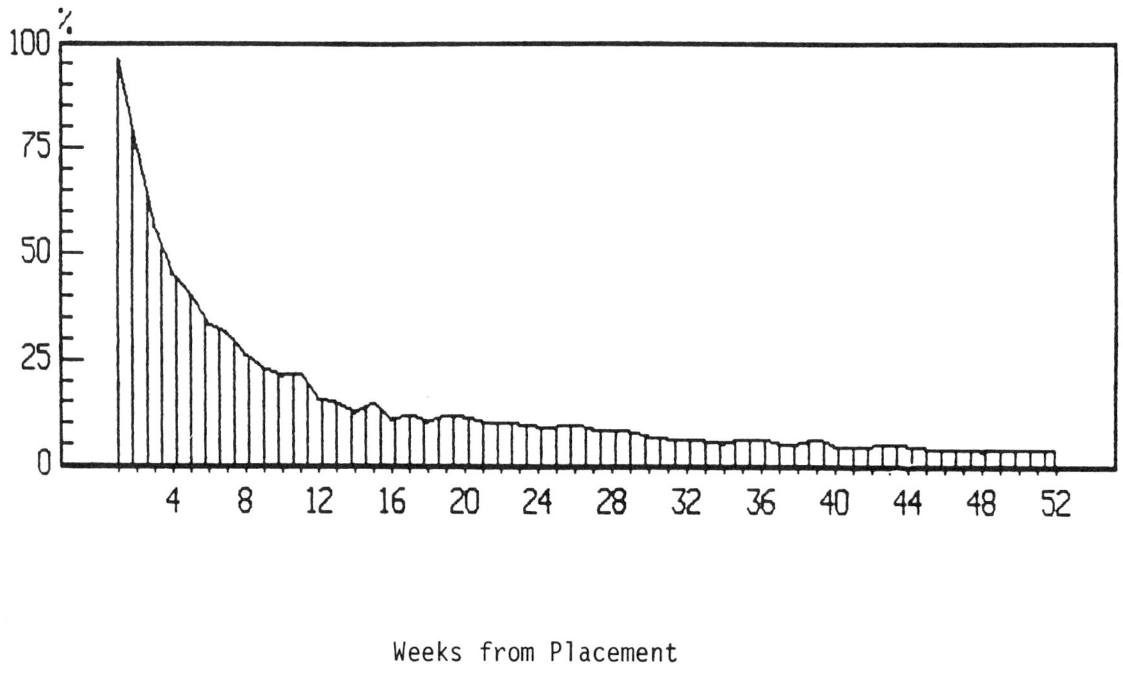

time, consumer training time, consumer program and job development, direct employment advocacy, indirect employment advocacy, and consumer screening/evaluation). Kregel (in press) reported that employment specialists spend 61.5 percent of their time engaged in activities that occur directly at the job site (time active and time inactive). By way of comparison, a very small percentage of time (2.4 percent) was devoted to consumer screening and evaluation, indicating that employment specialists in Virginia emphasize the delivery of intensive services to the target employee after placement in an actual job rather than evaluation and testing activities prior to placement.

Other major activities of employment specialists such as job development, transportation training, and advocating on behalf of the individual with employers, family members, and other agencies, are incorporated into intervention categories such as travel/transportation time, consumer program development, direct employment advocacy, and indirect employment advocacy and account for over one-third of all employment specialist activities. These data emphasize the fact that a large number of the services needed by target employees require the employment specialist to devote a significant amount of time away from the job site. These activities are crucial to the ability of employment specialists to provide the ongoing support services necessary to enable target employees to maintain employment successfully.

CONCLUSION

This chapter provides a data-based profile of the supported employment program development in Virginia. There has been a significant increase in the number of new programs developed, and yet persons with mental retardation have been by far the greatest beneficiaries. Furthermore, only persons with mild and moderate levels of mental retardation have participated to a significant extent. Over 30 percent of the instances in which a person separated from employment occurred because of the economic situation of the company, that the consumer did not want to work, or that the individual resigned to obtain a better job. The individual placement model of supported employment has easily been the most popular model utilized so far. It is anticipated that over the next several years the biggest change in these data will be that persons with a greater diversity of severe disabilities will participate in supported employment.

QUESTIONS (For answers see pp. 427)

1. When did efforts to redirect center based day programs for persons with mental retardation toward supported employment begin?

2. When did fee based participation by the Department of Rehabilitative Services in supported employment begin in Virginia?

3. What is the function of the Virginia Supported Employment Information System: (a) at the state level, and (b) at the local level?

4. Approximately how many data elements are tracked for each supported employment consumer by the Virginia Supported Employment Information System?

5. What disability group is served most frequently by supported employment programs in Virginia?

6. Besides people with mental retardation there has been a growing emphasis on placing people with other types of disabilities into supported employment settings. What types of disabilities are these people reported as having?

7. Other than wages, name two major considerations mentioned by the authors for evaluating supported employment in Virginia.

8. What percentage of individuals who have been placed in supported employment are no longer employed after twenty-four months?

REFERENCES

Brickey, M., Browning, L., & Campbell, K. (1982). Vocational histories of sheltered workshop employees placed in projects with industries and competitive jobs. *Mental Retardation*, *20*(2), 52–57.

Ford, L., Dineen, J., & Hall, J. (1984). Is there life after placement? *Education and Training of the Mentally Retarded, 19*, 291–296.

Greenspan, S. & Shoultz, B. (1981). Why mentally retarded adults lose their jobs: Social competence as a factor in work adjustment. *Applied Research in Mental Retardation, 2*, 23–28.

Hill, J. W., Hill, M., Wehman, P., Banks, P. D., Pendleton, P., & Britt, C. (1985). Demographic analyses related to successful job retention for competitively employed persons who are mentally retarded. In P. Wehman & J. W. Hill (Eds.), *Competitive employment for persons with mental retardation: From research to practice*. (Monograph, *1*). Richmond: Virginia Commonwealth University, Rehabilitation Research and Training Center.

Hill, J., Wehman, P., Hill, M., & Goodall, P. (1986). Differential reasons for job separation of previously employed persons with mental retardation across measured intelligence levels. *Mental Retardation, 40*(11–12), 330–334.

Hill, M., Banks, P. D., Handrich, R. R., Wehman, P. H., Hill, J. W., & Shafer, M. S. (1987). Benefit-cost analysis of supported competitive employment for persons with mental retardation. *Research in Developmental Disabilities, 8*(1), 71–80.

Hill, M., Hill, J., Wehman, P., Revell, G., Dickerson, A., & Noble, J. (1987). Supported employment: An interagency funding model for persons with disabilities. *Journal of Rehabilitation, 13*(4), 18–21.

Hill, M. L., Wehman, P. H., Kregel, J., Banks, P. D., & Metzler, H. M. D. (1987). Employment outcomes for people with moderate and severe disabilities: An eight-year longitudinal analysis of supported competitive employment. *Journal of the Association for Persons with Severe Handicaps, 12*(3), 182–189.

Inge, K. J., Banks, P. D., Wehman, P., Hill, J. W., & Shafer, M. S. (1988). Quality of life for individuals who are labeled mentally retarded: Evaluating competitive employment versus sheltered workshop employment. *Education and Training in Mental Retardation, 23*(2), 97–104.

Kregel, J. (1989). An analysis of the services provided by employment specialists in the individual placement model of supported employment. In P. Wehman & J. Kregel (Eds.), *Supported employment for persons with disabilities: Focus on excellence*. (pp. 115–135.) New York: Human Sciences Press.

Kregel, J., Hill, M., & Banks, P. D. (1988). Analysis of employment specialist intervention time in supported competitive employment. *American Journal on Mental Retardation, 93*(2), 200–208.

Revell, G., Wehman, P., & Arnold, S. (1984). Supported work model of competitive employment for persons with mental retardation: Implications for rehabilitative services. *Journal of Rehabilitation, 50*(4), 33–38.

Schalock, R. & Harper, R. (1978). Placement from community-based mental retardation programs: How well do clients do? *American Journal of Mental Deficiency, 86*, 170–177.

Shafer, M. S., Hill, J. W., Seyfarth, J., & Wehman, P. (1987). Competitive employment and workers with mental retardation: An analysis of employers' perceptions and experiences. *American Journal of Mental Retardation, 92*(3), 304–311.

Shafer, M. S., Kregel, J., Banks, P. D., & Hill, M. (1988). What's the boss think? An analysis of employer evaluations of workers with mental retardation. *Research in Developmental Disabilities, 9*(4), 377–391.

Shafer, M. S., Rice, M. S., Metzler, H. M. D., & Haring, M. (1989). A survey of nondisabled employees' attitudes toward supported employees who are mentally retarded. *Journal of the Association for Persons with Severe Handicaps, 14*(2), 137–146.

Wehman, P. & Hill, J. (Eds.). (1979). *Vocational training and placement of severely disabled persons: Project Employability* (Vol. 1). Richmond: Virginia Commonwealth University.

Wehman, P., Hill, J. W., Wood, W., & Parent, W. (1987). A report on competitive employment histories of persons labeled severely mentally retarded. *Journal of the Association for Persons with Severe Handicaps, 12*(1), 11–17.

Wehman, P. & Hill, M. (Eds.). (1980). *Vocational training and placement of severely disabled persons: Project Employability* (Vol. 2). Richmond: Virginia Commonwealth University.

Wehman, P., Hill, M., Goodall, P., Cleveland, P., Brooke, V., & Pentecost, J. (1982). Job placement and follow-up of moderately and severely handicapped individuals after three years. *Journal of the Association for Persons with Severe Handicaps, 7*, 5–16.

Wehman, P. & Kregel, J. (1985). A supported work approach to competitive employment of individuals with moderate and severe handicaps. *Journal of the Association for Persons with Severe Handicaps, 10*(1), 3-11.

Wehman, P. & Kregel, J. (1989a). Supported competitive employment: A decade later. In P. Wehman & J. Kregel (Eds.), *Supported employment for persons with disabilities: Focus on excellence* (pp. 115–135). New York: Human Sciences Press.

Wehman, P. & Kregel, J. (1989b). *Supported employment for persons with disabilities: Focus on excellence*. New York: Human Sciences Press.

Wehman, P., Kregel, J., Banks, P. D., Hill, M., & Moon, M. S. (1987). Sheltered versus supported work programs: A second look. *Rehabilitation Counseling Bulletin, 31*(1), 42–53.

Wehman, P., Kruetzer, J. S., Stonnington, H. H., Wood, W., Sherron, P., Diambra, J., Fry, R., & Groah, C. (1988). Supported employment for persons with traumatic brain injury: A preliminary report. *Journal of Head Trauma Rehabilitation, 3*(4), 82–94.

Wehman, P. & Moon, S. (1986). Critical values in employment programs for persons with developmental disabilities: A position paper. *Journal of Applied Rehabilitation Counseling, 18*(1), 12–16.

Wehman, P., Parent, W., Wood, W., Michaud, C., Ford, C., Miller, S., Marchant, J., & Walker, R. (in press). From school to competitive employment for young adults with mental retardation: Transition in practice. *Career Development for Exceptional Individuals.*

CHAPTER

3

Supported Employment in Illinois

Warren K. Ellis
Frank R. Rusch
Jho-Ju Tu
Wendy McCaughrin
University of Illinois at Urbana-Champaign

Writing about vocational training and employment of individuals with mental retardation, Marc Gold (1980) stated that the low expectancies held for these people perpetuates our failure to devise new and improved models. Gold felt so strongly about status quo adult services that he identified low expectancy as "the single most critical deterrent to progress in our field" (p. 168). Over the past 10 years we have learned much about providing support to persons with handicaps who are employed in the community. Our current expectations clearly have changed in relation to integrated employment; indeed the results of ongoing service demonstrations will continue to expand our expectations.

The purpose of this chapter is to describe supported employment as it has been implemented in the state of Illinois, providing first a brief history of the Illinois initiative and then a description of the Illinois Supported Employment Project (ISEP). The impact of model program development will be examined. The concluding section describes ongoing research at the University of Illinois, which is associated with the implementation of supported employment.

BRIEF HISTORY OF SUPPORTED EMPLOYMENT IN ILLINOIS

As discussed in Chapter 1, in the late 1960s the contributions of Marc Gold and others marked a dramatic change in vocational expectations for persons with severe disabilities. These researchers demonstrated that people with severe handicaps could learn and perform complex assembly tasks. This body of work led some individuals to begin to question models of vocational service then in existence. The 1970s saw the emergence of several new vocational training programs across the country. Indeed, new horizons were explored by Rusch, Wehman, Bellamy, and others. In 1978 a food service vocational training program began at a student residence hall at the University of Illinois. Funding came from a seed grant provided by the University's College of Education, and was supplemented later when the Illinois Department of Rehabilitation Services (DORS) provided reimbursement for "work adjustment training" in the community. The program replicated the Food Service Vocational Training Program initiated at the University of Washington in 1975 (cf. Rusch & Schutz, 1979). Both programs provided training in a university setting to individuals with mental retardation and utilized a survey, train, place, and follow-up format (Rusch, 1983; Rusch, Chadsey-Rusch, & Lagomarcino, 1986). Training with a staff/employee ratio of 1:4 was available in a variety of jobs, including dishwashing, bussing, and food preparation. Each trainee worked a 35-hour week, earned $3.24 per hour, and received all the benefits of a University employee.

In 1979 a second program, the Professional Housekeeping Program, began at the University of Illinois. This program was similar to the food services programs, except that the focus of the training was community employment of mentally retarded individuals as maids and janitors. As in the food service program, employees worked 35 hours per week and received University employee benefits, but in the professional housekeeping program they earned $3.98 per hour.

In order to support graduates from these two community-based training programs, a follow-up program was started in 1979, funded through Title XX funds. Direct observation of individuals at the job site, frequent communication with employers, and assessment of the results of work performance evaluations formed the basis of the long-term support services.

Upon entering the follow-up program, the individual became eligible for services from a fourth program also started in 1979. The Independent Apartment Training Program provided supervised placement into an apartment within the community, on-site skills training, and case coordination to individuals who were moving into the community because of employment. Before the existence of this program, the only residential alternative in the Champaign–Urbana area was a 60-bed intermediate care facility and an apartment follow-along program that required almost complete participant independence.

A total of 134 persons have participated in the "Community Services" programs begun in 1978 (see Table 3.1). Forty-three percent of those participating in the programs were diagnosed with multiple handicaps. Of the 134 persons who participated in training, 108 (81 percent) completed training and were placed in jobs in the community. The remaining 26 (19 percent) individuals did not complete training for a variety of reasons, including poor attendance, severe behavior problems, lack of interest in obtaining employment, and health problems.

Table 3.1 Job Placement Statistics

Length of time on job	*N*	%
Janitorial/Housekeeping	Placed: 82	
3 Months	75	91
6 Months	54	66
1 Year or more	40	49
Still employed—1986	36	44
Food Service	Placed: 26	
3 Months	20	77
6 Months	18	69
1 Year or more	16	62
Still employed—1986	12	46

Reprinted from Lagomarcino, T. R. (1986). Community Services: Using the supported work model within an adult service agency. In F. R. Rusch (Ed.). *Competitive employment issues and strategies.* Baltimore: Paul H. Brookes

Community Services constituted the first coordinated effort in Illinois to move individuals with mental retardation into the community using the survey, train, place, and follow-up support model. Interestingly, Schneider, Martin, and Rusch (1981) conducted a cost-benefit analysis of these programs which indicated that when they are compared to sheltered program alternatives, the yearly benefits of supported employment would begin to exceed costs after five years. It was projected that cumulative benefits would exceed cumulative costs after the eighth year, and after 10 years a net benefit of over $200,000 would be realized. Although projections indicated increasing benefits to the taxpayer and the supported employee, this information did not result in program expansion or replication in other parts of the state. It was not until 1984, when Susan S. Suter became the director of DORS, that supported employment became a priority in the state of Illinois. In 1984, the supported employment initiative resulted in an investment of $1,400,000 in integrated employment options for persons with severe disabilities.

Supported employment in Illinois formally began in 1985 with funding from the Illinois Department of Rehabilitation Services, the Governor's Planning Council on Developmental Disabilities, and the Department of Mental Health and Developmental Disabilities. (In 1986 Illinois also received a section III–B state change grant from the Office of Special Education and Rehabilitative Services under the 1986 amendments to the Rehabilitation Act.) In 1985, 31 model programs were funded in Illinois; in 1988, an additional 22 programs were funded.

Additionally, the Illinois Supported Employment Project (ISEP) at the University of Illinois was funded by DORS, the Governor's Planning Council, and the Department of Mental Health and Developmental Disabilities to (a) develop and implement an information system to gather and analyze program outcomes, (b) devise and implement a program evaluation model, and (c) provide technical assistance in the areas of model program development.

INFORMATION SYSTEM. The information management system developed by ISEP generates data on program and supported employee outcomes that are used for a variety of purposes. Reports are sent regularly to funding agencies and local programs in order to keep them abreast of activities at both the state and local levels.

In designing the system, ISEP staff members were sensitive to the extra burden that reporting requests place on community programs. At the same time they ensured that they collected the data necessary to track the impact and activities of the program across the state. Information is taken from four different sources for entry into the system. First, a *Worker Characteristics* form is completed for each individual who enters a supported employment program; the form requests demographic and assessment information as well as information about living arrangements, previous placements, the type of current placement, method of transportation, and an employment history.

Programs provide monthly updates on each individual using two separate forms. The first is the *Job Coach/Co-worker Involvement* form, which requests a breakdown of the hours spent in providing supportive services by the employment specialists, and the types of involvement co-workers have with the target employee. The second form is the *Benefit-Cost Analysis* form, requesting information on the status of the supported employee, the financial outcomes of employment, and additional programs or services the individual received.

When a change in employment occurs, a *Job Separation* form is completed. This form provides information on the type of employment from which the individual was terminated, the reason(s) for separation, the length of time the individual was employed before separation, the average hours per week of on-site assistance by the job coach during the month before separation, and a description of the individual's activities since job separation.

It is possible to have more than 103 data points for an individual during a month. The immensity of the task is apparent when it is remembered that in 1988, 700 individuals were enrolled in supported employment programs in Illinois.

PROGRAM EVALUATION. A primary focus of ISEP has been to evaluate the degree to which model programs have implemented supported employment-related services. The supported employment Degree of Implementation (DOI) instrument was developed through a review of model program services reported by Lagomarcino (1986), Wehman (1986), and Vogelsberg (1986). The DOI contains 26 items which are grouped into five components: (a) community survey and analysis, (b) job match, (c) job placement, (d) job maintenance, and (e) related job services/interagency coordination.

COMMUNITY SURVEY AND JOB ANALYSIS. Community survey and job analysis activities include surveying the community for potential job placement sites through telephone calls, mail correspondence, and personal contact. This component also involves identifying the vocational skills and social-interpersonal behavior requisites for a particular job. *Job match* services include assessing supported employee characteristics in relation to job requisites and documenting the use of psychometrically valid assessment instruments and ecological inventories in making accurate judgments resulting in a successful job match. *Job placement*, illustrated in Table 3.2, refers to the training of supported employees

Table 3.2 Job Placement

Evaluates target employees' performance to determine training needs.
Utilizes behavior management strategies.
Restructures job to adapt to target employees' skills.
Develops plan to maintain acceptable level of performance.
Develops plan for support services during Job Maintenance phase.
Obtains feedback from employer/supervisor through work performance evaluations.

Taken from Trach, J., Rusch, F., & DeStefano, L. (1987). Supported employment program development: Degree of implementation manual. In J. Trach & F. Rusch (Eds.). *Supported employment in Illinois: Program implementation and evaluation* (Vol. 1). Secondary Transition Intervention Effectiveness Institute, University of Illinois at Urbana-Champaign.

to perform a particular job. Training procedures typically require behavior management strategies and modifications to adapt the job to the supported employee's abilities. In addition, plans are made to maintain the performance acquired through training after the training period has ended. The placement period includes the first six months after actual job placement and before the *job maintenance* phase begins.

The final component, *related job services/interagency coordination*, is concerned with enhancing the quality of the employee's life through multiple agency cooperation and by ensuring that the supported employee keeps his or her position in society. Related job services consist of the actual programs, individuals, and subcomponents of participating agencies that provide the direct services needed to secure, train, and maintain a job placement. Interagency coordination convenes those agencies that, although functioning independently of each other, provide necessary services for a particular individual which may affect job placement and retention.

ISEP staff score the DOI during site visits, based on documentation provided by program staff and direct observation. The three-part scoring system requires the classification of an activity as nonexistent (score = 0), emergent (score = 1), or present (score = 2). For example, if a program had documented the development of individual plans to maintain acceptable levels of performance for at least 50 percent of the individuals placed at employment sites, that activity would be scored as 1, or emergent. The DOI is discussed in more detail in Chapter 5.

TECHNICAL ASSISTANCE. In order to meet technical assistance objectives, ISEP has developed a program that provides information pertaining to individual program needs. A contractual agreement with all of the model programs, identifying specific areas in which they request assistance, is documented and an ongoing general educational program is provided through a series of statewide conferences throughout the year. Conference topics, which are selected on the basis of participant feedback, have included generalization training, promoting autonomy at the work site, developing an effective follow-up program, and obtaining extended funding for supported employment. Data-based presentations have focused on such topics as the costs versus benefits of supported employment at individual program and state levels, the DOI and its use for both program development and evaluation, descriptions of the population being served in the state, and analysis of job termination factors.

IMPACT OF THE SUPPORTED EMPLOYMENT PROGRAM IN ILLINOIS

Employee characteristics

Between July 1, 1987 and June 30, 1988, 700 employees were provided with supported employment services. Table 3.3 indicates that 66 percent (n = 465) of the workers in Illinois were diagnosed with mental retardation, 62 percent of these with mild mental retardation, and 38 percent with moderate, severe, or profound mental retardation. There are 442 males and 256 females; the average age is 32 years. The group includes 557 whites, 98 blacks, 7 Asians, 24 Hispanics, and 1 American Indian.

Outcomes

Table 3.4 shows the placement models used throughout the state and indicates that 47 percent (n = 331) of all participants were in clustered placements, followed by 46 percent (n = 322) in individual placements, and 8 per-

Table 3.3 Demographic Characteristics—1988

Disability Categories	*N*		*N*
Learning disability	27	Trauamtic brain injury	9
Mild MR (IQ range 55–75)	288	Physical disability	24
Moderate MR (IQ range 40–54)	134	Health impairment	11
Severe MR (IQ range 25–39)	33	Substance abuse	1
Profound MR (IQ range 0–24)	10	Autism	14
Mental illness	97	Not reported	40
Sensory impairments	12	Total	700
Sex	***N***	**Race/Ethnicity**	***N***
Male	442	White	557
Female	256	Black	98
Not reported	2	Hispanic	24
Total	700	Asian	7
		American Indian	1
		Not reported	13
		Total	700

cent (n = 47) in mobile work crews. Additionally Table 3.4 shows that 85 percent of the placements came from sheltered programs offering a variety of services.

Table 3.4 also reflects outcomes by placement model, providing information on hourly wages, annual income, annual tax withheld, monthly work hours, and months employed. Employees in individual placements worked the most hours, had the highest incomes, and had the most taxes withheld, followed by clustered placements and mobile work crews. The average employee in a supported employment program in Illinois has been employed 6.1 months, works 80.83 hours per month at a wage of $3.02 per hour, earns $1,692.01 annually, and has $233.87 deducted in FICA and withholding taxes. The contribution of supported employees to the Illinois economy should not be ignored; the combined annual incomes of individuals working in these programs is approximately $1,040,586, with approximately $143,295 withheld in taxes. It is not known how many of these individuals have all or part of their withholding taxes refunded to them.

Table 3.5 shows average hours worked, gross hourly wages, and monthly income by category of disability and type of placement for the time period between April and June, 1988. As indicated earlier, the majority of individuals in supported employment programs have been diagnosed with mental retardation. Persons diagnosed with mild mental retardation worked an average of 87.4 hours per month, at a wage of $2.89 per hour, with a monthly gross income of $252.59. Individuals with moderate mental retardation averaged 74 hours per month, earning $2.64 per hour and $195.35 per month. Employees in the severe and profound category worked an average of 76 hours per month, at $1.73 per hour and $131.48 per month.

During 1988, workers were employed in a variety of occupations. Table 3.6 breaks down job categories by the different placement models and is illustrated in Figure 3.1 (p. 39). The nine different types of positions (light industry, laundry, warehouse, janitorial/maintenance, retail, grounds maintenance, food service, clerical, and health care) contain 19 different jobs. Janitorial/maintenance occupations employ the most individuals (n = 175) working primarily in clustered placements (n = 76). Light industry occupations employ the second largest number of individuals (n = 148), mostly as assembly-line workers in clustered placements (n = 100). These two job categories account for 46 percent of all

Table 3.4 Employee Characteristics by Model of Service Delivery

Employee Characteristics	Individual Placement	Clustered Placement	Mobile Crew	TOTAL
Average Age	31.2 (n = 322)	32 (n = 331)	35 (n = 47)	32 (n = 700)
Average FSIQ	62.6 (n = 209)	59.4 (n = 307)	66.5 (n = 42)	61.6 (n = 558)
Previous Placement Models				
Developmental training I	0	0	2	2
Developmental training II	30	73	13	116
Regular work*	107	98	15	220
Work adjustment training	28	33	9	70
Skill training	14	13	1	28
Vocational development	2	12	0	14
Evaluation	8	2	2	12
School	23	37	0	60
Community	40	4	0	44
Not reported				134
TOTAL				700
Outcome by Placement				
Average Hourly Wage	$3.51 ($n$ = 281)	$2.63 ($n$ = 311)	$2.69 ($n$ = 47)	$3.02 ($n$ = 639)
Average Hours Worked/Month	87.42 (n = 273)	77.39 (n = 311)	65.29 (n = 47)	80.83 (n = 631)
Average Months Employed	5.2 (n = 322)	6.7 (n = 331)	7.5 (n = 47)	6.1 (n = 700)
Average Annual Income	$1,912.12 ($n$ = 258)	$1,554.12 ($n$ = 310)	$1,393.17 ($n$ = 47)	$1,692.01 ($n$ = 615)
Average Annual Tax Withheld	$263.81 ($n$ = 258)	$212.73 ($n$ = 310)	$178.73 ($n$ = 47)	$233.87 ($n$ = 615)

*Regular work refers to sheltered employment in Illinois.

jobs in supported employment in Illinois. The next largest job category is food service occupations (n=97), accounting for 32 percent of the job categories.

An important part of an employment package is the fringe benefits an individual receives. As shown in Figure 3.2 (p. 39), 248 (35 percent) of the individuals who worked in supported employment projects in 1988 received some form of paid fringe benefit. The majority received paid vacations (65 percent), followed by paid sick leave (25 percent), and medical insurance (10 percent). Although many of the occupations typically identified with supported employment do not commonly include fringe benefits, it is not known at this point why some individuals receive paid benefits and others do not.

While the impact on the employment outcomes of supported employees is clear, a number of other issues associated with supported employment are not. Implementation issues such as reasons for job separation, effective instructional technology, cost-benefit analysis of supported employment, and program evaluation/development form the basis of ongoing research efforts at the University of Illinois at Urbana-Champaign. Cost-benefit analysis and program

Table 3.5 Average Hours Worked, Hourly Wages, and Gross Monthly Wages by Disability and Placement (April - June 1988)

Disability Category	Across All Placements		Individual Placements		Clustered Placements		Mobile Work Crew	
Average Hours Worked Per Month	***N***	**Hours**	***N***	**Hours**	***N***	**Hours**	***N***	**Hours**
Learning disability	17	93.9	9	114.2	7	79.5	1	13.8
Mental retardation								
Mild	207	87.4	70	86.2	119	89.9	18	76.0
Moderate	111	73.5	39	76.7	69	74.0	3	22.5
Severe	28	82.7	8	92.9	18	84.7	2	24.4
Profound	5	40.4	0	0	5	40.4	0	0
Mental illness	56	84.2	30	88.9	23	82.6	3	40.2
Sensory impairments	10	99.5	8	107.3	2	68.1	0	0
Traumatic brain injury	5	88.3	2	73.5	2	88.8	1	117.0
Physical disability	15	113.0	7	122.7	6	98.3	1	139.0
Health impaired	11	100.3	6	96.0	4	128.3	1	14.0
Substance abuse	1	134.7	1	134.7	0	0	0	0
Average Hourly Wages	***N***	$	***N***	$	***N***	$	***N***	$
Learning disability	17	3.03	9	2.92	7	3.35	1	1.86
Mental retardation								
Mild	209	2.89	71	3.21	120	2.73	18	2.70
Moderate	112	2.64	39	2.91	70	2.49	3	2.69
Severe	28	1.83	8	2.47	18	1.47	2	2.51
Profound	5	1.14	0	0	5	1.41	0	0
Mental illness	60	4.18	34	4.79	23	3.42	3	3.03
Sensory impairments	10	3.93	8	4.44	2	1.90	0	0
Traumatic brain injury	5	2.78	2	3.68	2	2.15	1	2.24
Physical disability	14	3.93	7	4.77	6	3.08	1	3.21
Health impaired	11	3.50	6	4.20	4	2.62	1	2.84
Substance abuse	1	4.50	1	4.50	0	0	0	0
Gross Monthly Income	***N***	$	***N***	$	***N***	$	***N***	$
Learning disability	17	301.50	9	343.79	7	286.58	1	25.73
Mental retardation								
Mild	205	254.70	69	253.97	118	257.09	18	213.68
Moderate	112	200.60	39	239.17	70	183.71	3	93.28
Severe	28	143.91	8	218.64	18	121.54	2	46.38
Profound	5	51.95	0	0	5	51.95	0	0
Mental illness	54	393.42	28	497.34	23	302.66	3	119.26
Sensory impairments	10	430.60	8	501.17	2	148.30	0	0
Traumatic brain injury	5	232.31	2	262.87	2	186.86	1	262.08
Physical disability	15	473.52	8	603.53	6	308.58	1	423.05
Health impaired	11	330.36	6	412.23	4	280.23	1	39.70
Substance abuse	1	756.00	1	756.00	0	0	0	0

evaluation/development are discussed in separate chapters in this text and will not be addressed here.

IMPLEMENTATION ISSUES

Kregel, Wehman, Revell, and Hill (in press) state that almost half of the individuals in supported employment in Virginia are not employed after two years. Lagomarcino and Rusch (1989) have found that approximately 30 percent of the employees working in Illinois supported employment programs since November 1985 have been separated from at least one job. These reports raise concern, given that a defining component of "supported" is the provision of follow-along services to assure success.

Table 3.6 Job Categories by Placement Models

	All Placements	Individual Placements	Clustered Placements	Mobile Work Crew
1. Janitorial/maintenance	175	77	76	22
2. Light industry	146	42	100	4
3. Food service	97	45	52	0
4. Grounds maintenance	65	31	19	15
5. Not reported	60	39	17	4
6. Clerical	59	46	13	0
7. Retail	37	18	19	0
8. Warehouse	27	5	22	0
9. Laundry	20	9	11	0
10. Health care	12	8	2	2

The major cause of job separation for the group Lagomarcino studied, as illustrated in Figure 3.3, are economic factors, which account for 33 percent of all separations. This conclusion must be viewed with caution, however, because two agencies accounted for many of these separations. Socially related reasons accounted for 23 percent of the separations, followed by other reasons (22 percent), job performance (12 percent), and individuals leaving for better jobs or no longer needing support (12 percent). The majority of the separations in the "other" category were due to individuals moving out of the area.

It is significant that social reasons were almost twice as often cited for job separation as job performance problems. Lagomarcino concluded that, without the opportunity to interact with a variety of individuals in community settings, supported employees will not learn the social skills they need. While this has implications during the time the employee is still in school, it is also important for those who have already left school and are not in community-based programming. Additionally, it must be noted that when combined, performance and social problems were the major cause of job separation (excluding economic factors as noted above). Both of these causes are directly affected by instructional technologies, which include behavior self-management, co-worker involvement, and factors associated with job coaches.

Instructional Technology

Instructional technology is an area that has been investigated in Illinois in an effort to reduce the number of negative job separations. Self-management techniques teach the target employee how to gain more control over his or her job and how to deal with co-workers. Instructional technology may become a powerful resource because of the importance of co-workers' presence in the work environment. The possibility that supported and non-supported employees may be performing the same or similar tasks has been the focus of an emerging instructional technology.

Self-management

Self-management seeks to develop autonomy in the employee in order to reduce the level of supervision required to maintain acceptable job performance. This is significant not only in the context of individual independence, but also because it has been found that the majority of intervention strategies currently used to provide ongoing support on the job foster dependence on the employment specialist rather than on the natural cues in the work environment for maintaining behavior (Mithaug, Martin, Agran, & Rusch, 1988).

Agran and Martin (1987) identified four self-management techniques that have proven to

FIGURE 3.1 Job Categories—1988 (N = 700)

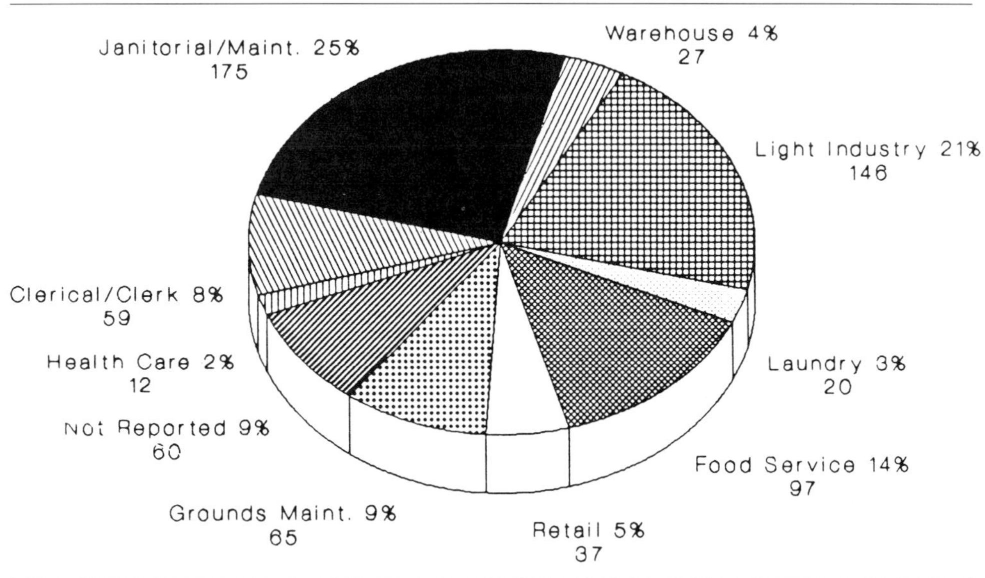

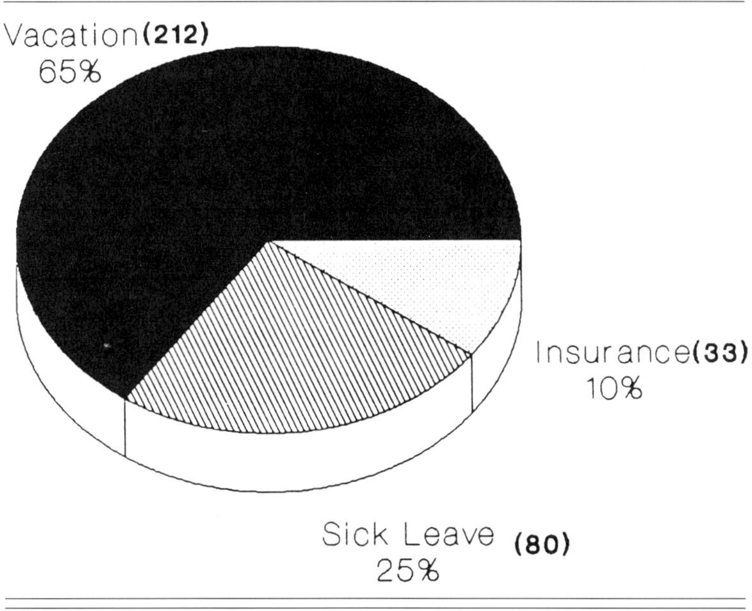

FIGURE 3.2 Fringe Benefits—1988 (N = 248)

FIGURE 3.3 **Primary Reason for Job Separation (N = 204)**

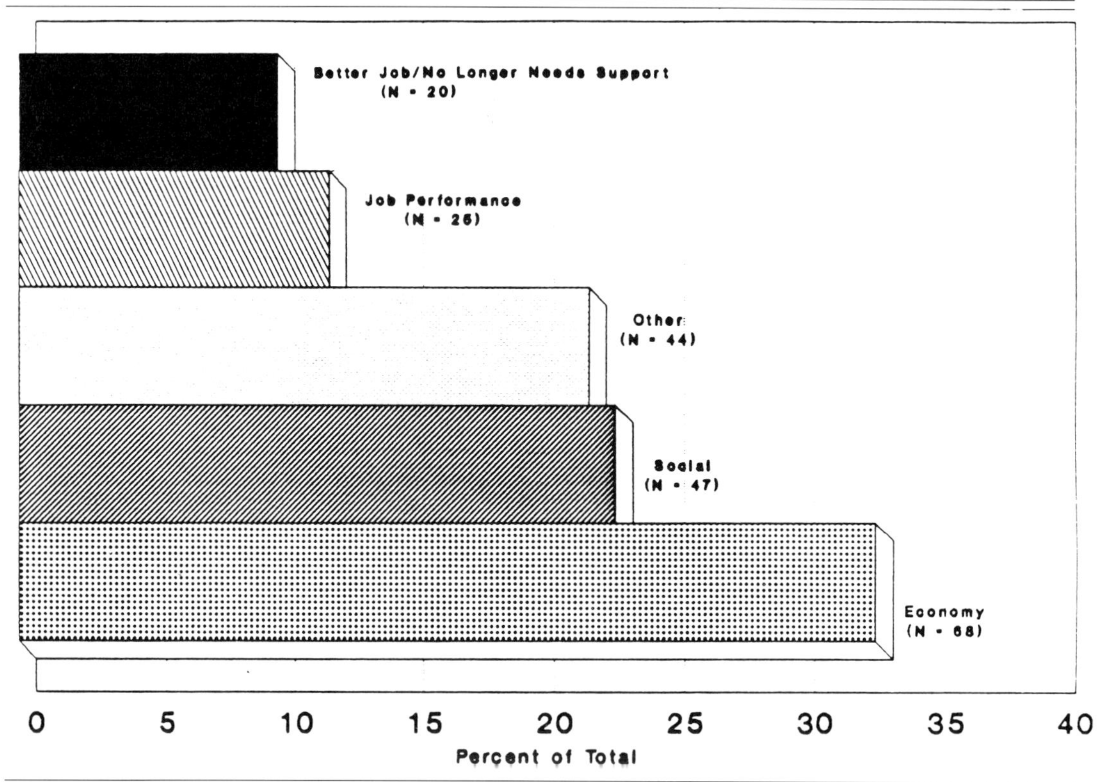

Used with permission from Winking, D., DeStefano, L., & Rusch, F. R. (1988). *Supported Employment in Illinois: Job Coach Issues* (Vol. 3). Champaign, IL: University of Illnois, The Secondary Transition Intervention Effectiveness Institute.

be effective in employment settings: picture prompts, self-instruction, self-monitoring, and self-reinforcement. *Picture prompts* are prearranged visual cues used by the supported employee to prompt desired behavior. *Self-instruction* utilizes verbal cues, produced by the employee, to guide subsequent behavior. *Self-monitoring* refers to individuals observing their own behavior and then reporting or recording their performance. Finally, *self-reinforcement* refers to reinforcement provided by employees for their own behavior contingent upon performance of target behaviors. Table 3.7 overviews recent recommendations made by Lagomarcino, Hughes, and Rusch (1988) when considering teaching supported employees to become more independent in the workplace.

Studies of the social ecology of the work site have demonstrated that employment sites are very social settings, with employees frequently interacting with their supervisors and co-workers about both job-related and non-job-related tasks (Chadsey-Rusch & Gonzalez, in press). Conversations at work sites are predominantly task related, and this pattern is true for workers with and without handicaps. Nisbet and Hagner (1988) recently concluded that promoting co-worker involvement as a natural support may be one means to providing consistent, ongoing follow-up services in integrated work settings.

Recent research reported by Rusch, Johnson, and Hughes (in press) suggests that co-workers (a) train, (b) associate, (c) befriend, (d) advocate, (e) collect data, and (f) evaluate performance.

Table 3.7 Steps in Self-Management

1. Identify the problem through evaluation.
2. Verify the problem through observation.
3. Establish a range of acceptable behavior.
4. Assess the work environment for naturally occurring stimuli and reinforcers.
5. Select self-management procedures:
   (a) Consider specific job requirements.
   (b) Consider the acceptability of the procedure within the work place.
6. Train self-management skills by withdrawing external assistance:
   (a) Task analyze target behavior and self-management procedures.
   (b) Train sequential steps through external assistance.
   (c) Withdraw external assistance.
7. Evaluate the effects of self-management:
   (a) Assess the maintenance of self-management procedures.
   (b) Validate change in target behavior.

Adapted from Lagomarcino, T., Hughes, C., & Rusch, F. R. (1988). Utilizing self-management to teach independence on the job. In T. Lagomarcino, C. Hughes, & F. R. Rusch (Eds.), Self-Management: Facilitating employee independence in supported employment settings (Vol. 4). The Secondary Transition Intervention Effectiveness Institute, The University of Illinois at Urbana-Champaign.

In the training relationship, the co-worker provides on-the-job training. An associating relationship exists when a co-worker merely interacts with the employee at some time, whereas befriending occurs when the co-worker interacts with the supported employee outside the work setting. When co-workers advocate, they protect, optimize, and support the supported employee's employment status. If co-workers evaluate performance, they provide feedback regarding social and work performance.

Over a five-month period, Rusch, Hughes, and Johnson (1988) indicated that supported employees (n = 309) tended to experience more co-worker associating (79 percent), followed by evaluating (62 percent), training (52 percent), advocating (37 percent), befriending (23 percent), and data collection (17 percent). Thirty-one persons with severe to profound handicaps were included in the sample. On the average, approximately 45 percent of all supported employees in the borderline, mild, and moderate mental retardation categories had experienced some type of co-worker involvement. In comparison, only 22 percent of the individuals with severe/profound handicaps had experienced some type of co-worker involvement. Only 2 percent of this group had experienced some type of befriending, 8 percent had had a co-worker advocate for them, and 28 percent had received some training from their co-workers.

In response to the question of whether or not co-worker involvement varies with respect to type of placement, Rusch et al. found a significant difference between the average frequency of occurrence and nonoccurrence of co-worker involvement with respect to individual, clustered, and mobile crew placements. A higher proportion (71 percent) of individuals in mobile crew placements did not experience co-worker involvement. Co-worker involvement did not increase over time in any of the settings.

Most recently, Rusch, Hughes, McNair, and Wilson (in press) developed the *Co-worker Involvement Index* containing the following items: physical integration, social integration, training, associating (frequency), associating (appropriateness), befriending, advocating, evaluating, and giving information.

Employment Specialists

Employment specialists are expected to perform multiple and often conflicting roles. Program coordinators, employers, co-workers, direct service agency employees, agency management, parents, and supported employees were interviewed in order to examine their perceptions of the roles and duties of employment specialists (Winking, DeStefano, & Rusch, 1988). The uniqueness of the position was reflected by all those interviewed, along with the impression that "the position could not be assumed effectively by someone not possessing sophisticated skills in the areas of management, communication and decision making" (p. 106). Parents' perceptions differed slightly from those of employers and program staff in that parents stressed the guidance and protection the job coach provides, rather than direct training to promote independence.

Regardless of any difference in perceptions,

FIGURE 3.4 Job Coach Intervention Time (N = 105 Job Coaches from 16 programs).

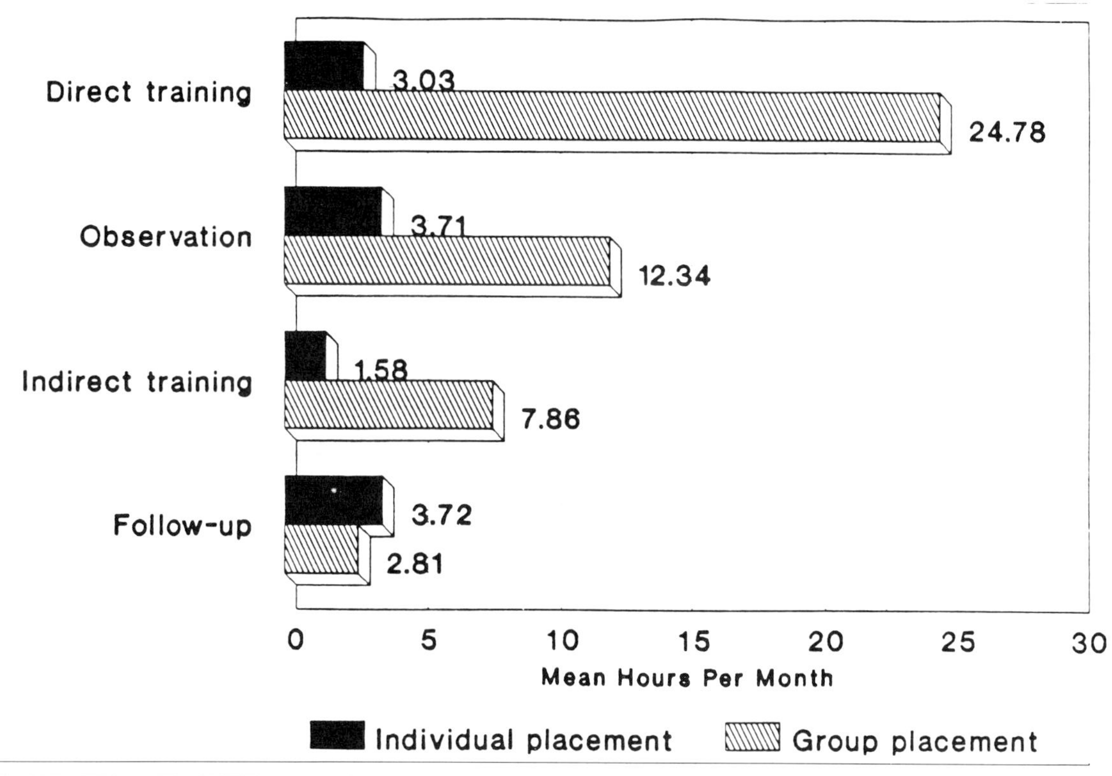

Used with permission from Lagomarcino, T. R. & Rusch, F. R. (1989). A descriptive analysis of reasons why supported employees separate from their jobs. In C. Hanley-Maxwell and D. Harley (Eds.), *Special report: An examination of the impact of supported employment on our nation's citizens with severe disablilities*. Washington, DC: President's Committee on Employment of Persons with Disabilities.

the primary activity of a job coach is the provision of direct training. In a study of sixteen programs involving 105 supported employees over a seven-month period, Rusch, Winking, Trach, Tines, and Johnson (1989) found that there appears to be a significant difference in the amount of time spent in direct training across program models. Figure 3.4 indicates that in one month, approximately twenty-five hours were spent in direct training, twelve hours in observation, eight hours in indirect training, and three hours in follow-up in group placements. In individual placements, however, an almost equal amount of time was spent in all categories. This difference warrants further investigation, particularly in light of a recent analysis of direct training hours, which has indicated that there is little reduction in the hours spent in direct training, across any supported employment model, over time (Johnson & Rusch, in press).

In an analysis of employment requirements for job coaches in Illinois, Rusch et al. (1989) found that almost 70 percent of the programs required some college hours, 52 percent required one to two years of work experience with persons with disabilities, and 39 percent required experience with disability groups as well as experience in business. Of the individuals actually employed as job coaches, 44 percent had a bachelor's degree, 57 percent had some work experience with a disability group, and 4 percent had experience with both disability groups and business. It is of interest to note that of those hired with a bachelor's degree, only 34 percent had a degree in a field of study related to social services. The fact that only 4 percent had experience with both disabilities and business reflects the uniqueness of the position.

The study showed that although almost 70 percent of the programs required some college hours, the mean salary for employment specialists in Illinois was $12,628 for those without experience and $13,482 for those with experience. Even with the recognition that the position requires unique skills and experiences, only 29 percent of the responding agencies reported that job coach salaries were higher than a comparison group of other direct service positions within the agency. It is not surprising that turnover for this position in Illinois is almost 47 percent a year. Of the individuals who left these positions, 61 percent reported that they left this position for offers of more money and promotions.

It appears, then, that we have created a different employment option with many of the same conditions that plagued its predecessor. Clearly, more research is needed, not only to understand the dynamics of the job coach position, but also to determine how to counteract the negative factors that lead to the high turnover rates reported.

CONCLUSION

This chapter provides a description of the development and impact of supported employment as it has been implemented in Illinois. Significant economic gains have been made by individuals in these programs. The majority of individuals in Illinois are working in clustered placements, performing janitorial or light industrial jobs. Although a wide majority of disabilities are represented, individuals diagnosed with mental retardation constitute 66 percent of the population. As reported in other states, people with mild and moderate levels of mental retardation constitute the majority of participants in supported employment. In Illinois they represent 90 percent of the segment labeled mentally retarded. This pattern is expected to continue in the future with the addition of an increasing number of individuals diagnosed with mental illness.

It is important to note that the majority of the job separations (65 percent) in Illinois are due to reasons other than job or social performance discrepancies (areas affected by direct training technology). This finding suggests that, although it is important to focus on training technologies, we must take a larger view of what contributes to successful employment.

QUESTIONS

(For answers see pp. 427–428)

1. When did supported employment formally begin in Illinois?

2. Name and describe the types of data included in the management information system of ISEP.

3. What are the components of the DOI instrument used to evaluate supported employment programs? Describe why each is important.

4. Name three placement models in use in Illinois and list the respective proportion of supported employees served by each model.

5. What two job categories account for nearly half of the supported job placements in Illinois?

6. List major reasons for job separation in Illinois.

7. List reasons why instructional technology has been investigated in Illinois.

8. Did Rusch et al. (1988) find that the amount of co-worker involvement varied with the level of retardation? Explain.

REFERENCES

Agran, M. & Martin, J. E. (1987). Applying a technology of self-control in community environments for individuals who are mentally retarded. In M. Hersen, R. Eisler, & P. Miller (Eds.), *Progress in behavior modification* (Vol. 12, pp. 108–151). Newbury Park, CA: Sage.

Chadsey-Rusch, J. & Gonzalez, P. (in press). Social ecology of the workplace: Employers' perceptions versus observation. *Research in Developmental Disabilities.*

Gold, M. W. (1980). *Did I Say That?*. Champaign, IL: Research Press.

Johnson, J. & Rusch, F. R. (in press). An analysis of the hours of direct training by employment specialists to supported employees. *American Journal of Mental Retardation.*

Kregel, J., Wehman, P., Revell, W. G., & Hill, M. (1989). Supported Employment in Virginia: 1980-1988. In F. R. Rusch (Ed.), *Supported employment: Models, methods, and issues*. Sycamore, IL: Sycamore Publishing Company.

Lagomarcino, T. R. (1986). Community services: Using the supported work model within an adult service agency. In F. R. Rusch (Ed.). *Competitive employment issues and strategies* (pp. 65–77).

Lagomarcino, T. R., Hughes, C., & Rusch, F. (1988). *Self-management: Facilitating employee independence in supported employment settings* (Vol. 4). Champaign, IL: University of Illinois, The Secondary Transition Intervention Effectiveness Institute.

Lagomarcino, T. R. & Rusch, F. R. (1989). A descriptive analysis of reasons why supported employees separate from their jobs. In C. Hanley-Maxwell and D. Harley (Eds.), *Special report: An examination of the impact of supported employment on our nation's citizens with severe disabilities*. Washington, DC: President's Committee on Employment of Persons with Disabilities.

Mithaug, D. E., Martin, J. E., Agran, M., & Rusch, F. R. (1988). *Why special education graduates fail. How to teach them to succeed*. Colorado Springs, CO: Ascent Publications.

Nisbet, J. & Hagner, D. (1988). Natural supports in the work place: A reexamination of supported employment. *The Journal of the Association for Persons with Severe Handicaps*, *13*, 260–267.

Rusch, F. R. (1983). Competitive vocational training. In M. Snell (Ed.), *Systematic instruction of the moderately and severely handicapped* (2nd ed., pp. 503–523). Columbus, OH: Charles E. Merrill.

Rusch, F. R., Chadsey-Rusch, J., & Lagomarcino, T. (1986). Preparing students for employment. In M. Snell (Ed.). *Systematic instruction of the moderately/severely handicapped* (3rd ed., pp. 471–490). Columbus, OH: Charles E. Merrill.

Rusch, F. R., Johnson, J. R., & Hughes, C. (in press). Analysis of co-worker involvement in relation to level of disability versus placement approach among supported employees. *The Journal of the Association for Persons with Severe Handicaps*.

Rusch, F. R., Hughes, C., McNair, J., & Wilson, P. (in press). *Co-worker involvement scoring manual and instrument*. Champaign, IL: University of Illinois, The Board of Trustees of the University of Illinois.

Rusch, F. R. & Schutz, R. P. (1979). Non-sheltered employment of the mentally retarded adult: Research to reality? *Journal of Contemporary Business*. *8*, 85–98.

Rusch, F. R., Winking, D., Trach, J., Tines, J., & Johnson, J. R. (1989). Supported employment in Illinois: Economics, industry, and the disabled worker. In W. Kiernan & R. Schalock (Eds.). *A look ahead: Economics, business, and industry*. Baltimore: Paul H. Brookes.

Schneider, K. E., Martin, M. E., & Rusch, F. R. (1981). Are we sacrificing quality? Costs versus benefits of sheltered and non-sheltered vocational training programs. *Counterpoint*, November, 1 and 28.

Trach, J., Rusch, F. R., & DeStefano, L. (1987). Supported employment program development: Degree of implementation manual. in J. Trach & F. R. Rusch (Eds.). *Supported employment in Illinois: Program implementation and evaluation* (Vol. 1). Champaign, IL: University of Illinois.

Vogelsberg, T. (1986). Competitive employment in Vermont. In F. R. Rusch (Ed.). *Competitive employment issues and strategies* (pp. 35–49). Baltimore: Paul H. Brookes.

Wehman, P. (1986). Competitive employment in Virginia. In F. R. Rusch (Ed.). *Competitive employment issues and strategies* (pp. 23–35). Baltimore: Paul H. Brookes.

Winking, D., DeStefano, L., & Rusch, F. R. (1988). *Supported Employment in Illinois: Job Coach Issues* (Vol. 3). Champaign, IL: University of Illinois at Urbana-Champaign, The Secondary Transition Intervention Effectiveness Institute.

CHAPTER

4

Supported Employment in Pennsylvania

R. Timm Vogelsberg
Temple University

This chapter provides a brief review of competitive supported employment in Pennsylvania. It also provides documentation of the actual process and individual outcomes that consumers have experienced within the first twenty-four months of actual service implementation. The final sections of the chapter identify future issues for service development, challenges to the existing developing system, and hopeful implications for a positive future for individuals who experience severe disabilities within the state of Pennsylvania.

HISTORY OF PENNSYLVANIA SUPPORTED EMPLOYMENT DEVELOPMENT

As a way to explore new approaches to providing community integrated vocational services to individuals with severe disabilities, a Supported Employment Task Force was convened in 1985. Members were charged to determine how Pennsylvania should initiate a plan to implement supported employment statewide. A long-term, developmental approach (five-year plan) was developed as a federal systems change grant. The grant required a consistent consumer outcome evaluation system that would serve as a basis for guidelines for statewide implementation of supported employment services.

Pennsylvania's approach is unique in a number of different ways. Perhaps the most important differences are the Supported Employment Task Force, single stream funding at the state level, multiple population focus, and the attempt to develop consensus at the state agency level as projects are implemented. While other state projects must seek funding from multiple state or local agencies with varying and diverse expectations, Pennsylvania provides an initial single stream of funds at the state level. This approach was taken to ensure consistent expectations across all involved state agencies and to provide the opportunity for long-term support to populations which do not at present have long-term options.

The multiple unique components of Pennsylvania's approach are included within Table 4.1. Each component was an attempt to guarantee an organized, accountable, and coordinated approach to the implementation of competitive supported employment.

Table 4.1 Pennsylvania's Approach to Supported Employment

Multiple agency consensus of all major departments (Education, Labor, and Welfare).
State-level combined funds in single stream to service providers.
Multiple population focus for those individuals with the most severe disabilities.
Comprehensive technical assistance centers in eastern and western Pennsylvania.
State-wide five-year plan for controlled growth, evaluation, and expansion.
Comprehensive consumer outcome micro-computer supported employment data system.

PENNSYLVANIA SUPPORTED EMPLOYMENT TASK FORCE

The Task Force consists of 18 departments, agencies, bureaus, and organizations (refer to Table 4.2). Members meet quarterly, and these meetings are chaired by the Executive Director of the Office of Vocational Rehabilitation.

Table 4.2 Supported Employment Task Force

List of Participating Organizations and State Agencies

Department of Public Welfare
  Office of Mental Health
  Office of Mental Retardation

Bureau of Blindness and Visual Services

Department of Labor and Industry
  Office of Vocational Rehabilitation
  Bureau of Job Training Partnership

Department of Education
  Bureau of Special Education
  Bureau of Vocational Education

Governor's Office of Policy Development
Developmental Disabilities Planning Council
Private Industry Councils
Pennsylvania Association of Rehabilitation Facilities
Pennsylvania Association for Retarded Citizens
Mental Health Association in Pennsylvania
United Cerebral Palsy of Pennsylvania
Pennsylvania Coalition of Citizens with Disabilities

Federal Systems Change Project

A federal proposal representing a five-year implementation plan for Pennsylvania was prepared and submitted to the Office of Special Education and Rehabilitative Services by the Task Force in 1986. This proposal (for $409,000 per year for five years) established a central administrative office and supported employment technical assistance centers in two locations. The Central Administrative Office is located within the Department of Labor, Office of Vocational Rehabilitation. The Western Technical Assistance Center is located at the University of Pittsburgh; the Technical Assistance and Data Center is located at Temple University.

Pennsylvania Supported Employment Definition

The Task Force identified criteria for supported employment, listed in Table 4.3, that parallel the federal definition. It should be noted that the definition adopted by the Task Force was accepted by all its members as a consensus for the definition of competitive supported employment in Pennsylvania.

Supported Employment Implementation Guidelines

Supported employment was intended to be recognized as a viable, new approach to providing integrated employment services to persons with severe disabilities. While some existing vocational placement programs did provide a sequence of evaluation, training, placement, and follow-up, supported employment combines the placement of persons with severe disabilities in competitive jobs with *training on-the-job and long-term support services* to help them remain on-the-job. Evidence of effectiveness with other populations is beginning to emerge (Sowers, Jenkins, & Powers, 1987; Vogelsberg & Richard, 1987; Wehman, Kregel, & Shafer, 1989).

Table 4.3 Supported Employment Criteria in Pennsylvania

Real work in a real work place.

Training on the job site.

Substantial pay.

Long-term support services.

Industry/business integration.

Coordination of local service system resources.

Consumer and advocate involvement.

A consistent issue within service development is the need to differentiate between time-limited and time-enduring services (Powers, 1987; Vogelsberg & Schutz, 1987). Work stations in industry, transitional employment programs, intensive on-the-job training for a short period, job clubs, expanded apprenticeship programs, and other short-term (time-limited) services are but a few of the multiple options for establishing community integrated employment that are very successful with individuals who have mild to moderate disabilities.

Through a comprehensive review of previous program development, multiple agency discussion, and the continual attempt to focus on consumer outcomes, implementation guidelines for providing services to individuals with more severe handicaps were identified. Some guidelines have been realized in practice; others are still challenges for growth and development for future projects in Pennsylvania. A short listing of selected guidelines is presented in Table 4.4.

Table 4.4 Implementation Guidelines in Pennsylvania

Program staff. Program managers, employment training specialists, and job developers must be full-time staff employed specifically to facilitate supported employment outcomes.

Compensation. Supported employment recognizes the value of staff who work directly with consumers. Salaries of employment training specialists must be adequate to demonstrate this value.

Administrative involvement. Project managers must be aware of the ongoing responsibilities of the employment training specialists and the importance of one-to-one contact with individuals. It is expected that all project administrative staff will engage in on-the-job training at least once a month.

Conversion. Projects must accept the expectation that traditional program directions and financial resources will be converted in the future.

Accessibility. Projects must be located in buildings that are accessible by status-enhancing methods.

Location. Project sites should be separate from other human service facilities. Preferably, projects will be located within reach of employment opportunities (such as an industrial complex).

Service coordination. The long range goal of competitive supported employment is to become a functional service that is incorporated into existing services.

Interagency agreements. Local agreements must be prepared in writing and revised each year.

Advisory boards. A county advisory board must be established to guarantee that all county agencies are represented and participate.

Time-enduring support. Those individuals placed into employment must be guaranteed long-term (time-enduring) support to maintain their employment.

Integration. Projects must adopt, develop, and implement the philosophy of community integration.

County education. Projects must provide educational assistance to local agencies and the private sector to guarantee that the concept of competitive supported employment is understood.

SERVICE DESIGN

The most documented form of supported employment continues to be the individual placement on-the-job training approach for individuals classified as severely disabled and mentally retarded (Barcus, Griffin, Mank, Rhodes, & Moon, 1988; Kiernan & Stark, 1986; McLoughlin, Garner, & Callahan, 1987; Moon, Goodall, & Wehman, 1985; Rudrud, Ziarnik, Bernstein, & Ferrara, 1984; Rusch, 1986; Rusch & Mithaug, 1980; Vogelsberg, 1986; Vogelsberg, Ashe, & Williams, 1986; Wehman, 1984, 1986). From numerous publications, project reports, and conference presentations a consistent model for program development has emerged.

Individual placement on-the-job training and support programs consist of four major components focused on community and consumer service development: referral, evaluation and job development, on-the-job training and placement, and follow-up. Figure 4.1 provides a flow chart of these activities. More detailed information about each stage in the process is available from several sources (Vogelsberg, 1986; Vogelsberg, Ashe, & Williams, 1986).

The four-component approach, although it appears cumbersome at first glance, actually represents an effective progression for the individual from initial referral through interagency agreement, evaluation and job development, actual placement and support, and finally to ongoing or follow-up support. As the approach has grown in sophistication, it has become focused on types of support and training. Previous component designs concentrated on training but have now been expanded to include many other forms of support.

State Fiscal Commitment

The total fiscal commitment for each year is as follows: 1986—$1,210,000; 1987—$2,648,000; and 1988—$4,181,000. Over a thirty-six-month period (1986–1988) the total commitment is expected to be $8,039,000. Table 4.5 provides a breakdown of funding amounts. It is interesting to compare contributions with the individuals benefiting from the program: Those individuals who have benefited most are classified as having mental retardation (Department of Public Welfare (DPW)/Office of Mental Retardation) or significant and persistent mental illness (DPW/Office of Mental Health).

Examining the department and agency support reveals that the agencies that have benefited most have not increased their contributions significantly over the three-year period. In 1988, the receipt of Title VIC ($1,096,000) and the General Fund ($829,000) allowed the Task Force contributors to reduce their level of fiscal commitment. The receipt of these funds has reduced the need to increase financial support from the separate departments for 1988, and this may also have decreased the level of involvement or commitment at the state level.

Table 4.5 also provides an indication of the various departments' agencies' and bureaus' levels of fiscal commitment to the projects. It is of additional interest to compare the total amount of funds available by department to the total amount of state-level commitment. Table 4.6 provides the percentages of contribution by office, bureau, council, and department.

The separate contributions of each agency must be evaluated in relation to actual outcomes for specific populations. A disheartening aspect of the funding contributions is that the Department of Public Welfare and the Department of Education have contributed a lower percentage of the funding in each of the three years, while the Department of Labor has increasingly accepted fiscal responsibility to expand, monitor, and maintain the projects. If the concepts of integration, conversion, and true multiple agency support are to become reality, then similar levels of contribution and involvement are necessary.

SUPPORTED EMPLOYMENT IMPLEMENTATION

Although many individuals continue to voice concern about employer receptivity, it has not been an issue with these projects. Over a two-year period beginning in 1986, 956 jobs were developed for 245 placements. Almost four times as many jobs were developed as were actually utilized. Two thousand and twenty-six service occupations and 1,558 other occupations were contacted over the twenty-four months of job development efforts in search of future employment sites.

Cost Information

the original funding intent was to establish an average cost per placement of $10,000. Each project was provided with the expectation of placing between twenty-five and thirty individuals and maintaining at least twenty individuals within each twelve-month period. This number, when compared to the average project funding level ($250,000), indicated initial fiscal and consumer outcome expectations.

The average cost per placement (as of July

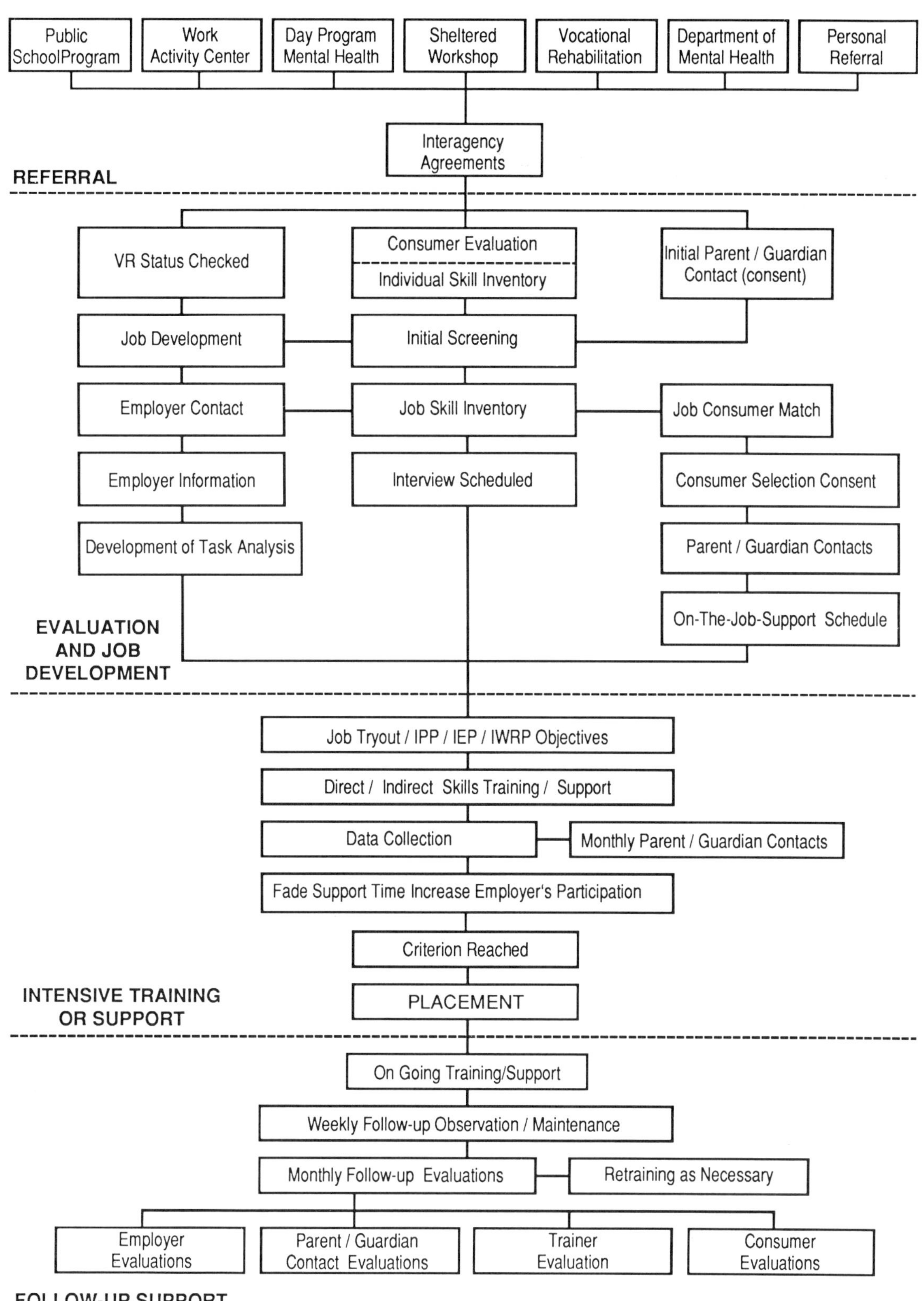

Figure 4.1 Components of Competitive Supported Employment

Table 4.5 Funding by Contributors

Year/ Contributor	1986(5)	1987(11)	1988(17)	Totals
Department of Public Welfare				
Office of Mental Retardation	$ 110,000	$ 229,000	$ 237,000	$ 576,000
Office of Mental Health	250,000	500,000	500,000	1,250,000
Bureau of Blindness and Visual Services	100,000	200,000	200,000	500,000
Developmental Disabilities Planning Council	110,556	219,000	219,000	438,000
TOTAL	460,000	1,148,000	1,156,000	2,764,000
Department of Education				
Bureau of Vocational Education	300,000	100,000	100,000	500,000
Bureau of Special Education	0	500,000	500,000	1,000,000
TOTAL	300,000	600,000	600,000	1,500,000
Department of Labor and Industry				
Office of Vocational Rehabilitation	250,000	500,000	500,000	1,250,000
Bureau of Job Training Partnership	200,000	400,000	0	600,000
Title VI C	0	0	1,096,000	1,096,000
General Fund	0	0	829,000	829,000
TOTAL	450,000	900,000	2,425,000	3,775,000
TOTALS	$1,210,000	$3,344,000	$4,181,000	$8,039,000

1, 1988) for all the projects is estimated at $9,139. This data can be divided into those projects that have twenty-four months of development (the 1986 projects) and those projects that have twelve months of development (the 1987 projects). With this division, the twenty-four-month projects' estimated cost per placement is $7,860 and the cost per placement for the twelve-month projects is $11,924. The information presented in Figure 4.2 may provide a better visual understanding of the difference that twelve additional months of development can make in the average cost per placement. It is important to note that the averages are weighted means (utilizing the total number of placements) rather than simple means: 1986 projects (twenty-four months)—$7,860; 1987 projects (twelve months)—$11,924; and Combined Average Cost Per Placement—$9,139.

Figure 4.2 provides a visual representation of this gradual reduction and leveling off of the cost per placement. The figures are notably different ($4,064 less per placement) when compared by total number of months in development. Those projects that have been operating for the twenty-four-month period have reduced their reported

Table 4.6 Percent of Funds Invested

	1986	1987	1988
Department of Public Welfare			
Office of Mental Retardation	9.1	8.6	5.7
Office of Mental Health	20.1	18.9	12.0
Bureau of Blindness and Visual Services	8.3	7.6	4.8
Developmental Disabilities Planning Council	9.1	8.3	5.2
TOTAL	47.2	43.3	27.6
Department of Education			
Bureau of Vocational Education	24.8	3.8	2.4
Bureau of Special Education	0	18.9	12.0
TOTAL	24.8	22.7	14.4
Department of Labor and Industry			
Office of Vocational Rehabilitation	16.5	18.9	12.0
Bureau of Job Training Partnership	16.5	15.1	0
Title VI C	0	0	26.2
General Fund	0	0	19.8
TOTAL	33.0	34.0	58.0

cost per placement to $7,860. This figure is actually $2,000 less per placement than originally anticipated. Many individuals are concerned about long-term retention and the fact that individuals lose their positions and must receive assistance for second and third placements—or find other services within the adult community. Although the long-term intent is to guarantee ongoing support, the adult service community still experiences fragmentation and difficulty in meeting this need. Although these projects were unable to change the service system totally in a twelve- or twenty-four-month period for every individual served, there is indication that, with effort and state-level support, these projects could improve and expand their ability to meet the comprehensive needs of the individuals who are receiving services.

The amount of salary earned is also important to consider. The cumulative amount of salaries earned over the twenty-four-month period is $655,340 (see Figure 4.3). This figure becomes even more important when the previous earning capacity of the individuals placed is analyzed. Few of the individuals placed had real community employment experience or fiscal earnings. Those individuals who were in sheltered workshops or work activities had average hourly wages that were significantly less than minimum wage, while all of the individuals working as a result of these projects are earning at least minimum wage.

FIGURE 4.2 Average Cost Per Placement July 1986–June 1988)

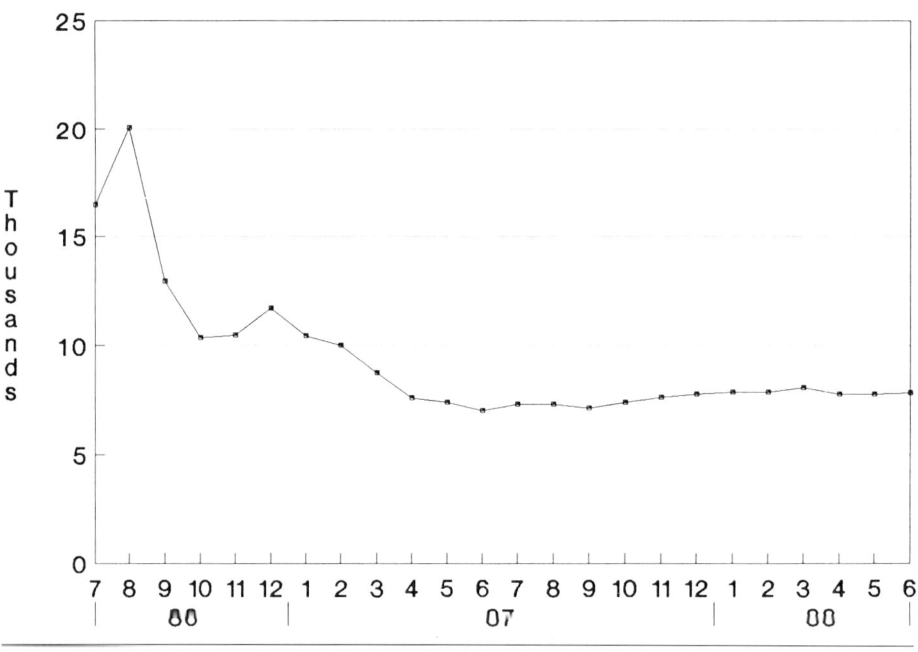

Additional financial figures that must be recognized include transportation reductions, social security benefit reductions, and the cost of existing programs that are no longer required. As these projects provide individuals in facility-based programs with services, they replace an existing service and thus reduce the cost to the community by that amount. The average cost per placement is currently $7,860 for the projects that have been operating for two years. This figure compares favorably to the average cost for partial hospitalization, sheltered employment, and adult day services. A major difficulty within Pennsylvania is gaining accurate cost figures of other forms of day support for comparison. Estimates ranging from $8,000 to $12,000 per year have been provided along with great discussion about the inaccuracy of the figures.

Cumulatively over the twenty-four-month period a total savings of $646,711 has been realized from those individuals who have been placed. Some cost-benefit analysts would suggest reducing the cost spent on the program by the above savings. Figure 4.4 provides a graphic representation of the combined savings over the twenty-four-month period.

1986 PROJECTS. In July of 1986 five projects (six counties) were funded to establish supported employment. Each project received approximately $250,000 for the first year to establish the program and maintain continual employment for at least twenty individuals with severe disabilities. As of July 1987, ninety-nine placements of individuals with severe disabilities had occurred (by July of 1988, 196). One of the projects was advised to relocate in an attempt to resolve performance issues.

1987 PROJECTS. An additional six projects were funded in July of 1987. The six new proj-

FIGURE 4.3 Total Salaries Earned (July 1986–July 1988)

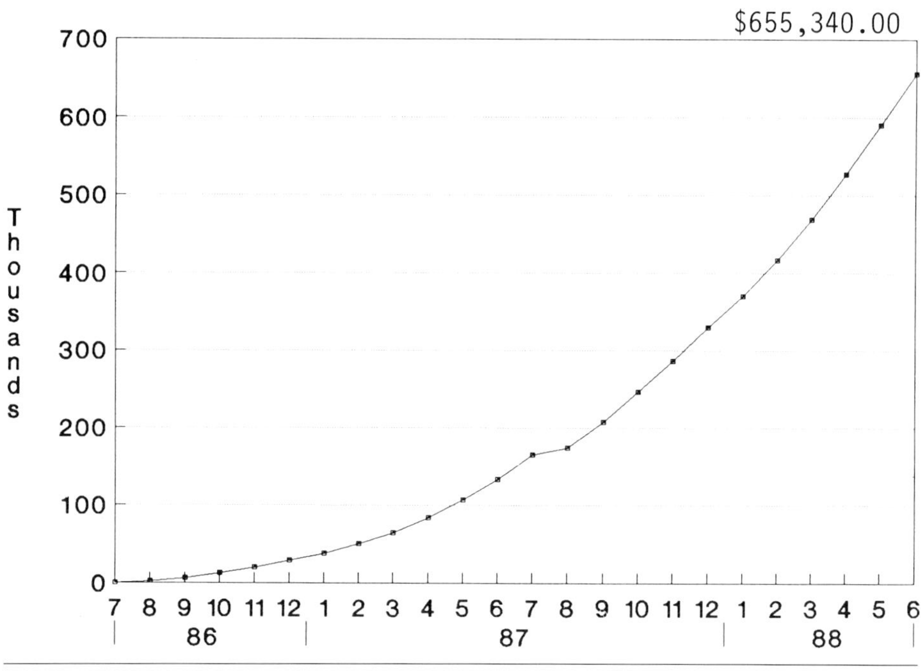

ects were selected on a competitive proposal basis and increased the total to eleven projects serving thirteen counties (two are multiple-county projects). At the end of twelve months, ninety-three placements had occurred (almost exactly the same number as the first twelve months of the 1986 projects). One project was discontinued due to serious performance problems.

CONSUMER OUTCOME DATA

Data are representative of individual specific outcomes in demographic, financial, support, training, follow-up, and employment-specific areas. The data provided by the eleven projects represent twenty-four months (five projects) and twelve months (six projects) of data. The micro-computer data system used by these projects (Vogelsberg, 1986) allows individual projects to enter data, generate their own reports, and share data as it is being compiled and presented at the state level.

From the limited amount of time that the data cover, it is dangerous to attempt to draw major conclusions. Certain tables (support, training, and follow-up) must be examined carefully and it must be recognized that the data represent information reported by individual projects. The data are checked for accuracy and frequent requests for edits and/or corrections are made to individual projects, but questions remain about the total accuracy of the data.

Demographic Information

Two hundred and eighty-nine placements of 245 people have occurred in the twenty-four and twelve months of program implementation. One hundred and fifty-two of these individuals over the total program period are still employed. At the sixty-day cutoff, 83 percent of these individuals were still employed. The average age of those

FIGURE 4.4 Transportation, SSA, and Program Costs Saved (July 1986–June 1988)

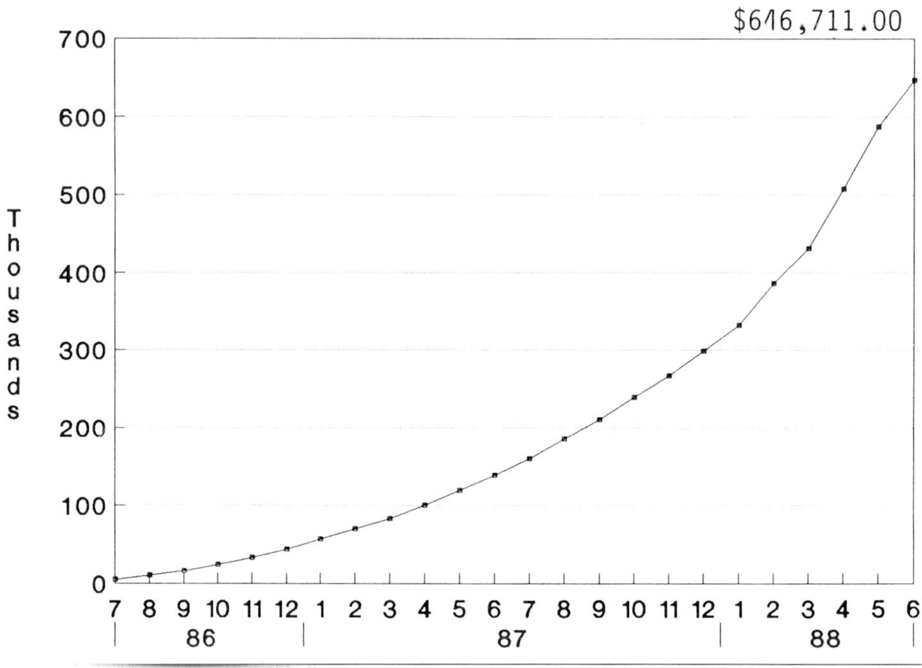

employed is thirty-two. The majority of the individuals live with their natural families or in their own apartment or home. One hundred of the individuals are classified as having mental retardation, ninety are classified as individuals experiencing significant and persistent mental illness, thirty-five experience physical disabilities, thirty-two are from special education programs, twelve experience blindness or visual impairments, and twenty experience other forms of severely disabling conditions.

Pennsylvania initiated separate supported employment codes to separate classifications of disability for funding purposes. Figure 4.5 provides a bar graph of the percentage of individuals who have benefited from competitive supported employment. Individuals experiencing mental retardation or mental illness were the largest group of service recipients.

A similar analysis by individual classification and retention over the twenty-four month period is graphically depicted in Figure 4.6. It is interesting to note that the individual who appears to have the best retention is the special education student. This is descriptive data and cannot be used empirically to verify cause and effect—but there are many opinions about the success of the special education student as opposed to the other individuals receiving support.

An additional ongoing issue for the establishment of successful competitive supported employment is that of residential support. Frequently, employment positions are developed that begin at early or late hours, or cover weekends. These types of positions require flexibility within residential settings and frequently cause staffing problems within community living arrangements. Some projects have been successful in working out the details with specific residential providers. Over time, the supported employment projects have come to realize that without residential support a successful placement will be difficult. Figure 4.7 below provides an indication of the living setting of the

FIGURE 4.5 Placements by Supported Employment Codes (July 1986–June 1988)

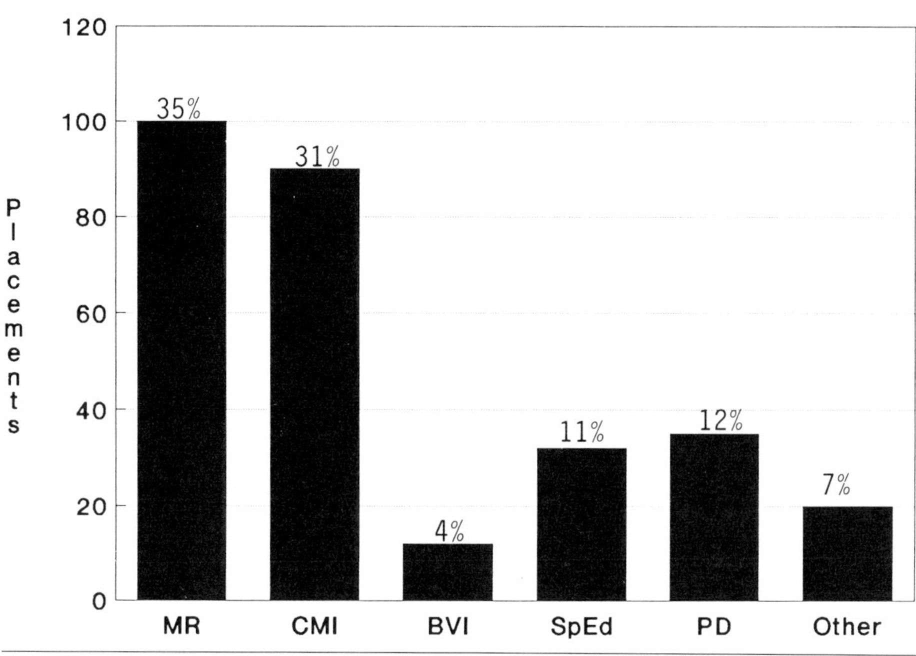

individuals placed. It is not surprising that a high percentage (53 percent) come from their natural homes.

Financial Information

All of the projects have allowed employers to claim targeted jobs tax credits (TJTC), and the average pay per hour is $3.84. Average salary per month is $396 and the average taxes paid per month are $79. Although these figures do not appear large, they represent a substantial increase over previous earnings. The figures also represent a total (see Figure 4.3) of $655,340 in earnings. Future issues within the financial arena include the establishment of improved opportunities and access to better positions.

The figures presented here represent an income increase for the majority of the individuals involved. They should also provide the service community with the knowledge that better paying and more challenging positions can be developed for individuals involved in competitive supported employment.

Support, Training, and Follow-Up Information

Data on support, training and follow-up must be considered with caution because many individuals are still in the "intensive support phase." The average total number of hours per individual per placement as of March 1988 was 116 for those projects that have been operating for twenty-four months and 142 for those projects that have been in operation for twelve months. Data on the number of support hours are being utilized to identify the amount of support time required by the individual, and to help projects identify certain characteristics of individuals who may require more intensive support time.

An analysis of average hours broken down

FIGURE 4.6 Percentage of Placements Still Employed (July 1986–June 1988)

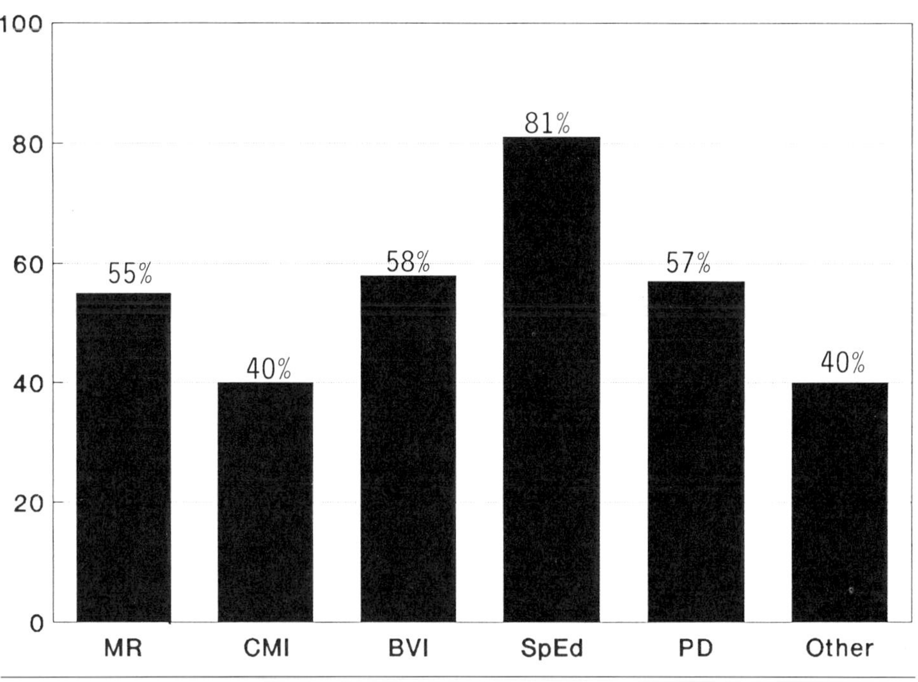

by classification of the individual indicates a substantial difference across individuals. This is an expected finding, and may be an indication that projects are beginning to understand the varied support needs of the people being provided with support. Persons with mental retardation received the most hours of service (415), followed by persons who are blind or visually impaired (357). Former special education students required 310 service hours, persons with mental illness 267 hours, and those with physical disabilities 195 hours.

An additional important evaluation consists of a breakdown of numbers of hours of support into the various categories of activity. Table 4.7 provides an analysis of the average number of hours spent in each type of support activity. As would be expected, individuals with mental retardation receive more support hours in direct training than other individuals receiving services. Although caution must be exercised with these data, the indications of numbers of support hours and types of support in relation to the individual classification may be useful in the future. It is interesting to note that those individuals with the highest retention rate (former special education students) also receive one of the highest levels of support hours.

Employment Information

Most individuals work part-time (an average of twenty-seven hours per week, or 104 hours per month), and have been absent or tardy an average of two times. The present issue is to maintain existing service occupations while developing other forms of employment as well. Figure 4.9 presents an analysis of positions by full-time and part-time. As of this report, 26 percent of the positions are full-time (at least thirty-five hours), and 74 percent are part-time. The graph indicates that most individuals have similar percent-

FIGURE 4.7 Living Arrangements of Individuals Placed (July 1986–June 1988)

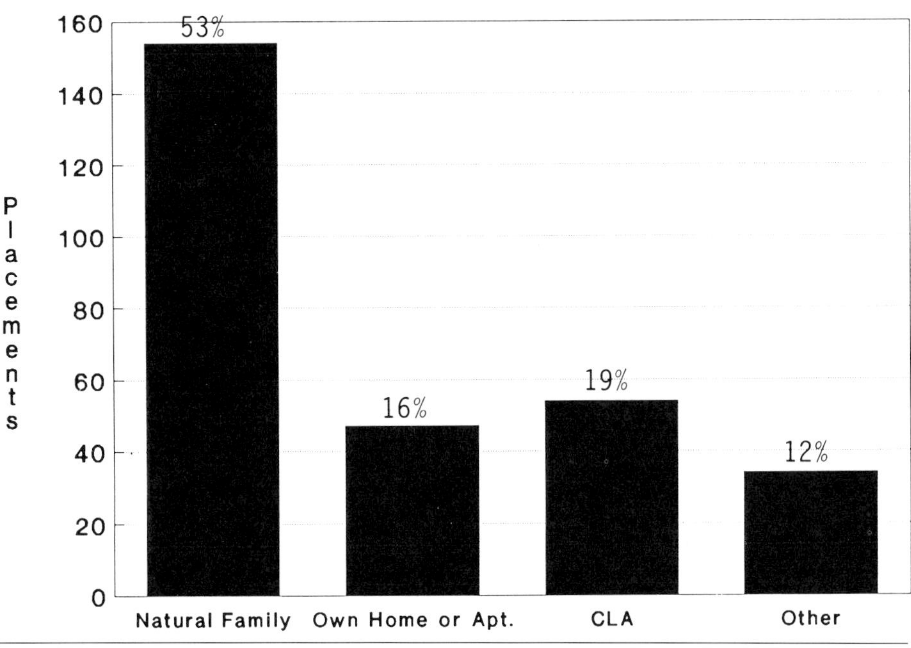

ages of full-time versus part-time employment, with the exception of special education students. Their larger percentage of part-time employment may be due to the fact that some of them are still receiving some school services while they are working. A separate analysis, conducted project-by-project, will indicate a wide range of percentages. Some projects have made an internal decision to place the majority of individuals into part-time employment with the hopes of eventually moving into full-time employment. Others have a

Figure 4.8 Average Number of Hours in Support Activities (July 1986–June 1988)

	MR	MI	SPED	BVI	PD	OTHER
Evaluation	8.7	5.6	8.2	9.4	6.1	4.9
Service coordination	42.5	38.4	47.4	51.5	22.7	40.8
Job development	20.7	16.8	15.4	16.7	8.5	13.4
Direct training	216.4	103.9	126.3	138.7	88.9	121.7
Indirect training	14.7	18.7	27.0	22.0	9.3	13.0
Observation	70.0	42.4	57.0	99.5	38.9	74.9
Follow-up	29.1	32.5	21.9	6.1	13.4	34.4
Co-worker or employer support	13.1	9.3	6.5	12.7	7.6	9.2
TOTALS	415.0	267.0	357.0	310.0	195.0	312.1

Table 4.7 Average Number of Hours in Support Activities (July 1986–June 1988)

	MR	MI	SPED	BVI	PD	OTHER
Evaluation	8.7	5.6	8.2	9.4	6.1	4.9
Service coordination	42.5	38.4	47.4	51.5	22.7	40.8
Job development	20.7	16.8	15.4	16.7	8.5	13.4
Direct training	216.4	103.9	126.3	138.7	88.9	121.7
Indirect training	14.7	18.7	27.0	22.0	9.3	13.0
Observation	70.0	42.4	57.0	99.5	38.9	74.9
Follow-up	29.1	32.5	21.9	6.1	13.4	34.4
Co-worker or employer support	13.1	9.3	6.5	12.7	7.6	9.2
TOTALS	415.0	267.0	357.0	310.0	195.0	312.1

much higher percentage of full-time employment.

SECOND GENERATION ISSUES

Supported employment in Pennsylvania has been developing for at least three years and has endured a state-level election which established new directors, deputy secretaries, and Task Force members. Consequently, it has lost the appeal of a "new concept" and is frequently seen as one of many service efforts. The challenge to Pennsylvania will be to maintain and improve implementation. As with most state-level programs addressing systems change that is fre-

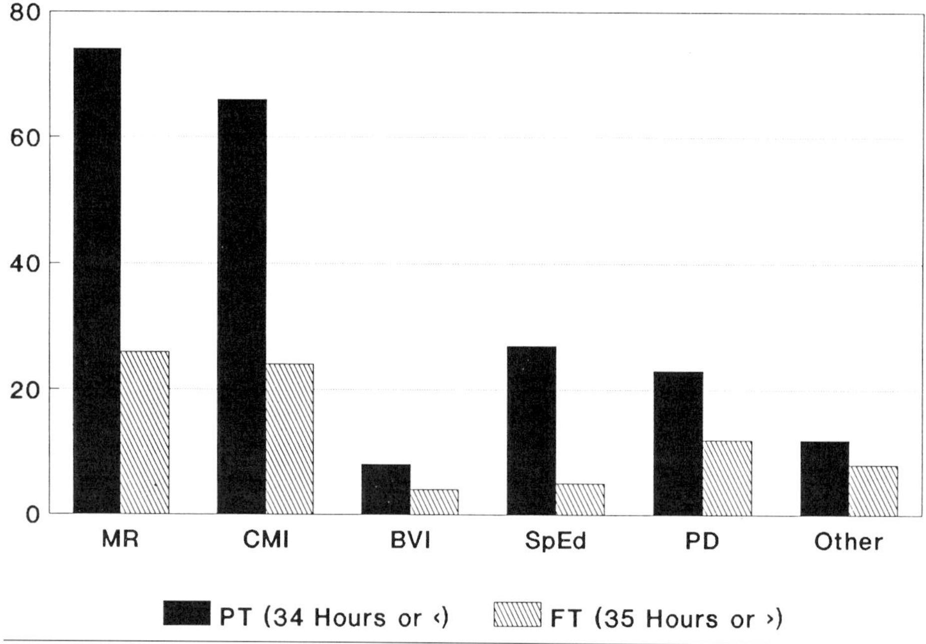

Figure 4.9 Part-time and Full-Time Employment by Individuals (July 1986-June 1988)

quently tied to a department initiative, elections and political change present a terrific challenge to the maintenance of effective programs. In addition, "second generation issues" can be identified and must be considered as areas for improvement. These issues include: multiple population services; multiple agency funding; employment mobility; service refinement and expansion; human resource development; quality of life verification; employer–private sector participation; accountability and documentation; consumer involvement; conversion; federal, state and local incentives; and legislation, regulations, and policy issues.

Multiple Population Services

Traditional services typically have been facility- or hospital-based and have segregated individuals with severe disabilities into similar groups (i.e., programs for people who are mentally retarded, mentally ill, etc.). One result of this orientation was the desire by the consumers (and service providers) to guarantee that individuals with similar conditions be placed together for reasons such as ease of service, socialization, and the general consensus that this was the best approach for service development.

Many of these reasons for single population services become irrelevant when the service is provided within a community-integrated setting. When this occurs, the other individuals present are people who do not experience disabilities (rather than similar—or dissimilar—"populations"). If individuals are provided with services that are integrated within their home communities, previous objections (such as the aversion to grouping individuals with mental illness with individuals with physical disabilities) are no longer valid.

Multiple Funding Agency

As in the well-known quotation "the sum of the parts is greater than each part separately," new directions focus on combined approaches that include combined funding to guarantee greater success. The present adult service system fragments finances and frequently duplicates services in the interest of population-specific services or federal and state agency autonomy. Individuals with severe disabilities frequently cannot gain access to services due to the inability of two offices or agencies to work cooperatively together. If adequate consensus can be gained, duplicated services combined, and funds shared, the results for the individual with disabilities have the potential to improve dramatically.

Employment Mobility

The issues of job mobility, career ladders, advancement in salary, and self-recognition are issues that we must all deal with during our working years. Many of us decide that our living environment is more important than career advancement. Others leave extremely positive living environments in the cause of professional advancement and increased salaries. These same options should be available to individuals with disabilities. The central issue is freedom of choice and a service system that is capable of providing the individual with that choice.

Service Refinement and Expansion

As many states develop an approach to supported employment, bureaucratic rigidity begins to set in. The concept of individualization is lost in the desire to provide equal services to everyone. Frequently, mistakes that occurred in other states are repeated. Many individuals do not believe that success or failure in other geographic areas has any relation to success or failure in their home state; they must therefore repeat the same mistakes before they accept the reality of known service difficulties.

The recent rejection of studies from Connecticut (Galloway, 1987), the National Association for Rehabilitation Facilities (Mason, 1989), combined states national overview (Wehman, Kregel, & Shafer, 1989), and other sources concerning the variation in the cost of individual placement, clustered placements, and mobile crews is an excellent example of this problem. Many individuals in Pennsylvania are convinced that mobile crews and clustered placements are less expensive and will provide services to larger numbers of individuals. Existing data do not, however, substantiate this belief, and it appears that Pennsylvania (like many other states) must revisit the problem rather than learn from existing data.

Perhaps the most crucial challenge to the Pennsylvania approach is the issue of combined local and state support. The present situation is one of state support and local resistance to fiscal participation. State-level officials have directed the local (project, regional, district, and/or county) settings to develop their own fiscal contributions for continuation. Local settings have similarly taken the approach that they cannot initiate true "conversion of funds" without state-level directives and support. It is a circuitous discussion that is jeopardizing future service development and refinement.

Human Resource Development

The reality of most of our existing university and college programs is that they are operating on curricula that are firmly anchored in traditional service delivery (segregated public school classrooms or adult service settings) rather than the contemporary approach which advocates total community integration in all areas of life.

As service options in community settings continue to expand, it is hoped that universities and colleges will recognize the manpower needs of the community and respond appropriately. The existing approach by universities appears to be one of cautious observation prior to actual commitment of programs or funds. The usual question asked is "Are sufficient students available to justify the curriculum change?"

As college and university personnel preparation programs evolve and service systems approach true community integration, it is evident that the technology being implemented within the service system is below known capabilities (the usual estimate is twenty years behind existing technology). The immediate approach to addressing this issue is to provide intensive technical assistance, inservice training, and ongoing data-based program assistance. This is not the total answer, but it does provide assistance as the multiple areas noted earlier begin to be realized.

Long-term human resource development issues such as professional growth, salaries, retention, and incentives must be addressed.

Pennsylvania initiated strong support for technical assistance and training in the first year (1986) when there were five projects in development. As the number of projects has expanded to seventeen, the amount of technical assistance support has decreased and may be one of the many contributing variables to ongoing performance discussions about the projects. If a true commitment to accountable and high quality program development is present, then human resource development issues must be addressed.

Quality of Life Verification

As we all talk, agree, and focus on the need to assist people to improve their quality of life, the service system must begin to verify these changes and to document that the consumers involved actually agree that their quality of life has expanded. Measurement of improved quality of life must include individualized consideration of such areas as health, employment, leisure, community, and family relationships. At different points everyone's life, these variables take different priorities. Adequate measurement of perceived quality of life changes must be individualized, as must service development.

Conversion

The concept of supported employment encompasses the term "conversion". Specifically, this means the conversion of segregated programs to community-integrated programs and (more important to some) the conversion of existing funds to support community-integrated activities. Many of our existing traditional services are expensive but do not result in maximum integration or independence for the individual.

Employer–Private Sector Participation

Earlier efforts focused on employer attitudes and incentives for employers to assist individuals with disabilities in gaining access to employment opportunities. There are now documented programs in which employers have assumed supervisory costs for supervisors in supported employment projects. This is an obvious positive result in a time of increasing numbers of individuals and decreasing amounts of financial support. Fast food services (including Pizza Hut, McDonald's, Wendy's, and Burger King) have initiated their own versions of support programs to afford access to employees within the service community. Department of Labor projections indicate that this is a positive time for the service community as business and industry begin their search for employees (Kiernan & Schalock, 1989).

Accountability and Documentation

The existing service system is still replete with programs that have not been verified as the most effective (in quality or cost) in producing outcomes for individuals with disabilities. Many approaches are still based on attitudes and opinions, rather than on empirical verification.

A continual issue within federal, state, agency, and academic programs is the organizational separation of data and research from actual program implementation. It is not unusual for the separation to be so severe that the program managers or training directors do not have access to the available data and therefore do not adequately address technical assistance and training needs, nor do they have the information necessary to consider the total situation.

A continual issue within supported employment across the nation and in Pennsylvania is the quantity versus quality debate. Despite careful definitions of appropriate populations for service, many individuals examining the data still believe that the lowest cost per placement is the final indicator of a quality program. This approach is understandable when there are huge waiting lists and limited resources, but it does not guarantee that a quality service is delivered to the intended population. It provides incentives to develop the least expensive service rather than the highest quality service. A compromise is necessary to recognize that the individual with the most severe disability will require more resources and it will therefore cost more to deliver high-quality services to that individual. Many programs recognize this, but few implement it without incentives.

Consumer Involvement

A very popular movement that was initiated in the 1960s is that of consumer power. Ralph Nader and his raiders, *Consumers Digest*, and other organizations have assisted the individual who does not experience a handicap to become a more sophisticated consumer.

These same efforts have begun to be identified and utilized by (and for) the consumer of the human service system. We are just beginning to understand the importance of choice and participation for consumers, significant others, and advocates. Continual focus on this issue could eventually lead to truly individualized service options that meet the needs and desires of the consumer.

Incentives for Community-Integrated Service Development

Within the issues raised above and elsewhere, the bottom line is frequently one of money, and the system will continue to have difficulty effecting change unless adequate incentives and assurances are developed to facilitate change. Financial incentives that assist service agencies to gain independence are a must for positive systems change. The current system includes financial disincentives and the amount of funds available is reduced and/or more difficult to access once a person moves from the workshop to the community, from an ICF to a group home, or from a hospital setting to a community setting.

The state of Colorado (St. Louis, Richter, Griffin, & Struxness, 1987) service community established a goal of 25 percent of all people with developmental disabilities in community integrated employment for 1988. They met this goal and are focusing on their next step, or the second generation issues. Although their approach was totally different from Pennsylvania's, it is interesting to report that many of their second generation issues are those identified in Pennsylvania.

Some states have initiated policies that direct all future funding into community expansion rather than facility expansion. Others have initiated a larger reimbursement rate for community integrated services than for facility-based services. These approaches are simple to implement and effective in the gradual process of systems change.

Legislation, Regulations, Policy

Pennsylvania has again initiated a Transition Bill (#1419) that has the potential to become law within this year. Regulations have been suggested on the state and federal levels that carry the concept of the "right to education" law (94–142) of 1975 into the adult service community as "right to employment" or "right to service" laws. Within the existing economic situation this will be a difficult but persistent issue. Gradual recognition of the cost effectiveness of employment as opposed to welfare or day services has slowly created support for expanding services that assist individuals to become contributing members of society.

Multiple federal and state fiscal disincentives must be addressed in order to guarantee adequate support for community integrated employment. If benefits are threatened, or if the system is difficult to understand and access, then artificial limits are placed on progressive movement towards independence. The 99th Congress accomplished many positive changes and removed (or reduced) many disincentives. There are, however, many more disincentives remaining.

ACKNOWLEDGEMENTS

This chapter was made possible through the assistance and support of the Pennsylvania State Task Force on Competitive Supported Employment, project personnel, and the individual consumers of services who continue to assist us to understand how we can benefit by mutually working towards true community integration.

Special acknowledgements must be offered Lynda Richard, Joan Nicoll, Carole Jesiolowski, and Reid Overturf for their assistance in statewide data system implementation and to Martha Ross and Jane Hill who assisted in the editing of data and data table preparation. No official support or endorsement of this report is intended or should be inferred.

QUESTIONS (For answers see p. 428)

1. Does funding for supported employment in Pennsylvania differ from patterns in other states? If so, how?

2. Describe the differences between time-limited and time-enduring services.

3. What has been the employer receptivity to the supported employment project?

4. Are supported employment costs (per placement) constant?

5. Other than wages, what factors have been included in the benefit-cost analysis in Pennsylvania?

6. What disability groups are most heavily represented in supported employment in Pennsylvania?

7. Of the populations placed in competitive employment, which group appears to have the best retention?

8. What problem exists between supported employment services and residential programs?. Explain.

9. According to the data from Pennsylvania, is there a difference in the amount of support required by individuals based on the classification of handicapping condition? Explain.

10. Which group requires the lowest level of support hours?

11. Do existing data (from Pennsylvania) suggest that individual placements are more expensive per placement than clustered placements and mobile crews?

12. Name two aspects of "conversion" described by the author in the text.

13. Note one of the positive trends in employer private sector participation.

14. Are the data from programs being properly used to address program development issues?

15. Name an argument for and one against using cost per placement as the criterion for selecting supported employment options. Explain your position.

REFERENCES

Barcus, M., Griffin, S., Mank, D., Rhodes, L., & Moon, S. (1988). *Supported employment implementation issues.* Richmond: Rehabilitation Research and Training Center, Virginia Commonwealth University.

Galloway, C. (1987). *Department of Mental Retardation funded supported employment opportunities.* Hartford: Connecticut Department of Mental Retardation.

Kiernan, W. E. & Schalock, R. L. (1989). *Economics, industry, and disability.* Baltimore: Paul H. Brookes.

Kiernan, W. E. & Stark, J. A. (1986). *Pathways to employment for adults with developmental disabilities.* Baltimore: Paul H. Brookes.

Mason, C. (1989). *National Association for Rehabilitation Facilities Report on Supported Employment.* Unpublished manuscript.

McLoughlin, C. S., Garner, J. B., & Callahan, M. (1987). *Getting employed, staying employed: Job development and training for persons with severe handicaps.* Baltimore: Paul H. Brookes.

Moon, S., Goodall, P., & Wehman, P. (1985). *Critical issues related to supported competitive employment.* Richmond: Virginia Commonwealth University Rehabilitation Research and Training Center.

Powers, M. D. (1987). *Expanding systems of service delivery for persons with developmental disabilities.* Baltimore: Paul H. Brookes.

Rudrud, E. H., Ziarnik, J. P., Bernstein, G. S., & Ferrara, J. M. (1984). *Proactive vocational habilitation.* Baltimore: Paul H. Brookes.

Rusch, F. R. (Ed.). (1986). *Competitive employment issues and strategies.* Baltimore: Paul H. Brookes.

Rusch, F. R. & Mithaug, D. E. (1980). *Vocational training for mentally retarded adults: A behavior analytic approach.* Champaign, IL: Research Press.

Sowers, J., Jenkins, C., & Powers, L. (1987). *The training and employment of persons with physical disabilities.* Unpublished manuscript.

St. Louis, D., Richter, C., Griffin, G., & Struxness, L. (1987). *Annual Report: Community integrated employment.* Wheat Ridge, CO: Rocky Mountain Resource and Training Institute.

Vogelsberg, R. T. (1986). Vermont's employment training programs. In F. R. Rusch (Ed.), *Competitive employment issues and strategies* (pp. 35–49). Baltimore: Paul H. Brookes.

Vogelsberg, R. T., Ashe, W., & Williams, W. (1986). Community based service delivery in rural Vermont: Issues and recommendations. In R. Horner, L. M. Voeltz, & B. Fredericks (Eds.), *Education of learners with severe handicaps: Exemplary service strategies.* Baltimore: Paul H. Brookes.

Vogelsberg, R. T. & Richard, L. (1987). *Implementation of supported employment for individuals with long-term mental illness.* Unpublished manuscript, Temple University Developmental Disabilities Center, Philadelphia.

Vogelsberg, R. T. & Schutz, R. (1987). Establishing community employment programs for persons with severe developmental disabilities: Systems designs and resolutions. In M. D. Powers (Ed.), *Expanding systems of service delivery for persons with developmental disabilities.* Baltimore: Paul H. Brookes.

Wehman, P. (1984). Transition for handicapped youth from school to work. In J. Chadsey-Rusch (Ed.), *Conference proceedings from "Enhancing transition from school to the workplace for handicapped youth."* Champaign, IL: Office of Career Development for Special Populations, University of Illinois.

Wehman, P. (1986). Competitive employment in Virginia. In F. R. Rusch (Ed.), *Competitive employment issues and strategies* (pp. 23–34). Baltimore: Paul H. Brookes.

Wehman, P., Kregel, J., & Shafer, M. S. (1989). *Emerging trends in the national supported employment initiative: A preliminary analysis of twenty-seven states.* Richmond: Virginia Commonwealth University Rehabilitation Research and Training Center.

CHAPTER

5

Supported Employment Program Characteristics

John S. Trach
University of Illinois at Urbana-Champaign

As discussed in Chapter 1, supported employment has been developing for more than a decade. Research and demonstration by Bates and Pancsofar (1981), Bellamy, Sheehan, Horner, and Boles (1980), Rusch and Mithaug (1980), Wehman (1981) and others has resulted in our better understanding of what constitutes supported employment. These demonstrations, along with newly developed statewide programs, suggest that supported employment programs share several common characteristics, including certain expectations for outcomes (e.g., wages). This chapter introduces these common characteristics in an effort to define the model for supported employment.

Three employment models for adults appear to have provided the conceptual framework for the emergence of supported employment (Bellamy et al., 1980; Rusch, & Mithaug, 1980; Wehman, 1981). Similarities between the models developed by Bellamy, Rusch, Wehman and their colleagues include the analysis of jobs, situational assessment, on-the-job training, job maintenance, and coordination of services. Horner and Bellamy (1979) outlined a model of "structured employment" that targeted individuals who are not candidates for competitive job placement. Characteristics of their model included extended employment with ongoing personal support and on-the-job training to promote productivity and wage earnings.

Rusch and Mithaug (1980) proposed a model to address the problems associated with "training and placing (persons with mental retardation) who failed to advance through the existing hierarchy of vocational training opportunities" (p. xvi). Rusch and Mithaug believed that their model applied to all persons, regardless of the severity of their mental retardation. They stated that "the greatest impediment to successful vocational training" was not due to the "lack of technological knowledge, but rather the lack of a cohesive, integrated, and coordinated application of our knowledge to the problems of vocational assessment, training, and placement" (p. 1). Their model proposed a problem-solving approach that prescribed specific training strategies for promoting employment integration (i.e., applied behavior analysis).

Wehman (1981) proposed a model for placing persons with severe disabilities in "nonsheltered employment options." He also focused on the design and implementation of employment services that resulted in community employment, outlining the role of parents and service coordination.

Concurrent with the development of employment models for adults with severe disabilities, researchers proposed a vocationally-oriented instructional curriculum for students who typically would enter traditional adult service programs after leaving school (i.e., sheltered workshops, day and work activity programs). Bates and Pancsofar (1981) and Wilcox and Bellamy (1982) proposed preparing students for community employment rather than sheltered employment. Bates and Pancsofar (1981, 1983) offered recommendations for the implementation of a model for students with severe disabilities that focused upon schools offering an employment and adult life-oriented curriculum. They proposed the development of an individualized transition plan that would ensure that students would obtain a functional and community-oriented program of study.

The school-based model proposed by Wilcox and Bellamy (1982) included productivity, participation, and independence as the foundation for curriculum development. They also recommended outcomes such as integration, age appropriateness, and community relevance. Wilcox and Bellamy advocated a comprehensive curriculum that addressed vocational preparation, independent living, and leisure and recreation.

These school and post-school employment models appear to have shared two basic premises: (1) the placement of consumers in real jobs in the community, and (2) the use of applied behavioral technology for systematic training. Common features included a survey of the community for potential jobs, a detailed analysis of jobs for placement that identified vocational and social requisites, situational assessments for evaluating consumer skills and directing individualized program development, systematic on-the-job training, and long-term follow-up.

RECENT SUPPORTED EMPLOYMENT MODEL PROGRAM CHARACTERISTICS

McLoughlin, Garner, and Callahan (1987) recently focused on job development and employment training. In the job development phase, program implementors identified community employment by surveying the community via telephone, correspondence, and visits to employment sites. Much attention is given to negotiations at potential employment sites and making decisions about the appropriateness of these sites for selected consumers.

The employment training component includes analyzing the job for vocational and social requisites, as well as situationally assessing the consumer. This component also outlines the provision of systematic training, monitoring progress, and addressing employer relations (e.g., increasing production rates, evaluating the employee, transferring supervision).

Although McLoughlin et al. (1987) differentiate between competitive employment and supported employment, their guiding philosophy is that, in developing jobs and placing persons with severe disabilities, program developers should not 'lock' themselves into "seeking a particular format or style of employment" (p. 35). They assume that competitive and supported employment should be interchangeable and that both should be available to the consumer.

More recently, Bellamy, Rhodes, Mank, and Albin (1988) proposed strategies for promoting change, developing leadership, involving secondary education, strengthening advocacy, training staff, and developing business participation. Their model utilizes a system consisting of five components or "organizational accomplishments." These five accomplishments include: (a) creating the opportunity to perform paid work, (b) assuring that the work is performed according to employers' requirements, (c) integrating employees with disabilities into the social and physical environment of the work place, (d) meeting the supported employee's ongoing support needs, and (e) maintaining the organization's capacity to offer supported employment. Creating the opportunity to perform paid work focuses on identification of employment options through surveying the community. The second component, meeting performance demands, entails analyzing employer expectations and teaching the consumer to learn the particular job to meet employer expectations. In addition to systematic training procedures, this may involve job redesign and adaptations in the work setting (refer to Chapter 7 for a complete overview

SUE RAUSCH

In 1943, Sue Rausch was born into a family of seven. At age nine, she was diagnosed as moderately mentally retarded (IQ 46). At this time, she was placed at the Dixon State School. While a resident at Dixon, she was described as being "shy" and "withdrawn." She was a resident at Dixon for 15 years, and was discharged at age 24. At the time of discharge, reports noted that she was capable of only simple vocational tasks.

After leaving Dixon, Sue rented a room in a boarding house and worked at a local sheltered workshop. After one year, she was placed in a community job through the workshop's vocational placement program. She worked as a maid and then as a dishwasher for several years, but was unable to maintain employment once support was phased out. Sue returned to the workshop, stating she never wanted to work in the community again.

After four years at the workshop, Sue is now working in the community as a dishwasher. Through the workshop's supported employment program and the ongoing support of a job coach, Sue is once again a contributing member of society. Recently, she increased her hours from 20 to 40 per week and was told by her supervisor that she was the best dishwasher he had ever hired. Sue is well-liked by her co-workers, and the regular customers greet her by name.

In mid-April, with money she saved from working, Sue moved out of her room at the boarding house (in which she had lived for 18 years) and into her own apartment. She also saved enough money to buy a new bed, couch, chair, and desk. When asked what she liked best about her new apartment, Sue said, "It's close enough so I can walk to my job!"

As a result of supported employment, Sue now receives support not only from her job coach, but from her supervisor, co-workers, and community. With this extended support and Sue's increased self-esteem, the supported employment staff is confident that Sue will continue to succeed.

of this strategy). The third component attempts to ensure that integration takes place. As the authors point out, success in creating integration for employees with disabilities is difficult to measure, but must be an integral part of the model. The fourth component addresses the need for ongoing support to maintain employment. The final component is primarily an administrative function to ensure that funding for services remains at a level that can sustain service requirements.

Gardner, Chapman, Donaldson, and Jacobson (1988) described the components of supported employment as job placement, job-site training and advocacy, ongoing assessment, and follow-up. In their model, *job placement* refers to identifying community jobs and requisite skills as well as matching target employees to jobs. Job-site training and advocacy provides the systematic training aspect of the services. Ongoing assessment and follow-up consist of services designed to maintain employment over time. In addition, coordination of related services (i.e., transportation, residential) are identified as major concerns that must be addressed.

Nisbet and Callahan (1988) developed an assessment tool based on twenty-one categories of quality indicators. Their instrument is organized into three sections: (1) administrative issues, (2) job matching and development issues, and (3) job training and support issues. Table 5.1 provides a list of these issues.

The activities they propose are similar to those of other supported employment models. For instance, job development activities include surveying the community for potential employment sites with concurrent activity in job analysis to identify requisite vocational and social skills.

Table 5.1 Assessing the Quality of Supported Employment Services

I. ADMINISTRATIVE ISSUES

A. Agency philosophy and mission
B. Agency administration
C. Fiscal management
D. Image enhancement and public relations
E. Interaction and coordination with school programs
F. Effective use of community resources
G. Positive relationships with employers
H. Effective utilization of personnel for job development and job training

II. JOB MATCHING AND DEVELOPMENT ISSUES

A. Employee selection procedures
B. Individualization in job matching: Applicant and family involvement
C. Use of job creation strategies
D. Use of a variety of payment mechanisms
E. Development of work sites that enhance the image of employees
F. Integrated work in typical businesses and industries that encourage interactions with non-disabled co-workers and supervisors
G. Development of quality jobs

III. JOB TRAINING AND SUPPORT ISSUES

A. Use of ecological and job analyses
B. Use of systematic instruction
C. Use of modifications, adaptations, and technology
D. Coordination with non-work life space areas
E. Emphasis on social and communication skills
F. Use of ongoing supports

Note. There are three to eight "quality indicators" per each of the items listed for the three components. Nisbet, J. & Callahan, M. (1988). *Assessing the quality of supported employment services.* Durham: University of New Hampshire, The Institute on Disability. Reprinted by permission of the author.

Job matching is included as part of the placement and evaluation process and systematic training in vocational, social, and communication skills is recommended. Ecological inventories, job modification and adaptation, and technology also are proposed. Coordination of services across all life skill areas is encouraged.

SUPPORTED EMPLOYMENT MODEL PROGRAMS

Boles, Bellamy, Horner, and Mank (1984) proposed the *Specialized Training Program Model Implementation Checklist* to assist with the dissemination of their "structured employment model," and to guide its replication. The offspring of this evaluation instrument was the *Supported Jobs Implementation Checklist* (Bellamy et al., 1988), which lists responsibilities for each accomplishment, duties related to each of the responsibilities, and tactics to address each of the duties (see Table 5.2). There are two responsibilities for each of the first four accomplishments, and three for the fifth accomplishment, a total of eleven responsibilities. There are thirty-eight duties related to the responsibilities, and a total of 187 tactics to address the duties and responsibilities, each of which is scored for presence or absence. Of the tactics listed, seventy-six address program administration, and eighteen address integration. The remaining ninety-three tactics address surveying the community for employment sites, analyzing jobs for requisite skills, matching target employees to jobs, and providing systematic training. Several of these tactics relate to program administration (e.g., developing policies and forms).

The *Utah Supported Employment Project Implementation Checklist*, developed by McDonnell, Nofs, Hardman, and Chambless (1986), has fourteen components with a total of eighteen procedural requirements to evaluate supported employment programs (see Table 5.3, p. 72). The authors explain that the development of the instrument is based on existing models of supported employment and field-tested procedures (i.e., Bellamy et al., 1988; Moon, Goodall, Barcus, & Brooke, 1986; Paine, Bellamy, & Wilcox, 1984; Rusch & Mithaug, 1980; Vogelsberg, Spaulding, Patterson, Schenck, & Phillips, 1984).

The instrument includes a worksheet with specific criteria for rating each of the procedural requirements. The worksheet inventories twenty discrete supported employment functions that define the procedural requirements and components, including wages, benefits, hours worked, integration, and administrative functions. Once more, the majority of functions that are assessed relate to surveying the community for employment, matching consumers to employment options, systematic training, and coordination of services. The worksheet lists each of the individual functions, delineates the standards for each function, and specifies a data source for evaluating the standards. The ratings are made on a three-point scale indicating that a standard has been met (2), there is progress towards a standard (1), or the standard has not been met (0). Scoring categories also allow for standards that are not applicable. The authors recommend quarterly evaluations.

The *Degree of Implementation* is a tool for evaluating supported employment services (Trach, Rusch, & DeStefano, 1987). The content for the instrument was identified through a review of model programs (Bates, 1986; Lagomarcino, 1986; Vogelsberg, 1986; Wehman, 1986). Employment services listed in this instrument are structured around 26 activities and classified by five categories of employment services (community survey and job analysis, job match, job placement, job maintenance, and related job services/interagency coordination). The Degree of Implementation Protocol is illustrated in Table 5.4.

COMMUNITY SURVEY AND JOB ANALYSIS. *Community survey and job analysis* refers to activities associated with surveying the community for potential job placement sites through telephone calls, correspondence, and personal contact, and identifying requisite vocational skills and social behavior for placement in those sites. For instance, a program might send out a letter or call a prospective employer and follow up with interested employers to determine, through observation, what a job might entail. A program would analyze a particular site for job requisites in both vocational and social areas.

JOB MATCH. *Job match* refers to assessing client characteristics in relation to job requisites. The program utilizes the information gathered during community survey and job analysis and then matches a target employee's assessment information on vocational and social skills to determine employment feasibility. The procedure must provide choice of employment options, be thorough enough to determine employment training needs, and must not exclude anyone from employment.

Table 5.2 Supported Jobs Implementation Checklist

Responsibilities	Duties
Accomplishment I: Paid Employment and Opportunities Available	
A. Jobs arranged and agreement(s) signed	1. Prospective employers identified and qualified.
	2. Process for negotiating job commitments established.
	3. Negotiations completed and commitments secured from employer.
B. Access to employment maintained	1. Employer relations planned.
	2. Employer relations implemented.
	3. Employer relations evaluated.
Accomplishment II: Work Requirements Met	
A. Work organized for performance	1. Job Analysis completed.
	2. Procedures for documenting employee performance organized.
B. Work performed	1. Workers trained to perform job.
	2. Job performance maintained.
Accomplishment III: Employee Integrated	
A. Integration opportunities identified	1. Systems established for identifying/analyzing physical and social integration opportunities.
	2. Physical integration opportunities developed/enhanced.
	3. Social integration opportunities developed/enhanced.
B. Integration achieved	1. Targeted integration opportunities analyzed.
	2. Performance in targeted integration opportunities is trained or supported.
Accomplishment IV: Service Coordination Completed	
A. Employees hired	1. Selection and hiring process for targeted individuals established.
	2. Screening and selection process implemented.
	3. Individuals matched with available jobs assuring the least restrictive approach to supported employment.
	4. Pre-employment logistics completed.
B. Employee services delivered	1. Individual plans completed.
	2. Programs developed and resources identified to meet planned objectives.

Table 5.2 (cont.)

	3. Individual plan implemented.
	4. Employment separation procedures developed and implemented.
Accomplishment V: Organizational Capacity Present to Provide Ongoing Support	
A. Organizational capacity to deliver support established	1. Organization legally structured.
	2. Initial funding established.
	3. Office organized.
	4. Financial policies and systems established.
	5. Personnel policies and systems established.
	6. Organizational planning and evaluation system established.
	7. Other policies and procedures established.
B. Organizational capacity maintained	1. Board operation, office, and legal status maintained.
	2. Personnel policies and systems maintained.
	3. Organizational planning and evaluation system maintained.
	4. Other policies and procedures maintained.
	5. Financial policies and systems maintained.
	6. Financial resources managed to maintain direct and overhead costs at or below income.
C. Perform mission	1. Constant improvement of support service.
	2. Maintain constancy or purpose.

Note. There are one to three "tactics" to address each duty listed. Bellamy, G. T., Rhodes, L. E., Mank, D. M., & Albin, J. M. (1988). *Supported employment: A community implementation guide.* Baltimore: Paul H. Brookes. Reprinted by permission of the author and the publisher.

JOB PLACEMENT. *Job placement* refers to procedures for training target employees to perform on the job. These procedures typically use systematic training techniques (e.g., applied behavior analysis), job modifications to adapt the job to target employees' particular handicap(s), and planning to maintain performance acquired through training once the training period has ended. Therefore, a program would task-analyze vocational and social aspects of a job, develop training strategies, determine criteria for determining acceptable performance, and plan for the continuance of the performance.

JOB MAINTENANCE. *Job maintenance* activities include procedures for assisting the individual in retaining employment once he or she has learned the job. Assessment of the match between the individual, the job, the quality of work, and the other life settings indicates the fit between the job and the individual. Job maintenance can be determined by reassessment of client performance during and after training, socially validating the quality of job performance, and modifying efforts to meet client, employer, and parent or guardian expectations. Typically, programs request Work Performance Evaluation Forms

Table 5.3 Procedural Components for Utah Supported Employment Project Implementation Checklist

Component		Procedural Requirement	
1.0	Individual program plan (IPP)	1.1	Specific goals on employment outcomes are established for each worker. These goals may include job placement, hours worked, and opportunities to interact with nondisabled co-workers.
		1.2	Participants in the development of the IPP include the worker, his or her guardian (if appropriate), caseworker from the Mental Retardation/Developmental Disabilities Agency, caseworker from the Vocational Rehabilitation Agency, residential service provider, and employment service provider.
2.0	Client assessment and job matching procedures	2.1	Assessment of the workers' social/communication, academic, physical, personal hygiene, and community mobility skills.
		2.2	Description of job tasks and demands.
		2.3	Systematic matching of worker skills to job demands.
3.0	Job analysis procedures	3.1	Detailed analysis of the demands of the job including identification of generic response components, environmental cues, speed criteria for each job task, quality criteria for each job task, and events that might prevent the worker's successful completion of the job.
4.0	Design of training programs	4.1	A written training program including a detailed task analysis of the job, specific response prompting and fading procedures, specific correction procedures, specific reinforcement procedures, and methods for tracking and summarizing worker performance.
5.0	Progress in training programs	5.1	Up-to-date summary of the worker's performance on assigned job tasks.
		5.2	Modification of training procedures after 10 training sessions with no worker progress.
6.0	Supervisor observation of training programs	6.1	Monthly observations of the job coaches effective in implementing the written training program.
7.0	Board of directors	7.1	An advisory board is established by the supported employment program to set policy and review operating procedures.
8.0	Nonprofit status	8.1	The supported employment program establishes itself legally as a nonprofit organization.
9.0	Workshop certification	9.1	The supported employment program obtains a Work Activity and/or Sheltered Workshop Certificate from the U.S. Department of Labor.
10.0	Formal marketing plan	10.1	The supported employment program develops a formal marketing plan to serve as a framework for obtaining employment opportunities for clients.

Table 5.3 (cont.)

Component	Procedural Requirement
11.0 Formal Services Contacts	11.1 The supported employment program establishes formal service contracts with each employer specifying the responsibilities of the employer and supported employment program during job placement, training, and follow-along.
12.0 Formal Accounting Procedures	12.1 Accounting procedures include mechanisms for tracking all accounts receivable, accounts payable, and state and federal taxes.
13.0 Standard Job Descriptions	13.1 Written descriptions are developed by the supported employment program specifying the roles and responsibilities of the program director, job developer, and/or coach.
14.0 Weekly Staff Meetings	14.1 The supported employment program conducts weekly staff meetings to review of worker outcomes (i.e., wages, work hours, progress in training programs, and integration), staff activities (i.e., job development efforts, employer contact and satisfaction, contact with parents/residential providers, administrative issues, and fiscal issues.

McDonnell, J., Nofs, D., Hardman, M., & Chambless, C. (1988). *An analysis of the procedural components of supported employment programs associated with worker outcomes.* Unpublished manuscript. Reprinted by permission of the author.

Table 5.4 Degree of Implementation Protocol (Revised)

SUPPORTED EMPLOYMENT PROGRAM DEVELOPMENT
DEGREE OF IMPLEMENTATION FORM

John S. Trach
Frank R. Rusch
Lizanne DeStefano

This degree of implementation form should be completed by the supported employment program coordinator or external evaluator as part of routine program evaluation. It will be necessary to examine job coach logs and other program documentation in order to complete this form. This evaluation will take between 1 and 2 hours to complete.

This instrument utilizes a 3-point scoring system to rate both the presence of a model component and the degree to which the component is established. Specific criteria are used to evaluate each component. The following scoring system is recommended:

2 YES	The component exists and is a routine activity of the program; also, this component is performed at an acceptable level.
1 EMERGENT	The component exists, but is carried out less frequently or at less than an acceptable level. Technical assistance/staff development is needed.
0 NO	The component is *not present* or is carried out *inappropriately*. Technical assistance/staff development is strongly needed. Those items considered "not applicable" to a program should be scored 0 and then explained.

Table 5.4 (cont.)

SUPPORTED EMPLOYMENT PROGRAM DEVELOPMENT
DEGREE OF IMPLEMENTATION FORM

	Yes	Emergent	No
Community Survey and Job Analysis			
1. Conducts a community survey to identify potential jobs.	2	1	0
2. Compiles a list of businesses willing to employ individuals with handicaps.	2	1	0
3. Obtains employer-validated job descriptions.	2	1	0
4. Conducts job analysis of targeted jobs.	2	1	0
5. Identifies job-specific work performance skills, including necessary job modifications.	2	1	0
6. Identifies job-specific social-interpersonal skills.	2	1	0
Job Match			
7. Administers standardized vocational assessment instrument to evaluate work performance skills.[1]	2	1	0
8. Administers standardized assessment to evaluate social-interpersonal skills.[1]	2	1	0
9. Observes work performance and social-interpersonal skills on-the-job.	2	1	0
10. Determines match of employees' strengths/weaknesses in relation to alternate job placements.[2]	2	1	0

[1] "Standardized" refers to those instruments for which administration procedures, reliability, and validity have been documented.

[2] This item focuses upon the best possible job match while assessing strengths and weaknesses in order to guide programming decisions. This item does not suggest that someone is unemployable or even less employable.

Table 5.4 (cont.)

	Yes	Emergent	No
Job Placement			
(first six months before Job Maintenance phase)			
11. Evaluates target employees' performance to determine training needs.	2	1	0
12. Utilizes behavior management strategies.	2	1	0
13. Restructures job to adapt to target employees' skills.	2	1	0
14. Develops plan to maintain acceptable levels of performance.	2	1	0
15. Develops plan for support services during Job Maintenance phase.	2	1	0
16. Obtains feedback from employer/supervisor through work performance evaluations.	2	1	0
Job Maintenance			
(continuous activity after Job Placement phase)			
17. Compares target employees' work performance and social-interpersonal skills to co-workers' through monthly observation.	2	1	0
18. Obtains feedback from employer/supervisor through work performance evaluations.	2	1	0
19. Provides on-the-job training to meet employers'/supervisors' expectations.	2	1	0
20. Annually assesses target employees' work performance with standardized assessment instruments.	2	1	0
21. Annually assesses target employees' social-interpersonal skills with standardized assessment instruments.	2	1	0

Table 5.4 (cont.)

	Yes	Emergent	No
Related Job Services/Interagency Coordination			
22. Identifies local agencies that provide employment services.	2	1	0
23. Identifies employment services within agencies that promote job maintenance.	2	1	0
24. Identifies local agencies to provide employment-related services.	2	1	0
25. Identifies employment-related services within agencies that promote job maintenance.	2	1	0
26. Revises Individualized Written Rehabilitation Plan to include interagency cooperation that focuses upon long-term employment through case management.	2	1	0

(WPEF) from employers monthly for the first 3 months, then at 6 months and a year, and then on a schedule determined by the employer. The WPEF is very similar to the standard personnel evaluation form used by all employers. In addition, interview data from guardians are collected, usually on a daily basis at first, then moving to a weekly, then monthly, and finally to the regular staffing pattern for the agency.

RELATED JOB SERVICES/INTERAGENCY COORDINATION. *Related job services* consist of the actual programs, individuals, and subcomponents of participating agencies that provide the direct services needed to secure, train, and maintain a job placement. *Interagency coordination* convenes those agencies that function independently of each other but provide necessary job services for a particular individual. These services and efforts incorporate (a) the ongoing coordination of all agencies involved and (b) the services within each agency that affect job placement and retention. The Individualized Written Rehabilitation Plan (IWRP) may function as the written document to coordinate services (Federal Register, August 1987). For students, the Individualized Education Plan (IEP) or Individualized Transition Plan (ITP) can serve the same purpose as the IWRP. In Illinois, for example, programs typically at least identify their local and regional rehabilitation department representative for employment services consultation and case openings, their social security agency for benefits planning, and the residential provider to ensure attendance and work readiness.

ADMINISTRATION AND SCORING. When evaluating each supported employment program, an evaluator or technical assistance staff scores the presence (absence) of each of the activities. The three-part scoring system requires classifying an activity as nonexistent (0), emergent (1), or present (2). The scores determine the level of employment service provided by a particular supported employment program. For example, if a program documents the development of individualized training plans for at least 50 percent of the individuals placed at employment sites (Item #12), that activity would score 1, or emergent. If that same program documents the development of training plans for *all* of the individuals placed at the employment sites, that activity would score 2, or present. Correspondingly, if a program documents the development of individualized training plans for less than 50 percent of the individuals placed at employment sites, the activity would score 0, or absent. A manual was developed with pre-established criteria to determine the scoring of the presence or absence of each component (Trach et al., 1987). Interrater reliability was assessed at .88.

MODEL PROGRAM INTERVENTION EFFECTIVENESS

Most researchers would agree that some evidence of viability is needed before attempting to replicate a model program. Replication on a large scale in a wide variety of settings would not only enhance that viability, but expedite implementation of the current supported employment initiative. Replicating model programs can reduce the cost of supported employment by decreasing the need for model development and increasing the use of existing research. With systematic replication of supported employment programs, cross-program evaluation designs would supplant internal evaluations. Furthermore, with systematic implementation of supported employment services, researchers developing program models could begin to evaluate services in relation to the expected outcomes of supported employment. In other words, the identification and evaluation of a constellation of employment services might provide some index for expected outcomes. Such systems analysis research has been conducted successfully in education (DeStefano, Wang, & Gordon, 1985; Leinhardt, 1974; Wang, 1980; Wang, Catalano, & Gromoll, 1983).

Until recently, evaluation of supported employment services and programs focused primarily on outcomes, particularly consumers served (e.g., IQ level), number of hours worked, wages earned, and integration. Integration is the most difficult of these outcomes to determine because there are no widely accepted, reliable methods for assessing whether employment is truly integrated (Lagomarcino, 1989). Contrary to Ball's (1981) assertion, evaluation of supported employment services seems to take process for granted when certain outcomes occur.

The manuals and guides described above have been evaluated by their respective developers. For example, Trach and Rusch (1989) found a relationship between supported employment services, as measured by the Degree of Implementation, and selected supported employment program outcomes. Two findings were significant. First, those programs that implemented more employment services (i.e., components) also served consumers with lower IQ scores than programs that implemented less services. Second, a significant positive correlation existed between the number of hours spent in job development, in job survey and analysis, and in job matching. In other words, those programs expending more time developing jobs were also spending more time surveying the community, developing jobs, and matching consumers to jobs.

McDonnell, Nofs, Hardman, and Chambless (1988) analyzed the procedural components of their model (c.f. *Utah Supported Employment Project Implementation Checklist*) in relation to program outcomes. They found that comprehensive individualized program plans were linked to supported employment benefits; functional assessment and job matching procedures improved consumer wages earned and hours worked; and training procedures (i.e., job anal ysis, written programs, frequent review of progress) contributed to the long-term employment of supported employees. McDonnell et al. (1988) also found that conducting structured weekly staff meetings, developing a specific marketing plan, establishing formal service contracts with employers, and defining staff roles were all strongly associated with improved worker outcomes.

Finally, Wacker, Fromm-Steege, Berg, and Flynn (in press) investigated supported employment as an "intervention package." They proposed a training and post-training package with 10 components. Their study found 3 of the 10 components were significantly related to long-term consumer employment: client advocacy, teaching collateral behavior (i.e., displaying social and communicative behaviors), and developing a follow-up plan (see Table 5.5).

Table 5.5 Components of the Iowa Supported Employment Model

Variable	Definition
1. Prior training	Client received part of job training at school or adult center prior to or in conjunction with on-site training.
2. On-site training	Client received training on-the-job by a job coach. Only clients who successfully completed the job task during the first training sessions, or who were trained entirely by co-workers, did not receive on-site training.
3. Previous work experience	Client has previous community work experience or had been placed previously in a community job for pay as part of the project.
4. Sufficient exemplars	Client received training on two or more examples of the job task, job materials, job setting, or trainers.
5. Permanent prompts	Client was trained to use a prompt to guide performance (e.g., pictures or a written list).
6. Client advocate	One or more co-workers were asked by project staff to advocate for the client by assisting with training or socializing with the client.
7. Program advocate	A supervisor, manager, or someone in authority served as an advocate for supported employment (e.g., served on an advisory council) but did not necessarily work closely with the client.
8. Follow-up	A consistent follow-up plan was initiated by the job coach that involved at least monthly follow-up calls or on-site contact other than for "crisis" intervention.
9. Maintenance plan	A specific maintenance procedure (other than follow-up) was developed to facilitate long-term employment, such as self-monitoring, soliciting of reinforcers, natural contingencies, etc.
10. Collateral behavior	Collateral behavior was defined as job-related social and communicative behaviors that were taught as part of job training. Clients who had opportunities for social interactions on the job site, and who engaged in social interactions, were scored as displaying collateral behavior.

Wacker, D.P., Fromm-Steege, L., Berg, W. K., & Flynn, T. H. (1988). *Supported employment as an intervention package: A preliminary analysis of internal validity.* Manuscript submitted for publication.

SUMMARY

Supported employment has developed from isolated demonstration projects to a national initiative. Examination of research related to supported employment indicates that, although labels for supported employment activities and services may vary among model developers, the procedures they describe and implement bear a marked resemblance to each other. Notably, these procedures include surveying the community for jobs, identifying and analyzing the requisite skills of potential employment sites, assessing the current skill levels of supported employees, matching jobs to prospective employees, providing systematic training in job-related skills, providing follow-up training and maintenance of learned skills, satisfying employers, and coordinating related services.

These models have also helped to identify the relationship between intervention (i.e., supported employment) and expected outcomes in wages, integration, and support. Supported employment service outcomes are well documented (Bellamy et al., 1988; Federal Register, 1987; Kiernan, & Stark, 1986; Rusch, & Hughes, 1989; Wehman, & Moon, 1988). However, until recently the relationship between supported employment models and expected outcomes was less clear. Recent research has begun to address supported employment process and outcomes (McDonnell et al., 1988; Trach, & Rusch, (1989); Wacker et al., 1988).

QUESTIONS (For answers see p. 428)

1. Name three components common to most supported employment models.

2. What is the most difficult outcome to determine and why?

3. Name three expected outcomes of supported employment.

REFERENCES

Ball, S. (1981). Outcomes, the size of the impacts, and program evaluation. In S. Ball (Ed.), *New directions for program evaluation: Assessing and interpreting outcomes* (Vol. 9, pp. 71–86). San Francisco: Jossey-Bass.

Bates, P. E. (1986). Competitive employment in Southern Illinois: A transitional service delivery model for enhancing competitive employment outcomes for public school students. In F. R. Rusch (Ed.), *Competitive employment issues and strategies* (pp. 51–63). Baltimore: Paul H. Brookes.

Bates, P. & Pancsofar, E. (1981). Longitudinal vocational training for severely handicapped students in the public schools. In R. York, W. K. Schofield, D. J. Donder, D. L. Ryndak, & B. Reguly (Eds.), *Organizing and implementing services for students with severe and multiple handicaps: Proceedings from the 1981 Illinois Statewide Institute for Educators of the Severely and Profoundly Handicapped* (pp. 105–122). Springfield: Department of Specialized Educational Services, Illinois State Board of Education.

Bates, P. & Pancsofar, E. (1983). Project EARN (Employment and Rehabilitation = Normalization): A competitive employment training program for severely disabled youth in the public schools. *British Journal of Mental Subnormality*, *29*, 97–103.

Bellamy, G. T., Rhodes, L. E., Mank, D. M., & Albin, J. M. (1988). *Supported employment: A community implementation guide*. Baltimore: Paul H. Brookes.

Bellamy, G. T., Sheehan, M. R., Horner, R. H. , & Boles, S. M. (1980). Community programs for severely handicapped adults: An analysis of vocational opportunities. *Journal of The Association for the Severely Handicapped*, *5*(4), 307–324.

Boles, S. M., Bellamy, G. T., Horner, R. H., Mank, D. M. (1984). *Specialized training program model implementation checklist*. Eugene: University of Oregon, Specialized Training Program.

DeStefano, L., Wang, M. C., & Gordon, E. W. (1985). An analysis of individual differences in student temperament characteristics and the implications for classroom processes and outcomes. In M. C. Wang (Ed.), *Temperament and school learning* (pp. 81–120). Symposium held at the April 1984 meeting of the American Educational Research Association, New Orleans, LA. Pittsburgh: University of Pittsburgh, Learning Research and Development Center.

Federal Register (August 14, 1987). The state supported employment services program, *52*(157), 30546–30552.

Gardner, J. F., Chapman, M. S., Donaldson, G. , & Jacobson, S. G. (1988). *Toward supported employment: A process guide for planned change*. Baltimore: Paul H. Brookes.

Horner, R. H. & Bellamy, G. T. (1979). Long-term structured employment: Productivity and productive capacity. In G. T. Bellamy, G. O'Conner, & O. Karan (Eds.), *Vocational habilitation for developmentally disabled persons: Contemporary service strategies* (pp. 85–101). Baltimore: University Park Press.

Kiernan, W. E. & Stark, J. A. (Eds.). (1986). *Pathways to employment for adults with developmental disabilities*. Baltimore: Paul H. Brookes.

Lagomarcino, T. R. (1986). Community services: Using the supported work model within an adult service agency. In F. R. Rusch (Ed.), *Competitive employment issues and strategies* (pp. 65–75). Baltimore: Paul H. Brookes.

Lagomarcino, T. R. (1989). *Assessing the multidimensional nature of integration in employment settings*. Unpublished doctoral dissertation, University of Illinois at Urbana-Champaign.

Leinhardt, G. (1974). Observation as a tool for evaluation of implementation. In M. C. Wang (Ed.), *The use of direct observation to study instructional-learning behaviors in school settings* (pp. 22–50). Pittsburgh: University of Pittsburgh, Learning Research and Development Center.

McDonnell, J., Nofs, D., Hardman, M. , & Chambless, C. (1986). *Utah supported employment project implementation checklist*. Salt Lake City: University of Utah.

McDonnell, J., Nofs, D., Hardman, M. , & Chambless, C. (1988). *An analysis of the procedural components of supported employment programs associated with worker outcomes*. Manuscript submitted for publication.

McLoughlin, C. S., Garner, J. B. , & Callahan, M. (Eds.). (1987). *Getting employed, staying employed: Job development and training for persons with severe handicaps*. Baltimore: Paul H. Brookes.

Moon, S., Goodall, P., Barcus, M. , & Brooke, V. (1986). *The supported work model of competitive employment for citizens with severe handicaps: A guide for job trainers*. Richmond: Virginia Commonwealth University, Rehabilitation Research and Training Center.

Nisbet, J. & Callahan, M. (1988). *Assessing the quality of supported employment services*. Durham: University of New Hampshire, The Institute on Disability.

Paine, S. C., Bellamy, G. T. , & Wilcox, B. (Eds.). (1984). *Human services that work: From innovation to standard practice*. Baltimore: Paul H. Brookes.

Rusch, F. R. & Hughes, C. (in press). Overview of supported employment. *Journal of Applied Behavior Analysis*.

Rusch, F. R. & Mithaug, D. E. (1980). *Vocational training for mentally retarded adults: A behavior analytic approach*. Champaign, IL: Research Press.

Trach, J. S. & Rusch, F. R. (1989). Supported employment program evaluation: Evaluating degree of implementation and selected outcomes. *American Journal on Mental Retardation, 94*, 134–139.

Trach, J. S., Rusch, F. R. , & DeStefano, L. (1987). Supported employment program development: Degree of implementation manual. In J. S. Trach, & F. R. Rusch (Eds.), *Supported employment in Illinois: Program implementation and evaluation* (Volume 1). Champaign, IL: University of Illinois at Urbana-Champaign, Illinois Supported Employment Project.

Vogelsberg, R. T. (1986). Competitive employment in Vermont. In F. R. Rusch (Ed.), *Competitive employment issues and strategies* (pp. 35–49). Baltimore: Paul H. Brookes.

Vogelsberg, R. T. & Richard, L. (1988). Supported employment for persons with mental retardation. In P. Wehman, & M. S. Moon (Eds.), *Vocational rehabilitation and supported employment* (pp. 253–268). Baltimore: Paul H. Brookes.

Vogelsberg, R. T., Spaulding, P., Patterson, D., Schenck, R. , & Phillips, R. (1984). Project Transition: Competitive employment case management system. *Center for Developmental Disabilities Monograph Series, 4*, 1–127.

Wacker, D. P., Fromm-Steege, L., Berg, W. K. , & Flynn, T. H. (1988). *Supported employment as an intervention package: A preliminary analysis of internal validity*. Manuscript submitted for publication.

Wang, M. C. (1980). *The degree of implementation assessment measures for the Adaptive Learning Environments Model*. Experimental edition. Pittsburgh:

University of Pittsburgh, Learning Research and Development Center.

Wang, M. C., Catalano, R. , & Gromoll, E. (1983). Training manual for the implementation assessment battery for adaptive instruction. Pittsburgh: University of Pittsburgh, Learning Research and Development Center.

Wehman, P. (1981). *Competitive employment: New horizons for severely disabled individuals*. Baltimore: Paul H. Brookes.

Wehman, P. (1986). Competitive employment in Virginia. In F. R. Rusch (Ed.), *Competitive employment issues and strategies* (pp. 23–34). Baltimore: Paul H. Brookes.

Wehman, P. & Moon, M. S. (1988). *Vocational rehabilitation and supported employment*. Baltimore: Paul H. Brookes.

Wilcox, B. & Bellamy, G. T. (1982). *Design of high school programs for severely handicapped students*. Baltimore: Paul H. Brookes.

PART

II

Introduction to Supported Employment Methods

Robert H. Horner
University of Oregon

Part Two presents nine chapters that offer an update on supported employment technology. Taken together, the chapters provide clear evidence that the enthusiasm accompanying the introduction of supported employment in the late 1970s is giving way to serious analysis of the means to maintenance of and improvement on initial advances. Supported employment has moved from an impressive infancy to a promising adolescence. This development is both appropriate and challenging. As the nine chapters in Part Two indicate, the challenge is being met with the same optimism that made supported employment initially successful.

Supported employment is both a theoretical approach and a behavioral technology for assisting people to be employed. Theoretically, it represented a move away from preparing people to be "ready" for employment to defining the type and level of support a person needed right now to be successfully employed. The significance of this shift is evidenced by the current moves to adopt a similar logic for "supported education" (TASH, 1989) and "supported living" (Bellamy & Horner, 1987; Taylor, 1985, April). People with disabilities are being acknowledged for the contributions they can make to individuals, communities, and society (Newton, Slovic, & Stoner, 1988). People with severe disabilities are being acknowledged for the capability they have to grow and learn, to build and control their own lives (Perske, 1988). Our expectations for a technology of support are changing, and the themes presented in Chapters 6–14 reflect those changes.

The nine chapters focus on three major aspects of supported employment methods: assessment and evaluation, employment support, and systems management.

ASSESSMENT AND EVALUATION

The first two chapters in Part Two focus on the assessment and evaluation needed to promote successful employment. Chapter 6 by James Martin provides a ten-step placement model that has been successful in Colorado. The key element of this chapter is the method for redesigning conventional supported employment procedures (assessment of the person with disabilities, assessment of the job, etc.) to maximize involvement and control by the person with disabilities. Chapter 6 exemplifies the growing recognition of special education and rehabilitation as "support" technologies. Our responsibility is not to control the individual with disabilities but to assist him or her to achieve personally defined, socially acceptable goals. As we have become more aware of the difference between controlling someone and supporting someone, a wave of humility has begun to sweep over our field. Our technology should not be guided by professionals; rather it should be used by professionals and guided by consumers. A critical part of our role in delivering support is assisting people with disabilities to participate in opportunities to express their choices. This is a difficult process and easy to oversimplify. As Martin discusses, however, it is the key to building supported employment opportunities that will endure and dramatically change the lives of people who receive support.

Building on these themes in their excellent analysis of vocational evaluation in Chapter 7, Menchetti and Flynn contrast our old approaches to evaluating a person for employment with the current technology developed in response to supported employment procedures. Traditional evaluation systems promised to assess a person's abilities and define the "right" job for him or her. This has proven to be a false promise. People are not the mechanical entities such a model of evaluation presupposes. They are dynamic, complex, elegant beings who are much more than the sum of an IQ test and a VALPAR score. Chapter 7 presents an ecological approach to assessment that emphasizes the array of variables to consider when attempting to match a person with a job. The reader is encouraged to attend to the important emphasis the authors place on assessing the social ecology of a workplace as well as the specific demands of the job. The evaluation model presented in Chapter 7 not only defines a new standard for vocational assessment but also suggests important features for job support and job satisfaction that apply to all persons, not just those with disabilities.

EMPLOYMENT SUPPORT

The importance of listening to worker preferences and acknowledging the complexities of individualized support carry over in the four chapters (8, 9, 10 and 11) that address specific procedures for supporting people in job settings. The single most important change affecting our technology of support has occurred in our expectations. In the early 1970s the field focused on whether people with severe disabilities could learn to perform vocational tasks. There was great excitement at demonstrations that learning had occurred and that learned tasks could be performed at nontrivial rates for nontrivial time periods. Expectations have risen. With supported employment, people are expected to learn real jobs in real job settings. The outcomes are not just positive trends on task analysis charts but real wages, social integration, personal independence, and the array of benefits that come to a person who is acknowledged as contributing to society. With the rise in expectations for supported employment outcomes has come an expansion in the technology of support.

In Chapter 8, Buckley, Mank, and Sandow provide an overview of the different elements of our current supported employment technology. They divide that technology into three classes: direct support, indirect support, and external support. The direct support technology is the most familiar to proponents of supported employment. The authors emphasize, however, the importance of self-management, social skills training, and communication training to the more traditional task analysis, training, and production support procedures. Even within the narrow area of direct support procedures, the demands on a job coach are growing.

In addition to direct support procedures, however, Buckley and colleagues emphasize the important "indirect" contributions of co-workers, supervisors, and employers. As more companies begin to implement their own supported employment efforts, these "indirect" roles will become less distinguishable from direct support efforts. The authors also acknowledge that a complete technology of supported employment must include the "external" support offered by parents, advocates, counselors, and case managers.

In Chapter 9, Berg, Wacker, and Flynn address the critical issues surrounding a technology of support that produces generalization and maintenance. It is not enough to teach skills that are important. People must be able to perform them across the range of situations they encounter and continue to do so for a significant period of time. The social validity of employment gains rests in part on the generalization and maintenance of employment successes. The authors emphasize the importance of teaching self-management skills and using preferred outcomes (worker choice) as critical elements in the development of effective gains.

Chadsey-Rusch in Chapter 10 and Hughes,

Rusch, and Curl in Chapter 11 further extend our knowledge concerning the technology of supported employment. Janis Chadsey-Rusch addresses the complex issue of social skills in employment settings. We have long known that employment success depends as much or more on social skills as on the skills required to perform specific jobs. What has been less clear is how to identify the critical social skills in work environments and what procedures to use for assisting people with disabilities to master those skills. The answers to these questions are not yet available, but the status of our current understanding and the directions for support procedures are provided in Chapter 10. A clear message by Chadsey-Rusch and expanded by the authors of Chapter 11 is that employment support requires ever-changing demands. As we moved beyond the "readiness" model of support, we accepted that, even when a person received the support needed for initial success on a job, the demands for support did not end. Employment is an ever-changing process. People outgrow jobs. Jobs change. Opportunities for new employment arise. With each of these developments, the need for employment support changes. An adequate technology of support must be responsive to ongoing changes in a person's life. As Hughes and colleagues suggest, the continuously changing nature of support needs fits well with the use of natural forms of employment support (e.g., from peers; co-workers, etc.).

Together, the authors of Chapters 8–11 offer an encouraging picture of the support technology that can (and should) be expected from supported employment. The technology is broadening. The skills of support personnel are becomimg more precise and diverse. These skills are consistent with the expanding outcomes discussed in earlier chapters, but they suggest increasing demands on job coaches, co-workers, and those delivering the support within supported employment. Expansion of service support expectations will require change in the systems that deliver support. The range of systems changes that can be expected are discussed in Chapters 12, 13, and 14.

SYSTEMS MANAGEMENT

The message from the final three chapters is that changes in support technology must be accompanied by changes in support systems. In Chapter 12, Szymanski and co-authors encourage movement to a transdisciplinary model of service delivery. This basic model has been the foundation of special education efforts for the past decade and fits well with the needs of supported employment consumers. If we are to build a truly trandisciplinary approach in which different professionals (and nonprofessionals) collaborate in the support of an individual, significant changes must occur in the way employment support is coordinated. Schalock and Kiernan provide an insightful analysis of the coordination demands that can be expected in the near future. They emphasize that, as supported employment moves from a social service-based effort to a private employer-based effort, our understanding of interagency coordination must expand to allow intersystem coordination. In addition, service delivery systems must adapt a form of evaluation based on the fundamental outcomes of employment on the lifestyle of the person with disabilities. DeStefano addresses this last message in depth with a discussion of the demands that will be placed on program evaluation efforts during the next decade. Traditional strategies of program evaluation used in special education and rehabilitation do not fit the demands and expectations of supported employment. The objectives of supported employment are not just employment but also change in the social and personal options a person enjoys. Supported employment is not just a way to obtain a job, it is a support strategy for re-establishing people with severe disabilities as viable, contributing members of society. This larger outcome should force continuous evaluation of the social validity of supported technology and result in a reaffirmation that supported employment is first and foremost a technology for people with very severe disabilities. As efforts to expand the technology of support continue, a central standard of evaluation should be the extent to which we succeed at employing those citizens with more severe developmental disabilities.

REFERENCES

Bellamy, G. T. & Horner, R. H. (1987). Beyond high school: Residential and employment options after graduation. In M. E. Snell, (Ed.). *Systematice instruction of persons with severe handicaps* (3rd ed.). Columbus, OH: Merrill Publishing Company.

Newton, S. J., Slovic, R., & Stoner, S. K. (1988). *"Contributions; and individuals with disabilities.* Eugene, OR: University of Oregon, Specialized Training Program.

Perske, R. (1988). *Circle of friends: People with disabilities and their friends enrich the lives of one another.* Nashville, TN: Abington Press.

TASH (The Association for Persons with Severe Handicaps), (1989). *Resolution on supported education*, February 14, 1989. Seattle: Author.

Taylor, S. (1985, April). In J. Knoll (Ed.), *The community integration project.* Syracuse, NY: Syracuse University, The Center on Human Policy, Division of Special Education and Rehabilitation.

CHAPTER

6

Consumer-Directed Placement

James E. Martin
Dennis E. Mithaug
University of Colorado

Supported employment programs unknowingly suspend basic employment rights that nonhandicapped workers enjoy. Providers and parents make most placement decisions (Mithaug, Martin, Husch, Agran, & Rusch, 1988). Consumer preference for particular jobs, tasks, or work conditions are often given little consideration (Martin, Mithaug, Husch, & Agran, in press; Mithaug, Martin et al., 1988). Guess and his associates claim:

> For most persons the ability and opportunity to make choices and decisions is an important and cherished component of their lives. The opportunity to make choices reflects favorably on one's perceived independence, dignity, and self-worth. Expressions of free choice are not only highly valued by our society, but are also protected and encouraged. According to the published literature, however, opportunities to make choices, decisions, and express preferences are conspicuously absent . . . . (Guess, Benson, & Siegel-Causey, 1985, p. 185)

Anthony and Blanch (1987) noticed this too. They characterize employment training as a "choose-get-keep" process. Unfortunately, they find supported employment programs all too often emphasize the get and keep stages, but *ignore* consumer-directed choice.

Consumers of supported employment services, not staff or parents, need to match their interests and abilities to available community jobs, and then make a choice. Work that matches interests increases motivation. These factors may be more critical to employment success than specific job skills (Berkell, 1987). But without consumer input directing the placement process, how can the match between consumer interests and job conditions be assured?

Consumer-directed supported employment empowers consumers to make reliable choices about their interests and the jobs they want (Mithaug et al., 1988). Consumers learn to reliably express their work preferences and match their work, social, and personal strengths to job requirements. This first occurs at self-planning sessions and during hands-on visits to numerous community work sites. Next, consumers test-out their choices during a job tryout. Last, placement in the preferred job follows. Of course, some individuals targeted for supported employment programs cannot exercise informed choice and decision making. In these cases, the staffing team, including parents or guardians, make all major placement decisions.

What is the structure and the role of staff in a consumer-directed program? How is a consumer-directed job match process implemented? Where do staff obtain job leads and determine what job tasks are like? How is a consumer-directed job match implemented with people who have severe disabilities? In this chapter, we present 10 steps to answer these and other questions concerning consumer-directed placement. To clarify many of the steps, we use examples from our consumer directed supported employment program at the University of Colorado.

STEP 1. ESTABLISH A CONSUMER REPRESENTED ADVISORY BOARD

Each community is unique. Its mix of economic conditions, and the relationships between providers, consumers, parents, schools, and employers are unlike those found in any other community. An advisory board, comprised of consumers currently employed in community jobs, parents, large and small employers, rehabilitation counselors, special educators, and community leaders, helps staff understand local conditions. The board provides the means to publicly monitor consumer-directed decision-making and, as Rusch (1983) suggests, "this committee might help a placement coordinator find job vacancies; gain entrance into various job sites; communicate with co-workers . . . and conduct local surveys" (p. 514).

Committee members are busy people. Meetings should be scheduled infrequently, start and end on time, and follow an established agenda.

STEP 2. DETERMINE JOB POSSIBILITIES

Each community possesses its own entry-level employment opportunities. For instance, a Colorado mountain resort community requires many motel, restaurant, and other service workers. The first task of the Advisory Board is to determine specific entry-level employment opportunities and formulate a list of the top six entry-level jobs. Information to help with this decision is readily available.

The Department of Labor in each state publishes current employment trends. Likewise, the local chamber of commerce or job service office provides local job market information. The program coordinator compiles these data, presents the results to the advisory board, asks them to consider the data in relationship to their knowledge of local employment needs, and facilitates the production of a list of the top jobs.

STEP 3. DEVELOP COMMUNITY JOB MATCH ASSESSMENT SITES

A consumer-directed employment program requires at least six job-match assessment sites within existing community firms. The six sites must represent the most available entry-level employment positions found in a community. (Job match assessment details are discussed in Step 5.)

Mithaug et al. (1988) suggest calling on previous or current employers, following leads provided by parents, employers, board members, or staff from other agencies or acquaintances, or making cold calls. Be sure to cover the following:

1. The purpose of the job match assessment site is to help trainees discover what types of work they like, learn what work they can do, and demonstrate their independence.
2. The schedule will be flexible so as not to interfere with normal business operations.
3. This opportunity helps trainees learn to make better decisions.
4. The business is not obligated to hire anyone.
5. All trainees will be under the supervision of program staff.

Unfortunately, only established programs have a pool of contacts. New supported employment programs must develop contacts before sites can be established. We recommend new programs start to build their network of contacts through the use of a mail survey.

MAIL SURVEY

A new supported employment program may use a mail survey to establish a number of potential sites quickly and inexpensively. First, send personalized letters to the firms that employ the targeted categories of workers. Develop a list of names by looking through the telephone book, or by asking the job service, chamber of commerce, local rehabilitation office, and advisory board members for suggestions.

When we first started our program at the University of Colorado, we called the firms on our list to check if the firm was still in operation. If so, we obtained the name of the person responsible for hiring entry-level staff. Second, we sent an original typed letter (produced on a word processor) addressed to the contact person from each firm (see Form 6.1 in the Appendix), and a self-addressed postage paid reply card (see Form 6.2 in the Appendix). We designed the card for quick response.

We also attached a fact sheet to the letter that explained the program in more detail. It highlighted the beneficial aspects of hiring a quality worker, and the associated financial benefits. We did not force attention through affirmative action policies or feelings of pity toward the handicapped. The informational handout we used initially is included as Form 6.3 in the Appendix. Note how the information is presented as if a service is being sold similar to any other service an employer purchases. The fact sheet used by On the Job Incorporated sells their service, too (see Form 6.4 in the Appendix). OJ Incorporated is not asking for handouts; it operates as any other service an employer may purchase.

To keep on the top of the flow of information, record in a ledger or computer database the names and addresses of individuals to whom letters were sent. As cards are returned, record data received, responses, and action notes. Keep the ledger or database readily available to record information on those who call. During a call, simply ask the questions contained on the response card and record this information in the ledger. These data will provide valuable information for many months.

TELEPHONE FOLLOW UP. Many people who receive the survey intend to reply but misplace the response card or forget to mail it. Call those who did not respond within two to three weeks. Briefly explain the program and then ask the questions included on the response card. Promptly record the information.

STEP 4. CONDUCT JOB ANALYSIS

A job analysis examines potential entry-level positions to determine required work skills, task demands, and employment conditions (Gannaway & Wattenbarger, 1979; Mithaug, Hagmeier, & Haring, 1977). Rusch and Mithaug (1980) suggest the job analysis be completed by: (1) interviewing the direct supervisor, (2) talking with the person who is currently doing the task, (3) observing the interaction and work environment while touring the job site, and (4) doing the job tasks.

Job Analysis Form

Each supported employment program requires its own job analysis form, one that reflects local needs and requirements. Included in the Appendix (Form 6.5) is a sample job analysis form. It consists of five sections. The items within each section are self-explanatory, but a few require additional comment.

POSITION TITLE (SECTION I). The *Dictionary of Occupational Titles* (DOT), produced by the U.S. Department of Labor (1977), provides a title and number for almost every job. Whenever possible, use the title listed in the dictionary, as many reports require its use. Also, several assessment and interest inventories key their results to DOT titles. However, to facilitate communication between the employer, co-workers, consumer, and follow-up staff the name of the position used by the firm may be the best choice.

STABILITY OF JOB (SECTION I). Calculate the position's two-year employee turnover rate. Note the figure in average monthly (or yearly, if the rate is very low) terms. For instance, in the example job analysis form, the average turnover rate is once very four months (twenty-four months divided by six turnovers = four per each four-month time period).

Reasons for previous firings and abandonments (Section I). Reasons for leaving can include supervisory style, task demands, or work conditions. Knowing why previous workers left may enable preventive actions to be taken. For example, most workers on the sample form left because of their dislike of required work. A worker considering this site needs to be aware of this requirement and agree to fulfill it.

Importance of speed (Section II). Workers must match their ability to work at a certain pace to specific job requirements. For instance, on the example form, a room must be cleaned in thirty minutes or less. Exceptions to established standards may be made for slower workers, but this requires employer support and may result in lower hourly wages.

General social environment (Section II). Note not only the social interactions associated with completing required tasks, but also those that occur during, before, and after work, and during breaks. Describe integration opportunities. List the ways and frequency in which the consumer comes into contact with nonhandicapped co-workers and customers.

Physical conditions (Section II). When a person moves from a sheltered workshop or classroom setting to competitive employment, a harsh physical environment may make the transition difficult. For instance, going from the workroom in a sheltered shop where the temperature is always in the 70s, to a meat-cutting room where the temperature is kept in the low 40s may cause problems for the individual. Record any possible physical barriers that may impede performance. For example, the sample analysis form indicates that the hotel work site is not wheelchair accessible.

Job task analysis (Section III). Some jobs key to time, others to changing environmental demands, and still others mix both time and sequences. The example form indicates that the first few steps at the start of a shift need to be in a specific order, but within a broad time frame. The remainder of the job requires doing each room in less than thirty minutes. Include, in the example form, the steps required to do each room-cleaning task.

Pay scale (Section IV). Resolve pay issues prior to placement, to avoid confusion later on. Note the agreed-upon starting salary, and schedule for future raises. Make sure placement details comply with all federal or state labor laws (see Martin & Husch, 1987 for detailed labor law discussion). If production is low and a decision is made to pay less than minimum wage, be sure to file the proper certificate. Contact the local Wage and Hour Division of the U.S. Department of Labor or a state rehabilitation counselor for additional information.

Union (Section IV). If a union is present, contact the local union steward (agent) and explain the program to obtain support. Request that the regional union office be informed. Most labor unions take pride in policy statements that commit them to advancing the employment conditions of workers who have handicapping conditions (see Weisgerber, Dahl, & Appleby, 1981). At times upper-level management may say that union policies prohibit hiring workers from a supported employment program, or their union contract prohibits any job restructuring. If local management wants to hire a worker but regional management does not, discuss the issues directly with regional union representatives. Our experience suggests that upper-level administration may use union contracts as a ploy to not hire.

Travel (Section IV). Describe car pools, mass transit, or other transporation possibilities. Be creative, for the lack of an adequate transportation plan can quickly stop a placement.

Criteria for promotion (Section IV). Many firms use a standard performance evaluation form. Try to obtain a copy of this form and use the items to evaluate the consumer. If formal promotion procedures do not exist, attempt to determine what performance categories the supervisor considers important.

FUNCTIONAL ACADEMIC SKILLS (SECTION V). Determine basic academic skill requirements and the employer's willingness to allow adaptations. For instance, on the example form the maid must check off on a written worksheet the items completed in each room. Determine whether a picture-coded checksheet could be used instead of the written form.

Verification

The consumer, vocational staff, and supervisor need to agree on the job tasks, duties, and conditions before the placement occurs. Requesting the job-site supervisor or manager to sign the analysis is an easy way to verify the details. This simplifies negotiating additional training time or other conditions when task, duties, or work conditions change. Our experience also suggests that this produces a more realistic worker-job match.

STEP 5. IMPLEMENT JOB MATCH ASSESSMENT PROCESS

During the job match process, consumers: (a) express what they like and match their preferences to available jobs, and (b) self-evaluate their work, social, and personal strengths and weaknesses. Consumers tell us what they like before and after a two-hour visit to one of six vocational sites. We repeat this process in a random order over an eight week period. After consumers have experienced each site, they become more reliable in expressing their preferences. For more information, see Martin, Mithaug, and Husch (1988) and Mithaug et al. (1988).

PREFERENCE ASSESSMENT. To express what they like, consumers complete three picture-based preference forms: (a) The Work Conditions I Like, (b) The Tasks I Like, and (c) The Jobs I Like. The Work Conditions I Like form provides an opportunity for consumers to express whether they like to work inside or outside, with people or things, and so on. An example of The Tasks I Like form is included as Form 6.6 in the Appendix. The Jobs I Like Form depicts the six most available entry-level jobs in Colorado Springs. Consumers complete the forms by circling their choice before a visit to a work site, then again after the visit. They then compare the two evaluations by counting the number of matches. Over time, they learn to express their preferences accurately and we learn if each individual can make a reliable, informed choice.

Consistency of choice is demonstrated in two ways. First, staff simply count the number of times consumers picked each item. The one picked most often is the obvious first choice. Second, consistency of choice is evident when comparing selection across the three forms. Consumer preference for conditions should match tasks. Their preference for tasks should match their job. For instance, a person who wants a laundry job should also want to work inside, with things, standing, and like washing clothes.

SELF-EVALUATIONS. The three self-evaluations focus upon consumer social, personal, and work strengths and weaknesses. Each person evaluates his or her own performance and then compares the assessment to that of a supervisor or employment specialist. These three assessments follow the same format. Individuals circle the pictures that best depict what they think. This provides an opportunity for consumers to become more realistic about what they can do and what they are like. A sample Work Strength and Weakness form is included as Form 6.7 in the Appendix.

STEP 6. CONSTRUCT A CONSUMER-DIRECTED EMPLOYMENT PLAN

In our supported employment program, consumers not only have input into their placement, they also make decisions. A consumer directed employment plan summarizes the outcome of the preference and self-evaluations. The plan depicts what the person likes and what he or she can do. Each consumer notes on the form the job he or she wants, as well as social, work, or personal behaviors that need improvement. Other forms such as the Can I Do The Job

Form feed into the Employment Plan. It compares job requirements to a person's strengths and weaknesses. Each consumer logically decides if he can do the job—staff or family *do not* make the decision. See Martin, Mithaug, and Husch (1988) and Mithaug et al. (1988) for a more detailed discussion and examples.

STEP 7. UNDERTAKE JOB TRYOUT

Job tryout follows job match assessment, but precedes placement. The employment plan directs tryout. During tryout, the consumer "testdrives" his or her first and second job choices. The consumer works a few hours a day to further evaluate the working conditions and preferences for the various tasks and duties. He or she also learns how to do much of the job. The tryout lasts eight weeks or less—four weeks at the first job, another four at the second job. When the consumer decides on the job he or she wants, placement staff secure a permanent position. To our surprise, many job tryout sites have converted into paid positions! Be sure to follow all labor laws. When the consumer's work benefits the firm, he or she must be paid. See Martin and Husch (1987) for a detailed labor law discussion.

STEP 8. SELF-MANAGED PERFORMANCE EVALUATION

Expect the employer to evaluate the worker toward the end of a job tryout (before it is converted into a placement), or during the probationary first few weeks of a placement. The assessment determines if the worker meets minimum employment criteria. Employers complete this initial process in different ways. Some employers complete informal evaluations based on observations and comments from the consumer's co-workers. Other employers complete a formal performance checklist.

To increase the likelihood of placement success, teach the worker to evaluate his or her own performance from the first day of tryout using evaluation items important to the employer. Ask the supervisor what he or she considers to be the top three evaluation factors associated with successful employment. An alternative is to ask the supervisor to name the worker's three biggest problems. As Martin, Mithaug, and Husch (1988) suggest, develop two 3"x5" cards. Title one "Supervisor Evaluation Card," and the other "My Evaluation Card." (See Form 6.7 in the Appendix for two sample cards.) At the end of the day, the worker picks up a completed "Supervisor Card," places it on a match contract, and compares it to his self-evaluation. The worker compares his or her own evaluations to those of the supervisor and asks, "Do they match?"

This process provides the worker with information to shape his or her self-evaluation. This is often sufficient to change problem behavior. If not, a more powerful problem-solving approach is used. A partial example of what we use in a problem situation is found as Form 6.8 in the Appendix. The person completes a problem identification process similar to the supervisor job match, then selects a solution from the Problem and Solution form. It is beyond the scope of this chapter to review on-the-job problem solving; see Mithaug et al. (1988) and Martin, Mithaug, and Husch (1988) for an in-depth discussion.

STEP 9. REDESIGN THE JOB

Job redesigning, or job engineering, is "the process by which jobs are constructed or modified to meet the specific needs of people" (Gannaway & Wattenbarger, 1979, p. 52). It is also where the nature of the work environments is altered to minimize work barriers (Vandergoot, Jacobsen, & Worrall, 1979). Job redesigning consists of two procedures. First, modify the job description. This includes altering the list of required tasks, changing the time allotted to complete the task, or sharing the job with another person. For instance, Brown et al. (1984) describe the modifications made to a consumer's hospital job. John folds towels, unpacks supplies, and attaches printed labels to supplies. He does not complete more complicated tasks such as setting dials on the washing and drying machines, operating sterilizers, or filling supply orders.

Second, use self-management procedures. Menchetti, Rusch, and Lamson (1981) surveyed the participants attending a professional food service conference to determine their opinions about different training modifications. The supervisors approved picture-coded task schedules, color coding of task equipment, and other self-management procedures. They disallowed lengthy intrusive physical training procedures. See Agran and Martin (1987) and Margin, Burger, Elias-Burger, and Mithaug (1988) for information about these and other types of self-management interventions.

STEP 10. CLARIFY PUBLIC SUPPORT FINANCIAL DETAILS

Many workers quit successful job placements because they fear losing Social Security eligibility or are confused over earned income and public support payments (Kochany & Keller, 1981). Since many supported employment participants receive Social Security payments, we *strongly* recommend holding a pre-placement staff meeting to examine *all* financial details. Include parents/guardians, residential providers, the consumer, and a counselor from the local state office of vocational rehabilitation at the meeting. To pay for work expenses and to retain Social Security payments, the staffing team may decide to write a Plan Achieving Self-Support (PASS) or to seek an Impairment Related Work Expense (IRWE).

An example PASS is included as Form 6.9 in the Appendix. Write the PASS *before* the person is placed. Basically, the pass requires that a certain amount of the Social Security or SSI payment be set aside monthly in a special bank account to pay for employment-related expenses. The PASS generally enables the worker to retain more of the Social Security or SSI payment than does the IRWE, but it is time-limited. The IRWE, on the other hand, requires less paperwork and is not time-limited. At the end of each month the worker or payee submits to the local Social Security Office receipts documenting his or her earnings and the amount of employment-related expenses. Contact your local Social Security or vocational rehabilitation offices for additional information.

SUMMARY

A consumer-directed supported employment program empowers consumers. It provides choice and facilitates decision making. If a person is unsure of his or her job preferences, the program provides exposure to a variety of real jobs to help the person decide. Choice and real decision making excites consumers, families, and staff.

Staff in a consumer-directed approach facilitate rather than direct decisions. Employment specialists still develop employment sites, but under the direction of expressed consumer preferences. Many logistical details remain in staff hands, but major decisions rest in the hands of the consumers that staff serve.

In this chapter we have provided an introduction to our consumer-directed supported employment model. We developed this approach in partnership with Colorado Rehabilitation Services, our local community-centered board, local workshops, schools, parents, and of course with many consumers. We tested the procedures across disability groups, including those with mental retardation, chronic mental illness, brain injury, and learning disabilities. Demonstration sites included schools, sheltered workshops, and supported employment programs. Hopefully, the points raised in this chapter will promote further development of a consumer-directed approach.

ACKNOWLEDGEMENT

The National Institute for Disability Rehabilitation Research, Colorado Rehabilitation Services, and the Colorado Division for Developmental Disabilities provided support for the preparation of this chapter. We wish to express our appreciation to James Husch, Eva Frazier, and Kathy Boeke for their thoughtful assistance.

QUESTIONS (For answers see pp. 428–429)

1. How does consumer-directed job choice (versus staff or family chosen) facilitate successful supported employment outcomes?

2. The authors mention ten steps to consumer-directed placement. List and describe each.

APPENDIX

Form 6.1

Current Date

Mrs. Betty Smith
Director of Human Resources Development
Penrose Community Hospital
3205 N. Academy Blvd.
Colorado Springs, Co. 80907

Dear Mrs. Smith:

Are the applications for your entry level positions well qualified? Do you have a high rate of turnover in these positions? If you are not satisfied with the answers to those and other similar questions, then please read on.

The University of Colorado at Colorado Springs in conjunction with the Special Education Program of School District #11 has started a project to facilitate the transition of mentally handicapped students from home and school into the world of work.

A primary goal of this project is to systematically train these students at community job sites to independently perform all of the specific tasks and to meet the social demands associated with entry level positions. These training sites will be under the supervision of the project.

However, we can provide you with these well-trained individuals only with your help. Please take a few minutes to fill out and return the pre-stamped reply card. This information will enable us to begin the process of training needed skills to fulfill the demands of potential entry level positions.

Thank you for your time and interest.

Sincerely,

James V. Husch
Placement Coordinator

Enclosures

From Rusch, F. R. (Ed.) (1986). *Competitive employment issues and strategies.* Baltimore: Paul H. Brookes. Reprinted by permission of the publisher.

Form 6.2

BUSINESS REPLY MAIL
FIRST CLASS PERMIT NO. 1387 COLORADO SPRINGS, CO

Postage will be paid by addressee.

School of Education
Department of Special Education
Attn: Jim Husch
University of Colorado at Colorado Springs
Austin Bluffs Parkway
Colorado Springs, CO 80907

REPLY CARD

Please check those that apply:

__________ I would like more information.
__________ I would like to be considered for a training site.
__________ I am willing to meet with you to discuss my entry level positions.
__________ I am willing to speak to your students with regard to careers.

Name: ____________________ Phone: __________

Address: ______________________________

City/State/Zip: __________________________

Form 6.3

Brochure used by the Comprehensive Transition Training Project

The Comprehensive Transition Training Project

The U.S. Office of Education, Department of Special Education and Rehabilitation Services is sponsoring, through the University of Colorado and School District # 11 a demonstration and research project to increase the independence of mentally handicapped youth. A primary goal of the project is to facilitate the transition of mentally handicapped students from home and school into the working community by improving their abilities to independently perform a wide range of tasks.

Major Project Objectives in Relationship to Employers:

* To establish a vocational training program that will facilitate the transition of students between school, supported work, and competitive employment settings.
* To survey community employers to determine potential jobs and job training stations.
* To conduct analyses of potential jobs from which identified, specific criteria can be developed for students to move from school to work.
* To develop curricula for training skills and behaviors necessary for advanced training and competitive employment.
* To involve well prepared students in appropriate community training sites.
* To place well trained students from the training sites into appropriate community jobs.

Needed Employer Involvement:

* To assist in the process of job analysis so the performance and behavioral requirements for various entry-level positions can be identified.
* To speak to special students about careers.
* To provide possible contract work and/or materials needed to set up simulated work stations in the schools.
* To provide community job training stations, so students can be taught specific job requirements at the work site.
* To assist in the process of matching well prepared students with appropriate jobs.

What Employers Can Expect from Project

* Development of well prepared students for specific entry-level jobs.
* Development of independent workers.
* Matching of appropriate students with appropriate jobs.
* Assistance, if eligible, in obtaining targeted jobs tax credit.
* Once placed, continued follow-up by project staff.

"On the Job Incorporated" Informational Brochure

Attention employers: Why take chances when you hire?

You wouldn't risk buying a new car
without a test drive . . .

Demonstrated Performance is the Key

On the Job, Inc.

Takes the risk out of hiring

And here's how . . .

Like buying, hiring is a major investment

When you buy a car . . .	When you hire through On the Job . . .
You shop around . . .	On the Job, Inc. (OJ) saves you shopping time. OJ recruits, screens, and trains entry level workers.
You consider the cost . . .	OJ's customers are eligible for substantial savings under the Targeted Job Tax Credit program. (We'll even do the paperwork!) OJ's workers are disabled and disadvantaged persons who truly want to work. OJ will save you money—by lowering your cost of recruiting, screening and training employees. Turnover goes down—productivity goes up.
You examine the track record . . .	OJ is bringing to California employers a service which has already proven highly effective in other states. We'll be happy to put you in touch with satisfied clients such as The Bank of Boston, Aetna Insurance Co., and Sheraton Corporation.
You choose the model you want . . .	Tell us the requirements of your jobs—OJ wil ensure that the applicants you see are the ones you're looking for.
You order custom options . . .	Your OJ worker will be trained—on the job, in your company with the help of OJ staff—to suit your specific needs.
You check the warranty . . .	OJ guarantees high quality, reliable, dedicated workers and good performance—at no risk to you. (During the training and "test-drive" period, your workers are on our payroll. You pay us, we pay them.)
You test drive . . .	OJ gives you a way to test a person's performance on the job—before you hire.

[Above portion of employer brochure reprinted with permission from On the Job, Inc., Berkeley, CA.]

Form 6.4 From Rusch, F. R. (Ed.) (1986). *Competitive employment issues and strategies.* Baltimore: Paul H. Brookes. Reprinted by permission of the publisher.

Completed Job Survey Analysis
from the Illinois Competitive Employment Project

JOB ANALYSIS

I. Firm and Position Overview

Name of Firm: Jumer's Castle Lodge

Address: 209 S. Broadway, Urbana, IL 61801 Phone: 384-8800 X119

Type of Industry: Hotel/motel industry

Name and Title of Person Interviewed: Betty Jones - Executive Housekeeper

Title of Position: Housekeeper/Maid

Total Number of People Employed: 167/Hotel Employees in Position 12 maids

Stability of Job: Turnover averages once every four months.

Reasons for Previous Firings/Abandonments: Firings have rarely occurred. Schedule default is the main reason. People leave their job to go to school, for more pay, problems at home, deciding not to work weekends. "Not a desirable job," says the supervisor, "the only thing is we work out of a basement and there is always work to be done."

II. Work Environment

Type of Firm: Hotel/lodge running at 60% occupancy per month. Football weekends, special weekends, (i.e. Mom's Day, Dad's Day, etc.) and shows in area increase occupancy.

Importance of Speed: Worker must be able to "to standard"* completely clean a room/bathroom in 1/2 hour.

Number of Co-workers Trainee Will Work Directly With: Direct contact will be with the Executive Housekeeper/2 assistants but trainee will be acquainted with 11 housekeepers/maids.

Supervision available: Executive housekeeper prorates minimal supervision. Runs checks from time to time as well as front desk checks to see if rooms are ready.

Probable Cooperation of Other Employees: Co-workers have their own work to complete in designated 8 hours but would be willing to help in necessity. Not doing trainee's work, however.

General Social Environment: "Family environment within department" - hotel friendly, warm, pleasant.

Physical Appearance: Maids wear white shoes, hose, Jumer's uniform: blue dress, white apron, white hat. Must wear hat and be well groomed; clean hair, no odor, must make good impression on public being served.

Physical Conditions: Work out of basement, no sunlight; noisy, hot in laundry. Requires use of elevator and some stairs. Rooms too small for a worker in a wheelchair - no room for making beds, cleaning bathrooms except in handicapped rooms.

* to standard - Jumer's guests pay higher rates for quality rooms done with a special flair (extras) and Lodge expects the utmost in cleanliness/neatness in rooms. Measured by guest approval (no comments) or complaints, as well as Executive Housekeeper.

Form 6.5 From Rusch, F. R. (Ed.) (1986). *Competitive employment issues and strategies.* Baltimore: Paul H. Brookes. Reprinted by permission of the publisher.

III. Job Task Analysis

Approximate Times	Task Performed
1. 8:00 a. m.	1. Punch in
2. 8:05 a. m.	2. Load cart with all maid supplies (see bottom)
3. 8:10 a. m.	3. Check vacuum to see if in working condition
4. 8:13 a. m.	4. Sign out master key for room entry/ sign time
5. 8:15 a. m.	5. Pick up linen sheet (see below)
6. 8:15 a. m.	6. Begin room check to see what rooms are vacant/ready to be cleaned
7. 8:30 a. m.	7. Begin cleaning 1st room on linen sheet that is vacant
8. 8:30 - 9:00 (see list attached)	8. Jumers' check list of things to be done in each room in 1/2 hour
9. 9:00 a. m.	9. Move to next room
10. 9:30 a. m.	10. Move to next room
11. 10:00 a. m.	11. Break 10 minutes in employee lounge
12. 10:10 a. m.	12. Move to next room
13.	13. And so on until lunch
14. 11:00 a. m.	14. Lunch
15.	15. Move to next room
16.	16. And so on until 10 minute break at 2:00
17. 2:00 p. m.	17. Move to next
18.	18. And so on until 4:30 p. m.
19.	19. Make sure all 15 rooms on sheet are vacant and ready to sell Clock out.

Comments: These times are approximate; Mrs. Steele emphasized importance of cleaning rooms quickly on day Lodge is booked.

Night maid works from 3:00-9:00 p.m. and has fewer rooms to clean. Take care of Lodge restrooms and central areas.

Maid Supplies - Camay, Safeguard, body towels, hand towels, washcloths, tissues, glasses, toilet paper, matches, sheets, chocolates (gift boxes) cleaning supplies, etc.

Linen Sheet - a listing of *15 rooms to be cleaned by shift's end. Used to account for what maid was in what room; when it is ready for occupancy, and to keep track of rooms done.

*15 - Could be reduced for efficient but slower handicapped employee. 8-10 rooms might be a possible goal for such an employee.

Form 6.5 (cont.)

JUMER'S CASTLE LODGE ROOM CHECKLIST
(can be picture cued)

GUEST ROOM:

1. Check bed pads, linens, blankets and spreads. Reject if torn or stained.
2. Make bed neatly and correctly. Corners hospital style with sheet (top) and blanket loose under quilt.
3. Empty wastebasket and wipe clean.
4. Wash ashtrays in bathroom with water. Place on table and one on desk and one in bathroom. Replace matches to standard. See example.
5. If a checkout, check drawers for lost and found items. If items found turn in to Executive House-keeper.
6. Check and replace in desk drawer; stationary, menu and phonebook.
7. Check and replace the Bible in the bedside drawer.
8. Clean and replace tray, ice bucket and four room glasses. Place on table or in the bat-room.
9. Check operation of radio, TV, lamps and drapery rods. May work with music or TV on.
10. Sweep down cobwebs on walls, large chandelier, and behind drapes.
11. Clean off mirror and TV screen with glass cleaner and paper towel.
12. Brush down all lamp shades, bed hangings and drapes.
13. Wipe out all drawers.
14. Wipe telephone and phone index.
15. Wipe fingermarks from all doors.
16. Replace coat hangers and place one laundry bag on top of the coat rack.
17. Dust all furniture and fixtures.
18. If a checkout, place doilies, candy and welcome card on the desk.

BATHROOMS:

1. Put liquid cleaner on brush and swab entire bowl.
2. Check faucets, toilet bowl, shower and lights for operation.
3. Remove all used soap if a checkout.
4. Empty waste basket. Wipe clean.
5. Scour and sanitize shower wall, tub, soap dish, wash basin, counter top, toilet seat and outside of toilet bowl.
6. Keep vent over tub free of dust.
7. Dust mirror frame and light globes.
8. Clean mirror and chrome tissue box cover with glass cleaner.
9. Dry all surfaces. Chrome should be free of water spots.
10. Check shower curtains and hooks. Replace if needed.
11. Check and replace soap (one bar of Camay and one bar of Safeguard), toilet tissue, Kleenex, one shoe shiner, two sanibags and one ashtray with matches.
12. Replace bathmat on towel holder over toilet.
13. Replace towels and washcloths to standard.
14. Scrub bathroom floor.
15. Turn off lights.
16. Spray with deodorant.

Must all be completed within 1/2 hour.

Each can be broken down into steps/maids may use this checklist.

Form 6.5 (cont.)

IV. Conditions of Employment

Work Hours Per Day: 8 1/2 hours Per Week: 35–40 hours (5 day work weeks)

Shift: 8:00 a.m. — 4:30 p.m. day maids 3:00 til about 9:00 or 10:00 when work is done.

Pay Scale: All maids begin at $3.35. After 90 days raise to $3.45: pay rate increases after this point are not common because of management.

Bonuses/Overtime Pay: Overtime — time and a half if one works a holiday and day before or day after and 20 or more hours a week.

Union operating

Name: none

Address:

Union Representative

Name: n/a

Address:

Travel Requirements: Worker can get to Lodge by Red, Green, Orange, Grey, Orchard Downs, and Yellow bus lines or must have own dependable source of transportation.

Training: Executive Housekeeper said experience is important but not necessary. Will train for 2 to 3 days working along with another maid. Trainers could work in room within Lodge on slow days. (under 60% occupancy).

Criteria for Promotion: To move up a person must be "aggressive," hard working, must take initiative to get work done, "to do work without being told," needs to be dependable and work weekends willingly.

Form 6.5 (cont.)

Form 6.5 (concluded)

V. Worker Requirements:

Education Requirements: Preferably high school graduate; will accept those with only 2 years high school. Age requirement – 20 years. Looking for maturity, social tact with guests.

Previous Experience: Not necessary but helpful. Training period is short (2-3 days).

Licenses/Certificates: None required.

Special Social/Functional Academic/Vocational Skills: It is necessary for the employee to be pleasant and tactful with guests. Some form of acceptable communication; writing or word cards or speaking mandatory.

Vocational Skills: Some knowledge of washing machines/dryers, vacuums for operation would be helpful. Skills needed: vacuum operation, elevator operation, dusting, scrubbing. Attention to detail (bedmaking).

Tests: None for day maid unless suspected of theft; the lie detector test may be required. Night maid is subject to lie detector test for security purposes. Night maid works "more alone." "Temptations are more easily given into at night."

Insurance and Other Benefits: One week paid vacation after one year. Free group insurance after 90 days. Employee gets one meal in shift — lunch in day shift, — dinner in night shift. It is the employee meal and it is free — entree, salad, soup, and milk or coffee.

THE TASKS I LIKE

NAME ______________

DATE ______________

BEFORE WORK 

BOXES

INSERTS

MAKE BED

VACUUM

LAUNDRY SORTING

LAUNDRY TICKET

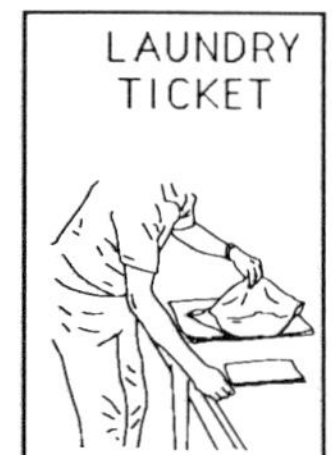

PULL DOWN

BOOKS

DUST MOPPING

CLEANING MATS

SILVERWARE WRAP-UP

TABLE WIPING

AFTER WORK

BOXES

INSERTS

MAKE BED

VACUUM

LAUNDRY SORTING

LAUNDRY TICKET

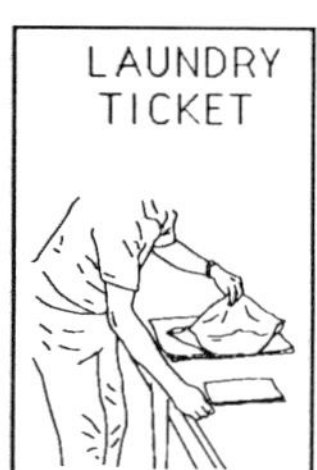

PULL DOWN

BOOKS

DUST MOPPING

CLEANING MATS

SILVERWARE WRAP-UP

TABLE WIPING

NUMBER OF MATCHES?

   1 2

DO I KNOW THE TASKS I LIKE?

Form 6.6

MY WORK STRENGTHS & WEAKNESSES

NAME ______________
DATE __________

WHAT I THINK 

COME TO WORK	MISS WORK A LOT	WORK SAFELY	WORK UNSAFELY	SAY "O.K." WHEN CORRECTED	GET MAD WHEN CORRECTED

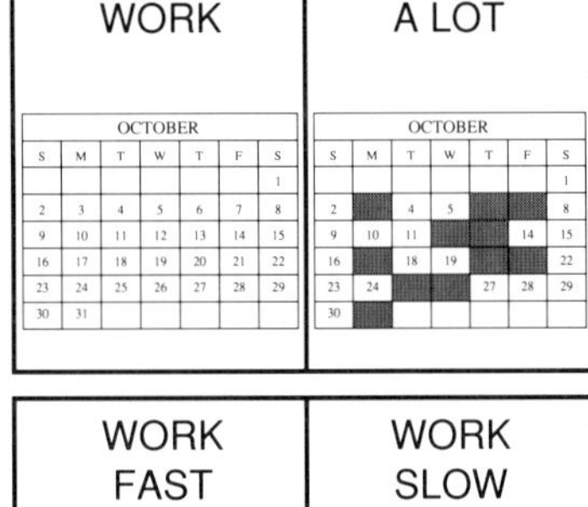

WORK FAST	WORK SLOW	WORK ACCURATELY	MAKE MISTAKES	COME TO WORK ON TIME	COME TO WORK LATE

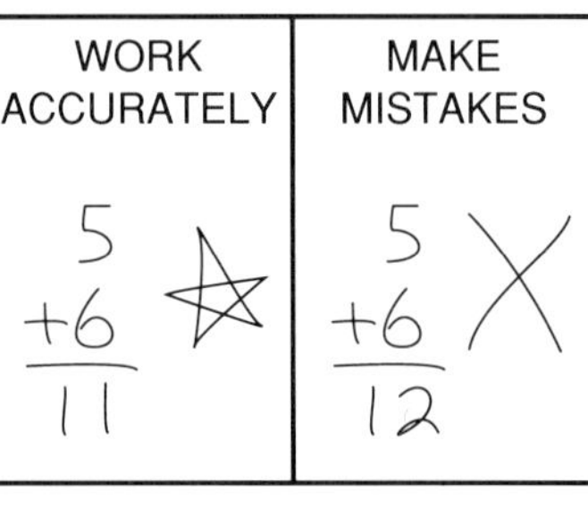

WHAT MY JOB COACH THINKS 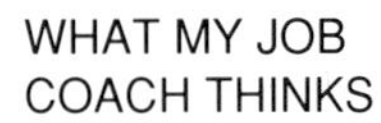

COME TO WORK	MISS WORK A LOT	WORK SAFELY	WORK UNSAFELY	SAY "O.K." WHEN CORRECTED	GET MAD WHEN CORRECTED

WORK FAST	WORK SLOW	WORK ACCURATELY	MAKE MISTAKES	COME TO WORK ON TIME	COME TO WORK LATE

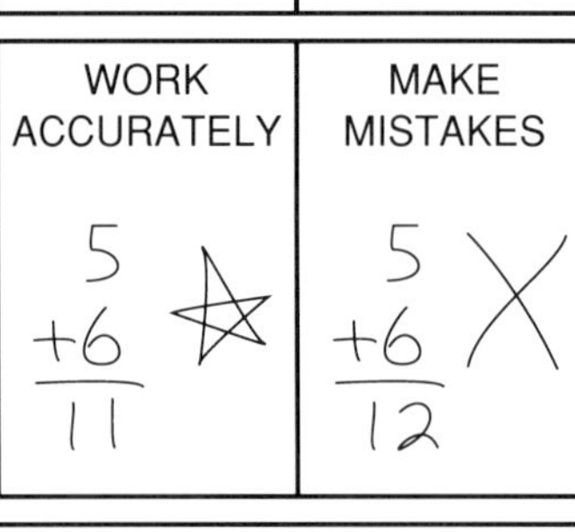

NUMBER OF MATCHES?

0 1 2 3 4 5 6

DO I MATCH MY JOB COACH?

?   =   

 YES

 NO

Form 6.7

INTRO MATCH CONTRACT

MY GOAL: | 0 | | 1 | 2 | 3 | MATCHES WITH SUPERVISOR

☆ ☆ ● = ●

NAME:________________ JOB:________________ DATE:__________

MY EVALUATION CARD

NAME:________________ JOB:________________ DATE:__________

WORK	Y N	
SOCIAL	Y N	
PERSONAL	Y N	

NAME:________________ JOB:________________ DATE:__________

SUPERVISOR'S EVALUATION CARD

NAME:________________ JOB:________________ DATE:__________

WORK	Y N	
SOCIAL	Y N	
PERSONAL	Y N	

HOW MANY MATCHES? | 0 | | 1 | 2 | 3 |

● = ●

MEET GOAL? ☆ ☆ | Y | | N |

MY NEXT GOAL IS | 0 | | 1 | 2 | 3 | MATCHES WITH SUPERVISOR

☆ ☆ ● = ●

Form 6.7 (cont.)

PROBLEMS AND SOLUTIONS	NAME:__________ DATE:__________
PROBLEMS	**SOLUTIONS**
ASK FOR HELP PROPERLY	1.WHEN NEED, WAIT TILL NOT BUSY AND ASK
	2.IF DON'T UNDERSTAND AND NEED HELP, ALWAYS ASK
	3.I DON'T WANT TO BOTHER ANYONE, I'LL MANAGE
	4.BUGGING PEOPLE TOO MUCH,BE MORE INDEPENDENT
	NAME DATE JOB 5.USE SELF INSTRUCTION / REMINDER CARDS

Form 6.8

Form 6.9

Plan for Achieving Self-Support

Name: ______________
SS Number: #____________

Part 1
SUPPORT NARRATIVE
Funding Support for Supported Employment Services

Issue Pre-Placement Interagency Cost Sharing Plan

Facts

1. __________ wants to become a __________ .(S)he is disabled due to __________________and needs a Supported Employment (SE) Specialist to provide one-on-one job training. The initial training and support (to begin _______, 1989) is being funded by Colorado Rehabilitation Services and will continue until ________is stabilized in the employment setting. Projected time frame to achieve stabilization for _______ is 4 months. During this period, __________will start with full-time SE support with gradual fading of intervention time. By ___________,1989, it is expected that (s)he will have stabilized in the employment setting and need "follow-along" SE intervention time, i.e., between 1 to 5 hours/week, averaging 3 hours/week.

2. The plan provides for an 18-month period of SE Specialist support.

3. (S)he will pay the SE Program $25.00 per hour. The number of hours will vary from month to month according to need.

Form 6.9 (cont.)

Objective

__________is a consumer of the University of Colorado-Colorado Springs Consumer-Directed Supported Employment Program (UCCS-CDSE). (S)he has been identified as appropriate for Supported Employment (SE) Services and chose to work in a position as_____________________ hours/wk at ___________on ______,1989. Currently, ___________lives in ______________, Colorado and supports him/herself with the funds (s)he recieves as an SSI (SSA) beneficiary.

This PASS involves sheltering earned income which will then be used to pay for supported employment follow-along services to be provided by UCCS-CDSE staff. UCCS-CDSE employment specialists will assess, place, train, and provide long-term follow-along support while on the job.

Justification

__________will benefit from SE services because of her/his disability and the fact that (s)he will require intensive support on the job. The SE specialist will provide intensive one-to-one job site training, social skills training, and advocacy to help both ___________and the employer overcome problems as they arise. The SE specialiat will teach___________to use an individualized problem-solving system that will increase her/his ability to independently perform at the job site.

Date the Objective will be Achieved

Intensive, full-time support will begin with ___________'s placement at _______________on_____,1989. The initial job-site training period is being funded by the State of Colorado Rehabilitation Services. Because of _______________disability category,__________________( ), he is not eligibile for long-term funding offered through other agencies. The initial support funded by the state CRS is expected to decrease to less than 20 hours per month, as stated in the objective, by____________,1989. Thereafter, _________will receive a contact of no less than 1 hour each week or 4 hours/month. Contacts are defined as personal visits

---

Form 6.9 (concluded)

with ____________at the job-site or his/her home and/or with his employer. The SE Specialist will be involved with _________for follow-along services for a period of 18 months at which point the PASS will be discontinued or an application for an extension will be made.

Total Amount of Money to Achieve the Objective

UCCS-CDSE Program will receive a fee of $25.00/hour for SE intervention time to be provided by a trained SE specialist.

Plan for disbursement

A. Items purchased: SE follow-along support.

B. Fulfillment of plan: UCCS-CDSE will submit a quarterly invoice to __________ and his/her payee___________ for SE services. ________(Payee) will have the responsibility of assisting ________ in maintaining a separate bank account and of seeing that UCCS-CDSE is paid the appropriate amount within a reasonable period of time (14 days).

We, the undersigned agree to this PASS and believe that it will result in _________________acheiving self support. We agree to cooperate to insure complaince with this contract.

_________________________________ ___________

Worker/SSI Recipient Date

_________________________________ ___________

SSA Claims Representative Date

_________________________________ ___________

Designated Payee Date

_________________________________ ___________

Kathleen Boeke, UCCS-CDSE Employment Specialist Date

REFERENCES

Agran, M. & Martin, J. E. (1987). Applying a technology of self-control in community environments for individuals who are mentally retarded. In M. Hersen, R. M. Eisler, & P. M. Miller (Eds.), *Progress in behavior modification* (Vol. 21, pp. 108–155). Newbury Park, CA: Sage Publications.

Anthony, W. A. & Blanch, A. (1987). Supported employment for persons who are psychiatrically disabled: An historical and conceptual perspective. *Psychosocial Rehabilitation Journal, 2*, 5–23.

Berkell, D. E. (1987). Vocational assessment of students with severe handicaps: A review of the literature. *Career Development for Exceptional Individuals, 10*, 61–75.

Brown, L., Shiraga B., York, J., Kessler, K., Strohm, B., Sweet, M., Zanella, K., VanDeventer, P., & Loomis, R. (1984). Integrated work opportunities for adults with severe handicaps: The extended training option. *Journal of the Association for Persons with Severe Handicaps, 9*, 262–269.

Gannaway, T. W. & Wattenbarger, W. (1979). The relationship of vocational evaluation and vocational placement functions in vocational rehabilitation. In D. Vandergoot & J. D. Worrall (Eds.), *Placement in rehabilitation* (pp. 43–58). Baltimore: University Park Press.

Guess, D., Benson, H. A., & Siegel-Causey, E. (1985). Concepts and issues related to choice-making and autonomy among persons with severe disabilities. *Journal of the Association for Persons with Severe Handicaps, 10*, 79–86.

Kochany, L. & Keller, J. (1981). An analysis and evaluation of the failures of severely disabled individuals in competitive employment. In P. Wehman (Ed.), *Competitive employment: New horizons for severely disabled individuals* (pp. 181–198). Baltimore: Paul H. Brookes.

Martin, J. E., Burger, D. L., Elias-Burger, S., & Mithaug, D. E. (1988). Application of self-control strategies to facilitate independence in vocational and instructional settings. In N. W. Bray (Ed.), *International review of research in mental retardation* (Vol. 15, pp. 155–193).

Martin, J. E. & Husch, J. V. (1987). U.S. Department of Labor rules in relation to school-based transition programs. *Journal of the Association for Persons with Severe Handicaps, 12*, 140–144.

Martin, J. E., Mithaug, D. E., Agran, M., & Husch, J. V. (in press). Consumer-centered transition and supported employment. In J. L. Matson (Ed.), *Handbook of behavior modification with the mentally retarded* (2nd ed.). New York: Plenum Press.

Martin, J. E., Mithaug, D. E., & Husch, J. V. (1988). *How to teach adaptability in community training and supported employment*. Colorado Springs, CO: Ascent Publications.

Menchetti, B. M., Rusch, F. R., & Lamson, D. S. (1981). Social validation of behavioral training techniques: Assessing the normalizing qualities of competitive employment training programs. *Journal of the Association for the Severly Handicapped, 6*, 6–16.

Mithaug, D. E., Hagmeier, L., & Haring, N. (1977). The relationship between training activities and job placement in vocational education of the severely and profoundly handicapped. *AAESPH Review, 2*, 89–109.

Mithaug, D. E., Martin, J. E., Husch, J. V., Agran, M., & Rusch, F. R. (1988). *When will persons in supported employment need less support?* Colorado Springs, CO: Ascent Publications.

Rusch, F. R. (1983). Competitive vocational training. In M. E. Snell (Ed.), *Systematic instruction of the moderately and severely handicapped* (2nd ed.) (pp. 503–523). Columbus, OH: Charles E. Merrill.

Rusch, F. R. & Mithaug, D. E. (1980). *Vocational training for mentally retarded adults: A behavior analytic approach*. Champaign, IL: Research Press.

U.S. Department of Labor. (1977). *Dictionary of occupational titles* (4th ed.). Washington, DC: Author.

Vandergoot, D., Jacobsen, R., & Worrall, J. D. (1979). New directions for placement practice in vocational rehabilitation. In D. Vandergoot & J. D. Worrall (Eds.), *Placement in rehabilitation* (pp. 2–41). Baltimore: University Park Press.

Weisgerber, R. A., Dahl, P. R., & Appleby, J. A. (1981). *Training the handicapped for productive employment*. Rockville, MD: Aspen Systems.

CHAPTER

7

Vocational Evaluation

Bruce M. Menchetti
Florida State University

Cynthia C. Flynn
Office of Programs for the Handicapped
South Carolina Department of Education

Recently, a new vocational opportunity has become available for persons with serious disabilities. Supported employment, with its focus on facilitating an individual's successful participation in integrated work settings, has provided an alternative to the traditional sheltered workshop service delivery model (Bellamy, Rhodes, Bourbeau, & Mank, 1986; Wehman, 1988). Supported employment offers occupational choices to persons who have had little or no personal autonomy, including those usually believed to be unemployable in the competitive labor market. Supported employment has been successfully implemented with individuals with mental retardation (Bates, 1986; Rusch, & Menchetti, 1981; Vogelsberg & Richard, 1988; Wehman, 1986); autism (McCarthy, Fender, & Fender, 1988; Wehman & Kregel, 1985); physical disabilities (Wood, 1988); and many other severe disabilities.

Supported employment includes several features that contrast greatly with the way services have traditionally been provided to individuals seeking entry into the labor market. As specified in federal regulations, supported employment has three distinguishing characteristics: (a) services should be targeted for individuals who traditionally have not succeeded in competitive employment; (b) services should be provided in integrated community settings; and (c) services should include the provision of long-term support from a variety of agencies and sources (*Federal Register,* August 14, 1987; Wehman, 1988). These zero reject, community integration, and continuous support features make supported employment a unique approach to employment training. In contrast, traditional employment services for persons with disabilities have developed through the years with restrictive eligibility requirements, an inclination toward services provided in sheltered facilities, and a proclivity for time-limited agency involvement. As supported employment programs spread across the nation, many traditional practices and procedures will have to be examined. The inherent differences between supported employment and traditional vocational services may necessitate the revision of many of these practices.

The genesis of supported employment has presented interesting challenges for vocational evaluation and its role in eligibility determination and program placement. For many years, vocational evaluation has played a key role in the rehabilitation and training process. The results of evaluation have been used to determine eligibility for rehabilitation services, recommend placement options, and plan an individual's program. Evaluation methods such as multiple aptitude batteries, work sample systems, and vocational rating scales or inventories have become widely accepted. These and other popular vocational evaluation techniques must be reviewed in the context of supported employment to determine what function they will play in this new employment training program.

This chapter addresses the issue of vocational evaluation in supported employment. The purposes of this chapter are to briefly describe popular vocational evaluation practices, analyze the appropriateness of these practices in relation to supported employment, and suggest changes needed to make evaluation a functional component of supported employment.

DESCRIPTION OF POPULAR VOCATIONAL EVALUATION PRACTICES

Vocational evaluation has a history almost as long as the development of the first standardized test. Some vocational evaluation practices are related to the mental testing approach that began with Alfred Binet in the early 1900s (Botterbusch, in press; Menchetti, Rusch, & Owens, 1983; Neff, 1966). These early techniques were adapted by the military and later by the private sector to select individuals for specific jobs and eventually evolved into some of the current practices used to evaluate persons with disabilities (Menchetti & Rusch, 1988a). Currently, there are three popular and widely used approaches in the vocational evaluation of persons with disabilities. These are: (a) the aptitude matching; (b) the work sample; and (c) the behavior inventory approaches. Other methods such as situational assessment (Dunn, 1973; Genskow, 1973) and job site analysis (Botterbusch, 1978), although available for many years, have never been widely accepted or used by vocational evaluation professionals (Botterbusch, in press).

The Aptitude Matching Approach

The aptitude matching approach is most directly related to military and civilian personnel selection techniques developed during and immediately after World War II. This approach is characterized by standardized instruments designed to measure general traits and compare an individual's performance to sixty-six occupational aptitude patterns which the U.S. Department of Labor suggests are related to various jobs. The multiple aptitude battery represents the most widely used kind of instrument in this trait measurement and matching approach.

The General Aptitude Test Battery, or GATB, developed by the U.S. Employment Service, is one of the most widely and frequently used multiple aptitude tests (Borgen, 1982), and has served as the conceptual model for several instruments developed specifically for use with special populations. Some examples of GATB "knock-off" instruments include the Nonreading Aptitude Test Battery, or NATB (U.S.E.S., 1981), the APTICOM (Vocational Research Institute, 1985), and to a lesser degree, the Talent Assessment Program, or TAP (Nighswonger, 1980). All of these instruments were designed to measure traits such as dexterity, spatial perception, and motor coordination and match an individual's performance with occupational aptitude patterns or worker trait groups described in the *Dictionary of Occupational Titles,* or *DOT*, published by the U.S. Department of Labor. For example, after administering the APTICOM, the evaluator can produce a profile which lists the examinee's score in each of ten Department of Labor aptitude areas including general intelligence, verbal aptitude, numerical aptitude, spatial aptitude, form perception, clerical perception, motor coordination, finger dexterity, manual dexterity, and eye-hand coordination. Based on these and other APTICOM interest and educational skill measures, the evaluator can prepare recommendations listing all the work groups for which an examinee's aptitude scores meet occupational aptitude pattern cutoffs established by the Department of Labor.

The Work Sample Approach

The work sample may be the most popular technique currently used in school programs, rehabilitation facilities, and job training programs to evaluate the vocational skills of persons with disabilities (Peterson, 1986). Work samples can be grouped into two large categories: (a) trait-oriented and (b) work-oriented. Trait-oriented work samples represented by systems such as the eighteen-part Valpar Component Work Sample Series (Valpar Corporation, 1981) are very similar to multiple aptitude batteries in that these work samples are designed to measure general worker characteristics such as size discrimination (Valpar Sample #2), multi-level sorting (Valpar Sample #7) and eye-hand-foot coordination (Valpar Sample #11). Three important differences between trait-oriented work samples and multiple aptitude batteries are: (a) the work samples almost exclusively measure motor responses through the use of complex and expensive apparatus rather than with paper and pencil; (b) there is less focus on general intellectual and academic abilities in the work samples as compared to the multiple aptitude batteries; and (c) many work samples are designed to be used independently rather than as part of a larger battery.

Work-oriented samples such as the Vocational Information and Evaluation Work Samples, or VIEWS (Vocational Research Institute, 1977), and the Singer Vocational Evaluation System (Singer, 1986), use simulated work to measure performance on specific tasks. Samples include tasks such as circuit board assembly, drill press operation, and bench assembly. Trait assessment and occupational aptitude pattern matching information are not typical outcomes of most work-oriented samples. Instead, work groups consisting of categories of occupations that are similar in terms of performance demands are reported, and the evaluator is left to decide which general traits the samples measure. After administration of the sixteen work samples comprising the VIEWS system (which promotional materials describe as appropriate for evaluating the "vocational potential" of persons with mild, moderate, and severe mental retardation) evaluators can make job recommendations in three work groups including machine tending and feeding, manipulating, and handling.

The Behavior Inventory Approach

A great many checklists, rating scales, and inventories have been developed over the years to measure the vocational and related behaviors of individuals with disabilities. Menchetti et al. (1983) have suggested that these instruments represent a specialized type of adaptive behavior scale. Indeed, most of the vocational inventories share the administration, scoring, and interpretation features of the more general adaptive behavior scales such as the popular AAMD Adaptive Behavior Scale-School Edition (Lambert & Windmiller, 1981) and the Vineland Adaptive Behavior Scales-Classroom Edition (Sparrow, Balla, & Cicchetti, 1985). Most vocationally oriented adaptive behavior scales are completed by an informed teacher, professional, or parent and result in scores for several behavioral areas or domains such as production, social, and self-help skills. These domain scores can then be compared to various norm groups or employment standards resulting in a profile of the examinee's performance.

Some of the more current vocational inventories have been developed through a process of surveying community members with the goal of identifying relevant behaviors to include in the checklist. This process, known as social validation (Kazdin & Matson, 1981; Van Houten, 1979), was used by Rusch and his colleagues (Rusch, 1979; Rusch, Schutz, & Agran, 1984) to survey employers representing the service industry in an effort to determine entry-level skill requirements for jobs in this area. These data were incorporated into the items comprising the Vocational Assessment and Curriculum Guide or VACG (Rusch, Schutz, Mithaug, Stewart, & Mar, 1982). The VACG and other vocational checklists such as the Prevocational Assessment and Curriculum Guide, or PACG (Mithaug, Mar, & Stewart, 1978), and the Social and Prevocational Information Battery, or SPIB (Halpern, Raffeld, Irvin, & Link, 1975), have become accepted components of supported employment evaluation efforts (DeStefano, 1987; Menchetti & Rusch, 1988a).

APPROPRIATENESS OF CURRENT EVALUATION PRACTICES

Recently, a few studies have examined the state-of-the-art in the evaluation of persons with disabilities. This research has provided information about the kinds of instruments used by practitioners in the field, how evaluation data are being applied to decision making, and the limitations of many current practices. Some studies have documented the current practice in general assessment of students with severe disabilities, while others have focused specifically on the area of vocational evaluation. This body of descriptive research has important implications for the provision of functional evaluation services in supported employment.

General Practices

Sigafoos, Cole, and McQuarter (1987) attempted to document the types of assessment instruments used with students with severe handicaps by reviewing the records of 143 pupils ranging in age from six years five months to twenty years ten months. These researchers found that only twenty-nine different instruments were used in the 229 separate test administrations recorded for their subjects. Our examination of the Sigafoos et al. (1987) data has revealed that of the twenty-nine instruments reported, thirteen were developmental or perceptual motor tests (e.g., the Denver Developmental Screening Test), eight were intelligence tests (e.g., Stanford Binet Form LM); four were adaptive behavior rating scales (e.g., the AAMD Adaptive Behavior Scale); and the remaining four instruments were tests assessing domains such as language development and reading achievement. It is interesting to note the complete absence of any test designed specifically to measure vocational skills in the Sigafoos et al. (1987) study, although it is not clear that these researchers would have included such instruments in their analysis. Nevertheless, the complete absence of any vocational evaluation instrument is disconcerting since the average age of subjects in this study was thirteen years and six months, an age approaching the time for transition planning to begin.

Sigafoos et al. (1987) also reported that the majority of the tests administered to their subjects were standardized, norm-referenced instruments. Although many professionals recommend the use of criterion-referenced tests with students who are severely handicapped, these instruments were used very infrequently with the subjects in this study. One possible explanation may be that criterion-referenced tests are not considered technically adequate by many psychometricians. Ironically, it was the norm-referenced instruments Sigafoos et al. (1987) found being used with students with severe handicaps that had highly suspect psychometric properties. They reported that none of the instruments found listed in students' records contained public school elementary or secondary age students with severe handicaps in the normative sample. Additionally, ninety-six of the 229 total test administrations (42 percent) were conducted with students who were older than the age range recommended for the instrument. Finally, many of the tests found in this study had very poor or missing reliability and validity information. The serious psychometric shortcomings Sigafoos et al. (1987) found in the tests they analyzed, "rendered them useless for making any educational decision affecting these 143 subjects" (p. 271). Most of the standardized, norm-referenced tests recorded in this study of general assessment practices were technically inadequate for the purposes for which they were being used. Making inappropriate decisions with tests having unrepresentative norm groups, poor reliability, and inadequate validity data is not limited to public school assessment practice. The inadequacy of standardized tests was also suggested in studies that specifically examined practices in vocational evaluation.

Vocational Practices

Peterson (1986) identified three recent trends in the provision of vocational evaluation services. These were: (a) an almost exclusive use of commercially published, standardized instruments; (b) an increased focus on the measurement of traits and aptitudes; and (c) a growing concern about the effectiveness of evaluation programs. These trends are reflected by the popularity of the aptitude matching, work sample, and behavior inventory approaches in the field of vocational evaluation. The vocational evaluation trends suggested by Peterson (1986) have been supported by the empirical research of Stodden and his colleagues (Stodden, Meehan, Hodell, Bisconer, & Cabebe, 1986) at the University of Hawaii.

Stodden et al. (1986) analyzed the vocational evaluation practices in two Hawaiian school districts and found that aptitude measures, work samples, and standardized behavior checklists were the most common approaches used. Surprisingly, Stodden et al. (1986) found that the mean number of vocational goals and objectives on students' individualized education plans, or IEPs, actually declined after vocational evaluation was completed. Generally, the Hawaii study found that there was little relationship between information collected through formal vocational evaluation and the training recommendations included in a student's IEP, leading Stodden et al. to question the validity of the popular evaluation approaches for program planning purposes.

There is also recent research investigating the evaluation methods practiced in employment training programs serving adults with disabilities. Agran and Morgan (1989) surveyed administrators of employment training programs such as sheltered workshops, work activity centers, and supported or competitive employment programs in seven Western states. These researchers were interested in determining the frequency with which certain evaluation approaches were utilized and the purposes for which the resulting data were used by the respondents. Agran and Morgan found that program administrators used a wide variety of evaluation approaches with direct observation, staff-developed tests, intelligence tests, motor performance tests, work samples, survival skill checklists, and adaptive behavior instruments all reported by some of the respondents. The administrators surveyed by Agran and Morgan also reported that evaluation data were used most frequently to make decisions regarding service eligibility, to assist in program planning, and to enhance communication between professionals and between parents and professionals.

These studies suggest that the popular vocational evaluation approaches represented by aptitude measurement, work sample, and behavior inventory instruments have been adopted by the new supported employment programs (Agran & Morgan, 1989; Stodden et al., 1986). It appears that evaluation data generated with these approaches are currently being used for two major purposes in supported employment: (a) to select legitimate candidates, and (b) to plan training programs for these individuals. The remainder of this section will examine whether some of the more popular evaluation measures are appropriate for determining eligibility and planning an individual's program of supported employment. In addition, the usefulness of screening and program planning as evaluation purposes in supported employment will be discussed.

Selecting Individuals for Supported Employment

Personnel selection has always been universally accepted as a primary purpose of vocational evaluation. Evaluation has usually been conducted to determine eligibility for vocational programs by attempting to measure variables that supposedly predict future employment potential such as IQ scores, vocational interests, aptitudes, and work traits. Those individuals who performed below specified levels were screened out of the program. Many popular evaluation instruments have claimed to be valid for the purpose of screening individuals for employment potential. Vocational evaluators have continued to call for selection decisions in supported employment, where some persons are chosen and others are not. Botterbusch (in press) has suggested that as long as there are more persons needing community-based services than there are jobs in the community, selection choices will continue to be necessary.

There are, however, both philosophical and methodological problems associated with the use of standardized tests to determine an individual's eligibility for supported employment. On a philosophical level, screening for eligibility seems inappropriate because supported employment has been conceptualized as a "zero-reject" program (Wehman, 1988). As discussed earlier in this chapter, the federal regulations for supported employment specifically call for the delivery of service to individuals who have not previously experienced successful community employment. The use of traditional, psychometric methods such as multiple aptitude batteries, work samples, and vocational rating scales to screen individuals will only result in the rejection of the very individuals the supported employment model was designed to serve. This represents a waste of valuable energy and resources that could be directed toward promoting the successful community employment of persons with severe disabilities. Acknowledging this situation, Botterbusch (in press) has suggested replacing the psychometric evaluation model with a "wholistic" approach consisting of job-site evaluations and situational assessment. Similarly, supported employment service providers must reconcile their evaluation practices with the philosophy of these programs and move toward an approach that recognizes that vocational success involves more than a worker trait profile. On a methodological level, there are also many reasons why the use of traditional evaluation methods to make screening decisions are inappropriate in the context of supported employment.

First, there is insufficient empirical evidence to suggest that performance on standardized, norm-referenced instruments is related to the eventual employment success of an individual with a severe disability. While it is true that many validation studies are used to justify the prediction claims made by test authors (Field, Sink, & Cook, 1978; Flenniken, 1975; Hull & Halloran, 1976; Jones & Lassiter, 1977; Parnicky, Kahn, & Burdett, 1971; Tryjankowski, 1987), these investigations generally have examined how popular instruments correlate with other standardized tests or with criteria having questionable vocational relevance.

A second problem with the prediction orientation to vocational evaluation is that many validation studies have failed to account for the influence of training and support on employment outcomes. As the success of supported employment has so clearly demonstrated, access to certain kinds of training programs and support services appear to be more indicative of an individual's employment success than performance on a standardized test. Finally, as evidenced by the Sigafoos et al. (1987) study, many widely used evaluation instruments were standardized using norm groups which have characteristics that are very different from the characteristics of persons seeking supported employment placement. Eligibility and placement decisions based on comparisons of different populations are invalid and capricious. The validation studies examining the relationship between employment potential and variables such as IQ, vocational interest, and adaptive behavior are illustrative of the methodological problems associated with popular evaluation practices.

IQ and Eligibility for Supported Employment

There has been a long debate over whether an individual's performance on a general intelligence test predicts employment success. Several studies have reported conflicting findings on this question (Albin, 1973; Bell, 1976; Fulton, 1975; Schreiner, 1978; Svendsen, 1980). Svendsen (1980) found a relationship between WAIS Full Scale IQ scores and an individual's receiving a disability pension for being unable to work in the community from the Norwegian National Insurance Institution. In the Svendsen (1980) study, 25 percent of the subjects scoring in the seventy-five to ninety-five IQ range received pensions, over 45 percent of the subjects scoring in the fifty-five to sixty-nine range received pensions, and 100 percent of the subjects scoring below fifty-five on the WAIS received occupational disability pensions. However, the author suggests that vocational training and residential experiences played a part in these findings. Most of the individuals receiving disability pensions had only sheltered work experiences, and either lived at home or in institutional settings. Svendsen concluded by stating that his subjects, "had obviously been socialized to a passive, protected role, and their disability may be explained on the basis of their environmental experiences" (p.199).

Failure to account for training and community exposure is a methodological weakness of most studies examining the relationship between IQ and employment potential. The success of many individuals with low IQs in supported employment programs is powerful evidence of the influence of training and experience on vocational success. Every case in which a person who performs poorly on intelligence tests and yet is still successful in employment is a refutation of the hypothesis that IQ is positively related to work potential. Successful supported employment programs have now provided thousands of refutations of the IQ-employment-potential theory.

However, even with the methodological weaknesses, the conflicting results, and the powerful demonstration of successful supported employment placements, IQ scores remain an almost impenetrable screen for persons with mental retardation seeking community employment. It is our experience that many agencies still use IQ information as an informal screen to decide eligibility and placement. The use of intelligence test scores to select individuals for supported employment is clearly inappropriate and must be strongly discouraged. Evaluation professionals must assume leadership in educating policy makers and practitioners about the irrelevance of IQ for predicting employment potential. The relevance of other variables measured with traditional vocational evaluation methods must also be examined in light of supported employment.

Vocational Interest and Eligibility for Supported Employment

Parnicky et al. (1971) conducted a study examining the reliability and validity of the Vocational Interest and Sophistication Assessment, or VISA, instrument with a large sample of persons classified as mild to moderately retarded (i.e., IQ scores ranging from forty-five to eighty-four with a mean of sixty-six). The VISA was designed to be a reading-free vocational interest test for use with persons with mental retardation. Parnicky et al. (1971) examined the validity of the VISA by collecting three criteria measures they felt documented the instrument's usefulness as a vocational evaluation tool: (a) the free-choice responses of subjects with mental retardation to the question, "If you could have any three jobs in the world, which ones would you pick?"; (b) the responses of teachers, workshop trainers, and institutional staff to a questionnaire rating the vocational interests of the subjects; and, (c) for subjects who had been placed in jobs, their employers' ratings of the subjects' vocational interests. Without presenting more than a range of T score values comparing only VISA and their subjects' free-choice responses, Parnicky et al. (1971) suggested that, "the general thesis that the VISA measures . . . have pertinence to vocational evaluation and programming appears further justified" (pp. 447–448). Domino (1982) has disputed this claim, suggesting that the sparse Parnicky et al. data are insufficient to validate the use of the VISA as an evaluation tool to make placement or other vocational decisions.

In another study of the predictive validity of a vocational interest instrument, Becker, Schull, and Cambell (1981) conducted a five-year follow-up of fifty individuals with moderate mental retardation who had completed the AAMD-Becker Reading Free Vocational Interest Inventory of RFVII. The RFVII includes a pictorial choice format designed to assess the job preferences of adolescents and adults with moderate mental retardation. Becker et al. (1981) found that thirty-two of the fifty subjects (64 percent) were still employed in jobs for which they had originally indicated a preference on the RFVII. These results could be interpreted as evidence that vocational interest is predictive of employment success for persons with mental retardation. Becker et al., however, cautioned that vocational interest data are more appropriately used in counseling and guidance decisions than in eligibility and placement decisions. These researchers recognized that, in follow-up studies, it is impossible to control for variables such as an individual's training and experience, and that these influences, rather than vocational interests, could have produced the job retention outcomes they observed.

Evaluation of vocational interests may serve a counseling and guidance function in supported employment. This function, however, must have a different emphasis than conventional counseling and guidance services. Interest data, when available, should be used to direct community survey and job development efforts. When individuals express a clear vocational preference, efforts should be made to match interest with a supported employment setting. However, the use of vocational interest information to determine eligibility for supported employment does not appear justifiable. Once again, evaluation professionals must be responsible for ensuring the appropriate use of vocational interest assessment in supported employment.

Adaptive Behavior and Eligibility for Supported Employment. A study attempting to validate the predictive capability of a vocational rating scale was conducted by Malgady, Barcher, Davis, and Towner (1980). These researchers asked workshop supervisors in Rochester, New York, to rate the behavior of 125 subjects with mild to severe mental retardation (i.e., an IQ mean score of 53.4) using the Vocational Adaptation Rating Scale, or VARS. The VARS, developed by Malgady et al. (1980), measured six areas of maladaptive behaviors that the researchers postulated could interfere with an individual's vocational success. VARS scores were correlated with the subjects' concurrent level of vocational placement and with subjects' placement one year after the study. Vocational placement was quantified using a seven-level hierarchical classification system ranging from sheltered day activity to independent community employment. Malgady et al. found statistically significant, low to moderate correlations between VARS scores and placement levels. Higher correlations were found with concurrent placements compared to one-year follow-up placements. Malgady et al. suggested that the VARS scores could be used as valid predictors of an individual's adjustment to sheltered workshop placements. However, since only 4 of the 125 subjects in this study moved from the sheltered workshop level to real jobs in the community, the authors could not suggest that VARS scores predict success in competitive or supported employment.

Menchetti and Rusch (1988b) also attempted a predictive validation of a vocational behavior scale, the Vocational Assessment and Curriculum Guide, or VACG. They evaluated the validity of the VACG for the purpose of differentiating among individuals with and without disabilities who were placed in a variety of sheltered and community jobs. In the Menchetti and Rusch study, raters completed the VACG with 139 subjects assigned to four different groups based on their employment level. Subjects with mental retardation consisted of fifty-nine individuals who had worked only in sheltered settings, thirty-four individuals who had once worked in a nonsheltered community job, but had returned to a sheltered setting, and nineteen individuals who had been successfully employed in a community job and were receiving varying levels of support. The fourth and final group was made up of twenty-seven subjects who did not exhibit or report a disability and were employed in the community. The results reported by Menchetti and Rusch suggested that VACG ratings could be used to discriminate between certain subject groups.

On all but one VACG domain (learning), Menchetti and Rusch (1988b) reported statistically significant differences between the average scores obtained by successful competitively employed subjects with mental retardation and subjects who had only been employed in sheltered settings. Conversely, VACG ratings were significantly different for subjects in sheltered workshops seeking their first competitive employment placement and successful competitively employed workers with mental retardation. Menchetti and Rusch suggested that these data were indicative of the validity of the VACG, but they did not suggest that the VACG be used for eligibility screening purposes. Instead, Menchetti and Rusch suggested the completion of the VACG be a starting point in an ecological job matching process. That is, ratings of adaptive behavior with instruments such as the VACG are most appropriately used to identify vocational and social skills that should be improved in order to increase the number of job matches between an individual and his or her community.

Other studies have examined the "validity" of vocational rating scales for planning vocational training programs (Giller, Dial, & Chan, 1986). Giller et al. correlated subjects' scores on the Street Survival Skills Questionnaire (SSSQ) with their scores on the Adaptive Behavior Scale-Public School Version (ABS-PSV) and with performance on the Wechsler Adult Intelligence Scale (WAIS). These researchers found that subjects' performance on the SSSQ was significantly correlated with both their ABS-PSV and WAIS scores. The Pearson Product-moment correlations for the SSSQ total raw score with the

ABS-PSV total raw score and the WAIS IQ were .74 and .84, respectively. Giller et al. suggested that these correlations were evidence that the SSSQ could provide functional information for developing rehabilitation plans, although they also cautioned that situational assessments should be used to augment the SSSQ data.

An individual's score on a vocational inventory such as the VARS, the VACG, and the SSSQ should not be used to determine eligibility for supported employment. Validation studies do not uphold the predictive validity of this type of evaluation approach. Instead, vocational inventory ratings should be used by vocational evaluators to facilitate a job match between an individual and the community. Inventory data are useful, however, for identifying skill areas that can be improved through community-based training. Once these skills are improved, the number of matches between the person seeking employment and the community increases substantially. Vocational evaluation professionals must promote the use of vocational rating scales for job matching rather than for eligibility determination. This will require a redefinition of the traditional roles of the vocational evaluator, including increased communication with policy makers and practitioners about the appropriate use of vocational behavior inventories in supported employment.

Job Matching and Program Planning

The use of traditional psychometric vocational evaluation methods to make supported employment eligibility decisions does not appear defensible because of serious philosophical and methodological problems. Many professionals have suggested that a more appropriate purpose for vocational evaluation in supported employment is to determine the congruence or goodness-of-fit between a target employee and the work setting (Chadsey-Rusch & Rusch, 1989; Menchetti & Rusch, 1988a; Renzaglia & Hutchins, 1988; Schalock & Jensen, 1986). That is, vocational evaluation in supported employment should have a "job matching" function designed to facilitate the compatibility between a target employee and a supported employment setting.

Vocational evaluation must broaden its focus if it is to effectively accomplish this new job matching function. Traditional measures focusing only on the aptitudes, interests, work behavior, and social skills of persons seeking supported employment must be supplemented with other information that can help promote a good match. Measurement of the characteristics of potential work sites can also produce useful job matching information. Until now, however, vocational evaluations have almost completely neglected the influence of work settings on success in supported employment. This neglect can be explained by the inherent differences in the conceptualization of traditional models of vocational evaluation and the broader ecological perspective. These differences are explained in the next section and a conceptual model for an ecological approach to vocational evaluation in supported employment is presented.

CONCEPTUAL DIFFERENCES IN MODELS OF VOCATIONAL EVALUATION

We conceptualize vocational evaluation as a process consisting of three components: measurement, analysis, and decision making. Within traditional perspectives on vocational evaluation of persons with disabilities, this tripartite process has been used to answer questions about an individual's eligibility and service needs (Menchetti & Rusch, 1988a). These have included determination of eligibility for rehabilitation services and identification of an individual's programming needs (Halpern & Fuhrer, 1984). In a broader ecological evaluation perspective, the same tripartite process has been designed to improve the goodness-of-fit or job match between the individual and his or her community. The conceptualization of vocational evaluation as a tripartite process is useful for comparing and contrasting traditional models with the ecological alternative.

A Conceptual Model of Traditional Vocational Evaluation

The purpose of measurement in traditional evaluation has been to collect the data needed to answer eligibility and programming questions and to predict employment success. The second component of the three-part process, analysis, has included the summary and study of the evaluation data. Finally, the vocational evaluation process has been concluded with decisions concerning whether an individual should be accepted for service (e.g., rehabilitation) or admitted to a certain program (e.g., supported employment).

Traditional evaluation models such as multiple aptitude batteries, work samples, and vocational behavior checklists have reflected the tripartite process consisting of measurement, analysis, and decision making. Measurement in traditional models has typically focused on two areas: (a) an individual's general abilities, aptitudes, or behaviors, and (b) the requirements of various jobs, vocational courses, or training programs. Ability, aptitude, and behavioral data have usually been summarized for analysis using developmental scores such as age and grade equivalents or with scores of relative standing such as percentile ranks.

For example, the Scales of Independent Behavior, or SIB (Bruininks, Woodcock, Weatherman, & Hill, 1984), is an adaptive behavior scale which reports age equivalency scores for four subtests including motor, social interaction and community, personal living, and community living skills. Similarly, the Talent Assessment Program, or TAP (Nighswonger, 1980), which is a popular system for assessing special needs vocational students, produces profiles based on percentiles from one of seven norm groups. In the traditional evaluation model, an individual's score has been analyzed by comparing it to the performance of a norm group or by matching it to job or course requirements using concepts such as the occupational aptitude pattern or level of training codes.

The Nonreading Aptitude Test Battery, or NATB (U.S.E.S., 1981), provides an example of a system that utilizes a job matching approach to analyze evaluation data. The NATB, which was developed as an alternative to the U.S. Employment Service's General Aptitude Test Battery, or GATB, for the "educationally deficient" individual, reports raw scores, standard scores, and pass-fail scores for occupational aptitude patterns. The occupational aptitude patterns are predictive norms designed to forecast occupational success (Borgen, 1982). The analysis of NATB and GATB data essentially consists of matching an individual's performance to cutoff points established for sixty-six occupational aptitude patterns. When a person scores above the cutoff point, a prediction of occupational success is made. Conversely, when an individual's performance is below the cutoff, a prediction of occupational failure is made.

Decision making in the traditional model of vocational evaluation has relied entirely on the dichotomous accept or reject approach. When measurement and data analysis have indicated that an individual has reached a certain cutoff point on a norm table, the person is accepted for service because the individual's abilities overlap to a high degree with job, course, or occupational requirements. When there is little or no overlap between an individual's ability and the requirements of a job, that person is rejected for service. When this situation occurs, rehabilitation counselors conclude that the individual has no potential for gainful employment and thus cannot benefit from their services. Similarly, in the vocational education system, the student whose performance was poor on traditional evaluation measures is viewed as not being able to benefit from the program. Figure 7.1 depicts a traditional evaluation model within the context of the tripartite process. Figure 7.1(a) illustrates the situation in which the person being evaluated has performed well. In this case, there will be a high degree of overlap between the individual's ability and the requirements of the job. The decision, of course, is to accept this individual for placement or service. Figure 7.1(b), however, depicts the more common situation when individuals with moderate to severe disabilities are evaluated within the traditional model. Generally, these individuals perform poorly resulting in an analysis that reveals little or no overlap between ability and requirements. In a traditional model of vocational evaluation, the decision is to reject the individual for service or placement.

A Conceptual Model of Ecological Vocational Evaluation

Ecological models of vocational evaluation may also be conceptualized as consisting of measure-

FIGURE 7.1 A Traditional Model of Vocational Assessment

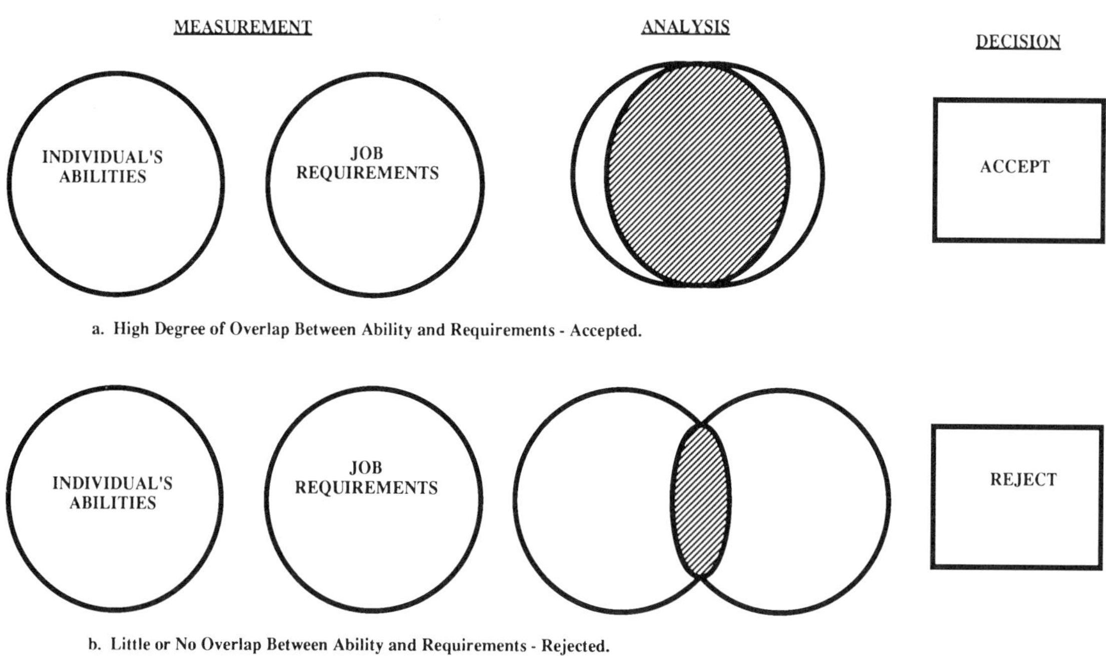

ment, data analysis, and decision making. There are important distinctions, however, between the ecological and traditional models in each of the three components.

Like its traditional counterpart, the ecological model of vocational evaluation is concerned with the measurement of an individual's abilities. Measurement, however, is expanded in the ecological model to include assessment of the social climate or ecology of the workplace. Moos (1974) has suggested that social environments have unique "personalities" just as people do. He has pointed out that just as some persons are more supportive than others, some social environments are more supportive than others. Moos (1974) has also stated that almost everyone acknowledges that the environment has a significant impact on the persons functioning in it. Moos and his colleagues at the Stanford University Social Ecology Laboratory have developed a series of Social Climate Scales to measure the personality or social climate of various environments, including work settings.

The construct of social climate has important implications for ecological evaluation practices in supported employment. Chadsey-Rusch and Rusch (1989) suggested that by accurately measuring the social climate or ecology of the workplace, evaluators can facilitate a better match between employees and their jobs. Increasing the match or goodness-of-fit between an individual with a severe disability and his or her community is, of course, the most appropriate function for evaluation in supported employment.

THE MEASUREMENT OF SOCIAL CLIMATE. There are several dimensions that should be considered when measuring the social climate or ecology of supported employment settings. Chadsey-Rusch and Rusch (1989) suggested three major dimensions should be assessed including: (a) the physical ecology; (b) the social ecology; and (c) the organizational ecology. Moos and Lemke (1983) have suggested that relationship dimensions (e.g., involvement, peer cohesion, and supervisor support); goal orientation dimensions (e.g., autonomy, task orientation, and work pressure); and system maintenance and change dimensions (e.g., clarity, control, innovation, and physical comfort) also be measured in an assessment of the social climate of the workplace.

Other dimensions such as transportation requirements, family support, and the availability of external incentives to employers should also be assessed to promote a good job match. Transportation can greatly influence employment success in rural and suburban areas. Family support, especially when an individual's SSI or SSDI benefits are threatened by community employment, is crucial to vocational adjustment. External incentives including the tax credits available to the company, salary subsidies available through state or local agencies, public relations opportunities, and job training support offered by public and/or private agencies, may determine the availability of a community placement. In larger companies or organizations, support of the concept of hiring people with handicaps at the regional, state, or national level can be viewed as an incentive for participation in supported employment.

The many dimensions of the social climate or ecology of a workplace are interactive and each element can change as a result of this interaction. For example, supervisors can have very positive attitudes about people with disabilities and be eager to work with them. In order to accommodate a target employee's needs, they may be willing to change the performance requirements of a job. Because these ecological dimensions interact and change, it is essential that they all be assessed. Assessment of the social climate of a workplace yields what could be called the *adaptability quotient* of the environment, or the capacity of the environment to change in order to meet the needs of an individual.

Measurement of the adaptability quotient is important regardless of the setting in which the person is to be placed. It is a concept that is equally meaningful whether it is in reference to acceptance into a training program, a service delivery program, or a specific job setting. The system, program, or job setting into which the person is trying to gain access will dictate the kind of variables that will be assessed; but the physical, social, organizational, relationship, goal orientation, and system maintenance and change dimensions suggested by Chadsey-Rusch and Rusch (1989) and Moos and Lemke (1983) should be included as well.

A comparison of an environment's adaptability quotient and the target employee's abilities are analyzed during the second phase of the ecological evaluation process to determine the areas of overlap. More specifically, the analysis indicates the capacity of the environment to adapt to meet the needs of the individual. The decision in the third step of the ecological process will be whether to accept the person, accept the person with support, or to recommend a specific alternative. Assessing only one element of the environment and matching it with the person's abilities will not allow for appropriate assessment. A person could be rejected when the adaptability of the organization or company would actually allow the individual a reasonable chance for success. There are no percentile cutoffs, standard scores, or norms attached to our concept of an adaptability quotient. It is merely a shorthand way of describing the capacity of the environment to adapt to meet an individual's needs. Table 7.1 is a comparison of the major features of both the traditional and the ecological evaluation models. Figure 7.2 depicts the ecological evaluation model.

NEW ROLES AND RESPONSIBILITIES FOR VOCATIONAL EVALUATORS IN THE ECOLOGICAL ALTERNATIVE

Vocational evaluation professionals wishing to advance supported employment efforts by conducting ecological assessments must fulfill many new and untraditional roles. These novel roles will include many of the responsibilities now assigned to job coaches and employment specialists, such as conducting community surveys and job analyses. It is our contention that vocational evaluators, by virtue of their training and background, are better suited for these tasks. It is also our belief that both vocational evaluators and the field of vocational evaluation have many important roles to play in the provision of effective supported employment services. In order for vocational evaluation to be a functional component of supported employment,

Table 7.1 Conceptual Differences in Vocational Evaluation Models

Model	Components of Evaluation		
	Measurement	**Analysis**	**Decision Making**
Traditional vocational evaluation	Two areas usually assessed: 1. General abilities, aptitudes, and/or behavior of the individual; and 2. Requirements of the job or vocational program.	Examination of degree of overlap between the individual and the job or program.	Dichotomous accept or reject approach.
Ecological vocational evaluation	Several areas assessed: 1. General abilities, aptitudes, and/or behavior of the individual; and social climate/ecological dimensions such as: 2. Physical variables, 3. Social variables, 4. Organizational variables, 5. Relationship variables, 6. Goal orientation, 7. System maintenance and change variables, 8. Transportation, and 9. Availability of external incentives.	Examination of both degree of overlap between the individual and setting requirements and the interaction of ecological dimensions.	Zero-Reject–some persons accepted with support as suggested by interaction of ecological dimensions with abilities.

however, evaluators must redirect their skills and energy to the seven activities described below.

1. Coordinate Community Surveys Identifying Potential Employers. Usually, the responsibility of coordinating community surveys is assigned to a job coach or job developer in supported employment service delivery models. Vocational evaluators, however, should become more involved with community survey efforts to familiarize themselves with locally available jobs. This involvement will also allow evaluators to make more informed judgments about the "face validity" of traditional psychometric measures that federal, state, and local agencies will not discard. Whenever possible, the results of vocational interest assessments should guide community survey efforts for specific individuals seeking supported employment services. This role shift will utilize the evaluator's expertise in measurement and data collection, thus freeing the often overburdened job coach to concentrate on training and maintenance issues.

2. Assess Reasons Why Employers Wish to Participate in Supported Employment. An interesting paradox of supported employment is that many business firms are willing to hire individuals that society has traditionally judged incapable of productive work because these employers perceive some benefit or profit potential from the arrangement. If the supported employment movement is to spread more widely, professionals must empirically determine exactly what benefits the employer perceives. Armed with this information, proponents of supported employment can focus their efforts on making programs accepted by more employers. Once again, vocational evaluators seem best prepared

FIGURE 7.2 An Ecological Model of Vocational Assessment

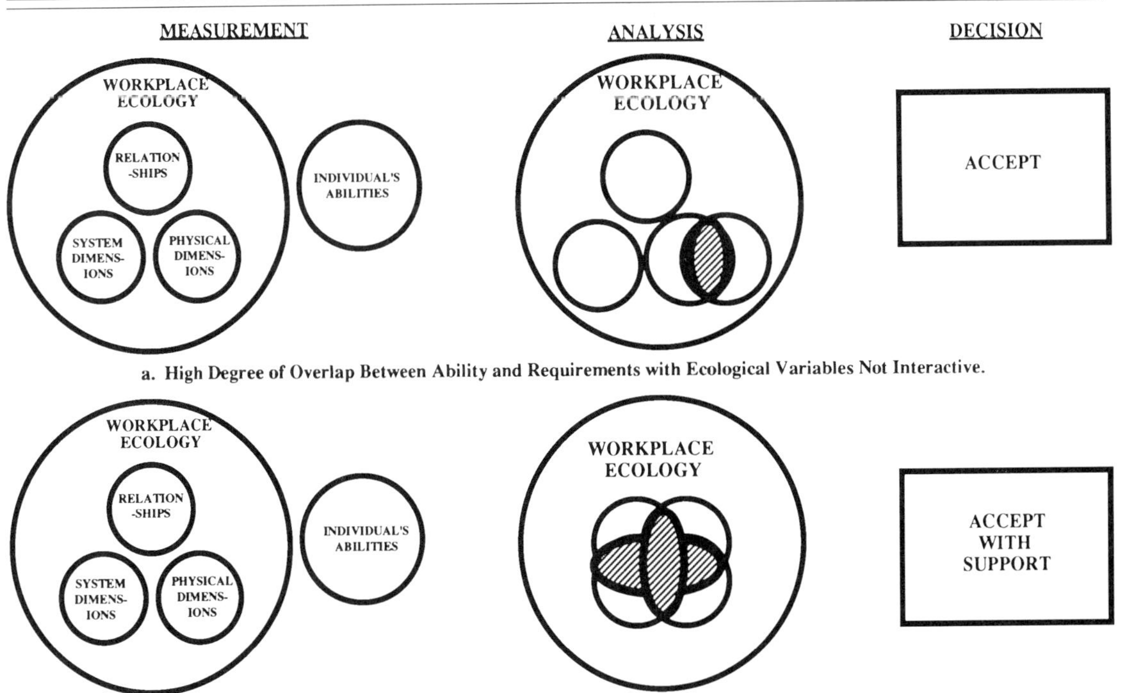

a. High Degree of Overlap Between Ability and Requirements with Ecological Variables Not Interactive.

b. Little or No Overlap Between Ability and Requirements with Ecological Variable Highly Interactive

to develop the data collection and analysis procedures required to fulfill this important role.

3. Conduct Behavioral Analyses of Local Job Sites. In most supported employment programs, the role of conducting behavioral analyses has been typically assigned to the job coach or employment specialist. Vocational evaluators, however, have training and experience in test design and data collection and are probably better suited for this responsibility. Vocational evaluators must use proven job analysis techniques (Chadsey-Rusch & Rusch, 1989; Menchetti & Rusch, 1988a) to identify the vocational and social skill requirements of a particular work setting. Once targeted, operationally defined, and put into checklist form, these skills can be used to match target workers to similar jobs in the community. The identification and quantification of survival skills, often called social validation (Kazdin & Matson, 1981; Menchetti, Rusch, & Owens, 1983; Rusch, Schutz, & Agran, 1982), has been a useful strategy in many supported employment programs and has led to the development of the Vocational Assessment and Curriculum Guide or VACG (Rusch, Schutz, Mithaug, Stewart, & Mar, 1982). The VACG is an instrument with tested reliability and validity (Menchetti & Rusch, 1988b) that can be used to identify the training needs of individuals interested in employment in the food service and janitorial industries. A useful role for vocational evaluators in supported employment programs is to develop socially validated behavioral checklists for the various occupational opportunities available in their communities.

4. Conduct Ecological Analyses of Local Job Sites. In addition to assessing the behavioral requirements of an employment setting, it is important to assess the ecological dimensions associated with successful and unsuccessful placements. Moos (1974) has developed the Social Climate Scales to measure the "personality" of work and other social environments. Jones, Risley, and Favell (1983) have suggested

that environmental and situational variables influence the effectiveness of behavioral training technology. They have written that when training is unsuccessful, "fault lies not only with the technology but also in settings that don't support the treatment. If researchers hope to understand why treatment fails, then it is necessary to gain a better understanding of how the environment influences treatment effectiveness" (pp.311-312). Jones et al. (1983) and others (Chadsey-Rusch & Rusch, 1989; Moos, 1974; Moos & Lemke, 1983; Rogers-Warren & Warren, 1977) have called the concern for environmental and situational variables in assessment the "ecological perspective." Vocational evaluators can facilitate supported employment efforts by using, developing, and validating instruments to assess the ecology of the workplace. Like the information produced through behavioral analyses of employment sites, ecological data can be very useful in promoting a match between the target employee and the job. It is very important that vocational evaluators play a leading role in this job matching process.

5. Identify Areas for Community Education and Intervention Programs. Most vocational programs for persons with disabilities have focused training and intervention efforts on the behavior of the individual. This person-oriented approach to education and training has produced a technology that has effectively changed the production rates, social skills, and a variety of other work-related behaviors of persons with disabilities. An assumption of the person-oriented approach to employment training was that an individual's behavioral deficits or excesses represented the major obstacles to successful adjustment to work settings, and that if the critical behaviors could be identified and changed, persons with disabilities would be more fully integrated into the work force. Widespread integration of persons with disabilities in community employment has not occurred even with the recent advances in training technology. Experiences in supported employment have demonstrated that the ecology of the workplace and the larger community context also influence successful vocational adjustment of persons with disabilities.

With this recognition have come attempts to describe, measure, and change the social climate of work settings to promote more meaningful participation of persons with disabilities. A broader ecological or social-systems orientation must replace the person-oriented approach to education and training.

One of the most functional roles vocational evaluators can play in supported employment is to be a source of reliable and valid information about the ecological variables most influencing successful placements. Once identified, these variables should form the basis of community education and intervention efforts aimed at changing work settings to make them more conducive to supported employment. Environmental and situational variables, as well as the behavior of individuals, are appropriate targets for change through intervention within an ecological model. Vocational evaluation professionals should coordinate community education and training efforts. This social-systems orientation may result in the employment integration of persons with more severe disabilities as employers and the community become educated about the benefits of supported employment.

6. Assist in the Development, Implementation, and Management of Training Data Systems. Adoption of an ecological perspective of supported employment does not mean that training individual workers will no longer be required. It is naive to believe that the behavior of the individual is unimportant to successful employment. Rather, the ecological perspective recognizes the balance and interaction of behavior and environment. Effective training will always be a characteristic of successful supported employment programs. Good training requires the systematic collection and analysis of data.

Usually vocational evaluators play little or no part in the development, implementation, and management of data collection procedures. In many programs, this responsibility falls on the job coach or employment specialist. Evaluators, however, are also suited for this role. Vocational evaluators must become familiar with behavioral observation techniques and repeated measures experimental designs that are useful tools in the analysis of work performance (Agran, 1986).

Continuous support is a defining feature of supported employment. Vocational evaluators can play an important role in the long-term follow-up of individuals placed in supported employment by coordinating data collection efforts that assist job coaches in making important training and fading decisions.

7. Assist in the Development, Implementation, and Management of Program Evaluation. Another area of supported employment in which vocational evaluators have traditionally had little or no responsibility is program evaluation. Given their expertise in data collection and interpretation, however, vocational evaluators seem ideally suited for this role.

Supported employment programs must be measurable, reportable, and accountable. Schalock (1988) has suggested eight critical performance indicators for evaluating supported employment programs: (a) participant demographics; (b) description of preplacement settings; (c) description of the employment placement environment; (d) employment data; (e) occupational category information; (f) level of integration, (g) hours of support services, and (h) job movement patterns. In addition, we believe employer satisfaction represents the ninth critical performance measure for evaluating supported employment programs.

Vocational evaluation professionals can facilitate supported employment efforts by playing a leading role in program evaluation. As Schalock (1988) has suggested, many programs have not yet standardized or implemented systematic evaluation systems. Vocational evaluators can play a pioneering role in this important endeavor.

SUMMARY

Supported employment represents a unique vocational opportunity for persons with disabilities. Characteristics of supported employment, such as its targeted consumers, emphasis on community integration, and provision of long-term support, present challenges to traditional vocational systems. In particular, vocational evaluation, with its tradition of psychometric testing to predict employment potential, must change to meet the challenge of supported employment.

This chapter has described the popular vocational evaluation approaches of aptitude matching, work sampling, and behavioral rating. Philosophical conflicts and methodological weaknesses of these approaches with supported employment were discussed. An ecological model of vocational evaluation was presented, that focuses not only on the abilities of the individual in relation to the requirements of the job, but also on the personality or social climate of the workplace. Ecological dimensions including the physical ecology, social ecology, organizational ecology, relationships variables, goal orientation, and system maintenance and change variables were described. The importance of ecological dimensions for successful supported employment was suggested, and corresponding vocational evaluation techniques were discussed. Finally, new roles and responsibilities for vocational evaluators in the ecological model were delineated.

We believe that vocational evaluation has an important contribution to make to supported employment. The knowledge and skills of vocational evaluation professionals must be redirected, however, to be more compatible with the features of this new occupational opportunity for persons with severe disabilities. This chapter has been an attempt to suggest ways in which vocational evaluators can contribute to the success of supported employment.

QUESTIONS (For answers see p. 429)

1. Name three distinguishing characteristics of supported employment.

2. Name the three widely used approaches in the vocational evaluation of persons with disabilities.

3. What is the most popular technique currently being used in schools, rehabilitation facilities, and job training programs to evaluate the vocational skills of persons with disabilities?

4. What are the important differences between trait-oriented work samples and multiple aptitude batteries?

5. Current vocational inventories such as the *VACG* have been developed using a process called social validation. Describe how social validation is used to develop vocational inventories.

6. What are the purposes of the popular vocational evaluation approaches in supported employment?

7. On what grounds is it philosophically inappropriate to select individuals for supported employment using standardized tests?

8. List three methodological problems using traditional vocational evaluation procedures to make screening decisions within the context of supported employment.

9. Is IQ a meaningful predictor of employment success? Explain.

10. What is the most appropriate use of instruments that yield a rating of adaptive behavior, e.g., *VACG*?

11. What is the most appropriate function for evaluation in supported employment?

12. Name three dimensions that should be considered when measuring the social ecology of supported employment settings.

13. Identify the activities necessary for vocational evaluation to become a functional component of the supported employment model.

REFERENCES

Agran, M. (1986). Analysis of work behavior. In F. R. Rusch (Ed.), *Competitive employment issues and strategies* (pp.153–164). Baltimore: Paul H. Brookes.

Agran, M. & Morgan, R. L. (1989). *Current transition assessment practices.* Manuscript submitted for publication.

Albin, T. J. (1973). Relationships of IQ and previous work experience to success in sheltered employment. *Mental Retardation, 11*, 26.

Bates, P. E. (1986). Competitive employment in Southern Illinois: A transitional service delivery model for enhancing competitive employment outcomes for public school students. In F. R. Rusch (Ed.), *Competitive employment: Issues and strategies* (pp.51-63). Baltimore: Paul H. Brookes.

Becker, R. L. , Schull, C., & Cambell, K. (1981). Vocational interest evaluation of TMR adults. *American Journal of Mental Deficiency, 85*, 350–356.

Bell, N. J., (1976). IQ as a factor in community lifestyle of previously institutionalized retardates. *Mental Retardation, 14*, 29–53.

Bellamy, G. T., Rhodes, L. E., Bourbeau, P. E., & Mank, D. M. (1986). Mental retardation services in sheltered workshops and day activities programs: Consumer benefits and policy alternatives. In F. R. Rusch (Ed.), *Competitive employment: Issues and strategies* (pp.257–271). Baltimore: Paul H. Brookes.

Borgen, F. H. (1982). A review of the U.S.E.S. General Aptitude Test Battery. In J. T. Kapes & M. M. Mastie (Eds.), *A counselor's guide to vocational guidance instruments* (pp.42–64). Falls Church, VA: American Personnel and Guidance Association.

Botterbusch, K. F. (1978). *A guide to job site evaluation.* Menomonie: Materials Development Center, University of Wisconsin-Stout.

Botterbusch, K. F. (in press). A model for vocational evaluation in community based employment. In R. Fry (Ed.), *Fourth national forum on issues in vocational assessment: The issue papers.* Menomonie: Materials Development Center, University of Wisconsin-Stout.

Bruininks, R. H., Woodcock, R. W., Weatherman, R. F., & Hill, B. (1984). *Scales of independent behavior.* Allen, TX: DLM Teaching Resources.

Chadsey-Rusch, J. & Rusch, F. R. (1989). Ecology of the workplace. In R. Gaylord-Ross (Ed.), *Vocational education for persons with special needs* (pp. 234–256). Mountain View, CA: Mayfield Publishing.

DeStefano, L. (1987). The use of standardized assessment in supported employment. In L. DeStefano & F. R. Rusch (Eds.), *Supported employment in Illinois: Assessment methodology and research issues* (Vol.2, pp.55–98). Champaign, IL: Transition Institute, University of Illinois at Urbana-Champaign.

Domino, G. (1982). Review of the VISA. In J. T. Kapes & M. M. Mastie (Eds.), *A counselor's guide to vocational guidance instruments* (pp.189–191).

Falls Church, VA: American Personnel and Guidance Association.

Dunn, D. J. (1973). *Situational assessment: Models for the future*. Menomonie: Materials Development Center, University of Wisconsin-Stout.

Federal Register. (August 14, 1987). The state supported employment services program: Final regulations (Vol. 52, pp.30546-30551). Washington, DC: Government Printing Office.

Field, T. F., Sink, J. M., & Cook, P. (1978). The effects of age, IQ, and disability on performance on the JEVS system. *Vocational Evaluation and Work Adjustment Bulletin, 11*, 14–22.

Flenniken, D. (1975). Performance on the 1973 revised Philadelphia JEVS work sample battery. *Vocational Evaluation and Work Adjustment Bulletin, 8*, 35–47.

Fulton, R. W. (1975). Job retention of the mentally retarded. Mental Retardation, *13*, 26.

Genskow, J. (1973). Evaluation: A multipurpose proposition. *Journal of Rehabilitation, 39*, 22–25.

Giller, V. L., Dial, J. G., & Chan, F. (1986). The Street Survival Questionnaire: A correlational study. *American Journal of Mental Deficiency, 91*, 67–71.

Halpern, A. S. & Fuhrer, M. J. (1984). *Functional assessment in rehabilitation*. Baltimore: Paul H. Brookes.

Halpern, A. S., Raffeld, P., Irvin, L. K., & Link, R. (1975). *Social and Prevocational Information Battery*. Monterey, CA: CTB/McGraw Hill.

Hull, M. & Halloran, W. (1976). The validity of the Nonreading Aptitude Test Battery for the mentally handicapped. *Educational and Psychological Measurement, 36*, 547–552.

Jones, C. & Lassiter, C. (1977). Worker non-worker differences on three VALPAR component work samples. *Vocational Evaluation and Work Adjustment Bulletin, 10*, 23–27.

Jones, M. L., Risley, T. R., & Favell, J. E. (1983). Ecological patterns. In J. L. Matson & S.E. Breuning (Eds.), *Assessing the mentally retarded* (pp.311–334). New York: Grune & Stratton.

Kazdin, A. E. & Matson, J. L. (1981). Social validation in mental retardation. *Applied Research in Mental Retardation, 2*, 39–54.

Lambert, N. & Windmiller, M. (1981). *AAMD Adaptive Behavior Scale-School Edition*. Monterey, CA: CTB/McGraw Hill.

Malgady, R. G., Barcher, P. R., Davis, J., & Towner, G. (1980). Validity of the Vocational Adaptation Rating Scale: Prediction of mentally retarded workers' placement in sheltered workshops. *American Journal of Mental Deficiency, 84*, 633–640.

McCarthy, P., Fender, K. W., & Fender, D. (1988). Supported employment for persons with autism. In P. Wehman & M. S. Moon (Eds.), *Vocational rehabilitation and supported employment* (pp.269–290). Baltimore: Paul H. Brookes.

Menchetti, B. M. & Rusch, F. R. (1988a). Vocational evaluation and eligibility for rehabilitation services. In P. Wehman & M. S. Moon (Eds.), *Vocational rehabilitation and supported employment* (pp.79–90). Baltimore: Paul H. Brookes.

Menchetti, B. M. & Rusch, F. R. (1988b). Reliability and validity of the Vocational Assessment and Curriculum Guide. *American Journal of Mental Retardation, 93*, 283–289.

Menchetti, B. M., Rusch, F. R. & Owens, D. M. (1983). Vocational training. In J. L. Matson & S. E. Breuning (Eds.), *Assessing the mentally retarded* (pp.247–284). New York: Grune & Stratton.

Mithaug, D. E., Mar, D. K., & Stewart, J. E. (1978). *Prevocational Assessment and Curriculum Guide*. Seattle: Exceptional Education.

Moos, R. H. (1974). *The social climate scales: An overview*. Palo Alto, CA: Consulting Psychologists Press.

Moos, R. H. & Lemke, S. (1983). Assessing and improving social-ecological settings. In E. Seidman (Ed.), *Handbook of social intervention* (pp.143–162). London: Age Publications.

Neff, W. S. (1966). Problems of work evaluation. *Personnel and Guidance Journal, 44*, 682–688.

Nighswonger, W. (1980). *Talent Assessment Program*. Jacksonville, FL: Talent Assessment.

Parnicky, J. J., Kahn, H., & Burdett, A. B. (1971). Standardization of the (VISA) Vocational Interest and Sophistication Assessment technique. *American Journal of Mental Deficiency, 75*, 442–448.

Peterson, M. (1986). Work and performance samples for vocational assessment of special students: A critical review. *Career Development for Exceptional Individuals, 9*, 69–76.

Renzaglia, A. & Hutchins, M. (1988). A community-referenced approach to preparing persons with disabilities for employment. In P. Wehman & M. S. Moon (Eds.), *Vocational rehabilitation and supported employment* (pp. 91–110). Baltimore: Paul H. Brookes.

Rogers-Warren, A. & Warren, S. (1977). *Ecological perspectives in behavior analysis*. Baltimore: University Park Press.

Rusch, F. R. (1979). Toward the validation of social/vocational survival skills. *Mental Retardation, 17*, 143–145.

Rusch, F. R. & Menchetti, B. M. (1981). Increasing compliant work behaviors in a non-sheltered work setting. *Mental Retardation, 19*, 107–111.

Rusch, F. R., Schutz, R. P., & Agran, M. (1982). Validating entry level survival skills for service occupations: Implications for curriculum development. *Journal of the Association for the Severely Handicapped, 8*, 32–41.

Rusch, F. R., Schutz, R. P., Mithaug, D. E., Stewart, J. E., & Mar, D. W. (1982). *Vocational Assessment and Curriculum Guide*. Seattle: Exceptional Education.

Schalock, R. L. (1988). Critical performance evaluation indicators in supported employment. In P. Wehman & M. S. Moon (Eds.), *Vocational rehabilitation and supported employment* (pp.163–174). Baltimore: Paul H. Brookes.

Schalock, R. L. & Jensen, C. M. (1986). Assessing the goodness-of-fit between persons and their environments. *The Journal of the Association for Persons with Severe Handicaps, 11*, 103–109.

Schreiner, J. (1978). Prediction of retarded adults' work performance through components of general ability. *American Journal of Mental Deficiency, 83*, 77–79.

Sigafoos, J., Cole, D. A., & McQuarter, R. J. (1987). Current practices in the assessment of students with severe handicaps. *The Journal of the Association of Persons with Severe Handicaps,* 12, 264–273.

Singer, T. (1986). The Singer Vocational Evaluation System. Rochester, NY: New Concepts.

Sparrow, S. S., Balla, D. A., & Cicchetti, D. V. (1985). *Vineland Adaptive Behavior Scales: Classroom Edition*. Circle Pines, MN: American Guidance Service.

Stodden, R. A., Meehan, K. A., Hodell, S,. Bisconer, S. W., & Cabebe, S. (1986). *Vocational assessment research project: A report of findings for project year 1985–86. Status study results*. Honolulu: University of Hawaii at Manoa, Department of Special Education.

Svendsen, D. (1980). Relationship of IQ and occupational disability of retarded adults in Bergen, Norway. *American Journal of Mental Deficiency, 85*, 197–199.

Tryjankowski, E. M. (1987). Convergent-discriminant validity of the Jewish Employment and Vocational Service System. *Journal of Learning Disabilities, 20*, 433–435.

United States Employment Service. (1981). *Non-Reading Aptitude Test Battery*. Washington, DC: U.S. Government Printing Office.

Valpar Corporation. (1981). *The Valpar component work sample series*. Tucson, AZ: Author.

Van Houten, R. (1979). Social validation: The evolution of standards of competence for target behaviors. *Journal of Applied Behavior Analysis, 12*, 581–592.

Vocational Research Institute. (1977). *Vocational information and evaluation work samples*. Philadelphia: Author.

Vocational Research Institute. (1985). *APTICOM*. Philadelphia: Author.

Vogelsberg, R. T. & Richard, L. (1988). Supported employment for persons with mental retardation: Programmatic issues for implementation. In P. Wehman & M. S. Moon (Eds.), *Vocational rehabilitation and supported employment* (pp.253–268). Baltimore: Paul H. Brookes.

Wehman, P. (1986). Competitive employment in Virginia. In F. R. Rusch (Ed.), *Competitive employment: Issues and strategies* (pp.23–33). Baltimore: Paul H. Brookes.

Wehman, P. (1988). Supported employment: Toward zero exclusion of persons with severe disabilities. In P. Wehman & M. S. Moon (Eds.), *Vocational rehabilitation and supported employment* (pp.3–14). Baltimore: Paul H. Brookes.

Wehman, P. & Kregel, J. (1985). A supported work approach to competitive employment of individuals with moderate and severe handicaps. *Journal of Autism and Developmental Disorders, 16*, 295–316.

Wood, W. (1988). Supported employment for persons with physical disabilities. In P. Wehman & M. S. Moon (Eds.), *Vocational rehabilitation and supported employment* (pp.341–363). Baltimore: Paul H. Brookes.

CHAPTER

8

Developing and Implementing Support Strategies

Jay Buckley
David Mank
Dennis Sandow
University of Oregon

Supported employment is predicated on the notion that access combined with individualized support will lead to integration (Wehman & Moon, 1988; Bellamy, Rhodes, Mank, & Albin, 1988; Martin, Mithaug, Agran, & Husch, in press; Rusch, 1986; Will, 1984a & 1984b). As described elsewhere in this text, the supported employment initiative is defined, in part, in terms of outcomes associated with access to stable employment in regular worksites where persons without disabilities are employed (Kiernan & Schalock, 1989; Bellamy et al., 1988; Wehman & Moon, 1988; Wehman, Moon, Everson, Wood, & Barcus, 1988; Wilcox & Bellamy, 1982; Will, 1984a & 1984b). The focus on outcomes suggests that each of these initiatives can and should involve a creative mix of strategies that enables individuals with severe disabilities to succeed in employment. Evidence for this can be found in federal statutes. The Developmental Disabilities Assistance and Bill of Rights Act of 1984 [PL98-527] and the Rehabilitation Act Amendments of 1986 [PL99-506], respectively, describe "support" in supported employment as:

> any activity needed to sustain paid work by persons with disabilities, including supervision, training, and transportation (Section 102 [iiif]) . . . services that are needed to support and maintain an individual with severe handicaps in employment. . . . (Section 103 [ib])

These open-ended descriptions of support imply that the support needed for an individual's integration should be a collection of individualized strategies selected and applied as needed. Too often in the past we defined our responsibility in terms of the application of a specific technique, or collection of techniques. Accordingly, the limits of our techniques came to define the limits of our commitment, and we included only those individuals for whom our techniques were known to be successful (Wehman, Kregel, & Shafer, 1989).

This chapter addresses identifying and applying individualized support strategies for persons with severe disabilities employed in integrated jobs. Before discussing specific support activities, the chapter attempts to arrive at a functional and comprehensive definition of support. Specific strategies designed to meet particular support needs are then analyzed and identified.

DEFINING SUPPORT AND SUPPORT STRATEGIES

Support needs are typically defined in terms related to the individual with disabilities. However, the recent past has enlarged our understanding of support issues to include an ecological context (Chadsey-Rusch, 1986, Chapter 10, this volume; Hughes, Rusch, & Curl, Chapter 11, this volume; Karan & Berger-Knight, 1986; Menchetti & Flynn, Chapter 7 this volume; Nisbet & Hagner, 1988; Pancsofar, 1986; Rogers-Warren & Warren, 1977; Wehman, 1981; 1986). This suggests that support might be defined in relation to three variables (a) the individual (i.e., the person's perceived strengths, experience, preferences, and social network); (b) the job (i.e., the informal culturally-specific willingness of co-workers to provide each other with assistance, and the more formal assistance available in some jobs through employee assistance programs; and (c) the support organization (i.e., the organization's willingness and ability to apply a variety of support strategies in response to different support challenges). The support provided to meet individual needs in specific jobs should utilize all three of these variables.

A complete range of support strategies can be organized into three major categories differentiated by the type of assistance provided and the individuals involved. These categories are identified and defined below. Table 8.1 presents the specific support strategies included in each category and the degree to which they influence commonly cited support needs. These strategies are discussed in considerable detail in the ensuing chapters.

Direct service strategies are instructionally-based activities that occur at or near the job site and directly involve the employee. This collection of strategies builds upon suggestions that a combination of direct interventions is necessary to enable individuals with severe disabilities to succeed in integrated settings (Mank & Buckley, 1988; Mank & Horner, 1988; Stokes & Osnes, 1986; Wacker & Berg, 1985).

Indirect service strategies include job site activities that do not directly involve the target worker. These strategies involve efforts taken to involve supervisors and co-workers as advocates and extensions of the employment training specialist. Another perspective is that indirect strategies include activities handled by the employment training specialist to facilitate integration and reciprocal relationships (Mank & Buckley, 1988).

External strategies include activities that typically take place away from the job site. These efforts seek to involve parents, advocates, and related professionals in activities that help the target worker maintain employment. Lack of support by these "external" agents has been identified as a significant factor in job retention and separation. These strategies help support staff use resources as efficiently as possible. (Table 8.1 presents direct, indirect, and external support strategies.)

Direct Service Strategies

Direct service strategies represent a range of instructional interventions identified in "best practice" literature and designed to address commonly cited sources of job loss (Berg, Wacker, & Flynn, Chapter 9 this volume; Gifford, Rusch, Martin, & White, 1984; Mank & Buckley, 1988; Mank & Horner, 1988; Martin et al., in press; Mcloughlin, Garner, & Callahan, 1987; Wacker & Berg, 1985). Table 8.2 defines seven categories of intervention and presents a brief description of procedures. Although these strategies are discussed separately, it is important to note that they can be used together to address different support needs. For example, a task analysis may be used to help a person learn to perform a task at the same time that a rate increase program is employed to meet the production demands of another task. These support strategies can also be used in concert to meet one specific need; that is, a task analysis can be developed and used to make sure that a target worker is able to use his or her self-management system. Readers are also referred to Berg, Wacker, and Flynn (Chapter 9) for a more complete overview of these strategies.

TASK ANALYSIS. The use of task analysis was instrumental in establishing that individuals with severe disabilities could achieve vocational success (Bellamy, Peterson, & Close 1975; Crosson, 1969; Gold, 1972; 1975). Employment training specialists employ task analyses to increase their understanding of a task, to assure consistency in training, and to facilitate and document the acquisition of small teachable steps. By including elements from general case programming (Horner, McDonnell, & Bellamy, 1986; Horner, Sprague, & Wilcox, 1982), such as identification of conditions that require performance variations and error analysis, task analyses can help the trainer provide instruction across the range of conditions encountered in integrated employment (Buckley, Sandow, & Smock, 1989). For detailed procedural information on task analyses, see Bellamy, Horner, & Inman (1979); Mcloughlin et al. (1987); Rusch and Mithaug (1980); Wehman (1981).

SELF-MANAGEMENT. The application of techniques that enable target workers to mediate their own responses is perhaps the most rapidly growing area of research in supported employment. Self-management includes systems that allow workers to provide themselves with cues, create records of their work, evaluate their own performance, and provide themselves with feedback. Procedural information is available in Buckley and Mank (1988); Gifford et al. (1984); Lagomarcino, Hughes, and Rusch (1989); and Martin et al. (in press), and in this text.

PRODUCTIVITY TRAINING. A number of constructs constitute the area commonly referred to as productivity. These include rate, pacing, and productivity. It is interesting to note that productivity, or the amount of work completed as compared to that completed (or potentially completed) by a co-worker, is typically not assessed at the individual worker level in business and industry. It is, however, the measure that the Department of Labor (May, 1988) requires. Information on issues associated with productiv-

Table 8.1 Support Strategies and Degree to which they Influence Identified Problems in Worker Retention.

	Direct Strategies										Indirect Strategies				External Strategies		
		Self-Management Training			Productivity Training												
Areas of Possible Problems*	General case task analysis	Antecedent cue regulation	Self-monitoring	Self-delivery of consequences	Rate	Pacing	Social skill training	Community referenced behavior management	Communication training	Mobility training	Advocate training	Discrete co-worker orientation	Supervision communication training	Ongoing employer support	Parent/advocate training	Parent/advocate counseling	Agenda setting for service coordination
Lack of autonomy	*	*	*	*	*	*		*	*	*				*			*
Lack of adaptability	*	*		*		*	*	*	*	*	*	*	*	*			*
Work quality problems	*	*	*	*	*	*		*			*	*	*	*	*		*
Attitude problems		*	*	*			*	*	*	*	*	*	*	*	*	*	*
Challenging behaviors			*	*			*	*	*		*	*	*	*	*	*	*
Economic layoffs																	*
Family issues											*	*		*	*	*	*
Co-worker relation problems							*	*	*	*	*	*	*	*	*	*	*

* Source Note: Derived from Gifford, Rusch, Martin, & White (1984) and Hill, Wehman, Hill, & Goodall (1985), respectively.

Table 8.2 Direct Service Strategy Definitions, Procedures, and Decision Rules

Support Strategy	Procedures	Decision Rules
Task analysis – Analysis of the stimulus and response requirements of each step in a task across the range of variability that occurs in the specific conditions in which the task is performed.	- Establish efficient task design. - Identify task-related stimulus for each response. - Articulate steps in terms of employer criteria. - Identify all conditions/variations. - Identify errors that occur. - Identify variations in criteria.	- Complete after job analysis. - Use in response to documented performance problems. - Analyze errors and error patterns to provide efficient assistance. - Criteria for mastery must be based on performance according to employer criteria across all relevant conditions encountered.
Self-management – The use of systems that enable the user to gain control of environmental events and/or work behaviors. Self-management is further defined by the particular component emphasized: antecedent cue regulation, self-monitoring, or self-recruited feedback.	- Define the performance requirement, i.e., some specific form of initiation, monitoring or feedback. - Select and teach a system that emphasizes the appropriate component. - Use standard instructional procedures (task analysis, assistance, reinforcement and error correction) to document that the user knows how to manipulate the system.	- Determine when to initiate by analyzing dependence and/or trainer presence. - System must be individualized for the target worker and job site. - Systems should be as unobtrusive as possible. - Systems should be easy for target worker, employment training specialist and employer to operate, maintain, and adapt over time. - Decisions regarding fading or withdrawing the system depend on obtrusiveness of the system, time involved in use, and worker and employer preference.
Productivity programming – Rate increase programs help target workers perform units of work according to time criteria specific to the task and work rate. Pacing programs help target workers identify varying environmental conditions that require different performance rates.	- Identify rate requirements for each task (beginning in job analysis). - Identify the frequency with which the pace changes. - Document the rate(s) at which the worker is able to perform. - Set incentives for increases in rate. - Select/identify cues for differences in pace. - Teach workers to respond to pacing cues.	- Rate issues depend on a system for identifying employer standards across varying production demands. - Task modification may increase productivity. - Self-managed systems can help workers increase rates of production and/or identify environmental cues requiring changes in pacing. - Criteria need to be validated for the job site according to the actual conditions the target worker encounters. - Production criteria change should therefore be assessed over time.
Community-referenced behavior management – Functional analysis to determine the relationship between difficult behavior (or classes of behavior) and events in the person's environment in order to apply an intervention that meets the unique demands of the individual, job site, and behavior under analysis.	- Observe and assess the individual in as many natural settings as possible. - Identify a range of stimulus conditions within and across environments. - Develop and test hypotheses regarding stimulus control factors. - Design a model for desired and excess responses. - Continue to analyze the behavior and presence or absence of various stimuli.	- Functional analysis should be used when extinction procedures are not successful. - Many individuals with challenging behaviors have little experience in employment settings. More natural stimuli may control more appropriate responses and obviate the need for intervention. - Support must be adequate for individuals with challenging behaviors. - Criteria need to be based on individual dignity, safety, security, and job site standards.

Table 8.2 Direct Service Strategy Definitions, Procedures, and Decision Rules

Support Strategy	Procedures	Decision Rules
Social skill training – The development of specific behaviors that occur in the context of interactions that take place in specific work sites.	- Identify specific activities and events and the social interactions involved. - Assess target worker participation and performance in these events. - Analyze targeted skills across the range of variation encountered in the work place. - Select performance alternatives. - Model the skill and allow the target worker to practice. - Shape, reinforce, and fade assistance.	- Target workers' preference in selecting activities and performance alternatives is critical. - Task analyses and/or self-management can be of assistance to the target worker and the trainer. - Social competence refers to perceived adherence to cultural rules. Co-worker orientation and support can be invaluable.
Communication training – Development of the modality or type of system used, the form or rules, and the content of the "language" (Stremel-Campbell & Matthews, 1987).	- Identify job-related communication requirements. - Designate a communication modality or system. - Ensure that critical communication requirements are covered. - Add work-related and social content as needed. - Test for ease of use. - Train the worker, co-worker and employer to operate the system.	- Existing and highly technical systems may not enable the worker to communicate with co-workers, employers and the public. - Systems and content should be introduced as needed. - Systems should be easy for the target worker, employment training specialist, co-workers, and employer to use, maintain, and adapt over time. - Due to skill and/or experiential deficits, some workers with no apparent communication disorders may need communication training.
Mobility training – Enabling a target worker to gain access to areas that are critical for worker performance and socialization in and around the work place.	- Identify environments in which the individual has optimum mobility. - Identify the amount and range of mobility required for the job. - Match mobility strategies to demands of the job. - Identify discrepancies and make modifications. - Teach the target worker, co-workers, and the employer to optimize mobility.	- Job match is the first issue. - The person must learn to enjoy full access to work and social opportunities. - Shaping and sensitization may help some individuals overcome reticence. - Due to skill and/or experiential deficits, some individuals with no apparent mobility impairments may need mobility training. - Co-worker orientation and training can help target workers feel welcome in new settings.

ity training is available in Bellamy et al. (1979); Mank and Horner (1988); Rusch and Mithaug (1980); and Mcloughlin et al. (1987).

COMMUNITY-REFERENCED BEHAVIOR MANAGEMENT. The growing need for training that can be conducted in public (Menchetti, Rusch, & Lamson, 1981) and for non-aversive behavior management (Horner & Dunlap, 1988) has created a new focus on procedures for facilitating the integration of persons with challenging behaviors. Functional analysis, the focus of community-referenced behavior management, emphasizes the relationship between environmental variables and the behavior (or class of behavior) in question (Horner, Albin, & Mank, 1989). Thus, it is directly applicable to supported employment where the emphasis is on support. The reader is referred to Gaylord-Ross (1980), Horner and Dunlap (1988), and Newton (1987) for procedural guidelines for community-referenced behavior management.

SOCIAL SKILL TRAINING. Social incompetence is frequently cited as a reason for job loss (Greenspan & Shoultz, 1981; Wehman et al., 1982). Individuals with disabilities have typically been denied access to situations in which they could develop many of the social abilities required for work. In terms of integration, the value of a given job is related to the degree to which it affords the opportunity to interact with others. Support is incomplete if it focuses only on the mechanical behaviors associated with work.

Chadsey-Rusch (Chapter 10) suggests that there is a critical difference between definitions and descriptions of social skill and social competence. Lists of social skills said to be important for hypothetical jobs may be combined to describe social competence. Employment training specialists will benefit more from an operational definition that helps to identify specific support needs. Social skills are behaviors related to specific interactions or events that occur in the context of specific cultures or worksites. Social competence refers to perceived adherence to the rules governing social interactions that can be identified within specific environments (also Chadsey-Rusch, 1986; McFall, 1982).

It is possible to identify three classes of work-related social interactions: (a) task-related interactions that are necessary for the completion of work tasks; (b) elective intra-task interactions, which occur during the completion of work tasks and are not required but often make jobs more interesting; and (c) break- and free-time interactions. These classes of interactions seem to build upon each other and progress from physical presence to social integration to the development of relationships. Participation across these types of interactions should be assessed and supported to allow the individual to meet his or her co-worker's definition of social competence.

COMMUNICATION TRAINING. If adequate performance in social interactions is the key to integration, then communication is the key to social interactions. Jobs that do not require communication probably involve a degree of isolation that is unacceptable. Communication involves the modality of the system (speech, sign, picture, or electronic), the form or rules for using the system, and the content of the "language." The content must include what is needed for full participation in the three types of social interactions noted above. Employment training specialists should assess and assure reciprocity in communication and social interactions since reciprocity, the development of peer relations, is the key to more meaningful integration (Bellamy, Newton, LeBaron, & Horner, 1986; Mank & Buckley, 1988).

MOBILITY TRAINING. Employment training specialists can ensure that employees with disabilities have access to locations in and around the worksite. In identifying locations, it is critical to include those required for job tasks and for socialization. Access should be defined as the removal of obstacles to movement, identification or augmentation of cues for movement, and arrangement of assistance as needed. Assistance can include that provided by co-workers or employment training specialists or the use of mobility aids such as canes and wheelchairs.

It is unlikely that any one individual would require all of the support strategies discussed in this chapter. The nature and intensity of supports will vary according to individual and environmental factors. Two variables serve as the foundation for the provision of direct support strategies: comprehensive job analysis and ongoing performance assessment (across job tasks, production demands, social skills, and self-management). Figure 8.1 shows the manner in which ongoing assessment, based on a thorough job analysis, leads to a determination of need for the direct strategies listed above. Table 8.3 presents assessment categories in terms of specific errors, possible causes and solutions.

Indirect Service Strategies

Indirect strategies are support functions that occur in and around the work setting and involve persons other than the individual with severe disabilities. Job coach intervention includes activities involving employers, supervisors, co-workers, and customers (Kregel, Hill, & Banks, 1987). Relations with co-workers are directly related to employment success and job tenure (Hill, Wehman, Hill, & Goodall, 1985). It is increasingly clear that company and co-worker support influences individual integration and success and the efficiency and effectiveness of the support organization (Buckley, Sandow, & Mank, 1989; Mank & Buckley, 1988; Nisbet & Hagner, 1988). Indirect strategies include support directed to co-workers and supervisors and ongoing employer relations.

CO-WORKER SUPPORT. The area of co-worker support includes a range of activities that can be organized through a number of arrangements. Nisbet and Hagner (1988) identify a number of models for establishing co-worker support. Co-workers can serve as observers, advocates, trainers, ongoing supervisors, and instructional program developers. Co-worker support can be (a) negotiated during job development activities; (b) arranged after the individuals with disabilities have begun employment; or (c) set up in response to problems that arise as the job coach begins to fade his or her presence (Buckley, Sandow, & Mank, 1989; Hughes, Rusch, & Curl, Chapter 11 this volume; Nisbet & Hagner, 1988; Shafer, 1986). Increasingly, employers are realizing that the skills co-workers learn when they assume support roles benefit the company as a whole. As a result, companies are beginning to negotiate with support organizations and university trainers for training in support skills.

SUPERVISOR SUPPORT. The employer-employee relationship is critical to employment success. It is unlikely that a supervisor will feel much commitment to an employee with whom he or she has limited contact. Job coaches should attempt to strengthen this relationship. Assistance in methods of supervising an individual with severe disabilities may include explanation or modeling in areas such as giving instructions, correcting or reinforcing worker performance and explaining variations in work routines. Supervisors' ability and willingness to work with their employees with disabilities may be enhanced by the use of practical and straightforward self-management and communication systems (Buckley & Mank, 1988; Mank & Horner, 1988). This support is easier to maintain when supervisors feel that they have access to assistance from employment training specialists when challenges occur (Rusch, Minch, & Hughes, in press).

ONGOING EMPLOYER RELATIONS. Support is marketed as a service to the employer. Employer relations are determined by the service the employers receive at all stages in supported employment. Sales and marketing efforts inform the employer of the nature of the services that are available from the support organization. Job analysis provides the employer (and employment training specialist) with a clearer understanding of the job and performance criteria that will be maintained (Buckley, Sandow, & Mank, 1989). Training and support activities demonstrate the ability of the individual with disabilities and the support organization to meet any agreements made. Maintaining positive employer relationships depends on responsive and timely methods for assessing their satisfaction, supporting their participation with the individuals with severe disabilities, and responding to issues and concerns they raise.

External Support Strategies

A third level of support strategies includes activities that do not directly involve the individual with disabilities and typically occur away from the workplace. These activities involve parents, families, friends, and related professionals. Since data indicate that the active involvement of these individuals is critical to employment success (Hill, Seyfarth, Banks, Wehman, & Orelove, 1987; Kochany & Keller, 1981; Schutz, 1986; Schalock, 1985) it seems appropriate that support personnel address this area by working to increase the role played by these external agents.

PARENT/ADVOCATE PARTICIPATION. Schutz (1986) classified parent involvement according to levels of participation that may increase individual autonomy and reduce the role played by paid support personnel. These include: (a)

Table 8.3 Assessment, Errors, Possible Causes, and Solutions

Assessment Areas	Specific Areas	Possible Causes	Possible Solutions
Initiation	Not initiating a task Initiating out of order	Stimulus problems - No message - Unclear messages	Self-managed cue regulation program - Developed - Upgraded to reflect individualization - Upgraded to reflect more accurate analysis of job requirements - Repositioned for better use
	Delaying initiation	Lack of motivation - Resistance - Dependence	Reward initiation
Quality, accuracy	Poor quality Failure to complete the task Inability to use task materials	Job analysis problems - Regarding employer criteria - Regarding variations	More precise training assistance - Cues (timely, salient, emphasizing rules) - Error correction - Reinforcement (natural, timely, individualized, scheduled appropriately)
	Erratic performance	Stimulus problems - Task design problems - Job (task) analysis problems - Confusion regarding discriminations	Task design/analysis - Developed - Upgraded
		Manipulation problems	Self-management systems - Cue regulation for steps in chain - Monitoring quality control
		Feedback problems - Confusion regarding intent - Schedule - Strength, individualization	Alter schedules for consequences/fading
		Fading problems	Reward independence
Production	Insufficient pace Irregular rate of production Inability to vary rate in response to work demands	Task design problems Job analysis problems - Regarding time allotted - Regarding rate variations	Modify task - Time - Time engaged without break - Location - Equipment used - Time allotted
		Stimulus problems - Amount/number required - Initiation and completion standards	Self-management - System for communicating amount/time required

Table 8.3 (cont.)

Assessment Areas	Specific Areas	Possible Causes	Possible Solutions
		Quality performance problems	- Record for tracking performance - Feedback and self-recruited feedback systems
		Feedback problems	Employer/co-worker training
		Fading problems	Rate increase program
			Pacing program
			Change/institute reinforcers
			Reward independence
Social behavior	Social skill deficit	Stimulus problems - Failure to "read" messages - Inability to make discriminations in/among behaviors	Modeling, shaping, and fading assistance Task analysis
		Feedback problems - Confusion regarding intent - Reinforcement for social problems or inadequacies - Schedule - Strength, individualization	Self-management - Self-instruction - Monitoring of new skills Functional analysis Employer/co-worker training and support

participating in training programs, (b) taking an active role in planning, (c) counseling other parents or advocates, and (d) becoming active in advocacy and policy making (Schutz, 1986). Clearly not all parents are interested in participating at these levels. It is not enough to have policies stating that parents, families, and advocates are welcome partners in the support team. Support organizations can facilitate involvement by working with individual families to establish the roles in which they feel most effective. These roles may change over time. Family members are more likely to participate if they believe that their priorities are valued, that their involvement in support is functional, that their views of the effectiveness of service is sought, and that their concerns for long-range planning are shared.

PARENT/ADVOCATE COUNSELING. Some parents and advocates may be ambivalent about integrated employment for their family member with disabilities. In some cases the reluctance may concern working conditions related to a specific job; in other cases the idea of integrated employment may be at issue. Given that family attitude is identified as a predictor of employment success (or failure) (Hill et al., 1985), it is important for support personnel to listen to parents' and advocates' concerns, respond to those that can be accommodated, and try to build a partnership. It may be that parents of individuals already employed will be more effective in providing information and increasing family support.

COORDINATION WITH OTHER PROFESSIONALS. The same range of levels of support identified above for parents exists for social service professionals. Some case managers, residential providers, and other support personnel, will help extend the autonomy of specific individuals

Figure 8.1 Relationship of Job Analysis and Performance Assessment to Support Strategies.

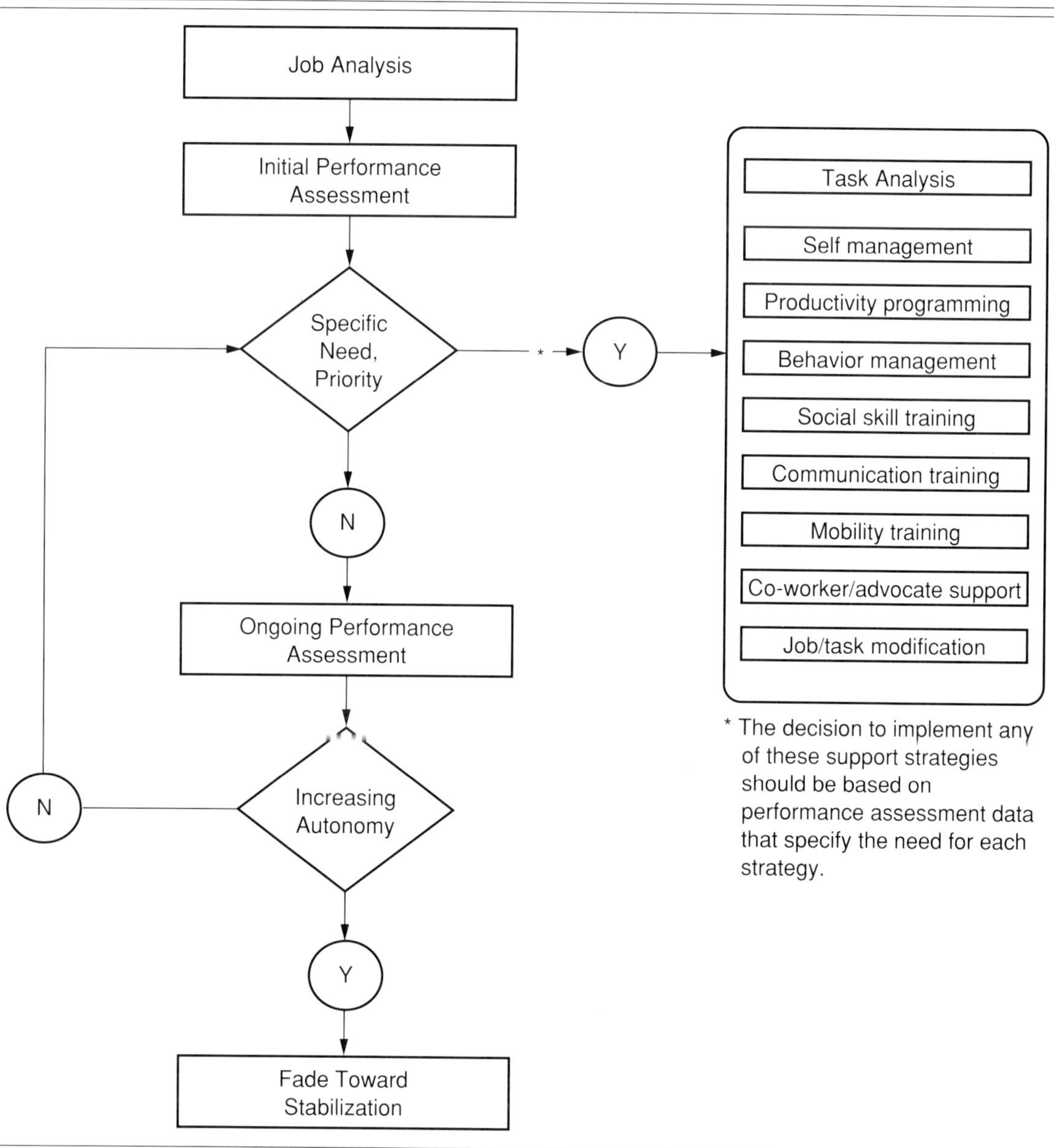

and advocate for increased access to integrated employment. Support programs and employment training specialists operate in a complex social service system environment. Support programs may find it easier to work with other professionals (and with parents) if mission statements, program descriptions, and actions clarify the purpose of the organization and the roles others can play.

The organization of support into direct, indirect, and external categories allows supported employment programs to identify and select specific strategies for individual success and for allocating program resources. Clearly, the implementation steps involved in allocating resources have a direct relationship on the program's ability to meet individual needs. Szymanski, Hanley-Maxwell & Parker (Chapter 12 this volume) and Schalock and Kiernan (Chapter 13 this volume) detail interagency coordination concerns.

SUMMARY

This chapter defined and analyzed support in terms of comprehensive ecological variables, including: the individual and his or her support network; the job and the support available within the worksite; and the support organization and its ability to apply a range of support strategies. Support strategies were identified according to three categories. The first involves instructionally-oriented strategies that directly involve the individual with disabilities. The second set of strategies is aimed at increasing co-worker and supervisor involvement. The third set of strategies is directed towards parents, advocates and other service providers.

A point emphasized in this chapter is that the selection and introduction of any of these support strategies depends on a foundation that consists of comprehensive job analysis, environmental and task modification, precise methods of instruction, and ongoing performance assessment. These interrelated variables set the stage for the support strategies described.

General procedures and decision rules for seven direct support strategies were presented, as was a format for using error analysis to make support decisions. Comprehensive, procedurally precise steps for the selection, introduction, maintenance, and fading of the support strategies discussed is beyond the scope of this chapter. References to more procedural sources are provided.

A critical point that is made throughout this chapter is that support organizations and individual employment training specialists need to implement those strategies that are needed to enable specific individuals to succeed in specific jobs. Implicit in this statement is the belief that programs and personnel should avoid expending resources on activities that are not needed to improve individual and program outcomes. Data systems that identify specific individual support needs help program staff differentiate between critical and non-critical activities.

The area of support requires continued emphasis and analysis. Efforts must be made to identify specific support strategies and the procedures involved in implementing these strategies. The involvement of co-workers, supervisors, and corporate management must be encouraged. Procedures for developing and using individual natural support networks must be developed. The interaction of these forms of support will most likely lead to improved individual and program-level outcomes and consumer, family, and employer satisfaction. Perhaps most importantly, procedurally specific information on support increases the likelihood that individuals who are perceived to have the most significant support needs will obtain access to integrated employment.

ACKNOWLEDGEMENTS

The authors would like to acknowledge the contributions of Andrea Cioffi, Lynn Greenwood, and Kristina Smock to the development of this chapter and the support strategies described.

QUESTIONS (For answers see pp. 429–430)

1. The authors suggest that support might be defined in relation to what three variables? Explain.

2. List and describe the three support service strategies discussed by the authors.

3. How might procedurally specific information on support improve supported employment outcomes?

REFERENCES

Bellamy, G. T., Horner, R. H., & Inman, D. P. (1979). *Vocational habilitation of severely retarded adults: A direct service technology*. Austin, TX: Pro-Ed.

Bellamy, G. T., Newton, J. S., LeBaron, N. M., & Horner, R. H. (1986). *Toward lifestyle accountability in residential services for persons with mental retardation*. Unpublished manuscript, University of Oregon, Eugene, OR.

Bellamy, G. T., Peterson, L., & Close, D. (1975). Habilitation of the severely and profoundly retarded: Illustrations of competence. *Education and Training of the Mentally Retarded*, 10, 174–186.

Bellamy, G. T., Rhodes, L. E., Mank, D. M., & Albin, J. M. (1988). *Supported employment: A community implementation guide*. Baltimore: Paul H. Brookes.

Buckley, J. & Mank, D. M. (1988). Self-management programming for supported employment. In D. Olson & P. Ferguson (Eds.), *Disability research: Issues in policy and practice* (pp. 63–90). Eugene: University of Oregon, Specialized Training Program, Center on Human Development.

Buckley, J., Sandow, D., & Mank, D. (1989, Spring). Extending service provider relationships with business and industry. *Innovation: Maryland Supported Employment Project News Update*. (Available from Maryland Supported Employment Project, Kennedy Institute, Baltimore, MD.)

Buckley, J., Sandow, D., & Smock, R. (1989). *Job analysis for supported employment*. Unpublished manuscript, University of Oregon, Specialized Training Program, Eugene, OR.

Chadsey-Rusch, J. (1986). Identifying and teaching valued social behaviors. In F. R. Rusch (Ed.), *Competitive employment issues and strategies* (pp. 273–287). Baltimore: Paul H. Brookes.

Crosson, J. E. (1969). A technique for programming sheltered workshop environments for training severely retarded workers. *American Journal of Mental Deficiency*, *73*, 814–818.

Gaylord-Ross, R. (1980). A decision model for the treatment of aberrant behavior in applied settings. In W. Sailor, B. Wilcox, & L. Brown (Eds.), *Methods of instruction for severely handicapped students* (pp. 135–158). Baltimore: Paul H. Brookes.

Gifford, J. L., Rusch, F. R., Martin, J. E., & White, D. M. (1984). Autonomy and adaptability: A proposed technology for maintaining work behavior. In N. Ellis & N. Bray (Eds.), *International review of research in mental retardation* (Vol. 12, pp. 284–314). New York: Academic Press.

Gold, M. (1972). Stimulus factors in skill training of the retarded on a complex assembly task: Acquisition, transfer and retention. *American Journal of Mental Retardation*, *76*, 517–526.

Gold, M. (1975). Vocational training. In J. Wortis (Ed.), *Mental retardation and developmental disabilities: An annual review* (Vol. 7, pp. 254–264). New York: Brunner/Mazel.

Greenspan, S. & Shoultz, B. (1981). Why mentally retarded adults lose their jobs: Social competence as a factor in work adjustment. *Applied Research in Mental Retardation*, *2*, 23–38.

Hill, J. W., Seyfarth, J., Banks, D. P., Wehman, P., & Orelove, F. (1987). Parent attitudes about working conditions of their adult mentally retarded sons and daughters. *Exceptional Children*, *54(1)*, 9–23.

Hill, J. W., Wehman, P., Hill, M., & Goodall, P. (1985). Differential reasons for job separation of previously employed mentally retarded adults. *Education and Training of the Mentally Retarded*, *15*, 179–186.

Horner, R. H., Albin, R. W., & Mank, D. M. (1989). Effects of undesirable, competing behaviors on the generalization of adaptive skills: A case study. *Behavior Modification*, *13(1)*, 74–90.

Horner, R.H., McDonnell, J.J., & Bellamy, G.T. (1986). Teaching generalized skills: General case instruction in simulation and community settings. In R. H. Horner, L. H. Meyer, & H.D. Fredericks (Eds.). *Education of learners with severe handicaps: Exemplary service strategies* (pp. 289–314). Baltimore: Paul H. Brookes.

Horner, R. H., Sprague, J., & Wilcox, B.G. (1982). General case programming for community activities. In B. Wilcox & T. Bellamy (Eds.). *Design of high school programs for severely handicapped students* (pp. 61–98). Baltimore: Paul H. Brookes.

Horner, R. H. & Dunlap, G. (Eds.) (1988). *Behavior management and community integration for individuals with developmental disabilities and severe behavior problems*. Eugene, OR: University of Oregon, Research and Training Center on Community-Referenced Behavior Management.

Karan, O. C. & Berger-Knight, C. (1986). Developing supported networks for individuals who fail to achieve competitive employment. In F. R. Rusch (Ed.), *Competitive employment issues and strategies* (pp. 241–256). Baltimore: Paul H. Brookes.

Kiernan, W. E. & Schalock, R. L. (1989). *Economics, industry, and disability: A look ahead*. Baltimore: Paul H. Brookes.

Kochany, L. & Keller, J. (1981). An analysis and evaluation of the failures of severely disabled individuals in competitive employment. In P. Wehman (Ed.), *Competitive employment: New Horizons for severely disabled individuals* (pp. 181–198). Baltimore: Paul H. Brookes.

Kregel, J., Hill, M., & Banks, P. D. (1987). An analysis of employment specialist intervention time in supported competitive employment: 1979–1987. In P. Wehman, J. Kregel, M. S. Shafer, & M. L. Hill (Eds.), *Competitive employment for persons with mental retardation: From research to practice* (Vol. II, pp. 84–111). Richmond: Virginia Commonwealth University, Rehabilitation Research and Training Center.

Lagomarcino, T. R., Hughes, C., & Rusch, F. R. (1989). Utilizing self-management to teach independence on the job. *Education and Training in Mental Retardation*, 24, 139–148.

Mank, D. M. & Buckley, J. (1988). Supported employment for persons with severe and profound mental retardation. In P. Wehman & M. S. Moon (Eds.), *Vocational rehabilitation and supported employment* (pp. 313–324). Baltimore: Paul H. Brookes.

Mank, D. M. & Horner, R. H. (1988). Instructional programming in vocational education. In R. Gaylord-Ross (Ed.), *Vocational education for persons with handicaps*. (pp. 142–173). Mountain View, CA: Mayfield.

Martin, J. E., Mithaug, D. E., Agran, M., & Husch, J. V. (in press). Consumer-centered transition and supported employment. In J. L. Matson (Ed.), *Handbook of behavior modification with the mentally retarded* (2nd ed.). New York: Plenum Press.

McFall, R. M. (1982). A review and reformulation of the concept of social skills. *Behavioral Assessment*, 4, 1–33.

Mcloughlin, C. S., Garner, J. B., & Callahan, M. (1987). *Getting employed, staying employed*. Baltimore: Paul H. Brookes.

Menchetti, B.M., Rusch, F.R., & Lamson, D.S. (1981). Social validation of behavioral training techniques: Assessing the normalizing qualities of competitive employment training procedures. *Journal of The Association for the Severely Handicapped,* 6(2), 6–16.

Newton, J. S. (1987). *Neighborhood Living Project behavior management package*. Eugene: University of Oregon, Center on Human Development.

Nisbet, J. & Hagner, D. (1988). Natural supports in the workplace: A reexamination of supported employment. *Journal of the Association for Persons with Severe Handicaps*, 13(4), 260–267.

Pancsofar, E. L., (1986). Assessing work behavior. In F. R. Rusch (Ed.). *Competitive employment issues and strategies* (pp. 93–102). Baltimore: Paul H. Brookes.

Public Law 98-527:Developmental Disabilities Assistance and Bill of Rights Act. (1984). Washington, DC: 98th Congress.

Public Law 99-506: Rehabilitation Act Amendments of 1986. (1986). Washington, DC: 99th Congress.

Rogers-Warren, A. & Warren, S. F. (1977). The developing ecobehavioral psychology. In A. Rogers-Warren & S. F. Warren (Eds.), *Ecological perspectives in behavior analysis* (pp. 3–8). Baltimore: University Park Press.

Rusch, F. R. (Ed.) (1986). Introduction. *Competitive employment: Issues and strategies* (pp. 3–6). Baltimore: Paul H. Brookes.

Rusch, F. R. & Mithaug, D. E. (1980). *Vocational training for mentally retarded adults: A behavior analytic approach*. Champaign, IL: Research Press.

Rusch, F. R., Minch, K., & Hughes, C. (in press). Evaluating job site supervisors role in the long-term employment of persons with severe disabilities. *The Journal of Vocational Special Needs Populations*.

Schalock, R. L. (1985). Comprehensive community services: A plea for interagency collaboration. In R. H. Bruininks & K. C. Lakin (Eds.), *Living and learning in the least restrictive environment* (pp. 32–62). Baltimore: Paul H. Brookes.

Schutz, R. P. (1986). Establishing a parent-professional partnership to facilitate competitive employment. In F. R. Rusch (Ed.), *Competitive employment issues and strategies* (pp. 289–302). Baltimore: Paul H. Brookes.

Shafer, M. S. (1986). Utilizing co-workers as change agents. In F. R. Rusch (Ed.), *Competitive employment issues and strategies* (pp. 215–224). Baltimore: Paul H. Brookes.

Stokes, T. F. & Osnes, P. G. (1986). Programming the generalization of children's social behavior. In P. S. Strain, M. J. Guralnick & H. M. Walker (Eds.), *Children's social behavior: Development, assessment, and modification* (pp. 418–441). Orlando, FL: Academic Press.

Stremel-Campbell, K. & Mathews, J. (1987). Development of emergent language. In M. Bullis (Ed.). *Communication development in young children with deaf-blindness: Literature review III* (pp. 165–201). Monmouth, OR: Teaching Research Publications.

U.S. Department of Labor. (1988, May). *Employment of workers with disabilities under special certificates* Part VI. Washington, DC: Author.

Wacker, D. P. & Berg, W. K. (1985). Use of peer instruction to train a complex photocopying task to moderately and severely retarded adolescents. *Analysis and Intervention in Developmental Disabilities*, 4, 219–234.

Wehman, P. (1981). *Competitive employment: New horizons for severely disabled individuals*. Baltimore: Paul H. Brookes.

Wehman, P. (1986). Competitive employment in Virginia. In F. R. Rusch (Ed.), *Competitive employment issues and strategies* (pp. 23–34). Baltimore: Paul H. Brookes.

Wehman, P., Hill, M., Goodall, P., Brooke, V., Cleveland, P., & Pentecost, B. (1982). Job placement and follow-up of moderately and severely handicapped individuals after three years. *Journal of The Association of the Severely Handicapped*. 7, (2) 5–16.

Wehman, P., Kregel, J., & Shafer, M. S. (1989). *Emerging trends in the national supported employment initiative: A preliminary analysis of twenty-seven states*. Richmond: Virginia Commonwealth University, Rehabilitation Research and Training Center.

Wehman, P. & Moon, M. S. (Eds.) (1988). *Vocational rehabilitation and supported employment*. Baltimore: Paul H. Brookes.

Wehman, P., Moon, M. S., Everson, J. M., Wood, W., & Barcus, J. M. (1988). *Transition from school to work: New challenges for youth with severe disabilities*. Baltimore: Paul H. Brookes.

Wilcox, B. & Bellamy, G. T. (1982). *Design of high school programs for severely handicapped students*. Baltimore: Paul H. Brookes.

Will, M. (1984a). Position paper. *OSERS programming for the transition of youth with disabilities: Bridges from school to working life*. Washington, DC: Office of Special Education and Rehabilitative Services.

Will, M. (1984b). *Supported employment for adults with severe disabilities: An OSERS program initiative*. Washington, DC: Office of Special Education and Rehabilitative Services.

CHAPTER

9

Teaching Generalization and Maintenance of Work Behavior

Wendy K. Berg
David P. Wacker
Thomas H. Flynn
University of Iowa

A variety of factors interact to affect the success and length of a job placement for any employee, regardless of the presence or absence of a disability. Such factors include issues related to the employer or work supervisor (e.g., expectations for performance, biases towards certain groups of people), the logistics of the job placement (e.g., acceptability of the work schedule, ease of transportation), and the employee (e.g., personal work habits, job satisfaction) (Rusch, 1986; Shafer, Kregel, Banks, & Hill, 1988; Wehman & Kregel, 1985). As supported employment opportunities are provided to persons who are severely disabled, the importance of each of these factors becomes increasingly apparent. Although all of these factors play a large role in the success of a job experience, the focus of this chapter is on those issues directly affecting the employee's behavior at the job site.

Within the supported employment model, the success of a job placement is typically defined in terms of length of paid employment. Although numerous investigations have documented that people who are severely disabled can learn to perform specific work tasks and to engage in social behaviors required for employment, long-term success in a community job setting requires more than the acquisition of specific behaviors. The employee also must respond to variations in the work setting that are encountered over an indefinite period of time (Rusch, Martin, & White 1985). In other words, acquiring specific work and social behaviors is a necessary, but not sufficient, goal of supported employment training (Martin, Burger, Elias-Burger, & Mithaug, in press).

As shown in Table 9.1, two interrelated components of behavior, generalization and maintenance, are required to facilitate long-term community employment. Generalization of behavior occurs when a target employee adjusts his or her behavior to respond appropriately to novel stimuli encountered in the work environment. Gifford, Rusch, Martin, and White (1984) referred to this component of behavior as adaptability and defined it as the ability to perform the needed behaviors across a range of task requirements and environmental conditions. Maintenance of behavior refers to the continued demonstration of the desired behavior over a period of time that is different from the time in which training occurred. Maintenance of behav-

Table 9.1 Components of Behavior Necessary for Success in Community Settings

Generalization of skills		Maintenance of performance	
Antecedent Training Procedures		**Consequence Training Procedures**	
Utilize stimuli contained within the task	**Utilize stimuli that are extra to the task**	**Establish effective reinforcers**	**Adjust schedule of reinforcement**
1. Common stimuli 2. Sufficient exemplars 3. General case	1. Antecedent cue regulation a. Verbal mediated cues b. External prompts	1. Natural contingencies 2. Premack Principle	1. Intermittent schedule 2. Indiscriminable contingencies 3. Engage available reinforcers 4. Solicit reinforcement 5. Consequence regulation

ior is also referred to as generalization across time (Drabman, Hammer, & Rosenbaum, 1979) and as independence (Gifford et al., 1984).

The purpose of this chapter is to describe those factors and procedures: (a) affecting generalization of behavior, and (b) affecting maintenance of behavior once the necessary skills have been acquired.

GENERALIZATION OF SKILLS

Generalization refers to the demonstration of behavior under conditions that differ from the training conditions and in which either no training has occurred, or substantially reduced amounts of training are required, for acceptable performance to occur (Stokes & Baer, 1977). There are two critical components to this definition; novel conditions and reduced training. The first component refers to the conditions for performance and includes a variety of factors that may affect behavior, such as changes in the setting in which the task is to be performed, the people present in the task setting, the materials to be used, the behaviors required for successful performance, and the time interval between the training situation and the generalization situation, as well as combinations of these changes (Drabman et al., 1979).

Typically, several types of generalization are required for a target employee to be successful in an employment setting. For example, in order for the employee to become independent at the job site, he or she must become less reliant on the job coach and more responsive to the employer, co-workers, or work supervisor (generalization across people). The target employee may also find it necessary to perform the assigned duties using equipment that has been updated or replaced since training was completed, or to use supplies that are different from the materials used for training (generalization across behaviors and materials). In addition, work areas may be rearranged or reassigned (generalization across settings), requiring the target employee to work in the company of different people with different materials (generalization across people and materials).

The second component of Stokes and Baer's (1977) definition for generalization relates to the amount of training a person requires to perform novel variations of a task. According to the definition provided by Stokes and Baer, generalization may be claimed when either: (a) the task is completed under novel (untrained) situations, or (b) the amount of training needed to perform subsequent variations of the task is substantially reduced. According to this definition, it is incorrect to assume that persons who are severely handicapped do not generalize across task variations if they do not perform at criterion during initial attempts to complete a novel task or after an extended period of time. Most people, disabled or nondisabled, typically require at least minimal instruction during generalization conditions when they are presented with a novel version of a task (e.g., using a new photocopying machine).

Inadequate generalization is reflected in problems resulting from the target employee's ability to perform desired behavior within the context of the work environment. Mager and Pipe (1970) referred to these types of problems in work behavior as skill-related problems. Skill-related problems indicate that the target employee does not know what behaviors are expected, does not know how to perform those behaviors appropriately, or is unable to determine when those behaviors are to be demonstrated. For example, skill-related problems are suggested when an employee reliably attempts to perform the correct task, but either performs certain steps incorrectly or deletes steps on an intermittent basis. Skill-related problems are also suggested when an employee is inconsistent in attempting or completing tasks at correct times, indicating that the employee is overly dependent upon cues provided by a supervisor or job coach for these behaviors. Although skill-related problems are often considered to reflect inadequate acquisition of target behaviors, they may instead reflect inadequate generalization to variations of behaviors that are required for success at the job site. Even subtle or minor changes in the work task or context can disrupt performance if training is not designed to promote generalization.

Skill-related problems that result from inadequate acquisition of the target task may occur because of training criteria that are insufficient for continued performance. These problems may reflect a training program that was too narrow in focus (i.e., that taught only one set of responses rather than a generalized skill), or that did not provide the target employee with the opportunity to acquire sufficient fluency or independence in performing the target task under the cues and consequences that are routinely available in the job setting. Both of these problems, narrow focus and lack of fluency or independence, actually reflect inadequate generalization from the training situation to the long-term employment situation. In other words, performance under training conditions, which usually involves extra resources, must eventually generalize to resources routinely available at the job site for long-term employment to be facilitated.

ANTECEDENT TRAINING PROCEDURES

Numerous antecedent stimuli are available within a work setting, any of which may control the target employee's behavior (Kirby & Bickel, 1988). These stimuli may be any feature of the environment that the target employee responds to as a guide for his or her behavior and may include the presence of specific people, the arrangement of work materials, the sound of a break whistle, and the sight of a clock on the wall, as well as cues and directions provided by a work supervisor. Training procedures that focus on teaching the individual to respond to the relevant stimuli that precede and signal desired behavior are referred to as antecedent training procedures.

As shown in Table 9.2, a number of antecedent training procedures are available for promoting generalization of performance, most of which can be placed within one of two categories: (a)procedures that utilize naturally occurring stimuli (i.e., stimuli contained within the task), and (b)procedures that utilize extra stimuli that are added to the task to either augment or replace the naturally occurring stimuli (Berg & Wacker, 1989). Programming common stimuli (Stokes & Baer, 1977), training sufficient exemplars (Stokes & Baer, 1977), and general case instruction (Horner & McDonald, 1982) are the most common methods that exemplify the first category.

Programming Common Stimuli

In order to be successful at a particular work site, the target employee must learn to respond to the discriminative stimuli that are specific to that work site. One method to ensure that the target employee's behavior is under the control of stimuli routinely available within the work setting is to utilize these stimuli (or very similar stimuli) during training. This method of training is referred to as programming common stimuli (Stokes & Baer, 1977). Providing instruction under conditions that match those of the targeted long-term employment setting facilitates generalization from training to long-term employment conditions because the stimuli used to guide behavior are common across the two conditions.

Table 9.2 Training Strategies for Skill Problems

Strategy	Definition	Description
Common stimuli	Stimuli that will guide behavior in the generalization conditions are incorporated into training.	The employment setting is analyzed to determine the antecedent stimuli that will be available to guide the employee's behavior. These stimuli are incorporated into training.
Sufficient exemplars	Training is conducted on at least two examples of the desired response.	Possible variations of the target task, work materials, or work supervisors are used as additional training examples.
General case	Training is conducted on known variations of the desired response.	Variations of the task are analyzed in terms of their stimulus properties and response requirements. Examples from each set of variations are selected as additional training examples.
Antecedent cue regulation	The target employee is taught to follow cues that are extra to the desired response to guide responding.	Instructions for performing the task are produced verbally by the target employee, or for tasks requiring long, complex chains of behavior, are provided to the employee in a visual, auditory, or tactual format that is controlled by the employee.

In some cases, observed decreases in the employee's behavior following the removal of the job coach from the employment setting may reflect a lack of commonality between the discriminative stimuli that guided the employee's behavior during training (e.g., the job coach) and the stimuli routinely available within the employment setting (co-workers or stimuli available within the task). For example, the target employee may appear to be independent during training but is actually relying on the job coach for subtle cues (e.g., marking a score sheet, closing a work folder, or moving to the next work area) to determine the adequacy of performance. Once the job coach is removed from the work setting, the additional cues provided by the job coach are not available, and the target employee may be unable to discriminate acceptable from unacceptable performance (e.g., when to begin or complete a task). In this case, the employee has not generalized from the training situation, in which the job coach was present, to the actual work condition, in which he or she is expected to rely on the cues provided by the task or by co-workers. To facilitate generalization, job coaches should first determine what stimuli will be present to continue to guide behavior following training, and should then terminate training only after the employee is responding to those stimuli. This may require much less prompting by the job coach during training and, instead, require that the job coach permit the employee to respond to the natural stimuli before feedback is provided (Wacker et al., 1986).

Sufficient Exemplars

A second natural antecedent training procedure is the use of a sufficient exemplars training approach. Stokes and Baer (1977) reported that one method for promoting generalization to novel situations is to provide training on multiple (sufficient) examples of relevant antecedents, target responses, settings, and/or trainers during training. Providing training on more than one example exposes the target employee to variations of the stimuli that may be encountered in the work setting. Increasing the employee's exposure to variations in the target task increases the likelihood that the target employee will continue to demonstrate desired responses following any changes that may occur in work arrangements, materials, supervisors, or coworkers. Training is considered to be sufficient once the employee generalizes across changes in antecedent stimuli.

Hunt, Alwell, and Goetz (1988) used a sufficient exemplars training approach to teach three high school students who were severely mentally retarded to initiate and maintain conversations as a socially appropriate way to gain and maintain attention. The three students in the Hunt et al. study had limited verbal skills and obtained attention through the frequent display of inappropriate behavior. Each student was taught to use a pictorial communication book to initiate and maintain conversations with a minimum of four peers who were not disabled. In addition to providing training with multiple examples of nondisabled conversation partners, Hunt et al. ensured that training occurred in a minimum of three community sites and three school sites for each student. The students learned to initiate conversations independently and to maintain those conversations by asking questions or making comments through the use of their conversation books. In addition, two of the three students generalized their skills to other visual materials (such as magazines and photo albums) as a conversation referent, and all three students were able to use their conversation books with different adults when prompted. Providing training with multiple peers and in a variety of settings varied the irrelevant stimuli across training sessions; the only stimuli that remained constant were the conversational cues provided by the peers and the conversation books. Thus, the likelihood of the students' behavior coming under the control of extraneous or irrelevant stimuli was reduced, and the control of the targeted antecedent stimuli (conversational cues and conversation book) was maximized (Kirby & Bickel, 1988).

The number of examples necessary to produce generalization must be defined empirically for any given person. A sufficient number of examples have been trained when the person performs the desired behaviors under untrained conditions. In many cases, three examples are sufficient to produce generalization (Hupp, 1986).

One method for determining if the target employee has reached an adequate level of independence is to assess the employee's ability to perform the tasks in a different but similar work setting under post-training conditions. An employee who can perform the target task in the employment setting, but not in a similar setting, is most likely relying on cues that are extraneous to the work task but which have come to control his or her behavior (through pairing with reinforcement) (Kirby & Bickel, 1988). For example, a target employee in a clerical setting may be using an irrelevant cue (e.g., a crack in the wall behind the photocopier) to correctly align the papers that are to be copied, rather than following the guides provided on the machine. Although the crack in the wall may be an effective cue initially, it is not the cue that will lead ultimately to long-term independence in completing photocopying tasks. If the machine is moved, the wall is painted, or different sized materials (such as books) are to be copied, this extraneous cue will no longer be effective. Training on multiple examples and testing the employee's independence in different settings, or under different work conditions, provides useful information to the job coach regarding the target employee's ability to respond to relevant stimuli.

General Case

An extension of the sufficient exemplars approach is the use of what Horner and McDonald (1982) referred to as general case instruction. With general case instruction, the potential variations of the target task that the trainee is likely to encounter are analyzed in terms of the stimulus features (stimulus class) that either guide the same response (response class) or guide different responses. Once the relevant stimulus features for the task are defined, examples that sample the range of relevant stimulus features and response demands are selected for training. Providing training on representative samples of the relevant stimuli and response demands increases the likelihood of the person responding correctly to untrained examples. General case instruction is successful when all members of a given stimulus class produce specific responses.

Pancsofar and Bates (1985) used a general case training paradigm to teach four students with moderate to severe mental retardation to operate liquid soap dispensers. During a survey of sixty-six fast food restaurants, liquid soap dispensers were observed to be the most commonly used type of dispenser. The liquid soap dispensers (forty-one) were selected as the target task and were analyzed for the stimulus features that resulted in different responses. Based on this analysis, the dispensers were divided into three groups: (a) lift operated dispensers, (b) push operated dispensers, and (c) pull operated dispensers. Within each group, four representative exemplars were selected which varied in terms of color, shape, and size (extraneous stimuli), but which remained consistent in terms of the motoric responses required to operate the machine (relevant stimuli). The results of the investigation indicated that the students required training on exemplars from at least two of these categories before generalization occurred to the third category. Once the students reached acquisition on one or two exemplars from at least two categories, they were then able to operate the remaining exemplars within those categories, with some students also being able to operate exemplars from the third (untrained) category. The findings of Pancsofar & Bates support the conclusion that for generalization of even relatively simple responses to occur, well-chosen exemplars of training stimuli must be selected.

The training of multiple exemplars becomes increasingly important as the length of employment increases. Most community work sites change over time to incorporate new materials, the hiring of different personnel, or the expansion of work and break areas. Not all of these changes can be anticipated or systematically incorporated into training. However, by training multiple exemplars and by focusing on generalization rather than on acquisition, the job coach can facilitate the adaptability of the employee over time.

Antecedent Cue Regulation

The antecedent procedures discussed thus far rely on developing a functional relationship between the antecedent stimuli contained within the task or setting and the target employee's behavior. In each case, the antecedent stimuli likely to be encountered following the completion of training are systematically introduced during training, with the purpose of training being to increase the employee's responsiveness to those antecedent stimuli. A different approach is to teach the target employee to respond to antecedent stimuli that are external to the task or setting. These stimuli are either produced by the target employee (self-generated procedures) or are provided to the employee from an external source (externally generated procedures). In either case, these procedures are used to augment or replace existing antecedent stimuli, which, for a variety of reasons, never exert functional control over responding.

When extra antecedent stimuli are added to the task or setting, an antecedent cue regulation procedure (Gifford et al., 1984) is being selected in which the employee controls the presentation of the cues. This procedure has also been referred to as mediated generalization (Stokes & Baer, 1977), because the cues are used by the employee to mediate his or her subsequent behavior in generalization conditions. Antecedent cue regulation refers to responses the target employee makes to limit the range of stimuli guiding his or her behavior (Martin, Rusch, James, Decker, & Trtol, 1982). Providing the target employee with a system for producing or controlling the presentation of discriminative stimuli increases the likelihood of the employee continuing to follow these stimuli across variations in the work situation. The procedures used to mediate generalization include establishing a response (e.g., stating task directions, looking at a picture) as part of the training paradigm, which is then used by the employee in other situations requiring the same target behavior (Stokes & Baer, 1977).

VERBAL MEDIATORS. Self-instructions and self-labeling are the two most commonly used forms of self-generated antecedent cue regulation procedures. When self-instructions are used, the target employee is taught a sequence of statements to verbalize when performing the target task. This series of statements constitutes the directions for performing the target task or responding appropriately to the situation.

Whitman, Spence, and Maxwell (1987) demonstrated that adults with mild to moderate mental retardation who were taught to use self-instruction procedures demonstrated better maintenance and generalization of performance than a similar group of adults who received training with instructions provided by another adult. Following the completion of training, both groups of adults were assessed for maintenance of performance over a two-day period and for generalization to a second (untrained) task. The adults trained with the self-instruction procedure achieved higher levels of performance for the training and generalization tasks than did the adults receiving external training. Furthermore, additional analyses indicated that a higher frequency of self-verbalizations across all of the assessment conditions was positively related to higher ability level, self-instruction training, and acquisition of the training criteria.

Self-labeling is a second training procedure that relies on speech as a mediator. Self-labeling procedures promote generalization by providing a verbal label to highlight the stimuli that are normally available within the task. This is in contrast to self-instruction training, in which the client provides verbal directions regarding the behavior to be performed to complete the task. With self-labeling, the target employee states the relevant stimuli of the target task to make those stimuli more salient. For example, Wacker, et al. (1989) taught students who were moderately mentally retarded to enter data into a computer by verbally stating the numbers written on the program sheet as they entered them into the computer. By stating the numbers in the correct sequence, the students focused on the salient stimuli (numbers) for performing the task correctly. The use of this procedure resulted in generalization across novel computer programs, data sets, and settings.

EXTERNAL PROMPTING SYSTEMS. External prompting systems provide extra stimuli (stimuli that are added to the task or setting) that the individual learns to control to guide behavior across task variations (Gifford et al., 1984). These prompting systems function by providing individuals with a stable set of stimuli that either augment or highlight the stimuli occurring naturally within the task.

The most common example of an external prompting system is picture prompts. Picture prompts control behavior by depicting each step in a chain of responses. The pictures, usually bound together in a book, are controlled (regulated) by the target employee, who is trained to perform the step depicted, to turn the page, and to perform the next step depicted. Once a target employee learns to use the pictures, the potential for generalization may be increased, because the same chain of behaviors originally trained (look-then-do) are required, and the same antecedent stimuli (pictures) continue to guide behavior. The utility of picture prompts has been documented in numerous investigations (Connis, 1979; Johnson & Cuvo, 1981; Martin et al., 1982; Sowers, Rusch, Connis, & Cummings, 1980; Wacker & Berg, 1983; Wacker & Berg, 1984; Wacker, Berg, Berrie, & Swatta, 1985).

Wacker et al. (1985) taught three adolescents who were severely disabled to use picture prompts to complete complex vocational and domestic living tasks. Following training on one set of pictures, the participants were able to use novel pictures to perform novel tasks in novel settings with substantially reduced amounts of training. Furthermore, the students' performance on the generalization tasks did not appear to be affected by the tasks' similarity or dissimilarity to the original training task.

External prompting systems are not limited to visual stimuli. Alberto, Sharpton, Briggs, and Stright (1986), for example, reported on the advantages and efficiency of utilizing self-operated auditory prompting systems as an alternative to picture prompt systems. In their investigation, prerecorded tapes were used to teach four adolescents who were moderately to severely mentally retarded to complete a vocational and a daily living task. All four adolescents learned to complete both tasks quickly using the taped instructions and, following training, were able to complete the tasks accurately without the prerecorded tapes. Alberto et al. listed several advantages associated with the use of prerecorded instructions, including the ease with which the cues can be adapted to meet the individual needs of the student and the social acceptability of miniature cassette tape players as evidenced by their use in public by nonhandicapped persons.

In the Alberto et al. (1986) investigation, the adolescents were able to perform the target tasks without the prompting system following training. In other investigations, the participants continued to rely on the prompting system to maintain correct behavior even after extensive training was provided. For example, Berg and Wacker (1989) taught a young woman who was deaf, blind, and mentally retarded to follow tactual prompts to perform a variety of envelope-stuffing tasks. In this investigation, raised tactual cues were placed in front of stacks of items to be collated and stuffed into envelopes. Matching tactual cues were placed, one per page, into a tactual cue book. The woman was taught to select the correct envelopes and fillers by matching the tactual cue found in the book to the cues located in front of her, taking one item from the stack behind that cue, placing that item in an envelope, turning the page, and repeating the sequence. Once trained, the woman was able to use different sized envelopes, different types of fillers, and even different sets of tactual cues to complete the envelope stuffing tasks. However, the woman continued to depend on the tactual prompting system to guide her performance on the training and generalization tasks. These results are consistent with those of Wacker et al. (1985), who evaluated the use of picture prompts. In cases in which the use of an external prompting system remains an integral component of performance, arrangements must be made for inclusion of the system in generalization conditions if generalized performance is to occur (Kirby & Bickel, 1988). Thus, for long-term employment, the acceptability of prompting systems to the employer must be established.

With each of these investigations, the participants were able to perform variations of the target task by following the same sequence of behaviors originally trained; a look-then-do (picture prompts), a listen-then-do (prerecorded instructions), or a touch-then-do (tactual prompts) behavioral chain was trained. The results of these investigations indicate that the effectiveness of an external prompting system is not determined by the mode of cue presentation but, instead, appears to be related more to the ability of the system to provide stimuli in a fixed sequence that is interpretable to the individual.

Summary

Antecedent training procedures promote generalization of behavior to variations in the work task or setting, thus increasing the likelihood that the target employee will continue to demonstrate the desired behaviors over time. Generalization of behavior is facilitated by the target employee's previous experience with the relevant stimuli (common discriminative stimuli, sufficient exemplars, general case instruction), and by the target employee's ability to produce or control the relevant stimuli (antecedent cue regulation/ mediated behavior). The decision as to which type of procedure to use is based first on the employee's ability to learn to respond to naturally available antecedent stimuli. If extra stimuli are needed, then an antecedent cue regulation approach may be successful, if it is acceptable to the employer and employee.

MAINTENANCE OF PERFORMANCE

The second component of behavior needed for success within community work settings, maintenance of performance, is the independent demonstration of the desired behaviors over time. Maintenance of performance requires that the target employee perform desired behavior within the reinforcement contingencies available at the work site. Mager and Pipe (1970) referred to problems associated with this aspect of work behavior as performance or motivation problems.

Performance or motivation problems are indicated when an employee has the skills needed to perform the required behaviors but does not perform those behaviors consistently. Specifically, the target employee performs the required behaviors well under certain conditions of reinforcement but not under other systems. Reinforcement at work can include social attention, participation in preferred activities, and the termination of undesired activities, as well as tangible reinforcers, such as money.

Performance problems might be determined by first evaluating the target employee's attempt to complete certain tasks. If the target employee consistently fails to even attempt a task, or if the employee engages in inappropriate behaviors to solicit or to augment available reinforcement (e.g., calls out co-workers' names), the normally available reinforcers at that job site, or the schedule of reinforcement, may not be sufficient to maintain the employee's performance over time. When a target employee is capable of performing the required behaviors, but does not display those behaviors consistently, it is necessary to evaluate the available contingencies for work behavior. In some cases, it may be necessary to adjust the use of various reinforcers or to augment the normal reinforcement schedule.

CONSEQUENCE PROCEDURES

Consequence procedures are used to promote maintenance of behavior by adjusting the contingencies that maintain behavior. Some consequence procedures function by providing feedback to the individual regarding the accuracy of performance; others serve to motivate continued responding, with most procedures providing both correction and motivation. As illustrated in Table 9.3, we have focused on those consequence procedures that are intended to motivate continued performance and that appear to be applicable to community employment settings.

Consequence procedures maintain behavior by: (a) adjusting the reinforcers that are provided following the display of desired behavior, (b) adjusting the individual's responsiveness to potential reinforcers, or (c) adjusting the schedule with which the reinforcers are delivered. Maintenance of employment is dependent, in part, on the target employee's generalization of performance from the reinforcement conditions provided during training to the reinforcement conditions that are available within the employment setting. Once the employee learns to complete the job tasks and to display job-relevant responses, then maintenance is frequently a function of identifying and incorporating consequence conditions that reinforce behavior.

Natural Maintaining Contingencies

Just as generalization of behavior across stimuli is facilitated by using natural antecedent stimuli, generalization across consequence conditions is facilitated by utilizing the reinforcers and contingencies during training that continue to occur in the work setting. Target employees typically receive large amounts of praise and attention during training, and, as the target employee's accuracy in performance increases, the amount of positive feedback also increases. The praise provided by the job coach may be delivered at such a high rate that other sources of reinforcement (e.g., attention from co-workers) are not pursued by the employee, or the regular reinforcers provided through the employment situation (e.g., paycheck) become secondary to the praise received from the job coach. It may be necessary in these instances to pair the effective reinforcer (praise from the job coach) with the normally available reinforcer (praise from co-workers or paycheck). Once the target employee's behavior is under the control of the paired

Table 9.3 Training Strategies for Performance Problems

Strategy	Definition	Description
Natural contingencies	Normally available reinforcers are paired with currently effective reinforcers. The currently effective reinforcers are gradually reduced (through fading) until the normally occurring reinforcers control behavior.	The reinforcers that remain available within the employment setting are utilized in conjunction with reinforcers that currently control the employee's behavior.
Premack Principle	Engagement in preferred activities is used as a reinforcer for completion of less preferred activities.	Required activities at the work site are identified as either preferred or nonpreferred activities. The employee's schedule is arranged so that nonpreferred activities are completed prior to preferred activities.
Intermittent schedules of reinforcement	Reinforcement is provided on an intermittent rather than continuous schedule.	Reinforcement is provided on a schedule that more closely mirrors the frequency of reinforcement that will occur at the job site.
Indiscriminable contingencies	Reinforcement is provided on a schedule that is not predictable to the employee.	Reinforcement is provided for work completed on a schedule that is unknown to the employee.
Engage normally available reinforcement	The employee augments the amount of reinforcement typically received at the job site by engaging in behaviors that are likely to be reinforced.	Employees are taught to demonstrate social or work-related behaviors that will increase the likelihood of receiving positive feedback from co-workers or the work supervisor.
Consequence regulation	The employee augments the amount of reinforcement received by delivering reinforcers to himself or herself on a preestablished basis.	The employee is taught to monitor his or her own work performance and then, based on that performance, to deliver reinforcers to himself or herself.

reinforcers, the extraneous reinforcer (e.g., praise from the job coach) is gradually reduced until the target employee is responsive to normally available reinforcers.

In some instances, the target employee may remain unresponsive to the reinforcers that are typically provided at the work site, perhaps because of a lack of familiarity with those reinforcers. When a paycheck is the main form of reinforcement at the work site, the target employee who does not have previous experience in earning and spending money is at a disadvantage. Frequently, paychecks are provided on a bi-weekly schedule and are automatically deposited into a bank account. Payment under these conditions may not function as a reinforcer, and maintenance of performance would not be expected. In this case, it is necessary to make the connection between work and money more salient for the target employee during training. For example, the employee might be given cash immediately after work is completed, thus establishing the connection between work performed and money received. Similarly, the money received might be used immediately to purchase a desired item, thereby establishing money as a reinforcer. Once the relationship between work performed and money earned is established, the provision of money can be faded gradually to transpire at the naturally occurring time (e.g., bi-weekly) and in the naturally occurring form (e.g., paycheck). However, if the money earned by an employee is subsequently withheld, then there is a reduced reason to work;

in other words, the major, natural reinforcer for working is not available, and maintenance problems should be anticipated. Most people work, in part, to receive money and to spend at least part of their wages on preferred goods or activities.

Preferred Activities at Work

In some instances the completion of certain job tasks may be punishing to the employee (Mager & Pipe, 1970). For example, an employee who completes the regular photocopying job ahead of schedule may be assigned to clean the office restroom in the remaining time. Cleaning the restroom may not only represent more work, but may very well be less desirable to the employee than the regularly assigned tasks. In other cases, there may be several regularly assigned tasks (e.g., an office job with several duties to be completed daily), some of which are preferred by the employee over others. To accommodate preferences among job tasks, the employee may find that performing the preferred tasks (e.g., photocopying) first, and at a slower rate, eliminates the need to perform the less preferred tasks (e.g., cleaning the restroom).

The use of preferred activities, or the Premack Principle, (Whaley & Malott, 1971) may be applied in situations where both preferred and nonpreferred tasks must be completed. This approach involves using engagement in preferred activities as reinforcers for the completion of less preferred activities. In a supported employment setting, job duties might be identified as being either preferred or nonpreferred tasks by asking the target employee or by observing which tasks the employee chooses to perform when given a choice. Once preferred tasks are identified, the work schedule might be arranged so that a highly preferred task (or a work break) follows the completion of a less preferred task. In the above example, the preferred task of photocopying might be performed only after the restroom has been cleaned, thus providing a simple solution to a potentially complex problem. Changes in the schedule in which work tasks are performed must be acceptable to employers and co-workers; if they are acceptable, immediate benefits in employee performance may occur. The use of preferred activities may prove to be substantially easier to implement than continued use of direct instruction procedures intended to teach the employee to perform tasks under the original work schedule.

Intermittent Schedules of Reinforcement

Another issue affecting the effectiveness of reinforcement concerns the delivery of the reinforcer. Typically, reinforcement is provided on a continuous schedule throughout much of the training period at a job site. Although such a schedule may be effective in promoting the employee's acquisition or accuracy of performance, it does not lead to independence of performance if it does not reflect the schedule of reinforcement available following training. When an employee has received a spuriously large amount of praise and attention during training, the praise and attention available following the completion of training may be insufficient to maintain behavior; in other words, the employee experiences an extinction condition. Similarly, reinforcement that is response-based (contingent on accuracy and rate of performance) may be effective during training, but because it does not reflect the type of schedule typically available at a work site (time-based), it may not be effective for promoting long-term independence at the job site. In addition to establishing functional control between naturally available reinforcers and the employee's behavior at the work site, it is also necessary to consider the schedules of reinforcement that are in effect at the work site.

One approach to facilitating maintenance of performance is to change from a continuous to an intermittent schedule of reinforcement during training. Intermittent schedules of reinforcement may be more effective than continuous schedules for two reasons. First, to the degree that the intermittent schedule of reinforcement more closely resembles the normal reinforcement schedule at the work site, the employee receives training under more natural (similar) conditions. Second, intermittent schedules of reinforcement are more resistant to extinction. As the target employee becomes increasingly independent at the work site, it is likely that the degree of supervision and frequency of work-related interactions with the work supervisor or co-workers will decrease or vary over time. Target employees who are trained to work for reinforcement that is provided on an intermittent basis are more likely to maintain their levels of performance, even when the schedule of reinforcement becomes more lean or variable.

Indiscriminable Contingencies

Although intermittent schedules can facilitate maintenance, the target employee may need further adjustments to that schedule to increase consistent performance over time. In some cases, these adjustments are made to augment available reinforcement, whereas in other cases, the adjustments are used to make the delivery of reinforcement less predictable. For example, some target employees may perform the desired behaviors independently in the presence of a job coach, but discontinue working when the job coach is absent from the work setting. In this case, the target employee may have learned that the presence of the job coach is a stimulus that good work performance will result in praise. Although the presence of the job coach may be a reliable cue to continue working, it is not the cue that will eventually lead to independence at the job site and long-term employment. The employee is unlikely to be successful unless he or she relies on cues associated with the work task or co-workers as guides to either continue or stop working. One method for reducing the employee's reliance on extraneous stimuli (job coach) to continue working and to promote more consistent performance is to use what Stokes & Baer (1977) referred to as indiscriminable contingencies.

The use of an indiscriminable contingencies approach relies on providing reinforcement for performance on a schedule that the target employee cannot predict. In the above example, the target employee had learned that reinforcement was forthcoming when he or she worked consistently in the presence of the job coach. The conditions for reinforcement for this employee consisted of two cues: (a) performance of the work task, and (b) presence of the job coach. In this case, the goal of an indiscriminable contingencies approach is to reduce the functional control established by the presence of the job coach on the employee's behavior and to promote the employee's reliance on the work to be performed to guide his or her behavior.

Dunlap, Plienis, and Williams (1987) used three conditions of supervision to teach a man who was profoundly mentally retarded to display appropriate task-related behaviors in unsupervised or loosely monitored settings. The first condition of supervision utilized a continuous schedule of reinforcement in which a trainer provided the participant with reinforcement following each correct response. During the second supervision condition, the participant worked alone and received reinforcement at the end of the session. This condition was labeled as a post-session contingency condition. The third condition consisted of a variable ratio fading procedure in which the trainer provided reinforcement on a variable ratio schedule that was not predictable to the client. The results of the investigation indicated that the participant demonstrated appropriate work behaviors in the unsupervised condition only after the feedback and the presence of the trainer were withdrawn on a variable ratio schedule; in other words, the participant was unable to predict when reinforcement would be provided for the work performed.

The conditions of this investigation are similar to those often found within supported employment settings. The target employee is frequently on a continuous schedule of reinforcement during training, followed by a sudden decrease in both reinforcement and supervision when the job coach is removed from the employment setting. Three procedures can facilitate more consistent performance using indiscriminable contingencies. First, the follow-up schedule of the job coach should be unpredictable to the employee and should be decreased gradually over time. Second, when the job coach is on-site, praise should be delivered for work previously completed, not for work completed in the presence of the job coach. In this way, if praise is reinforcing, the employee must work consistently to receive praise. Third, the job coach should ask co-workers to deliver praise intermittently to augment the praise of the job coach. In addition to increasing the overall amount of praise delivered, the use of co-workers makes the delivery of praise less predictable (i.e., not tied specifically to the presence of one person).

Engage Normally Available Reinforcement

In cases in which the employee requires more reinforcement than is typically available at the work site, it may be more effective to teach the employee to augment the amount of reinforcement received than to attempt to train the employee to work under the reinforcement conditions that are currently available. One method to increase the schedule of reinforcement is to teach the employee to engage in behaviors that are likely to be reinforced (Stokes & Baer, 1977). For example, an employee who greets co-workers with brief prompts for conversation is more likely to receive positive attention from co-workers than an employee who merely says, "Good morning." Similarly, an employee who straightens and tidies up the work area at the end of the work day is more likely to receive positive feedback regarding work behavior than one who does not engage in these behaviors, even if the behaviors are not specifically required as part of the job task (Wacker et al., 1986).

Shafer et al. (1988) reported three factors of work behavior that were strongly related to positive employer evaluations: (a) good attendance, (b) punctuality, and (c) consistent task performance. Employees who demonstrated these behaviors consistently received higher performance evaluations by their employers and were more likely to retain their jobs than were workers who did not demonstrate these behaviors. Teaching employees to perform behaviors that are correlated with employer satisfactions increases the opportunities for positive feedback to the employee.

In some work sites, it may not be possible to augment reinforcement through extra praise by the supervisor or co-workers. In these cases, it may be more effective to teach the employee to solicit reinforcement at the appropriate times (Seymour & Stokes, 1976). For instance, Mank and Horner (1987) taught three young adults attending a program for students with severe handicaps to monitor their work rate at community job sites, to compare their work against the standard for acceptable performance, to score their performance with a (+) if they met or exceeded the standard or a (−) if they did not meet the standard, and to show their score to their work supervisor to recruit feedback. The employer responded with praise when the student displayed a plus for acceptable performance and expressed disapproval when the student displayed a minus for work behavior. Each of the three participants demonstrated improved work behavior when the self-recruited feedback phase of the training package was implemented, suggesting that a package of self-monitoring and self-recruited feedback may be an effective method for employees to augment the reinforcement they typically receive at the job site. In other situations, the employee might check off completed job tasks on a card and show the card at the end of the work day to parents or job coaches. Again, this procedure results in increased reinforcement that is recruited by the employee.

Consequence Regulation

A final approach to augment normal amounts of reinforcement is to teach employees to deliver a previously established reinforcer to themselves based on appropriate performance. For example, target employees might be taught to deliver a tangible reinforcer (such as money for a snack) to themselves at specified intervals throughout the work day for work completed. In this case, the employee learns to buy a snack contingent on the completion of specific work behaviors. This strategy may have particular utility in situations where break time can be scheduled by the employee.

Summary

Maintenance of behavior (and employment) is dependent upon the target employee's generalization of performance across the cues and contingencies provided within the training condition to the cues and contingencies that remain available for long-term employment. Generalization across conditions of reinforcement can be facilitated by training the target employee to perform under the reinforcement conditions and schedules that are in effect at the work site, promoting the employee's responsiveness to the reinforcement contingencies at the work site, or adjusting the schedule of reinforcement.

General Summary

Generalization and maintenance of performance are two interrelated components of behavior, both of which may be necessary if persons with severe disabilities are to retain employment in paid community job sites. To maximize the potential for generalization from the conditions associated with training to those in which long-term performance is necessary, three issues need to be considered (Kirby & Bickel, 1988). First, the settings and conditions in which future performance is expected to occur should be examined for the antecedent stimuli and reinforcement contingencies that will be present to guide and maintain behavior. The training situation needs to be arranged to promote both the employee's responsivity to these stimuli and reinforcers and his or her ability to adapt behavior to accommodate variations in stimuli and reinforcers. Second, the training situation should be analyzed to determine if any extraneous stimuli are controlling the employee's behavior. If these stimuli are not available in the long-term employment setting, steps need to be taken to reduce the control established by extraneous stimuli. Finally, if adequate generalization does not occur from the training to the long-term employment condition, analyses of when acceptable behavior does and does not occur are needed to determine the conditions that are guiding and maintaining the employee's behavior. A lack of generalization across conditions indicates: (a) the stimuli or reinforcers that controlled behavior during training are not present in the long-term employment situation, or (b) the controlling stimuli are present but are not sufficient. Once the factors contributing to a lack of generalization and maintenance have been determined, retraining can be implemented to promote the employee's ability to function under the relevant antecedent and consequence stimuli available at the employment site. As discussed by Wacker and Berg (1986), what is needed in most cases is a package of these procedures, which promote both adaptability and independence.

QUESTIONS (For answers, see p. 430)

1. Is the acquisition of specific work and social behaviors the ultimate goal of supported employment? Explain.

2. Name two interrelated components of behavior required to facilitate long-term community employment and briefly describe each.

3. Define generalization.

4. If an individual is inconsistent in attempting or completing tasks at correct times, what may be the problem?

5. What is an antecedent cue regulation procedure?

6. Name two categories of antecedent training procedures named by the authors. Briefly describe and give examples of techniques of each.

7. Define maintenance of trained behaviors.

8. What type of problem is indicated when a person has the needed skills to perform a target behavior but does not do so consistently?

9. What is the primary reason for using consequence procedures?

10. Why is it important to try to pair extraneous (trainer delivered) reinforcement with naturally occurring reinforcers and/or fade them altogether?

REFERENCES

Alberto, P. A., Sharpton, W. R., Briggs, A., & Stright, M. H. (1986). Facilitating task acquisition through the use of a self-operated auditory prompt system. *The Journal of The Association for Persons with Severe Handicaps, 11*, 85–91.

Berg, W. & Wacker, D. (1989). Evaluation of tactile prompts with a student who is deaf, blind, and mentally retarded. *Journal of Applied Behavior Analysis, 22*, 93–99.

Connis, R. (1979). The effects of sequential pictorial cues, self-recording, and praise on the job task sequencing of retarded adults. *Journal of Applied Behavior Analysis, 12*, 355–361.

Drabman, R. S., Hammer, D., & Rosenbaum, M. S. (1979). Assessing generalization in behavior modification with children: The generalization map. *Behavioral Assessment, 1*, 203–219.

Dunlap, G., Plienis, A., & Williams, L. (1987). Acquisition and generalization of unsupervised responding: A descriptive analysis. *The Journal of The Association for Persons with Severe Handicaps, 12*, 274–279.

Gifford, J., Rusch, F., Martin, J., & White, D. (1984). Autonomy and adaptability: A proposed technology for maintaining work behavior. In N. Ellis & N. Bray (Eds.), *International review of research on mental retardation* (Vol. 12, pp. 285–314). New York: Academic Press.

Horner, R. & McDonald, R. (1982). Comparison of single instance and general case instruction in teaching a generalized vocational skill. *The Journal of The Association for the Severely Handicapped, 7*, 7–20.

Hunt, P., Alwell, M., & Goetz, L. (1988). Acquisition of conversation skills and reduction of inappropriate social interaction behaviors. *The Journal of The Association for Persons with Severe Handicaps, 13*, 20–27.

Hupp, S. (1986). Use of multiple exemplars in object concept training: How many are sufficient. *Analysis and Intervention in Developmental Disabilities, 6*, 305–317.

Johnson, B. & Cuvo, A. (1981). Teaching mentally retarded adults to cook. *Behavior Modification, 5*, 187–202.

Kirby, K. & Bickel, W. (1988). Toward an explicit analysis of generalization: A stimulus control interpretation. *The Behavior Analyst, 11*, 115–129.

Mager, R. & Pipe, P. (1970). *Analyzing performance problems or "You really oughta wanna."* Belmont, CA: Fearon Pitman.

Mank, D. & Horner, R. (1987). Self-recruited feedback: A cost-effective procedure for maintaining behavior. *Research in Developmental Disabilities, 8*, 91–112.

Martin, J., Burger, D., Elias-Burger, S., & Mithaug, D. (in press). Application of self-control strategies to facilitate independence. *International Review of Mental Retardation.*

Martin, J., Rusch, F., James, V., Decker, R., & Trtol, K. (1982). The use of picture cues to establish self-control in the preparation of complex meals by mentally retarded adults. *Applied Research in Mental Retardation, 3*, 105–119.

Pancsofar, E. & Bates, P. (1985). The impact of the acquisition of successive exemplars on generalization. *The Journal of The Association for Persons with Severe Handicaps, 10*, 3–11.

Rusch, F. R. (Ed.), (1986). *Competitive employment issues and strategies*. Baltimore: Paul H. Brookes.

Rusch, F., Martin, J., & White, D. (1985). Competitive employment: Teaching mentally retarded employees to maintain their work behavior. *Education and Training of the Mentally Retarded, 20(3)*, 182–189.

Seymour, F. & Stokes, T. (1976). Self-recording in training girls to increase work and evoke staff praise in an institution for offenders. *Journal of Applied Behavior Analysis, 9*, 41–54.

Shafer, M., Kregel, J., Banks, D., & Hill, M. (1988). An analysis of employer evaluations of workers with mental retardation. *Research in Developmental Disabilities, 9*, 377–391.

Sowers, J., Rusch, F., Connis, R., & Cummings, L. (1980). Teaching mentally retarded adults to time-manage in vocational settings. *Journal of Applied Behavior Analysis, 13*, 119–128.

Stokes, T. & Baer, D. (1977). An implicit technology of generalization. *Journal of Applied Behavior Analysis, 10*, 349–367.

Wacker, D. & Berg, W. (1983). Effects of picture prompts on the acquisition of complex vocational tasks by mentally retarded adolescents. *Journal of Applied Behavior Analysis, 16*, 417–433.

Wacker, D. & Berg, W. (1984). Training adolescents with severe handicaps to set up job tasks independently using picture prompts. *Analysis and Intervention in Developmental Disabilities, 4*, 353–365.

Wacker, D., Berg, W., Berrie, P., & Swatta, P. (1985). Generalization and maintenance of complex skills by severely handicapped adolescents following picture prompt training. *Journal of Applied Behavior Analysis, 18*, 329–336.

Wacker, D., Berg, W., McMahon, C., Templeman, M., McKinney, J., Swarts, V., Visser, M., & Marquardt, P. (1988). An evaluation of labeling-then-doing with moderately handicapped persons: Acquisition and generalization with complex tasks. *Journal of Applied Behavior Analysis, 21*, 369–380.

Wacker, D., Berg, W., Visser, M., Egan, J., Berrie, P., Ehler, C., Short, B., Swatta, P., & Tasler, B. (1986). A preliminary analysis of independence in a competitive employment setting. *The Journal of The Association for Persons with Severe Handicaps, 11*, 246–254.

Wehman, P. & Kregel, J. (1985). A supported work approach to competitive employment of individuals with moderate and severe handicaps. *The Journal of The Association for Persons with Severe Handicaps, 10*, 3–11.

Whaley, D. & Malott, R. (1971). *Elementary principles of behavior*. New York: Appleton-Century Crofts.

Whitman, T., Spence, B., & Maxwell, S. (1987). A comparison of external and self-instructional teaching formats with mentally retarded adults in a vocational setting. *Research in Developmental Disabilities, 8*, 371–388.

CHAPTER

10

Teaching Social Skills on the Job

Janis Chadsey-Rusch
University of Illinois at Urbana-Champaign

One of the defining characteristics of supported employment is its emphasis upon integration. This implies that persons with disabilities will have opportunities to work in employment settings with workers who are not disabled. Broadly speaking, there are two types of integration—physical and social. When employees with disabilities are physically integrated, they work in close physical proximity to workers without disabilities; they may perform job tasks in the same room, pass by each other frequently during the same working period, or sit in the same room or at the same table during lunch or break times.

Social integration implies that employees with and without disabilities are incorporated into and share equal membership in the same social network in the workplace. As with physical integration, social integration may take many forms. Workers may converse together about job- and nonjob-related matters, participate in holiday parties, or interact with co-workers outside of the job setting. Although physical integration is a necessary condition for social integration, it is not a sufficient condition.

It is likely that workers who are socially integrated possess a repertoire of skills that enable them to participate effectively in the social network at work. Research suggests that many individuals have lost their jobs because they displayed inappropriate social skills (Brickey, Campbell, & Browning, 1985; Ford, Dineen, & Hall, 1984; Greenspan & Shoultz, 1981; Hanley-Maxwell, Rusch, Chadsey-Rusch, & Renzaglia, 1986; Hill, Wehman, Hill & Goodall, 1986; Kochany & Keller, 1981; Lagomarcino, Chapter 18 this volume; Martin, Rusch, Lagomarcino, & Chadsey-Rusch, 1986; Wehman, Hill, Goodall, Cleveland, Brooke, & Pentecost, 1982). Because work is such an important aspect of adult life (Terkel, 1972), methods must be found to teach the social skills workers use to get and keep jobs, and become a part of the social network. But what are the social skills needed in employment settings? And how does one teach them? As Chadsey-Rusch (1986) indicated, little agreement has been reached on how to define, measure, assess, and teach social skills.

This chapter discusses the results from recent research that contribute to our knowledge about social skills in employment settings. Specifically, information will be presented regarding the general interaction patterns found in work settings, the types of social skills identified as valuable, and the strategies used to teach these skills to workers with disabilities. Before these areas are discussed, the term "social skill" is defined.

A DEFINITION OF SOCIAL SKILLS

Sometimes, concepts lend themselves easily to one-sentence definitions. The concept of social skills, however, is not one of these. Social skills are very complex and are composed of many components. Cartledge and Milburn (1983) described several of the elements that seemed to be present in most definitions of social skills. These elements can be combined to form a comprehensive definition of social skills. This definition consists of four parts and is discussed below.

Social Skills are Socially Acceptable Learned Behaviors that Elicit Positive or Neutral Responses

Successful social skills can be viewed as socially acceptable learned behaviors that enable an individual to interact with others in ways that elicit positive or neutral responses and assist in avoiding negative responses from others. This part of the definition implies that there are acceptable and unacceptable social skills, that social skills are learned, and that success in using these skills is judged by others.

Certain social settings and contexts influence both acceptable and unacceptable social behaviors. For example, when workers have conversations with their co-workers, most know to listen and not to speak until there is a pause in the conversation—that is, they take turns talking. As a negative example, many workers know that when they meet a new co-worker for the first time, they should not ask personal questions, such as "how much do you weigh?" or "how much money do you make working here?" Even though they may be hard to define, there are rules for our social behavior and most people would recognize and agree upon these rules (McFall, 1982). The rules that surround particular social settings and contexts dictate acceptable and unacceptable behavior.

Social skills are learned. The best evidence that we have for knowing that these skills are learned is to study the social skills used by individuals in foreign countries. For example, workers in Japan are likely to be more formal in their interactions with one another than workers in the United States (Schein, 1981). These social conventions or rules are likely shaped by parents and societies in general. If we know that social skills are learned, then it logically follows that social skills can be taught, which is good news for workers who display unacceptable behaviors.

Social skills are judged by others, and it is probable that we are judged as being either socially competent or incompetent (McFall, 1982). If our social skills are judged as competent, we will likely receive positive responses, or at least avoid receiving negative responses from others. The unfortunate thing about having our social skills judged by others is that this judgment is subject to error and bias. Such things as the personal history of the judge (e.g., previous interactions with persons who are disabled) and the person being judged (e.g., age, sex, experience) may influence the type of judgment made (McFall, 1982).

Social Skills are Instrumental, Goal-Directed Behaviors

Social skills are used for a reason—we exhibit social behaviors in order to affect others and the impact we have will influence future interactions. Social skills are used to achieve certain goals or purposes. Questions may be used by employees at work in order to find out information that is related to completing a specific job task. A worker may tell a joke in order to draw positive attention to himself/herself. A work direction might be followed in order to avoid being criticized. These goals are determined by the individual. If engaging in a specific social skill results in a goal being met, then the same social skill will probably be used in future interactions. It is important for workers to understand that their social behaviors can effect environmental and personal change.

Social Skills are Situation-Specific and Vary According to Social Context

The types of social skills that are exhibited by individuals will vary depending upon the physical setting, the people in the setting, and the

CYNTHIA WINGATE

Cynthia Wingate is a 36-year-old woman diagnosed in the moderate range of mental retardation (IQ 40–54). She lives on the southwest side of Chicago with her father and younger sister. An older sister lives with her husband and daughter in a nearby suburb. Cynthia attended public schools, where she was placed in special education classes until age 16. Before starting in a local developmental training program in February, 1986, Cynthia had been home for 17 years, receiving no habilitation or social services. She lived vicariously through her family with very few activities that could truly be called her own.

On June 25, 1986, Cynthia started her job at Oak Lawn National Bank in Oak Lawn, Illinois. When she started, Cynthia's job involved maintenance/janitorial tasks—cleaning the grounds, straightening the cafeteria, wiping tables, stocking supplies, and shredding documents. Now her job involves almost all kitchen/cafeteria tasks including operating the dishwasher, preparing entrees for cooking, baking, setting up the cold counter, serving on the cafeteria line, and making bank deposits.

Socially, Cynthia has evolved from a shy, retiring young woman who found it nearly impossible to make eye contact or respond with more than "yes" or "no" to an outgoing young lady who takes breaks and lunch with co-workers, initiates conversations, and tells jokes freely. She greets bank staff, from the bank president to the mail clerk, with a friendly "hello" and a broad smile whether she sees them daily or rarely at all. She participates in 80 percent of the bank-sponsored social events, including the annual Christmas dinner dance, bowling party, company picnic, dinner cruise on Lake Michigan, and White Sox baseball games, just to name a few.

Since she became involved in SEP, Cynthia has become far more active in her leisure time, making plans for many of her activities herself, both at home and with friends. She plans sleepovers and pizza parties, and has taken her sisters out to eat. She also participates in monthly outings with peers sponsored by a local job club including horseback riding, shopping trips, movies, dining out, plays, bowling, and dances.

Cynthia is eagerly anticipating the opportunity to move into a Community Integrated Living Arrangement with two other developmental training center clients, when placement becomes available. In preparation, Cynthia is learning how to cook one new meal a week at work, then shopping for the ingredients and preparing the same meals for her father and sister at home. Through her job she has also learned to use a checking account and become responsible for paying many of her own bills.

Cynthia, her family, and the SEP staff have been both thrilled and awed by the changes in her personality and lifestyle since placement in the Supported Employment Program.

social context or occasion for the interaction. Physical setting exerts direct influence on social skills. For example, consider the effects that a gym and a library have on social skills. It is appropriate to shout and yell during a basketball game at a gym, but if these same behaviors were exhibited at the library, patrons and librarians would quickly give negative feedback. According to McFall (1982), setting accounts for a major portion of the variance found in judgments of social performance.

The social occasion associated with interactions can also influence the type of social skills demonstrated, and social occasions can be different from physical settings. That is, two social occasions can occur in the same physical setting but have a differential influence on the types of behaviors exhibited. For example, a funeral and a party can both be held in a work setting (e.g., a church), but individuals at funerals appear sad and subdued, while individuals at parties are more likely to appear happy and gay.

Skills also vary depending upon the individuals involved in the interaction. For example, the types of social skills used with co-workers may be very different from the skills used with the boss. Workers would probably feel comfortable asking a close friend personal questions, but would not feel comfortable asking a casual acquaintance the same type of questions. The skills used with others will likely vary depending on the age, sex, prior interactions, and relationships experienced with others. As with the other components, workers must be taught that social skills vary depending upon the physical setting, the people in the setting, and the social context or occasion for the setting.

Social Skills Involve Both Specific Observable and Nonobservable Cognitive and Affective Elements

The last component of the definition of social skills states that: (a) the specific behaviors used to exhibit social skills are both observable and nonobservable; (b) these behaviors are influenced by the form of communication and the affect used; and (c) the ability to make fine discriminations and solve problems influences the judgments of others and the achievement of social goals. In the massive literature on social skills training (e.g., Cartledge & Milburn, 1986; Goldstein, Sprafkin, Gershaw, & Klein, 1980; Hollin & Trower, 1988; Matson & Ollendick, 1988), a number of behaviors have been taught which were observable and could be discreetly defined and reliably counted. Some of the trained behaviors included such skills as asking questions, following directions, accepting criticism, and greetings; these behaviors have been referred to as social tasks by McFall (1982). The communicative form used in the majority of these studies has been verbal. That is, study participants have been asked to exhibit the various social skills through verbal forms, or talking.

Other behaviors or processes that we use when we engage in social skills are not observable, but are no less important. These are the behaviors used to perceive or decode social contexts, make decisions about the observable behavior to exhibit, and evaluate the effectiveness of the behavior used based on the feedback from others and whether or not our social goal was met. Inherent in this process is the ability to make fine discriminations based on setting, social occasion, and the people involved in the social interaction. Although it is difficult to measure this problem-solving process, several researchers who have proposed social-skill models are convinced the process is essential to being viewed as socially competent (Argyle & Kendon, 1967; Ladd & Mize, 1983; Greenspan, 1981; McFall, 1982; Trower, 1982). There are also data to suggest that the lack of this process has led to workers with mental retardation getting fired (Greenspan & Shoulz, 1981; Martin et al.; Hanley-Maxwell et al., 1986). In addition, there is at least one study that suggests that components of this process can be trained, resulting in improved social skills (Park & Gaylord-Ross, in press).

Summary

Social skills can be defined as goal-directed, socially acceptable, learned behaviors that are situation-specific and vary according to social context. They also involve both observable and nonobservable cognitive and affective elements that assist in eliciting positive or neutral responses and avoiding negative responses from others. This definition of social skills reveals how complex it can be to interact with others, particularly if one looks at the component parts. Yet many of us learn these behaviors easily without much direct instruction. This should not imply, however, that all people are good in all social contexts all of the time. Our abilities vary depending upon our past experiences and reinforcement history; the social occasion, setting, and people in the setting; and the strengths and weaknesses of observable and nonobservable behaviors used to exhibit a particular social skill.

A word of caution must be expressed before moving on to the next section of the chapter. There is little empirical evidence to validate the social skill components suggested here. Yet, some definition or framework would seem to be essential if we want to train social skills—that is, it seems to make sense to know what something is and how it might work before it is trained. Nonetheless, research is needed to verify the validity of the definition suggested in this chapter.

The remainder of the chapter will focus on recent research that contributes to our knowledge about social skills in work settings. Two areas have received the most research attention: the types of social skills that are valued, observed, and trained in work settings, and the methods used to teach these skills. Within the definition proposed above, these two areas concern (primarily) the observable behaviors used when exhibiting a social skill and illustrate how social skills vary according to social context.

RESEARCH IDENTIFYING VALUED SOCIAL BEHAVIORS IN EMPLOYMENT SETTINGS

Employer Surveys

A number of studies have used survey methodology to determine the social behaviors that are valued in nonsheltered employment settings. Typically, employers have been sent surveys asking them to rate behaviors according to their importance and to the frequency with which they occur.

In one of the first studies of this type, Rusch, Schutz, and Agran (1982) sent questionnaires to 120 potential employers from food service and janitorial/maid service occupations in Illinois to solicit information about their expectations for those they hire. Survey results indicated that respondents (66 percent of the sample) considered seventy behaviors to be necessary for entry into competitive employment. Of these seventy behaviors, sixteen social behaviors were agreed upon by 90 percent of the employers as being important. Two social behaviors (verbally reciting full name on request and following one instruction provided at a time) were mentioned by every employer as being critical for competitive employment.

In another study, Salzberg, Agran, and Lignugaris/Kraft (1986) surveyed employers from five different jobs to obtain their opinions regarding social behaviors important for entry-level work and behaviors that may differ in importance across jobs. The results from this study indicated that social behaviors related to worker productivity (e.g., asking supervisors for assistance, following directions, responding to criticism, getting information before a job, offering to help co-workers) were rated higher in importance than general personal social behaviors (e.g., listening without interrupting, acknowledging and expressing appreciation to co-workers). Interestingly, the mean rating for nonsocial production-related behaviors (e.g., getting to work on time) was significantly higher than the mean rating for task-related social behaviors and personal social behaviors. Furthermore, little relationship was noted between the frequency of occurrence of a behavior and its rated importance.

While Salzberg et al. (1986) confirmed the assumption that social factors are critical for success in all the jobs studied, differences between jobs emerged. For example, social behaviors were considered more important for kitchen helpers and food service workers than for janitors, dishwashers, and maids. Such differences were attributed to the fact that some jobs (i.e., kitchen helpers and food service workers) were carried out in a more social context where workers frequently interacted with co-workers and customers.

Most recently, Salzberg, McConaughy, Lignugaris/Kraft, Agran, & Stowitschek (1987) surveyed employers from manufacturing businesses (e.g., clothing, electronics/computers, construction, printing companies) to determine the social-vocational skills important for employment. Although the size of the sample was small ($n = 20$), their interesting results extended the findings from previous research.

Employers in the Salzberg et al. (1987) study were first asked to rank-order their employees, to rate their employees on whether or not twenty-seven different behaviors were a positive or negative quality, and lastly, to rate how important each behavior was in determining the employees' ranks. Generally, importance ratings were related to productivity. Task-related social behaviors, such as following directions, offering to help co-workers, getting necessary information for a job, requesting assistance, and clarifying ambiguous or incomplete instructions were rated most important. Nontask-related social behaviors, such as asking about others' personal affairs and praising co-workers, were rated least important. This finding is similar to the results reported in prior research (Salzberg et al., 1986).

Other results from the Salzberg et al. (1987) study indicated that top-ranked employees had a greater total number of positive behaviors attributed to them than bottom-ranked employees. However, some behaviors that were rated high in importance were not always those that separated the top from the bottom-ranked workers. For example, several nontask social behaviors (i.e., ignoring grumbling and complaining, praising co-workers, and expressing appreciation to co-workers) were rated low in importance but were significant characteristics of top-ranked workers. Additionally, some social behaviors were considered positive for both top and bottom-ranked employees—acknowledging what others are saying, using an appropriate tone of voice, using social amenities, and not being nosy. These findings led Salzberg et al. (1987) to conclude that workers may need a broad behavioral repertoire if they want to become highly-valued workers.

Table 10.1 Valued Social Skills Reported By Employers

Asking for assistance
Responding to criticism
Following directions
Offering to help co-workers
Providing information about the job
Answering questions
Greetings
Conversing with others
Using social amenities
Giving positive comments

Summary and Future Directions

When asked, employers have been willing to indicate the types of social behaviors they believe to be important for entry-level positions. A list of the behaviors that seem to be the most valued is included in Table 10.1.

The results from the studies discussed above are important for several reasons. First, the behaviors specified begin to form the list of observable social behaviors, or social tasks (McFall, 1982), that employers believe are important for work. According to McFall, the social task serves as the unit with which to organize or chunk events. The task must be easily observable and amenable to being broken down into subtasks by analyzing its component parts. Behaviors that can be observed, analyzed, and defined are easier to teach than behaviors that are not easily observed, analyzed, and defined (Mager, 1962).

This research is also important because it has focused upon the perceptions of employers. It is important to know what employers think because they will be making judgments and decisions about who gets hired, who gets fired, and who gets promoted. Although employer judgments about social competence will likely be influenced by error and bias (McFall, 1982), it is still critical to know what they value. Clearly, from the results presented above, employers value the social skills that are associated with job performance; they value these skills more than they value the skills associated with the interpersonal relationships between co-workers. It is not clear whether or not the social skills associated with job performance will enhance the social integration between workers with and without handicaps (Chadsey-Rusch, Gonzalez, Tines, & Johnson, 1989); however, it is clear that social integration on the job is not even a possibility if one does not have a job or is fired from a job.

Although these studies provide a useful list of valued behaviors, further research is needed to document whether or not different social skills are required for different jobs. The types of jobs that have been sampled have primarily been in the food service, janitorial, and some manufacturing occupations—representation is needed from other jobs as well. Future researchers should incorporate similar categorization systems for the types of skills they assess. A beginning point for uniformity would be to develop questionnaires consisting of the same types of behaviors reported in past research (e.g., Salzberg, et al., 1986), or reflecting the definition proposed in this chapter, as well as making certain that the behaviors listed are observable and definable. Although it may be important for employers to rate the importance of "peer relationships," it is nearly impossible to know what a high (or low) rating for this means. Unless there is some uniformity in the way that social skills are defined and categorized, it will be difficult to make comparisons and generalizations between future research efforts (Martin, et al., 1986).

Surveys from employers have been important in identifying valued social behaviors associated with a variety of jobs; however, there is little assurance that this information is accurate—that is, there have been few direct observations of social skills in employment sites to confirm these reports. The next section of this chapter discusses research findings related to the types of social skills that have been observed directly in employment settings. In addition, studies comparing the social patterns exhibited by workers with and without disabilities are discussed.

DIRECTLY OBSERVED INTERACTION PATTERNS

Recently, a number of investigators have begun to describe the types of interaction patterns present in settings employing workers with disabilities. Lignugaris/Kraft and his colleagues (Lignugaris/Kraft, Rule, Salzberg, & Stowitschek, 1986; Lignugaris/Kraft, Salzberg, Stowitschek, & McConaughy, 1986; Lignugaris/Kraft, Salzberg, Rule, Salzburg, & Stowitschek, 1988) have conducted a number of these investigations. In Lignugaris/Kraft, Rule et al. (1986), the social interactions used by a group of workers with and without disabilities who were employed in a nonprofit business for refurbishing household goods were described. Both groups of workers were observed directly for five ten-minute sessions. At the end of each observation session, the observers used a social skill checklist to indicate if a behavior had occurred, had not occurred, or was not applicable to the observational session. Thirty-five items were included on the checklist.

The results from this study revealed that both groups of workers were highly social when they were completing work tasks. The majority of the interactions were with co-workers rather than supervisors, and the bulk of the conversations concerned work-related topics. Certain social behaviors were found to occur infrequently (e.g., requests for assistance and criticism) while others were more frequent (e.g., giving assistance and working cooperatively). Only one statistically significant difference was found between the two groups of workers—workers with disabilities joked and laughed significantly less than their nonhandicapped counterparts.

In a later study, Lignugaris/Kraft, Salzberg et al. (1986) used the same subject sample as in the study reported above, but examined a broader array of contextual variables during break as well as during work times. Employees were observed during five- to ten-minute observation periods for a minimum of thirty minutes during break and sixty minutes during work times using a fifteen-second interval recording technique. The social context of the workers' interactions, their initiation patterns, and the general structure of the interactions were measured.

The results from Lignugaris/Kraft, Salzberg et al. revealed no significant differences in the interaction patterns between the workers with and without developmental disabilities; consequently, the data from both groups were combined to describe the general interaction patterns in the setting. The combined data indicated that workers interacted more frequently and for longer durations during break than during work. In addition, group interactions were observed more frequently during break, while dyadic interactions occurred more frequently during work. Few interactions were initiated by supervisors; however, workers with disabilities initiated just as many interactions as their nondisabled co-workers.

In their most recent study, Lignugaris/Kraft et al. (1988) again compared the interaction patterns between a group of workers with mild and moderate disabilities and a group of workers without disabilities who were working in the same setting as in the studies described above (i.e., nonprofit businesses). In this investigation, however, Lignugaris/Kraft et al. used a different research methodology (i.e., anecdotal recordings) to collect information. The findings from this study indicated that interactions were frequent, that the target workers interacted more with co-workers than with supervisors, and that commands and asking for information were the most frequently observed skill areas. Additionally, differences in the interaction patterns between the workers with and without disabilities were found. Employees with disabilities were more likely to interact with other employees with disabilities, and nondisabled employees interacted more frequently with their own counterparts. Workers with disabilities received more commands, and were less involved in teasing and joking interactions. Workers without disabilities were involved in fewer greetings and were asked for information more often during work than employees with disabilities.

Chadsey-Rusch and her colleagues (Chadsey-Rusch & Gonzalez, 1988; Chadsey-Rusch, et al., 1989) have conducted similar investigations to observe directly the types of social behaviors exhibited in work settings. In contrast to the settings used in the Lignugaris/Kraft studies, all of the workers observed by Chadsey-Rusch and her colleagues were working in competitive employment settings, and the workers with disabilities were individually placed and received occasional follow-up services from a local rehabilitation agency.

In their first study, Chadsey-Rusch and Gonzalez (1988) observed the social interaction patterns of nondisabled employees across seven different competitive employment sites using narrative recording procedures. Each of the workers without disabilities worked at the same time as a worker with disabilities and performed a similar job. The workers were observed during four time periods: when they arrived at work, during break, and during two different work periods.

Data from the observations indicated that the majority of interactions observed were used to share information, tease and joke, ask questions, and give directions. In addition, there were more work-related interactions displayed than nonwork-related interactions. However, most interactions used during arrival and break were unrelated to work. The targeted employees were involved in more interactions with their co-workers than with their supervisors.

Recently, Chadsey-Rusch et al. (1989) analyzed the social interaction patterns between eight workers with and without disabilities. The nondisabled workers were the same workers observed by Chadsey-Rusch and Gonzalez (1988). The workers with disabilities were primarily male, mildly mentally retarded, and had been successfully employed at the same job site for approximately three years; they worked at the same time as the nondisabled workers and performed the same job.

The findings from this study indicated that there were significant differences in the frequencies of interactions between co-workers and supervisors. In all observations, employees engaged in more interactions than did supervisors. There were no significant differences between supervisors' interactions with workers with and without disabilities, but interactions did vary significantly between co-workers. Nondisabled workers interacted more with co-workers without disabilities than with co-workers with disabilities.

Interactions also varied depending upon the context of the interactions (e.g., lunch) and who was engaging in the interactions. Task-related interactions (or interactions related to work or work tasks) occurred more frequently during the two work observation periods, while nontask interactions (i.e., interactions unrelated to work or work tasks) occurred more frequently during lunch and break observations. There were no differences in the types of interactions used by workers when they first arrived at work.

Across all observation conditions and types of interactions, there were no instances in which supervisors interacted more with workers without disabilities than with workers with disabilities. However, co-workers were engaged in significantly more nontask interactions with workers without disabilities than workers with disabilities during lunch/break and during both work conditions.

Storey and Knutson (1989) also directly observed social interactions in integrated work settings. The majority of their participants with disabilities, however, were high school students with moderate and severe handicaps who were receiving vocational training services. Each student was matched with a nonhandicapped worker who had similar job responsibilities.

Data were collected using a twenty-one-item a priori code. Participants were observed on ten different days for fifteen minutes per day during work periods. An interval recording system was used to record the observed social behaviors. Although there was no statistically significant difference in social interactions between the workers with and without disabilities, Storey and Knutson did compare individual categories of behaviors. This analysis showed: (a) the workers without disabilities were involved in more interactions with their nondisabled co-workers; (b) the students with disabilities were involved in more interactions with their school supervisor; and (c) students with disabilities received more compliments and directions than the workers without disabilities.

Summary and Future Directions

The information from the research described above provides information on the types of social skills exhibited in employment settings, validates many of the skills described by employers as being important, and begins to delineate some of the differences between workers with and without disabilities. Despite different methodologies, different settings, and different subjects, both Lignugaris/Kraft and his colleagues and Chadsey-Rusch and her colleagues have consistently found that workers exhibit both task-related and nontask-related social skills throughout the work day. In addition, it appears that the frequency of social skills exhibited varies depending upon the context of the interaction (e.g., nontask-related social skills are likely to occur more often than task-related skills during lunch). Another finding from both groups is that supervisors seem to be involved in fewer interactions than co-workers; however, individual variation does occur (Chadsey-Rusch et al., 1989).

As further validation for the results reported by Lignugaris/Kraft et al. (1988) and Chadsey-Rusch et al. (1989), Kirmeyer (1988) reported similar findings, even though her study had nothing to do with the employment of individuals with disabilities. In her study, the communication styles of police dispatchers (who were nonhandicapped) were observed with direct observation methodology. Kirmeyer reported that both task-related and nontask-related skills occurred and that employees interacted twice as much with their co-workers as with their supervisors. Thus, although these studies are few in number, there appears to be a consistent pattern of interactions that occur in work settings with respect to task and nontask interactions and with respect to the frequencies of interactions exhibited by supervisors and co-workers.

The studies described above also indicate that many of the skills identified as being important by employers actually do occur with regular frequency in employment settings. In particular, giving directions, sharing information, and asking questions were found to occur regularly (Chadsey-Rusch & Gonzalez, 1988; Lignugaris/Kraft et al. 1988). Some skills cited as being important by employers, however, do not occur very often. These skills included offering assistance, requesting assistance, accepting criticism, and using social amenities (Chadsey-Rusch & Gonzalez, 1988). The fact that these skills occurred infrequently should not imply that they are unimportant.

As mentioned above, a variety of nontask-related social skills were observed frequently in employment settings even though employers have not rated these types of behaviors as being critical on the job. One behavior, teasing and joking, was found to occur with great regularity even though it was never mentioned by employers. Although more research is needed to determine whether social nontask-related interactions are crucial to employment success, it is possible that these types of interactions may influence social integration.

Interestingly, from the studies reviewed, there appear to be more similarities than differences between workers with and without disabilities. This may be because many of the workers observed had been successfully employed and were not at risk of losing their jobs. Several differences were found, though, which could potentially have an adverse impact on social integration. Chadsey-Rusch et al. (1989), Lignugaris/Kraft et al. (1988) and Storey and Knutson (1989) all found that nonhandicapped co-workers were less likely to interact with workers with disabilities. Chadsey-Rusch et al.(1989) qualified this finding by reporting that differences were only apparent in nontask-related interactions. Lignugaris/Kraft et al.(1988) also reported that workers with disabilities received more commands and were less involved in teasing and joking interactions.

Although this research begins to describe the kinds of social skills that are likely to occur in employment settings, further research is needed that describes interaction patterns with more workers with severe disabilities across diverse work settings. In addition, it is very important to sample the types of interactions exhibited across different contextual variables (e.g., lunch versus work, supervisor versus co-worker) because of the influence these variables exert upon interaction patterns.

Because social skills are so complex, continual research is needed that addresses the best way to measure these behaviors in the natural environment. Although a priori codes, narrative records, anecdotal records, and checklists have been used in past research, there is no assurance that these techniques are the best way to capture such complex behaviors. In particular, researchers using these methods have reduced complex interaction patterns into simple frequency counts of behavior. It may be that other measures (e.g., duration, sequential analyses) may be more appropriate to describe ongoing interactions (Bakeman & Gottman, 1986).

One way to more accurately describe interaction patterns may be to augment observational recording techniques with other types of measures. For example, because the evaluation of social skills is influenced by the judgment of others, it is important to assess the perceptions of co-workers, supervisors, and the workers with disabilities. Chadsey-Rusch et al. (1989) reported that, while workers with disabilities were observed to be involved in few nontask social interactions with their co-workers, only three of the eight workers stated that they wished they had more friends at work. Six workers, however, responded that they wished they had more friends in general. Augmenting direct observational procedures with more qualitative measures is particularly important when decisions are being made for training. If frequency counts reveal low rates of interaction but workers are satisfied with their position in the social network at work, then the low rates of interaction alone should not automatically dictate workers as candidates for social-skill training.

The direct observation of social skills and the surveys of employer perceptions begin to identify the type of social skills that are valued and likely to occur in employment settings. The next section of this chapter reviews the methods that have been used to teach these skills.

INTERVENTION STRATEGIES

Several individuals have proposed that social-skills training be studied from an ecobehavioral perspective (Chadsey-Rusch, 1986; Walker & Caulkins, 1986). The goal of the ecobehavioral approach is to maximize the fit (Rappaport, 1977) or congruence (Thurman, 1977) between the person and his or her environment. According to Thurman, congruence occurs when an individual's behavior is in harmony with the social norms of his or her environment. When individuals with disabilities enter into integrated employment settings, they may display behaviors that vary considerably from established social norms, or they may lack the skills necessary to function adequately. If incongruences occur, three options exist: (a) the behavior of the worker with disabilities can be changed, (b) the context (e.g., work setting, supervisors, co-workers, job task) can be altered, or (c) both the worker and the context can be transformed. Ecological congruence does not necessarily imply "normal"; instead it should be viewed as "maximal adaptation to the environment" (Thurman, 1977, p. 332).

It is the premise of this chapter that social-skills training should be viewed from an ecobehavioral perspective. That is, the individual can be trained, the context or environment can be altered, or both can be modified. Due to page limitations, and the paucity of information on contextual modifications, the focus of training in this chapter will be on strategies designed to alter the individual's social abilities rather than on changing the demands of the environment. However, readers are referred to Hughes, Rusch, and Curl (Chapter 11, this volume) for an overview of how to promote social acceptance.

This chapter will only review research that has been designed to increase appropriate work-related social skills in employment settings. Another line of research has investigated strategies to decrease inappropriate social behaviors (e.g., Dwinell & Connis, 1979; Rusch, Weithers, Menchetti, & Schutz, 1980; Schutz, Rusch, & Lamson, 1979), but that research will not be reviewed here.

This section will be divided into two parts. First, recent research related to teaching social skills to workers with disabilities in (primarily) integrated employment settings will be reviewed. Second, an analysis of these studies will be presented with respect to how closely they match the definition of social skills that was presented at the beginning of this chapter.

Social-Skill Training Studies

In a prior review, Chadsey-Rusch (1986) discussed several studies that had been conducted to train employment-related social skills to individuals with developmental disabilities. Most of these investigations used all or parts of a training package to teach social skills which typically consisted of the following components: (a) a rationale as to why a given social behavior was desirable; (b) an opportunity to observe examples of the behavior (i.e., modeling); (c) an opportunity to practice the behavior, usually in role-play situations; and (d) feedback regarding performance. Most of the studies discussed by Chadsey-Rusch trained skills in analogue settings, but several researchers had trained and taken measures in the natural environment.

The studies reviewed by Chadsey-Rusch (1986) using social skill training (SST) packages had trained a variety of skills, including: job interview skills (Hall, Sheldon-Widgen, & Sherman, 1980; Kelly, Wildman, Urey, & Berler, 1980), compliance to directions (Karlan & Rusch, 1982; Rusch & Menchetti, 1981), question-asking during conversations (Chadsey-Rusch, Karlan, Riva, & Rusch, 1984), and handling criticism, taking a joke, and soliciting assistance (Shafer, Brooke, & Wehman, 1985). Although all studies had been successful in training social skills, generalization was mixed. In addition, the majority of participants involved in these studies were mildly handicapped, which is not the group of individuals for whom supported employment was intended (Rusch, Chadsey-Rusch, & Johnson, in press).

Work-related social skills have also been trained using strategies other than the typical SST package. In a study conducted by Breen, Haring, Pitts-Conway, and Gaylord-Ross (1985), a break-time sequence, or script, of social behaviors was taught to four high school students with autism. Nonhandicapped high school students were used as trainers and generalization effects to an in vivo break time with natural co-workers were measured. During the simulated break time, the task-analyzed sequence of social behaviors was taught using instructional assistance along with massed practice for steps that were difficult to learn in the sequence. Once the sequence was learned, generalization to a natural co-worker was measured. When generalization did not occur, a second peer was used as a training co-worker until generalization effects were demonstrated. All four youths learned the social skill sequences and achieved generalization to natural co-workers. However, the experimenter was present during all generalization probes (which could have served as a prompt for the trained behaviors to occur) and the training was conducted in the same situation as the probe setting.

Stowitschek, McConaughy, Peatross, Salzberg, and Lignugaris/Kraft (1988) recently conducted a study to determine if supervisors' statements of rules for appropriate social responses prior to the work day, paired with supervisors' reminders during the work day and preceding staged occasions for responding, were associated with the use of social amenities by adults with mental retardation. The results from this study indicated that some workers did increase the frequency with which they used social amenities and further increased their rate when they were asked to repeat the rules prior to the work day. It was not possible for Stowitschek et al. to measure generalization across settings and individuals because the study was conducted in a work activity center.

Because generalization and maintenance are such critical issues in social skills training, several recent studies have focused on ways to enhance these stages of learning. In particular, self-control and process training approaches have been investigated. With these techniques, learners are taught to generate their own problem-solving strategies so they can self-mediate (Stokes & Baer, 1977) and manage their own behavior. Self-control strategies have been shown to be effective for training task-related job skills in supported employment settings (e.g., Rusch, Morgan, Martin, Riva, & Agran, 1985; Hughes & Rusch, in press) and several studies have recently investigated the use of this approach for training social-related job skills (Agran, Salzberg, & Stowitschek, 1987; Rusch, McKee, Chadsey-Rusch, & Renzaglia, 1988; Storey & Gaylord-Ross, 1987). Also, readers are referred to Berg, Wacker, and Flynn (Chapter 9, this volume).

Self-Control Training

Self-control strategies typically involve the individual performing one or more functions, including: (a) recognizing a problem, (b) indicating an action and instructing oneself to resolve the problem, (c) monitoring the performance of the action, and (d) evaluating the performance. Agran et al. (1987) used a combination of two of these components (e.g., recognizing a problem and indicating an action and instructing oneself to resolve the problem) and the typical SST package (rationale, modeling, practice, and feedback) to teach four adults with moderate mental retardation to initiate interactions with a supervisor when they ran out of work materials or when they needed assistance. Their results indicated that the self-control strategy plus the SST package led to the generalization and maintenance of employee's responses across different settings. However, because the self-control components were used in combination with the SST package, it was difficult to ascertain the specific effects of the self-control procedures.

Rusch et al. (1988) used training procedures similar to those of Agran et al. (1987) in teaching an adolescent with severe handicaps to request needed materials under two stimulus conditions: (a) when there were not enough materials, and (b) when materials were missing. Unlike the Agran et al. study, the Rusch et al. study was conducted in a nonsheltered setting.

In the Rusch et al. study, all but one of the components of self-control (monitoring of performance) were used in combination with the SST package. When performance did not generalize to the work or probe situation, corrective feedback was delivered immediately following the error. Generalization only occurred when corrective feedback was always used in combination with the SST package and self-control procedures.

Storey and Gaylord-Ross (1987) attempted to isolate the effects of one of the components of self-control (monitoring of performance) for affecting the maintenance of positive statements. In this study, a group of twelve youths with mild and moderate handicaps were taught to emit positive verbal statements while playing pool during break at a branch office of the AT & T company. The generalization setting was a different break area adjacent to the training area.

A multiple-component treatment package, which included role-playing, graphic feedback, contingent positive reinforcement, and self-monitoring, was implemented across three experiments and was found to be successful in increasing the rate of positive verbal statements among the youth while they were playing the game of pool. In addition, when the components of the treatment package were withdrawn systematically, self-monitoring and contingent reinforcement were found to be effective in maintaining the rate of positive statements made across two of the experiments, and self-monitoring alone was found to be effective for three of the four students in the third experiment. However, in all three experiments, there was little generalization of treatment effects to the other break area. Storey and Gaylord-Ross (1987) concluded that the lack of generalization effects may have been due to the fact that only one leisure activity (pool) was used during training, and that if training had occurred across a variety of leisure activities, more generalization might have occurred.

In summary, it is difficult to ascertain the specific effects that self-control strategies have had on the acquisition and generalization of social skills. In all of the studies reported above, self-control strategies were always used in combination with other intervention approaches. Even with the use of self-control components, however, generalization effects were only demonstrated in one study (Agran et al., 1987).

Process Training

Closely related to the use of self-control strategies is the concept of process training. With process training, individuals are taught a generative process of social behavior rather than specific component behaviors (Hollin & Trower, 1988). Argyle and Kendon (1967) originally conceptualized a social skills model which consisted of a series of stages; this process model has also been discussed by McFall (1982). Figure 10.1 presents a social-skills model that is a combination of the theoretical thinking suggested by Argyle and Kendon (1967) and McFall (1982).

The first stage in this model is the *goal* that the individual wants to achieve. Within an employment context, an individual may want to share work-related information, accept criticism, or make friends. Social goals can be viewed as social tasks. As McFall (1982) has stated, social skills need to be chunked into some kind of unit, and the key is to find the best unit with which to categorize and organize events. Social goals or tasks must be observable and amenable to being broken down into subtasks. For example, the goal of "making friends" might be broken down into smaller tasks or goals such as "meeting potential friends," "conversing," and "developing a relationship." It is important to understand the social goals of workers. If direct service providers choose goals for workers and institute training programs to achieve these goals, training programs may be unsuccessful because workers do not have vested interests in the goals of training.

The second stage of the model begins with the perception or *decoding* of cues from the environment. An individual must be able to discriminate and interpret the verbal and nonverbal behavior of others, as well as the cues and rules associated with the social occasion and environment (McFall, 1982). After decoding, the individual uses *decision* skills (McFall, 1982) to search for responses that will meet the requirements of the social task, and to decide on the most appropriate response(s)—i.e., the individual must translate his or her perceptions into plans for action (Hollin & Trower, 1988). After making a decision, the individual then carries out or *performs* a specific behavior.

The third stage in the model is the external consequences of the performance which causes some sort of *environmental change* (Hollin & Trower, 1988). Here, the individual judges whether or not the performed behavior appropriately met the demands of the social task or goal. Future response selection is then modified based upon the *feedback* encountered.

An example may help to clarify the process approach. Let's assume that a female worker is at risk for losing her job because she does not accept criticism well from her supervisor. The worker does not want to lose her job and knows that she will be more valued as an employee if she learns to accept criticism from others. Thus, her *goal* (and the social task) is to learn to accept criticism from her supervisor.

With *decoding* skills, the worker is taught to interpret and discriminate cues in the environment when she is criticized. The worker needs to understand what is happening, who is criticizing her, why the person is criticizing her, and how the person might feel.

With *decision* skills, the worker generates several response alternatives (e.g., ignoring the person, crying, blaming others, apologizing and promising to remedy the situation) and selects

Figure 10.1. Process Model adapted from Argyle and Kendon (1967), McFall (1982), and Hollin and Trower (1986).

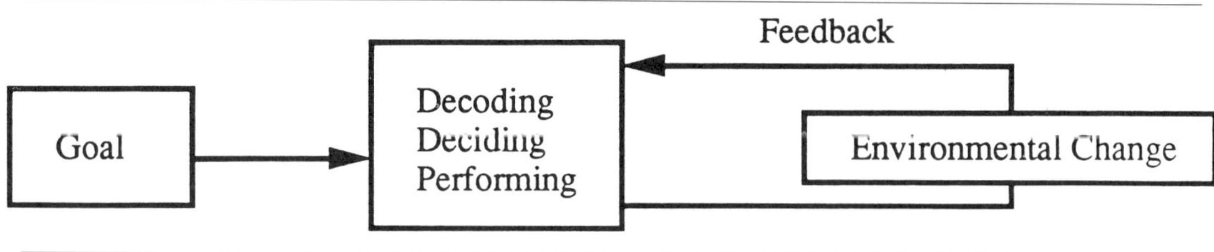

the response that has the highest probability of eliciting positive feedback from her environment.

With *performance* skills, the worker displays a response to the criticism (e.g., apologizes and says she will remedy the situation). Then, the worker evaluates the *feedback* from her environment in response to the behavior she displayed. She notes how the person feels, how she feels, and decides if she did the right thing. If her behavior resulted in positive feedback from her environment, then she would have met her social goal and would be likely to emit the same behavior under similar circumstances in the future.

It appears that the components of process training are very similar to the components of self-control strategies. That is, with each approach, individuals are taught to discriminate stimuli in order to recognize that a response is needed. They must decide upon a response, perform the response, and then evaluate the effectiveness of the response. However, there do appear to be differences between the two approaches. Advocates suggesting that the process approach be used for social skills training (e.g., McFall, 1982; Hollin & Trower, 1988) believe that when an individual is confronted with a social task, each step in the process must be followed. Researchers who have employed self-control strategies (e.g., Agran et al., 1987; Rusch et al., 1988) have only used specific components, and seem to view the strategies individually rather than as a unit or process. Additionally, in the process approach, individuals generate their own solutions to a social task, whereas in self-control strategies, trainers provide the appropriate solutions. Finally, in the process approach, individuals are trained to discriminate a variety of social cues during the decoding process, whereas in self-control strategies, individuals have only been trained to recognize that a problem exists.

Unfortunately, very little research has investigated the effectiveness of training job-related social skills using a process approach. Recently, Park and Gaylord-Ross (in press) conducted two experiments. One experiment sought to determine the efficacy of a process-training package for enhancing generalization. The other experiment compared results of the traditional SST procedures to those of the process approach.

In the first experiment, two youths with mild mental retardation were trained to either increase or decrease a variety of social skills—greetings, making polite and negative comments, mumbling, initiations, and expansions. Contingent effects were seen in the training setting with the onset of process training and the effects generalized to the nontraining or work settings. In the second experiment, two additional youths with mild mental retardation were trained to exhibit initiations, expansions, and terminations in conversations. First, the youths were trained to exhibit these behaviors with a traditional SST package, and then they were trained to exhibit the same behaviors using a process approach. No generalization effects appeared in the criterion work setting until process training was instituted. Thus, Park and Gaylord-Ross (in press) demonstrated that youths with mild mental retardation could learn the process for generating social behaviors, and that the process approach did lead to the generalization of behaviors across settings. Additionally, this study suggests that the process approach may be more effective for training job-related social skills than the traditional SST package.

Summary

The first and most obvious conclusion from this review of social skill training studies is that very little research has been conducted. In the twelve studies reported, most subjects were employees with mild mental retardation. Considering that two of the studies were conducted in sheltered employment settings, and that two studies trained job interview skills, only eight investigations trained social skills directly in supported employment environments. Clearly, it is difficult to draw any generalizations about the best approaches to training based on the limited amount of research that has been done.

However, from the studies reported above, it appears that researchers have incorporated five different types of intervention approaches: (a) training using an SST package, (b) training in an employment setting and/or using co-workers and supervisors, (c) training via the use of a situational script, (d) training using self-control strategies, and (e) training using a process approach. Except for several of the early studies that used SST packages only (e.g., Kelly et al, 1980; Chadsey-Rusch et al., 1984), most other studies have incorporated several of these approaches into their training paradigms, making it even more difficult to speculate which single approach may be the best method for training social skills.

Although it is difficult to specify the best method for training social skills at this time, these methods can be analyzed with respect to how closely they focus upon teaching the elements of the social skills definition which was presented at the beginning of this chapter. An analysis is presented below.

ANALYSIS OF TRAINING STUDIES AND THEIR RELATIONSHIP TO THE DEFINITION OF SOCIAL SKILLS

In this chapter, social skills were defined as goal-oriented, socially acceptable learned behaviors that are situation specific, vary according to social context, and involve both observable and nonobservable cognitive and affective elements that assist in eliciting positive responses and avoiding negative responses from others. Each of the five approaches to training discussed above typically focused on training observable behaviors within the context of specific situations or scenarios presented to study participants. In this respect, all of these approaches meet at least two of the elements included within the definition of social skills—a focus on observable behaviors that are situation-specific. However, except for the studies incorporating aspects of self-control strategies or the process approach, little attention has been paid to the goal of training (or what the participant might want to achieve) or the nonobservable cognitive and affective elements that are associated with social skills. Specifically, within most of the training approaches, participants have not been trained to perceive and interpret social contexts, nor have they been trained to generate and decide upon effective responses that would best meet the demands of a social situation. Additionally, they have not been trained to evaluate their own social behavior because environmental consequences are generally provided by the trainer. In fact, it appears that it is only the process approach that addresses most of the components specified in the definition.

But is the process approach the answer to training social skills? Clearly, there has been so little research regarding this approach that an answer cannot yet be given. There are still many unanswered questions about how to operationalize and teach the process. For example, if the decoding process is taught, it is not clear which specific social cues individuals should be taught to discriminate. That is, what are the most salient social cues that set the occasion for responding? Using the definition given above, we know that social skills vary depending upon the physical setting, the people in the setting, and the social context or occasion for the interaction. If individuals are taught to respond to cues related to each of these three variables, will they be more likely to decode social tasks accurately? Also, what is the best way to teach the decision component of the process, especially if individuals generate few alternatives for responding, or only generate inappropriate responses? Additionally, how can we be certain that the cognitive aspects of the process approach are being used in the performance setting since it is difficult to measure "thinking?" Thus, it may be that before we can answer the question about the effectiveness of the process approach for facilitating social skills, we need to ask questions about the best method(s) to operationalize the process so it can be taught.

Another pressing issue with regard to the process approach is how best to use it (or whether it can be used) with individuals who have severe language impairments. Because the process approach is taught primarily through language, there may be some question whether it can be used with individuals with severe disabilities. Many researchers who work with individuals with severe handicaps (Brown et al., 1983; Coon, Vogelsberg, & Williams, 1981; Marchetti, McCartney, Drain, Hooper, & Dix, 1983), recommend that skills be taught in the natural environment so that generalization effects will be enhanced. However, it is frequently unnatural and inconvenient for direct service providers to intervene and provide instruction to workers when they are engaged in social interactions with supervisors, co-workers, or customers. Additionally, some social skills, while very important (e.g., responding to criticism) occur infrequently, and the probability of a trainer being in close proximity when an episode like this occurs is small. Even though others (e.g., Nisbet & Hagner, 1988; Rusch & Menchetti, 1981) have recommended that co-workers could be trained to provide quick instructions and/or feedback, participants in training would still not have the advantage of being trained in all components of the definition (e.g., establishing goals, cognitive elements) that may be important for the development of generative social skills. Also, if co-workers are used as trainers, it is not clear what kind of effects this would have on the establishment of other types of relationships (e.g., friendships).

The steps in the process could possibly be simplified, or externally generated mediators other than language (e.g., picture cues) could be used to teach the process. Picture cues have been used successfully to teach workers with moderate and severe mental retardation a variety of task-related job skills (e.g., Wacker & Berg, 1983).

If the definition of social skills presented in this chapter is accepted, then it can be concluded that few training approaches, with the possible exception of the process approach, incorporate all aspects of the definition into their procedures. It may be that the definition proposed lacks validity; however, elements of this definition have come from researchers teaching social skills to children (e.g., Cartledge & Milburn, 1986), as well as a variety of other clinical populations, including persons with schizophrenia, phobias, mental retardation, depression, and substance abuse (Hollin & Trower, 1988). The goal of social skills training in employment settings should be to train generative skills that enable employees to participate equally in the social network of the workplace. It is possible that a combination of training approaches will be needed to help workers with severe disabilities meet this goal. Regardless of the approach chosen, it may be helpful to attend to the definition proposed herein so that time is not spent teaching isolated behaviors that fail to generalize.

SUMMARY

Social skills are important for employment success. Not only do they assist workers in getting and keeping their jobs, but they also enable workers to form social relationships with others. It is clear that employers value social skills, and many of the skills they value have been verified by direct observation methods. Broadly speaking, there are two categories of social skills that occur in employment settings—those related to a job task (e.g., following a work direction) and those unrelated to job tasks (e.g., talking about baseball). Both task-related and nontask-related social skills vary depending upon the context of the work situation. Additionally, employers seem to value task-related social skills more than they value nontask skills; however, nontask-related social skills may be more important for forming intimate relationships with others.

Although social skills are valued, there have been few attempts to train these behaviors. Upon review, it appears that five different approaches, or combinations of approaches, have been used in training, each of which has met with varying degrees of success. These approaches were analyzed with respect to a definition of social skills which was proposed in this chapter. Social skills are complex; they can be viewed as goal-oriented, socially acceptable, learned behaviors that are situation-specific and vary according to social context. In addition, they involve both observable and nonobservable cognitive and affective elements that should assist in eliciting positive responses and avoiding negative responses from others. Clearly, further research is needed to determine the best methods to teach these complex behaviors.

The goal of social skills training in employment settings should be to enable employees to participate as equals in the social network of the workplace. This implies that workers have the skills to engage in task-related and nontask-related interactions, and that they can use these skills to form relationships with others, if they so desire. Hopefully, future research efforts will aid those lacking in social skills to achieve this goal.

QUESTIONS (For answers see pp. 430–431)

1. Define social integration.

2. Define social skills.

3. Research has identified a number of social behaviors employers seem to value. List at least five of them.

4. Summarize the similar findings of Lignugaris/Kraft and Chadsey-Rusch and their associates.

5. Identify several differences found between workers with and without disabilities that could potentially have an adverse impact on social integration.

6. Identify the goal of social skills training from an ecobehavioral perspective.

7. What components are typically involved in SST packages?

8. In general terms, how is process training different from other forms of social skills training?

9. Why is it important to understand the social goals of supported employees?

REFERENCES

Agran, M., Salzberg, C. L., & Stowitschek, J. J. (1987). An analysis of the effects of a social skills training program using self-instructions on the acquisition and generalization of two social behaviors in a work setting. *The Journal of the Association for Persons with Severe Handicaps, 12*, 131–139.

Argyle, M. & Kendon, A. (1967). The experimental analysis of social performance. In L. Berkowitz (Ed.). *Advances in experimental social psychology* (Vol. 3, pp. 55–98). New York: Academic Press.

Bakeman, R. & Gottman, J. M. (1986). *Observing interaction: An introduction to sequential analysis.* Cambridge, England: Cambridge University Press.

Breen, C., Haring, T., Pitts-Conway, V., & Gaylord-Ross, R. (1985). The training and generalization of social interaction during breaktime at two job sites in the natural environment. *The Journal of the Association for Persons with Severe Handicaps, 10*, 41–50.

Brickey, M. P., Campbell, K. M., & Browning, L. J. (1985). A five-year follow-up of sheltered workshop employees placed in competitive jobs. *Mental Retardation, 23*, 67–73.

Brown, L., Nisbet, J., Ford, A., Sweet, M., Shiraga, B., York, J., & Loomis, R. (1983). The critical need for nonschool instruction in educational programs for severely handicapped students. *The Journal of the Association for Persons with Severe Handicaps, 8*, 71–77.

Cartledge, G. & Milburn, J. F. (1983). Social skills assessment and teaching in the schools. In T. Kratochwill (Ed.). *Advances in school psychology* (pp. 175–235). Hillsdale, NJ: Earlbaum.

Cartledge, G. & Milburn, J. F. (1986). *Teaching social skills to children* (2nd ed.). New York: Pergamon.

Chadsey-Rusch, J. (1986). Identifying and teaching valued social behaviors in competitive employment settings. In F. R. Rusch (Ed.). *Competitive employment: Issues and strategies* (pp. 273–287). Baltimore: Paul H. Brookes.

Chadsey-Rusch, J. & Gonzalez, P. (1988). Social ecology of the workplace: Employers' perceptions versus direct observation. *Research in Developmental Disabilities, 9*, 229–245.

Chadsey-Rusch, J., Gonzalez, P., Tines, J., & Johnson, J. R. (1989). Social ecology of the workplace: An examination of contextual variables affecting the social interactions of employers with and without mental retardation. *American Journal of Mental Retardation, 94*, 141–151.

Chadsey-Rusch, J., Karlan, G. R., Riva, M., & Rusch, F. R. (1984). Competitive employment: Teaching conversation skills to adults who are mentally retarded. *Mental Retardation, 22*, 218–225.

Coon, M., Vogelsberg, R. T., & Williams, W. (1981). Effects of classroom public transportation instruction on generalization to the natural environment. *Journal of the Association for Persons with Severe Handicaps, 6*, 46–53.

Dwinell, M. A. & Connis, R. T. (1979). Reducing inappropriate verbalizations of a retarded adult. *American Journal of Mental Deficiency, 84*, 87–92.

Federal Register, August 14, 1987. The state supported employment services program. *52*, 30546-30552.

Ford, L., Dineen, J., & Hall, J. (1984). Is there life after placement? *Education and Training of the Mentally Retarded, 19*, 291–296.

Goldstein, A. P., Sprafkin, R. P., Gershaw, N. J., & Klein, P. (1980). *Skill streaming the adolescent: A structured learning approach to teaching prosocial skills*. Champaign, IL: Research Press.

Greenspan, S. (1981). Defining childhood social competence: A proposed working model. In B. Keogh (Ed.). *Advances in special education* (Vol. 3, pp. 1–39). Greenwich, Conn.: JAI Press.

Greenspan, S. & Schoultz, B. (1981). Why mentally retarded adults lose their jobs. Social competence as a factor in work adjustment. *Applied Research in Mental Retardation, 2*(1), 23–38.

Hall, C., Sheldon-Wildgen, J., & Sherman, J. A. (1980). Teaching job interview skills to retarded clients. *Journal of Applied Behavior Analysis, 13*, 433–442.

Hanley-Maxwell, C., Rusch, F. R., Chadsey-Rusch, J., & Renzaglia, A. (1986). Factors contributing to job terminations. *The Journal of the Association for Persons with Severe Handicaps, 11*, 45–52.

Hill, J. W., Wehman, P., Hill, M., & Goodall, P. (1986). Differential reasons for job separation of previously employed persons with mental retardation. *Mental Retardation, 24*, 347–357.

Hollin, C. R. & Trower, P. (1988). Development and application of social skills training: A review and critique. In M. Hersen, R. M. Eisler, & P. M. Miller (Eds.). *Progress in behavior modification* (Vol. 22, pp. 165–214). Newbury Park, CA: Sage.

Hughes, C. & Rusch, F. R. (in press). Teaching employees with severe mental retardation to solve problems in a supported employment setting. *Journal of Applied Behavior Analysis.*

Karlan, G. R. & Rusch, F. R. (1982). Analyzing the relationship between acknowledgement and compliance in a nonsheltered work setting. *Education and Training of the Mentally Retarded, 17*, 202–208.

Kelly, J. A., Wildman, B. G., Urey, J. R., & Berler, E. S. (1980). Small group behavioral training to improve the job interview skills repertoire of mildly retarded adolescents. *Journal of Applied Behavior Analysis, 13*, 461–471.

Kirmeyer, S. L. (1988). Observed communication in the workplace: Content, source, and direction. *Journal of Community Psychology, 16*, 175–187.

Kochany, L. & Keller, J. (1981). An analysis and evaluation of the failures of severely disabled individuals in competitive employment. In P. Wehman (Ed.). *Competitive employment: New horizons for severely disabled individuals.* Baltimore: Paul H. Brookes.

Ladd, G. W. & Mize, J. (1983). A cognitive-social learning model of social-skill training. *Psychological Review, 90*, 127–157.

Lignugaris/Kraft, B., Rule, S., Salzberg, C. L., & Stowitschek, J. J. (1986). Social interpersonal skills of handicapped and nonhandicapped adults at work. *Journal of Employment Counseling, 23*, 20–30.

Lignugaris/Kraft B., Salzberg, C. L., Rule, S., & Stowitschek, J. J. (1988). Social-vocational skills of workers with and without mental retardation in two community employment sites. *Mental Retardation, 26*, 297–305.

Lignugaris/Kraft, B., Salzberg, C. L., Stowitschek, J. J., & McConaughy, E. K. (1986). A descriptive analysis of social interaction patterns among employees in sheltered and non-profit business settings. *The Career Development Quarterly*, *35*, 123–135.

Mager, R. (1962). *Preparing instructional objectives.* Palo Alto, CA: Fearon.

Marchetti, A., McCartney, J., Drain, S., Hooper, M., & Dix, J. (1983). Pedestrian skills training for mentally retarded adults: Comparison of training in two settings. *Mental Retardation*, *2*, 107–110.

Martin, J. E., Rusch, F. R., Lagomarcino, T., & Chadsey-Rusch, J. (1986). Comparison between workers who are nonhandicapped and mentally retarded: Why they lose their jobs. *Applied Research in Mental Retardation*, *7*, 467–474.

Matson, J. L. & Ollendick, T. H. (1988). *Enhancing children's skills: Assessment and training.* New York: Pergamon.

McFall, R. M. (1982). A review and reformulation of the concept of social skills. *Behavioral Assessment*, *4*, 1–33.

Nisbet, J. & Hagner, D. (1988). Natural supports in the workplace: A reexamination of supported employment. *Journal of the Association for Persons with Severe Handicaps*, *13*, 260–267.

Park, H. & Gaylord-Ross, R. (in press). Process social skill training in employment settings with mentally retarded youth. *Journal of Applied Behavior Analysis.*

Rappaport, J. (1977). *Community psychology: Values, research and action.* New York: Holt, Rinehart, & Winston.

Rusch, F. R., Chadsey-Rusch, J., & Johnson, J. R. (in press). Supported employment: Emerging opportunities for employment integration. In L. Meyer, C. Peck, & L. Brown (Eds.). *Critical issues in the lives of people with severe disabilities.* Baltimore: Paul H. Brookes.

Rusch,. F. R., McKee, M., Chadsey-Rusch, J., & Renzaglia, A. (1988). Teaching a student with severe handicaps to self-instruct: A brief report. *Education and Training of the Mentally Retarded*, *23*, 51–58.

Rusch, F. R. & Menchetti, B. M. (1981). Increasing compliant work behaviors in a non-sheltered work setting. *Mental Retardation*, *19*(3), 107–111.

Rusch, F. R., Morgan, T. K., Martin, J. E., Riva, M., & Agran, M. (1985). Competitive employment: Teaching mentally retarded employees self-instructional strategies. *Applied Research in Mental Retardation*, *6*, 389–407.

Rusch, F. R., Schutz, R. P., & Agran, M. (1982). Validating entry-level survival skills for service occupations: Implications for curriculum development. *Journal of the Association for Persons with Severe Handicaps*, *7*, 32–41.

Rusch, F. R., Weithers, J. A., Menchetti, B., & Schutz, R. P. (1980). Social validation of a program to reduce topic repetition in a nonsheltered setting. *Education and Training in Mental Retardation*, *15*(3), 187–194.

Salzberg, C. L., Agran, M., & Lignugaris/Kraft, B. (1986). Behaviors that contribute to entry-level employment: A profile of five jobs. *Applied Research in Mental Retardation*, *7*, 299–314.

Salzberg, C. L., McConaughy, K., Lignugaris/Kraft, B., Agran, M., & Stowitschek, J. J. (1987). Behaviors of distinction: The transition from acceptable to highly-valued worker. *The Journal for Vocational Special Needs Education*, *10*, 23–28.

Schein, E. H. (1981). SMR Forum: Does Japanese management style have a message for American managers: *Sloan Management Review*, *23*, 55–68.

Schutz, R. P., Rusch, F. R., & Lamson, D. S. (1979). Evaluation of an employer's procedure to eliminate unacceptable behavior on the job. *Community Serviçes Forum*, *1*, 4–5.

Shafer, M. S., Brooke, V., & Wehman, P. (1985). Developing appropriate social-interpersonal skills in a mentally retarded worker. In P. Wehman & J. W. Hill (Eds.). *Competitive employment for persons with mental retardation: From research to practice* (Vol. 1, pp. 358–375). Richmond: Virginia Commonwealth University, Rehabilitation Research and Training Center.

Stokes, T. F. & Baer, D. M. (1977). An implicit technology of generalization. *Journal of Applied Behavior Analysis*, *10*, 349–367.

Storey, K. & Gaylord-Ross, R. (1987). Increasing positive interactions by handicapped individuals during a recreational activity using a multicomponent treatment package. *Research in Developmental Disabilities, 8*, 627–649.

Storey, K. & Knutson, N. (1989). A comparative analysis of social interactions of workers with and without disabilities in integrated work sites: A pilot study. *Education and Training of the Mentally Retarded, 24*, 265–273.

Stowitschek, J. J., McConaughy, E. K., Peatross, D., Salzberg, C., & Lignugaris/Kraft, B. (1988). Effects of group incidental training on the use of social amenities by adults with mental retardation in work settings. *Education and Training of the Mentally Retarded, 23*, 202–212.

Terkel, S. (1972). *Working*. New York: Pantheon.

Thurman, S. K. (1977). Congruence of behavioral ecologies: A model for special education. *Journal of Special Education, 11*, 329–333.

Trower, P. (1982). Toward a generative model of social skills: A critique and synthesis. In J. P. Curran & P. M. Monti (Eds.). *Social skills training* (pp. 399–427). New York: Guilford.

Wacker, D. & Berg, W. (1983). Effects of picture prompts on the acquisition of complex vocational tasks by mentally retarded adolescents. *Journal of Applied Behavior Analysis, 16*, 417–433.

Walker, H. M. & Calkins, C. F. (1986). The role of social competence in the community adjustment of persons with developmental disabilities. *Remedial and Special Education, 7*, 46–53.

Wehman, P., Hill, M., Goodall, P., Cleveland, V. B., & Pentecost, J. H. (1982). Job placement and follow-up of moderately and severely handicapped individuals after three years. *Journal of the Association for Persons with Severe Handicaps, 7*, 5–15.

CHAPTER

11

Extending Individual Competence, Developing Natural Support, and Promoting Social Acceptance

Carolyn Hughes
Frank R. Rusch
University of Illinois at Urbana-Champaign
Rita M. Curl
Utah State University

In introducing a follow-up services model in this chapter, we contend that the post-placement process consists of three complementary goals: (a) *extending individual competence*, (b) *developing natural support* in the workplace, and (c) *promoting social acceptance*. Based on these goals, the follow-up model that we propose significantly extends approaches that we have introduced in the past (cf. Rusch, 1986; Rusch & Mithaug, 1980; Rusch, Chadsey-Rusch, & Lagomarcino, 1987). Contrary to the present model, prior proposals have focused on the supported employee primarily as a recipient of services (cf. Hanley-Maxwell, Rusch, & Rappaport, 1989). Our model focuses on the employee as an active participant in his or her adjustment on the job. Additionally, setting characteristics and co-workers are considered viable "support" alternatives to employment specialists providing training and evaluation. Over the past few years we also have learned how to promote employer and co-worker acceptance of supported employees. These important developments are now the salient ingredients that define the responsibilities of employment specialists.

As a result of our increasing understanding of how people learn, combined with a better understanding of work environments, our current view of the post-placement process assumes that individuals grow and change as a result of their employment experiences, often in ways that are unpredictable. Past approaches to follow-up have assumed that people are "static" and, provided appropriate support systems, will develop their competencies within a predictable range (French & Bell, 1984).

We contend that in fact we have not been good at predicting the competence that will emerge once an individual is employed in an integrated environment. Due to our continuing inability to predict emerging competencies (Gold, 1975), we recommend that employment specialists "set the occasion" for long-term success or, as recommended by Stokes and Baer (1977), plan for generalization and maintenance. Employment specialists should set the occasion for individuals to adjust to their target work settings and then manage the expectations, often also unpredictable, held by significant others (i.e., co-workers, work supervisors, employers). Because individuals grow and change in relation to their work experiences, we hold that the rationale for providing follow-up services is not simply to maintain acceptable work behavior, but also to provide opportunities to the supported employee that result in career advancements (Curl & Rule, 1987) (e.g., increased wages, modified work schedules, new job responsibilities). This chapter describes our follow-up model based on the goals of extending individual competence, developing natural support in the workplace, and promoting social acceptability.

Assumptions of the Proposed Model

Our model is based on the following assumptions. First, we assume that changes in the workplace occur as soon as an employee is placed in a work environment (Rusch, Chadsey-Rusch, White, & Gifford, 1985). These changes include (a) the assignment of new work tasks and (b) changes in expectations for performance of these work assignments. Furthermore, because expectations within the work environment probably continue to change over time, the goals of follow-up must be longitudinal (Rusch & Mithaug, 1985). Additionally, follow-up services must take into account nonwork-related environments in which a supported employee is a participant (Chapters 7 and 10, this volume; Rusch & Mithaug, 1985). Therefore, employment specialists must become knowledgeable of the demands that work places upon an individual's residential placement, leisure activities, and so forth.

Finally, we assume that most traditional "job coach" models foster dependent interactions between the job coach and the supported employee (Agran & Martin, 1987; Shafer, 1986; Winking, DeStefano, & Rusch, 1988). Consequently, our model proposes a new role for these job coaches as "employment specialists" that includes extending individual competence and "tying-in" to existing support alternatives within the workplace, rather than imposing an external structure on the work environment. Also, we propose managing individual and work group expectations that pervade all work settings by utilizing emerging social validation methodology (French & Bell, 1984; Hanley-Maxwell et al., 1989; Lippitt & Lippitt, 1984; Nisbet & Hagner, 1988; Rappaport, 1981; Rusch & Mithaug, 1985; White, 1986).

EXTENDING INDIVIDUAL COMPETENCE

Extending employee competence requires that we focus on teaching individuals strategies that they can use to adapt to their roles as employees and to the expectations that exist in all human performance situations. Our research over the past ten years (see Chapter 1) has shown that employees encounter new expectations for performance and often new responsibilities throughout their employment. These new expectations require that employees adapt their performance in ways that will result in acceptable judgments by work supervisors and co-workers—the significant others in the workplace. Therefore, extending individual competence requires the use of procedures that promote acceptable work behavior. These procedures are reviewed by Berg, Wacker and Flynn in some detail in Chapter 9. We extend their discussion here to a very narrow application, that is, adjustment on the job after placement.

We propose two strategies that employment specialists should use in extending individual competence. These strategies are: (a) identifying independence objectives for supported employees in relation to the demands of the workplace, and (b) teaching employee independence.

Identifying Independence Objectives

Employment specialists typically conduct situational assessments to determine job-related requirements and supported employees' abilities in relation to meeting these requirements. (See Chapter 7 for a more thorough discussion of situational assessment.) Methods that employment specialists often use include interviews and observation of actual performance of job tasks. For example, Crouch, Rusch, and Karlan (1984) asked supervisors in a food service setting to specify the times that work tasks were to be started and completed. Supervisor evaluations indicated that three employees failed to get their work done on time. Next, these supported employees were observed (observation) to identify the time they started and completed their required job tasks. Direct observation indicated that the supported employees rarely met the supervisors' criteria. Figure 11.1 displays the observed performance of the target employees before intervention (baseline) and during the intervention period. Using a self-instructional strategy, these employees learned to begin and end their work assignments on time.

Teaching Employee Independence

When problem areas are identified in which the supported employee is not performing independently, strategies should be implemented by the employment specialist that will result in improved employee performance independent of ongoing specialist assistance. Procedures have emerged as a result of recent research showing that supported employees may be active participants in promoting their own independent performance (Mithaug, Martin, Husch, Agran, & Rusch, 1988). These procedures consist of the supported employee (a) making a decision, (b) performing independently, (c) evaluating performance, and (d) adjusting future performance as a result of self-evaluation (Mithaug et al., 1988).

During *decision-making*, employees are taught to identify the tasks they are assigned; during *independent performance*, the employee completes the work assignment by performing the work as scheduled. Typically, supported employees are assisted initially in the acquisition of planning, scheduling, and managing their own behavior (cf. Rusch, Martin, & White, 1985). During *self-evaluation*, employees monitor their own performance by self-recording work outcomes, such as the time they begin and end work, the amount of work completed, and the accuracy of the work (Connis, 1979). By comparing these outcomes with their own expectations, they learn to determine if they have met their own goals, which allows the employee an opportunity to evaluate and plan for future work performance.

During *adjustment*, employees decide if changes need to be made the next time they perform the task(s). Adjustments may consist of changes in starting or ending times, task selection or set-up, or accuracy of task completion. If an employee's performance meets the goals established during decision-making, little or no adjustment will be required. Performance that does not meet these goals will require a change in task or method of task completion.

Summary

By extending employee competence, employment specialists help supported employees adapt to changing expectations for performance and increasing responsibilities and opportunities on the job. We recommend two strategies that employment specialists should use to extend individual competence: (a) identifying independence objectives, and (b) teaching employee independence. Extending individual competence by promoting independence allows supported employees to adjust their performance in relation to the varying demands and expanding opportunities of their jobs.

PROMOTING NATURAL SUPPORT IN THE WORKPLACE

Sometimes assistance provided by the employment specialist cannot be extended solely to the supported employee. Consequently, behavior management must be transferred to stimuli or significant others in the work environment (Rusch & Kazdin, 1981). We contend that natural support, including both setting variables and significant others such as co-workers, exists in abundance in the workplace. Thus, employment specialists should be able to identify and enlist necessary support from either the work environment or co-workers. The following three sections introduce methods that we have implemented to foster the long-term

FIGURE 11.1. Number of minutes taken (task duration) to complete each task for subjects and co-workers. The horizontal, dashed line is the supervisor-established time allowed to complete the task.

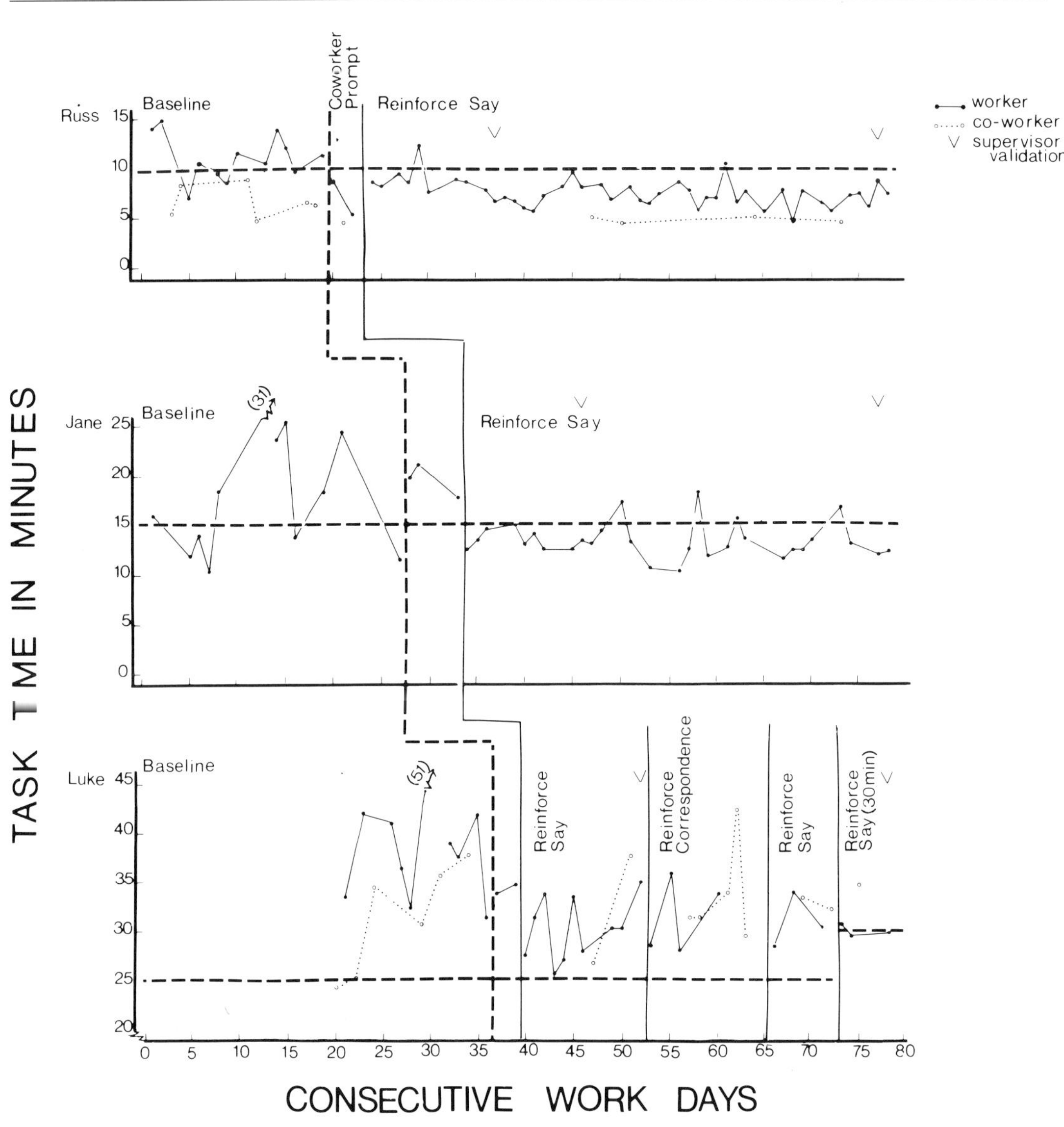

Crouch, K.P., Rusch, F.R., & Karlan, G.P. (1984). Competitive employment: Utilizing the correspondence training paradigm to enhance productivity. *Education and Training of the Mentally Retarded, 19,* 268–275. Reprinted by permission of the publisher.

"support" employees need in order to remain employed. Two strategies are described: (a) identifying natural support, including setting variables and co-workers, and (b) matching available support to employees' identified needs.

Identifying Natural Support in the Workplace (Setting Variables)

Identifying work-related stimuli that maintain independent performance is accomplished through ecological inventories performed by employment specialists (Martin, 1986). Possible stimuli in the work environment that may promote independent work performance include *clocks or whistles* to prompt going to a job station and beginning work, *co-workers leaving a job station* to prompt going on break, or *food scraps on tables* that remind the employee to wipe the table surface clean. Table 11.1 provides examples of possible stimuli in the workplace that may be used to prompt acceptable work behavior (Lagomarcino, Hughes, & Rusch 1989).

Sowers, Rusch, Connis, and Cummings (1980) used clocks located in the workplace to teach supported employees to manage their time on the job. The supported employees, who could not tell time, were taught to use pictured clock faces to go to and from lunch and break independently (see Figure 11.2).

Identifying Natural Support in the Workplace (Co-workers)

Based on their analysis of the literature investigating the interactions of non-professional, non-managerial employees, Nisbet and Hagner (1988) concluded that (a) considerable social interaction is characteristic of work environments, (b) patterns of social interaction vary across and within work environments, and (c) support is available naturally within employment settings. Nisbet and Hagner concluded that social interaction in the workplace provides considerable support for persons with or without disabilities, and that support is associated with job satisfaction and job performance. Several other researchers also have argued that co-worker involvement may provide the support needed for supported employees to maintain independent performance (Chadsey-Rusch & Gonzalez,

Table 11.1 Stimuli in the Workplace

	Stimulus	Response	Consequence
1.	Clock	Go to job station	Begin work
2.	Co-workers leave job station	Go to break	Take break
3.	Food scraps on table	Wipe table	Table is clean
4.	Out of job materials	Get job materials	Continue working
5.	Equipment breakdown	Seek maintenance personnel	Equipment is repaired
6.	Window is sprayed with cleaner	Wipe off cleaner with squeegee or towel	Window is clean
7.	Office is occupied	Move on to next unoccupied office	Followed supervisor instructions
8.	Usual transportation to work is unavailable (co-worker is sick)	Check bus schedule	Take bus to work
9.	Customer comes to counter	Greet customer	Customer returns greeting
10.	Dirty dishes are piling up	Increase rate of dishwashing	Dishes are cleaned in time

Lagomarcino, T.R., Hughes, C., & Rusch, F.R. (1989). Utilizing self-management to teach independence on the job. *Education and Training in Mental Retardation,* 24, 139–148. Reprinted by permission of the publisher.

FIGURE 11.2. Clock faces used by supported employees.

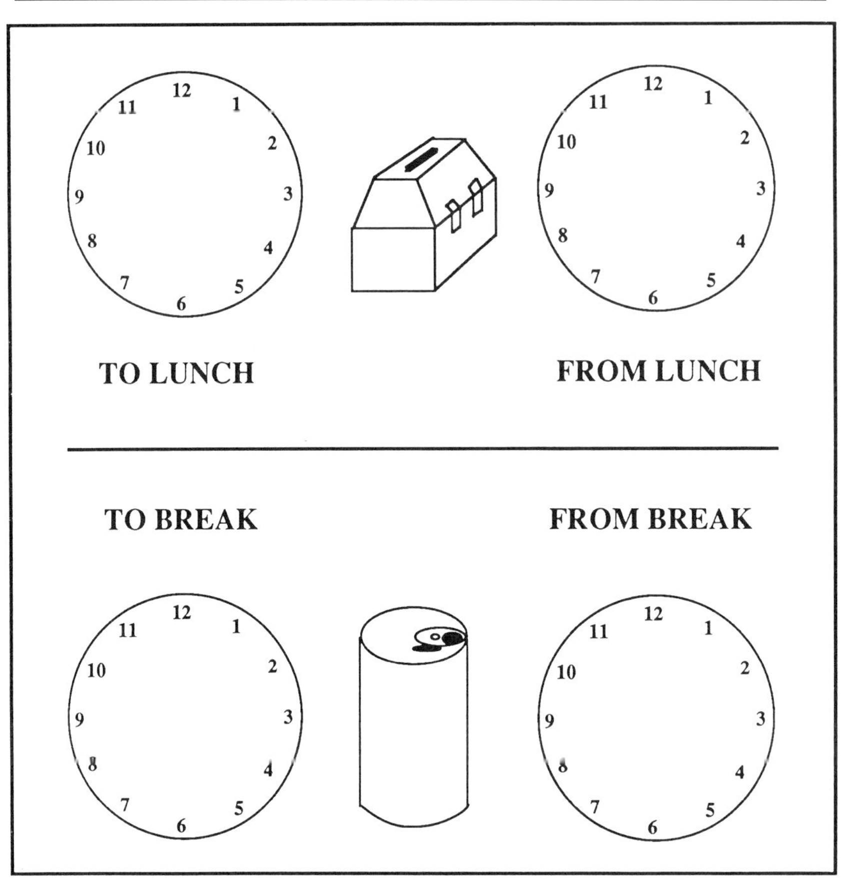

1988; Chadsey-Rusch, Gonzalez, Tines, & Johnson, 1989; Likins, Salzberg, Stowitschek, Lignugaris/Kraft, & Curl, 1989; Nisbet & Hagner, 1988; Rusch, Johnson, & Hughes, in press; Rusch & Minch, 1988; Shafer, 1986).

Co-workers are employees who meet one or more of the following criteria: (a) work in the proximity of the supported employee, (b) perform the same or similar duties as the supported employee, and (c) take breaks or eat meals in the same area as the supported employee (Rusch, Johnson, & Hughes, in press). Rusch and Minch (1988) identified five types of co-worker support that have been reported by applied researchers who have enlisted the involvement of co-workers. This involvement included: (a) *validating instructional strategies* (Haught, Walls, & Crist, 1984; Rusch & Menchetti, 1981; Schutz, Rusch, & Lamson, 1979); (b) *collecting subjective evaluations* (Crouch et al., 1984; Schutz, Jostes, Rusch, & Lamson, 1980; White & Rusch, 1983); (c) *implementing training procedures* (Curl, McConaughy, Pawley, & Salzberg, 1987; Kochany, Simpson, Hill, & Wehman, 1982; Rusch, Weithers, Menchetti, & Schutz, 1980; Stanford & Wehman, 1982); (d) *collecting social comparison information* (Crouch et al., 1984; Rusch, Morgan, Martin, Riva, & Agran, 1985); and (e) *maintaining work performance after skill acquisition* (Kochany et al., 1981; Rusch et al., 1985). For example, Stanford and Wehman (1982) taught co-workers to respond to social interactions initiated by supported employees who worked as dishwashers. Initially, the employment specialist prompted the supported employees to interact. Following

Table 11.2 Types of Co-worker Involvement (Definitions)

Advocating. A co-worker advocates for a supported employee by *optimizing*, *backing*, and *supporting* a supported employee's employment status. *Optimizing* refers to encouraging a supervisor to assign high-status and relevant tasks to a supported employee, *backing* refers to supporting a supported employee's rights, for example, by attempting to prevent practical jokes aimed at a supported employee. It also includes speaking up for a supported employee or offering explanations during differences of opinion. *Supporting* relates to providing emotional support to a supported employee in the form of friendship, association, etc.

Associating. A co-worker interacts socially with a supported employee at the work place.

Befriending. A co-worker interacts socially with a supported employee outside the workplace.

Collecting Data. A co-worker collects data by observing and recording social and/or work performance.

Evaluating. A co-worker appraises a supported employee's work performance and provides (written/oral) feedback to him or her.

Training. A co-worker supports a supported employee by providing on-the-job skill training.

From *Co-worker involvement scoring manual and index* by F. R. Rusch, C. Hughes, J. McNair, and P. G. Wilson, 1989, Champaign: University of Illinois, The Board of Trustees of the University of Illinois. Adapted by permission.

prompting, the social interactions of both the co-workers and the supported employees increased.

Rusch, Hughes, Johnson, and Minch (1988) extended the findings of Rusch and Minch (1988) by describing types of co-worker involvement reported among supported employees in model supported employment programs in Illinois. Findings indicated that co-workers were involved with supported employees as described in the literature. Specifically, Rusch, Hughes et al. (1988) indicated that the greatest percentage of supported employees had co-workers who served as associates (87 percent), followed by evaluators (70 percent), trainers (61 percent), advocates (42 percent), friends (20 percent), and data collectors (17 percent). (See Table 11.2 for definitions of these types of co-worker involvement.)

Subsequently, Rusch, Johnson, and Hughes (in press) described patterns of co-worker involvement in relation to level of disability versus placement approach. Specifically, this study sought to describe the type of co-worker involvement reported by employment specialists who place their supported employees individually or in groups. Supported employees who were employed in mobile work crews were much less involved with co-workers. Supported employees who were individually placed or who worked in clustered placements were more involved with co-workers. Differences in levels of co-worker involvement provided were observed to relate less to level of disability than to type of placement. These findings suggest that supported employees associate extensively with their nonhandicapped co-workers when the opportunity for co-worker involvement exists.

In support of the findings of Rusch, Johnson, and Hughes (in press), Table 11.3 indicates the percentage of supported employees who reportedly received co-worker support. These data were reported by employment specialists associated with model programs in Illinois from October through December, 1988.

Additionally, based on interviews with supervisors in businesses that employ individuals with disabilities, several procedures for providing co-worker support have emerged (Menchetti, Rusch, & Lamson, 1981; Rusch, Minch, & Hughes, in press). These procedures include pairing a new employee with a veteran employee who answers questions, demonstrates job tasks, provides information, and shows the new employee around the workplace. Furthermore, co-workers have been allowed to physically assist and to repeat instructions to new employees.

We identify co-worker involvement at the worksite by scoring the *Co-worker Involvement Index* (Rusch, Hughes, McNair, & Wilson, 1989). This instrument is used to assess co-worker involvement within a worksite in relation to: (a) physical integration, (b) social integration, (c) training, (d) frequency of associating, (e) appropriateness of associating, (f) befriending, (g) advocating, (h) evaluating, and (i) giving information. By administering the *Co-worker Involvement Index*, the employment specialist identifies how co-workers are involved with supported employees in a workplace.

Table 11.3 Percentage of Supported Employees Receiving Co-worker Involvement

Type of Co-worker Involvement	October 1988 (n = 423) %	November 1988 (n = 445) %	December 1988 (n = 419) %
Training	75	64	68
Associating	84	82	86
Befriending	17	20	20
Advocating	36	45	43
Collecting Data	15	19	17
Evaluating	65	66	69

Teaching co-workers to provide training

Although co-workers provide some support naturally, research shows that they often need formal instruction to become effective training and maintenance agents (Curl, Pawley, DeFrancesco, & Salzberg, 1987; Walls, Zane, & Thvedt, 1980). Previous research has shown that many entry-level job trainers provide instructions or model job tasks, but do not systematically use both procedures during training (Curl, Pawley et al., 1987). Further, most co-worker-trainers do not ask trainees to demonstrate tasks taught or systematically evaluate tasks completed. Inadequate instruction impacts trainees in two ways: (a) trainees with handicaps may not benefit from instructions without demonstrations, and (b) trainees continue to complete jobs incorrectly without the benefit of immediate monitoring and correction. Subsequent performance deficits often result in job termination (Ford, Dineen, & Hall, 1984; Wehman, Hill, Wood, & Parent, 1987).

In research on co-workers as trainers and maintenance agents, entry-level co-workers who were working in community businesses were selected to complete job training for individuals with developmental disabilities (Curl, Pawley et al., 1987). For example, Figure 11.3 shows how Wendy, a co-worker, was taught to use instruction, modeling, observation, and coaching to teach Ben, a supported employee, to clean bathrooms. The use of the combined training procedures in addition to the use of a timer and performance contingencies resulted in acceptable work performance in terms of rate and accuracy for this supported employee.

Matching Available Support to Employees' Identified Needs

Once behaviors are identified that need support and available support has been measured, the employment specialist must develop a "support match" between the employee's needs and support available at the worksite. As a result of identifying independence objectives for the supported employee in relation to the demands of the workplace (see section on Extending Individual Competence, this chapter), the employment specialist has identified specific areas in which an employee needs continued support. These needs should be "matched" to the natural support, including both setting variables and co-workers, that the employment specialist has identified as available within the work environment.

For example, some employees may fail to take their breaks on time. These individuals could be taught that when co-workers leave their job stations (a natural cue) they also should take a break. In this case, a setting variable (co-workers leaving their job stations) serves as a natural support for prompting acceptable behavior. Also by example, the employment specialist may determine that an employee consistently is assigned the least desirable jobs in a workplace. This employee then may be paired with a co-worker who has been observed to advocate for fellow workers, in order to prompt the supported employee to "speak up" for his or her rights. To promote co-worker involvement, co-workers

FIGURE 11.3. Percentage of intervals during which the co-worker-trainer, Wendy, instructed, modeled, observed, and coached the trainee during daily work sessions. Completion times and accuracy percentages are for the trainee, Ben. Shaded areas represent

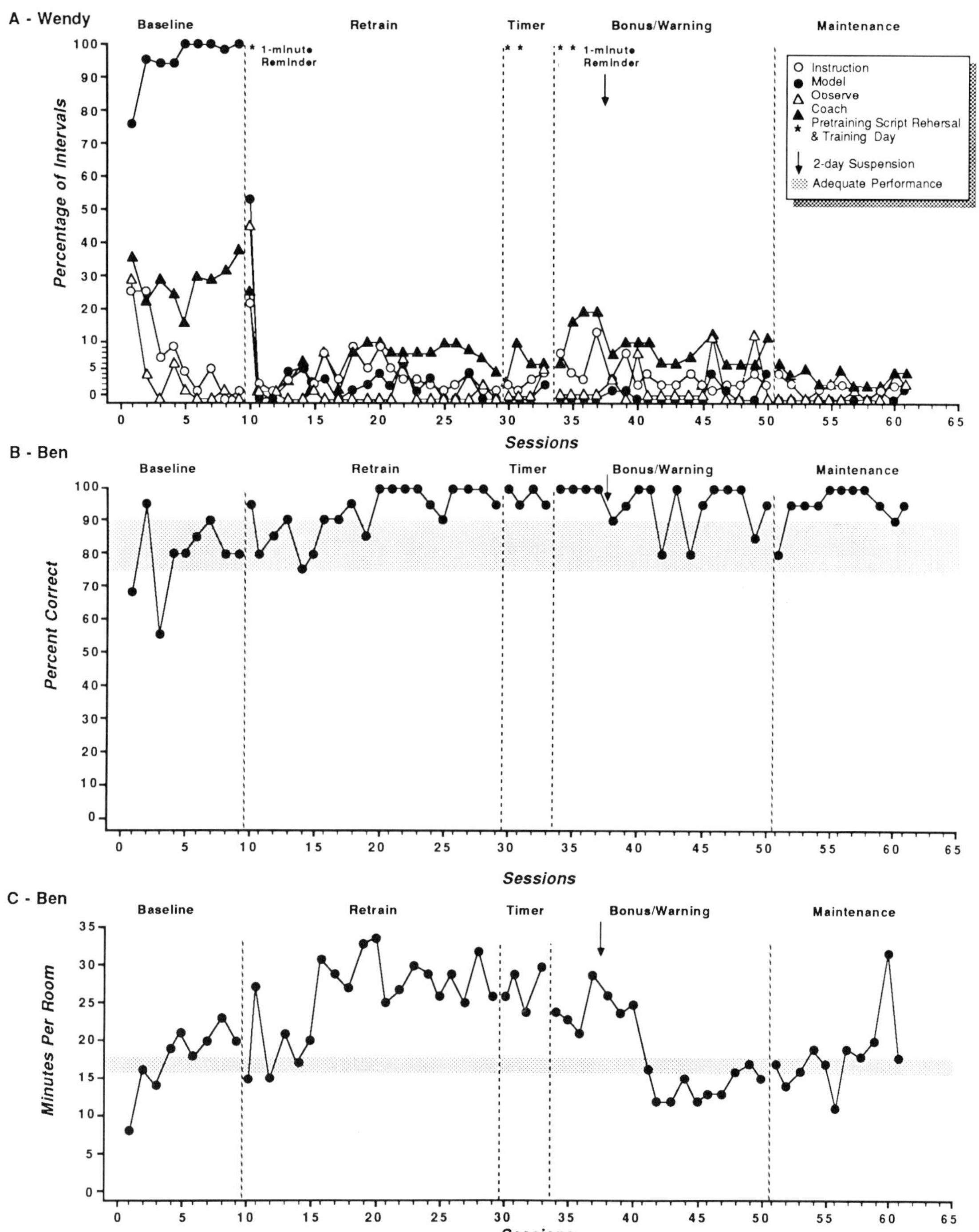

may be taught in brief 10-minute sessions during breaks or before or after work how to provide support to employees (cf. Rusch, Chadsey-Rusch, & Lagomarcino, 1987).

Rusch, McKee, Chadsey-Rusch, and Renzaglia (1988) observed that an employee with severe mental retardation who worked in a university film center failed to complete orders when he ran out of supplies. Consequently, Rusch, McKee et al. (1988) taught the employee to respond to the natural stimulus of running out of supplies by requesting more materials from an assistant. The use of a setting variable (no materials) as a natural support allowed this employee to complete his orders correctly. Schutz et al. (1980) observed that two food service employees with moderate mental retardation were not meeting their supervisor's criteria for sweeping and mopping floors. Co-workers then were asked to evaluate the quality of the employees' performance. Co-workers serving as evaluators provided the natural support for the employees to improve their performance.

Summary

Based on our awareness that different employees require varying types and levels of support, we described a method that employment specialists should use to match employees' needs to support naturally available in the workplace. Two strategies were described: (a) identifying natural support in terms of setting variables and significant others (co-workers), and (b) matching available support to employees' identified needs.

PROMOTING SOCIAL ACCEPTANCE

Supported employment is associated with three outcomes: integration, wages, and ongoing support. Of these three outcomes, integration is supported employment's most distinguishing feature.

In our view, *employment integration* refers to the participation of employees with and without disabilities as equal members within a workplace. An *integrated workplace* is formed when individual differences are accepted and individual competence is maximized by providing opportunities and support.

If participation within the workplace by employees with and without disabilities exists, and if individual differences are accepted and individual competence maximized, the work environment need not be modified. However, if employment integration is not characteristic of a workplace, the employment specialist must promote participation by managing expectations. Indeed, *unmanaged expectations of supported employees, co-workers, supervisors, and employers may be the major deterrent to successfully integrated employment.* We contend that employment specialists promote social acceptance of supported employees by (a) utilizing social validation methodology, and (b) managing social acceptance across time.

Utilizing Social Validation Methodology

Significant others within the workplace must be consulted to provide information regarding the acceptance of changes that occur when individuals are placed into the work environment, or regarding the acceptance of changes that have been made in supported employee performance. A major advancement in how to utilize opinions to gauge acceptance that promotes employment integration has been the emergence of social validation methodology (Kazdin, 1977; Kazdin & Matson, 1981; VanHouten, 1979; White, 1986; Wolf, 1978). *Social validation* is a methodology that assesses the acceptability of an individual's performance to significant others (Wolf, 1978). We assume that employers and co-workers have diverse expectations regarding the abilities of previously segregated individuals who become employees in integrated work sites. Social validation methodology has provided us with guidelines for evaluating social acceptance.

Using social validation, an employee's performance is evaluated by obtaining the opinions of significant others with whom the employee has contact (e.g., co-workers, supervisors, employers). For example, Rusch et al. (1980) used subjective evaluation to assess the acceptability of the conversational speech of a food service employee. Initially, the employee's supervisors and co-workers were consulted to determine if topics discussed by the supported employee were considered a problem (subjective evaluation). Social comparison data also revealed that before training, the employee repeated topics approximately five times as often as his co-workers. After training, the employee decreased his repetitions in relation to total topics to levels approximating his co-workers (see Figure 11.4).

Managing Social Acceptance Across Time

Obtaining subjective evaluations is critical for determining the social acceptance of a supported employee's performance. We recommend that employment specialists administer work performance evaluations that are routinely completed by supervisors in order to manage social acceptance. Table 11.4 presents work performance measures that have been used across a variety of integrated worksites to evaluate supervisors' perceptions of employee independence (Rusch & Hughes, 1988). These measures are similar to those used by Hill and Wehman (1979) in assessing co-workers' and supervisors' acceptance of the work performance of supported employees in community job sites in Virginia.

There are three considerations in the administration of work performance evaluations. First, behaviorally-based work performance evaluation forms should be completed by an employee who has responsibility for staff evaluations. It should not be filled out solely by co-workers employed in positions similar to those held by supported employees or by the supported employee alone. Research has revealed gross discrepancies between evaluations conducted by experienced supervisory staff and those completed by supported employees or co-workers

Rusch, F.R., Weithers, J.A., Menchetti, B.M., & Schutz, R.P. (1980). Social validation of a program to reduce topic repetition in a non-sheltered setting. *Education and Training for the Mentally Retarded, 15,* 208–215. Reprinted by permission of the publisher.

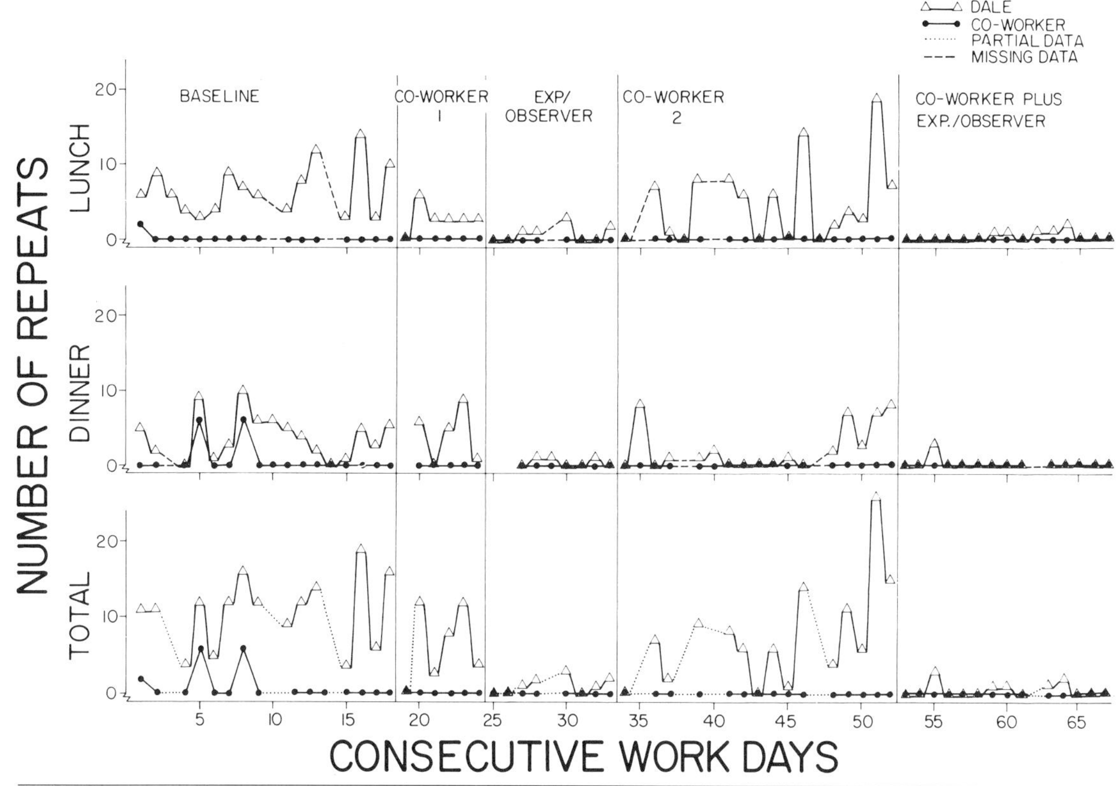

FIGURE 11.4 Number of repeats for Dale (the supported employee) and a designated co-worker.

Table 11.4 Measures of Employee Independence

A. Performance Measures

1. Works independently.
2. Completes all assigned tasks.
3. Attends to job tasks consistently.
4. Meets company standards for quality of work.
5. Meets company standards for rate of work performance.
6. Follows company procedures.
7. Maintains good attendance and punctuality.
8. Takes care of equipment and materials.
9. Maintains acceptable appearance.

B. Adaptability Measures

1. Obtains/returns materials for tasks.
2. Adjusts rate of performance according to job demands.
3. Works safely.
4. Follows a schedule.
5. Manages time appropriately.
6. Is able to adjust to changes in routine.
7. Solves work-related problems independently.

C. Social Skills Measures

1. Follows directions.
2. Accepts criticism.
3. Asks for assistance when necessary.
4. Gets along with fellow workers.
5. Interacts appropriately with customers.

From "Supported employment: Promoting employee independence" by F. R. Rusch and C. Hughes, 1988, *Mental Retardation, 26,* 351-355. Reprinted by permission.

(White & Rusch, 1983). Supported employees and co-workers evaluate performance significantly higher than work supervisors.

Second, work performance evaluations must be completed routinely. Typically, the employment specialist obtains performance evaluations from the work supervisor shortly after an employee begins work. These evaluations may be obtained as often as once a week during the first month, then once a month for the next five months, and at least twice a year thereafter (Rusch, 1986). Finally, once the evaluations are gathered, the work supervisor provides verbal feedback to the supported employee. The importance of the work supervisor completing and reporting the measures should not be underestimated. Research has shown that supported employees perform differently in the presence of employment specialists who have assumed these supervisory roles (Rusch, Menchetti, Crouch, Riva, Morgan, & Agran 1984). Because we are attempting to transfer responsibility for work performance to the employee and to natural support that exists in the workplace, we believe that significant others present in the work environment should be associated with positive and negative feedback.

Work performance evaluations provide information to employment specialists directly related to the extent to which supported employees are accepted in a new job. Although supported employees may fail to meet some acceptance criteria, employment specialists will be able to increase the likelihood of the employer, supervisor, and/or co-worker accepting the performance of the supported employee, even though the employee's performance may be different from the performance of co-workers.

Summary

Integrated employment is participation within a work environment by employees both with and without disabilities. Integration within a workplace is enhanced by managing significant others' social acceptance of supported employees' participation. Employment specialists manage social acceptance by: (a) utilizing social validation methodology, which is a major factor influencing the successful integration of a supported employee into the work environment; and (b) managing social acceptance across time.

GENERAL SUMMARY

In this chapter, we contend that supported employment placements are not "stagnant." Individuals continue to grow and change (adapt) when they are employed in integrated work environments. Accordingly, expectations for these individuals change across time, as responsibilities and opportunities increase. We propose a follow-up services model that takes into account changing expectations for supported employees. Our model incorporates the three complementary goals of (a) extending individual competence, (b) developing natural support in the workplace, and (c) promoting social acceptance. Each of these goals has corresponding objectives that guide the employment specialist in implementing post-placement support services (see Table 11.5). Extending individual competence requires that the employment specialist identify independence objectives for the supported employee in relation to the demands of the workplace and then teach independent performance. Developing natural support includes identifying natural support in the

Table 11.5 Goals and Objectives of Long-term Follow-up

1. Extend individual competence
    - Identify independence objectives for supported employee in relation to the demands of the workplace
    - Teach employee independence
2. Develop natural support in the workplace
    - Identify natural support in the workplace
        - Setting variables (clocks, schedules)
        - Co-workers
    - Match support to employee needs
3. Promote social acceptance
    - Utilize social validation methodology
    - Manage social acceptance across time

Table 11.6 Step-by-Step Implementation of Long-term Support

Step 1.	Identify independence objectives.
Step 2.	Extend individual competence.
Step 3.	Identify areas in which employee needs continued support.
Step 4.	Identify natural supports.
	- Use ecological inventory to identify setting variables.
	- Use *Co-worker Involvement Index* to identify available co-worker support.
Step 5.	Match support available to employee needs.

workplace and matching that support to identified employee needs. Promoting social acceptance requires utilizing social validation methodology and managing social acceptance across time.

We recommend expanding the role of job coach to that of an "employment specialist" who extends employee competence, rather than fosters dependence on externally-introduced assistance. Employment specialists enhance individual competence by coordinating their services with existing support within the workplace and by managing the social acceptance of significant others in relation to the supported employee. Furthermore, we hold that as employee competence continues to emerge, performance expectations for the employee must be managed across time. The actual steps the employment specialist follows in implementing long-term support are shown in Table 11.6.

Long-term employment is enhanced by our ability to adjust our own expectations for individuals with disabilities. Because we cannot predict the extent to which these individuals will change in relation to the demands of an integrated work environment, we must, accordingly, learn to become careful observers and managers. In order to achieve employment integration, we must learn to let the "unexpected" become the "expected." By promoting the acceptance of individual differences and maximizing individual competence, we can enhance the participation of employees with disabilities as equal members within an integrated workplace.

QUESTIONS (For answers see p. 431)

1. Name the three complementary post-placement goals of the follow-up services model. Explain each.

2. Previous models have seen the supported employee primarily as a recipient of services. How does the present model differ?

3. What is the role of the job coach in this model?

4. List four components of the procedures for teaching employee independence described by the authors.

5. Name the strategies that foster the long-term support employees need to remain employed.

6. Name five types of co-worker involvement listed by the authors.

7. Differences in co-worker involvement are related more to level of disability than type of placement. True or False?

8. To what does the term "support match" refer?

9. Of the three outcomes associated with supported employment (integration, wages, and ongoing support), which is the most distinguishing feature of supported employment?

10. Define employment integration and integrated workplace.

11. How can employment specialists promote social acceptance of supported employees?

12. To what does social validation refer?

13. How is social validation achieved?

14. List three considerations in the administration of work performance evaluations.

REFERENCES

Agran, M. & Martin, J. E. (1987). Applying a technology of self-control in community environments for individuals who are mentally retarded. In M. Hersen, R. Eisler, & P. Miller (Eds.), *Progress in behavior modification* (Vol. 14, pp. 108–151). Newbury Park, CA: Sage Publications.

Chadsey-Rusch, J. & Gonzalez, P. (1988). Social ecology of the workplace: Employers' perceptions versus observation. *Research in Developmental Disabilities, 9*, 229–245.

Chadsey-Rusch, J., Gonzalez, P., Tines, J., & Johnson, J. R. (1989). Social ecology of the workplace: An examination of contextual variables affecting the social interactions of employees with and without mental retardation. *American Journal on Mental Retardation, 94,* 141–151.

Connis, R. T. (1979). The effects of sequential pictorial cues, self-recording, and praise on the job task sequencing of retarded adults. *Journal of Applied Behavior Analysis, 12*, 355–361.

Crouch, K. P., Rusch, F. R., & Karlan, G. P. (1984). Competitive employment: Utilizing the correspondence training paradigm to enhance productivity. *Education and Training of the Mentally Retarded, 19*, 268–275.

Curl, R. M., McConaughy, E. K., Pawley, J. M., & Salzberg, C. L. (1987). *Put that person to work! A co-worker training manual for the co-worker transition model.* Logan, UT: Developmental Center for Handicapped Persons, Utah State University.

Curl, R. M., Pawley, J. M., DeFrancesco, D. P., & Salzberg, C. L. (1987). *Teaching co-workers to train new workers with developmental disabilities and mental retardation: Data from direct observation.* Unpublished raw data.

Curl, R. M. & Rule, S. (1987). *A demonstration project for teaching entry-level job skills to youths with mild and moderate handicaps by employing co-workers as trainers.* (Grant No. H078C80034-89). Washington, DC: U. S. Department of Education.

Ford, L., Dineen, J., & Hall, J. (1984). Is there life after placement? *Education and Training of the Mentally Retarded, 19*, 291–296.

French, W. & Bell, C. (1984). *Organizational development: Behavioral science interventions for organizational improvement.* Englewood Cliffs, NJ: Prentice-Hall.

Gold, M. W. (1975). Vocational training. In J. Wortis (Ed.), *Mental retardation and developmental disabilities: An annual review* (Vol. 7, pp. 254–264). New York: Brunner/Mazel.

Hanley-Maxwell, C., Rusch, F. R., & Rappaport, J. (1989). A multi-level perspective on community employment problems for adults with mental retardation. *Rehabilitation Counseling Bulletin, 32*, 266–280.

Haught, P., Walls, R. T., & Crist, K. (1984). Placement of prompts, length of task, and level of retardation in learning complex assembly tasks. *American Journal of Mental Deficiency, 89*, 60–66.

Hill, M. & Wehman, P. (1979). Employer and nonhandicapped co-worker perceptions of moderately and severely retarded workers. *Journal of Contemporary Business, 8*, 107–112.

Kazdin, A. (1977). Assessing the clinical or applied importance of behavior change through social validation. *Behavior Modification, 1*, 427–437.

Kazdin, A. & Matson, J. (1981). Social validation in mental retardation. *Applied Research in Mental Retardation*, 2, 39–54.

Kochany, L., Simpson, T., Hill, J., & Wehman, P. (1982). Reducing noncompliance and inappropriate verbal behavior in a moderately retarded food service worker: Use of a systematic fading procedure. In P. Wehman & M. Hill (Eds.), *Vocational training and job placement of severely disabled persons* (pp. 128–139). Richmond: Virginia Commonwealth University, School of Education.

Lagomarcino, T. R., Hughes, C., & Rusch, F. R. (1989). Utilizing self-management to teach independence on the job. *Education and Training in Mental Retardation, 24*, 139–148.

Likins, M., Salzberg, C. L., Stowitschek, J. J., Lignugaris/Kraft, B., & Curl, R. (1989). *Co-worker implemented job training: The use of coincidental training and quality-control checking procedures on the food preparation skills of employees with mental retardation.* Manuscript submitted for publication.

Lippitt, G. & Lippitt, R. (1984). The consulting function of the human resource development professional. In N. Nadler (Ed.), *Handbook of human resource development* (5.1–5.16). New York: John Wiley & Sons.

Martin, J. (1986). Identifying potential jobs. In F. R. Rusch (Ed.), *Competitive employment issues and strategies* (pp. 165–185). Baltimore: Paul H. Brookes.

Menchetti, B. M., Rusch, F. R., & Lamson, D. S. (1981). Social validation of behavioral training techniques: Assessing the normalizing qualities of competitive employment training procedures. *Journal of the Association for the Severely Handicapped, 6*, 6–16.

Mithaug, D. E., Martin, J. E., Husch, J. V., Agran, M., & Rusch, F. R. (1988). *When will persons in supported employment need less support?* Colorado Springs, CO: Ascent Publications.

Nisbet, J. & Hagner, D. (1988). Natural supports in the workplace: A reexamination of supported employment. *Journal of the Association for Persons with Severe Handicaps, 13*, 260–267.

Rappaport, J. (1981). In praise of paradox: A social policy of empowerment over prevention. *American Journal of Community Psychology, 9*, 1–25.

Rusch, F. R. (1986). Developing a long-term follow-up program. In F. R. Rusch (Ed.), *Competitive employment issues and strategies* (pp. 225–232). Baltimore: Paul H. Brookes.

Rusch, F. R., Chadsey-Rusch, J., & Lagomarcino, T. (1987). Preparing students for employment. In M. E. Snell (Ed.), *Systematic instruction for persons with severe handicaps* (3rd ed.) (pp. 471–490). Columbus, OH: Charles E. Merrill.

Rusch, F. R., Chadsey-Rusch, J., White, D. M., & Gifford, J. L. (1985). Programs for severely mentally retarded adults: Perspectives and methodologies. In D. Bricker & J. Filler (Eds.), *Severe mental retardation: From theory to practice* (pp. 119–140). Reston, VA: Council for Exceptional Children.

Rusch, F. R. & Hughes, C. (1988). Supported employment: Promoting employee independence. *Mental Retardation, 26*, 351–355.

Rusch, F. R., Hughes, C., Johnson, J. R., & Minch, K. E. (1988). *A descriptive analysis of co-worker involvement in supported employment.* Manuscript submitted for publication.

Rusch, F. R., Hughes, C., McNair, J., & Wilson, P. G. (1989). *Co-worker involvement scoring manual and instrument.* Champaign: University of Illinois, The Board of Trustees of the University of Illinois.

Rusch, F. R., Johnson, J. R., & Hughes, C. (in press). Analysis of co-worker involvement in relation to level of disability versus placement approach among supported employees. *Journal of the Association for Persons with Severe Handicaps.*

Rusch, F. R. & Kazdin, A. E. (1981). Toward a methodology of withdrawal designs for the assessment of response maintenance. *Journal of Applied Behavior Analysis, 14*, 131–140.

Rusch, F. R., Martin, J. E., & White, D. M. (1985). Competitive employment: Teaching mentally retarded employees to maintain their work behavior. *Education and Training of the Mentally Retarded, 20*, 182–189.

Rusch, F. R., McKee, M., Chadsey-Rusch, J., & Renzaglia, A. (1988). Teaching a student with severe handicaps to self-instruct: A brief report. *Education and Training in Mental Retardation, 23*, 51–58.

Rusch, F. R. & Menchetti, B. M. (1981). Increasing compliant work behaviors in a non-sheltered work setting. *Mental Retardation, 19*, 107–111.

Rusch, F. R., Menchetti, B. M., Crouch, K., Riva, M., Morgan, T., & Agran, M. (1984). Competitive employment: Assessing employee reactivity to naturalistic observation. *Applied Research in Mental Retardation, 5*, 339–351.

Rusch, F. R. & Minch, K. E. (1988). Identification of co-worker involvement in supported employment: A review and analysis. *Research in Developmental Disabilities, 9*, 247–254.

Rusch, F. R., Minch, K. E., & Hughes, C. (in press). Evaluation of the role of job site supervisors in the supervision of employees with severe disabilities. *The Journal for Vocational Special Needs Education.*

Rusch, F. R. & Mithaug, D. E. (1980). *Vocational*

training for mentally retarded adults: A behavior analytic approach. Champaign, IL: Research Press.

Rusch, F. R. & Mithaug, D. E. (1985). Competitive employment education: A systems-analytic approach to transitional programming for the student with severe handicaps. In K. C. Lakin & R. M. Bruininks (Eds.), *Strategies for achieving community integration of developmentally disabled citizens* (pp. 177–192). Baltimore: Paul H. Brookes.

Rusch, F. R., Morgan, T. K., Martin, J. E., Riva, M., & Agran, M. (1985). Competitive employment: Teaching mentally retarded employees self-instructional strategies. *Applied Research in Mental Retardation*, 6, 389–407.

Rusch, F. R., Weithers, J. A., Menchetti, B. M., & Schutz, R. P. (1980). Social validation of a program to reduce topic repetition in a non-sheltered setting. *Education and Training of the Mentally Retarded, 15*, 208–215.

Schutz, R. P., Jostes, K. F., Rusch, F. R., & Lamson, D. S. (1980). Acquisition, transfer, and social validation of two vocational skills in a competitive employment setting. *Education and Training of the Mentally Retarded, 15*, 306–311.

Schutz, R. P., Rusch, F. R., & Lamson, D. S. (1979). Evaluation of an employer's procedure to eliminate unacceptable behavior on the job. *Community Services Forum, 1*, 4–5.

Shafer, M. S. (1986). Utilizing co-workers as change agents. In F. R. Rusch (Ed.), *Competitive employment issues and strategies* (pp. 215–224). Baltimore: Paul H. Brookes.

Sowers, J., Rusch, F. R., Connis, R. T., & Cummings, L. E. (1980). Teaching mentally retarded adults to time manage in a vocational setting. *Journal of Applied Behavior Analysis, 13*, 119–128.

Stanford, K. & Wehman, P. (1982). Improving social interactions between moderately retarded and nonretarded coworkers: A pilot study. In P. Wehman & M. Hill (Eds.), *Vocational training and job placement of severely disabled persons* (pp. 141–159). Richmond: Virginia Commonwealth University, School of Education.

Stokes, T. F. & Baer, D. M. (1977). An implicit technology of generalization. *Journal of Applied Behavior Analysis, 10*, 349–368.

VanHouten, R. (1979). Social validation: The evolution of standards of competency for target behaviors. *Journal of Applied Behavior Analysis, 12*, 581–592.

Walls, R. T., Zane, T., & Thvedt, J. E. (1980). Trainers' personal methods compared to two structured training strategies. *American Journal of Mental Deficiency, 84*, 495–507.

Wehman, P., Hill, J. W., Wood, W., & Parent, W. (1987). A report on competitive employment: Histories of persons labeled severely mentally retarded. *The Journal of the Association for the Severely Handicapped, 7*, 11–17.

White, D. M. (1986). Social validation. In F. R. Rusch (Ed.), *Competitive employment issues and strategies* (pp. 199–213). Baltimore: Paul H. Brookes.

White, D. M. & Rusch, F. R. (1983). Social validation in competitive employment: Evaluating work performance. *Applied Research in Mental Retardation, 4*, 343–354.

Winking, D. L., DeStefano, L., & Rusch, F. R. (1988). *Supported employment in Illinois: Job coach issues.* Champaign: University of Illinois, The Board of Trustees of the University of Illinois.

Wolf, M. M. (1978). Social validity: The case for subjective measurement or how applied behavior analysis is finding its heart. *Journal of Applied Behavior Analysis*, 11, 203–214.

CHAPTER

12

Transdisciplinary Service Delivery

Edna Mora Szymanski
University of Wisconsin–Madison
Cheryl Hanley-Maxwell
Southern Illinois University
Randall M. Parker
The University of Texas at Austin

Assisting people with severe disabilities to obtain and maintain competitive employment requires the integration of information from a variety of sources and the collaboration of a number of disciplines. In this chapter, we introduce a framework to assist professionals in understanding the complex processes involved in enabling competitive employment and promoting independence of supported employees. The focus of this chapter is on the coordinated planning and service delivery of professionals, caregivers, and supported employees. (Kiernan and Schalock address similar issues from a systems perspective in Chapter 15.)

The framework introduced in this chapter has two major components: transdisciplinary collaboration and an ecological approach. This framework is designed to assist practitioners and educators in special education, rehabilitation counseling, and related fields in understanding the complexities of preparing people with severe disabilities for employment. This framework is presented through the following topics: (a) background and rationale for a transdisciplinary, ecological framework; (b) transdisciplinary service delivery; (c) ecological framework for habilitation and rehabilitation; and (d) transdisciplinary, ecological planning and service delivery.

BACKGROUND AND RATIONALE

Habilitation, rehabilitation, and special education services for persons with severe disabilities have changed dramatically in the last decade, posing new challenges for professionals and university-based preservice educators (Renzaglia, 1986; Renzaglia, Chapter 24 this volume). Changes in four major areas have contributed to the need for the integrative framework presented in this chapter. These areas are: (a) disability models, (b) service delivery philosophies, (c) service delivery strategies, and (d) service delivery environments.

Disability Models

Disability models influence the concept of disability and the nature of appropriate interventions. According to Hahn (1985), a shift in rehabilitation service delivery has begun and is the result of an evolution of disability models which may be described as

> A shift from a medical definition of disability, which focused on physical impairments, to an economic perspective which emphasized vocational limitations, and finally to a sociopolitical orientation which regards disability as the interaction between the individual and the environment. (pp. 53–54)

Similarly, Wright (1983) emphasized the importance of the professionals considering the environmental dimensions of disability. She indicated that such considerations are often obscured by a variety of factors including a psychological tendency to view problems as residing within the individual rather than the environment and the tendency of professionals to use labels (e.g., educational classifications, diagnoses) to "underscore personal attributes while ignoring environmental factors that contribute to the problem" (p. 73).

Philosophy of Service Delivery

Changes in models of disability and rehabilitation were accompanied by changes in the philosophies and ideologies of intervention. Normalization, civil rights, and consumerism have permanently changed the way habilitation, rehabilitation, and special education services are delivered (Heal, 1988; Szymanski, Rubin, & Rubin, 1988). Whereas the precursors of current special education and rehabilitation practices emphasized protecting people with disabilities from harm or protecting society from its members with significant differences, currently evolving practices emphasize the rights of such individuals and focus on enabling independence, self-determination, and productive participation in society (Bruininks & Lakin, 1985; Heal, Haney & Amado, 1988; Rubin & Roessler, 1987). Although professional wisdom once dictated segregated (protected) interventions, it is now understood that isolating people with disabilities from their nondisabled peers abrogates their acquisition of independence and productivity (Daniels, 1988). This philosophical shift is best reflected by the concluding phrase in the purpose of the Rehabilitation Act (Section 2) in the 1986 Amendments: "The purpose of this Act is to develop and implement . . . comprehensive and coordinated programs of vocational rehabilitation and independent living for individuals with handicaps in order to maximize their employability, independence, and integration into the workplace and the community" (Rehabilitation Act Amendments of 1986, Section 101).

Service Delivery Strategies

Improvements in service delivery strategies have accompanied changes in disability models and philosophies of intervention. Demonstration projects throughout the country have shown that persons previously considered unemployable can become valued employees of community businesses and industries (Bellamy, Rhodes, Mank, & Albin, 1988; Rusch, 1986; Wehman, 1986a). Concurrently, the prevailing "train and place" model characteristic of traditional sheltered workshops has been shown to be ineffective in promoting community integrated employment of persons with mental retardation (Bellamy, Rhodes, Bourbeau, & Mank, 1986). The training concepts underlying these traditional programs have also been questioned in light of research on generalization and maintenance of behavior (Rusch, Gifford, & Chadsey-Rusch, 1985; Szymanski, Hanley-Maxwell, Hansen, & Myers, 1988). Even in supported employment, the single-case task analytic models of recent years have been shown to mitigate against generalization and maintenance of work behavior (Wacker & Berg, 1986), and thus against the autonomy and adaptability of target employees (Rusch, et al., 1985).

Service Delivery Environments

Many of the recent improvements in service delivery reflect shifting service delivery paradigms (Szymanski, Rubin, & Rubin, 1988). Deficit-based and individual-centered services have given way to ecologically oriented approaches that take into consideration the environmental dimension of behavior and intervention (Chadsey-Rusch, 1985, 1986a,b; Hanley-Maxwell, 1986; Szymanski, Dunn, & Parker, 1989). Additionally, where most services were previously provided in a controlled environment (e.g., self-contained classroom or sheltered workshop), modern service delivery provides interventions in the multiple environments that constitute the total, integrated life space of the individual, such as a competitive workplace, public transportation, shopping mall, and a supervised living situation (Orelove & Sobsey, 1987; Rusch, 1986; Snell, 1987).

The increasing complexity of service delivery has been accompanied by increases in the number of agencies and professionals involved in individual service provision (see Kiernan & Schalock, Chapter 15, this volume). Because such complexity may confuse service providers, caregivers, and target employees alike, some of the major disciplines are described and a framework for integrating members from multiple disciplines into focused service delivery teams is presented in the next section.

TRANSDISCIPLINARY SERVICE DELIVERY

Although there are a variety of disciplines involved in the employment preparation of supported employees (Tooman, Revell, & Melia, 1980), it often appears that each discipline knows very little about the expertise and qualifications of the others (Johnson, Bruininks, & Thurlow, 1987). Lack of knowledge may lead to service gaps and overlaps, thus potentially contributing to role strain (Szymanski, Parker, Hanley-Maxwell, & Koch, in press). In an effort to ameliorate this situation, the President's Committee on Employment of Persons with Disabilities (PCEPD, 1988) has included an integrative literature review in the work plan of the employment preparation committee. It is essential that professionals, target employees, and their caregivers understand the roles, functions, and qualifications of the various professionals involved in service delivery. To assist in this understanding, the roles of the major disciplines involved in facilitating and enabling the employment and independence of target employees are described below.

REHABILITATION COUNSELING. The goal of rehabilitation counseling is to optimize the congruence between individuals and their chosen environments by environment-centered interventions (e.g., job modifications, job restructuring) and person-centered interventions (e.g., adaptation, compensation) (Szymanski, Dunn, & Parker, 1989). In community integrated employment services, rehabilitation counselors serve in a variety of roles, most often planning and coordinating the efforts of direct service providers (Szymanski & Parker, 1988).

Rehabilitation counselors work in a variety of settings, including state and federal vocational rehabilitation (VR) agencies, schools, rehabilitation facilities, and insurance companies. Their graduate training provides them with a sequence of courses including: (a) counseling; (b) case management; (c) medical aspects of disabilities and resultant functional limitations; (d) psychosocial aspects of disabilities; (e) vocational evaluation and career development; (f) rehabilitation planning; (g) job analysis, job modification, and job restructuring; and (h) job placement and follow-up (Council on Rehabilitation Education, 1983; Szymanski & King, 1989).

Although there is national certification of rehabilitation counselors (Commission on Rehabilitation Counselor Certification, 1986) and recent evidence of a positive relationship between rehabilitation counselor education and service outcomes for state VR clients with severe disabilities (Szymanski & Parker, 1989), many agencies and facilities still hire persons without preservice education into rehabilitation counseling positions (Hershenson, 1988; Kuehn, Crystal, & Ursprung, 1988). Thus, unlike the title of Special Education Teacher, the title of Rehabilitation Counselor does not yet mean that the bearer holds specific training and expertise. However, where such training is present, it is clear that rehabilitation counselors are unusually well suited for a major role in community integrated employment services for target employees.

SPECIAL EDUCATION. With the new emphasis on transition, special education has become specifically "an outcome-oriented process encompassing a broad array of services and experiences" intended to lead to employment upon school leaving (Will, 1986, p. 10) and to successful community living (Halpern, 1985). In community integrated employment it is critical that this process lay the foundation for adult life by teaching functional, community-based survival skills (Everson, Moon, & Williams, 1986; Wehman, 1986b; Will, 1986).

Special educators can be found in a variety of school and community settings. Although their roles vary depending on their work situation, their professional training backgrounds are remarkably similar. Before special education teachers can start their course sequence in foundations and general methods for special education, they must take foundation courses in general education. Completion of these courses allows entry into disability-specific teaching methods courses and student teaching (Ysseldyke & Algozzine, 1982). Certified teachers are expected to be competent in: (a) curriculum development, (b) basic skills instruction, (c) class management, (d) professional consultation and communication, (e) teacher-parent-student relationships, (f) student-student relationships, (g) exceptional conditions, (h) referral, (i) individualized teaching, and (j) professional values (Ysseldyke & Algozzine, 1982, p. 93).

Although many states require special training for teachers who work with students with disabilities, as reflected in special certification standards for special education teachers, few states require evidence of special preparation to teach secondary special education. In general, personnel preparation programs for special educators have focused primarily on kindergarten through sixth grade (Weisenstein, 1986). The obvious mismatch has resulted in secondary-level programs that look more like elementary school programs in curriculum content, location of instruction, and teaching techniques. Many students have not been taught the skills critical to survival in employment and in other adult arenas (Chadsey-Rusch, 1986b). However, educators who are appropriately prepared to provide instruction to secondary special education students can produce meaningful employment and community outcomes for their students by providing systematic training of vocational, domestic, leisure/recreation, and community skills in the natural settings of skill performance; evaluation input by assisting in the collection and interpretation of data; community/school education; and coordination of services while the student is in school (Everson, Moon, & Williams, 1986).

EMPLOYMENT SPECIALIST. Employment specialists provide direct job training services and related services to target employees in community work settings (Szymanski, Hanley-Maxwell, & Parker, 1988). They possess a wide range of academic and practical experiences (Siegel & Loman, 1987; Winking, DeStefano, & Rusch, 1988) resulting in the demonstration of different skills for different populations of target employees (Buckley, Mank, & Cioffi, 1988). Nonetheless, there is standardization of function, as suggested by the seven basic functions identified in a 1985 study by Harold Russell Associates: (1) providing on-the-job training, (2) analyzing job tasks, (3) providing supervision, (4) managing behavior, (5) advocating for integrated relations, (6) fading assistance, and (7) negotiating work related issues (McDaniel, 1986).

Research at the Rehabilitation Research and Training Center (RRTC) at Virginia Commonwealth University found employment specialists' roles to be similar to those identified by the Harold Russell Associates study 67.4 percent of the employment specialist's time is composed of on-the-job-site activities (orienting, assessing, training, collecting data, advocating, and fading); the remaining 32.6 percent of the time is spent in such off-site activities as screening and evaluation, program development, employment and nonemployment advocacy, consumer training, and traveling and transporting (Kregel, Hill, & Banks, 1988).

OTHER INVOLVED DISCIPLINES. Although the above disciplines are the major team members in community integrated employment services, there are a variety of other disciplines that may be involved. Such disciplines include, but are not limited to, vocational education, school counseling, orientation and mobility, psychology, medicine, nursing, occupational therapy, and rehabilitation engineering. Specific roles and involvement depend on individual needs of target employees, agency configurations, and environmental requirements. Whatever disciplines are included, it is clear that coordination of planning and activities is a major ingredient of service delivery.

A Transdisciplinary Framework

For many years, the multidisciplinary and interdisciplinary team models were the major methods of service delivery coordination. In recent years, these models have been recognized as impeding assessment and intervention in natural environments; for example, physical therapy (PT) was done in the PT room and unrelated to classroom or work activities. The transdisciplinary model (see Figure 12.1) has emerged as a partial solution to the need to provide coordinated services in the natural environment (Orelove & Sobsey, 1987).

The transdisciplinary model has the following characteristics: (a) assessment and service delivery in natural environments; (b) "sharing, or transferring, of information and skills across traditional disciplinary boundaries"; and (c) indirect service delivery, "whereby one or two persons are primary facilitators of services and other team members act as consultants" (Orelove & Sobsey, 1987, p. 9).

Tooman, Revell, and Melia (1988) observed that role changes of service providers are inevitable correlates of community integrated employment services. Throughout the employment preparation of targeted individuals, direct service leadership may shift from the special education teacher to the rehabilitation counselor and the employment specialist. Clearly, the transdisciplinary concept allows for such shifts while promoting the consultative involvement of those disciplines not in a direct service role at any specific time. Thus, the special education teacher involved in employment preparation is enriched by the coordination skills and labor market knowledge of the rehabilitation counselor and the job training skills of the employment specialist. Conversely, the employment specialist's skills are bolstered by specific training strategies of the special education teacher and the counseling and coordination skills of the rehabilitation counselor.

In summary, "coordination of these [professional roles] into a focused effort understood by the service consumer [target employee] and valued by the employer is central to a successful program" (Tooman, Revell, & Melia, 1988, p. 91). It appears that the transdisciplinary model offers the flexibility necessary to transcend disciplinary boundaries and focuses the skills of multiple professionals on job skill training and employment-related services for target employees in multiple natural environments (e.g., work setting, bus, home).

An Ecological Framework for Habilitation and Rehabilitation

After reviewing a wide range of special education and rehabilitation literature, Szymanski, Dunn, and Parker (1989) described an ecological framework for rehabilitation of persons with learning disabilities that was designed to be applicable to a wide range of disability groups. The major tenets and dimensions of this model follow.

1. Each individual is a part of many different but interrelated ecosystems, such as home, work, and school (Wallace & Larsen, 1978).
2. Environmental factors influence individual behaviors (Cummins, 1984; Wacker & Berg, 1986; Wallace & Larsen, 1978; Wright, 1983).
3. Individual characteristics influence environmental factors (Cook, 1987; Wallace & Larsen, 1978).
4. The interactions between individuals and their environments are determined not only by present environments, but also by past experiences and interactions (D'Alonzo, Arnold, & Yuen, 1986; Turner, 1987).
5. Individuals differ in their perceptions of similar situations (Hoffman et al., 1987; Wright, 1983).
6. Individual ecosystems are dynamic. Individual actions or factors cannot be considered in isolation, without reference to the sur-

FIGURE 12.1 Transdisciplinary employment service delivery

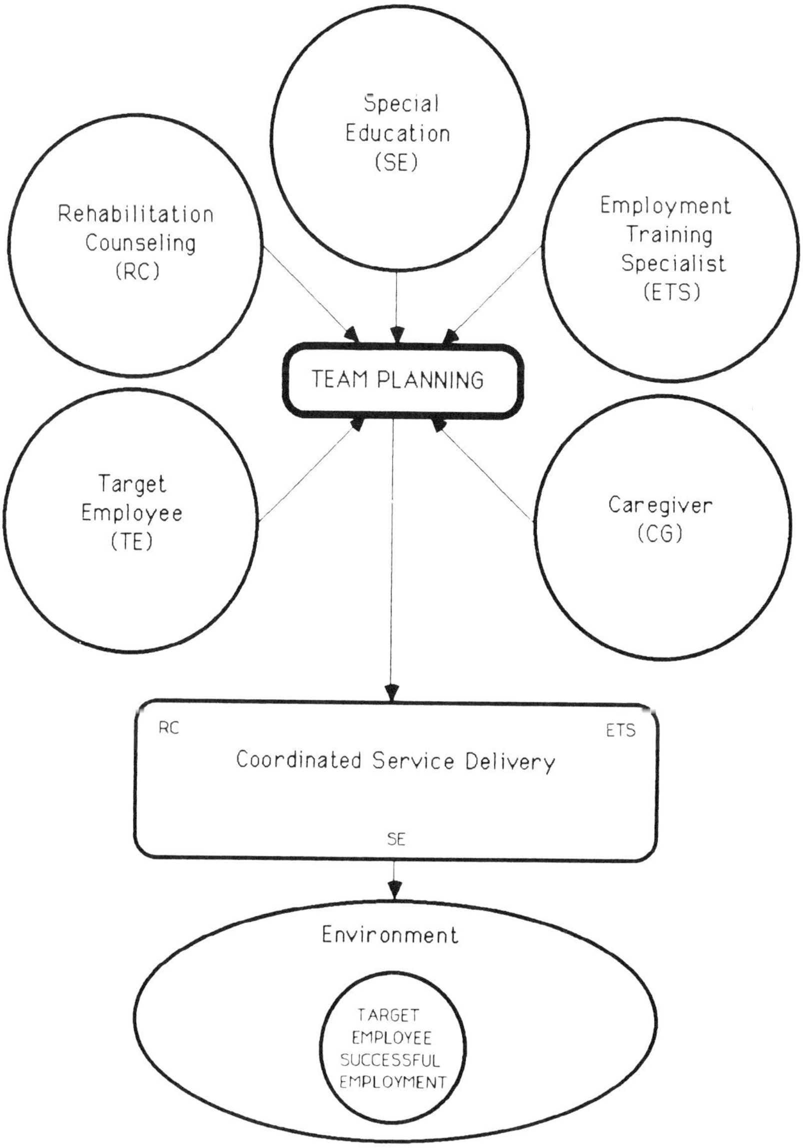

rounding actions or factors (Shonkoff, 1983; Snell & Grigg, 1987).

7. Assessments are rarely neutral in value and may have detrimental effects on clients (Amado, 1988; Pancsofar, 1986; Shonkoff, 1983).

The fundamental tenets of the ecological framework form the philosophical foundation for all assessments and interventions. They are applied to rehabilitation and habilitation planning through the following dimensions: (a) individual attributes; (b) environmental attributes; (c) nature, quality, and sequence of interactions; and (d) perceptions of involved individuals. The dimensions of the framework form the basis of habilitation and rehabilitation planning by providing dimensions along which information is integrated and planned activities are focused.

TRANSDISCIPLINARY ECOLOGICAL PLANNING FOR SERVICE DELIVERY

The dimensions and tenets of the ecological model form the background for the framework introduced in Table 12.1 to assist target employees, their families, and professionals to integrate the diverse sources of information necessary to plan effective habilitation and rehabilitation services. The framework can be used to design rehabilitation plans that utilize a variety of desired activities, desired environments, and success criteria.

Furthermore, Table 12.1 highlights the importance of considering the many facets of individual interaction with the environment and the discrepancies between current behaviors and desired outcomes. The framework, and the interactions described therein, may be used to specify the desired activity in the desired environment and to interpret the effect of current and past interactions on observed behaviors.

A critical feature of the planning framework is that the perceptions of all involved individuals are considered in each goal area, thus identifying perceptual discrepancies that need to be addressed. Table 12.2 illustrates some perceptual discrepancies regarding goal characteristics that are relatively common among target employees, their families, and professionals (Hoffman et al., 1987). In considering physical disabilities, Wright (1983) attributed part of the perceptual discrepancy to the different frames of reference of the target employee (insider) and others (outsider). It is suspected that Wright's observations are as valid for persons with cognitive limitations as they are for those with physical limitations. Nonetheless, this aspect of discrepancy is often not considered in habilitation, rehabilitation, or educational planning, and professionals are often surprised that the target employee had in mind a different goal activity, desired environment, or success criteria than did the professionals.

Perceptual discrepancies among the target employee, family, and professionals are further complicated by potential philosophical differences among the involved professionals (see Table 12.2), which could easily result from the rapid shifts in service delivery philosophies described earlier in this chapter. Nonetheless, clarification of professional frames of reference and perceptions appears to be rare. Many professionals may not recognize that such discrepancies exist and thus fail to clarify the perceptions and expectations of other team members. A frequent result is the failure of coordinated service delivery, and, unfortunately too often, the target employee rather than the professionals are blamed for the failure (Szymanski, Hanley-Maxwell, & Parker, 1988).

Once a number of alternative goal possibilities are identified and their characteristics clarified among all parties, the second part of the framework allows for examination of discrepancies between the target employee's current skills and resources and those required by particular desired jobs in specific environments. This process can be accomplished systematically for each major goal; an example is provided in Table 12.3 for one goal. Once discrepancies are listed, their magnitude is evaluated by considering the following questions:

1. Can the job be modified or restructured, for example, through assistive devices, changes in task sequence, or insertion of additional steps (Bellamy, Horner, & Inman, 1979; Hanley-Maxwell, Rusch, & Rappaport, 1989)?
2. Can the job be shared by two individuals with complementary abilities (Hanley-Maxwell et al., 1989)?
3. Can person-job congruence be enhanced, for example, through cue highlighting or mediation, verbal or pictorial (Wacker & Berg, 1986)?

Such information enables target employees and professionals to rank various goals in terms of magnitude of effort required for attainment. A discrepancy analysis is illustrated in Table 12.4.

The information identified in Table 12.1 provides the foundation for the integrated planning framework proposed in Table 12.5, which is a planning format in which the enabling activities and responsibilities are specified for the professionals, target employee, and caregiver(s) for each mutually agreed-upon-goal. Such specification is provided for each activity that assists the target employee to attain the specified goal.

Table 12.1 Ecological Assessment

Goal Dimension/Perceiver	Perception
Desired Activity[a]	
Target employee	
Family	
Professional 1	
Professional 2	
Professional 3	
Desired Environment[a] **(for specified activity, including required work-related and social interactions)**	
Target employee	
Family	
Professional 1	
Professional 2	
Professional 3	
Success Criteria (for desired activity in desired environment)	
Target employee	
Family	
Professional 1	
Professional 2	
Professional 3	
Environmental Barriers (for desired activity in desired environment)	
Target employee	
Family	
Professional 1	
Professional 2	
Professional 3	
Current Skills and Behavior (related to desired activity and environment)	
Target employee	
Family	
Professional 1	
Professional 2	
Professional 3	

Table 12.1 (cont.)

Discrepancies[b] Between Current Situation and Desired Situation
Target employee
Family
Professional 1
Professional 2
Professional 3

Adapted from Rehabilitation counseling with persons with learning disabilities: An ecological framework by E. M. Szymanski, C. Dunn, and R. M. Parker (1989). *Rehabilitation Counseling Bulletin.*
[a]Multiple activities and related environments can be considered and compared for relative discrepancies.
[b]Once discrepancies have surfaced, each is examined for potential of environmental modification (e.g., job modification, job restructuring) and individual adaptation (e.g., learning new skills, compensation).

Planning for target employee independence must also be considered an integral part of each activity. Lead professionals should consider this aspect when identifying activities and success criteria. Table 12.5 includes independence by specifying space for the identification of independence criteria.

The activities of Table 12.5 should be as specific as possible in order to guide coordinated service delivery. For overall coordination and management purposes, such information can easily be summarized in a management matrix as discussed by Schalock and Kiernan (see Chapter 15 of this volume). To enhance communication and coordinated service delivery, a written copy of the plan for each individual involved in planning, including the target employee and caregiver is provided. (Szymanski, Hanley-Maxwell, & Parker, 1988). In addition, when the target employee's and caregiver's responsibilities in each activity are fully explained, the written plan can foster a sense of partnership in the planning and implementation process.

SUMMARY

This chapter introduced a transdisciplinary framework intended to assist professionals in conceptualizing the complex processes necessary to facilitate the competitive employment and independence of target employees. The model not only promotes coordinated planning and service delivery by professionals, caregivers, and target employees, it also fosters the provision of coordinated services in the natural environment.

The ecological approach, which considers the environmental dimension of behavior, may be used to design interventions that optimize the congruence between supported employees and their chosen environments. The major contribution of this chapter, then, is the coordinated presentation of a transdisciplinary and ecological approach to habilitation and rehabilitation. The tabular material presented herein may be used by rehabilitation professionals as a guide in planning the activities and behaviors within the desired environment that will maximize the target employee's probability of achieving the desired outcome.

Professionals must provide effective, coordinated planning. The ecological, transdisciplinary model provides one vehicle to achieve this end. The ultimate result will be improved outcomes for target employees.

QUESTIONS (For answers see pp. 431–432)

1. Changes in what areas have contributed to the need for a transdisciplinary ecological framework?

Table 12.2 Ecological Assessment

Goal Dimension/Perceiver	Perception
Desired Activity	
Target employee	Helping in a restaurant kitchen
Family	A food service job
Professional 1	A food service job
Professional 2	Any job
Professional 3	Sheltered employment
Desired Environment (for specified activity, including required work-related and social interactions)	
Target employee	Any Burger (a local fast food chain) [interactions with boss]
Family	A restaurant close to home [interactions with boss]
Professional 1	A restaurant with a slow work pace [interactions with supervisors and co-workers]
Professional 2	Any safe structured work environment [interactions with benevolent co-workers and supervisors]
Professional 3	ABC sheltered workshop [interactions only with people with disability and paid staff]
Success Criteria (for desired activity in desired environment)	
Target employee	Wearing a uniform
Family	Being on time for work every day
Professional 1	Meeting employers' standards for work speed and quality
Professional 2	Being in some program every day
Professional 3	Attending ABC sheltered workshop every day

Table 12.3 Ecological Assessment—Discrepancy Analysis

Goal Dimension/Perceiver	Perception
Agreed upon desired activity	Working as a janitor
Agreed upon desired environment	XYZ bank building
Agreed upon success criteria	Meet quality and quantity standards of employer with respect to work performance and work behavior (exact details known to all parties)

Table 12.3 (cont.)

Goal Dimension/Perceiver	Perception
Environmental Barriers (for desired activity in desired environment)	
Target employee	Doesn't see any problems
Family	Transportation to and from work
Professional 1[a]	Must use elevator between floors (number recognition); vending machines used for food and beverage at break time
Professional 2	Mirrors are too high to reach for cleaning; only three of seven light switches are to be turned off after finishing cleaning a floor; soap dishes are to be kept full (how to judge when to refill)
Professional 3	Cleaning supplies must be replenished from large supply room
Current Skills and Behavior (related to desired activity and environment)	
Target employee	Loves to work
Family	Persistent in finishing tasks
Professional 1	Good work quality in janitorial work trail
Professional 2	Persistent in structured janitorial work situations
Professional 3	Accepts supervision reasonably well
Discrepancies Between Current Situation and Desired Situation	
Target employee	Doesn't see any
Family	Transportation availability
Professional 1	Number recognition for elevator use; coin recognition and use for vending machines
Professional 2	Reaching mirror; turning off only the correct three light switches; being sure soap dishes are full (judgment task)
Professional 3	Recognizing which cleaning supplies are replenished from which container

[a]Table 12.3 represents a different group of involved professionals than those in Table 12.2. In Table 12.3, all professionals are actively working towards a specific supported employment goal. This group might include the rehabilitation counselor, the employment training specialist, and the special education teacher.

2. How is disability currently conceptualized?

3. Name three influences on the change in the philosophy and ideology of intervention in habilitation and rehabilitation.

4. What is the prevailing belief in regard to the utility of the "train and place" approach to promoting integrated employment of persons with mental retardation?

5. What have deficit-based and individual-centered services given way to? Describe.

6. What do the authors suggest the role of special education has become since the new emphasis on transition has emerged?

Table 12.4 Discrepancy Analysis—Resolution

Discrepancy	Possible Resolution(s)
Transportation availability	Travel training; taxi; arrangement with co-worker
Number recognition for elevator use	Using a chart to match floor destination with elevator panel (pictorial mediation)
Coin recognition for use in vending machines	Work with family to use different change wallets, each with a picture of the desired item (e.g., soda, ice cream) and containing correct change (pictorial mediation) until exact change amounts are learned.
Reaching mirror	Carry lightweight non-slip stool on cleaning cart (compensation strategy)
Turning off only the correct three (of seven) light switches	Put colored tape under those light switches to be turned off (cue highlighting)
Being sure soap dishes are full	Insert marker inside soap dishes at minimum level which constitutes "full." Teach target employee to fill soap dishes until marker doesn't show (cue highlighting and inserting extra job step to teach difficult task).
Recognizing which cleaning supplies are replenished from which container	Take label from used large container used for replenishing and place on smaller container used in daily cleaning. Teach target employee to match labels to replenish (pictorial mediation, cue highlighting)

Table 12.5 Habilitation /Rehabilitation Planning Guide

Mutually Agreed Goal

Desired acitivity (including required behaviors and interactions)

Desired environment

Success criteria (for desired activity in desired environment)

Independence criteria

Enabling Activities and Responsibilities

Activity 1 (include related environment)

Target employee

Family

Professional 1/Role (lead or support)[a]

Professional 2/Role

Table 12.5 (cont.)

Professional 3/Role
Activity 2 (include related environment)
Target employee
Family
Professional 1/Role (lead or support)[a]
Professional 2/Role
Professional 3/Role

Adapted from *Rehabilitation counseling with persons with learning disabilities: An ecological framework* by E. M. Szymanski, C. Dunn & R. M. Parker (1989). *Rehabilitation Counseling Bulletin.*
[a]Roles of professionals as lead and support will be likely to vary across activities and over time.

7. Why has special education had trouble fulfilling its role?

8. What seven basic functions for employment specialists have been identified?

9. Identify the characteristics of the transdisciplinary model?

10. List the fundamental tenets of the ecological framework.

11. Name the two phases of implementing the transdisciplinary framework.

REFERENCES

Amado, A. N. (1988). A perspective on the present and notes for new directions. In L. W. Heal, J. I. Haney, & A. R. N. Amado (Eds.), *Integration of developmentally disabled individuals into the community* (2nd ed. pp. 299–305). Baltimore: Paul H. Brookes.

Bellamy, G. T., Horner, R. H., & Inman, D. P. (1979). *Vocational habilitation of severely retarded adults: A direct service technology*. Austin, TX: Pro-Ed.

Bellamy, G. T., Rhodes L. E., Bourbeau P. E., & Mank, D. M. (1986). Mental retardation services in sheltered workshops and day activity programs: Consumer benefits and policy alternatives. In F. R. Rusch (Ed.), *Competitive employment issues and strategies* (pp. 257–271). Baltimore: Paul H. Brookes.

Bellamy, G. T., Rhodes, L. E., Mank, D. M., & Albin, J. M. (1988). *Supported employment: A community implementation guide*. Baltimore: Paul H. Brookes.

Bruininks, R. H. & Lakin, K. C. (Eds.) (1985). *Living and learning in the least restrictive environment.* Baltimore: Paul H. Brookes.

Buckley, J. Mank, D. M., & Cioffi, A. R. (1988, May). *Supported employment for individuals with "other" disabilities.* Panel presentation at the Supported Employment Forum at the annual meeting of the President's Committee for Employment of People with Disabilities, Washington, DC.

Chadsey-Rusch, J. G. (1985). Community integration and mental retardation: The ecobehavioral approach to service provision and assessment. In R. H. Bruininks & K. C. Lakin (Eds.), *Living and learning in the least restrictive environment* (pp. 245–260). Baltimore: Paul H. Brookes.

Chadsey-Rusch, J. (1986a). Identifying and teaching valued social behaviors. In F. R. Rusch (Ed.), *Competitive employment issues and strategies* (pp. 273–287). Baltimore: Paul H. Brookes.

Chadsey-Rusch, J. (1986b). Roles and responsibilities in the transition process: Concluding thoughts. In J. Chadsey-Rusch & C. Hanley-Maxwell (Eds.), *Enhancing transition from school to the work place for handicapped youth: Issues in personnel preparation* (pp. 221–235). Urbana. University of Illinois, College of Education, Office of Career Development for Special Populations.

Commission on Rehabilitation Counselor Certification (1986). *Guide to rehabilitation counselor certification*. Arlington Heights, IL: Author.

Cook, D. (1987). Psychosocial impact of disability. In R. Parker (Ed). *Rehabilitation counseling: Basics and beyond* (pp. 97–120). Austin, TX: Pro-Ed.

Council on Rehabilitation Education. (1983). *Accreditation manual for rehabilitation counselor education programs*. Chicago: Author.

Cummins, J. (1984). *Bilingualism and special education: Issues in assessment and pedagogy*. Clevedon, England: Multilingual Matters.

D'Alonzo, B. J., Arnold, B. J., & Yuen, P. C. (1986). Teaching adolescents with learning and behavioral differences. In L. F. Masters & A. A. Mori (Eds.), *Teaching secondary students with mild learning and behavior problems* (pp. 1–12). Rockville, MD: Aspen.

Daniels, S. (1988, November). *Rehabilitation manpower development and training*. Paper presented at Orientation to Rehabilitation, a regional training meeting sponsored by the Rehabilitation Services Administration, Dallas, TX.

Everson, J. M., Moon, M. S., & Williams, D. (1986). Transition services for young adults with severe disabilities: Professional roles and implications for inservice training. In J. Chadsey-Rusch & C. Hanley-Maxwell (Eds.), *Enhancing transition from school to the work place for handicapped youth: Issues in personnel preparation* (pp. 175–192). Urbana: University of Illinois, College of Education, Office of Career Development for Special Populations.

Hahn, H. (1985). Changing perception of disability and the future of rehabilitation. In L. G. Perlman & G. F. Austin (Eds.), *Social influences in rehabilitation planning: Blueprint for the 21st century*, (pp. 53–64). A report of the Ninth Mary E. Switzer Memorial Seminar. Alexandria, VA: National Rehabilitation Association.

Halpern, A. S. (1985). Transition: A look at the foundations. *Exceptional Children, 51*, 479–486.

Hanley-Maxwell, C. (1986). Curriculum development. In F. R. Rusch (Ed.), *Competitive employment issues and strategies* (pp. 187–197). Baltimore: Paul H. Brookes.

Hanley-Maxwell, C., Rusch, F. R., & Rappaport, J. (1989). A multi-level perspective of community employment problems for adults with mental retardation. *Rehabilitation Counseling Bulletin, 32*, 266–280.

Heal, L. W. (1988). The ideological responses of society to its handicapped members. In L. W. Heal, J. I. Haney, & A. R. N. Amado (Eds.), *Integration of developmentally disabled individuals into the community* (2nd ed. pp. 59–68). Baltimore: Paul H. Brookes.

Heal, L. W., Haney, J. I., & Amado, A. R. N. (Eds.) (1988). *Integration of developmentally disabled individuals into the community* (2nd ed.). Baltimore: Paul H. Brookes.

Hershenson, D. B. (1988). Along for the ride: The evolution of rehabilitation education. *Rehabilitation Counseling Bulletin, 31*, 204–217.

Hoffmann, F. J., Sheldon, K. L., Minskoff, E. A., Sautter, S. W., Steidle, E. F., Baker, D. P., Bailey, M. B., & Echols, L. D. (1987). Needs of learning disabled adults. *Journal of Learning Disabilities, 20*, 43–52.

Johnson, D. R., Bruininks, R. H., & Thurlow, M. L. (1987). Meeting the challenge of transition service planning through improved interagency cooperation. *Exceptional Children, 53*, 522–530.

Kregel, J., Hill, M., & Banks, P. D. (1988). Analysis of employment specialist intervention time in supported competitive employment. *American Journal of Mental Retardation, 93*, (200–208).

Kuehn, M. D., Crystal, R. M., & Ursprung, A. (1988). Challenges for rehabilitation counselor education. In S. E. Rubin & N. M. Rubin (Eds.), *Contemporary challenges to the rehabilitation counseling profession* (pp. 273–302). Baltimore: Paul H. Brookes.

McDaniel, R. (1986). Preservice implications for delivering effective transitional services in vocational rehabilitation. In J. Chadsey-Rusch & C. Hanley-Maxwell (Eds.), *Enhancing transition from school to the work place for handicapped youth: Issues in personnel preparation* (pp. 193–211). Urbana: University of Illinois, College of Education, Office of Career Development for Special Populations.

Orelove, F. P. & Sobsey, D. (1987). *Educating children with multiple disabilities: A transdisciplinary approach*. Baltimore, MD: Paul H. Brookes.

Pancsofar, E. L. (1986). Assessing work behavior. In F. R. Rusch (Ed.), *Competitive employment issues and strategies* (pp. 93–102). Baltimore: Paul H. Brookes.

President's Committee for Employment of Persons with Disabilities (1988). Employment Preparation Committee: 1989 Work Plan. Washington, DC: Author.

Rehabilitation Act Amendments of 1986, 29 U.S.C. 701.

Renzaglia, A. (1986). Preparing personnel to support and guide the emerging contemporary service alternatives. In F. R. Rusch (Ed.), *Competitive employment issues and strategies* (pp. 303–316). Baltimore: Paul H. Brookes.

Rubin, S. E. & Roessler, R. T. (1987). *Foundations of the vocational rehabilitation process* (3rd ed.). Austin, TX: Pro-Ed.

Rusch, F. (Ed.). (1986). *Competitive employment issues and strategies*. Baltimore: Paul H. Brookes.

Rusch, F. R., Gifford, J. L., & Chadsey-Rusch, J. (1985). Behavioral training strategies and applied research in competitive employment. In S. Moon, P. Goodall, & P. Wehman (Eds.), *Critical issues related to supported competitive employment: Proceedings from the first RRTC symposium on employment for citizens who are mentally retarded* (pp. 82–99). Richmond: Rehabilitation Research and Training Center, Virginia Commonwealth University.

Shonkoff, J. P. (1983). The limitations of normative assessments of high-risk infants. *Topics in Early Childhood Special Education, 3*(1) 29–43.

Siegel, G. L. & Loman, L. A. (1987). Enhancing employment opportunities for persons who are developmentally disabled. *Journal of Job Placement, 3*(2), 16–20.

Snell, M. E. (Ed.). (1987). *Systematic instruction of persons with severe handicaps* (3rd ed.). Columbus, OH: Charles E. Merrill.

Snell, M. E. & Grigg, N. C. (1987). Instructional assessment and curriculum development. In M. E. Snell (Ed.), *Systematic Instruction of Persons with Severe Handicaps* (pp. 64–109). Columbus, OH: Charles E. Merrill.

Szymanski, E. M., Dunn, C., & Parker, R. M. (1989). Rehabilitation of persons with learning disabilities: An ecological framework. *Rehabilitation Counseling Bulletin, 33*, 38–53.

Szymanski, E. M., Hanley-Maxwell, C., Hansen, G. M., & Myers, W. A. (1988). Work adjustment training, supported employment, and time-limited transitional employment programs: context and common principles. *Vocational Evaluation and Work Adjustment Bulletin, 21*, 41–45.

Szymanski, E. M., Hanley-Maxwell, C., & Parker, R. M. (1988). Quality dimensions of supported employment: A guide for rehabilitation educators. *Rehabilitation Education, 2*, 75–84.

Szymanski, E. M. & King, J. (1989). Rehabilitation counseling in transition planning and preparation. *Career Development for Exceptional Individuals, 12*(1), 3–10.

Szymanski, E. M. & Parker, R. M. (1989). Competitive closure rate of vocational rehabilitation clients with severe disabilities as a function of counselor education and experience. *Rehabilitation Counseling Bulletin, 32*, 292–299.

Szymanski, E. M. & Parker, R. M. (1988). Supported employment and time-limited transitional employment training: Options for rehabilitation counselors. *Journal of Applied Rehabilitation Counseling, 19*(2), 11–15.

Szymanski, E. M., Parker, R. M., Hanley-Maxwell, C., & Koch, W. (in press). Dimensions of role strain between rehabilitation counselors and job coaches. *Rehabilitation Counseling Bulletin.*

Szymanski, E. M., Rubin, S. E., & Rubin, N. M. (1988). Contemporary challenges: An introduction. In S. E. Rubin & N. M. Rubin, (Eds.), *Contemporary challenges to the rehabilitation counseling profession* (pp. 1–14). Baltimore: Paul H. Brookes.

Tooman, M. L., Revell, W. G., & Melia, R. P. (1988). The role of the rehabilitation counselor in the provision of transition and supported programs. In S. E. Rubin & N. Rubin (Eds.), *Contemporary challenges to the rehabilitation counseling profession* (pp. 77–92). Baltimore: Paul H. Brookes.

Turner, K. D. (1987). *Birth to six interactions: Implications for Special Education.* Unpublished manuscript. University of Texas at Austin, Special Education Department.

Wacker, D. P. & Berg, W. K. (1986). Generalizing and maintaining work behavior. In F. R. Rusch (Ed.), *Competitive employment issues and strategies* (pp. 129–140). Baltimore: Paul H. Brookes.

Wallace, G. & Larsen, S. C. (1978). *Educational assessment of learning problems: Testing for teaching.* Boston: Allyn & Bacon.

Wehman, P. (1986a). Supported competitive employment for persons with severe disabilities. *Journal of Applied Rehabilitation Counseling, 17*(4), 24–29.

Wehman, P. (1986b). Transition for handicapped youth from school to work. In J. Chadsey-Rusch & C. Hanley-Maxwell (Eds.), *Enhancing transition from school to the work place for handicapped youth: Issues in personnel preparation* (pp. 26–43). Urbana: University of Illinois, College of Education, Office of Career Development for Special Populations.

Weisenstein, G. (1986). Preservice implications for secondary special education: preparing teachers to enhance the transition effort. In J. Chadsey-Rusch & C. Hanley-Maxwell (Eds.), *Enhancing transition from school to the work place for handicapped youth: Issues in personnel preparation* (pp. 143–158). Urbana. University of Illinois, College of Education, Office of Career Development for Special Populations.

Will, M. (1986). OSERS programming for the transition of youth with disabilities: Bridges from school to working life. In J. Chadsey-Rusch & C. Hanley-Maxwell (Eds.), *Enhancing transition from school to the work place for handicapped youth: Issues in personnel preparation* (pp. 9–25). Urbana: University of Illinois, College of Education, Office of Career Development for Special Populations.

Winking, D. L., DeStefano, L., & Rusch, F. (1988). Supported employment in Illinois: Job coach issues. Urbana-Champaign, IL: Secondary Transition Intervention Effectiveness Institute, University of Illinois.

Wright, B. A. (1983). *Physical disability—A psychosocial approach* (2nd ed.). New York: Harper & Row.

Ysseldyke, J.E. & Algozzine, B. (1982). *Critical issues in Special and remedial education* (pp. 63–67). Boston: Houghton Mifflin.

CHAPTER

13

Interagency Service Delivery Coordination

Robert L. Schalock
Hastings College
William E. Kiernan
Children's Hospital
Boston, Massachusetts

This chapter addresses four changes in our service delivery system that have occurred in recent years. It then discusses how two programs (one rural and one urban) have addressed the challenges imposed by these changes as each program has dealt with the larger issue of *service delivery coordination*. Throughout the chapter, the term service delivery coordination refers to the coordination (across public and private components) of programs, resources, clientele and information in ways that: (a) minimize duplication and fragmentation; and (b) maximize cross component cooperation, efficiency and effectiveness.

Rehabilitation historians will undoubtedly look back on the last five to ten years and marvel at the service delivery changes that we have all experienced. Four of these significant changes include:

1. A shift to integrated employment with time-limited or ongoing support services.
2. A shift to agency interfacing as we move toward transitioning persons to more productive, independent and community-integrated environments.
3. An increased need for on-site evaluation, training and habilitation practices to maximize the individual's skills to meet workplace demands.
4. An increased need for program reportability and accountability that focus on individual cost and outcome data.

As with any change, there is both good and bad news. The good news is that more persons with severe disabilities are being placed into non-sheltered workshop environments. For example, a recent two-year national employment study (Kiernan, McGaughey, & Schalock, 1988; Schalock, McGaughey, & Kiernan, 1989) found that about 19 percent of persons with developmental disabilities who are in day habilitation, work activity, and sheltered workshops are currently being placed yearly into either transitional, supported or competitive employment. Similar trends are reported by Kregel, Hill, and Banks (1988) and Noble and Conley (1987).

The bad news is that the service delivery system has become very complex and poorly understood by most people (Conley & Noble, 1989). Additionally, despite the dramatic changes in the magnitude and comprehensiveness of the service system, much remains to be accomplished for persons with severe disabilities. Buckley and Bellamy (1985), for example, found that large numbers of such persons are still in day care or work activity centers.

The remaining sections of the chapter are not meant to be panaceas for all service delivery coordination problems. They do, however, summarize how a rural (Nebraska) and an urban (Boston) program have addressed the challenges imposed by these four changes, as each program has attempted to coordinate its employment services with the larger service delivery system.

SHIFT TO INTEGRATED EMPLOYMENT WITH SUPPORT SERVICES

Three internal program changes have accompanied the shift to integrated employment: (1) training employment staff in marketing principles; (2) developing employment specialist competencies; and (3) focusing on the program's capacity to provide long-term, job-related support.

Developing a Marketing Orientation

Marketing consists of much more than advertising; indeed, it identifies needs, translates these needs into production and accounting components, and directs and coordinates all the activities of the company (that is, agency). Basic to all of these functions is the need to orient and train employment staff in marketing principles. The two critical components that we have stressed in this marketing orientation and training include marketing planning guidelines and marketing mix considerations. Relevant features of each are presented in Table 13.1.

It is important in establishing any strategic marketing plan that one makes a clear identification of the market segments. In expanding integrated employment for persons with severe disabilities there are four distinct market segments: (1) the individual with a severe disability; (2) the employer; (3) the family; and (4) the human services provider. The marketing planning guide and marketing mix considerations noted in Table 13.1 deal with the employee and employer market segments. Similar approaches should be utilized in developing a marketing strategy for parents as well as professionals in the field of rehabilitation. The establishment of a comprehensive marketing plan must respond to these four key market segments. The marketing mix considerations (that is, the product, price, placement/distribution, and promotion) will vary depending on what market segment is being addressed. Specific marketing mix considerations for the family and human service provider are provided in Table 13.2.

Developing Employment Specialist Competencies

Organizationally, we have adapted to the increasing emphasis on integrated employment with support services by training employment specialist staff to demonstrate the following employment specialist competencies (Sale, Wood, Barcus, & Moon, 1989): job development, consumer assessment, program marketing, job placement, job-site training, ongoing support, support fading, and coordinating services with intersector participants.

Focusing on Long-Term Program Capacity

The ecological (person-environment) orientation in rehabilitation programs stresses the need to focus on both the person and his or her environment in the planning and delivery of employment services (see Chapters 7 and 10, this volume). Very recently, however, we have begun to focus also on factors that significantly affect the match between the features of an agency and its habilitation practices and the ecology of the service delivery system within which the agency operates (Schalock, 1989). Work by Calkins, Schalock, Griggs, Kiernan, and Gibson (1988) has identified critical factors that occur at each of three phases of rehabilitation programming, including: (a) creating job opportunities; (b) training and job placement; and (c) maintaining job placement. Within each of these three phases one finds seven critical factors: agency characteris-

Table 13.1 Marketing Planning Guidelines and Marketing Mix Considerations for Employment Specialists

Marketing Planning Guidelines	Marketing Mix Considerations
1. Research customer needs a. employee (challenging, productive job with good working conditions and career advancement) b. employer (stable, productive work force)	1. Product Job match On-site training, assistance, and support Work design Environmental modification Prosthetic Job restructuring Customer service (follow-up and agency services)
2. Develop target markets a. consists of studying and aggregating groups of customers with similar needs b. employment specialists unite these targeted markets by developing a "marketing mix"	2. Price Target tax credits Vocational Rehabilitation funds Job Training Partnership Act funds On-the-Job Training Funds (ARC) Credit terms
3. Identifying marketing mix considerations (see adjacent column)	3. Placement/distribution Employment services training-placement component(s) Individual transition plan Intersector agreement Not-for-profit corporations Vendor/brokerage functions
4. Complete strategic marketing plan a. describes the marketing mix offered to a specific target market b. describes the resources that will be needed c. includes sales projections	4. Promotion Advertising (media) Publicity Promotional blend Personal selling Public relations
5. Establish monitoring and evaluation variables	

Adapted from Johnsen, Schik, Koehler, & Schalock (1987); Johnsen & Schalock (1989); Kiernan, Carter, & Bronstein (1989); Elliott, Schalock, & Ross (1989).

tics, vocational [training] competence, employee expectations, systems interface, [accessing] the natural environment, quality of work life, and other external conditions. Relevant features of each factor are summarized in Table 13.3.

We have begun using *The Program Capacity Checklist and Manual* (Calkins et al., 1988) as an assessment procedure designed both to support an agency's rehabilitation practices and to allow it to interface better with other components of the service delivery system. The procedure involves defining the degree of agreement between the feature of the agency on each critical factor and the ecology of the service delivery system. For example, in the section on systems interface, a question reads, "Are you directly involved with other adult service providers in the provision of services to your clients?" The employment specialist or respondent then evaluates the services provided by his or her agency in terms of (1) Not in place, (2) Somewhat in place, or (3) Fully in place. The employment specialist also indicates the perceived importance for employment success as (1) Not important, (2) Somewhat important or (3) Very important. This evaluation results in the identification of significant mismatches to long-term employment suc-

Table 13.2 Marketing Mix Considerations for the Family and Human Service Provider

Product

- Job matching
- On-site social supports
- Positive work experience
- Increased earnings
- Increased independence

Price

- Increased wages
- Company benefits (when available)
- Loss of or reduction in Social Security benefits

Placement/distribution

- Job coach on-site
- Designated company supervisor

Promotion

- Security in job matching and job training
- Increased social contacts
- Ongoing support in training and replacement if necessary
- Coordination of other sources

cess that then serve as the basis for an agency's plan of action.

Agency Interfacing

Previous publications (Schalock, 1985, 1986) have both discussed the importance of interagency collaboration and outlined the critical features of such collaboration. Over the last few years, however, we have found that it is more effective to use task groups (as opposed to interagency groups) that focus on a particular problem such as the transition from school to work, private sector interfacing, or individual judicial plans (Schalock, 1987). Correspondingly, our management strategy has evolved into the use of matrix management (Lawrence, Kolodney, & Davis, 1977) whose key features include:

- the development of a clear plan with objectives stated in terms of measurable results and strategies for achieving them;
- a management structure of shared resources and defined responsibilities to address the problems; and
- a plan for monitoring and assessing its effectiveness.

An example of how the task group and matrix management approach work is outlined in a table shell format presented in Table 13.4.

Table 13.3 Critical Factors Involved in Creating Job Opportunities, Training/Job Placement and Maintaining Job Placement

1. **Agency Characteristics**
   Philosophy
   Organization
   Structure/staffing patterns
   Program resources
   Program practices
   Program evaluation strategies
   Resources (financial, manpower, training)
2. **Vocational Competence**
   Job responsibilities
   Job-related competence
   Social competence
3. **Employee Expectations**
   Towards hiring persons with disabilities
   Previous experiences with persons with disabilities
4. **Systems Interface**
   Relationships
   Agreements
   Task forces
5. **Natural Environment**
   Use of naturally assuring persons, settings, and social supports
   Normal range of community services
   Integrated settings
   Involvement of friends, co-workers, or family members
6. **Quality of Work Life**
   Employee decision making
   Employee satisfaction
   Opportunities for increased job responsibilities
   Opportunities for pay increases, benefits, promotion(s)
7. **External Factors**
   Seasonal variations
   Economic disincentives
   Transportation
   Regulatory environment

Adapted from Calkins et al. (1988)

The specific problem addressed might relate to transitioning students with severe disabilities into integrated employment with ongoing support services, combining the activities and resources of the public schools, community-based mental retardation programs, vocational rehabilitation, Job Service, Job Training Partnership Act personnel, and the local college. The matrix shows along the left side the four primary objectives regarding the task: completing the transition process, obtaining employment, maintaining employment, and evaluating outcomes. Across the top one sees the major strategies that specific agencies need to use to accomplish the objectives. These strategies relate to transition planning, assessment/eligibility, obtaining employment, on-the-job training, and funding. The matrix is then completed, summarizing the tasks associated with each agency. Thus far, we have found this task group/matrix management approach very effective in overcoming many of the problems and barriers that one finds frequently in the traditional interagency approach.

Assessment and Habilitation Strategies

The third change facing employment programs is the increased need for on-the-job evaluation and training strategies that both maximize the success of integrated employment and are consistent with the following two current programmatic trends (Schalock & Jensen, 1986).

• Person-environment (or ecological) assessment strategies with which one evaluates a person's behavioral capabilities in light of the (work) environment's requirements. Once identified, significant mismatches between capabilities and requirements are addressed through behavioral skill training techniques, prosthetic usage and/or environmental modification (Chapters 6 and 7).

• Training in the natural environment (Chapters 8, 9, 10, and 11).

Our employment-related assessment system currently uses two instruments that were developed in response to these two trends. The

Table 13.4 Management Matrix for Task Group Focusing on Transition from School to Work

Objectives	Strategies/Agency Responsibilities				
	Transition Planning	Assessment Eligibility	Obtain Employment	On-the-Job Training/Supervision	Funding
1. **Complete transition process**					
a. at 16 years of age					
b. 2-3 years before graduation					
c. 1 year before graduation					
2. Obtain employment					
3. Maintain employment					
a. initial training					
b. ongoing assistance					
4. Evaluate outcomes (process evaluation)					

first instrument, the *Employment Screening Test* (Schalock, Johnsen, & Schik, 1985), incorporates the critical skills and temperament requirements associated with most jobs (U.S. Department of Labor, 1982). The second instrument is the *Enhancing Employment Outcomes (EEO) Match Tool* (Boles, Griggs, Walker, Schalock, & Calkins, 1988). An example of the latter is presented in Figure 13.1. The 16 items composing the *EEO Match Tool* were developed, field tested and validated based on the current research literature on individual social competence factors that enhance or impair successful job placement. As shown in Figure 13.1, the sixteen items are divided into two groups: eight "enhancer" items and eight "impair" items. Within each group, there are four behaviors that are either critical or unacceptable, and four that are either desirable or tolerated. The "Employee" column contains boxes for the job coach or placement specialist to check if the corresponding behavior is present (exhibited) or absent (not exhibited). The "Work Environment" column contains boxes for the employer, job supervisor, or employment specialist to check to indicate whether a behavior is required to be present, required to be absent, or simply not required of a supported employee. The "mismatch" column is checked whenever an employee–work-environment mismatch occurs. Such a mismatch occurs when either: (1) a particular behavior is checked as "present," but is also checked as "required absent" in the work environment, or (2) a behavior is "absent," but is "required present" in the work environment.

Once significant mismatches are identified, the employment specialist must decide the best strategy to use to reduce the mismatch between the supported employee's behavioral/skill capabilities and the job's performance requirements. Readers are referred to chapters 7 and 10 this volume for a thorough discussion of work design and environmental modification. The following discussion relates to the training strategies and decision-making guidelines associated with the *EEO Match Tool* presented in Figure 13.1.

We have found that both facility-based and generic employment specialists become easily frustrated and potentially burned out because of the unavailability of an easy-to-use (and teach) decision-making tool for providing support on the job. Thus, we have recently implemented the *EEO Intervention Selection Guide* (Calkins et al., 1988) whose major purpose is to provide the employment specialist with nonaversive intervention/skill training strategies and decision-making guidelines that can be used to reduce the mismatches identified through the *EEO Match Tool*. An example of the *Guide* is presented in Figure 13.2, showing a mismatch on critical behavior #2, "follows job-related instructions from co-workers/supervisor." The decision-making steps that then follow ask the respondent to answer three questions related to the impact of this behavior on the work environment, other considerations, classes of (previous) interventions,

Employee Name *Joe S.* ID *000-00-0000* Date *6/20/89*

Work Environment *Valley Industries* Rater *A.A.*

DESCRIPTORS	EMPLOYEE		WORK ENVIRONMENT				
ENHANCER ITEMS	ABSENT	PRESENT	REQUIRED PRESENT	REQUIRED ABSENT	NOT REQUIRED	MIS-MATCH	MATCH
CRITICAL BEHAVIORS							
1. Asks questions for directions, information, personal needs.	—	✓	✓	—	—	—	(2)
2. Follows job-related instructions from co-workers/ supervisors.	—	✓	✓	—	—	—	(2)
3. Accepts criticism without anger or disruptive outbursts.	✓	—	✓	—	—	✓	2
4. Follows established workplace rules and procedures.	—	✓	✓	—	—	—	(2)
DESIRABLE BEHAVIORS							
5. Is neatly groomed and physically clean.	—	✓	✓	—	—	—	(1)
6. Adapts to changes in occupants of co-worker/ supervisor roles.	—	✓	—	—	✓	—	1
7. Interacts appropriately with co-workers/supervisor in informal situations (e.g. breaks).	✓	—	✓	—	—	✓	1
8. Is courteous to co-workers/ supervisor while on job.	✓	—	✓	—	—	✓	1
IMPAIR ITEMS							
UNACCEPTABLE BEHAVIORS							
9. Steals	✓	—	—	✓	—	—	(4)
10. Is physically aggressive toward self and others.	✓	—	—	✓	—	—	(4)
11. Argues/ refuses to cooperate with co-workers/supervisor.	—	✓	—	✓	—	✓	4
12. Consistently late/absent.	✓	—	—	✓	—	—	(4)
TOLERATED BEHAVIORS							
13. Lacks social awareness (ignores others, overly affectionate, incessant talking, etc.)	—	✓	—	✓	—	✓	2
14. Whines, complains, has tantrums.	✓	—	—	✓	—	—	(2)
15. Is easily distracted from job duties.	✓	—	—	✓	—	—	(2)
16. Displays bizarre behaviors (rocking, hand waving, other stereotypic movements).	✓	—	—	✓	—	—	(2)

NOTES:

TOTAL *25* *69.4* % MATCH QUOTIENT

TABLE A

MATCH TOTAL	MATCH QUOTIENT
1	2.7
2	5.6
3	8.3
4	11.1
5	13.9
6	16.7
7	19.4
8	22.2
9	25.0
10	27.8
11	30.6
12	33.3
13	36.1
14	38.9
15	41.6
16	44.4
17	47.2
18	50.0
19	52.3
20	55.6
21	58.3
22	61.1
23	63.9
24	66.7
25	69.4
26	72.2
27	75.0
28	77.8
29	80.6
30	83.3
31	86.1
32	88.9
33	92.7
34	94.4
35	97.3
36	100.0

FIGURE 13.1 Enhancing Employment Outcomes Match Tool

EEO Intervention Selection Criteria

(A)

Employee Name ______________________ Date ______________________

Work Environment ______________________ (EXAMPLE) Planner ______________________

MISMATCH #2. FOLLOWS JOB–RELATED INSTRUCTIONS FROM CO–WORKERS/SUPERVISOR

(B)

Impact on the Work Environment:

(C) KEY: 25% — 50% — 75%

PLEASE RATE TO WHAT DEGREE THE PRESENCE OF THIS BEHAVIOR . . .

EXPERT RATINGS ON THE DEGREE THE PRESENCE OF THIS BEHAVIOR INFLUENCES THEIR DECISION TO INTERVENE:

Minor 1	2	*Moderate* 3	4	*Major* 5		*Minor* 1	2	*Moderate* 3	4	*Major* 5
					. . . DISRUPTS THE WORKER'S ROUTINES					
					. . . DISRUPTS THE CO-WORKERS' ROUTINES AND PRODUCTIVITY					
					. . . REDUCES SOCIAL CONTACTS BY CO-WORKERS					

Weekly or Less 1	*2–3 x per Wk.* 2	*About Daily* 3	*2–3 x per Day* 4	*More than 3 x per Day* 5		*Weekly or Less* 1	*2–3 x per Wk.* 2	*About Daily* 3	*2–3 x per Day* 4	*More than 3 x per Day* 5
					OBSERVED FREQUENCY OF MISMATCHED BEHAVIOR					

Based upon the overall ratings, would you intervene? ☐ Yes ☐ No

(D)

Other Considerations:

1. Has the worker ever been able to follow job-related instructions?
2. Have you ruled out problems in health that might be contributing?
3. Are other significant events occurring in the worker's life?
4. Are there systematic responses to this person when he or she fails to follow job-related instructions?
5. Have attempts been made previously to teach this skill?
6. Is the worker able to follow instructions from anyone in any other setting?

Notes:

After considering the above, would you still intervene for this mismatch? ☐ Yes ☐ No

(E)

Classes of Interventions:

1. Have you considered changing aspects of the work environment? ☐ Yes ☐ No

   What, if any, accommodations or adaptations might be made? ______________________

2. Have you considered any training exercises/curricula? ☐ Yes ☐ No

   What, if any, training might be provided outside of the work environment? ______________________

3. Have you considered changing the behavior of the employee? ☐ Yes ☐ No

   What, if any, interventions might be attempted at the work site? ______________________

(F)

Recommended Interventions:

PERCENT OF EXPERTS SELECTING INTERVENTIONS (0 5 10 15 20 25 30 35)

SELECTED INTERVENTIONS

- Control of natural reinforcers ☐
- Change tasks/tools/routines ☐
- Self-monitoring ☐
- Social/verbal reinforcers ☐
- Preferred activity/money ☐
- DRO/DRI ☐
- Control of natural antecedents ☐
- Points/tokens ☐
- Shaping/chaining ☐

(G)

Intervention Implementors:

After considering all desirable/preferable interventions, who is the best person to intervene?

☐ Planner (Job Coach, Employment Specialist) ☐ Behavior Management Specialist

☐ Supervisor and/or Co-workers ☐ Other Agency Staff (specify) ______________________

FIGURE 13.2 Equal Employment Opportunity Intervention Solution Criteria

and the person who is the best one to intervene. In the development of the *Guide*, a panel of employment training experts also suggested the impact of the mismatch on the work environment (C) and the recommended interventions (F). Additionally, for each recommended intervention (see Figure 13.3), the *Guide* presents a definition of the strategy, expert ratings on six attributes of the strategy (social acceptability, effectiveness, cost, undesirable side effects, intrusiveness and an overall composite rating), recommendations regarding specific mismatches, and published references on the strategy.

The perceived utility of these assessment and habilitation strategies to employment specialists and employers has resulted in several catalysts to effective service delivery coordination, including a common language; a natural environment orientation; attractiveness and ease of use by employment specialists/job coaches; and marketability to employers who can see their feasibility and use across their employer populations.

Program Reportability and Accountability

Current rehabilitation services are being buffeted by powerful forces including service recipient empowerment, cost containment, and outcome analysis. These forces are causing us to focus increasingly on the issue of what rehabilitation actually achieves for service recipients, and how those achievements can be identified and measured (Fuhrer, 1987). Our task in this last section of the chapter is to discuss briefly the premise and components of our approach to outcome analysis as we have attempted to coordinate employment services within the larger contexts of generic integrated employment with support services and agency interfacing.

Our premise to outcome analysis is that we need to develop data sets that can address both the needs of each agency or component within the system *and* the employment objectives of the participant, program, and larger system, including funding sources and policy makers. In that regard, we have developed the following four outcome analysis components: (1) standard recipient characteristics; (2) longitudinal data sets; (3) individual cost data; and (4) individual employment-related outcomes. A summary of these components is presented in Table 13.5 and described more fully in Kiernan et al. (1988), Schalock (1988) and Schalock and Thornton (1988).

There is an increasing expectation that rehabilitation programs will be required to do more formal program evaluation as they are impacted further by reportability and accountability requirements. Although this topic is beyond the scope of this chapter, we suggest that individual programs are currently able to do process analysis, wherein one describes the program and the general environment within which it operates, including the persons served, what services are provided, individual cost and outcome data, and how the program can be replicated. As a service delivery system, however, we have yet to establish standard outcome analysis data sets, such as those presented in Table 13.5, that will allow for either impact or benefit-cost analysis. Impact analysis involves, for example, making the comparison between what happens in the program or system and what happens in the comparison (such as no program or an alternate program) state. Nor do we yet have the necessary data sets in place to do benefit-cost analysis that involves determining whether a program has impacts that are sufficiently large to justify its costs.

The complexity of impact and benefit-cost analysis is beyond the current capability of most programs and service delivery systems. However, the continued emphasis on reportability, accountability and policy analysis will force us to implement data systems that cross agencies and service delivery components. Thus, it makes sense to think about strategies within the immediate future to increase our data collection and analysis efforts so that we can respond appropriately to policy analysis and program evaluation questions that are sensitive and responsive to the empowerment, cost containment, and outcome analysis forces impacting (re)habilitation services.

SUMMARY AND CONCLUSION

In summary, we have presented a number of issues reflecting the changes in the service delivery system over the last ten years. The movement toward accessing integrated employ-

Intervention Strategy Profile

INTERVENTION D: CONTROL OF NATURAL REINFORCERS

DEFINITION:

Reinforcement is frequently *not* given in the work environment each time an appropriate social competency is exhibited. Most social behaviors performed daily are only reinforced occasionally in the natural work environment. Moreover, some behaviors receiving reinforcement only some of the time tend to persist longer when reinforcement is withdrawn (e.g., being consistently late/absent, being easily distracted from job duties). Controlling natural reinforcers, such as attention, is critical if excessive or problem behaviors are to be reduced in frequency. In addition, different reinforcement schedules affect the acquisition of desirable social competencies, such as following instructions. For this reason also it may be important to control naturally occurring reinforcers provided by supervisors and co-workers, whenever possible and feasible.

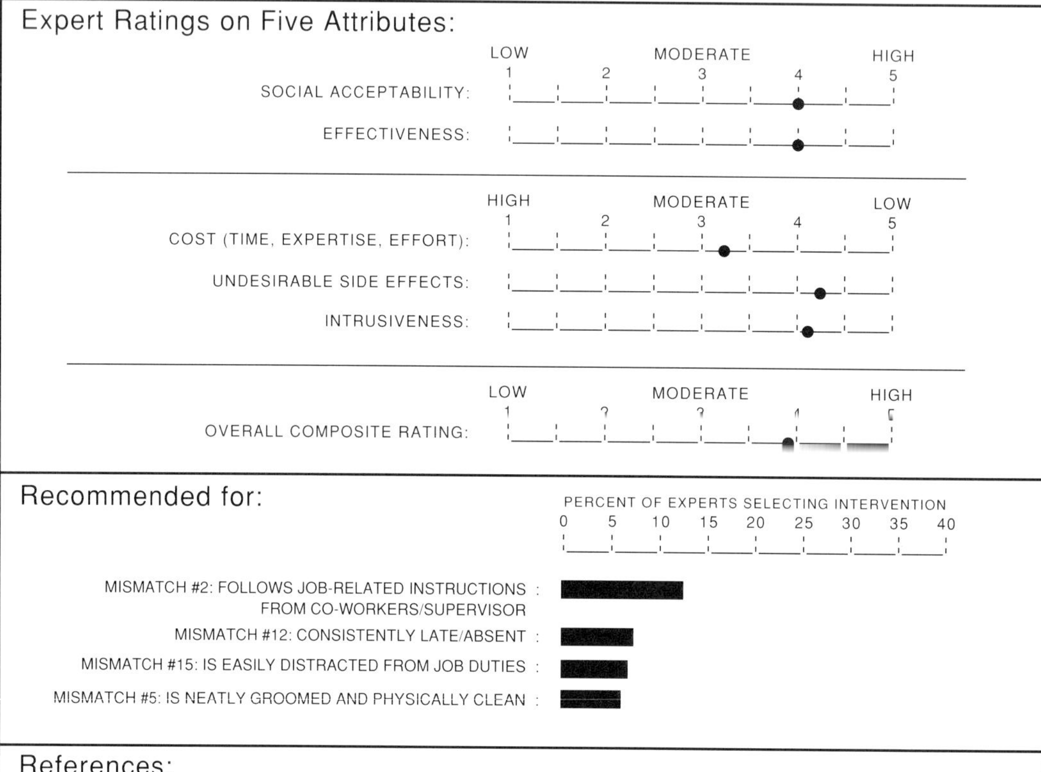

References:

Marr, J. N., & Roessler, R. T. (1986). Behavior management in work settings (Richard J. Baker Memorial Monograph). Vocational Evaluation and Work Adjustment Bulletin, (Special edition, 2).

FIGURE 13.3 Intervention Strategy Profile

Table 13.5 Outcome Analysis Data Sets

Recipient Characteristics
- Name/ID number
- Age
- Gender
- Level of disability

Longitudinal Data Sets[a]
- Setting prior to placement
- Employment placement environment
- Job support type and hours
- Occupational category
- Individual outcomes data (see next column)
- Job movement patterns

Individual Cost Data[b]
- Average cost per participant month of service

$$[\text{Average cost per participant}] = \frac{\text{Total cost for period}}{\text{Total months of participation for period}} \times [\text{Average months of participation per participant}]$$

or

- Average cost per enrollee:

$$[\text{Average cost per participant}] = \frac{\text{Total cost for time period}}{\text{Number of people enrolled during that period}}$$

Individual Employment Outcome Data
- Wages/hours
- Hours/week
- Duration of employment
- Benefits (health, unemployment, vacation)
- Level of integration

[a]Presented in more detail in Kiernan et al. (1988).

[b]Presented in more detail in Schalock (1988) and Schalock & Thornton (1988).

ment by utilizing transitional, intermittent and ongoing supports has clearly provided opportunities for persons with severe disabilities to increase their independence, productivity, and integration in the community. The current emphasis on supported employment has led to a clearer understanding of the capacity of persons with severe disabilities in integrated work settings. In the next five years, the authors believe that the movement will be focused on generic, integrated employment opportunities for persons with severe disabilities and ongoing services will be provided as needed. Thus, the distinctions that are currently made among supported employment, transitional employment, and competitive employment may be considerably less dramatic as the entire service delivery system moves toward the concept of generic supports for persons with severe disabilities in integrated work settings.

The changes in the service delivery system that we have recently seen have meant changes in staff training, agency directions, and long-term planning approaches. The authors have pointed out that staff and agency directors need to be more responsive to the concepts of marketing, and that staff who provide job coaching services must develop skills and competencies that will allow them to provide on-site training in the least intrusive fashion possible in integrated work settings.

The shift in employment emphasis has also led to an expanded need for agency collaboration and coordination. Specific models and concepts of coordination have been offered by the authors. Coordination must include not only employment needs but residential and recreational needs for persons with severe disabilities. (Schalock & Kiernan, in press). Additionally, coordination must be viewed longitudinally; it has a focus on total needs during a specific time period (i.e., day, week, month) as well as over several years. The focus on the needs of the individual with severe disabilities over a longer period of time has clearly meant that agencies and programs must be more effective at working together (Schalock & Kiernan, in press).

Assessment techniques utilizing person-environment matching strategies and habilitation training approaches that are effective in integrated work settings will be the key to integration for persons with severe disabilities. The accurate identification of abilities of the individual and then matching those abilities to the demands of the marketplace while offering training and intervention strategies that are compatible with the social and cultural environment of the work setting is critical.

Finally, in the area of accountability, measurement of program outcomes solely by dollars earned will not document the changes in the quality of life that an individual realizes through integrated employment (Schalock, in press). Thus, a broader view of accountability must include not only measures of outcome for the individual with regard to economic gains, but also measurements regarding changes in the person's quality of life. Documentation of changes in levels of independence, productivity, and integration for persons with severe disabilities will serve not only as a strategy for verifying program impact, but also as an effective marketing tool for reaching persons with disabilities, employers, families and professionals (Schalock, in press).

In conclusion, we have "revisited" the issue of service delivery coordination and suggested that employment-related rehabilitation programs and interagency arrangements in the 1990s will look very different from those of today. The foci will be less on "interagency" than "inter-system"; more on generic employment with support services than either supported or competitive employment; and more on outcome evaluation than service description. It is a challenging future, and one that hopefully will see current agencies and programs becoming part of a larger mosaic that reflects recipients wishes to achieve the goals of increased productivity, independence, and real community integration.

QUESTIONS (For answers see pp. 432–433)

1. What is service delivery coordination?

2. Outline the four significant service delivery changes in the last decade.

3. What changes have accompanied the shift to integrated employment for support services?

4. To obtain expanded integrated employment for persons with severe disabilities, what four market segments require attention?

5. What do the authors identify as the three phases of habilitation programming?

6. To achieve agency interfacing, the authors state that they no longer suggest using interagency groups that focus on a particular problem. What do they now propose? Explain.

7. Briefly describe how ecological assessment works.

8. What forces are causing rehabilitation services to increasingly focus on reportability and accountability?

9. Do the authors suggest any unit of measure other than dollars earned? If so, what and why?

REFERENCES

Boles, S. M., Griggs, P. A., Walker, H. M., Schalock, R. L., & Calkins, C. F. (1988). *Social competence match scale*. Kansas City: University of Missouri, Institute for Human Development, Enhancing Employment Outcome Project.

Buckley, J. & Bellamy, G. T. (1985). *National survey of day and vocational programs for adults with severe disabilities: 1984 profile*. Eugene: University of Oregon Specialized Training Program, College of Education.

Calkins, C. F., Schalock, R. L., Griggs, P. A., Kiernan, W. E., & Gibson, C. A. (1988). *Program planning manual*. Kansas City: University of Missouri, Institute for Human Development, Enhancing Employment Outcomes Project.

Conley, R. W. & Noble, J. H., Jr. (1989). Changes in the service system for persons with disabilities. In W. E. Kiernan and R. L. Schalock (Eds.), *Economics, industry and the disabled: A look ahead* (pp. 37–45). Baltimore: Paul H. Brookes.

Elliott, B., Schalock, R. L., & Ross, I. (1989). *Handbook for transition planning and implementation*. Hastings, NB: Educational Service Unit #9.

Fuhrer, M. J. (1987). *Rehabilitation outcomes: Analysis and measurement*. Baltimore: Paul H. Brookes.

Johnsen, D. A. & Schalock, R. L. (1989). Meeting consumer needs by developing a marketing orientation. In W. E. Kiernan and R. L. Schalock (Eds.), *Economics, industry and the disabled: A look ahead* (pp. 57–66). Baltimore: Paul H. Brookes.

Johansen, D. A., Schik, T. L., Koehler, R. S., & Schalock, R. L. (1987). *Customer-oriented employment services: A field guide.* Hastings, NE: Mid-Nebraska Mental Retardation Services, Inc.

Kiernan, W. E., Carter, A., & Bronstein, E. (1989). Marketing and marketing management in rehabilitation. In W. E. Kiernan and R. L. Schalock (Eds.), *Economics, industry and disability: A look ahead* (pp. 49–56). Baltimore: Paul H. Brookes.

Kiernan, W. E., McGaughey, M. J., & Schalock, R. L. (1988). Employment environments and outcomes for adults with developmental disabilities. *Mental Retardation*, *26*(5), 279–288.

Kregel, J., Hill, M., & Banks, P. D. (1988). Analysis of employment specialist intervention time in supported competitive employment. *American Journal on Mental Retardation*, *93*(2), 200–208.

Lawrence, P. R., Kolodney, H. F., & Davis, S. M. (1977). The human side of the matrix. *Organization Dynamics*, *15*(3), 46–59.

Noble, J. H., Jr. & Conley, R. W. (1987). Accumulating evidence on the benefits and costs of supported and transitional employment for persons with severe disabilities. *The Journal of the Association for Persons with Severe Handicaps*, *12*(3), 163–174.

Sale, P., Wood, W., Barcus, J. M., & Moon, M. S. (1989). The role of the employment specialist. In W. E. Kiernan and R. L. Schalock (Eds.), *Economics, industry and the disabled: A look ahead* (pp. 169–178). Baltimore: Paul H. Brookes.

Schalock, R. L. (1985). Comprehensive community services: A plea for interagency collaboration. In R. H. Bruininks and K. C. Lakin (Eds.), *Living and learning in the least restrictive environment* (pp. 37–63). Baltimore: Paul H. Brookes.

Schalock, R. L. (1986). Service delivery coordination. In F. R. Rusch (Ed.), *Competitive employment issues and strategies* (pp. 115–127). Baltimore: Paul H. Brookes.

Schalock, R. L. (1987). The individual transition plan: A 10-year reunion. Paper presented at the Secondary Transition Institute Conference, San Diego, CA. January 20, 1987.

Schalock, R. L. (1988). Critical performance evaluation indicators in supported employment. In P. Wehman and M. S. Moon (Eds.), *Vocational rehabilitation and supported employment* (pp. 163–174). Baltimore: Paul H. Brookes.

Schalock, R. L. (1989). Person-environmental analysis: Short- and long-term perspectives. In W. E. Kiernan and R. L. Schalock (Eds.), *Economics, industry and the disabled: A look ahead* (pp. 105–116). Paul H. Brookes.

Schalock, R. L. (Ed.) (in press). *Quality of life: Issues and perspectives.* Washington, D.C: American Association on Mental Retardation.

Schalock, R. L. & Jensen, C. M. (1986). Assessing the goodness-of-fit between persons and their environments. *The Journal of the Association for Persons with Severe Handicaps*, *11*(2), 103–109.

Schalock, R. L., Johnsen, D. A., & Schik, T. L. (1985). *Employment screening test and standardization manual.* Hastings, Nebraska: Mid-Nebraska Mental Retardation Services, Inc.

Schalock, R. L. & Kiernan, W. E. (in press). *Habilitation planning for adults with disabilities.* New York: Springer–Verlag.

Schalock, R. L., McGaughey, M. J., & Kiernan, W. E. (1989). Placement into non-sheltered employment: Findings from the 1984–85 and 1985–86 national employment surveys. *American Journal on Mental Retardation 94*(1), 80–87.

Schalock, R. L. & Thornton, C. V. D. (1988). *Program evaluation: A field guide for administrators.* New York: Plenum.

CHAPTER

14

Designing and Implementing Program Evaluation

Lizanne DeStefano
University of Illinois at Urbana-Champaign

In order to be effective, program evaluation of social service programs must be grounded in everyday realities. Evaluations should be comprehensive enough to contain information to answer a variety of important questions as they arise in the life of a program, yet be of reasonable size so as not to tax the data collection and management capabilities of those responsible for their operation. Evaluation should be targeted to the specific information needs of the program staff and administration, yet flexible enough to accommodate additional requests which may arrive from funders and other sources. Evaluation should be able to provide information at individual, agency, and aggregate levels. It should be sophisticated enough in design to effectively capture the complex, multifaceted nature of supported employment programs, yet easily understood and implemented by persons who may have limited background in program evaluation and related activities.

In order to be maximally implemented and useful to the various stakeholders, program evaluation systems in supported employment must take into consideration the information needs, evaluation expertise, personnel and monetary resources, and level of interest associated with the supported employment project or group of projects being evaluated. Because these project characteristics are apt to vary considerably, it is difficult to put forth a single or generic design or program evaluation system which would be equally feasible and useful in all circumstances. An extensive analysis of the various approaches to program evaluation, design, and techniques is beyond the scope of this chapter. (Detailed reviews can be found in Attkisson, Hargreaves, Horowitz, & Sorenson, 1978; Rossi, Freeman, & Wright, 1975; Madaus, Scriven, & Stufflebeam, 1985; Worthen & Sanders, 1987). Instead, this chapter presents a series of considerations or organizing principles and a collection of resources that can be used by program administrators and other persons planning evaluations of supported employment programs to shape the evaluation. In addition, the chapter offers a framework for constructing a management information system (MIS) for use as a primary evaluation tool.

CONSIDERATIONS IN EVALUATION OF SUPPORTED EMPLOYMENT PROGRAMS

A good evaluation system is one that is well integrated into the program's daily operation and well suited to its information needs. In order to maximize the utility and feasibility of a program evaluation system, several issues must be considered during the design phase of the evaluation:

1. The focus of program evaluation may differ based on the interests, information needs, and capabilities of evaluators and their clients.
2. Supported employment involves the interaction of individual, employment, and program characteristics to produce a set of outcomes.
3. Evaluations can be used summatively and formatively.
4. Evaluation can be multi-level and multi-user.

EVALUATION FOCUS

The focus of program evaluation can depend upon the information needs, level of expertise, and personal preference of the evaluator or the evaluation client. The chosen focus will determine what questions are asked and answered during the course of an evaluation. In turn, evaluation questions will affect the way in which information is collected, analyzed, and interpreted. Evaluation foci in supported employment can be organized into four broad categories: 1) compliance monitoring; 2) process evaluation; 3) outcome evaluation; 4) efficiency or benefit cost analysis.

Compliance Monitoring

At the very minimum, a program administrator must be concerned as to whether or not a program adheres to certain regulations set forth by federal, state, or local authorities. Federal regulations regarding supported employment implementation are found in the amendments to the Rehabilitation Act of 1973 made public by PL 99-506, the Rehabilitation Act Amendments of 1986. The regulations set standards for the nature and extent of supported employment services and the population to be served. These standards have important implications for the compliance monitoring of supported employment programs.

The statute defines supported employment to mean *competitive work* in an *integrated work setting* for *individuals with severe handicaps* for whom competitive employment *has not occurred* or for whom competitive employment has been *interrupted* or *intermittent*. Individuals who are eligible for services under the program must not be able to function independently in employment without intensive ongoing support services and must require these on-going support services for the duration of employment (Federal Register, *52* (157) August 14, 1987). The regulations go on to set an average twenty hours per week work requirement to define competitive work.

Integrated work settings are defined as "job sites where most co-workers are not handicapped and individuals with handicaps are not part of a work group of other individuals with handicaps, or are part of a small work group of not more than eight individuals with handicaps. If there are no co-workers or the only co-workers are members of a small group of not more than eight individuals with handicaps, individuals with handicaps must have regular contact with non-handicapped individuals, other than personnel providing support services, in the immediate work setting" (Federal Register, *52* (157) August 14, 1987). Further, the regulations require that job skill training must be provided at least twice monthly at the job site, except in the case of individuals with chronic mental illness.

Given the above information, in order to evaluate the extent to which a supported employment program is in compliance with federal requirements, certain standards, data, and criteria must be considered. Table 14.1 lists four standards that correspond with federal regulations. Also, Table 14.1 lists the data and criteria that should be considered. For example, federal guidelines suggest a population (the standard) that evaluators should consider when collecting information that satisfies published regulations. Consequently, it is necessary to collect data on handicapping condition and previous work history to determine if the population consists of persons for whom employment has not occurred or has been intermittent or interrupted.

Program evaluation focused upon compliance monitoring of a supported employment program would involve collecting data relevant to each of the standards and applying the criteria to determine whether or not the standard has been met.

Table 14.1 Standards, Data to be Collected, and Criteria to Consider When Evaluating Supported Employment

Standard	Data	Criteria
Population	Primary/secondary handicapping condition Previous work history	Persons with severe handicaps for whom employment has not occurred or has been intermittent or interrupted
Competitive work	Hours worked for each individual per pay period	Averaging at least 20 hours per week for each pay period
Integrated work setting	Extent of contact with nonhandicapped co-workers	Workgroup of not more that eight individuals with handicaps; regular contact with nonhandicapped co-workers
Ongoing support services	Number of contacts and nature of support services provided to employee at the job site	Continuous or periodic job skill training services provided at least twice monthly at the job site (except for individuals with chronic mental illness)

Unmet standards may call for revision of program practice or policy. Compliance information is often collected by or reported to a supervisory or funding agency.

Compliance monitoring simply assesses the extent to which a program adheres to a set of standards. It does not in and of itself give a comprehensive picture of the program or evaluate program effectiveness. While compliance monitoring is often essential for accreditation and funding purposes, the information it requires is not always useful to program managers for decision making and program improvement. These activities most often require information on program process and outcomes, to be discussed in the next two sections.

Process Evaluation

Evaluation of program process considers the extent to which the program is implemented and the manner in which services are delivered to clients (Posavac & Carey, 1980). Process evaluation requires the identification of critical components associated with supported employment and the development of criteria to detect their presence and absence in a specific supported employment program. The Degree of Implementation (DOI) (Trach, Rusch, & DeStefano, 1987) is an instrument designed to measure the extent to which program activities are carried out in a supported employment program. Table 14.2 lists 26 program activities that are divided into five major areas:

COMMUNITY SURVEY AND JOB ANALYSIS. (Items 1–6). These activities are associated with surveying the community for potential job placement sites through telephone calls, mail correspondence, and personal contacts. This component also involves identifying the vocational skills and social interpersonal behavior requisites for a particular job.

JOB MATCH. (Items 7–10). The job match component concerns assessing target employee characteristics in relation to job requisites and includes documenting the use of standardized norm and criterion-referenced instruments along with ecological inventories as a basis for making accurate judgments resulting in a successful job match.

JOB PLACEMENT. (Items 11–16). Job placement refers to procedures utilized when training employees to perform on the job. These procedures typically require vocational training techniques and job modifications as well as planning

Table 14.2 Supported Employment Program Development Degree of Implementation Form

	Yes	Emergent	No
Community Survey and Job Analysis			
1. Conducts a community survey to identify potential jobs.	2	1	0
2. Compiles a list of businesses willing and unwilling to employ individuals with handicaps.	2	1	0
3. Obtains employer-validated job descriptions.	2	1	0
4. Conducts job analysis of targeted jobs (enclaves/work sites).	2	1	0
5. Identifies job-specific work performance skills, including necessary job modifications.	2	1	0
6. Identifies job-specific social-interpersonal skills.	2	1	0
Job Match			
7. Administers standardized vocational assessment instrument to evaluate work performance skills.[1]	2	1	0
8. Administers standardized assessment to evaluate social-interpersonal skills.[1]	2	1	0
9. Observes work performance and social-interpersonal skills on the job.	2	1	0
10. Determines match of target employees' strengths/weaknesses in relation to alternative job placements.[2]	2	1	0
Job Placement			
(First six months before Job Maintenance phase)			
11. Evaluates target employees' performance to determine training needs.	2	1	0
12. Utilizes behavior management strategies.	2	1	0

[1] "Standardized" refers to those instruments for which administration procedures, reliability, and validity have been documented.

[2] This item focuses on the best possible job match while assessing strengths and weaknesses in order to guide programming decisions. This item does not suggest that someone is unemployable or even less employable.

Table 14.2 (cont.)

	Yes	Emergent	No
13. Restructures job to adapt to target employees' skills.	2	1	0
14. Develops plan to maintain acceptable levels of performance acquired through on-the-job training.	2	1	0
15. Develops plan for support services during job maintenance phase.	2	1	0
16. Obtains feedback from employer/supervisor through work performance evaluations.	2	1	0
17. Compares target employees' work performance and social-interpersonal skills to coworkers' through monthly observation.	2	1	0
18. Obtains feedback from employer/supervisor through work performance evaluations after job placement period.	2	1	0
19. Provides on-the-job training to meet employers'/supervisors' expectations.	2	1	0
20. Annually assesses target employees' work performance with standardized vocational instruments.	2	1	0
21. Annually assesses target employees' social-interpersonal skills with standardized assessment instruments.	2	1	0
Related Job Services/Interagency Coordination			
22. Identifies local agencies that provide employment services.	2	1	0
23. Identifies employment services within each potential agency that could promote continuation in present placement.	2	1	0
24. Identifies agencies to provide employment-related services.	2	1	0
25. Identifies employment-related services within each agency that could promote continuation in present placement.	2	1	0
26. Revises Individualized Written Rehabilitation Plan to include interagency cooperation that focuses on long-term employment through case management.	2	1	0

ANTHONY MEISNER

Anthony Meisner is a 28-year-old man who was born in Chicago as an only child. Anthony attended O. W. Wilson Occupational High School and was graduated in 1979. After graduation, he began attending a local work activities program. He was diagnosed as developmentally disabled with a secondary medical condition. Anthony remained in work activities for two and a half years. He was then able to enter the work adjustment training program with the motivation to improve his skills and eventually find a "real" job.

After three and a half years, Anthony was placed in an on-the-job training situation with Chicago City-Wide Colleges hospital services. Upon completion of the program, Anthony was placed in a job as a dishwasher at the Art Institute of Chicago. He was laid off from this job after six months and was referred to another workshop that in turn enrolled him into the job training program, which he completed in 1984. From this program he was placed into another dishwashing position at a nursing home. Anthony was laid off again because, he says, he was "too slow."

After these experiences, Anthony decided to re-enter a work adjustment training program. During the next few years he was placed into several competitive jobs, such as dishwashing at a bakery and janitorial work at a local tavern.

Although Anthony's motivation and enthusiasm never wavered, each of his employment experiences terminated because of his extremely slow work pace and "poor concentration." Anthony could not hold a job on his own and always returned to the workshop. He continued to attend interviews with the aid of a placement specialist, but was never offered a job. When asked how he felt about being fired, Anthony replied, "I was upset and angry, but I always would think about getting another job."

A local program obtained funding in 1985 for supported employment. In January, 1987, an assembly job at a lamp company on the south side of Chicago became available through supported employment. Anthony was referred for the position because he would have constant supervision by a one of the program's employees and could set his own work pace. Anthony has now been working eight hours each day, three days a week, for more than two years. In the beginning he worked very slowly and awkwardly. Today Anthony works at a steady pace, and is one of the fastest, most reliable workers not only in the supported employment enclave but also in the company. Anthony is a perfect example of an individual who couldn't "make it" in the competitive job market but is an excellent worker with the assistance of an on-site job coach and a successful job match based on his strengths and abilities.

When asked how he feels about supported employment, Anthony replied, "I feel pretty good; the job is staying with me." Lois Meisner, Anthony's mother, also feels very positive about Anthony now, and about the supported employment program. She says, "This job is suitable for Anthony because he is learning and accomplishing something. It makes him feel good that he can think and use his hands!"

to maintain performance acquired through training once the training period has ended.

JOB MAINTENANCE. (Items 17–21). A primary consideration in supported employment is whether the target employee maintains his or her job. Job maintenance is conducted by reassessment of target employee performance, social validation of the quality of job performance, and modification of efforts to meet target employee and employer expectations.

RELATED JOB SERVICES/INTERAGENCY COORDINATION. (Items 22–26). The items included in the last component of the DOI relate to enhancing one's quality of life through multiple agency cooperation. The overall focus of this component is to ensure that the employee keeps his or her position in society. Related job services consist of the actual programs, individuals and subcomponents of participating agencies that provide the direct services needed to secure, train, and maintain a job placement. Interagency coordination convenes those agencies that provide necessary job services for a particular individual but function independently of each other. The services within each agency work in conjunction with each other in order to attain work placement, train for and maintain work placement, and develop skills outside work placement that may promote continued employment.

The DOI form can be completed by the supported employment program coordinator or external evaluator as part of routine program evaluation. It is necessary to examine employment specialists' logs and other program documentation in order to complete the form.

The instrument utilizes a three-point scoring system to rate both the presence of an activity and the extent to which it is carried out. Criteria and data sources specific to each item are detailed in the accompanying manual. The scores are as follows:

2—Yes The component exists, is a routine activity of the program, and is performed at an acceptable level.

1—Emergent The component exists, but is carried out less frequently or at less than acceptable levels. Technical assistance or staff development is necessary.

0—No The component is not present, or is carried out inappropriately. Technical assistance is strongly needed.

By summing individual item scores, overall implementation and component scores are obtained.

Research conducted with the DOI has shown it to be a reliable and valid means of assessing the extent to which the twenty-six critical activities are documented as operational in a supported employment program (Trach & Rusch, in press). Scores on the DOI can be used to document a supported employment program's fidelity to a particular model of supported employment. Multiple programs can be compared in terms of their level of implementation by using global or component DOI scores.

Process evaluation using the DOI can also be used to target aspects of the program that need improvement. Low scores on the overall instrument, in a particular component, or on individual items can indicate program needs. These needs can result in program or policy modifications, requests for technical assistance, or staff development activities. By examining program process in light of the outcomes achieved by the program, the elements associated with successful supported employment programs can be identified.

Outcome Evaluation

An essential element in outcome evaluation is to specify objective, measurable, and relevant outcomes associated with supported employment (Rockart, 1979). The outcomes can be considered at the individual, agency or employer, and community levels and may include both social and economic benefits associated with the program (Long, Mallar, & Thornton, 1981). It may be desirable to set criterion levels for each outcomes (i.e., ten individuals will be placed during the next fiscal year) or it may be left to the evaluation stakeholders (i.e., funders, consumer groups, or program staff) to determine the merit of outcomes achieved.

INDIVIDUAL LEVEL. At the individual level, the outcomes that come most quickly to mind are the economic benefits derived from the job placement such as job tenure, hourly or monthly wage, hours worked per month, and benefits received. It is important, however, to consider the social and personal impact of the job placement on the worker. Because these outcomes are more difficult to operationalize and quantify than economic benefit data, they are often not included in outcome evaluations of supported employment programs, yet their relevance to job success, family involvement, and to philosophical mission of supported employment is unquestionable (Goode, 1988).

Recent developments in the measurement of employment integration, consumer satisfaction, and quality of life now make it possible to include personal and social impacts in outcome evaluation of supported employment programs. The Employment Integration Index (Integration Index) (Lagomarcino, 1989) is an evaluation instrument that identifies the nature and extent of integration during the workday for persons with disabilities who work in competitive settings. The Integration Index can be used for two purposes: 1) to evaluate the current status of employment integration for a specific employee, and 2) to assist direct service providers to assess opportunities for integration for prospective worksites.

Developed through a review of the research literature related to the integration of persons with disabilities, an analyses of approximately fifty existing supported employment programs, and a survey of service providers and "experts" in supported employment, the Integration Index consists of twenty-three indicators of worksite integration. The indicators are grouped into three dimensions: 1) physical integration, 2) social integration, and 3) organizational integration. Table 14.3 lists these indicators.

Designed to be used by persons familiar with a specific employment site, items are scored based

Table 14.3 Twenty-three Indicators of Worksite Integration

Physical Integration

Item 1. General work environment ratio (company).
Item 2. General work environment ratio (shift).
Item 3. Immediate work environment ratio.
Item 4. Transportation utilized by the target employee for arrival to and departure from work.
Item 5. Arrival time of the target employee.
Item 6. Work tasks performed by the target employee.
Item 7. Departure time of the target employee.
Item 8. Number of hours worked per day by the target employee.
Item 9. Number of days worked per week by the target employee.
Item 10. Accessibility and use of company facilities (e.g., work areas, restrooms, locker rooms, break areas).
Item 11. Work attire.

Social Integration

Item 12. Work-related social interactions occur between the target employee and *company supervisors* during work.
Item 13. Work-related social interactions occur between the target employee and *nonhandicapped co-workers* during work.
Item 14. Nonwork-related social interactions occur between the target employee and *company supervisors* during work.
Item 15. Nonwork-related social interactions occur between the target employee and *nonhandicapped co-workers* during work.
Item 16. Nonwork-related social interactions occur between the target employee and *nonhandicapped co-workers* during lunch or break.
Item 17. The target employee interacts with nonhandicapped co-workers at company-sponsored activities.
Item 18. The target employee interacts with nonhandicapped co-workers outside of work at *informal* social activities.

Organizational Integration

Item 19. The target employee receives on-the-job training.
Item 20. The target employee is supervised and evaluated.
Item 21. The target employee is reimbursed for work performed.
Item 22. The target employee receives company benefits.
Item 23. Potential for vocational growth.

on whether integration exists (score = 2); partial integration is evident (score = 1); or the opportunity for integration does not exist (score = 0). Scores for each dimension can be obtained by summing the scores for each item within the dimension. A global integration score can be obtained by summing the raw scores for each dimension.

Internal consistency, interrater, and test-retest reliability estimates are high (range-.87 to .98). Reliability and validity studies support the use of the Integration Index as a measure of employment integration in both prospective and current employment sites (Lagomarcino, 1989). In a program evaluation, individual and aggregate Integration Index scores can be reported to document the level of integration of job placements in a supported employment program. Low overall Integration Index ratings indicate a need for improved job development strategies that emphasize the identification or creation of opportunities for integration in job development.

Despite the importance of consumer satisfaction in evaluating the impact of supported employment programs, few instruments exist to measure that construct. Lifestyle satisfaction assessment can include measurement of the degree of residential, work, and leisure integration, financial independence, extent of support network, presence of family and friendships, feelings of security and satisfaction with life, and degree of personal control. Some of these areas may be captured by measures of adaptive behavior, but others are not commonly found in any standardized measure. Some programs may choose to develop informal questionnaires or semi-structured interviews to assess the level of satisfaction of their employees. A small number of standardized measures are available.

One such instrument is the Lifestyle Satisfaction Survey (LSS) (Heal, Chadsey-Rusch, & Novak, 1982). The LSS consists of twenty-nine items that are asked of the client in an interview format to assess satisfaction with residence, community, work, friends, and opportunities. Mean scores are available for a sample of thirty-eight individuals with mental retardation. An acquiescence subscale makes it possible to correct satisfaction scores for acquiescence bias. Empirical data indicate the experimental version of the LSS has internally consistent subscales and good test-retest and inter-rater reliabilities.

The Quality of Life Questionnaire (Schalock, 1986) is a 28-item instrument that can be completed by the examinee or by two staff members who are familiar with the examinee. Items relate to living conditions, personal control, social contact, financial independence, and job satisfaction, and are scored on a 3-point scale.

The Co-worker Involvement Index (R) (Rusch, Hughes, McNair, & Wilson, 1989) provides another way of assessing the quality of work life by assessing the extent to which co-workers affiliate with target employees at specific job placements. This instrument is based on research that assumes that co-worker involvement with supported employees enhances job performance. Greater co-worker involvement in conjunction with employment training specialist assistance may be associated with an increased likelihood of job retention, greater work productivity, and enhanced cost effectiveness of employee training methods. Psychometric properties of the instrument show good interrater (r = .80) and test-retest (r = .88) reliability. Table 14.4 displays a copy of the Co-worker Involvement Index (R).

Quality of life information enables program personnel to assess the impact of supported employment placement on aspects of workers' lives in and outside of work. Ideally, recreational, residential, and social opportunities should be enhanced by participation in supported employment. If negative repercussions are associated with participation, the program personnel, families, and the worker himself or herself must strive to alleviate them. In any case, information on quality of life is an essential part of outcome evaluation.

Unfortunately, the outcomes associated with supported employment are not always positive; supported employees sometimes lose their jobs. Understanding the reasons why they do may enable program staff to improve job analysis, job match, job maintenance, or interagency coordination to reduce job separation. As supported employment program personnel gain experience

Table 14.4 Co-worker Involvement Index (Items Only)

Co-worker Involvement Items				
Item 1:	*Physical Integration.* The target employee works, takes breaks, and eats meals in the same areas at the same time as the co-worker(s). 2 – Works, eats, takes breaks in the same area at the same time. 1 – Does not work in the same area at same time but takes breaks and/or eats in same area at same time (or vice versa). 0 – Does not work, take breaks, or eat in same area at same time.	2	1	0
Item 2:	*Social Integration.* While completing his/her work or during breaks, the target employee regularly has opportunities to interact with co-workers without negative effects on job performance. 2 – Regularly occurring opportunities for interaction. 1 – Few opportunities for interaction. 0 – No opportunities for interaction.	2	1	0
Item 3:	*Training.* The co-worker supports a target employee by providing on-the-job skill training. 2 – Co-worker independently provides on-the-job training to target employee. 1 – Co-worker provides on-the-job training when prompted and/or assisted. 0 – Co-worker does not provide on-the-job training to target employee.	2	1	0
Item 4:	*Associating (frequency).* A co-worker socially interacts with the target employee at the work place. 2 – Co-worker socially interacts with target employee typically on a daily basis. 1 – Co-worker socially interacts with target employee typically only 2 to 3 times per week. 0 – Co-worker socially interacts with target employee once a week or less.	2	1	0
Item 5:	*Associating (appropriateness).* A co-worker socially interacts with the target employee in a manner considered appropriate within the context of the workplace. 2 – Most social interactions are appropriate. 1 – Some social interactions are appropriate. 0 – Few social interactions are appropriate.	2	1	0

Table 14.4 (cont.)

Item 6:	*Befriending.* A co-worker befriends the target employee by interacting socially with the target employee outside of the workplace.	2	1	0
	2 – Interaction occurs at least once a month. 1 – Interaction occurs less than once a month. 0 – Interaction does not occur.			
Item 7:	*Advocating.* The co-worker advocates for the target employee by optimizing, backing, and supporting the target employee's employment status.	2	1	0
	2 – Co-worker advocates independently. 1 – Co-worker advocates with assistance or prompting. 0 – Co-worker does not advocate.			
Item 8:	*Evaluating.* The co-worker evaluates and provides (written/verbal) feedback to the target employee.	2	1	0
	2 – Co-worker evaluates and provides feedback. 1 – Co-worker evaluates without providing feedback. 0 – Co-worker does not evaluate or provide feedback.			
Item 9:	*Giving Information.* The co-worker spontaneously provides information to the target employee.	2	1	0
	2 – Co-worker spontaneously gives information. 1 – Co-worker gives information only when asked by target employee. 0 – Co-worker does not give information even when asked.			
	TOTAL SCORE________(0 - 18)			

at placing and maintaining persons in supported employment, it is expected that job separation rates will decrease. Routine collection of job separation data allows the documentation of these trends over time. Chapter 18 in this volume presents information regarding job separation among supported employees.

AGENCY/EMPLOYER LEVEL. As mentioned above, individual data on hours worked, wages, benefits, job tenure, job separation, level of integration, and quality of life can be aggregated and used to represent the supported employment program in terms of the number of workers placed, average hours worked, average earnings, and so on. When comparing programs, it is important to remember that outcomes must be considered in conjunction with a number of other factors such as employee, program, and job characteristics. This will be discussed in a later section.

Employers' ratings of supported employment workers and the services they receive may be considered as an important piece of evaluative information both for the individual and the program. The Worker Performance Evaluation Form (see Table 14.5) provides one way of collecting employer satisfaction information (White & Rusch, 1986).

COMMUNITY LEVEL. Benefits to the community as a result of supported employment can include taxes paid by supported employment workers as well as alternate program costs or public assistance saved by their participation in supported employment. These variables are typically included in efficiency evaluation.

Efficiency Evaluation

Efficiency describes the extent to which a program achieves its successes at reasonable cost in terms of resource inputs and comparative programs. As efficiency or benefit-cost analysis of supported employment programs is the topic of Chapter 16 of this volume, it will not be discussed here.

THE INTERACTIVE NATURE OF SUPPORTED EMPLOYMENT

Up to this point evaluation of the various aspects of supported employment programs (i.e., process, outcomes) have been discussed separately. As mentioned earlier, it may be misleading to assess the outcomes of a program without considering other variables such as the level of employee disability served or the amount of employment specialist support available. For this reason it may be desirable to conceptualize a supported employment program as an interactive system made up of individual, employment, and agency variables coming together to produce a set of outcomes. These outcomes will, in turn, influence subsequent individual, employment, and agency variables.

A comprehensive evaluation of supported employment includes monthly or quarterly collection of data on many or all of the variables listed in Table 14.6. The variables to be included should relate directly to the evaluation questions of interest and the focus of the evaluation. Complete descriptive statistics (i.e., mean, range, standard deviation, frequency) of each variable category can be reported along with analyses depicting the interactions among variables. For example, descriptive statistics concerning the average level of functioning of supported employees served by the program, average wages earned, and level of integration might be reported for a particular supported employment program. However, merely reporting averages may not present a clear picture of what is happening in a supported employment project. A second analysis might be performed to demonstrate the interaction between the level of employee functioning and level of integration or wages earned. Longitudinal data collection collected over the life of a supported employment program or group of programs will allow the observation of trends over time.

Obviously, the need to organize and manipulate an ongoing data set in the ways described here demands the capabilities of a computer and a database software package. Creation and maintenance of a management information system for a supported employment program may seem like a considerable outlay of time and resources, yet the benefit of having information readily available to aid in decision making may be well worth the initial expenditure.

As stated in the introduction, if the information system is to be maximally useful, it must be grounded in everyday realities. One important consideration is how current information must be in order to meet the needs of evaluation stakeholders. This is the topic of the next section.

FORMATIVE AND SUMMATIVE EVALUATION UTILIZATION

For many programs, evaluation is a yearly event describing a project's accomplishments, activities, goals, and expenditures for the purpose of justifying past or securing future funding. This type of evaluation is often referred to as a summative evaluation. Although it fulfills the requirements for securing funding, compliance monitoring, or accountability, the preordinate timeline may limit its usefulness as an aid to daily decision making.

Table 14.5 Worker Performance Evaluation Form

Employee______________________ Employer______________________

Job Title______________________ Supervisor______________________

Months Employed______________

Please rate employee in the following categories:	Excellent	Good	Average	Below Average	Does Not Apply
1. Attendance and punctuality					
2. Work rate					
3. Work quality					
4. Accepts responsibility					
5. Accepts criticism from supervisor					
6. Works independently					
7. Follows directions					
8. Takes initiative					
9. Judgment/problem solving skills					
10. Adjusts to changes in routine					
11. Safety conscious					
12. Interacts well with co-workers					
13. Courteous to customers					
14. Personal appearance					

Is the job coach maintaining an acceptable amount of contact with you as the employer?

_____ yes _____ no

Comments:

____

____

____

______________________ Supervisor ______________ Date

THANK YOU

Table 14.6 The Illinois Supported Employment Project Job Separation Form

(1) AGENCY NUMBER:____________ (2) WORKER NUMBER:____________

(3) REPORTED JOB SEPARATION DATE:____________

(4) EMPLOYER:____________

(5) TYPE OF JOB:

_____ Light industrial
_____ Laundry
_____ Warehouse
_____ Janitorial/maintenance
_____ Retail
_____ Grounds maintenance
_____ Food service
_____ Clerical
_____ Health care
_____ Other (specify)____________

(6), (7), & (8) REASONS FOR JOB SEPARATION: Please check the primary reason for separation. If a single reason cannot be determined, check *one* additional reason for job separation. Rank order reasons based on importance (e.g., "1 - low quality work, 2 - maladaptive behavior).

_____ Transportation problem
_____ Does not want to work
_____ Economic situation of employer
_____ Low-quality work
_____ Poor social skills
_____ Insubordinate behavior
_____ Parent/guardian initiated
_____ Continual prompting required
_____ Criminal behavior
_____ Supervisor(s) or co-workers are "uncomfortable" with employee
_____ Poor job match
_____ Parental interference
_____ Poor attendance/tardy
_____ Deceased
_____ Work rate too slow
_____ Poor appearance
_____ Maladaptive behavior
_____ Poor work attitude
Financial aid threatened
_____ Medical/health problem
_____ Seasonal layoff
_____ Moved away
_____ Took better job (e.g., better wages, more hours)
_____ Hired by company
_____ No longer needed supported employment services
_____ Retired

(9) PLEASE PROVIDE BRIEF CLARIFICATION OF THE REASON(S) CHECKED:

Reason #1:____________

Reason #2: (if applicable)____________

(10) AMOUNT OF TIME EMPLOYED PRIOR TO JOB SEPARATION: _____ Months _____ Weeks

Table 14.6 (cont.)

(11) AVERAGE HOURS OF JOB COACH ON-SITE ASSISTANCE PER WEEK DURING MONTH PRIOR TO JOB SEPARATION (Time spent by job coach with the target employee at the job site engaging in training, retraining, data collection, or observation): ______

DESCRIPTION OF WHAT HAS HAPPENED TO INDIVIDUAL FOLLOWING JOB SEPARATION: Please check the category that most closely describes the placement of the individual following his or her separation from supported employment.

(12) INDIVIDUAL WAS PLACED INTO A VOCATIONAL PROGRAM OFFERED BY *YOUR* AGENCY: Please check the vocational program the person entered immediately following the job separation.

________ Another supported employment site
________ Adult day care (DT I, Illinois)
________ Work activity (DT II, Illinois)
________ Work adjustment training
________ Skills training program (Training for a limited time in a specific occupational area. For example, janitorial or food service)
________ Extended sheltered employment (Regular Work, Illinois)
________ Competitive employment with time-limited follow-up
________ Other (specify):____

(13) INDIVIDUAL WAS PLACED INTO A VOCATIONAL PROGRAM OFFERED BY *ANOTHER* AGENCY: Please check the vocational program the person entered immediately following the job separation.

________ Another supported employment site
________ Adult day care (DT I, Illinois)
________ Work activity (DT II, Illinois)
________ Work adjustment training
________ Skills training program (Training for a limited time in a specific occupational area. For example, janitorial or food service)
________ Extended sheltered employment (Regular Work, Illinois)
________ Competitive employment with time-limited follow-up
________ Other (specify):____

(14) INDIVIDUAL IS NO LONGER RECEIVING VOCATIONAL SERVICES FROM AN ADULT SERVICE AGENCY: If applicable, please check the appropriate category.

________ Working without support from an adult service agency (specify):
Type of job________________________ Employer________________________

________ Receiving only nonvocational services (e.g., counseling, case management)
________ Not working
________ No record on individual

(15) POSITION OF PERSON COMPLETING FORM

________ Job Coach/Employment Training Specialist
________ Program Coordinator
________ Other (specify):________________________________

14.1 Diagram Showing the Interactive Nature of Individual, Employment, and Agency Variables to Produce Outcomes in Supported Employment Program Evaluation.

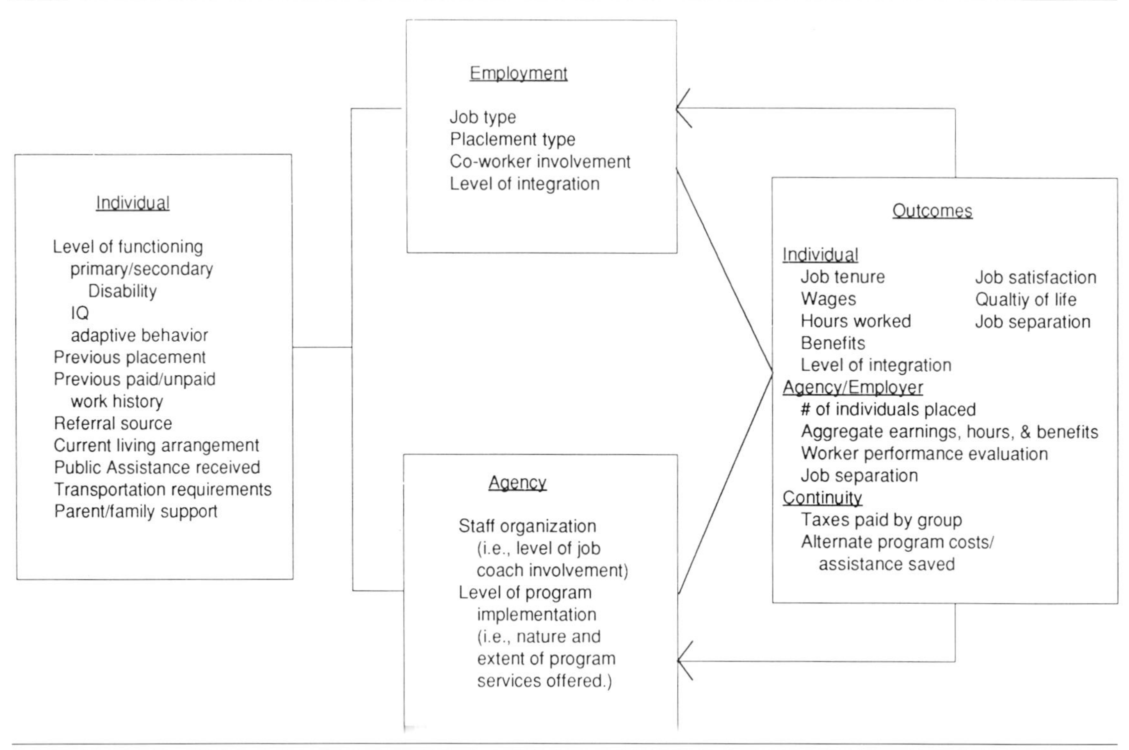

Program administrators and staff make decisions about the course of a program throughout its life, not merely in the advent of refunding. If these day-to-day decisions are to be influenced by data describing what is happening in the supported employment program, these data must be recent, relevant, and easily accessible to the decision-maker. Evaluation data collection must therefore be an ongoing and continuous event. Data on worker characteristics, employment and agency variables, and outcome can be collected monthly, bimonthly, or quarterly, depending on the data needs and data collection capabilities of the project's personnel. In this way, evaluation data can be used to guide and give feedback on program development or program improvement efforts in the manner of formative evaluation.

A computerized management information system allows for continuous entry and updating of evaluation information, greatly enhancing a project's capability to conduct ongoing formative evaluation as an aid to program management and decision making. Maintaining such a database and using evaluative data in an ongoing manner also makes it easier to respond to requests for summative evaluation as the information is readily available and easily aggregated across time.

Persons in different positions within supported employment programs (i.e. funders, program administrators, job placement specialists) are likely to have differing ongoing information needs. In order to be maximally useful, a supported employment management information system must meet the multi-level, multi-user information needs of evaluation stakeholders.

MULTI-PERSON/MULTI-LEVEL UTILIZATION

A state agency that funds many supported employment programs is interested in knowing the relative effectiveness of these programs in placing workers with severe mental retardation into food service positions. A program administrator in a supported employment program wants to determine the average number of employment training specialist hours necessary to place and train workers in a local hotel laundry. An employment training specialist would like to determine the level of co-worker involvement experienced by a particular supported employee in an effort to identify naturally occurring cues in the work environment. Each of these examples represents different levels and information needs, yet each can be accommodated by the information system presented in this chapter.

Several factors facilitate multi-person/multi-level utilization of evaluation information in supported employment. First, if information is to be aggregated or compared across programs, a subset of variables, their definitions, and method and timelines for collection must be common to all programs. For example, if a variable such as level of employment specialist involvement is to be compared across projects, a standard operational definition such as "number of hours per week spent in training, observing, or interacting with the worker, his or her employer or supervisor, or co-workers" must be adopted. A common form and specified time (i.e., third week of each month) would serve to improve the quality of data collected. Failure to standardize definitions and means of reporting may result in data that are misleading or uninterpretable when aggregated.

A second factor that encourages multi-person/multi-level use is the degree to which the data are complete and current. The period of time between data collection and entry should be minimized. An ideal situation is one where data are entered directly into the computer as collected, eliminating the need for pencil-and-paper coding.

Direct entry of data by employment training specialists, program coordinators, and program administrators necessitates that each is familiar with and has access to the management information system software and a computer terminal. This access and familiarity is likely to increase the use of the system to answer questions as they arise in the life of the program. Multi-level staff training in the use of the management information system is a vital part of the adoption of such a system. In fact, in terms of variables to be included, timelines for data collection and methods for data entry and analysis may increase the responsiveness of the system to its user groups.

SUMMARY

Supported employment programs are emerging as the preferred method of service delivery in schools and adult service agencies across the nation. As with any rapidly growing initiative, evaluation activities play an important role in the development and "fine tuning" of supported employment programs. Evaluation is also needed to determine the outcomes of supported employment at individual, agency/employer, and community levels and to assess the impact of supported employment on the quality of life of workers. In order to address these multiple purposes, an evaluation system must be reasonable in scope, flexible, ongoing, and easily accessible to its various stakeholders.

While compliance monitoring satisfies the most basic need to know if a support employment program is operating in accordance with federal and state statutes, program evaluation can take on different foci depending on the curiosity and information needs of evaluation stakeholders. These foci can include an emphasis on process, outcomes, or the interactive nature of supported employment.

Whatever its focus, an evaluation system is one that is well suited to the information needs and the evaluation capabilities of its users. For this reason, users must be involved in planning and maintaining all aspects of the evaluation system. The system itself should undergo periodic evaluation to ensure that it is sufficiently meeting the needs of its users.

Effective evaluation can be critical in advancing the success of individual supported employment programs and the entire supported employment initiative. Documenting and disseminating what works and what doesn't in supported employment will enable others to develop programs based on past experience. If supported employment is to continue to grow as a service option, evidence of its benefits for workers, agencies, employers, and the community must be readily available and well publicized. Program evaluation can provide that evidence.

QUESTIONS (For answers see p. 433)

1. How does the author describe a good evaluation system?

2. Name and describe key elements of each of the four supported employment evaluation foci suggested by the author.

3. What is the purpose of the Degree of Implementation instrument?

4. Name three types of outcome variables that comprise supported employment from an interactive system perspective.

5. Identify some important individual outcome variables.

6. What is the purpose of the Integration Index?

7. What is the purpose of the Worker Performance Evaluation Form?

8. What advantages accrue from having a computerized management information system?

9. Name factors that facilitate multi-person/multi-level utilization of evaluation information in supported employment.

REFERENCES

Attkisson, C. C., Hargreaves, W. A., Horowitz, M. J., & Sorenson, L. E. (Eds.) (1978). *Evaluation of human service programs*. New York: Academic Press.

Federal Register, *52* (157), August 14, 1987.

Goode, D. A. (1988). Quality of life and quality of work life. In W. E. Kiernan and R. L. Schalock (Eds.). *Economics, Industry and Disability*. Baltimore: Paul Brookes.

Heal, L. & Chadsey-Rusch, J. (1985). *Lifestyle satisfaction scale* (LSS): Assessing individuals' satisfaction with residence, community setting, and associated services. *Applied Research in Mental Retardation, 6*, 475–490.

Lagomarcino, T. L. (1989). *Assessing integration in supported employment contexts*. Unpublished doctoral dissertation. Urbana: University of Illinois at Urbana-Champaign.

Long, D. A., Mallar, C. D., & Thornton, C. V. D. (1981). Evaluating the benefits and costs of the Job Corps. *Journal of Policy Analysis and Management, 1*(1), 55–76.

Madaus, G., Scriven, M., & Stufflebeam, D. (1985). *Evaluation models: Viewpoints on educational and human services evaluation*. Boston: Kluwer-Nijhoff Publishing.

Posavac, E. J. & Carey, R. G. (1980). *Program evaluation: Methods and case studies*. Engelwood Cliffs, NJ: Prentice Hall.

Rockart, J. F. (1979). Chief executives define their own data needs. *Harvard Business Review, 79*(3), 81–83.

Rossi, P. H., Freeman, H. E., & Wright, S. R. (1975). *Evaluation: A systematic approach*. Beverly Hills, CA: Sage Publications.

Rusch, F. R., Hughes, C., McNair, J., & Wilson, P. (1989). *Co-worker involvement scoring manual and instrument*. Champaign: University of Illinois.

Shalock, R. (1986). Defining and measuring the quality of work and outside life. Paper presented at the 1986 Annual TASH Conference, San Francisco.

Trach, J. S., Rusch, F. R., & DeStefano, L. (1987). Supported employment program development degree of implementation manual. In J. S. Trach and F. R. Rusch (Eds.). *Supported employment in Illinois: Program implementation and evaluation*. Champaign: University of Illinois, Illinois Supported Employment Project.

Trach, J. S. & Rusch, F. R. (in press). Supported employment program evaluation: Degree of implementation and selected outcomes. *American Journal on Mental Retardation*.

Worthen, B. R. & Sanders, J. R. (1987). *Educational evaluation: Alternative approaches and practical guidelines*. New York: Longman.

White, D. & Rusch, F. (1983). Social validation in competitive employment. Evaluating work performance. *Applied Research in Mental Retardation, 4*, 343–354.

PART

III

Introduction to Supported Employment Issues

Robert Gaylord-Ross
San Francisco State University

Supported employment is in its second decade of operation since the founding of the University of Washington Food Service Program (Connis, Sowers, & Thompson, 1978; Rusch & Schutz, 1979; Wehman, 1981). The first phase of supported employment demonstrated that persons with the more severe disabilities could be successfully employed in nonsheltered settings. Concurrent with these demonstrations, a political movement emerged that advocated the expansion of supported employment programs throughout the nation. Indications of this movement were the passage of the federal transition initiation (98-199) in 1985 and the supported employment amendment to the Vocational Rehabilitation Act in 1986. Although advocacy rhetoric and bandwagon demonstration is probably necessary for the advancement of a political movement, it appears that we may be entering a more sober phase in the history of supported employment. Larger data bases are emerging from regional and state efforts. As supported employment attains a more statutory position, investigators may wear their scientific coats more often than their advocacy ones. The chapters in this book in general, and in this issues section in particular, reflect this attempt to objectively appraise the accomplishments and shortfalls of supported employment. The authors address broad issues of policy and economics, as well as more practical matters of improving the technology of supported employment programs. Thus the chapters offer a nice balance of appraising the past while forecasting the future.

ECONOMICS

As an aggregate of supported employment programs appears, economists may begin to index outcome data in terms of its costs and benefits to society, and this task is no easy matter. Although costs may be more objectively determined, it is not always clear how they are absorbed by different agencies. Estimating benefits may easily trap the investigator in a quagmire. Monetary benefits to what people or agencies? Quality-of-life advantages to whom?

The authors in this volume present a lucid and informative presentation of benefit-cost factors in supported employment. Walls, Dowler, and Fullmer (Chapter 15) clearly explain price indexing. They portray the consumer as a rational being who will analyze fiscal matters to determine whether it makes economic sense to work or remain unemployed. They make a convincing case that, when economic forces are favorable for the individual, people will choose to work. It might be pointed out that Halpern (1973) showed how, even in undesirable economic circumstances, rehabilitation programs can place individuals into competitive employment.

The Conley and Noble piece (Chapter 16) is a true *tour de force* because of their precise exposition in their analysis of the State of Illinois data base. They point out that their current analyses of supported employment costs are not as sanguine as originally proposed. It appears that, as programs attain longevity, their costs are reduced in terms of level of supervision and other cost-cutting measures (e.g., space rental mentioned by Parent & Hill, Chapter 19). It appears that economists like Conley and Noble will have to integrate consumer and societally based estimates of benefit costs.

THE DYNAMICS OF WORKING

From a client-based perspective, the Lagomarcino piece (Chapter 18) is both telling and provocative. A long-standing goal in vocational special education has been to identify the main causes of job termination. In analyzing a statewide survey from Illinois, Lagomarcino offers the field its largest data base yet for isolating the factors that contribute to job separation. In the past, researchers interpreted their survey findings in relation to job production (accuracy, rate, duration) and social skills (interaction, role-following, outbursts, conduct). Although most studies have reported on the importance of these two factors, investigators oftentimes emphasize social factors in their conclusions and recommendations. Lagomarcino suggests the lack of job responsibility as the primary cause for job terminations. Job responsibility means commitment to a job, and the lack of it is reflected in poor attendance, poor work attitudes, or absence of work motivation. Lack of responsibility accounted for 17 percent of separations, whereas inadequate task production accounted for 12 percent and poor social skills for 10 percent of all terminations. Thus motivation is a variable that must receive increasing attention. Lagomarcino cites Turner (1984) in pointing out that individuals leaving a sheltered workshop rarely choose competitive employment and often suffer "peer group displacement." Yet Jones (1989) recently found that the quality of work life improved for developmentally disabled adults who moved from sheltered to supported employment.

Persons may also lack work motivation because of a poor match between the ecological work demands and individual preferences and abilities (Calkins & Walker, 1989). Practitioners and researchers thus need to further explore job selection, work reinforcement, and job accommodation variables. In examining these variables, we notice certain interesting relationships. For example, almost all jobs for persons with developmental disabilities have been simple, repetitive entry-level positions. The lack of intrinsic reinforcement in these jobs appears more directly to affect persons with mild disabilities. Wehman and colleagues (1982) have shown that persons with more severe disabilities are more likely to be terminated for external reasons like economic lay-offs. Mildly disabled persons are terminated for internal variables of their own doing, such as lack of motivation and social skills. Also, severely disabled persons have lower rates of termination.

These facts might lead us to certain tentative conclusions. First, motivational and job-matching variables ought to receive more attention, especially for those persons with mild disabilities. Although Mank, Buckley, and Rhodes (Chapter 17) are rightfully concerned that 85 percent of those receiving supported employment are in the mild/moderate level, this group may in fact have the highest termination rates. Persons in the mild group may in some cases be offered more job coaching than they need (Mank et al.), yet they might need more off-site counseling and assessment. Similarly, the more time-consuming on-site services might be better deployed to place and train substantially more persons with severe disabilities.

THE FUTURE

Whitehead (Chapter 20) optimistically points to the many employment opportunities for disabled persons in the future. In spite of the growth in technological professions, numerous lesser-skilled positions will be embedded within technical settings and related service industries. Already a number of industries have targeted senior citizens and disabled persons to fill a variety of positions, particularly those that are part-time and those that have a high turnover.

Supported employment will continue to expand as it engenders political support (Gaylord-Ross, 1987). Although Mank, Buckly, and Rhodes report on the innovative state initiatives to institutionalize supported employment, they state that only 10 percent of adults with developmental disabilities are accessing this service. This 10 percent figure is even more dismal when one considers that it does not include the many individuals on waiting lists for adult services. This waiting list phenomenon is one that potentially undercuts the benefit-cost analyses that compare supported employment to alternative segregated programs. Although Conley and Noble believe that some programs are becoming normative, Ward and Halloran (in press) report otherwise, citing growing waiting lists for adult services.

We will extricate ourselves from this economic morass only by generating most creative solutions. Parent and Hill suggest that one such solution could involve redefining supported employees so as to "pay" for their vocational services through social security adjustments. Although current benefit-cost analyses may show increasing gains, these economic benefits seldom flow back to the individual program. Johnson (Chapter 21) reports that supported employment professionals responding to a survey state that their greatest concern is continued and adequate resources to fund their programs. Shoestring program budgets lead to low-paid job coaches with 47 percent turnover rates (Johnson). Creative fiscal solutions will permit benefit monies (tax contributions, lower SSI payment) to flow back to vocational programs, perhaps through a client voucher (Gaylord-Ross, in press).

Supported employment is a program model that works. As this book well documents, persons with disabilities can be successfully employed in nonsheltered work settings, with subsequent fiscal and lifestyle benefits. The universal appearance of supported employment is likely to depend on forces larger than those of this profession. The broader society must express a political will to fund social programs in general and supported employment in particular. Unfortunately, supported employment emerged in the politically conservative 1980s when program cutbacks were commonplace. Yet nations in both the East and West are currently experimenting with admixtures of capitalism and socialism, attempting to maximize business gains while advancing principles of social justice for their citizens. Disabled persons can play a critical role in business and service ventures. The motivation of clients and corporations appears to be crucial in the unfolding of this vision.

REFERENCES

Calkins, C. F. & Walker, H. M. (1989). Enhancing employment outcomes through habilitation planning for social competence. In W. E. Kiernan & R. L. Schalock (Eds.), *Economics, industry, and disability*. Baltimore: Paul H. Brookes Publishing Co.

Connis, R. T., Sowers, J., & Thompson, L. E. (1978). *Training the mentally handicapped for employment*. New York: Human Science Press.

Gaylord-Ross, R. (1987). Vocational integration for persons with mental handicaps: A crosscultural perspective. *Research in Developmental Disabilities, 8*, 531–548.

Gaylord-Ross, R. (in press). Review of *Economics, industry, and disability*, W. E. Kiernan & R. L. Schalock (Eds.). Baltimore: Paul H. Brookes Publishing Co., *American Journal of Mental Retardation*.

Halpern, A. S. (1973). Several unemployment and vocational opportunities for EMR individuals. *American Journal of Mental Deficiency, 78*, 123–127.

Jones, C. (1989). *Quality of work life experiences, segregated and integrated*. Unpublished masters thesis, San Francisco State University.

Rusch, F. R. & Schutz, R. P. (1979). Nonsheltered employment of the mentally retarded adult: Research to reality? *Journal of Comtemporary Business, 8,* 85–98.

Wehman, P. (1981). *Competitive employment: New horizons for severely disabled individuals.* Baltimore: Paul H. Brookes.

Wehman, P., Hill, J., Soodall, R., Cleveland, R., Brooke, V., & Pentecost, J. (1982). Job placement and follow-up of moderately and severely handicapped individuals after three years. *Journal of the Association for Severely Handicapped, 7,* 5–16.

Ward, M. & Halloran, W. (in press). Government report on services for developmentally disabled adults. *Career Development for Exceptional Individuals.*

C H A P T E R

15

Incentives and Disincentives to Supported Employment

Richard T. Walls
Denetta L. Dowler
Steven L. Fullmer
West Virginia University

What do supported employees want? What do their parents/guardians/caretakers want? What do their employment specialists want? What do employers want? What does the Social Security Administration want? Each of these questions ends with the word "want." These are questions of incentive. If we ask what these key actors in supported employment want to avoid, disincentives are the topic.

In this chapter, incentives and disincentives are considered from both a psychological and an economic perspective. These dominant theoretical views contain summaries and explanations of why people do or do not engage in productive employment as well as predictions about what should happen when supported employees, their parents/guardians, employment specialists, employers, and social service agencies are faced with economic decisions. Further, the context in which these decisions are made is partially created by rules according to which cash and in-kind benefit programs operate. The success of supported employment depends on the synergy of key actors operating in a beneficial environment to create a system that encourages rather than discourages integration into the workforce.

THEORETICAL PERSPECTIVES

Incentives and disincentives: Psychological theory.

An incentive is on the stimulus end of the stimulus-response-consequence contingency (Figure 15.1). It is an object or condition perceived as capable of satisfying a motive or drive. Because of past experience with the object or condition, the person learns that attainment of that goal object or condition should satisfy the motive or drive. It is desirable. Such expectancies may be learned either through direct experiences with reinforcing consequences or through vicarious experiences. Although a person may never have experienced a particular reinforcing consequence of his or her own behavior, the effects can be generalized from similar experiences or from observation or hearing about the consequences that other people have experienced.

Modern expectancy theory (Bolles, 1972; 1978) holds that the person will make a response if the perceived value of the consequence is sufficiently high. Most people would be more likely to buy a $1 raffle ticket for the giveaway of a new car than for a new potholder. Most peo-

Figure 15.1 Incentives and disincentives in psychological theory

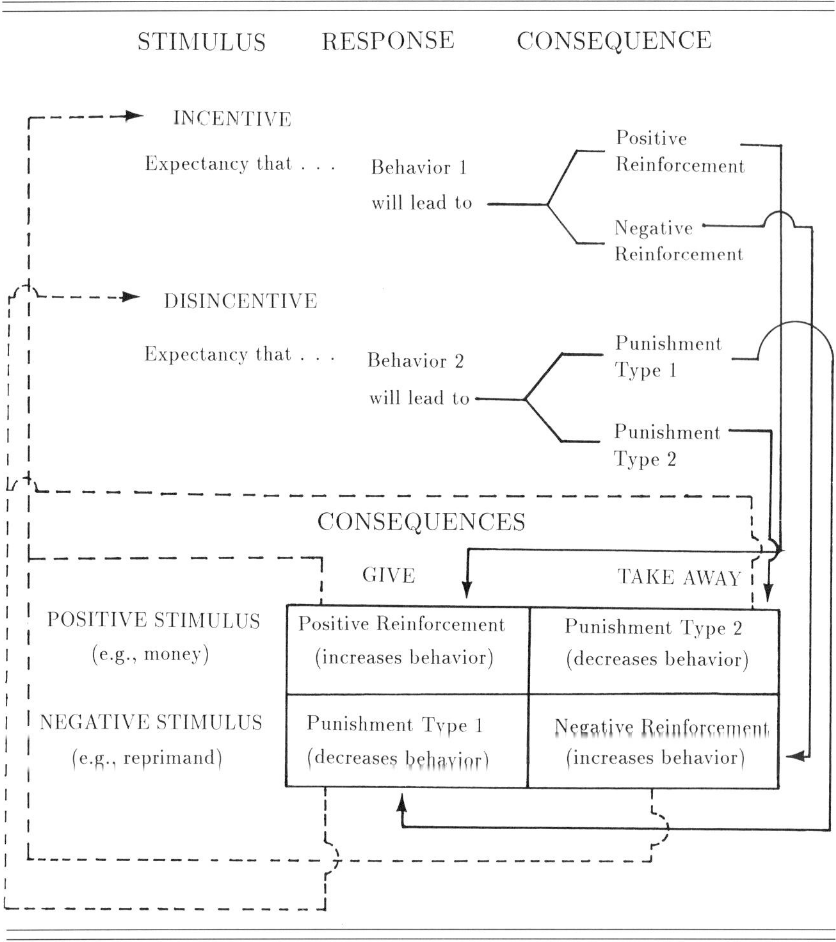

ple who buy raffle tickets for new car give-aways have never won a car before. They can, however, anticipate the reinforcing consequence of winning. This anticipation comes from such sources as riding in new cars, hearing about other people winning big prizes, and reading magazine ads. The perceived chances (expectancy) of attaining the reinforcing consequence (object or condition) also influence whether or not the response will be made. If the chances are one in a million of winning the car, some potential buyers would be discouraged, although people tend to overestimate their chances of winning a lottery (Kahneman & Tversky, 1984).

It sounds confusing to say that perception (anticipation or expectancy) of the consequence can serve as a stimulus leading to a response. Simply, if the person has learned from direct or vicarious experience to expect (stimulus), that doing something (response) will likely lead to a reinforcing outcome (consequence), and if the response cost is not too high, the person will try to do it. The expectancy has become a stimulus, an incentive, for action.

A disincentive can also serve as a stimulus; it is an expectancy about a consequence that the person wants to avoid. As with incentives, these expectancies may be learned either through direct experience or vicariously. The perceived (a) aversiveness of the punishing consequence, (b) response cost (difficulty in making the avoiding response), and (c) chances of the response being successful in avoiding the noxious object or condition likewise contribute to the decision to act or not to act.

A person at the beach would likely put on shoes or sandals before walking on hot sand if other people are observed wincing and stepping lightly. The expectancy of discomfort serves as a disincentive for going barefoot. People often avoid a particular group at lunch or in a gathering if they anticipate having to talk with abrasive or boring people. The expectancy of an unpleasant encounter is a disincentive for contacting this group. An appropriate response may be made to an inaccurately perceived consequence. For example, historical avoidance of individuals who were psychologically disabled was based on a faulty expectancy.

Again, anticipation that a response will allow a person to avoid a punishing consequence serves as a stimulus for that avoiding response. Simply, if a person has learned from direct or vicarious experience an expectancy (stimulus) that doing something (response) will likely avoid a punishing outcome (consequence), the person will try to do it. The expectancy has become a stimulus, a disincentive, for action.

As noted, incentive and disincentive effects are related to direct or vicarious experience with reinforcing or punishing consequences. In positive reinforcement, the consequence of a person's response increases the probability that the response will be emitted again. In negative reinforcement, the removal of a negative stimulus after a response increases the probability of that response. In punishment, the consequence of the person's response decreases the probability of that response being emitted in the future. This punishing consequence may be in the form of either presentation of an aversive event (punishment Type 1) or removal of a positive circumstance (punishment Type 2) (see Figure 15.1).

EXAMPLE 1: EXPECTANCIES OF REINFORCEMENT AND PUNISHMENT. Suppose Amy is a 23-year-old woman who has never worked outside her home. Her education included a certificate of graduation in special education. Amy receives $354 per month in SSI benefits. She lives with her mother who has always managed her affairs for her. Amy was evaluated by Vocational Rehabilitation (VR) and found to be too severely disabled to be a good candidate for vocational rehabilitation services. The prospect of a minimum wage job at a local grocery store excites Amy and scares her mother. Amy would like to have her own checking account, meet people, get out of the house more often, and be viewed by her family as a responsible adult. Her mother, on the other hand, does not want Amy to participate because Amy may fail in her attempt at competitive employment. She is also concerned that Amy will lose her SSI benefits and that her wages will not replace them.

In this example, work and the resultant wages are incentives for Amy. She expects that working will lead to (a) earnings (positive reinforcement), (b) new respect from her family (positive reinforcement), and (c) getting out of the house more often (negative reinforcement). Expectancies (a) and (b) were learned vicariously through seeing or hearing about others attain similar objectives. The last expectancy was learned through direct experience in the community.

Fear that Amy will fail and the potential loss of SSI benefits are disincentives for Amy's mother. She expects that if her daughter tries to work in the community she may be treated badly and may suffer emotionally from the experience (punishment Type 1). She also knows that the family needs the income from Amy's SSI check and is afraid those benefits will be lost (punishment Type 2). The first expectancy was learned through direct experience of observing her daughter's capabilities and the reactions of others over the years. The second expectancy was learned vicariously through stories she has heard about others who went to work and lost their benefits.

Incentives and disincentives: Microeconomic theory.

In microeconomic terms, incentives and disincentives may be viewed as sets of economic circumstances that influence utility maximization decisions. Maximizing utility means that people choose the set of circumstances that gives them the highest satisfaction possible within their budget constraints. People will not voluntarily enroll in a public benefit program or a supported employment program unless they think they will profit from it (Hanks, 1986). Walls, Zawlocki, & Dowler (1986) expressed the concepts of utility function (preference curve) and price (income) line as related to utility maximization with the following example. A child goes into a candy store with a dime in her pocket. She chooses two Mary Janes (2 cents), one Tootsie Pop Drop (3 cents), and one jaw breaker (5 cents). This combination has highest utility for her, given her budget constraint. She would rather have this combination than two jaw breakers or ten Mary Janes or any other combination that she can afford. A preference curve is used in microeco nomics to represent the points at which a person is equally satisfied with the possible combinations of circumstances. All the choices represented by the points on this utility or preference curve are equally acceptable. In the example, the child's utility function is such that she would just as soon have an ice cream bar (25 cents), three jaw breakers (15 cents), or two jaw breakers and a Tootsie Pop Drop (13 cents) as what she chose. All four choices have equal satisfaction value for her. She maximized utility by choosing the only one of these four combinations she could afford. Economically speaking, the point at which her utility function (preference curve) touched her price or income line dictated her decision.

Although the stakes are much higher in supported employment, the concepts are the same. In any utility function (preference curve), there is a trade-off. In the following example, if people work more hours and earn more money, they will have fewer leisure hours, and vice-versa.

Example 2: Maximizing Utility. Suppose, in this example, that three people have the same preferences associated with work, leisure time, and income, and they have the same ability to earn money. In other words, even though their utility functions will be at different levels, they will have the same shape. All three are men who can work at the minimum wage ($3.35 per hour, or $536 per month before taxes). We will say that their take-home pay after 20 percent taxes and withholding is $536 × .20 = $429 per month for 160 hours of work (Figure 15.2).

Person 1 can earn minimum wage ($3.35 per hour, or $2.68 after taxes) for various numbers of hours of work, as illustrated by his income opportunity line ABC. He prefers to work full-time (160 hours per month). Although all points on the Person 1 preference curve are equally attractive to him, this full-time position is the one that touches his preference curve (point B). So, Person 1 will work 160 hours and take home $429.

Person 2 is not working and is receiving $354 per month in benefits (point D). If he goes to work and loses all benefits, his income line is DABC. His preference curve touches his income opportunity line only at point D, and so he chooses not to work. He will not work a full-time job and lose all benefits including leisure time for a gain from $354 (tax-free benefits) to $429 (after taxes and withholding).

In a second scenario, instead of the precipitous 100 percent loss of benefits, suppose Person 2 is allowed to retain his benefits at a benefit-loss rate of 50 percent of earnings. That is, half of $3.35 (minimum wage) is subtracted from his benefits for every hour he works up to a breakeven point when he has lost the equivalent of all benefits. In this situation, if he chooses to work, he would essentially work for half wages for all 160 hours because he would not reach the breakeven point by working this job. That is, his benefits are $354; his salary is $536 gross ($429 after taxes); his breakeven point is $708 per month.

Looked at in one way, the extra money may be an incentive to work. He would now have $429 (take-home pay) + $86 (remaining benefits) = $515 (total). Looked at in another way, he is working a full month (160 hours) for $515 − $354 = $161. Most people would view a salary of only $161 for a month of work as a major disincentive. These views, of course, are predicated only on economic considerations; they do not consider social incentives or disincentives to work.

Person 3 has personal wealth that yields $354 each month in nonlabor income. His income opportunity line is DEF because he would not

Figure 15.2 Incentives and Disincentives in Microeconomic Theory

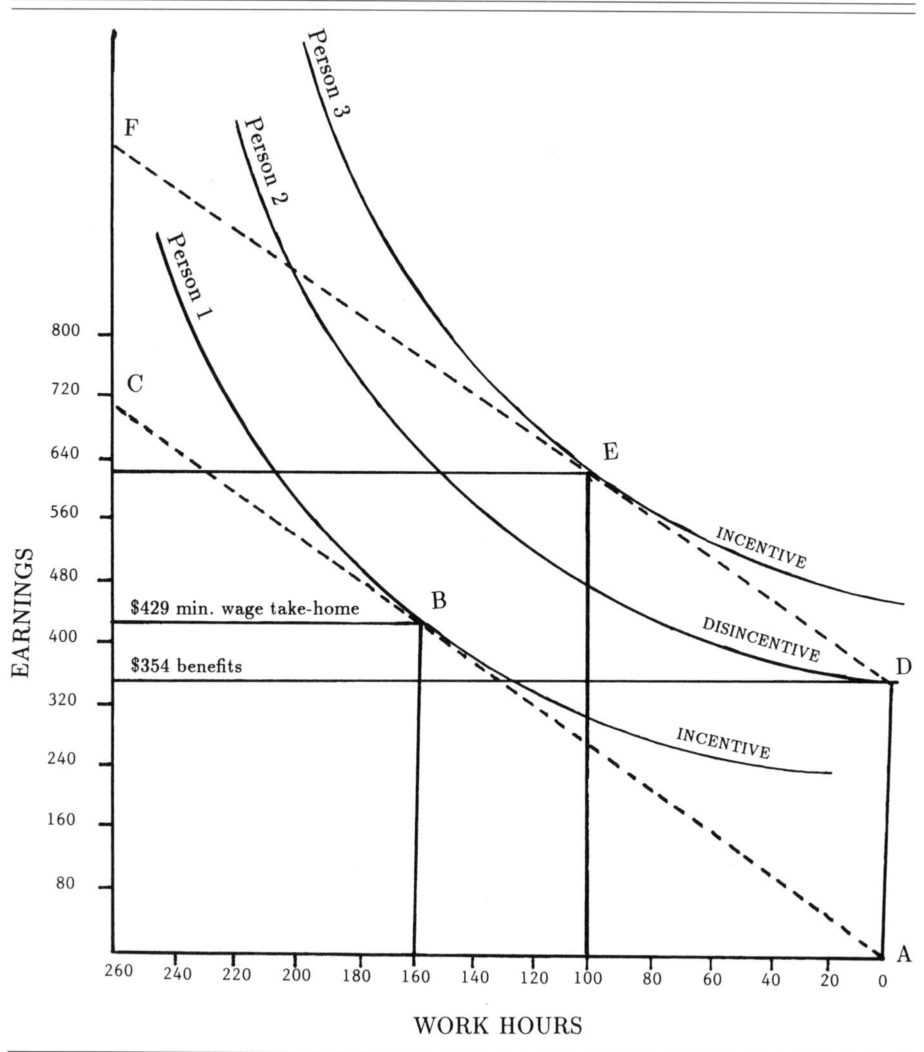

lose any of that $354 if he goes to work. His preference (utility) curve touches his income line at point E. He will maximize utility by working 100 hours (point E) to supplement his income. Expectancy of the extra income is an incentive rather than a disincentive. If Person 2 could work but chose not to, he might be labeled a chiseler. Even though Person 3 elected to work less than Person 1, he would never be called a chiseler. Remember, all three people have the same opportunity and ability to work and earn money. Because of the presence or absence of money from wealth and benefits, however, their preference curves are at different levels. These are decisions influenced by incentives and disincentives that may be described and explained through microeconomic or psychological theory. They involve no moral or ethical turpitude (Walls, Masson, & Werner, 1977).

A number of essays and research efforts have referred to economic disincentives that result when public support programs create obstacles to competitive employment (e.g., Berkowitz, 1981; Berkowitz, Horning, McConnell, Rubin, & Worrall, 1982; Conley, Noble, & Elder, 1986; Rusch, Mithaug, & Flexer, 1986; Walls, 1982;

Worrall, 1983). People often feel it is in their own best interest to remain dependent on public benefits, and economically speaking, this may indeed be the case.

Conley, Noble, and Elder (1986) cited reduction of net gain from work as a work disincentive created by income support and health care programs. The gains and losses in income must be weighed carefully by SSDI beneficiaries who are attempting employment. The loss in income associated with work activity is less severe for SSI beneficiaries owing to the $1 for $2 benefits reduction rule discussed later. Poole (1987) reported that for 120 individuals with cerebral palsy, there was a negative relationship between beneficiary status (receipt of SSI and/or SSDI benefits) and competitive employment.

Having to prove you are disabled and not able to do any substantial work activity starts the spiral of disincentive effects. Even before applicants are accepted as beneficiaries or recipients in a public benefit program, they must not work as partial demonstration that they can't work. Thus, planning to participate in income maintenance programs requires diminished work capacity and encourages reduction of commitment to employment (Greenblum & Bye, 1987). Accordingly, expectancy from psychological theory and utility maximization from microeconomic theory may be used either separately or in concert to interpret as well as forecast incentive and disincentive producing circumstances.

NUMBERS AND AMOUNTS

There are more than fifty cash and in-kind benefit programs from which target employees and their families might gain (Walls, Zawlocki, & Dowler, 1986). Supplemental Security Income (SSI) is the predominant benefit program for target employees, but many have Social Security Disability Insurance (SSDI) (Whitehead, 1988). There were an estimated 1,041,180 persons with developmental disabilities receiving SSI in December, 1987 (Office of Supplemental Security Income of the Social Security Administration). In 1984, there were 362,000 receiving Social Security Disability Insurance (SSDI) payments (Braddock, 1985, cited in Whitehead, 1987). The Office of Research and Statistics of the Social Security Administration estimated as of December, 1987 that there were 765,490 adult SSI recipients who were developmentally disabled. In addition, 275,690 people under age twenty-one were estimated to be SSI recipients. These recipients were projected to require lifelong support (Helms, 1988).

Aggregate data from seventy-two supported employment programs (N = 1,026) indicated that 60 percent of target employees were receiving SSI at referral, 47 percent were receiving Medicaid, 20 percent were receiving SSDI, 18 percent were receiving Medicare, 11 percent were receiving food stamps, 3 percent were receiving welfare, and 12 percent were receiving aid from other sources (J. Kregal, personal communication, August 16, 1988). They worked an average of twenty-six hours a week at $3.46 an hour ($360 per month). In one state, data for the first quarter of 1987 indicated that 212 target employees in individual supported jobs earned an average of $446 per month (28.2 hours per week at $3.95), and 200 individuals in clustered placements made an average of $237 per month (26.1 hours per week at $2.27) (Goodman, 1987). A national survey concerning adults with developmental disabilities who were placed in employment was conducted by Kiernan, McGaughey, Schalock, & Rowland (in press). Of those who received SSI or SSDI or both, 55 percent had their benefits affected by employment.

Examples of two states are provided to demonstrate the idea of wages, fringe benefits, and reasons for separation of supported employees from their jobs. In North Dakota, 229 target employees had worked at 305 positions averaging twenty hours a week and $2.72 an hour ($218 per month). Of these employees, 10 percent had sick leave, 15 percent had paid vacation, 9 percent had medical insurance, 5 percent had dental insurance, 18 percent had employee discounts, 32 percent had free or reduced-cost meals, 6 percent had other benefits, and 52 percent had no fringe benefits. Of the 109 separations reported,

41 percent resigned, 17 percent were laid off, and 39 percent were terminated. Reasons for separation were psycho/social (24 percent), took better job (22 percent), did not want to work (13 percent), work quality/quantity (11 percent), economic situation (9 percent), and other (21 percent) (VCU-RRTC, 1988a).

In Virginia, 831 supported employees had worked at 1,072 positions averaging 28 hours a week and $3.63 an hour ($407 per month). Among these employees, 33 percent had sick leave, 45 percent had paid vacation, 33 percent had medical insurance, 8 percent had dental insurance, 15 percent had employee discounts, 28 percent had free or reduced-cost meals, 12 percent had other benefits, and 35 percent had no fringe benefits. Of the 509 separations reported, 42 percent resigned, 15 percent were laid off, and 41 percent were terminated. Reasons for separation were psycho/social (23 percent), work quality/quantity (14 percent), does not want to work (12 percent), economic situation (12 percent), took better job (10 percent), and other (29 percent) (VCU-RRTC, 1988b).

Whitehead (1988) reported the findings of a survey concerning supported employment to which more than 300 professionals from 44 states responded. Increased wages to supported employment participants was reported as one benefit of the program. Griss (1985) also reported that fringe benefits, including health coverage, often were not provided to workers with severe chronic disabilities. Low wages and loss of medical coverage are often cited as primary disincentives for individuals with disabilities. Several respondents in Whitehead's (1988) survey indicated that the changes in SSI and other legislation were not fully understood either by recipients or professionals. Another problem reported by Whitehead is that the jobs obtained in integrated employment were often dead-end jobs with little chance of upward mobility.

Thus, the early reports of progress are encouraging but also highlight areas of concern. Higher wages are obviously an incentive to workers. Assurance of medical coverage, whether through Medicaid or employer insurance, is an obvious incentive for those who want to work. Misunderstanding of the complexities of earning wages and receiving reduced benefits or no benefits is a disincentive. The seasonal or dead-end nature of some supported employment placements is a disincentive. A success of supported employment programs has been an increase in wages for supported employees. In one sense, more money is an incentive to go to work. In another sense, higher earnings put the worker's social service benefits at risk and thus may act as a disincentive.

SOCIAL SECURITY DISABILITY INSURANCE (SSDI)

Historically, there has been philosophical disagreement about "benefits." The Disability Advisory Council (1988) to the Social Security Administration (SSA) reported that their study of the legislative history convinced them that the Social Security Disability Insurance (SSDI) program was designed to make monthly payments to insured workers who became "totally and permanently disabled." They cited a report of the House Ways and Means Committee saying that the monthly check would go to those who were "forced into premature retirement" because of disability. A contradictory second aspect of the legislation encouraged referral of SSDI beneficiaries for vocational rehabilitation services. The GAO (1987) claimed that, from its inception in 1954, a focus of SSDI has been to rehabilitate as many beneficiaries as possible and return them to the work force.

This philosophical dichotomy between premature retirement from the work force and rehabilitation to productive employment is alive and well today for target employees and their families. Across time for the same person, there may first be pressures to demonstrate an inability to work and later pressures to return to work. Across people at the same time, there are some who view benefits as retirement and use them for a ticket out of the work arena while others use benefits as a bootstrap to gain education and improved employment opportunity (Walls, Dowler, & Fullmer, 1989).

SSDI (Title II of the Social Security Act) gives income support (partial replacement of earnings lost due to disability) and Medicare insurance (health care for workers who were covered by Social Security, their spouses, and dependent children including disabled adult children) to workers who became disabled and unable to continue working. Although SSDI benefits are usually associated with former workers (disabled insured beneficiary, age eighteen to sixty-five), many supported employees in supported employment are "childhood disability beneficiaries." A disabled "adult child" beneficiary is aged eighteen years or older, was disabled before age twenty-two, and is the son or daughter of an SSA-covered former worker who is disabled, retired, or deceased.

Not more than 10 percent to 15 percent of all beneficiaries are thought to be realistic prospects for rehabilitation, and less than 1 percent are actually returned to the work force and removed from SSDI rolls (GAO, 1987). General Vocational Rehabilitation (VR) counselors with at least two years of experience (N = 1,560) were surveyed in the GAO study to help determine (a) why SSDI beneficiaries participate or do not participate in VR, and (b) what changes in SSDI rules might result in more beneficiaries returning to work. A substantial majority of counselors indicated that SSDI referrals were (a) more severely disabled, (b) less motivated to participate in rehabilitation, (c) more time-consuming for counselors, (d) more expensive to serve, and (e) less likely to succeed than other people referred for VR services.

In the ten states surveyed by GAO (1987), about 13 percent of the SSDI beneficiaries were referred to VR by SSA. When a separate study was conducted to see what happens to such referrals, the GAO found that about half of the referrals were considered unpromising and were not contacted by VR. Less than 25 percent responded to contacts from VR, and only 13 percent actually made application for VR services. Less than 1 percent are typically removed from the SSDI rolls through VR intervention (GAO, 1987). It does not appear to matter how active a state is in referring SSDI beneficiaries to VR; the outcomes remain about the same.

VR counselors believed the main reason for nonparticipation by SSDI beneficiaries was fear of losing SSDI benefits and Medicare coverage. Some counselors commented that many health insurance plans carried by potential employers exclude pre-existing conditions from coverage. Health insurance is not offered by some employers. Additionally, small companies fear the effect of hiring individuals with disabilities on their health insurance premiums. Counselors said that fewer than one-third of SSDI beneficiaries would be better off economically after completing rehabilitation services and taking a job. Even those who successfully complete a VR program often do not earn enough to make returning to work a viable alternative to SSDI benefits (GAO, 1987). Kiernan and Brinkman (in press) reported results from an earlier investigation surveying experts in the area of employment. They perceived the number one barrier to employment for adults with developmental disabilities to be "economic and benefit disincentives" (p. 19).

Traditionally, people were either too disabled to work and received SSDI benefits or they worked and received no benefits. This all-or-none dilemma can serve as a disincentive to people who are unsure of their ability to function in the workplace. Most VR counselors agreed that extended Medicare coverage and an extended period of eligibility instituted by SSA act as incentives to employment. For those beneficiaries who are motivated to return to work, they can serve to smooth out the transition from benefits to earnings. Additionally, however, they suggested that adopting a sliding benefit scale (such as the scale now used by SSI) for working beneficiaries and indefinitely extending Medicare coverage would encourage even more fearful beneficiaries to attempt working (GAO, 1987). Griss (1985) remarked, "By substituting a gradual reduction in benefits in the SSDI program as earned income rises below a breakeven point as exists in the SSI program, one can ensure that SSDI beneficiaries are always better off working than not working" (p. 87). In a randomly selected sample of 437 working-aged people with physical disabilities, about 20 percent claimed to have limited their work efforts to avoid losing

Medicaid or Medicare (Wisconsin Department of Health and Social Services, 1986).

1. Under the SSDI program, a worker who becomes disabled must wait five months after the disability begins before receiving disability benefits (SSA, 1987). This is an *incentive* to work if viewed as "that is too long to wait." It is a *disincentive* to work if viewed as "I can't work during this five-month period because I have to demonstrate disability so I can get benefits."

2. There is no new waiting period if a disabled worker returns to the disability rolls within five years of leaving them (SSA, 1987). This is an *incentive* to work if viewed as "I can get my benefits back without waiting if my disability later gets worse and prevents me from working."

3. There is a trial work period (nine months, not necessarily consecutive) in which each month that the target employee earns more than $75 (or fifteen hours of work for the self-employed) is counted as one of those nine months. Earnings, which average over $300 per month ($740 for persons who are blind) during or after the trial work period, are considered evidence of ability to perform substantial gainful activity and signal to SSA that this beneficiary is no longer disabled. Some groups have suggested that $300 is too low for substantial gainful activity and should be raised (Disability Advisory Council, 1988; Michigan Interagency Task Force on Disability, 1987). The reasoning is that the substantial gainful activity level should be high enough that people will not be afraid to try to work, thereby risking loss of SSDI or failure to qualify for SSI. An alternative that is often suggested is complete elimination of the substantial gainful activity level. Under this latter arrangement, eligibility is based solely on disability, not income, and the benefits received from public support programs would be adjusted (e.g., $1 reduction for $2 in earnings) up to the breakeven point. The Disability Advisory Council also recommended that the monthly earnings amount that counts toward the trial work period should be raised from $75 to the substantial gainful activity level. In the current system, SSDI checks may be stopped (with a three-month grace period) after the trial work period because of a month of substantial gainful activity during or after the trial work period (SSA, 1987). This is an *incentive* to work if viewed as "I can test my ability to work without losing benefits." This is a *disincentive* to work if viewed as "If I make more than $300, I'm going to lose my SSDI check." This is a well known disincentive to go to work for some people (e.g., Kiernan & Brinkman, in press; Walls, 1982; Walls, Zawlocki, & Dowler, 1986). Similarly, the limit on the maximum family benefit may encourage work reduction in order to keep the family under the limit.

4. SSA allows an extensive list of "impairment-related work expenses" (e.g., medical devices, attendant care, special transportation) to be deducted from the person's earnings when determining whether or not the individual's earnings exceeded the substantial gainful activity level. In addition, the dollar value of "employer wage subsidies" (for extra training or supervision) can be deducted from earnings that the Social Security Administration will count toward substantial gainful activity. This is an *incentive* to work if viewed as "I can subtract these expenses and subsidies from my earnings and retain my benefits." This is a *disincentive* to work if viewed as "I'm not going to take any chances with all these confusing rules." Legitimate disability-related work expenses and subsidies may help keep countable income under $300 and thus allow the worker to retain benefits. Sometimes wages are intentionally kept down and impairment-related work expense up; for example, a recipient might have earnings of $500 less $210 of impairment-related work expense, which equals $290 earnings for determining substantial gainful activity. Add to this the SSDI benefits of $483, which was the average SSDI check in Ohio for a single individual in 1987 (Whitehead & McCaffrey, 1988). This total of $983 is substantially better than the minimum wage level of $536 (or $429 after taxes). Further, the person will not lose the monthly SSDI check because he or she stayed below the substantial gainful activity level. Thus, people who can manipulate the system may work less than their physical or mental condition allows in order to retain benefits. The

Wisconsin Department of Health and Social Services (1986) commented that, "As long as their access to health care coverage is dependent on earning less than SGA, many persons with disabilities cannot afford to work" (p. 1).

5. There is an extended period of eligibility of thirty-six months beyond the trial work period for beneficiaries who have not medically recovered. If the person demonstrated the ability to perform substantial gainful activity during or after the trial work period, he or she will still get an SSDI check for the grace period and for any month earnings fall below the substantial gainful activity amount for three years after the trial work period ends (SSA, 1987; Whitehead & McCaffrey, 1988). This is an *incentive* to work if viewed as "If I can't work much during some months in the next three years I'll have my original SSDI amount those months to fall back on." This is a *disincentive* to work if viewed as "I can play games and still get my check for three years."

6. There is a twenty-four-month waiting period after SSDI benefits begin plus the initial five-month wait (for disabled insured beneficiaries) after disability onset to get Medicare coverage (SSA, 1987). This is an *incentive* to work if viewed as "I've got to get a job that has medical insurance as a fringe benefit because I can't wait twenty-nine months to get Medicare." This is a *disincentive* to work if viewed as "If I can hold out until I get Medicare (by using cash from SSDI or Medicaid from SSI), I'll have both cash to live on and medical coverage, without working." Medicare consists of automatic hospital insurance (Part A) and physician/outpatient insurance (Part B). Recipients can choose to have $24 per month subtracted from their SSDI check to cover the cost (Whitehead & McCaffrey, 1988). If SSDI benefits are lost because of earnings at the substantial gainful activity level but the person is not medically recovered, then Medicare eligibility continues throughout the three-year extended period of eligibility. As noted, a person's SSDI benefits might be stopped because of substantial gainful activity earning $300 (or medical recovery). But if a former disabled insured beneficiary becomes eligible again within five years (seven years for childhood disability beneficiaries), there is not a new Medicare waiting period. Further, disability beneficiaries who become disabled again more than five years later, based on the same (or directly related) impairment, do not have to go through another Medicare waiting period (Disability Advisory Council, 1988).

7. Policies and regulations of SSDI as well as SSI are "complex" (Division of Mental Health and Community Rehabilitation Services, 1988). There are "intricate technical aspects" (Whitehead, 1988). Most target employees and their parents are not students of the Social Security laws. There is major confusion about waiting periods, trial work periods, substantial gainful activity, impairment-related work expenses, countable income, pre-existing conditions, grace periods, extended period of eligibility, and the like. Parenthetically, there is also widespread lack of mastery of the details by rehabilitation workers and SSA professionals. The Social Security Administration is concerned about the confusion. J. K. McGill (Personal communication, January 27, 1989) noted the following.

> . . . we [Social Security Administration] would like to stress that we are aware of the difficulties in maintaining a high level of technical expertise in our local offices, and are continually working to remedy shortcomings in this area. Our extensive July 1987 training effort and our more recent mandatory training package on Plans for Achieving Self Support are good examples. We have also established a network of Work Incentive Liaisons in our local offices to be the key contact points for professionals, organizations, and agencies who work with disabled people . . . the Social Security Administration is aware of the complexity of these various rules and is anxious to work with service provider organizations and others to help clarify and spread the word on these important provisions.

Hubbard (1987) said, "Unfortunately, tracking down reliable information on SSI and SSDI is difficult . . . I do not recommend calling the 800 numbers, or numbers which connect to a general switchboard of Social Security information operators. Each time I used this resource, I received information that was contradictory or, in several cases, simply wrong" (p. 17).

The volume and interconnection of regulations defies accurate recall and interpretation by all but the highly competent few. Although specialists knowledgeable about the law may argue that consumer education is the answer, more pamphlets will provide only marginal improvement. The confusion, fear, distrust, and even anger will continue to act as a major *disincentive* to work.

SUPPLEMENTAL SECURITY INCOME (SSI)

Supplemental Security Income (SSI) (Title XVI of The Social Security Act) provides a minimum standard or floor of income and is designed to help people with disabilities who have little or no other income or resources. To qualify for SSI, (a) a medical examiner must determine that the person's disability is severe enough to warrant SSI, (b) the person must not be working at the substantial gainful activity level, and (c) the person may not have more than $2,000 in countable resources per individual in 1989, or $3,000 for a couple.

Recent legislation has modified the rules governing earnings for SSI recipients in an attempt to reduce disincentives to employment. The base monthly SSI cash payment in 1989 was $368 to an individual or $553 to a couple. The size of the check to a particular individual is related to that person's earned income, unearned income, impairment-related work expenses, resource limitations, and participation in a Plan to Achieve Self-Support.

Section 1619 of the Social Security Act allows people with disabilities to retain SSI benefits even though they are working. SSI recipients who earn more than $300 per month (substantial gainful activity level in 1988) are eligible for "special" 1619(a) benefits. In June 1987, there were 1,436 participants in Section 1619(a) (Section 1619 works, 1988). In June 1988, there were 16,241 people in Section 1619(a) earning an average of $496 a month (Division of Program Management and Analysis, September 1988). Whereas Noble (1984) found that the impact of 1619 had been minimal up to that time, there is considerable use of 1619 today. Of the 1619(a) participants in June 1988, 40 percent had mental retardation and 24 percent had a psychotic condition. The majority (58 percent) were under age thirty (Division of Program Management and Analysis, 1988). Their SSI entitlement is adjusted to their income, they retain Medicaid benefits, and they will not be removed from the SSI rolls unless they medically improve or are terminated for a nondisability-related reason. Earnings for "regular" (those who earn $300 or less) and "special" 1619 recipients are treated in the same way. That is, in addition to any other exclusions, they receive an $85 exclusion ($20 general plus $65 earned income exclusion), and for each $2 of earnings above the $85, their SSI benefit amount is reduced by $1. The point at which earnings cancel out benefits (breakeven point) was $793 in 1988. A full-time worker earning the minimum wage would still receive an SSI payment of $128.50 per month (in 1988), as illustrated in Figure 15.3.

Even though those worker/recipients who earned more than $793 in 1988 no longer received cash benefits, they retained their Medicaid coverage under Section 1619(b) (the Social Security Act) if they needed Medicaid. As soon as a person qualifies for SSI cash payments, he or she also gets Medicaid coverage (Title XIX of the Social Security Act) in many states because there is no waiting period. Special SSI disability status under Section 1619(b) gives continued Medicaid coverage for those who have continuing disability but go to work and have earnings too high for SSI cash payments to continue (e.g., above the $793 breakeven point in 1988). They can keep Medicaid if the disability continues and they can't afford to get "a reasonable equivalent" to Medicaid coverage.

A threshold is used to define when a recipient's earnings are high enough to replace Medicaid coverage. This threshold is reached when a worker earns the equivalent of the base SSI payment ($354 per month in 1988), plus impairment-related work expenses, plus resources set aside under a "Plan to Achieve Self-Support," plus the reasonable equivalent of the estimated cost of medical coverage similar to Medicaid plus the cost of attendant care services. This threshold varies from state to state as the cost of health care varies. It was $1,134 per month in Ohio in 1987 (Whitehead, 1988). Special threshold calculations are made for people who have unusu-

Figure 15.3 SSI benefit computation for monthly earnings at the minimum wage of $536 ($3.35 × 160 hours)

SSI Benefit at Minimum Wage

$ 3.35	per hour (minimum wage)
x 160	hours worked in a month (4 x 40 hours)
$ 536.00	earned income
$536.00	earned income
- 20.00	general income exclusion
- 65.00	earned income exclusion
$451.00	

$451.00 ÷ 2 = $225.50 total countable income

$354.00	SSI benefit rate (in 1988)
- 225.50	total countable income
$128.50	net SSI payment
$536.00	earned income
+ 128.50	net SSI payment
$664.50	total income

SSI Breakeven Point

$354.00	SSI benefit rate (in 1988)
x 2	
$708.00	
+ 20	general income exclusion
+ 65	earned income exclusion
$793.00	breakeven point where earnings cancel out SSI benefits

ally high medical expenses. In a Plan to Achieve Self-Support, SSI recipients can set aside (accumulate) money for a specified period of time if they have a formal (SSA approved) plan for eventually becoming self-sufficient. Like SSDI, SSI benefits continue if the person recovers medically but is in a Vocational Rehabilitation (VR) program. If SSA is informed of the VR plan, benefits will continue until the plan is completed.

Together, the provisions of SSI and Section 1619(a) and 1619(b) are designed to encourage disabled people to work as they are able without fear of losing benefits and medical coverage unless they can earn enough to replace them. People will work if they can afford to work (Walls et al., 1986). Because of extensive testimony about disincentives and the sincere desire of Congress and SSA to encourage work, the SSI program dropped the trial work period and substantial gainful activity tests for termination of benefits (Disability Advisory Council, 1988). The provisions of 1619 creating a sliding scale of benefits (two for one) eliminated the need for a trial work period and substantial gainful activity. As a consequence of these and other provisions (e.g., Plan to Achieve Self-Support), SSI has more built-in incentives to work than does SSDI. Some might say that no disincentives remain in the SSI program, but this is not true for many target employees and their families.

1. The person must not be earning more than $300 per month at the time of the initial SSI eligibility determination. This is a *disincentive* to work if viewed as "I can't make more than

$300 and get SSI." This kind of thinking might persist after being declared eligible, even though the substantial gainful activity level is not a basis for termination of benefits. A similar scenario might apply to the amount of allowable resources available to the person.

2. Under Section 1619(a) (The Social Security Act), cash SSI payments continue even though earned income is above the substantial gainful activity level. After the $20 general income exclusion plus $65 earned income exclusion and other special exclusions, benefits are reduced by $1 for every $2 earned. At the breakeven point ($793 in 1988) the person receives no SSI cash. Even if the person exceeds the breakeven point in a given month, SSI benefits are not terminated for future months. This is an *incentive* to work if viewed as "I can work all I am able and not lose SSI benefits." This is a *disincentive* to work if viewed as "I'm losing a dollar for every two I make so I'm working for half-wages."

3. As noted, when a person makes enough money to exceed the substantial gainful activity level or even the breakeven point in a particular month, SSI benefits continue in subsequent months. When a person starts making more than $300 (not to mention $793), however, his or her case folder is sent back over to the disability determination section of SSA. They review the case (redetermination) to see if the person has "medically improved." This is an *incentive* to work if viewed as "Even though I made too much money (more than the breakeven point) to get an SSI check this month, if I can't work as much next month, I'll get a check again." This is a *disincentive* to work if viewed as "If I start making too much money, they're going to look at my case again."

4. Section 1619(b) (The Social Security Act) protects Medicaid benefits when earnings are too high to get cash SSI (above the breakeven point) but are not high enough to offset the loss of Medicaid. Medicaid is retained unless the person earns more than the state threshold (described earlier) or has comprehensive coverage and does not need Medicaid. This is an *incentive* to work if viewed as "I can work and still not lose my medical card." This is a *disincentive* to work if viewed as "I can't make more than the threshold or I will lose my medical card." Whitehead (1988) noted a potential discouragement associated with Medicaid-certified Intermediate Care Facilities for persons with mental retardation. Because Medicaid pays for their care, residents contribute all their income (except a personal needs allowance) toward the cost of their care. States must allow a minimum of $30 per month for this personal needs allowance but can allow more. Setting a larger allowance would reduce this *disincentive* to work.

5. Under a Plan to Achieve Self-Support the person can set aside income or resources for a specific vocational objective in a specific time period (an initial period of not more than 18 months maximum, but extensions can be granted). Such a plan can help set aside otherwise countable income (such as SSDI cash or earnings) to make the person eligible, keep the person eligible for SSI, or increase the current SSI payment (Whitehead, 1988). The savings (amount set aside) put in a special bank account might be used for vocational education, paying a job coach, or starting a business. For example, an SSI beneficiary who wanted to open a flower stand could write up (with or without assistance) a plan for achieving self-support which would describe the vocational goal, the time projected to reach the goal, and the specific savings and spending plan that provides for clearly identifiable accounting of funds which are set aside (Disability Advisory Council, 1988). The amount set aside is not counted under SSI income and resources tests, thereby allowing the person to accumulate some savings as well as maintaining eligibility and increasing his or her SSI check. This is an *incentive* to work if viewed as "My plan lets me save money toward my vocational goal." This is a *disincentive* to work if viewed as "If I reach the vocational goal, I will lose benefits." Without an approved plan, the countable resource limitation ($2,000 in 1989) is a *disincentive* for saving or investing because such resources will make a person ineligible for SSI (Hubbard, 1987).

6. SSI eligibility first must be established without any deductions for impairment-related work expenses. Impairment-related work expenses for such things as medical devices, attendant care, and special transportation then

can be excluded to compute SSI cash payments. This is an *incentive* to work if viewed as "I have a lot of expenses that can be deducted so as to allow me to keep more of the money I earn."

7. The requirements and jargon associated with substantial gainful activity, eligibility, case redetermination, resource limitations, earned income, unearned income, work expenses, Plan to Achieve Self-Support, regular (SSI), special 1619 provisions, breakeven point, reasonable equivalent, and threshold are virtually unintelligible to most target employees and their families. They are afraid that anything they do may make their situation worse (Walls et al., 1986). If remedial or add-on legislation, designed to reduce disincentives, instead compounds existing confusion, that legislation actually reduces the intended incentive. Feelings of ambiguity, misunderstanding, and frustration still run rampant and continue to be a major *disincentive* to work. Fredericks (1988) has stated, "As I talk to parents around the country, they have voiced two major concerns about supported employment. Can my child succeed, and will my child lose Social Security income benefits, and most importantly, medical benefits?"

BENEFITS FROM MORE THAN ONE PROGRAM

Eligibility for other benefits (e.g., workers' compensation) will affect the amount of money received from SSI or SSDI. For example, SSI applicants eligible for other programs (e.g., SSDI) must try to get those benefits and use such cash income to reduce the SSI benefit amount. If the SSDI monthly check is low enough, the person can also get cash from SSI. If a parent is eligible for both SSI and Aid to Families with Dependent Children, the person must choose the one that will be most beneficial. He or she can't have both. Most people who get SSDI or SSI also receive health benefits (Medicare or Medicaid). The list of other potential benefits includes food stamps, WIC (Women, Infants, and Children), housing assistance, and social services.

Of the people who received SSI in 1982, about 91 percent received Medicaid, 45 percent received food stamps, 12 percent received school lunches, and 15 percent lived in public housing (Conley, Noble, & Elder, 1986). The loss of benefits from all these sources can be caused by taking a full-time job. Even minor adjustments to income, however, can cause considerable complications within a given benefit source as well as across sources. Additions to income such as holiday bonuses or overtime would be viewed as *incentives* for employees. For those who must be careful not to exceed substantial gainful activity, a breakeven point, or other benefit program criteria, however, additional earnings are a *disincentive*.

The effects of any changes in benefit program rules can be viewed by recipients as either incentives or disincentives. This determination is based on an individual's perception of the complex rules governing the different programs and the relationships among those programs. This complexity highlights the need for coordination of benefit programs. Lack of coordination among agencies creates considerable problems. "Clients, staff and the general public lack a clear picture of available services and how they fit together because programs were established at different times for different purposes and have complicated rules, conflicting goals and insufficient public information support" (Disability Advisory Council, 1988, p. 25). At the federal level, the Social Security Administration and the Departments of Education, Health and Human Services, Justice, and Labor, and several administrative offices under these departments (e.g., Rehabilitation Services Administration and Human Development Services) have rules and procedures for providing services. At the state level, these programs may be supplemented (e.g., Medicaid changes and SSI supplements) and state level programs (e.g., family services) may be initiated, each with its own rules and procedures for providing services. Finally, at the local level, community-based programs (e.g., housing authorities, transportation services, and soup kitchens) address needs they see and work from additional rules and procedures. This multilayered morass of programs, rules, agencies, services, and agendas has little logical integrity.

SUMMARY

More firms are hiring workers with disabilities. Yet, a presidential committee says that 8.2 million people with disabilities who are willing to work are still jobless (A Special News Report, 1988). When benefit programs are made more attractive by extending benefits to try to reduce disincentives, more people will be attracted to benefits. Murray (1988) noted that there is no way to make it easier to get off benefits without simultaneously making benefit programs more attractive. There are a lot of people on the edge who could be nudged from marginal self-sufficiency to dependence on benefits. In discussing welfare reform legislation, Murray described this nudge that the new day care and Medicaid provisions give to marginal working women who have never been on Welfare before. Although these reforms undoubtedly make it easier for a woman on Welfare to take a job, the danger lies in the trap it sets for the single working mother who is supporting her family and has managed to stay off the welfare rolls. By losing her job, qualifying for Welfare benefits, and waiting a few months before going back to work, she can retain free child care and Medicaid benefits.

Although most target employees in supported employment are unlikely to be faced with this welfare reform situation, the parallel to other benefit programs is apparent. When employment disincentives are removed for those currently receiving benefits (e.g., by totally eliminating the substantial gainful activity provision or by making SSI have fewer disincentives by passing Section 1619), those programs by definition take on stronger drawing power.

From a rehabilitation perspective, we want target employees to receive all the benefits to which they are entitled, but we also want them to find employment that frees them from public benefits. We may find third-party payments for client services that reduce the cost to the rehabilitation agency but increase reliance on benefits for the individual. The dilemma becomes all the greater when one tries to use medically determined disability as the only eligibility criterion (rather than earnings). It has been argued for years that medical labels should be replaced or at least supplemented by measures of functional capacity to operationalize ability and disability.

Earnings per se, unconstrained by social and economic context, might be considered an index of functional capacity. Economic self-sufficiency is a functional outcome that takes that context into consideration and thus may vary in terms of the amount of earnings (Kiernan, Smith, & Ostrowsky, 1986). The Disability Advisory Council (1988) wrote, "The essential problem in disability is that it is not possible to construct a set of medical and vocational standards that will distinguish perfectly between those who are able to work and those who are not able to work" (p. 23).

Children and adults are often reinforced for undesirable behaviors and punished for desirable ones, even though it is not rational to do so. It is difficult to create a responsive social service system for helping those in need while maintaining incentives for competitive employment. Employment outcome will be a function of (a) the employability of the individual, (b) the intervention and support services provided, and (c) employment opportunity (including incentives, disincentives, and availability of jobs) (Moriarty, Walls, & McLaughlin, 1987). Given the opportunity, individuals with and without disabilities will maximize utility in trading time, effort, and losses in one area for food, money, and gains in another area.

Legislative "incentives" are created with the people in mind who are currently receiving benefits. These "incentives" (like the trial work period) are to encourage those already in the benefit program to go to work and, one hopes, to gain independence from public benefit programs. Yet, although the number of SSDI beneficiaries continues to increase and the "replacement rate" of benefits for earnings has continued to climb, virtually no one goes back to work and leaves the SSDI rolls. Once they begin receiving benefits, only 0.5 percent leave the rolls each year as a result of work activity (Disability Advisory Council, 1988). This figure has remained relatively constant over the past 10 years. Are the "incentives" working to put people back into substantial employment? Clearly, they are not. To argue that only 0.5 percent of SSDI beneficiaries have medically recovered enough to return to work is ludicrous. For SSI recipients, Section 1619 will undoubtedly encourage more work activity, as the data are beginning to indicate. It is doubtful, however, that it will create a substantial exodus from the SSI roll. It certainly makes SSI more attractive for those disabled and marginally destitute people for whom it would take only a nudge to push them into dependency.

At this point it is traditional to paint with broad brushstrokes the picture of the new social solution that will eliminate disincentives and create incentives to work. Suggestions for reform have included: (a) eliminate the substantial gainful activity level; (b) increase the substantial gainful activity level; (c) create a sliding earning-benefit scale up to a breakeven point for SSDI similar to that operating in SSI now; (d) provide Medicare to beneficiaries for life unless they medically recover before age sixty-five; (e) redefine the trial work period; (f) eliminate the trial work period; (g) provide long-term vocational support for target employees through the Vocational Rehabilitation system; (h) directly subsidize employers who hire target employees, (i) discontinue the Targeted Jobs Tax Credit program; (j) eliminate federal funding that supports restrictive housing; (k) eliminate special provisions for blind individuals; (l) institute the special provisions, now applicable only to blind individuals, for all disability categories; (m) eliminate the 24-month waiting period from Medicare; (n) make Medicare coverage as comprehensive as Medicaid coverage; (o) modify the dependent, spouse, and widow(er) criteria; (p) revise the continuing disability review procedure; (q) develop a work incentive package for individuals eligible for both SSI and SSDI; (r) funnel SSI funds through an employer so that target employees receive only one check, which increases as the number of hours worked increases; (s) permit former beneficiaries to purchase health insurance coverage from the federal government if it is not available through the private sector; (t) pass legislation to bar employers and insurance companies from refusing to cover pre-existing conditions; (u) simplify current incentive provisions; (v) create new work incentive provisions; (w) train SSA field office employees to provide accurate information (e.g., Disability Advisory Council, 1988; Noble et al., 1986).

Our only recommendation is not a novel one. Each person with a disability should have a single service plan which considers medical, vocational, and social well-being. There should be a single eligibility determination process based on functional capacity. We should acknowledge that, in spite of good intentions, we have created a series of service structures so cumbersome, fragmented, and unwieldly that no one understands the entire system. Professionals misinterpret and misadvise. Consumers cannot use the system effectively. Piecemeal attempts to fix this system are certain to fail. Until a more streamlined system with centralized service planning can be instituted, we will continue to struggle with programs that work at cross-purposes, catching target employees in the crunch.

ACKNOWLEDGEMENTS

Preparation of this chapter was supported, in part, by the National Institute of Disability and Rehabilitation Research through the West Virginia Rehabilitation Research and Training Center (West Virginia University and West Virginia Division of Rehabilitation Services). For supplying information and/or advice, appreciation is expressed to Ronald Conley, Lee Faris, Dale Hanks, William Kiernan, John Kregel, David Mank, Kenneth McGill, Katherine Oliver, Craig Thornton, Timm Vogelsberg, Paul Wehman, and Claude Whitehead. Appreciation for manuscript preparation is expressed to Mandy Maziasz and Karen Redmond.

QUESTIONS (For answers see p. 431)

1. According to the authors, the success of supported employment depends on what?

2. What is an incentive?

3. What is a disincentive?

4. In microeconomic theory, what does a preference curve represent?

5. Explain how participation in income maintenance programs negatively affects employment for persons with disabilities.

6. Name at least two possible incentives and disincentives for supported employment identified through research.

7. What reasons did the 1,560 VR counselors surveyed by the GAO give to explain why SSDI beneficiaries do not tend to participate in VR?

8. Summarize the major provisions of 1619(a) concerning wages for persons with disabilities who are working.

9. What are two major concerns about supported employment that parents express?

10. What do the authors recommend to resolve the problem of incentives/disincentives in (re)habilitation?

REFERENCES

A special news report on people and their jobs in offices, fields, and factories. (1988, August 2). *The Wall Street Journal*, p. A1.

Berkowitz, M. (1981). Disincentives and the rehabilitation of disabled persons. In E. Pan, T. Backer, & C. Vosh (Eds.), *Annual review of rehabilitation* (pp. 40–57). New York: Springer.

Berkowitz, M., Horning, M., McConnell, S., Rubin, J., & Worrall, J. D. (1982). An economic evaluation of the beneficiary rehabilitation program. In J. Rubin (Ed.); *Alternatives in rehabilitating the handicapped: A policy analysis* (pp. 1– 87). New York: Human Sciences Press.

Bolles, R. C. (1972). Reinforcement, expectancy, and learning. *Psychological Review*, *79*, 394–409.

Bolles, R. C. (1978). Whatever happened to motivation? *Educational Psychologist*, *13*, 1–13.

Conley, R. W., Noble, J. H., Jr., & Elder, J. K. (1986). Problems with the service system. In W. E. Kiernan & J. A. Stark (Eds.), *Pathways to employment for adults with developmental disabilities* (pp. 67–83). Baltimore: Paul H. Brookes.

Disability Advisory Council. (1988). *Report of the Disability Advisory Council*. Baltimore: Social Security Administration.

Division of Mental Health and Community Rehabilitation Services. (1988). *SSI/SSDI: A manual for behavioral health case managers and advocates.* Charleston, WV: Office of Behavioral Health Services, Department of Health.

Division of Program Management and Analysis. (September, 1988). *Section 1619: Quarterly statistical report*. Washington, DC: SSA, Office of Supplemental Security Income.

Fredericks, B. (1988). *Supported employment: It works*. National satellite teleconference sponsored by The Office of Special Education and Rehabilitative Services. Morgantown, WV: The Job Accommodation Network.

GAO. (1987). *Social Security: Little success achieved in rehabilitating disabled beneficiaries* (Report No. GAO/HRD 88–11). Washington, DC: General Accounting Office.

Goodman, L. (1987). DMR's quarterly progress report. *Interact*, *1*(2), 2.

Griss, B. (1985). *Report on health care coverage for working-aged persons with physical disabilities: A key to reducing disincentives to work*. Madison, WI: Department of Health and Social Services.

Greenblum, J. & Bye, B. (1987). Work values of disabled beneficiaries. *Social Security Bulletin*, *50*, 67–74.

Hanks, D. (1986). Costs and other economic considerations in transition programming. In L. G. Perlman & G. F. Austin (Eds.), *The transition to work and independence for youth with disabilities* (pp. 67–92). Alexandria, VA: National Rehabilitation Association.

Helms, R. B. (1988). *Report to the secretary from the working group on policies affecting mentally retarded and other developmentally disabled persons.* Unpublished manuscript, Department of Health and Human Services.

Hubbard, T. S. (1987). *What advocates and service providers should know about the effects of employment on Social Security Disability Insurance and Supplemental Security Income*. Eugene, OR: Rehabilitation Research and Training Center.

Kahneman, D. & Tversky, A. (1984). Choices, frames, and values. *American Psychologist*, *39*, 341–350.

Kiernan, W. E. & Brinkman, L. (in press). Disincentives and barriers to employment. In P. Wehman & M. S. Moon (Eds.), *Vocational rehabilitation and supported employment*. Baltimore: Paul H. Brookes.

Kiernan, W. E., McGaughey, M., Schalock, R., & Rowland, S. (in press). *Employment outcomes for adults with developmental disabilities: A national survey*. Boston: Training and Research Institute for Adults with Disabilities, Boston College.

Kiernan, W. E., Smith, B. C., & Ostrowsky, M. B. (1986). Developmental disabilities: Definitional issues. In W. E. Kiernan & J. A. Stark (Eds.), *Pathways to employment for adults with developmental disabilities* (pp. 11–20). Baltimore: Paul H. Brookes.

Michigan Interagency Task Force on Disability. (1987). *Substantial Gainful Activity (SGA) as a work disincentive*. (Available from Author, 6th Floor, Lewis Cass Building, Lansing, MI 48913).

Moriarty, J. B., Walls, R. T., & McLaughlin, D. E. (1987). The Preliminary Diagnostic Questionnaire (PDQ): Functional Assessment of Employability. *Rehabilitation Psychology*, *32*, 5–15.

Murray, C. (1988, October 13). New welfare bill, new welfare cheats. *Wall Street Journal*, p. A16.

Noble, J. H. (1984). Rehabilitating the SSI recipient: Overcoming disincentives to employment of severely disabled persons. In *The Supplemental Security Income program: A 10-year overview* (pp. 55–102). Washington, DC: U.S. Senate, Special Committee on Aging.

Poole, D. L. (1987). Competitive employment of persons with severe physical disabilities: A multivariate analysis. *Journal of Rehabilitation*, *53*, 20–25.

Rusch, F. R., Mithaug, D. E., & Flexer, R. W. (1986). Obstacles to competitive employment and traditional program options for overcoming them. In F. R. Rusch (Ed.), *Competitive employment issues and strategies* (pp. 7–21). Baltimore: Paul H. Brookes.

Section 1619 works. (1988, July). *Independent News*, Huntington, WV: Huntington Center for Independent Living.

SSA. (1987). *A summary guide to Social Security and Supplemental Security Income work incentives for the disabled and blind*. Baltimore: Social Security Administration, Office of Disability.

VCU-RRTC. (1988a). *Quarterly report: Successful outcomes in supported employment, Quarter 2, North Dakota*. Richmond: VCU Rehabilitation Research and Training Center.

VCU-RRTC. (1988b). *Quarterly report: Successful outcomes in supported employment, Quarter 2, Virginia*. Richmond: VCU Rehabilitation Research and Training Center.

Walls, R. T. (1982). Disincentives in vocational rehabilitation: Cash and in-kind benefits from other programs. *Rehabilitation Counseling Bulletin*, *26*, 37–46.

Walls, R. T., Dowler, D. L., & Fullmer, S. L. (1989). *Cash and in-kind benefits: Incentives rather than disincentives for vocational rehabilitation. Rehabilitation Counseling Bulletin, 33*, 118–126.

Walls, R. T., Masson, C., & Werner, T. J. (1977). Negative incentives to vocational rehabilitation. *Rehabilitation Literature*, *38*, 143–150.

Walls, R. T., Zawlocki, R. J., & Dowler, D. L. (1986). Economic benefits as disincentives to competitive employment. In F. R. Rusch (Ed.), *Competitive employment issues and strategies* (pp. 317–329). Baltimore: Paul H. Brookes.

Whitehead, C. W. (1987). Supported employment: Challenge and opportunity for sheltered workshops. *Journal of Rehabilitation*, *53*(3), 23–28.

Whitehead, C. W. (1988, June). *Ensuring stable and continuing funding for employment support through state and local action*. Paper presented at the Pennsylvania Conference on Supported Employment, Harrisburg, PA.

Whitehead, C. W. (1988). *National study of Vocational Rehabilitation facilities and their response to the integrated employment initiatives* (Progress report and preliminary analysis of findings). Unpublished manuscript.

Whitehead, C. W. & McCaffrey, F. D. (1988). *A guidebook for the employment initiatives of the 99th Congress: Opportunities for persons with disabilities*. Columbus, OH: Ohio Legal Rights Services; Ohio Rehabilitation Services Commission; Governor's Office of Advocacy for People with Disabilities.

Wisconsin Department of Health and Social Services. (1986). *Report on health care coverage for working-aged persons with physical disabilities: A key to reducing disincentives to work*. Madison, WI: Author.

Worrall, J. D. (1983). Compensation costs, injury rates, and the labor market. In J. D. Worrall (Ed.), *Safety and the work force: Incentives and disincentives in workers' compensation* (pp. 1–17). Ithaca, NY: ILR Press, Cornell University.

CHAPTER

16

Benefit-Cost Analysis of Supported Employment

Ronald W. Conley
Administration on Developmental Disabilities
Washington, DC
John H. Noble, Jr.
SUNY at Buffalo

Although the importance of conducting benefit-cost or evaluation studies[1] relating to the effectiveness of social programs has been stressed for many years, benefit-cost techniques have been primarily used in evaluating programs that lead to employment. The reasons for the emphasis on employment or manpower development programs—particularly federal-state vocational rehabilitation programs and employment programs funded by the Department of Labor—are obvious. Earnings, the primary objective of employment programs, are unambiguously established by market forces and can be reliably and inexpensively measured in terms of dollars and cents.

Supported employment programs are the most recent innovations in the manpower development sphere. They have been devised to assist persons with severe disabilities to attain integrated employment. They particularly focus on people who were formerly thought incapable of competitive employment and, therefore, largely relegated to sheltered workshops, work activity centers, adult day care, or to complete idleness. Although originally designed to serve persons with mental handicaps, supported employment programs appear applicable to all persons with severe disabilities. Persons with mental retardation, however, continue to be the largest group of beneficiaries. In the near future we anticipate seeing many benefit-cost analyses of supported employment programs because of their surging popularity, the ease with which data on supported employee earnings can be collected, and the keen interest of professionals, politicians, and the public in knowing about outcomes. This chapter discusses (a) methods for conducting benefit-cost analyses of supported employment programs and how they differ from the traditional approach to benefit-cost analysis; (b) limitations in the validity and utility of benefit-cost analysis as a guide to decision making; and (c) early statistical data on the effectiveness of a supported employment program.

THE IMPORTANCE AND USES OF BENEFIT-COST ANALYSES

It is important to carry out benefit-cost studies of supported employment programs for many reasons. First, supported employment programs represent a recent major policy initiative on the part of federal and state governments.

The U.S. Department of Education has awarded expansion grants to twenty-seven states to stimulate development of transitional and supported employment programs. In addition, the federal Rehabilitation Services Administration has recently been given authority to fund supported employment programs in each of the states. Moreover, throughout the federal government, programs such as Social Security Disability Insurance, Supplemental Security Income, Medicare, and Medicaid programs are being examined to determine if they have adverse effects on employment. Significant changes have been made in these programs to encourage employment among beneficiaries (Conley & Noble, 1989), and we anticipate that additional changes for this purpose will be made.

Second, transitional and supported employment programs are perhaps the fastest growing segment of the service system for persons with severe disabilities. On the basis of survey reports from 952 facilities, Kiernan, McGauphey, Schalock, & Rowland (1988) reported that 16,453 adults with developmental disabilities were placed into transitional, supported, or competitive employment in 1987 in the United States. On the basis of a 27-state survey, Wehman, Kregel, & Shafer (1989) reported that 20,817 adults with disabilities were placed in supported employment in 1988, a two-year increase of about 50 percent in the states surveyed.

If account is taken of differences in the surveys, there is substantial consistency between them. Because of definitional ambiguities, it is probable that persons reported as in transitional or competitive employment in the Kiernan et al. (1988) survey would be regarded as supported employees in the Wehman et al. (1989) survey. Another difference was that the Wehman et al. survey encompassed persons with diverse disabilities while the Kiernan et al. survey included only persons with developmental disabilities. Neither study encompassed all situations involving supported employment since the facilities in the Kiernan et al. survey represent about one half of the total number of facilities to which questionnaires were sent and the Wehman et al. survey included just over half of the fifty states.

Taking into account these data limitations, one can surmise that the total number of persons in supported employment in 1988 was between 40,000 and 50,000.

A third reason why it is important to conduct benefit-cost analyses lies in their value as a guide to public policy; that is, in determining whether supported employment is worthwhile, whether it should be expanded or contracted, and whether it can be made more effective and less costly. It must be emphasized that the importance of conducting benefit-cost studies goes far beyond their customary use. Most benefit-cost studies have addressed the question of whether a program is worthwhile and, assuming a favorable answer, have been used to support budget requests. In passing, it should be noted that benefit-cost studies that do not "prove" that a program is economically justified are likely to be quickly criticized for being flawed or incomplete and quietly discarded.

Benefit-cost analyses should also be used to address the question of whether a program should be expanded or perhaps even contracted. This is sometimes referred to as the "how much" issue. The answer is obviously not dependent on an overall benefit-cost ratio of a program. Whether or not a program should expand depends upon whether the *additional* benefits that accrue from program expansion exceed the *additional* costs that are incurred. These additional benefits and costs are technically known as "marginal" program benefits and costs. Clearly, it is this marginal information on benefits and costs that should accompany requests for increases or decreases in budget, but such information is rarely available.

In addition, benefit-cost analyses can and should be used to identify methods of improving the operation and management of programs. For example, carefully crafted studies may assist in identifying which supported employees could be shifted to less costly or more productive types of employment. This is sometimes referred to as the "how to" issue. Although these types of analyses are sometimes described as "cost-effectiveness" analyses, this can be misleading. Cost effectiveness analysis usually assumes a fixed or stable outcome. In supported employment programs it is frequently impossible to establish a fixed or stable outcome insofar as the productivity of the supported employee varies as a function of the job and the type and level of support that is provided. Accordingly, benefit-cost analyses oriented to program improvement must consider both benefits and costs, not just costs in relation to a fixed or stable outcome.

Designing and implementing studies that focus on "how to" issues is essential if a system of supported employment is to be established that is dynamic, i.e., susceptible to continuous improvement over time. Lacking data to ascertain the effectiveness of alternative program approaches, the tendency of program managers is to provide similar services to all clients while continuing to do business in the same old way year after year. There is also the tendency to select only clients who "fit" into the standard program.

The need for studies that focus on program improvement is highlighted by the slow evolution of programs that serve persons with disabilities. Over the years, legislators have created a large array of expensive programs for persons with disabilities. Unfortunately, these programs are usually poorly coordinated and often have conflicting and sometimes counterproductive goals. For example, the income support and health care financing programs create major work disincentives for beneficiaries. Moreover, more public funds are still directed to day care and institutional care than to work programs and community based services. We believe that the slowness with which programs have evolved into effective and efficient means of fostering the independence of persons with disabilities is largely the result of the dearth of information about the effectiveness of these programs and the general failure to adequately compare program outcomes and costs. In the absence of a marketplace in which failure to produce efficiently marks the demise of the enterprise, information about benefits and costs should be the principal tool for program improvement. This assumes that legislative and executive branch officials are willing to rely on such information for decision making rather than basing decisions on short-term political advantage.

METHODS OF CONDUCTING BENEFIT-COST STUDIES

Benefit-cost analysis can be defined as the systematic comparison of the benefits of a program with its costs. A rigorous benefit-cost analysis should have the following components:

1. Specification and measurement of the major relevant tangible and intangible benefits from the perspectives of individuals, employers, government, and society;
2. Specification and measurement of the major relevant costs associated with the provision of program services from the four perspectives noted above;
3. Identification and measurement of factors other than employment services that affect outcomes, such as the unemployment rate and the availability of other services (housing, transportation);
4. Specification of the relevant disability and/or functional limitation categories (e.g., type and level of disability) as well as other personal characteristics that affect costs and outcomes (e.g., age, level of education) in order to carry out class-specific comparisons of costs and benefits.
5. Specification of the major variations in methods of providing services and site-level operational differences, if appropriate, to assist in explaining differences in outcomes and costs.

The underlying purpose of evaluating programs for persons with disabilities is to identify the effectiveness of these programs in reducing the negative consequences of disabling conditions, such as mental retardation. Among the negative consequences that may ensue are:

- A need for services such as medical care, rehabilitation, social services, counseling, respite care, and special education. To provide these services, society must give up other types of consumption (or work longer).
- A reduction in ability to work which may cause a loss of earnings, reductions in the ability to perform housework, yard and home maintenance, and volunteer activities, and a reduction in ability to provide child care.
- A reduction in the ability to engage in normal

social activities such as visiting friends and relatives, attending shows, camping, etc.

- An increase in other negative effects such as less stable marriages, reduced savings (which may affect long-term economic growth), loss of opportunities for children of persons with disabilities to advance themselves (e.g., by going to college).
- A reduction of intangible, yet crucial, desired attributes such as self-esteem, or an increase in equally critical intangible undesirable attributes such as frustration, anger, and fear.

The complete list of all of the possible effects of a severe disability is quite extensive, and must be seen as having ripple effects that extend over many years affecting the lives of individuals and families and the welfare of communities and society at large. Obviously, the number and size of these effects varies substantially among persons with disabilities.

Let us assume that we can: (a) identify all of the effects of disability on people; (b) measure the extent to which people are affected; and (c) place a numerical (i.e., dollar) value on these effects. The dollar total of all of these effects would represent the total social cost of disability. Although it is clearly impossible to measure all of the effects of disability, partial estimates are frequently calculated, such as the costs of alcoholism, cancer, road accidents, and so on. These estimates can be made specific to a particular type of disability, or even to a particular individual. Individual estimates are most often made in cases involving litigation in order for the court to determine the appropriate amount of indemnification to award to a person who is injured as the result of negligence by another party or because the injured party is insured.

Returning now to benefit-cost analysis, suppose society decides to initiate a new program such as supported employment. Some of the types of costs that are involved in calculating the social costs of disability will increase. It is the *increase* in costs required to establish a program that defines costs for purposes of benefit-cost analysis. These costs are obviously different in concept and nature from the social costs resulting from a disabling condition described above. The term "social costs," has been used by various writers to refer both to the costs relevant to benefit-cost analysis and to the total costs associated with disability, even though the two cost concepts are quite different.

The purpose of incurring program costs is to reduce some of the other effects of disabling conditions. For example, if people are helped to engage in work, the loss of productivity will decline and this decline can be roughly approximated by the resulting increase in earnings. Similarly, social skills may improve, and the ability to care for children may be enhanced, each of which represents a reduction in a component of the social cost of a disabling condition. The total value of all of the positive effects represents the benefits resulting from a given program. Collectively, these benefits are sometimes described as the increase in social well-being.

This approach to defining benefit-cost analysis makes clear that benefit-cost analysis encompasses many variables for which monetary values are difficult (and sometimes impossible) to derive. In fact, any outcome that increases social well-being is relevant to policy, program, and budgetary decision making and, as such, is the legitimate concern of benefit-cost analysis. As an example of how a comprehensive benefit-cost study may be defined, Figure 16.1 sets forth the measures of benefits and costs by the analytic perspectives that will be used in New York State in its evaluation of supported employment for persons with severe disabilities (Noble, Swaninathan, Shankar, Goodman, & Peters, 1989).

In comparing benefits and costs, most studies utilize the benefit-cost ratio (B/C), which calculates the level of benefits per dollar of costs. Other ways of comparing benefits and costs include calculation of: (a) the total net benefits (i.e., the difference between benefits and costs (B − C)); (b) the payback period (i.e., the amount of time before the original cost is recaptured in benefits); and (c) the internal rate of return (i.e., the average annual benefit as a percent of the original cost).

Analysts tend to prefer the benefit-cost ratio, largely because it is relatively easy to calculate and understand. In addition, if alternative programs are being compared, the benefit-

Figure 16.1 Measures of benefits and costs of supported employment: New York State

	Analytic Perspective			
Benefits and Costs	**Individuals/ families**	**Employers/ private sector**	**Government**	**Society**
A. Increased tangible benefits (all disabilities)				
i. Hours worked	X			X
ii. Hourly wage rate	X			X
iii. Total earnings				X
a. Net of taxes	X			
b. Taxes			X	
iv. Fringe benefits	X			X
a. Health insurance				
b. Sick leave				
c. Transportation				
v. Reduced public dependency				
a. SSDI			X	X
b. SSI			X	X
c. Medicare			X	X
d. Medicaid			X	X
e. Other sources			X	X
B. Increased intangible benefits (all disabilities)	X			X
i. Employability (all disabilities)	X			X
a. Cognitive functioning				
b. Disposition to work				
c. Emotional functioning				
d. Physical functioning				
ii. Community living (all disabilities)	X			X
a. Personal management				
b. Nutrition management				
c. Money management				
d. Home management				
e. Medical management				
f. Time management				
g. Community use				
h. Problem solving				
i. Safety management				
iii. Emotional/behavioral functioning (traumatic brain injury/developmental disabilities)	X			X
a. Anxiety				
b. Depression				
c. Withdrawal				
d. Low self-esteem				
e. Somatic concerns				
f. Thought/behavior disorder				
g. Physical aggression				
h. Noncompliance				
i. Distractability				
j. Hyperactivity				
k. Verbal aggression				
l. Sexual malajustment				

Figure 16.1 (cont.)

iv. Psychiatric symptomatology (mental illness)	X			X
a. Somatization				
b. Obsessive-compulsive				
c. Interpersonal sensitivity				
d. Depression				
e. Anxiety				
f. Hostility				
g. Phobic anxiety				
h. Paranoid ideation				
i. Psychoticism				
v. Neuropsychological functioning (traumatic brain injury)	X			X
a. Adaptive functioning				
b. Single and choice reaction time				
c. Digit span				
d. Verbal learning				
e. Problem solving				
f. Language comprehension				
g. Perceptual organization				
h. Fine motor control				
i. Planning ability				
j. Writing skills				
k. Word fluency				
l. Arithmetic				
m. Spatial visualization				
n. Reading				
vi. Work Integration (all disabilities)	X			X
a. Physical				
1. 50' ratio of workers with handicaps to total workers				
2. Visibility to consumers/public				
b. Social (contact frequency with workers without handicaps)				
1. During job				
2. During work breaks				
3. During lunch				
c. Social network (contact frequency in "offsite" social/recreational activities)				
vii. Employee stability/labor market turnover (all disabilities)		X		X
viii. Family/household derivative benefits (all disabilities)	X			X
a. Time for self				
b. Getting along together				
c. Paid work				
d. Unpaid/volunteer work				
e. Household/yard work				
f. Social/recreational activities				
C. Costs				
1. Case service expenditures (a + b + c = 1)	aX	bX	cX	X
2. Administrative and overhead (a + b = 1)		aX	bX	X
3. Income loss/foregone earnings during program				X
a. Net of taxes	X			
b. Taxes			X	
4. Research, training, and facility costs (a + b + 1)		aX	bX	X
5. Targeted job tax credit (TJTC)			X	X

cost ratio is superior to other methods of comparing benefits and costs for the following reasons. (a) It adjusts for differences in the size of the initial expenditure, which the *total net benefits* approach fails to do. (b) It takes account of all future benefits, which the *payback period* approach may fail to do. (c) Finally, the benefit-cost ratio, which usually does not make allowance for the replacement of lost capital, is the preferred approach when measuring the return on human capital, while the *internal rate of return* calculation, which allows for depreciation, is preferred when measuring the return on physical capital.[2] Investments in employment programs are a form of investment in "human capital" which lasts only as long as the individual lives. In contrast, physical capital is depreciated and replaced at the end of its useful life.

The best procedures for calculating and comparing benefits and costs differ significantly among programs because of differences in their operating characteristics. Consider the major differences in employment programs for persons with disabilities. *Vocational rehabilitation* services consist of the provision of a wide range of services (e.g., physical restoration, training, assistance in locating employment) are provided on a time-limited basis. There is *no* provision for long-term services or follow-up to assure successful job placement. It is assumed that the individual will be self-sustaining once placed on a job.

Supported employment services, on the other hand, must consider support-related costs for as long as the individual remains on the job. Support can be provided on the job (e.g., on-the-job supervision, training, counseling) as well as apart from the job, such as when transportation, community living skills training, and counseling are provided to other family members. These services are deemed necessary to successful job placement and maintenance. The support may be continuous or provided on an irregular, as-needed basis.

Supported employment poses several definitional issues that make a benefit-cost analysis difficult to conduct. For example, how much "integration" is necessary in order to define a program as providing supported employment. The Specialized Training Program (STP), initiated in Oregon and Washington, is located in workshop settings where only a few persons without disabilities are hired as co-workers. STP programs nevertheless maintain a strong work orientation and serve persons with severe disabilities who require extensive support and, in our opinion, should be regarded as providing supported employment services.

Supported employment programs will become increasingly diverse in the future as programs are individualized to serve persons with enormous variations in capabilities as a consequence of differences in the extent and characteristics of their intellectual, physical, and emotional handicaps. These differences create a need for jobs with different levels and types of supervision and other service supports. Another reason for diversity in supported employment programs is that the opportunities for work vary substantially among different regions of the country; individuals placed in one type of job in one area may need to be placed in a different type of job in another area which, in turn, will require differences in the types and levels of support services provided. For example, the logistics of finding jobs and transporting supported employees to work in rural areas are quite different from those in industrialized areas.

The characteristics of supported employment make possible a major change in the way that benefit-cost ratios are calculated, both simplifying and reducing the extent of conjecture involved in estimating benefits and costs. In a mature supported employment program, average annual costs per person served will remain roughly constant from year to year as the number of persons entering the program stabilizes as a relatively fixed proportion of the total caseload. Program stabilization is a necessary assumption because we anticipate that the cost of the initial process of job placement and training will usually be considerably more than the costs required to maintain supported employees on the job after acquisition of job skills and improvement of work habits.

Although it is possible to project benefits and costs into future years for a cohort of supported employees, the average costs for a given cohort of new supported employees over time should be identical with the average costs for the supported employees of a matured program (adjusting for inflation and changes in the level of staff salaries). If projections of benefits and costs are made into the future, then both benefits and costs must be discounted and adjusted for productivity changes in the economy. Since both the numerator (benefits) and denominator (costs) would contain the same adjustments for discounting and productivity change, they cancel each other out. Consequently, the ratio of benefits to costs measured for one year of *mature* program operation will be approximately equal to the ratio of benefits to costs that would be derived if these calculations were extended into the future for each cohort of clients.

Another way of arriving at the same conclusion is to recognize that supported employment services are the *sine qua non* for the attainment of earnings by supported employees. If services end, so too will employee earnings. In this sense, only the earnings for the year in which costs are incurred are attributable to those costs.

This enormously simplifies benefit-cost calculations for supported work programs as compared to the models for vocational rehabilitation or transitional employment programs. No longer is there the need to project future changes in earnings or rates of job separation, or to adjust for inflation, or to select an arbitrary discount rate (or a range of discount rates).

The simplified method for computing benefit-cost ratios begins to break down, however, if some of the supported employees progress to the point where they can remain in competitive employment without additional support. In such cases, their future increased earnings should be projected and attributed to the program costs up to that point. This contingency restores all of the uncertainty surrounding the estimation of the benefits of time-limited services. However, the bulk of the supported employees served are believed to have disabilities sufficiently severe to require lifelong services, although in some cases, these services may not be continuous. In theory, a few supported employees may be able to work without support for months or years at a time, but still remain on the supported employment rolls because of the likelihood that they will require additional services at some future date. Despite these reservations, we anticipate that most benefit-cost analyses of supported employment programs will compare benefits and costs for a single year. In the next section, we further elaborate on the assumptions underlying this benefit-cost model, and describe possible problems of interpreting these analyses.

CHANGE IN ASSUMPTIONS ABOUT ALTERNATIVE SERVICES

The traditional vocational rehabilitation benefit-cost model (e.g., Conley, 1965, hereafter referred to as the Traditional Model) generally makes the implicit assumption that clients would not be placed in alternative programs in the absence of vocational rehabilitation. Although it is never made explicit, the logic of the Traditional Model requires that, in the absence of rehabilitation services, clients would essentially remain idle and dependent on some combination of their own resources, their families, benefits from the Social Security Disability Insurance (SSDI) program or other insurance fund, or payments from the Supplemental Security Income (SSI) program. For this reason, the primary benefit that is measured by the Traditional Model is increased earnings.

In recent years, however, there has been an enormous expansion of adult programs (e.g., sheltered workshops, work activity centers, adult day care) so that many persons who are not in competitive employment are placed in one of these alternate programs. This is particularly true for persons with severe disabilities. Consequently, an important benefit of supported employment is the savings in the costs that would have been incurred if the supported employees had been placed in alternative programs. Although such benefits were frequently mentioned in earlier benefit-cost studies (Conley, 1965), it has only recently become realistic to assume that most clients will, in the absence of supported employment, be placed in an alternative program. Thornton (1980) lists a large number of alternative programs in which such savings may occur. For adults with severe disabilities, the most important are sheltered workshops, work activity centers, and adult day activity programs.

Of course, not all clients entering into supported employment will come directly from an alternate program. Some clients will enter from school, others may have been on a waiting list for an alternative program, and still others may apply directly for services. It is, nevertheless, reasonable to assume that the majority of clients would have been placed in alternate programs if they had not been placed in supported employment.

Because there is a shortage of services for adults with severe disabilities in many areas of the country, we cannot assume that *all* persons in supported employment would have been placed in alternative programs. As a consequence, savings in alternate programs do not always accrue. This raises an ethical question: Should we decline to count savings in alternative programs as a benefit when it is the inadequacy of the service system itself that would force some clients in supported employment to forego alternate program services if they were not in a supported employment program? The importance of taking account of the savings in alternate programs becomes apparent through available data, which frequently indicate that the costs of supported employment programs are often significantly greater than the earnings of clients. Looked at in isolation, many supported employment programs may not appear economically justified. But these programs may be shown to have substantial economic benefits when compared to alternative programs which tend to result in lower earnings and higher costs of services (Noble & Conley, 1987).

Evaluating supported employment by considering *both* increased earnings and savings in alternative program costs is fundamentally different from traditional methods of evaluating the federal-state vocational rehabilitation program and employment programs funded by the U.S. Department of Labor. Consequently, if traditional benefit-cost ratios for vocational rehabilitation programs are compared with benefit-cost ratios for supported employment programs that utilize the above premises, the results should be cautiously interpreted and fully qualified.

Insofar as there are many techniques for comparing the benefits and costs of a program or for comparing the benefits and costs of different programs with each other, the precise procedure utilized will often depend on the particular question being asked. For example, in comparing the benefits and costs of supported employment with respect to the benefits and costs of alternative programs, it would be inappropriate to include savings in the costs of alternative programs as a benefit of supported employment programs (unless alternative programs are correspondingly perversely conceptualized as providing savings in the costs of supported employment services). A comparison of earnings and costs alone would suffice to judge the relative efficiency of sheltered workshop and supported employment programs.

PROBLEMS IN CONDUCTING BENEFIT-COST ANALYSES

There are numerous problems that generally affect the accuracy of calculations of benefits and costs as well as the way in which these estimates are used. The following discussion in no way surveys all of them. It does, however, identify the more important ones and examines several problems in which the technology of supported employment permits novel and reasonably accurate solutions.[3]

Lack of Data

The lack of accurate and comprehensive data with which to conduct rigorous evaluations of human service programs, whether employment-related or not, is often noted. As previously mentioned, information on the primary benefit, earnings, is usually collected for supported employment programs. There are, however, many other positive effects of enabling people with severe disabilities to work in integrated employment. Many of these benefits are psychological, such as increased self-esteem. Others are more easily observed, such as an increase in unpaid work performed at home or in the neighborhood, return to paid work by a member of the family, and the reduced need for daily supervision. The lack of this information is not due to an inability to collect it but rather a reluctance to incur the additional costs of obtaining it. Collecting information about possible intangible benefits often requires asking a number of questions or even administering a battery of tests. In many cases, the technology for obtaining this information is not well developed.

Marginal Benefit-Cost Analyses

Most benefit-cost studies calculate an *average* per client benefit-cost ratio by dividing the total of all estimated benefits by the total of all estimated costs. This is not, however, the relevant criterion for determining whether or not a program should expand or contract since it does *not* indicate what the effects on benefits and costs would be if the program were to expand (or contract) by a small amount. Suppose, for example, that expanding a supported employment program would result in recruitment of clients with more severe disabilities than before. This would probably result in higher costs and lower benefits. Although calculations of the overall average benefit-cost ratio would still exceed one, the *marginal* benefit-cost ratio (the ratio for the additional clients only) would not necessarily exceed one. In principle, programs should expand only if the marginal benefits associated with the expansion are greater than the marginal costs of the expansion, regardless of the overall relationship of benefits to costs. Similarly, programs should contract only if marginal benefits are less than marginal costs.

Unfortunately, it is much less difficult to estimate the average benefit-cost ratio for a program than the marginal benefit-cost ratio. This is because, in most cases, there is no way of knowing which clients would be served because of program expansion, or which clients would not be served if the program contracted.

The inability to calculate marginal benefit-cost ratios is often cited as a major weakness of benefit-cost analyses of large employment programs, such as the vocational rehabilitation program. There are, however, ways of addressing the issue of whether or not supported employment programs should expand without making formal calculations of marginal benefits and marginal costs.

Let us first assume that the number of persons receiving supported employment services is a small percentage of the total number who could benefit from this program. Second, let us assume that even though clients are selected on the basis of their likelihood of success, the personal characteristics and work potential of enrollees into supported employment will probably not change significantly for the next few years. The latter assumption is based on the premise that there exists a large pool of persons in sheltered workshops, work activity centers, and adult day care programs who, but for lack of supported employment funding, could be selected under existing criteria to receive supported employment services. It follows from these two assumptions that the average benefit-cost ratio for many supported employment programs will be similar to the marginal benefit-cost ratio of expanding these programs because the additional enrollees will be comparable to persons already being served.

This theoretical construct can be tested by examining the characteristics of persons in supported employment programs as compared to persons in alternative programs such as sheltered workshops, work activity centers, and adult day care, or to persons who are receiving no services at all. It is important to emphasize that these comparisons should not be made between all clients of a supported employment program and all clients of an alternative program. Instead, the comparison should ascertain if there are clients in the alternative program who are so similar to those in the supported employment program that they could profitably be switched to supported employment. Of course, the validity of the presumption should be subjected to empirical proof, paying attention to the relative frequency of false positive and false negative decisions.

There are many opportunities for comparing clients in supported work programs with clients in sheltered workshops, work activity centers, and adult day programs. Undertaking such comparisons would overcome two of the most persistent criticisms of benefit-cost studies, namely that they do not identify the marginal benefits and marginal costs of expanding programs, nor do they have a reliable control group (see below) with which to determine what would have happened in the absence of the program. To reiterate, the logic for proceeding in this way is valid to the extent that the number of clients served by supported employment programs is small relative to the total who could benefit from these programs, and that there remains a large number of persons in alternative programs (or in no program) with disabilities comparable to those in supported employment. We recognize, of course, that as the program expands, and as the pool of "more employable" persons with severe disabilities diminishes, marginal benefits will eventually decline and marginal costs rise.

Control Group

The benefits of any employment program should theoretically be measured by the difference in actual earnings after or while receiving the services of that program and what earnings would have been in the absence of services. Ideally, a control group should be identified that is similar to those receiving services in every respect except for the provision of services, making possible the inference that statistically significant differences in earnings between the two groups are attributable to the provision of services rather than to other possible factors. Randomization is the key to the formation of a valid control group, although a number of less rigorous options are possible (Campbell & Stanley, 1963; Cook & Campbell, 1979).

Only in recent years has there been any serious effort to rigorously select a follow-up group with which to evaluate the effectiveness of employment programs (e.g., Kerachsky & Thornton, 1987). For the most part, benefit-cost studies of vocational rehabilitation programs have attempted to approximate "with and without" studies by comparing the earnings made by clients "before and after" services (Conley, 1965; Noble, 1977) or by comparing the earnings of clients with those of a group of applicants to the program that did not receive services. However, the use of any substitute for a "with and without" services comparison has been strongly contested by researchers. To date, the findings of almost every benefit-cost study of vocational rehabilitation and other employment programs must be regarded as compromised and suspect because of uncertainty as to what the employment experience of successful clients would have been in the absence of services.

The problem of determining what the earnings of clients would have been in the absence of services may be much less problematic when evaluating supported work programs. If we make the reasonable assumption that most, if not all, clients in supported work programs would otherwise be placed in an alternative program (e.g., sheltered workshop, work activity center, adult day care), then a close approximation to what their earnings would have been in the absence of the supported work program is available by ascertaining the average earnings of the alternative programs in which they would otherwise have been placed. Of course, earnings vary broadly among the types of alternative programs, but even here the characteristics of supported work programs as currently evolving provide an answer to much of this problem. Many clients of supported work programs are taken directly from an alternative program so that the type of alternative program into which the client would have been placed is known with reasonable certainty. Of course, there will be cases in which the client enters the supported work programs directly after leaving school, requiring that estimates be made of what earnings would have been in an alternative program. Nevertheless, the potential error in estimating earnings in the absence of services is much less in supported work programs than has been the case for vocational rehabilitation and other employment programs.[4]

Targeted Jobs Tax Credit

In order to encourage employers to hire persons with severe disabilities, the U.S. Department of the Treasury administers the Targeted Job Tax Credit (TJTC) program which provides a tax subsidy for the first two years of employment of persons who qualify. It is unclear, however, whether the TJTC should be added into measures of program costs for purposes of benefit-cost analyses.

Consider three possibilities. First, does the TJTC compensate employers for additional costs arising from employment of persons with severe disabilities (e.g., extra training, modification of the work station, additional supervision)? If so, then expenditures under the TJTC program should be included as part of the total cost of providing supported employment services. A second possibility views the TJTC as a public subsidy to augment the earnings of these new employees with the expectation that their productivity will rise sufficiently to justify the normal wage after two years. If so, then the TJTC is not part of the social costs of providing supported employment services. It is a cost to taxpayers and an income transfer benefit to clients that has *zero* net social cost. If the second interpretation of the TJTC is accepted, then that portion of the earnings of clients that is subsidized by the TJTC program should not be counted as a social benefit. The final possibility is that the productivity of workers is equal to their earnings and that the employer incurs no additional costs in hiring the supported employee so that the TJTC becomes equivalent to a payment to the employer for providing the job.

In the first possibility, costs are increased; in the second, benefits are decreased. While the choice of either the first or second of the above possibilities would have some effect (probably small in most cases) on the size of the benefit-cost ratio, it would have no effect on the measure of total net benefits. The third possibility leads to several different ways of adjusting costs or benefits, all confusing. Lacking clear justification for interpreting the TJTC one way or the other, we recommend that any TJTC expenditures for clients be considered part of the cost of supported employment. It is the least difficult concept to explain.

Distribution of Benefits and Costs

The costs of most employment programs are born out of tax funds while a large part of the benefits accrue to clients. In consequence, even a favorable benefit-cost ratio may not unambiguously indicate that a program is worthwhile and/or should expand. There is always the need to justify taxing one group of citizens to benefit another. There are a number of ways of justifying such actions. First, employment programs can be considered a form of social insurance since the onset of disability cannot be predicted and may happen to any family. Second, employment programs can reflect a social belief that all citizens are entitled to certain services if they need them. Third, it can be argued that employment programs may yield sufficient nonmonetary benefits to taxpayers to justify their support. Of course, where evidence exists that an employment program produces monetary benefits to taxpayers exceeding the costs of their attainment, the program has unambiguous justification.

Program Phaseout

If the evaluation of supported employment programs is based on the assumption that clients would be placed in alternative programs, then the savings in the costs of alternative programs is an important benefit of supported employment. This raises an immediate problem of how to quantify alternative program cost savings. The usual approach is to determine the *average* cost of the alternative placement and to assume that this amount constitutes the savings. Unfortunately, this is not always the case. The actual savings is the *marginal* cost of serving one or more fewer clients in the alternative program, not the average cost of serving all clients. The difference between average and marginal costs can be substantial. For example, the loss of some of the clientele of an alternative program does not mean that costs will be reduced proportionately. Fixed costs, such as rent, property insurance, and licenses will be unchanged and many variable costs, such as electricity, water, and heating, may only decline slightly, if at all. Even staff costs do not necessarily decline in proportion to the reduction in personnel. In consequence, estimates of savings in alternative program costs that are based on average costs may overstate these benefits. In fact, the use of average costs can be justified only if there are special circumstances, for instance, if some alternative facilities are closed down (as should occur as supported employment programs expand) or if the alternative program itself is altered so that it provides both supported work and the alternative program so that fixed and semi-fixed costs are used to benefit the supported employee.

EXPANSION OF ALTERNATIVE PROGRAMS

It is possible, even likely, that as clients are moved from alternative programs to supported employment, the alternative program will fill the slot with another client so that there is no net decrease in their clientele. Under these circumstances, should supported employment be credited with creating savings in alternative employment programs? The answer is yes. Benefits must be measured in the basis of what would have happened in the absence of supported employment. If the supported employment programs did not exist, the most likely scenario would be an expansion of the alternative programs. Thus supported employment programs enable society to avoid the cost of expanding alternative programs.

THE ILLINOIS EXPERIENCE

The state of Illinois commissioned the University of Illinois at Urbana-Champaign to collect data from state-funded vendors of supported employment services. Data collected during the period July 1, 1986 to June 30, 1987 (FY 1987) from twenty-five of the thirty-one local vendors are analyzed here. The state of Illinois terminated the funding of several of the agencies that are not included in this analysis. The reporting agencies were all private nonprofit and all provided some combination of alternate program services in addition to supported employment. A total of 394 individuals were in supported employment in Illinois during the study period. Almost all had mental retardation, about half of whom were functioning at the mild and borderline levels of mental retardation (some of whom had associated physical or emotional disabilities). (Readers are referred to Chapter 3 for a detailed description of supported employee characteristics.)

Costs

The cost of supported employment was estimated by adding together the funds paid to vendors specifically for the purpose of providing supported employment services and the reimbursement to employers provided by the Targeted Jobs Tax Credit (TJTC) program. At the state level, supported employment funds were provided by the Illinois Department of Rehabilitation Services (DORS) and the Illinois Department of Mental Health and Developmental Disabilities (DMH-DD). In addition, some municipal and local agencies allocated funds for supported employment. During FY 1987, only fifty-six individuals in supported employment participated in the TJTC program. The total costs of supported employment in Illinois were $1,668,752 in 1987.[5]

Increased Earnings

The gross wages of the 394 supported employees in FY 1987 came to $703,264. To estimate what portion of these earnings are attributable to supported employment services, the amount they would have earned in the absence of supported employment must be determined and subtracted. The assumption that these supported employees would have been placed in alternative programs in the absence of supported employment is particularly strong in this case insofar as almost all of the 394 employees had been placed in alternative programs before embarking on supported employment.

Table 16.1 lists the alternative programs in which the 394 supported employees had previously participated, together with an estimate of the earnings that would have accrued had they remained in their former programs instead of entering supported employment. The alternative programs include sheltered workshops, work activity centers, and other work-oriented programs in Illinois.

From these data, we estimate that the supported employees, had they remained in their alternate programs, would have earned $423,832 in 1987.[6] The estimated *increase* in the earnings as a result of supported employment in 1987 was $279,412, or almost $710 per employee.

Table 16.1 Estimated earnings and costs of supported employment clients had they remained in their alternative program

Alternative Program	Number of Clients	Estimated Average Annual Earnings	Estimated Average Annual Costs[c]
Developmental Training I (adult day care)[a]	2	$ 116.50	$2712.50
Developmental Training II (work activities)[a]	92	260.10	2611.87
Regular work or extended employment (sheltered workshop)[b]	146	1445.05	1140.01
Work adjustment training[b]	57	1265.47	793.09
Skill training[b]	14	2530.90	3393.29
Vocational training[b]	12	1168.17	2215.17
Evaluation[b]	11	1061.91	3399.09
Transitional employment[b]	6	2508.50	7430.33
School STEP program or community[b]	50	1075.76	2475.00

[a] The earnings of clients in the Developmental Training I and II programs averaged $16.21 and $36.13 per month, respectively (Taylor Institute, 1988). These monthly earnings were multiplied by 7.2, which was the average number of months in employment of supported employment clients during 1987.

[b] Average hourly earnings in other alternative employment programs were based on the average hourly wage rates reported by these organizations to the U. S. Department of Labor. These hourly rates were: $1.93 for regular work or extended employment programs, $1.69 for the work adjustment and skill training programs; and $1.56 for the vocational development and evaluation programs. Earnings for clients coming from the community or schools were based on an average of the above rates. These hourly rates were multiplied by 26, the average number of hours worked per week, and then by 4 to estimate total monthly earnings. Finally, total monthly earnings were multiplied by 7.2 to estimate total annual earnings.

[c] The cost that would have been incurred had clients remained in supported employment was estimated as follows. The average annual cost for each form of alternative program was assigned on the basis of the rates reported by the Department of Rehabilitation Services and the Department of Mental Health and Developmental Disabilities in Illinois. This average cost was then adjusted downward by the ratio of 7.2/12 to reflect the average time of participation by clients in the supported employment programs in 1987.

Savings in Alternative Program Costs

Using the data presented in Table 16.1, an estimated savings of $975,075 as a result of not providing alternate program services in 1987 was calculated for persons who entered supported employment. The estimate was derived by multiplying the number of clients in each alternative program category by the average alternative program costs. As previously explained, the use of the average cost of alternative programs will usually overstate the actual savings of switching individuals to supported employment unless the alternative program closes down or, as is the case here, expands its operations to provide supported employment along with other alternative programs.

The Social Benefit-Cost Ratio

A social benefit-cost ratio for the first year of operation of the supported employment program in Illinois was derived by dividing the estimate of increased earnings and the savings in alternative program costs, $1,254,487, by total costs, $1,668,752. This benefit-cost ratio indicated that society received a return of $.75 for each dollar of expenditure on supported employment, indicating a net loss of $.25 per dollar spent.

The relatively unfavorable benefit-cost ratio, which takes into account only increased earnings and none of the intangible benefits of supported employment, is inconsistent with previous conclusions on the benefits and costs of supported employment by the authors (Noble & Conley, 1989). This may be partly explained by the newness of the program. As the supported employment program matures, average benefits/earnings should rise and average costs should fall, yielding a more favorable benefit-cost outcome. Earnings should rise as employees gain experience and seniority on their jobs and become more productive in their work. Moreover, supported employment staff should become more adept in placement as they gain experience and have access to an increased number and variety of jobs resulting from the favorable response of employers to job development campaigns.

Costs, in contrast, should fall for several reasons: (a) the level of support and oversight required will decline as employees become accustomed to their jobs; (b) supported employment programs, when stabilized, will incur fewer start-up costs (e.g., staff training, new transport, initial job development); and (c) supported employment programs themselves will become more efficient through experience and discovery of more effective means of rendering services. Evidence from several studies supports the expectation that benefits continue to increase while costs decrease over time (Hill, Wehman, Kregel, Banks, & Metzler, 1987; Hill & Wehman, 1983; McCaughrin, 1988; Tines, Rusch, McCaughrin, & Conley, in press).

The Taxpayer Benefit-Cost Ratio

Although taxpayers bore 100 percent of supported employment costs, a substantial part of the increase in earnings is received by participants. Nonetheless, taxpayers receive a surprisingly large percentage of the benefits of supported employment. To begin with, some supported employees receive public payments from tax supported programs such as the Social Security Disability Insurance program, the Supplemental Security Income program, Medicare, and Medicaid. The Illinois data indicate that there was an aggregate reduction of $26,138 in these payments in 1987. In addition, supported employees pay taxes out of their earnings. In 1987, it was estimated that these employees paid almost $98,457 in taxes. Almost all of this total represented new taxes since supported employees in alternative placements are not required to pay Social Security or Medicare taxes, and they are exempt from state taxes in Illinois.

Adding together the estimate of reduction in public payments, increased taxes, and the savings in alternative program costs of over $975,000, we conclude that the total monetary benefit to taxpayers resulting from the supported employment program in 1987 was $1,099,670. This amounts to a return of $.66 for each tax dollar spent on supported employment, indicating a net loss of $.34 per dollar spent.

Over time, the return to taxpayers should become even greater as supported employees experience further increases in earnings and pay taxes on them. In addition, while the initial savings in public payments are small they may rise substantially in the future. For one thing, the earnings of supported employees will rise, causing further reductions in public income support. In addition, increasing numbers may qualify for employer-provided medical insurance. Moreover, some employees will use up the nine month trial work period that is granted under the SSDI program with no change in benefits. Finally, some supported employees would probably have had to apply for additional public support had they not engaged in supported employment. The Illinois data do not capture possible future savings from these sources.

SUMMARY

The measured monetary benefits were less than costs of the supported employment program in Illinois in 1987. Of course, additional intangible and psychological benefits may have accrued that could not be quantified at this stage. But more importantly, it appears likely that changes in benefits and costs of supported employment over the next few years will result in a more favorable benefit-cost ratio.

It must be emphasized, however, that the savings in the cost of alternative programs represented more than three-fourths of the benefits ascribed to supported work. Supported employees' earnings were only about 37 percent greater than their earnings would have been in alternative employment programs, representing about a $60-per-month increase. Clearly, despite stunning successes in gaining public acceptance of supported employment for persons with severe disabilities, advocates cannot afford to become complacent. The Illinois data argue for aggressive and continuing efforts to upgrade and refine the supported employment programs that have been initiated. The future of supported employment in the U. S. may well depend on demonstrating continuing improvements in program effectiveness and efficiency over time. The data also argue for serious efforts to obtain reliable evidence of the possible intangible benefits that may flow from supported employment. Evidence of such intangible benefits is needed to bolster arguments for maintaining and expanding supported employment options for persons with severe disabilities.

NOTES

[1] The qualifiers, "benefit-cost" and "evaluation," are used synonymously, although other analysts have attempted to distinguish between them. Both terms emphasize the assessment of outcomes resulting from identifiable program interventions.

[2] See Conley (1973) for further discussion on the strengths and weaknesses of each of these approaches to comparing benefits and costs.

[3] See Noble (1977) for systematic review and critique of the methods, assumptions, and results of the 18 earliest benefit-cost studies of the federal-state vocational rehabilitation program.

[4] In order to avoid confusion in terminology, it is important to emphasize that the marginal benefit-cost ratio described above refers only to the benefit-cost ratio associated with the additional clients who will be served if a program expands. By the same token, the average benefits for all clients are measured by the increment in earnings and other variables that occurs as a result of services. The notion of incremental change is inherent in the measurement of benefits for all clients (i.e., the increase in earnings) and to the marginal benefit-cost ratio (i.e., the increased earnings associated only with additional clients served).

[5] This somewhat understates actual costs since administrative costs borne by state- and local-level authorities are not included. In addition, there is no allowance for current or past research expenditures on supported employment. Finally, some part of the costs of supported employment programs that failed in Illinois and are not included in the cost data should be allocated to the cost of supported employment programs. After all, even unsuccessful activities are a part of the cost of doing business.

[6] Estimated foregone average annual earnings were derived by multiplying the estimated earnings of clients in each alternative program by the number of supported employment clients who were originally in those programs.

QUESTIONS (For answers see p. 434)

1. How can benefit-cost analyses guide public policy?

2. What is the major reason why effective rehabilitation programs for persons with severe disabilities have been slow to develop?

3. Identify the major components of a rigorous cost benefit analysis.

4. What is the purpose of evaluating programs for persons with disabilities?

5. How does a benefit/cost ratio compare benefits and costs?

6. Assuming that most persons with severe disabilities will be placed in either day programs or supported employment, what would the major source of savings be if supported employment replaced traditional day programs?

7. When looked at in isolation, many supported employment programs may not appear economically justified. How do the authors justify supported employment strictly from an economic point of view?

8. From an economic perspective, when should programs expand? Explain.

9. Explain why estimates of savings in alternative program costs that are based on average costs may overestimate benefits.

10. Explain why the authors claim average benefits/earnings should increase and costs should fall as supported employment programs mature.

REFERENCES

Campbell, D. & Stanley, J. (1963). *Experimental and quasi-experimental designs for research.* Chicago: Rand McNally.

Conley, R. W. (1965). *The economics of vocational rehabilitation*. Baltimore: The Johns Hopkins University Press.

Conley, R. W. (1973). *The economics of mental retardation*. Baltimore: The Johns Hopkins University Press.

Conley, R. W. & Noble, J. H. (1989). Changes in the service system for persons with disabilities. In W. Kiernan & R. Schalock (Eds.), *Economics, industry, and disability: A look ahead* (pp. 37–45). Baltimore: Paul H. Brookes.

Cook, T. & Campbell, D. (1979). *Quasi-experimentation*. Chicago: Rand McNally.

Hill, M. & Wehman, P. (1983). Cost-benefit analysis of placing moderately and severely handicapped individuals into competitive employment. *Journal of the Association for the Severely Handicapped, 8*, 30–32.

Hill, M., Wehman, P., Kregel, J., Banks, P. D., & Metzler, H. M. D. (1987). Employment outcomes for people with moderate and severe disabilities: An eight-year longitudinal analysis of supported competitive employment. *Journal of the Association for the Severely Handicapped, 12*, 182–189.

Kerachsky, S. & Thornton, C. (1987). Findings from the STETS Transitional Employment Demonstration. *Exceptional Children, 53*(6), 515–521.

Kiernan, W. E., McGauphey, M. J., Schalock, R. L., & Rowland, S. M. (1988). *Employment survey for adults with developmental disabilities*. Boston: The Children's Hospital, The Training and Research Institute for Adults with Disabilities.

McCaughrin, W. B. (1988). *Longitudinal trends of competitive employment for developmentally disabled adults: A benefit-cost analysis*. Unpublished doctoral dissertation, University of Illinois, Urbana-Champaign.

Noble, J. H. (1977). The limits of cost-benefit analysis as a guide to priority-setting in rehabilitation. *Evaluation Quarterly, 1*(3), 347–380.

Noble, J. H. & Conley, R. W. (1987). Accumulating evidence on the benefits and costs of supported and transitional employment for persons with severe disabilities. *Journal of the Association for the Severely Handicapped, 12*(3), 163–174.

Noble, J. H., Swaninathan, S., Shankar, Y., Goodman, S., & Peters, A. V. (1989). *New York State Office of Vocational Rehabilitation supported employment management information system (SEMIS)*. Version 1.3. Buffalo: State University of New York.

Taylor Institute (1988). An assessment of the effectiveness of developmental training programs in Illinois: A report for The Governor's Planning Council on Developmental Disabilities, Chicago, Illinois: Author.

Thornton, C. (1980). Benefit-cost analysis of social programs. In R. H. Bruinincks & C. K. Lakin (Eds.), *Living and learning in the least restrictive environment* (pp. 225–244). Baltimore: Paul H. Brookes.

Tines, J., Rusch, F. R., McCaughrin, W. B., & Conley, R. W. (in press). *Longitudinal benefit-cost analysis of a supported competitive employment program: The Schneider et al. study revisited. Journal of Applied Behavior Analysis* (in press).

Wehman, P., Kregel, J., & Shafer, M. S. (1989). *Emerging trends in the national supported employment initiative: A preliminary analysis of 27 states*. Richmond: Rehabilitation Research and Training Center on Supported Employment, Virginia Commonwealth University.

CHAPTER

17

National Issues for Implementation of Supported Employment

David Mank
Jay Buckley
Larry Rhodes
University of Oregon

Since the formation of a national initiative to end joblessness among persons with severe disabilities, every state in the nation has attempted to redesign its service delivery system. This new initiative has affirmed the principle that support should be provided to individuals with severe disabilities to allow participation in typical community activities. Supported employment has required a new partnership between employers and organizations that serve persons with disabilities. And, perhaps most significantly, it has been directed toward persons whom many considered inappropriate for employment, even within the context of a sheltered workshop (e.g., Barcus, Griffin, Mank, Rhodes, & Moon, 1988; Kiernan & Schalock, 1989; Wehman & Moon, 1989).

Seekins and Fawcett (1984) describe four separate phases in the policy development process: agenda-setting, policy development, policy implementation, and policy review. Legislation on supported employment, notably the Developmental Disabilities Act of 1984 and the Rehabilitation Act Amendments of 1986, reflect the movement from setting an agenda to formulation of national policy direction. Implementation is far from complete but has moved from local demonstration to more widespread state system change activities (e.g., Oregon Supported Employment Initiative, 1987; Virginia Department of Rehabilitation Services, 1988; Wehman, Kregel, & Shafer, 1989; Whitehead, 1989). The focus of attention is beginning to include calls for policy review as progress reports emerge. Review of progress to date allows for adjustment of policy and expanded implementation.

The fundamental strategy for implementing supported employment has involved changing systems for funding, regulating, and operating services at all levels, from government to local service providers. The central objective of systems change activities has been to shift services from a variety of segregated day programs to integrated employment by redirecting resources already available in the system (U.S. Department of Education, 1985; National Association of Rehabilitation Facilities, in press; Public Law 99-506; Wehman, Kregel, & Shafer, 1989).

The acceptability of the current pace of implementing supported employment may be debated. Yet, there is little doubt that thousands of individuals with severe disabilities, who just a few years ago had little chance of a job, now have access to integrated employment. The questions for future action relate to expanding access to a greater number of persons with severe disabilities, while improving both quality and opportunities for choice.

The purpose of this chapter is to review highlights of the systems change approach and discuss issues faced by states individually and collectively. In addition, this chapter will argue that supported employment has begun to, and indeed must, shift from strategies for initiating a movement to strategies for widespread expansion and implementation. Finally, strategies for expanded systems change will be discussed in terms of three needed features: ongoing improvement in *quality*; significant expansion of *access*; and building *stability* into the system.

CURRENT STATUS AND STRATEGIES FOR SYSTEMS CHANGE

The progress of the national initiative may be considered in at least two ways: the emerging data about individuals in supported employment, and the nature of the systems change strategies used in various states. Together these suggest something about the progress of the initiative, its effectiveness to date, and the needs for future implementation across states.

Available Data

Data on progress of the implementation of supported employment are increasingly available. Reports from Virginia Commonwealth University (Wehman, Kregel, & Shafer, 1989), and the National Association of Rehabilitation Facilities (in press) provide the best available markers of national progress. Combined with reports from a number of states, these reports provide needed information about progress to date and help define future implementation issues (e.g., Lyon, Domaracki, & Alexy, 1988; North Dakota Department of Human Services, 1988; Northwest Instructional Design, 1987; St. Louis, Richter, Griffin, & Struxness, 1987). These data provide information about the direction of the initiative and the issues for the next few years. Based on the data available, several observations regarding current trends can be made.

ACCESS IS EXPANDING BUT IS STILL SEVERELY LIMITED. Documentation of placements of thousands of individuals with severe disabilities in less than four years provides evidence of significant expansion in a relatively short time. Estimates suggest, for example, that about 10 percent of adults with developmental disabilities currently served in day services now have access to supported employment. The flipside of these data must also be considered. That is, nine of ten individuals with developmental disabilities do not yet have access to integrated employment. This 90 percent includes neither those adults with severe disabilities who are on states' waiting lists for service, nor persons currently residing in institutions.

PERSONS WITH MILD AND MODERATE MENTAL RETARDATION HAVE THE GREATEST ACCESS. The available data suggest that as much as 85 percent of those placed are moderately and mildly mentally retarded. While support for these individuals is necessary for employment success, persons with more severe developmental disabilities, persons with long-term mental illness, severe and multiple physical disabilities, traumatic head injuries, and others are far less represented. As supported employment continues, equal access will be at issue.

FACILITY PROGRAMS ARE INVOLVED IN IMPLEMENTATION OF SUPPORTED EMPLOYMENT. Available state and national reports suggest that most programs involved in supported employment implementation are programs that have formerly served persons with disabilities in segregated settings. While some facility programs are making commitments to total conversion to integrated employment, others have only "added on" supported employment (e.g., National Industries for the Severely Handicapped, 1989). This suggests the beginnings of possible change in the mission and service strategies of established programs toward more integrated employment. At issue will be the extent to which existing facility programs actually serve all individuals who will benefit in integrated jobs.

Access to Vocational Rehabilitation Resources is Expanding in Title VI-C and Also in Title I. The persons for whom supported employment is considered appropriate include those who were previously ineligible for vocational rehabilitation services because of the severity of their disability. Estimates for 1988 suggest rapid growth in the numbers receiving services through states' vocational rehabilitation agencies in combination with long-term funding from other sources. In some states, vocational rehabilitation general funds (Title I) have been invested in addition to the newer resources earmarked specifically for supported employment. The pace of future implementation will depend in part on the extent to which all persons who could benefit from supported employment will have access to vocational rehabilitation support.

Costs are Variable. Available cost data suggest a range of ongoing support costs from less than \$1,000/year to more than \$16,000/year. The variables accounting for cost are complex, with key reasons including local economic conditions, public opinion about the right of individuals with severe disabilities to work, the competence of local support organizations, geographic location, state rate structures, and the perceived support needs of individuals. Establishing an appropriate rate to cover costs of supported employment seems desirable and necessary for adequate planning; however, establishing a fixed rate in the early years of supported employment is difficult, inexact, and may well discourage flexibility and innovation in local communities.

Federal Funds have Provided Incentives, But State Resources are Providing the Greater Share of Funding. By design, vocational rehabilitation resources and federal incentives have provided the opportunity to begin the initial investment in supported employment for many individuals. Support over time must come largely from state day services funds. While federal investment appears substantial, it has begun to leverage multimillions in long-term resources in states.

Implementation Strategies Include Some Variety. The data available suggest variety in the nature of the jobs in which individuals are placed and in the approaches for providing support. Future implementation should be expected to show even greater variety while maintaining a focus on employment outcomes. The discrete labels of individual placements, clustered placements, or crews no longer describe many supported employment placements. "Institutionalizing the model" by requiring strict adherence to process standards might be expected to stifle rather than encourage continued innovation.

THE FOCUS OF STATE SYSTEMS CHANGE EFFORTS

The notion of creating change in the system that supported segregation and day activity at a national level was created formally in 1985 via incentive money to states in the form of Title III demonstration grants (U.S. Department of Education, 1985). This request for proposals called for two notable conditions of application. First, indication of interagency coordination was required. Second, applications were to propose methods to demonstrate change in the basic day services system. These changes were to include policy and funding change, rather than just the creation of new direct service programs. Where deinstitutionalization efforts often have been driven by legal action, supported employment as a broad systems change initiative began with a relatively small incentive to states. In 1985, ten states were awarded five-year grants as an incentive to leverage the multimillion dollars in the day services and day treatment programs in mental retardation and mental health. In 1986 systems change incentive grants were awarded to an additional seventeen states and the Vocational Rehabilitation Act of 1986 was amended to provide funds (Title VI-C) to all states in the nation.

One interesting upshot of the state demonstrations was how change and innovation were encouraged. If the task were defined as setting up demonstration programs, it might be expected that a small number of local programs would be recruited and supported, perhaps with fanfare, perhaps in a rather quiet fashion, but without addressing policy and systems issues statewide. Instead, the demonstration states embarked on a broad set of strategies that included setting up training and technical assistance projects, testing interagency funding, reviewing policy and regulations, developing statewide and sometimes interagency information systems, and creating public information campaigns. This occurred in addition to funding demonstration programs across each state. Within states these strategies marked the beginning of an initiative for supported employment that sought to rapidly increase the number of people with severe disabilities who work in integrated jobs. Of equal importance, the states began building long-term capacity and expanding ownership for the concept of supported employment.

The question, of course, is this: Will the strategy work in transforming a billion dollar system of segregation and day activity into integrated employment with long-term support? Several years into the initiative, it is too soon to say. The data generated within and across states provide some idea of the direction and rate of implementation. Another view provides a somewhat different but complementary perspective for considering progress in capacity-building in states. Changes in state strategies have been monitored by the Employment Network Technical Assistance Project on supported employment.

The Employment Network project was funded in 1985, funded again in 1987 as a technical assistance resource in tandem with the Title III state change projects, and then later with Title VI-C projects. The purpose of the project is to provide on-site technical assistance, dissemination of emerging information and training institutes on supported employment. While the project's point of entry is defined as the state supported employment project, a primary focus of the assistance to states has been overall systems change, planning, and assistance in capacity-building. This has developed based on ongoing technical assistance planning with each state. A review of the nature of the technical assistance request by states and the changes in focus of these requests across four years makes possible a few observations about states' systems change efforts (Employment Network, 1988). Table 17.1 depicts noted changes in the nature of state initiatives' efforts.

1. Many Early Requests Focused on Building Consensus and Providing Basic Information. In the early months of most state projects, one important focus area of activity involved providing basic information to as many people as possible. These activities were important in terms of establishing a baseline level of information to interested people and building consensus about the direction of integrated employment services for the future.

2. Early Requests Included a Focus on Demonstrating Features of State Change. One important aspect of state projects addressed the matter of systemic issues for supported employment. In 1985 1986, the now familiar strategies of joint funding and interagency agreements specifying roles for agencies in the employment of people with severe disabilities were first tested. In some states an important beginning in this area involved demonstrations of agencies working together and jointly funding a small number of integrated employment projects. Initially demonstrating that this was even possible was as difficult as it was important. These successful efforts can serve to lay the groundwork for later, more thorough, application of systems change features across states.

3. Recent Requests Include a Focus on Expansion to Other Disabilities. Clearly, the majority of persons with access to supported employment have been persons with mental retardation. Perhaps this is no surprise given the advocacy community's calling for integrated employment in the late 1970s and the early and mid-1980s. More recently, however, advocates of persons with disabilities other than mental retardation have begun to call for integrated employment with long-term support. As a result, states

Table 17.1 Changes in the Nature of Assistance Requests

The Employment Network Project
Technical Assistance for Systems Change in Supported Employment

1985-1986	1987	1988-1989
Marketing for access to jobs	-----------------------	Corporate and economic development
Establish local training and technical assistance centers	-----------------------	Expand availability of training and technical assistance
		Extend training and technical assistance to other disability programs
Define and demonstrate roles in interagnecy coordination	-----------------------	Refine roles and extend collaboration and ownership
Demonstrate joint funding of projects	-----------------------	Change funding policies and mechanisms for stable co-funding
Develop an information system	-----------------------	Build a quality assurance system
Create public information campaigns	-----------------------	Develop consensus among stakeholders
Plan project strategies	-----------------------	Conduct long-term planning for stability over time

have initiated programs and requested technical assistance for creating supported employment for persons with long-term mental illness, persons with severe physical disabilities and persons with traumatic head injuries as well as persons with severe and profound mental retardation.

4. RECENT REQUESTS SEEK TO REFINE AND EXPAND FEATURES OF SYSTEMS CHANGE FOLLOWING SUCCESSFUL DEMONSTRATIONS. States' efforts to show what was possible regarding changes in policy, funding, and interagency collaboration have been successful inasmuch as constructive systems change was demonstrated. These demonstrations have been followed by efforts to implement policy, funding, and regulation changes across some entire states.

5. OVERALL, THE CHANGES SUGGEST A FUNDAMENTAL SHIFT FROM EFFORTS TO BEGIN AN INITIATIVE TO BROAD SYSTEMS CHANGE. Naturally, development within and across states is highly variable. Even so, many states have broadened implementation, attempted new strategies, and learned from each other. Together, these changes suggest that states have reached a milestone toward more widespread implementation.

The emerging data about progress in supported employment, coupled with system change strategies, help make the argument that the supported employment initiative has long since begun. The issue now is one of extending access and changing the heart of state systems, where the responsibility rests for long-term success. At issue for states individually and collectively is to capitalize on early efforts in order to accomplish three future goals: *quality* in implementation; expanded *access* to the thousands of people who will benefit; and *stability* for integrated employment over time. The next section of this chapter discusses these features in terms of strategies for both state and national implementation.

FOCUS ON QUALITY, ACCESS, AND STABILITY IN SUPPORTED EMPLOYMENT IMPLEMENTATION

An early structure for statewide change to supported employment in states was defined by Bellamy, Rhodes, Mank, and Albin (1988). This state change approach identified four primary areas of accomplishment for systems change to supported employment: creating employment opportunities; developing local service providers; establishing state management systems; and building consensus and participation. Each of these accomplishment areas is organized into objectives and specific strategies to develop supported employment outcomes. Figure 17.1 presents the state change approach.

This structure has been useful as states begin supported employment implementation. It has also served as a reference point for state-supported employment project personnel. An adaptation has been used for ongoing review of the progress of implementation and priority needs in states in cooperation with technical assistance planning with the Employment Network project. In many states the self-assessment has been developed across agencies in order to realize a broader-based perspective on continued state change.

The opportunity in the coming months and years is to reconsider such a systems change approach for more thorough implementation. Three critical areas will create the future focus: ongoing improvement in the *quality* of individual outcomes; increased *access* to integrated employment; and *stability* of the initiative over time. Table 17.2 suggests some strategies for increasing quality, access, and stability across system change accomplishment areas.

Building Quality into Supported Employment

The "bottom line" in the ongoing implementation of supported employment is the quality of outcomes realized by individuals with disabilities. Supported employment is predicated on the notion that access combined with support will result in meaningful outcomes. Implementation over the last few years has

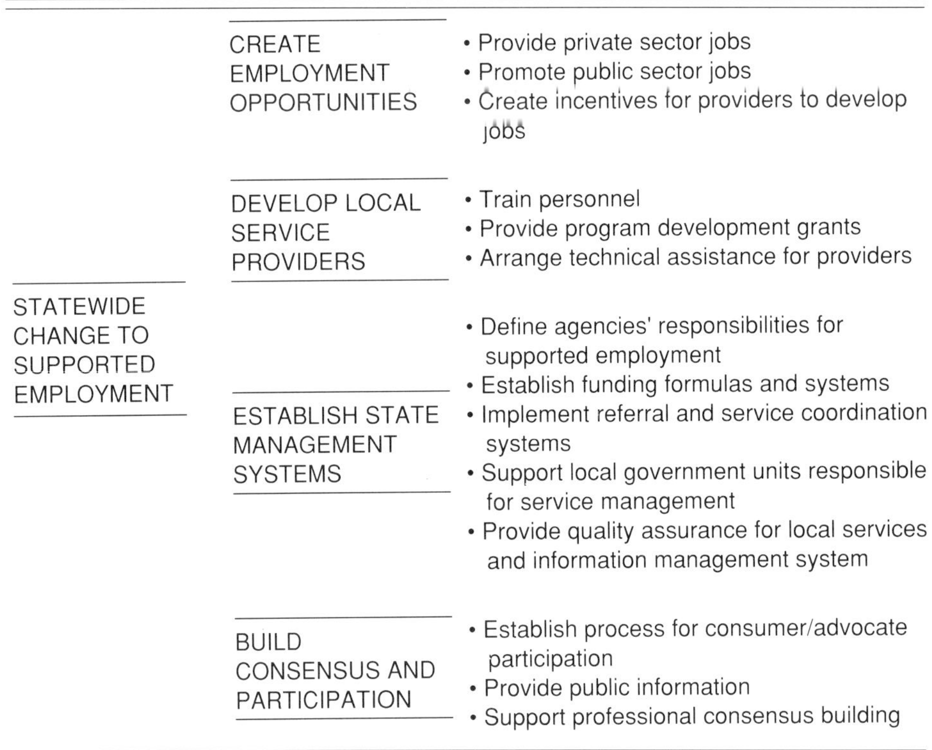

Figure 17.1 An overview of the accomplishments necessary for statewide change to supported employment (from Bellamy, G. T., Rhodes, L. E., Mank, D. M., & Albin, J. M. (1988). *Supported employment: A community implementation guide*. Baltimore: Paul H. Brookes. Reprinted by permission of the author and the publisher.

Table 17.2 State System Change: Possible Strategies for Future Implementation

	Quality	Access	Stability
Create employment opportunities	- Provide incentives to promote with increasing wages; jobs with benefits; individual choice; greater variety of jobs; and career advancement opportunities.	- Provide for equal access for all persons with severe disabilities. - Extend private sector leadership and partnership in supported employment. - Expand across public sector employment.	- Extend involvement of business community. - Develop policies for full employment of people with disabilities.
Develop local service providers	- Provide role-specific training and individualized technical assistance. - Reward innovation and improved outcomes. - Promote new processes for ongoing improvement.	- Expand implementation across: - all areas of state. - different disability labels. - different support labels. - the number and type of total programs involved.	- Support community ownership of integrated employment. - Address direct service staff turnover needs. - Create stable policy for integration at local levels. - Expand conversion of existing program.
Establish state management systems	- Refine interagency roles and agreements.- Close gaps between systems. - Align funding policy and mechanisms with integration. - Maintain flexibility and accountability in funding and policy. - Provide for ongoing review and change in state policy. - Extend involvement of long-term funding. - Review and respond to emerging data.	- Develop access for school-leavers. - Identify and revise policy, funding, and regulation barriers. - Extend conversion of segregated programs. - Explore new sources of long-term funding. - Extend use of existing day service resources for integrated employment.	- Ensure participation of all state agencies. - Establish policy and statutes that stabilize integration and employment into the future. - Extend long-term funding of integrated employment. - Maintain within-state training and technical assistance. - Revise and monitor data systems to track progress.
Build consensus and participation	- Ensure that advocacy groups and familiies are part of decision-making processes. - Encourage individual choice and decision-making. - Extend consensus-building to all interested groups. - Encourage consumer monitoring efforts.	- Promote self-advocacy. - Increase involvement of families and advocates in all areas of operation.	- Build community ownership of employment of people with disabilities. - Extend consensus on replacing segregation with integration.

shown some similarity of efforts, yet a creative range of job and support options has also been developed. Individuals with severe disabilities will benefit directly if the lessons learned in the last few years are incorporated into ongoing implementation (Barcus, Griffin, Mank, Rhodes, & Moon, 1988). The strategies for supporting quality seem especially important for within- and across-state implementation.

DEVISE SYSTEMS FOR IMPROVEMENT OVER TIME RATHER THAN RELIANCE ON MONITORING PROCESSES. The relationship of innovation to quality can hardly be overstated. Innovations that show promise for improving quality come from a number of sources including (a) quality assurance systems developed in business and industry (e.g., Deming, 1975; Ishikawa, 1976; Zeleny, 1989) and how they have been applied to supported employment programs (e.g., Sandow & Rhodes, 1989); (b) state development personnel who have differentiated between monitoring and quality assurance and focus on steps for promoting internal improvement rather than external compliance (e.g., Sandow, Rhodes, Mank, Ramsing, & Lynch, in press; Virginia Department of Rehabilitation Services, 1988); (c) leadership exercised by the business community resulting in the development of "better" jobs (e.g., Washington Supported Employment Initiative, 1989); (d) the growth in self-advocacy (e.g., Allen, 1988; Gould, 1987) and the promise it holds for increasing the likelihood that the outcomes individuals with severe disabilities achieve are those they themselves select; and (e) the many creative ways service providers have found to provide services to individuals with a variety of severe disabilities (e.g., McCarthy, Fender, & Fender, 1988; Sowers, Jenkins, & Powers, 1988; UCPA, 1988; Wehman, Kreutzer, Wood, Morton, & Sherron, 1988) in a wide range of business settings. The recent past has also demonstrated the value of continued consensus building. As states seek widespread implementation, the clarity of advocates and others on what defines quality and improvement can frame future agendas for improvements.

REGULARLY COLLECT AND USE DATA FOR DECISION MAKING. Decisions made in the absence of data are less likely to anticipate problems and capitalize on progress. Regular review of progress, including successes and failures, helps ensure that those involved in the initiative learn from their experience. In addition, data review allows for the information collected to be adjusted and enlarged over time (Wehman & Hill, 1989). In just a few years the standards for quality have changed and increased. Early in the initiative, outcomes focused almost exclusively on wages and presence as defined by the number of hours spent in community jobs. More recently, a greater emphasis has been placed on improved wages over time, benefits, evidence of individual choice, career advancement, and meaningful social integration.

SUPPORT INNOVATION EFFORTS. Supported employment has demonstrated the importance of implementation efforts that include a number of people in different roles in communities and states. Innovation has come from families and self-advocates (e.g., Gould, 1987; Allen, 1988), and service providers as well as government agencies. Interest in ongoing improvement of quality is important from the individual to the state systems' levels. Individuals with severe disabilities can be encouraged to define preferences. Providers can be supported to promote ongoing improvement in outcomes. Training and technical assistance projects can maintain a focus on competency-based training while investing in innovation and documenting new strategies. Federal, state, and regional funders and program developers can seek methods of developing and supporting implementation so that the focus is on individual outcomes rather than agency convenience.

Innovators in many different roles have contributed significantly to developing the reality of supported employment in many communities. Support for continued risk-taking in innovation can build improved quality into supported employment.

Increasing Access to Supported Employment

In addition to improved implementation of supported employment, the number of individuals who have access to integrated employment must expand over time. The pace of implementation to date has involved many thousands of individuals. Even so, most people with severe disabilities do not have access to supported employment. While attention to quality will define individual success, the numbers of people with access may well be used to define the success or failure of the initiative as a whole.

Four strategies appear critical to improving access for the thousands who are still waiting.

EXPAND CONVERSION OF EXISTING LONG-TERM RESOURCES. Continued focus on using existing day services resources in state agencies is needed for increasing access to supported employment. Leadership in using existing dollars to support integrated employment rather than segregation and day activity can come from local programs as well as state agencies. This important strategy has been the basis of many states' systems change initiatives from the outset.

SEEK NEW RESOURCES. Some states have increased access by passing legislation that appropriates new dollars. Waiting lists remain for any day service in most states. This need will not be met only by using existing resources differently. The first strategy focuses on change in present systems, the second focuses on providing access for people currently unserved. Both needs are worthy of attention.

ENCOURAGE EMPLOYER LEADERSHIP AND FULL PARTICIPATION. Recent developments in employer-led supported employment hold promise for increasing access (e.g., Rhodes, Ramsing, & Bellamy, 1988). Some employers are working closely with state project personnel and providers to expand business involvement (e.g., Washington Supported Employment Initiative, 1989). Employers are also increasingly interested in acquiring the support technology used to train and support target workers (e.g., Buckley, Sandow, & Mank, 1989), a development that could positively affect the use of public funds in community implementation.

In addition, natural supports in the workplace, that is, the ability and willingness of co-workers to assume some of the responsibility for assisting employees with disabilities (Nisbet, & Hanger, 1988), also holds promise for increasing access. When programs are able to reduce the costs they incur in providing support, they increase their ability to improve quality and increase access.

CONTINUE TRANSITION PROJECTS. Another strategy for increasing access is to ensure that individuals who leave school possess the skills to succeed in community jobs. More extensive vocational experience in schools means that some individuals with milder disabilities will be able to make the transition to employment with time-limited services. Students with severe disabilities who work in integrated jobs with support while in school appear to have more chance of gaining access (Hasazi, 1987).

Stability in Supported Employment

Supported employment will be stable over time if the systems that define services support rather than allow integrated employment. Strategies that encourage stability include state activities on policy and funding, expanded business participation, and local ownership of integrated employment for all citizens with severe disabilities.

ADJUST POLICY AND FUNDING. Statements about the direction of the development of community services provide clarity about how services develop over time. For example, Connecticut and Oregon state mental retardation agencies have developed mission statements focusing on integration, individual rights, and agency participation. Policy, legislation, and funding define stability in states and make it possible for integrated employment to expand and improve. However, inflexible regulations, fixed funding formulae, and compliance monitoring may only create a sense of immediate order while hindering long-term stability.

EXPAND BUSINESS PARTNERSHIPS. Recent innovations in business and industry suggest that long-term success is best served by flexibility and commitment to change (Deming, 1975; Ishikawa, 1976; Peters, 1988; Sandow, & Rhodes, 1989). Recent developments in employer leadership and participation bring opportunities for stability not previously considered. That is, if the business community regularly and routinely expects to hire people with disabilities, then steady and stable growth over time can be expected. State systems can both create and support stability. Employer commitment can make supported employment more commonplace.

SUPPORT LOCAL OWNERSHIP. Stability is also defined by community ownership of the idea and direction of community employment. State and national incentives provide encouragement, but local communities ultimately define implementation. When people with disabilities succeed in jobs, their security and options improve, and co-workers and friends become their strongest advocates. Rich and varied social networks provide the strongest hope for individual stability (O'Connell, 1988).

SUMMARY

As a nationwide initiative, supported employment is growing rapidly from a budding idea to availability in most states. Thousands of individuals have tried it with success. Many thousands more wait. Will supported employment succeed? Will joblessness of people with severe disabilities end? Supported employment is still an opportunity, not a mandate. Five years ago segregation, unemployment, and underemployment for people with severe disabilities were virtually guaranteed in the system. New and difficult issues remain, but the opportunity now exists for real jobs in regular settings for people with severe disabilities.

ACKNOWLEDGEMENTS

Preparation of this paper was supported, in part, by USDOE Contract #300-87-0057. The views here are those of the authors. No official endorsement should be inferred.

QUESTIONS (For answers see p. 435)

1. Describe the central objective of systems change activities.

2. Summarize the conclusions the authors make based on currently available data on supported employment.

3. What is the problem with establishing a cost for supported employment in the early years of implementation?

4. When and how did the notion of creating change in the system that supported segregation and day activity at a national level occur?

5. What are the authors' major observations in regard to changes in the nature of states' system change efforts?

6. List and describe the three future goals discussed by the authors.

7. List four strategies for improving access.

REFERENCES

Allen, W. T. (1988). *The right to be heard: A resource guide for developing consumer-based service plans*. Provided to the Employment Network Project, University of Oregon, Eugene, OR.

Barcus, M., Griffin, S., Mank, D., Rhodes, L., & Moon, S. (Eds.). (1988). *Supported employment implementation issues*. Richmond: Virginia Commonwealth University, Rehabilitation Research and Training Center.

Bellamy, G. T., Rhodes, L. E., Mank, D. M., & Albin, J. M. (1988). *Supported employment: A community implementation guide*. Baltimore: Paul H. Brookes.

Buckley, J., Sandow, D., & Mank, D. (1989, spring). Extending service provider partnerships with business and industry. *Innovation: Maryland Supported Employment Project News Update*. (Available from Maryland Supported Employment Project, Kennedy Institute, Baltimore, MD.)

Deming, W. E. (1982). Why productivity increases with improvement of quality. *Quality, productivity, and competitive position*. Cambridge: Massachusetts Institute of Technology, Center for Advanced Engineering Study.

Employment Network. (1988). *Annual Report on the Employment Network Technical Assistance Project*. Contract #300-87-0057. Washington, DC: National Institute on Disability and Rehabilitation Research.

Gould, M. (1987). *Issues in self-advocacy for individuals in supported employment*. Unpublished manuscript. Philadelphia: Temple University, Community Integration Research and Training Institute.

Hasazi, S. B. (1985). Facilitating transition from high school: Policies and practices. *American Rehabilitation, 11*(3), 9–11, 16.

Ishikawa, K. (1976). *Guide to quality control*. Tokyo: Asian Productivity Organization.

Kiernan, W. E. & Schalock, R. L. (1989). *Economics, industry, and disability; A look ahead*. Baltimore: Paul H. Brookes.

Lyon, S. R., Domaracki, J. W., & Alecky, S. L. (1988). *A study of job retention in the Pennsylvania Competitive Supported Employment Program.* Pittsburgh, PA: University of Pittsburgh, Program in Severe Disabilities. (p. 4).

McCarthy, P., Fender, K. W., & Fender, D. (1988). Supported employment for persons with autism. In P. Wehman, & M. S. Moon (Eds.), *Vocational rehabilitation and supported employment* (pp. 269–290). Baltimore: Paul H. Brookes.

National Association of Rehabilitation Facilities (NARF). (in press). *NARF survey of supported employment: Executive Report.* Washington, DC: Author.

National Industries for the Severely Handicapped. (1989). The Jafits-Wagner-O'Day Program and supported employment [Special edition]. *NISH Newsletter, 14*(4).

Nisbet, J. & Hagner, D. (1988). Natural supports in the workplace: A reexamination of supported employment. *Journal of The Association for Persons with Severe Handicaps, 13*(4), 260–267.

North Dakota Department of Human Services, Division of Vocational Rehabilitation, Supported employment Program. (1987). *Project data summary, March 1986 to August 1987.* Bismarck, ND: Author.

Northwest Instructional Design, Oregon Developmental Disabilities Council. (1987). *Report on supported employment in Oregon.* Salem, OR: Author.

O'Connell, M. (1988). *The gift of hospitality: Opening the doors of community life to people with disabilities.* Evanston, IL: Northwestern University, Center for Urban Affairs and Policy Research.

Oregon Supported Employment Initiative. (1987). *Request for proposals: Solicitation of program proposal to counties for the expansion of supported employment opportunities for persons with developmental disabilities.* Salem, OR: Author.

People First of Washington. (1986). *What we want from supported employment programs.* Tacoma, WA: Author.

Peters, T. (1988). *Thriving on chaos.* New York: Alfred A. Knopf.

Public Law 98-527: Developmental Disabilities Assistance and Bill of Rights Act. (1984). Washington, DC: 98th Congress.

Public Law 99-506: Rehabilitation Act Amendments of 1986. (1986). Washington, DC: 99th Congress.

Rhodes, L. E., Ramsing, K. D., & Bellamy, G. T. (1988). Business participation in supported employment. In G. T. Bellamy, L. E. Rhodes, D. M. Mank, & J. M. Albin. (Eds.), *Supported employment: A community implementation guide* (pp. 247–261). Baltimore: Paul H. Brookes.

Rusch, F. R. (1986). On integrated work: An interview with Lou Brown. In F. R. Rusch (Ed.), *Competitive employment issues and strategies* (pp. 339–346). Baltimore: Paul H. Brookes.

St. Louis, D., Richter, C., Griffin, C., & Struxness, L. (1987). *Colorado Division for Developmental Disabilities Annual Report: Community integrated employment.* USDOE (OSERS) Grant No. G00-86-35508. Wheat Ridge, CO: Rocky Mountain Resource and Training Institute.

Sandow, D., & Rhodes, L. (1989, Winter). Assuring quality in supported employment. *Employment News.* (Available from University of Oregon, Specialized Training Program, Eugene, OR).

Sandow, D., Rhodes, L. E., Mank, D. M., Ramsing, K., & Lynch, W. F. (in press). Assuring quality in supported employment. *Journal of Rehabilitation Administration.*

Seekins, T. & Fawcett, S. B. (1984). Planned diffusion of social technologies for community groups. In S. C. Paine, G. T. Bellamy, & B. Wilcox (Eds.), *Human services that work: From innovation to standard practice* (pp. 247–260). Baltimore: Paul H. Brookes.

Sowers, J. A., Jenkins, C., & Powers, L. (1988). Vocational education of persons with physical handicaps. In R. Gaylord-Ross (Ed.), *Vocational education for persons with handicaps* (pp. 387–416). Mountain View, CA: Mayfield.

United Cerebral Palsy Associations. (1988). *National demonstration project on supported employment: An update.* Unpublished manuscript. Washington, DC: Author.

United States Department of Education, Office of Special Education and Rehabilitative Services (1985). *Request for Proposals: Special projects and demonstrations for providing vocational rehabilitation services to severely disabled individuals.* Washington, DC: Author.

Virginia Department of Rehabilitation Services (DRS). (1988). *Guidelines for DRS utilization of transitional employment programming for persons with long-term mental illness*. Richmond, VA: Author.

Washington Supported Employment Initiative. (1989). *Initiative: Business leadership and supported employment*. Seattle, WA: Author.

Wehman, P. & Hill, M. L. (1989). Competitive employment for persons with mental retardation: A benefit-cost analysis of outcomes. In W. E. Kiernan, & R. L. Schalock (Eds.), *Economics, industry, and disability: A look ahead* (pp. 287–298). Baltimore: Paul H. Brookes.

Wehman, P., Kregel, J., & Shafer, M. S. (1989). *Emerging trends in the national supported employment initiative: A preliminary analysis of twenty-seven states*. Richmond: Virginia Commonwealth University, Rehabilitation Research and Training Center.

Wehman, P., Kreutzer, J., Wood, W., Morton, M. V., & Sherron, P. (1988). Supported work model for persons with traumatic brain injury: Toward job placement and retention. *Rehabilitation Counseling Bulletin, 31*(4), 298–312.

Wehman, P. & Moon, M. S. (Eds.). (1988). *Vocational rehabilitation and supported employment*. Baltimore: Paul H. Brookes.

Whitehead, C. (1989). Influencing employment through federal and state policy. In W. E. Kiernan, & R. L. Schalock (Eds.), *Economics, industry, and disability: A look ahead* (pp. 17–25). Baltimore: Paul H. Brookes.

Zeleny, M. (1988). Quality management systems: Subject to continuous improvement? *Human Systems Management, 8*(1), 1–3.

CHAPTER

18

Job Separation Issues in Supported Employment

Thomas R. Lagomarcino
University of Illinois at Urbana-Champaign

Over the past ten years we have learned that providing support to target employees in varying intensities over time may result in long-term, competitive employment for persons with disabilities. In fact, these findings provided the database that contributed most significantly to the Rehabilitation Act Amendments of 1986. A review of the published findings of work performance research suggests that the majority of this was contributed by investigators who served a wide range of persons with disabilities. The results indicated that employment retention for persons with moderate and, in some instances, severe mental retardation exceeded statistics reported by the U.S. Department of Labor for persons with lesser disabilities (USDOL, 1977).

Today, legislative intent recognizes the unique contribution made by competitive employment methods developed and tested over the last ten years. The provision of on-the-job training that results in good adjustment to jobs by individuals who have not traditionally been employed competitively or for whom competitive employment has been interrupted or intermittent is an important and timely addition to the Rehabilitation Act. There are several concerns, however, that have been expressed by several different consumer groups. It is the purpose of this chapter to address one of these concerns.

The intent of supported employment is to provide assistance to individuals with severe disabilities who are not able to function in competitive employment without support. These persons require extensive ongoing support to participate in integrated community services and to enjoy a quality of life that may be realized by people with few or no disabilities. Historically, legislative intent has not paralleled implementation, and the history of supported employment may prove to be no different. Supported employment has been conceptualized and implemented by State Vocational Rehabilitation agencies to varying degrees and to a wide range of persons with and without severe disabilities. Unemployment results from two possibilities. The first is that support is provided to persons who do not need it; the second is that we fail to provide support to target employees who need "ongoing support" in order to remain employed.

Supported employment poses problems to the field because, as a profession, we are not technically capable of predetermining likely support. We know that individuals adapt to their work environments. As they become more skilled, they should in turn require less support. Of interest, however, is research that suggests that ongoing support does not decrease or increase over time (Johnson & Rusch, in press). It seems that we do not systematically withdraw our support regardless of whether we are serving persons with severe mental retardation or mild mental retardation, placed individually or placed in groups.

We also know that integration, which is mandated by the Rehabilitation Act, results in new opportunities for persons with and without disabilities to interact. For example, co-workers without disabilities are assuming non-prescribed roles, including associating with target employees during breaks, training target employees to perform new tasks, and providing feedback to target employees to perform new tasks, and providing feedback to target employees about their work performance (Rusch, Johnson, & Hughes, in press).

This chapter presents recent findings about why supported employees with disabilities are separating from their jobs, even though ongoing support is intended to continue their employment. The conclusions about the extent to which support is an issue are based on the termination or separation records of previously supported employees.

JOB SEPARATION FINDINGS

Since its inception, the intent of supported employment has been to focus on providing integrated employment opportunities for individuals who have never been employed, either because they were considered too severely disabled to be employed in the community or because someone may have thought they were not quite "ready" for employment in the community. With respect to these individuals, agencies in the past were unable to provide the ongoing support needed for them to be competitively employed. In addition, supported employment has focused on individuals who have been unable to hold a job for an extended period of time. These individuals usually have a checkerboard employment pattern, for they may not have received the support necessary to remain employed. The supported employment initiative was developed to meet the needs of these consumers.

We have witnessed the many successes that have resulted from this most recent provision of rehabilitation services. However, we must also examine the reasons individuals with severe disabilities are leaving supported employment. This information is a key aspect in the evaluation of the supported employment initiative and could contribute valuable information in the future delivery of support services to persons with severe disabilities in community employment settings.

A number of studies were conducted in the past which attempted to identify the behavioral factors that contribute to successful and unsuccessful placements. These earlier efforts were case studies of programs that focused on individual placements of persons with mental retardation. Greenspan and Shoultz (1981) developed a conceptual framework for job separation analysis by identifying three categories of social factors (temperament, character, and social awareness), two categories of production factors (quantity and quality of work), and health factors. Their study, which reported on the primary reason for involuntary termination from competitive employment for thirty individuals with mild to moderate mental retardation, found that social incompetence played at least as important a role in explaining job failure as poor production. Two additional job separation studies utilized the same conceptual framework in their analyses. Hanley-Maxwell, Rusch, Chadsey-Rusch, and Renzaglia (1986) reported similar findings in their investigation of factors contributing to the job terminations of fifty-one adults with disabilities. Martin, Rusch, Lagomarcino, and Chadsey-Rusch (1986) extended these earlier studies by comparing the terminations of food service employees with and without mental retardation. Interestingly, they found no significant differences between the two groups, with social and production problems contributing almost equally to job terminations.

Hill, Wehman, Hill, and Goodall (1986) examined 107 reasons for job separation of persons with mental retardation who had been employed in the community. In contrast to the previous studies, they examined the primary reasons for job separation according to client-related and externally-related separations. The results indicated that persons with higher IQ scores (in the mid 50s) tended to be the "actor" who frequently caused his or her own job separation due to skill or behavioral deficits. In addition, this group experienced significantly more separations due to behaviors expressing poor work attitudes (e.g., poor attendance, not wanting to work). These results contrast with persons with lower IQ scores (in the mid 40s) who separated from their jobs primarily due to external, environmental factors (e.g., economic situation of employer, external parental interference).

Characteristics of Individuals Separated from Supported Employment

Our research analyzed seventy agencies implementing supported employment across the State of Illinois that serve a diverse population of persons with disabilities who are employed through individual placements, clustered placements, and mobile work crews. We identified 285 individuals who have separated from a total of 318 jobs between November 1, 1985 and December 31, 1988. Table 18.1 provides a summary of the individuals who separated from supported employment.

DISABILITY CATEGORY. Individuals from a number of different disability groups experienced separations from their jobs. Persons with mild mental retardation represented approximately 46 percent of those individuals separated from supported employment. Persons with psychiatric disabilities represent the second largest group leaving their jobs (16 percent). Persons with moderate mental retardation account for only 14 percent of all job separations. Persons with severe or profound mental retardation account for 7 percent of all job separations. Persons with physical disabilities, sensory impairments, autism, traumatic brain injury, and learning disabilities account for the remaining 17 percent of the job separations. In comparison to earlier data presented on persons currently employed, it appears that persons with mild mental retardation or psychiatric disabilities are leaving their jobs at a faster rate than persons with moderate, severe, or profound mental retardation.

PREVIOUS PLACEMENT. Approximately 65 percent of the persons leaving their jobs had come from some form of sheltered vocational service delivery (e.g., work activity, sheltered workshop). The majority of these individuals had previously been employed in a sheltered workshop (n = 72). Eight percent of those separating from supported employment had been previously employed in the community, whereas 6 percent had been in school, and 4 percent had been at home.

PLACEMENT APPROACH. Approximately 47 percent of the job separations resulted from persons individually placed into jobs, whereas 46 percent were in clustered placements and 6 percent in mobile work crews.

LENGTH OF EMPLOYMENT PRIOR TO JOB SEPARATION. Of those reporting (n = 298), 67 percent left their jobs within the first six months of employment. In fact, 44 percent of *all* job separations occurred within the first three months of employment. Eighteen percent of all job separations occurred between seven and twelve months of employment. Finally, 11 percent of the job separations occurred between one and two years of employment, while 4 percent occurred after being on the job for over two years.

Data Collection Procedures

Job separation data were reported on a monthly basis by all of the agencies participating in the Illinois Supported Employment Project from November 1, 1985 through December 31, 1988. A job separation form was completed by the employment specialist most familiar with the individual case. The following information was collected on each job separation: (a) date of job separation, (b) type of job, (c) placement approach, (d) number of months employed prior to job separation, and (e) brief description of what happened to the individual following the job separation. In addition, twenty-seven reasons for job separation have been identified based on descriptors that were used in previous studies (see Table 18.2). The employment specialist was required to indicate the primary reason for job separation and provide a brief clarification of the reason that was checked. A secondary reason for

Table 18.1 Characteristics of Individuals Separated from Supported Employment.

Disability Categories	
Mild mental retardation (IQ range 55-75)	126
Psychiatric disabilities	43
Moderate mental retardation (IQ range 39-54)	39
Severe or profound mental retardation (IQ range 0-38)	20
Autism	8
Learning disabilities	6
Sensory impairments	5
Physical disabilities	4
Health impairments	4
Traumatic brain injury	3
Not reported	27
Previous Placement	
Work activity	61
Evaluation	10
Work adjustment training	37
Sheltered workshop	72
School	16
Community employment	21
Home	10
Other/not reported	58
Placement Approach	
Individual placement	131
Clustered placement	128
Mobile work crew	14
Not reported	43
Length of Employment Prior to Job Separation	
1 to 3 months	130
4 to 6 months	69
7 to 9 months	36
10 to 12 months	19
13 to 17 months	20
18 to 24 months	13
Over 24 months	11
Not reported	18

Table 18.2 Primary Reasons for Job Separation by Category

Lack of job responsibility Does not want to work Poor attendance/tardy Poor work attitude Criminal behavior	Economy Economic situation of employer Seasonal layoff
Task production Low quality work Work rate too slow Continual prompting required	Change in job status Took a better job Hired by company No longer needed supported employment services
Social-vocational behavior Poor social skills Insubordinate behavior Poor appearance Maladaptive behavior	Other external factors Medical/health problem Transportation Parent/guardian initiated Financial aid threatened Moved away Program termination Retired

job separation was checked if a single reason could not be determined.

Job Separation Categories

Six major job separation categories were identified for analysis purposes: (1) lack of job responsibility, (2) task production, (3) social-vocational behavior, (4) economy, (5) health, and (6) change in job status. Job responsibility includes behaviors that suggest job commitment (Salzberg, Lignugaris–Kraft, & McCuller, in press). Therefore, a *lack of job responsibility* was indicated by employees who had poor attendance, poor work attitudes, or a lack of motivation to work. *Task production* refers to the performance of required tasks to company standards (e.g., work quality, production). Furthermore, it includes the ability to learn and perform a variety of tasks. Reasons for job separation in this category included working too slowly, requiring continual prompting to complete the job, or poor work quality. *Social-vocational behavior* addresses the social interactions that occur at the employment site. This domain is divided into task-related social competence and personal-social competence. Task-related social competence refers to social skills that directly affect the performance of job tasks, such as following directions and responding to criticism. In contrast, personal-social competence refers to social skills that are not directly related to performance of tasks. Reasons for job separation in this category included insubordinate behavior, maladapative behavior, and poor social skills. *Economy* refers to a separation due to the economic conditions of a company that affect employees with and without disabilities (Greenspan & Shoultz, 1981). Reasons for job separations in this category included permanent or temporary layoffs due to the seasonal nature of the work, and the economic situation of the employer. Health refers to changes in an employee's physical condition that are serious enough to make continuation in a particular job impossible (Greenspan & Shoultz, 1981). Primary reasons for job separation related to health included physical problems that restricted work activity and hospitalization due to the reoccurrence of symptoms related to specific psychiatric disabilities. *Change in job status* refers to a positive change in the employment status of a person with a disability (i.e., took a better job, no longer needed support services, hired by company).

Job Separations for All Disability Categories

Table 18.2 shows the primary reasons for job separation across all disability categories. Lack of job responsibility was most often cited as

PETER FINCH

Peter Finch is a 23-year-old man with Down's Syndrome. His IQ is diagnosed in the moderate range of 39–43 (TMH). He lives in Champaign, Illinois, with his mother and older brother. His father died 13 years ago. Other members of his family include three brothers and one sister. They do not live at home but reside in the Champaign area. Peter attended a local TMH facility, where he received vocational training. Peter has always had a problem with weight and in May 1985 he was 90 pounds overweight, although generally in good health.

In August, 1984, Peter was trained to improve on his community skills at a local hospital, concentrating on work tasks, behavior, and good social language skills. He successfully completed the training program in May, 1985. Peter was also successfully involved in several other community skills training programs.

On October 8, 1986, Peter began to work at Disk-Tec, Inc., a supported employment worksite in cooperation with a local developmental training facility. Peter had several problems: He could not learn to ride the mass transit bus and exit at the proper location, and he became frustrated and confused when he exited the bus. Peter's interactions were very limited, and his speech was difficult to understand. Peter also needed assistance in learning to tell time and improving his counting skills. As a materials handler, Peter's responsibility was twofold. First, he had to prepare the stacks of disks by removing the packages from the box, remove the disks from the packages, and place them on the table. Next he had to count the disks and stack them. Because Peter lacked counting skills, this task was difficult for him.

By spring of 1988, Peter was ready to graduate and become the "butterfly coming out of his cocoon." He had shed 100 pounds and was feeling great about himself. This attitude carried over into his work performance, which greatly improved. Peter's production percentage climbed from 53 to 60 percent, and he earned a 25¢ raise. He is very proud of himself and satisfied with his vocational adjustment. Peter began working with a very small crew that has increased to include eight members. He is very involved with the group and interacts with all the members socially.

Since Peter's involvement in the SEP, he has become more sure of himself and his environment. His speech has improved and is more easily understood. He participates in monthly activities sponsored by his supervisor for all the crew members, including hayrides, picnics, movies, roller skating, and holiday parties. Peter has also been active in all areas of Special Olympics.

Peter, his family, and the developmental training facility's staff have all marvelled at the tremendous change that has come about in Peter's life as a direct result of the supported employment program.

---

the reason for persons separating from supported employment ($n = 57$; 18 percent). Within this category, thirty individuals indicated that they no longer wanted to work. Poor attendance ($n = 15$), poor work attitude ($n = 8$), and criminal behavior ($n = 4$) were other identified job responsibility problems. Economy accounted for 17 percent of all job separations. Economic situation of the employer was the most frequent reason given in this category ($n = 41$) followed by seasonal layoffs ($n = 14$). Thirteen percent of the individuals leaving their jobs did so because of a change in their job status. Twenty-one individuals no longer needed the ongoing support services to remain employed. Seventeen individuals took better jobs with better pay and more hours. Three individuals were hired by the company. Production-related reasons accounted for approximately 12 percent of all job separations (e.g., work rate too slow, poor work quality, or continual prompting required to complete work). Poor social-vocational behavior accounted for 10 percent of all job separations. Social-related reasons that were most frequently

Table 18.3 Reasons for Job Separation by Disability Category

	Mild Mental Retardation		Moderate Mental Retardation		Sev/Profound Mental Retardation		Psychiatric Disability	
	N	%	N	%	N	%	N	%
Lack of job responsibility	22	17	11	26	4	20	13	30
Task production	20	15	3	7	6	30	5	12
Social-vocational behavior	16	12	2	5	3	15	2	5
Economy	23	17	12	28	2	10	1	2
Health	12	9	-	-	-	-	9	21
Change in job status	21	16	4	9	2	10	4	9
Other external factors	19	14	11	26	2	15	9	21

cited for job separation included insubordinate behavior, maladaptive behavior, and poor social skills. The Other category includes employees who had to leave their jobs for a variety of reasons, including (a) moving away, (b) program termination, (c) parents, or (d) transportation.

Job Separations by Disability Category

Table 18.3 examines job separation by disability category. Due to the small number of individuals representing certain disability groups (e.g., traumatic brain injury, physical disabilities), this analysis is based on the job separations of persons with mental retardation or psychiatric disabilities.

PERSONS WITH MILD MENTAL RETARDATION. One hundred and twenty-six persons with mild mental retardation accounted for 133 job separations. The data indicate that these individuals left their jobs for a wide variety of reasons. Economy was cited in 17 percent ($n = 23$) of the cases. The majority of these job separations were due to the economic situation of the employer. Lack of job responsibility was also cited in 17 percent of all the job separations for this category. Twelve of the twenty-two separations in this category were due to the fact the individual no longer wanted to work. Poor attendance or tardiness was the second most frequent reason noted in this category ($n = 6$). Change in job status accounted for 16 percent of all job separations in this group. Thirteen of the employees no longer needed supported employment services and eight individuals took better jobs (i.e., more hours, better pay). Persons with mild mental retardation tended to lose their jobs equally for social-related (12 percent) and production-related (11 percent) reasons. Finally, 9 percent of the separations for this group were due to medical or health problems. This may be due to the fact that many of the individuals who have been diagnosed as having mild mental retardation also have secondary handicapping conditions (e.g., physical disabilities, epilepsy).

PERSONS WITH MODERATE MENTAL RETARDATION. Thirty-seven persons with moderate mental retardation accounted for forty-three job separations over the three-year time period. Twenty-eight percent ($n = 12$) lost their jobs for economic reasons (i.e., layoffs). Twenty-six percent of the job separations were due to a lack of job responsibility (i.e., does not want to work, poor attendance). Three individuals lost their jobs for production-related reasons, while two individuals lost their jobs for social-related reasons. Finally, three individuals experienced a change in job status.

PERSONS WITH SEVERE OR PROFOUND MENTAL RETARDATION. Of the twenty individuals with severe or profound mental retardation who separated from jobs, the majority ($n = 6$; 27 percent) lost their jobs for production-related reasons (i.e., work rate too slow, continual prompting required). By contrast, only 14 percent ($n = 3$) lost their jobs for social-related reasons. Lack of job responsibility was cited in 18 percent ($n = 4$) of the job separations. The primary reasons listed in this category were poor work attitude and no longer wanting to work. Two individuals (9 percent) took a better job. In examining other external factors contributing to the job separations of persons with severe or profound mental retardation, we found that 15 percent left supported employment for fear of losing their financial aid.

PERSONS WITH PSYCHIATRIC DISABILITIES. Twenty-seven percent ($n = 13$) of persons with psychiatric disabilities separated from supported employment due to a lack of job responsibility. These individuals usually indicated that they no longer wanted to work or had poor attendance. Of the four groups analyzed, persons with psychiatric disabilities experienced far more medical and health-related problems which affected their employment status ($n = 9$; 17 percent). Twelve percent ($n = 5$) of persons with psychiatric disabilities lost their jobs for production-related reasons, while only 7 percent ($n = 2$) lost their jobs for social-related reasons. Two individuals decided to leave supported employment because the earnings gained from their job jeopardized other public support income (i.e., Social Security Disability Income, Public Aid).

Implications of Job Separation Findings

Earlier studies identified a variety of factors related to the success of individuals with severe disabilities in competitive employment sites (Greenspan & Shoultz, 1981; Hanley-Maxwell, et al., 1986; Hill, Wehman, Hill, & Goodall, 1986). Most of the variables found to be related to lack of success on the job were individual-centered problems that included skill deficits and behavioral excesses, or individual characteristics (e.g., sex, IQ). Interestingly, Lagomarcino and Rusch (1988), in their analysis of applied research that had been conducted on adults with mental retardation in competitive employment settings, found that all of the studies dealt exclusively with changing the behavior of the adults with mental retardation. The unidimensional nature of these studies results in a restricted view of the factors impeding community employment as well as the identification of subsequent solutions.

Karan and Knight (1986) contended that the problems experienced by individuals with severe disabilities in employment settings are a reflection of the individual's interaction with the setting and with other persons present in these settings. Consequently, implications of job separation findings should reflect consideration of the employment context, potential service providers, employers, peers, co-workers, and society. A multi-level perspective is required to thoroughly analyze the myriad of problems that affect the community employment of persons with severe disabilities (Hanley-Maxwell, Rusch, & Rappaport, 1989). Four major levels have been identified: (a) individual, (b) small group, (c) organizational, and (d) the community level. The individual level includes the employee with a disability. The small group level includes family members and the individuals who comprise the employment setting (i.e., co-workers, employer). The organizational level refers to the agency, and more specifically the personnel, responsible for delivering supported employment services (e.g., job developer, employment training specialist). The community level represents characteristics of the local community including: (a) size, (b) members and their attitudes towards persons with disabilities, (c) types of industry, and (d) the economic climate. In addition, the community level refers to policy at the local, state, and federal levels that affects services for persons with disabilities.

This section will discuss the major reasons for job separation as they relate to these four levels. In addition, solutions are offered to overcome the factors that impede the provision of equal employment opportunities for persons with severe disabilities.

Lack of Job Responsibility

Lack of job responsibility was the most frequent reason cited for the separation of persons with severe disabilities from supported employment during the three year period that was investigated. There are a number of factors that potentially contribute to these results.

Employees with severe disabilities may experience a variety of problems at the small group level which can include family members, residential staff, or co-workers in the employment setting. For example, parents may not place a great deal of value on employment, thus affecting the perceptions and attitudes their son or daughter may have towards the world of work.

A second factor contributing to the lack of job responsibility noted in the job separation findings is the widespread placement of persons with severe disabilities in entry-level service occupations where historically there has been a great deal of turnover. The National Hotel and Restaurant Association indicated that over 2300 individuals in comparable entry-level positions retained their jobs for less than five months (Wehman Kregal, 1985). Burnout caused by staff shortage and the stressful fast-food work environment lead many workers to seek alternative employment. In fact, Wagel (1989) reports that fast-food industry turnover rates average 300 percent annually. Furthermore, recent data on the meaning of work and job satisfaction attest to the fact that workers, particularly those in positions that require little skill and involve much repetition, frequently have trouble adjusting to their jobs (Halle, 1984; Locke, 1983). Given low pay, part-time hours, and the absence of benefits, is it surprising that persons with severe disabilities choose to leave these positions?

At the organizational (i.e., agency) level, there are several problems that may contribute to individuals no longer wanting to work in the community. Turner (1983) points out that leaving the workshop is seldom a function of an individual's expressed dissatisfaction with this setting. In fact, he suggests most individuals leave the sheltered workshop reluctantly. Furthermore, Hill et al., (1986) noted that individuals who separated from supported employment frequently did so in order to return to the sheltered workshop. But why? First, service providers ignore the impact that community employment may have on existing friendships and social networks these individuals have established with peers in their previous vocational settings (e.g., sheltered workshops, work activity centers). As a result, individuals frequently experience social isolation even within the context of community employment settings. Second, individuals with severe disabilities typically have little input into where they are ultimately placed. That is, matching the person to the job is done *to* them rather than *with* their participation. If service providers ignore the interests and career aspirations of persons with severe disabilities in the job placement process, they should expect at least some of them to become disenchanted with the employment opportunities that have been selected for them.

Dependence oriented programs such as Social Security Disability Insurance (SSDI) and Medicaid are two prime examples of barriers at the community or societal level that contribute to the lack of job responsibility inherent in many persons with severe disabilities. These are programs that are entitlements by nature; that is, persons with disabilities who are unable to work or engage in "substantial gainful activity" are entitled to benefits so long as they continue to be "unable to support themselves." The SSDI program gives beneficiaries who return to work a nine-month trial work period. At the conclusion of the trial work period, the beneficiaries are reevaluated, and if they are found capable of earning more than the SGA level of $300 per month they will be terminated from the program. Since the average benefit for individuals in this program is approximately $500 per month, and since the beneficiary must consider the loss of other benefits, such as Medicaid, the disincentives to work are strong (Conley & Noble, 1989). Furthermore, the penalty for working is particularly strong for persons who live in Medicaid-certified-facilities such as intermediate care facilities for persons with mental retardation. In these cases, residents are entitled to keep a personal needs allowance that must be at least $25 a month. Any amount over the personal needs allowance must be paid to the facility to reduce the costs charged to Medicaid (Conley & Noble, 1989). Given these work disincentives, is it unreasonable for certain individuals with disabilities to choose not to work?

Possible Solutions

Several things could be done at the organizational or agency level to address the problems that have been cited. First, agency personnel need to acknowledge that with supported employment comes peer group displacement. Supported employment programs must identify potential social support systems available in community settings and develop strategies that enable persons with disabilities to more actively participate in these social support networks (Nisbet & Hagner, 1988). In addition, employment training specialists may have to work closely with case management and residential staff in providing opportunities for individuals with disabilities to get together with their peers outside of work. Second, agency personnel must develop strategies enabling the consumer to more actively participate in the job selection process (Mithaug, Martin, Husch, Agran, & Rusch, 1989). For most persons the ability and opportunity to make choices and decisions is an important component of their lives. Choice, as a decision-making process, involves the expression of preferences (Guess, Benson, & Siegal-Causey, 1985). Within the context of employment, it implies the ability to actively select among two or more occupational alternatives. Therefore, persons with severe disabilities must have the opportunity to actively choose the job that is most compatible to their known interests, abilities, and background experience. Third, potential placements should be evaluated carefully with respect to wages, work characteristics, and work culture (Moseley, 1989). Greater job satisfaction has been related to (a) a person's increased control over his or her task and conditions of work; (b) the ability to function as part of a work team, and living in a community in contact with one's co-workers (Blauner, 1966; Friedman, 1964); (c) higher and more equitable pay (Locke, 1983); and (d) the ability to perform work tasks sufficient to hold one's interest (Blauner, 1966; Friedman, 1964; Locke, 1983). Along with offering consumers choices comes the identification of employment opportunities that offer individuals security and vocational growth. Changes at the community or societal level are also needed. The passage of legislation which made 1619(a) and 1619(b) a permanent part of the Social Security program helped to alleviate many of the concerns that SSI recipients had towards seeking employment. Clearly, the equivalents of the 1619(a) and (b) need to be enacted for SSDI recipients, not only because of the desire of Congress to encourage work among persons with disabilities, but also because of the "glaring inconsistencies" in the way persons on SSDI are treated in comparison to SSI recipients (Conley & Noble, 1989). In addition, changes are needed that enable residents of Medicaid-certified facilities to retain a greater amount of the money that they have earned.

Economy

Economy was the second most frequently cited reason for job separation. Several factors at the organizational and community levels may play a role in these job separations. First, individuals with severe disabilities have been primarily placed in service-related occupations, with the majority of these individuals being placed in the food service industry. Although the restaurant industry is still outgrowing the overall economy, there are increasing indications that the United States now has more eating outlets than even our mobile society can readily absorb. After a decade or more of rapid growth, some of the large chains have retrenched and scaled down their operations (Standard & Poor's Industry Survey, 1989). A number of large chains are closing down less profitable units and opening fewer new restaurants than in the past.

In addition, agency personnel need to be cautious about establishing supported employment placements with new companies. New companies frequently look for financial incentives when they first get started to help offset expensive start-up costs (Targeted Jobs Tax Credit, Job Training Partnership Programs). However, almost 61 percent of all the businesses that fail are new businesses, and between 53 percent and 60 percent of all businesses that fail do so within the first five years of operation (Mayers, 1984).

Finally, unemployment rates of counties in the State of Illinois where supported employment programs are in operation ranged from a low of 4.4 percent to a high of 17.2 percent in 1987. These data indicate that certain counties in the state were affected by employment downturns more than others, particularly in agriculture-related industries.

Finally, it is possible that employees in clustered placements in industrial settings may be hired at a time of high production or when special packaging contracts have been secured. These employees may be more susceptible to layoffs when production demands decrease.

POSSIBLE SOLUTIONS. Individuals responsible for job development need to be aware of a number of issues when surveying potential employers. These include: (a) length of time that the company has been in operation, (b) employment record, (c) identification of company personnel currently performing targeted tasks, and (d) seasonal nature of work. Special attention to these issues may help guarantee more stable working conditions for persons with severe disabilities.

Production

Production was cited as a factor contributing to the job separations of persons with severe disabilities. This category includes individuals who lost their jobs because of working too slowly, poor work quality, or the need for continual prompting to complete assigned tasks. Interestingly, production was the most frequently cited reason for job separation for persons with severe or profound mental retardation. This may be due to a number of factors, including poor job match procedures, unavailability of rehabilitation or mechanical engineering resources, or the role of the employment training specialist.

Inadequate job analysis and consumer assessment information may result in a poor job match. Placement decisions are often based on information about a job provided by the employer without directly observing a person performing the job during "peak" times. This may result in misconceptions of the actual work demands of the position. Also, the job demands of a position may differ over time from those originally agreed upon between the employer and the employment training specialist. The potential discrepancies between the actual demands of the position and an individual's capabilities may be so great as to jeopardize the employment status of a person with severe disabilities.

In addition, rehabilitation and mechanical engineers are not always available to assist employment training specialists in the development of prosthetics. As a result, inefficient work performance impedes the productivity of employees with severe disabilities in community employment settings.

A recent study conducted by Winking, DeStefano, and Rusch (1989) revealed that the typical duties of employment training specialists included "prompting workers to complete tasks," "checking the quality of work," and "helping the workers if the job is not done." Promoting consumer independence was not an expectation in job descriptions for employment training specialists. If this is the case, we will continue to see persons with disabilities being dependent on others for assistance.

POSSIBLE SOLUTIONS. Careful job analysis coupled with job redesign and rehabilitation engineering are often critical to the employment success of persons with disabilities. A careful analysis which includes direct observation of individuals performing the targeted job provides employment training specialists with a complete description of the equipment and materials needed to perform the tasks, time frames in which the work is to be completed, the level of supervision available, and work-related skills that are needed (Rusch, Chadsey-Rusch, & Lagomarcino, 1987). This information is invaluable when attempting to match a person's interests and abilities to the job requirements that have been identified. It is also recommended that the employment training specialist have the employer sign an agreement outlining the specific job responsibilities of the targeted position. This may help to reduce the possibility of major changes in the job responsibilities expected of a person in an identified position.

The 1986 Amendments to the Rehabilitation Act also emphasize the need to utilize rehabilitation engineering. Unfortunately, these services have not always been readily available, yet are essential for persons with physical and cognitive disabilities who are striving to become independent, productive employees. Employment training specialists could work with rehabilitation engineers in identifying critical mismatches between the target employee and the job requirements. Furthermore, these critical mismatches could be reduced through environmental modification or prosthetics, thus increasing productivity and the likelihood of successful, independent performance.

Expectations are important in service delivery because they influence outcomes. Mithaug et al. (1989) stated: "If we expect persons to be productive, eventually they become more productive" (p. 55). This will require the utilization of self-management techniques which allow persons with disabilities to control their own work behavior, thus reducing their dependency on the employment training specialist (Lagomarcino, Hughes, & Rusch, 1989).

Change in Job Status

Changes in job status were most frequently experienced by persons with mild mental retardation. These individuals probably possess many of the skills required for entry-level, part-time positions prior to job placement. Therefore, these individuals are being provided with opportunities to enhance their vocational growth by taking new jobs that offer more hours and increased wages. In addition, it is being determined that many of these individuals no longer need the support that persons with severe disabilities typically receive through supported employment.

POSSIBLE SOLUTIONS. There is a long-standing precedent for too little support; only recently has legislation allowed us to consider too much support to be an issue. Given the population currently being served in supported employment nationally, one wonders if persons with mild mental retardation are in their "least restrictive environment." Vocational rehabilitation counselors may have to become more selective in the criteria used to determine the eligibility of persons with severe disabilities for supported employment.

Social Reasons

Social reasons have frequently been cited as a reason for job separation among persons with mental retardation (Greenspan & Shoultz, 1981; Hanley-Maxwell et al., 1986; Martin et al., 1986). Although the data from this study indicate that it may not be one of the primary reasons for job separation, it was identified as a problem experienced by persons with severe disabilities in adjusting to community employment. Furthermore, although the lack of social skills may not result directly in job loss, it may hinder the opportunities for persons with severe disabilities to interact with co-workers without disabilities during the course of a working day (Lagomarcino, 1989). The data from this study indicated that most of the problems were related to interpersonal interactions with co-workers versus the absence of task-related social skills (e.g., acknowledging requests). Two reasons may explain these results. First, the individual may not possess the social skills needed in community employment settings (Chadsey-Rusch, 1986). Second, employment training specialists often pay closer attention to teaching the vocational skills required in community employment settings while failing to address necessary social skills.

POSSIBLE SOLUTIONS. The ecology of employment settings must be studied in order to define the continuum of social behaviors that will maximize person-environment congruence (Chadsey-Rusch, 1986). A careful analysis will result in the identification of task-related social and personal-social skills required in potential employment settings. This information can be used for job matching purposes as well as in the identification of goals and objectives for training.

Other External Factors

Similar to Hill et al. (1986), a number of external factors contributed to the job separations of persons with severe disabilities, including: (a) medical/health problems, (b) parent or guardian interference, (c) financial aid being threatened, and (d) transportation difficulties. Interestingly, persons with psychiatric disabilities experienced more job separations (percentage-wise) than any of the four other groups. Chronic mental illness is accompanied by chronic medical illness (Talbot, 1984). National data indicate that each person with a psychiatric disability will have a 60 percent chance of being readmitted within two years of his or her discharge from the hospital. Furthermore, fewer than 50 percent continue to take their medication (Talbot, 1984). These data, in combination with the everyday stresses of community employment, explain at least in part why almost 16 percent of all job separations for this group were due to medical or health problems.

The employment status of persons with psychiatric disabilities and persons with severe or profound mental retardation were most affected by the possible loss of their financial aid. Persons with psychiatric disabilities often receive Social Security Disability Insurance (SSDI). Due to current legislation, community employment may actually jeopardize the SSDI income that is being received. As a result, persons with psychiatric disabilities often choose not to work. Individuals with severe or profound mental retardation who are placed in intermediate care facilities for persons with mental retardation (ICFs/MR) also may have their financial aid threatened. The federal ICF/MR program will fund day care and nonvocational services, but not vocational services. Therefore, many states, including Illinois, place most residents of ICFs/MR in adult day care rather than employment, making no effort to provide service that could lead to employment (Conley & Noble, 1989).

Available data suggest that employment programs will not be successful without parental support (Kochany & Keller, 1981). In the current study, there were few job separations initiated by parents or guardians. This could be because parental support is frequently required prior to a person being placed into supported employment. Therefore, sons and daughters of parents with reservations concerning community employment may not have the opportunity to participate in supported employment. Similarly, transportation has frequently been identified as an obstacle to community employment, yet the unavailability of public transportation may keep certain individuals from participating in supported employment as well.

Possible Solutions. Unfortunately, several external factors may have adverse effects on the provision of equal employment opportunities for persons with severe disabilities. For persons with psychiatric disabilities, medication and continuing contact (e.g., counseling, person-to-person contact) have been identified as the two variables that appear to prevent both relapse and readmission (Talbot, 1984). Continuity of care by personnel sufficiently trained in modern treatment methods is needed to ensure the support that is needed. In addition, current work disincentives need to be addressed to eliminate the financial risks currently experienced by persons with psychiatric disabilities who are trying to make a living by working in the community. Furthermore, although recent passage of legislation has provided limited circumstances under which vocational services can be funded by Medicaid, this legislation still does not provide the much-needed flexibility to promote integrated community services.

SUMMARY

Individuals with severe disabilities have to a large degree been excluded from employment as evidenced by the 50 to 80 percent who are unemployed (U. S. Commission on Civil Rights, 1983). Furthermore, it is estimated that 60 percent of adults with disabilities who are of working age are at or near the poverty level (Bowe, 1980). In response to these growing concerns, supported ployment has emerged as an important policy development that must also be seen as a significant departure from previous service delivery and policy. As a result, thousands of individuals with severe disabilities are now working in local communities across the country because of the support services now available to them. However, there still remain many barriers which deny or impede thousands of others from community employment. It is essential that we identify potential solutions at the individual, small group, organizational, and community levels if we are to provide equal employment opportunities for *all* persons with severe disabilities.

Evaluation of supported employment outcome data, in combination with the job separation data, raises several concerns about the impact of this initiative on the quality of life of individuals with severe disabilities. First, we must question the extent to which individuals with severe disabilities are receiving these services. Are these programs simply an alternative funding source for individuals with mild handicaps? Second, equal employment opportunity is not synonymous with community employment. Rather, it means that individuals with severe disabilities have opportunities to grow vocationally and experience the benefits available to persons without disabilities in society. The majority of the individuals receiving supported employment services are currently employed in part time entry level positions in which they frequently earn minimum wage or below. Given these outcomes, individuals with severe disabilities will continue to hover around the poverty line and be dependent on government support programs to survive in the community. Finally, equal employment opportunity means that individuals with severe disabilities have the right to pursue their career aspirations and be involved in the job selection process. Given the number of individuals who indicated they "no longer wanted to work," one must question if they are involved at all in choosing their employment situation.

The reasons why individuals leave supported employment provide us with valuable information about the barriers to community employment. Efforts must be made to break down these barriers that exist at the state and federal levels. In addition, we must become more sensitive to the vocational interests of individuals with severe disabilities while identifying jobs that provide opportunities for vocational growth and greater financial security. It is only through these activities that we will begin to achieve the ultimate goal of supported employment, which is to integrate individuals with severe disabilities into all facets of life in their local communities.

QUESTIONS (For answers see pp. 435-436)

1. What does the author state the intent of supported employment has been since its inception?

2. What factor, other than production problems, has been shown by research to be a major contributor to job separation for persons with severe disabilities?

3. Of the following disability groups, which have been identified by research as leaving their jobs at a higher rate: psychiatric, mild MR, moderate MR, severe, or profound MR?

4. When do the majority of job separations occur?

5. Identify the major job separation categories identified by the author.

6. Results of research by the author indicate the primary reason for job separation across all disability categories was . . . ?

7. What was the major reason within the job responsibility category that people were separated from supported employment?

8. Identify the major reason that individuals with mild mental retardation were separated from supported employment.

9. Identify the major reason why persons with severe or profound mental retardation were separated from their jobs.

10. Name at least one factor that contributes to job separation at each of the four levels identified by the author.

11. What does the author suggest can be done at the organizational/agency level to address problems which may lead to job separation?

12. List four factors the author says should be considered when performing job development. Explain the importance of each.

13. List examples of factors contributing to production problems resulting in job separation.

REFERENCES

Blauner, R. (1966). Worker satisfaction and industrial trends in modern society. In R. Bendix & S. M. Lipset (Eds.), *Class status and power: Social stratification in comparative perspective* (pp. 473–487). New York: The Free Press.

Bowe, F. (1980). *Rehabilitating America: Toward independence for disabled and elderly people*. New York: Harper & Row.

Chadsey-Rusch, J. (1986). Identifying and teaching valued social behaviors. In F. R. Rusch, (Ed.), *Competitive employment issues and strategies* (pp. 273–288). Baltimore: Paul H. Brookes.

Conley, R. W. & Noble, J. H. (1989). Contradictions and inconsistencies in the service system for adults with disabilities. In W. E. Kiernan & R. L. Schalock (Eds.), *Economics, industry, and disability* (pp. 299–316).

Friedman, G. (1964). *The anatomy of work: Labor, leisure, and the implications of automation*. New York: Free Press of Glencoe.

Greenspan, S. & Shoultz, B. (1981). Why mentally retarded adults lose their jobs: Social competence as a factor in work adjustment. *Applied Research in Mental Retardation, 2*(1), 23–38.

Guess, D., Benson, H. A., & Siegal-Causey, E. (1985). Concepts and issues related to choice-making and autonomy among persons with severe disabilities. *The Journal of the Association for Persons with Severe Handicaps, 10*, 79–86.

Halle, D. (1984). *America's working man: Work, home and politics among blue collar property owners*. Chicago: University of Chicago Press.

Hanley-Maxwell, C. H., Rusch, F. R., Chadsey-Rusch, J., & Renzaglia, A. (1986). Reported factors contributing to job terminations of individuals with severe disabilities. *Journal of the Association for Persons with Severe Handicaps, 11*(1), 45–52.

Hanley-Maxwell, C., Rusch, F. R., & Rappaport, J. (1989). A multi-level perspective on community employment problems for adults with mental retardation. *Rehabilitation Counseling Bulletin, 32*, 266–280.

Hill, J. W., Wehman, P., Hill, M., & Goodall, P. (1986). Differential reasons for job separation of previously employed persons with mental retardation. *Mental Retardation*, 24, 347–351.

Johnson, J. R. & Rusch, F. R. (in press). Analysis of direct training hours received by supported employment consumers. *American Journal on Mental Retardation*.

Karan, O. C. & Knight, C. (1986). Developing support networks for individuals who fail to achieve competitive employment. In F. R. Rusch (Ed.), *Competitive employment: Service delivery models, methods, and issues* (pp. 241–256).

Kochany, L. & Keller, J. (1981). An analysis and evaluation of the failure of severely disabled individuals in competitive employment. In P. Wehman (Ed.), *Competitive employment: New horizon for severely disabled individuals* (pp. 181–198). Baltimore: Paul H. Brookes.

Lagomarcino, T. R. & Rusch, F. R. (1988). Competitive employment: Overview and analysis of research focus. In V. B. VanHasselt, P. S. Strain, & M. Hersen (Eds.), *Handbook of developmental and physical disabilities* (pp. 150–158). New York: Pergamon Press.

Lagomarcino, T. R. (1989). *Assessing the multidimensional nature of integration in employment settings*. Unpublished doctoral dissertation, University of Illinois at Urbana-Champaign.

Lagomarcino, T. R., Hughes, C., & Rusch, F. R. (1989). Utilizing self-management to teach independence on the job. *Education and Training in Mental Retardation*, 24(2), 139–148.

Locke, E. A. (1983). The nature and causes of job satisfaction. In M. D. Dunnette (Ed.), *Handbook of industrial and organizational psychology* (pp. 1297–1349). Chicago: Rand McNally.

Martin, J., Rusch, F. R., Lagomarcino, T. R., & Chadsey-Rusch, J. (1986). Comparison between nonhandicapped and mentally retarded workers: Why they lose their jobs. *Applied Research in Mental Retardation, 7*(4), 467–474.

Mayers, H. S. (1984). *Minding your own business: A contemporary guide to small business success.* Homewood IL: Dow Jones-Irwin.

Mithaug, D. E., Martin, J. E., Husch, J. V., Agran, M., & Rusch, F. R. (1989). *When will persons in supported employment need less support?* Colorado Springs, CO: Ascent Publishing.

Moseley, C. R. (1989). Job satisfaction research: Implications for supported employment. *Journal of the Association for Persons with Severe Handicaps, 13* (3), 211–219.

Nisbet, J. & Hagner, D. (1988). Natural supports in the workplace: A reexamination of supported employment. *Journal of the Association for Persons with Severe Handicaps, 13*(4), 260–267.

Rusch, F. R., Chadsey-Rusch, J., & Johnson, J. R. (in press). Supported employment: Emerging opportunities for employment integration. In L. Meyer, C. Peck, & L. Brown (Ed.) *Critical issues in the lives of people with severe disabilities*. Baltimore: Paul H. Brookes.

Rusch, F. R., Chadsey-Rusch, J., & Lagomarcino, T. R. (1987). Preparing students for employment. In M. E. Snell (Ed.), *Systematic instruction of persons with severe handicaps* (pp. 171–190). Columbus, OH: Charles E. Merrill.

Rusch, F. R., Johnson, J. R., & Hughes, C. (in press). Analysis of co-worker involvement in relation to level of disability versus placement approach among supported employees. *The Journal of the Association for Persons with Severe Handicaps.*

Saltzberg, D. L., Lignugaris-Kraft, B., & McCuller, G. L. (in press). Reasons for job loss: A review of employment termination studies of mentally retarded workers. *Research and Intervention in Developmental Disabilities.*

Standard & Poor's Industry Survey. (1989, July). Volume 1, p. 34.

Talbot, J. A. (1984). The chronic mental patient: A national perspective. In M. Mirabi (Ed.) *The chronically mentally ill: Research and services* (pp. 3–22). Spectrum.

Turner, J. L. (1983). Workshop society: Ethnographic observations in a work setting for retarded adults. In K. Kernan, M. Begab, & R. B. Edgerton (Eds.), *Environments and behavior: The adaptation of mentally retarded persons* (pp. 147–172). Baltimore: University Park Press.

Wagel, W. H. (1989). Hardees: One step ahead in the race for employees. *Personnel*, 66, (4), 20–22.

Wehman, P. & Kregal, J. (1985). A supported work approach to competitive employment of individuals with moderate and severe handicaps. *Journal of the Association for Persons with Severe Handicaps*, 10(1), 3–11.

Winking, D. L., DeStefano, L., & Rusch, F. R. (1988). *Supported employment in Illinois: Job coach issues.* Champaign: University of Illinois, The Secondary Transition Intervention Effectiveness Institute.

U. S. Commission on Civil Rights. (1983, September). *Accommodating the spectrum of disabilities.* Washington, DC: U. S. Commission on Civil Rights.

U. S. Department of Labor. (1977). *A nationwide report on sheltered workshops and their employment of handicapped individuals.* Washington, DC: U. S. Department of Labor.

CHAPTER

19

Converting from Segregated Sheltered Employment to Supported Employment

Wendy S. Parent
Virginia Commonwealth University
Mark L. Hill
Office of Supported Employment
Richmond, Virginia

The vocational rehabilitation system has undergone significant change during the last fifteen years, making a major impact on employment services for persons with severe disabilities (Rubin & Rubin, 1988; Wehman & Moon, 1988). The federal vocational rehabilitation program was established after World War I to provide employment assistance for veterans who had become disabled during the war. Since that time, legislation has mandated the extension of services to persons with physical disabilities, blindness, mental retardation, mental illness, behavior disorders, substance abuse problems, and those who are socially disadvantaged. The passage of the Rehabilitation Act of 1973 has placed an additional priority on providing services for persons with severe disabilities. The goal of the rehabilitation program is to help persons with a disability become productive members of society by providing the necessary services that will enable them to achieve gainful employment.

It is assumed that individuals who meet the eligibility criteria for rehabilitative services will progress through the phases of the rehabilitation process, from evaluation, to program planning, to treatment and service delivery, and finally to termination from rehabilitation services after placement into employment (Rubin & Roessler, 1987). But individuals with severe disabilities typically do not move past the evaluation phase, where they are often denied eligibility to receive services or are placed in extended evaluation for eighteen months or more to determine their employment potential (Bitter, 1979). This is reflected in the high unemployment rates of 50 percent to 90 percent for persons who have a severe disability (Louis Harris Poll, 1986; U.S. Commission on Civil Rights, 1983).

Sheltered workshops and day activity programs were developed in the 1960s to provide long-term evaluation services, job skill training, and work adjustment for the purpose of preparing individuals for remunerative work in the business community (Hill, Revell et al., 1987). It is estimated that approximately 1.6 million persons receive services annually from the over 5,500 sheltered workshops and 2,000 activity centers in operation today (Menz, 1987). Yet statistics show that only 7 percent of the individuals in activity centers and 12 percent of those in sheltered workshops move into competitive employment annually, with only 3 percent exiting after two years in such programs (Bellamy, Rhodes, Bourbeau, & Mank, 1986).

Supported employment has emerged as an alternative vocational option for persons with severe disabilities (Kiernan & Stark, 1986; Rusch, 1986; Wehman & Moon, 1988). In contrast to traditional rehabilitation services, supported employment is based on the philosophy that individuals do not have to work independently in order to be successfully employed. Instead of training to become ready for competitive employment, persons with severe disabilities are trained directly at the job site after placement into paid employment and are provided with support services for as long as they remain employed. Supported employment is targeted to those individuals who are receiving services in sheltered work and day programs or who have been excluded or are waiting for vocational rehabilitation services, and who also require ongoing services to remain in integrated employment situations (Parent, Hill, & Wehman, in press). Supported employment was authorized as an acceptable employment outcome in the federal rehabilitation program with the passage of the Vocational Rehabilitation Act Amendments of 1986 (*Federal Register*, May 27, 1987; Shafer, 1988). In 1985 and 1986, the Office of Special Education and Rehabilitative Services funded twenty-seven states to convert their service delivery systems from sheltered to supported employment services. In addition to the statewide conversion projects, numerous rehabilitation facilities have demonstrated that conversion can be successfully accomplished on an individual level when the necessary steps for organizational change have been implemented (Gardner, Chapman, Donaldson, & Jacobson, 1988; Sither, 1988; Wehman, Kregel, & Shafer, 1989).

Beneficial organizational change is a planned, systematic process that involves identifying problems and implementing solutions to enhance outcomes (Lippitt, Langseth, & Mossop, 1985). The first step in the change process is the *diagnosis* of a problem and the commitment to make changes in an effort to solve the problem (Lippitt et al., 1985); this requires a critical evaluation by rehabilitation facilities of the present services and outcomes in comparison to the desired services and outcomes. Incongruencies between the two—for example, low wages, low retention in competitive employment positions, and little social integration—indicate a need for problem identification and the implementation of problem-solving changes within the organization. Johnson & Friedian (1986) propose a three-stage process for organizational change that involves information gathering, planning, and implementation. Program evaluation has been suggested as a fourth component in other change models (Lynn & Lynn, 1984). This chapter discusses the issues associated with conversion and the resources available to rehabilitation facilities during each phase of the organizational change process, including planning for conversion, implementing the conversion process, and evaluating supported employment outcomes.

PLANNING FOR CONVERSION

Planning is the next critical step of the change process. It is during this stage that the present state of the facility is assessed, the future state is defined, and the strategies for reaching the desired future state are identified (Beckhard & Harris, 1987; Bellamy, Rhodes, Mank, & Albin, 1988). Planning provides the foundation and direction for implementing the conversion process (Gardner et al., 1988). One advantage of thorough planning is the identification of potential problems so that strategies can be designed and resources allocated to facilitate a smooth conversion. One important source of information for facility providers is communication with other facility administrators who are involved in converting their service delivery system. A second resource is professional publications and workshops related to supported employment and conversion. The information identified during the planning phase is used to develop the goal and mission statement of the facility (Gardner et al., 1988). Combined with the resources available, specific activities and objectives are incorporated into a formal change plan for guiding the conversion process.

Goals are specific statements that determine the kinds of services the organization will provide, who is eligible to receive services, and what the desired outcomes will be (Brager & Holloway, 1978). Goals establish a set of standards that guide the operation of the facility, provide a framework for decision making, and establish a mechanism for assessing progress (Szilagyi & Wallace, 1983). The goals should reflect the values associated with supported employment: integration, decent wages, real work, individual choice, and increased opportunity (Chernish & Beziat, 1988). Objectives provide a means for specifying the activities that will occur, the timeline for completion, and the standards for evaluating the results (Kettner, Daley, & Nichols, 1985). For example, the facility will place thirty workshop participants in supported employment situations and demonstrate a 75 percent retention rate by the end of the first year. Responsibility should be assigned to the person who will be held accountable for completion of the activity (Gardner et al., 1988). Often, the facility manager is responsible for monitoring the completion of the objectives and coordinating the conversion activities (McDaniel & Flippo, 1988).

A major part of the planning phase is the analysis of resources needed for conversion and supported employment implementation. Lawrence & Dyer (1983) suggest that organizational change and survival depend on an organization's efficient use of resources. The determination of resources will assist with the development of a realistic and obtainable conversion plan as well as effective strategies for achieving the facility's goals. Other supported employment and conversion projects in the community can share information based on their experiences in the specific locality through telephone contacts, written resources, audiovisual materials, and on-site visits. In addition, monthly or bimonthly meetings can be scheduled as a source of information-sharing among programs. Many states that have received funds to implement statewide conversion have established an office of supported employment, with regional representatives to answer questions and disseminate materials. On a national level, federal funding opportunities, staff training and technical assistance programs, and manuals for conversion or supported employment implementation are available. Table 19.1 provides a summary of many currently available resources.

IMPLEMENTING THE CONVERSION PROCESS

Gaining Participant Support

The support of professionals, facility board members and staff, persons with severe disabilities, family members, local businesses, and other agencies is critical for successful conversion (Parent, Hill, & Wehman, in press). Often, the response to change will be negative, which may actually be a reflection of individuals' doubts, fears, or misconceptions. Still others may voice an eagerness to participate in supported employment, only to back away hesitatingly when actually provided with the option to deliver or receive services. Brager & Holloway (1978) suggest that the more the change goal is perceived as threatening or unfamiliar, the more likely it is that it will be met with resistance. One strategy to gain support is to encourage input and feedback from all participants throughout the change process, including the planning, implementation, and evaluation phases (Howes & Quinn, 1978). Another way to promote positive attitudes is to provide information that carefully describes what the change will entail, the effect that the change will have on each individual, and the benefits associated with supported employment services. Although some degree of resistance can be expected as a natural reaction to change, education, involvement, support, and negotiation

Table 19.1 Conversion Resources

Resource	Reference/ Name/Contact	Purpose/ Content	Target Audiences
Rehabilitation facility conversion planning/implementation	McDaniel, R. H. & Flippo, K. F. (1987). *Managing facility initiated supported employment.* San Francisco: Rehabilitation Administration, University of San Franciso.	Discusses the issues and strategies for the implementation of supported employment services from a rehabilitation facility. Specific content areas include: philosophical foundation, planning & implementation, change management, staff roles, budgeting, program evaluation, and interagency planning teams.	Facility managers
	Gardner, J. F., Chapman, M. S., Donaldson, G. & Jacobson, S. G. (1988). *Toward supported employment: A process guide for planned change.* Baltimore: Paul H. Brookes.	Describes the issues involved in converting from a sheltered or day activity program to a supported employment program. The factors addressed are: planning, change management, worker needs, staff development, facility utilization, organizational structure, financing, implementation, and quality control.	Facility managers
Supported employment implementation	Barcus, M., Brooke, V., Inge, K., Moon, S. & Goodall, P. (1987). *An instructional guide for training at a job site: A supported employment resource.* Richmond: Virginia Commonwealth University, Rehabilitation Research & Training Center. Dr. Paul Wehman, Director.	Describes job training strategies that have been utilized to train individuals with severe disabilities to perform competitive jobs in the community. Instructional strategies and intervention techniques for all phases of job site training are presented.	Direct service providers
	Moon, S., Goodall, P., Barcus, M. & Brooke, V. (Eds.), (1986). *The supported work model of competitive employment for citizens with severe handicaps: A guide for job trainers.* (rev. ed.) Richmond: Virginia Commonwealth University, Rehabilitation Research & Training Center. Dr. Paul Wehman, Director.	Describes the activities involved with implementation of the supported work model. The components discussed are: job development, consumer assessment, job placement, job site training, on-going follow-along and time management.	Direct service providers
	Chernish, W A., Britt, C., Nutter, S. O. & Sakry, L. A. (1987). *Components of a supported work model for private rehabilitation facilities.* Norfolk, VA: Louise W. Eggleston Center.	Provides a summary of facility manager considerations and guidelines for implementation of the supported work model of competitive employment. A summary of the components and activities of each phase are discussed.	Direct service providers, facility managers

Table 19.1 (cont.)

Staff training and technical assistance	The Employment Network Project University of Oregon 135 College of Education, Eugene, OR 97403 Contact: David Mank, Jay Buckley, Larry Rhodes.	Supported employment training areas include: program management, support strategies, and agency roles.	Program managers, local government personnel, state decision makers
	University of San Francisco Rehabilitation Administration C-4 Campion Hall 2130 Fulton Street San Francisco, CA 94117 Contact: Richard Robinson, Karen Flippo (Collaborator with The Employment Network Project).	Supported employment training areas include: agency conversion, role in rehabilitation system, and state implementation.	Rehabilitation agencies, program managers, state decision makers
	University of Vermont Department of Special Education 405A Waterman Building Burlington, VT 05405 Contact: Michael Collins (Collaborator with The Employment Network Project).	Supported employment training areas include: rural implementation, technical assistance models, organization management, interagency relationships, and transition planning.	Employment training specialists, rural program managers, in-state decision makers, transition teams
	Wisconsin Community Development Finance Authority 14 West Mifflin Street, #312 Madison, WI 53703 Contact: Dale Verstegen (Collaborator with The Employment Network Project).	Supported employment training areas include: agency management, business development, and support strategies.	Direct service staff, program managers, program staff
	Boston University Psychiatric Rehabilitation Center 1019 Commonwealth Avenue Boston, MA 02215 Contact: Karen Danley (Collaborator with The Employment Network Project).	Supported employment training areas: agency management, strategies for individuals with psychiatric disabilities, and support strategies.	Providers and decision makers in supported employment, programs for persons with chronic mental illness
	Virginia Commonwealth University Rehabilitation Research and Training Center VCU Box 2011 Richmond, VA 23284 Contact: Michael Barcus (Collaborator with The Employment Network Project).	Supported employment training areas include: program management, model implementation, strategies for persons with head injuries, and job coach approaches.	Direct service staff, program managers, state managers, programs for persons with head injuries

Table 19.1 (cont.)

	Virginia Commonwealth University Rehabilitation Research and Training Center VCU Box 2011 Richmond, VA 23284 Contact: Vicki Brooke.	Training areas include: supported work model implementation, data management, and employment specialist competencies.	Direct service providers, program managers
	The Association for Persons in Supported Employment 5001 West Broad Street Suite 34 Richmond, VA 23230 Contact: Wendy Wood	Provides national alliance of persons interested in furthering supported employment. Resources include: newsletters, policy updates, work incentive training, and networking information.	Consumers, parents/guardians, employment specialists, rehabilitation counselors, mental health/mental retardation case managers, facility managers, state decision makers, sheltered workshop staff, administrators, and educators
Funding	Hill, M. L. (1986). *Outline and support materials to assist in the preparation of proposals to provide time-limited and ongoing services within a program of supported employment.* Richmond: Virginia Commonwealth University, Rehabilitation Research and Training Center.	Describes an interagency funding model of time-limited (TES) and ongoing (OES) employment services. It is designed as a "how to" manual for assistance in receiving funds for supported employment services by becoming a vendor of TES and OES services.	Workshop and activity program directors, community service board staff, vocational rehabilitation staff, private agencies
	Rehabilitation Research and Training Center Newsletter. (1987). *Funding supported employment.* Richmond: Virginia Commonwealth University, *4*(1).	Identifies possible funding sources for supported employment and interagency strategies for funding services. A section of commonly asked questions related to funding issues and their answers is included.	Facility managers, rehabilitation administrators & counselors, employment specialists, mental health/mental retardation case managers & administrators
	Hill, M. L., Banks, P. D., Handrick, R. R., Wehman, P., Hill, J. W., & Shafer, M. S. (1987). Benefit-cost analysis of supported competitive employment for persons with mental retardation. *Research on Developmental Disabilities, 8*, 71-89.	Describes the benefits and costs of supported employment from the perspective of the taxpayer and the consumer. The financial benefits discussed are increased revenue, decreased service expenditures, and decreased government subsidy. An analysis of consumer and taxpayer costs/-expenditures includes operational costs, lost workshop earnings, decreased government subsidy, and taxes paid/credited.	Mental health/mental retardation agencies, vocational rehabilitation agencies, sheltered workshops, day programs, schools, consumers, taxpayers

Table 19.1 (cont.)

	Hill, M. L., Wehman, P. H., Kregel, J., Banks, P. D., & Metzler, H. M. D. (1987). Employment outcomes for people with moderate and severe disabilities: An eight year longitudinal analysis of supported competitive employment. *The Journal of the Association for Persons with Severe Handicaps, 12*(3), 182-189.	Presents the results of 8 years of longitudinal data obtained from individual supported competitive employment placements by the Rehabilitation Research and Training Center at Virginia Commonwealth University. A benefit/cost analysis for consumers and taxpayers is discussed.	Mental health/mental retardation agencies, rehabilitation agencies, sheltered workshops, day programs, schools, taxpayers, consumers

are strategies that can be used to increase acceptance of the proposed change (Gardner et al., 1988). The more persons who support the facility's decision to convert, the greater the resources that will be available to the facility.

PERSONS WITH SEVERE DISABILITIES. As consumers of supported employment services, it is important for persons with severe disabilities to understand what supported employment is and to be actively involved throughout the placement process. A careful job match which takes into account the individual's interests, skills, and desires is essential for job satisfaction and retention. Ongoing input and feedback from the consumer as well as evaluation of the services provided will contribute to effective and successful supported employment programming.

Frequently, concerns are raised that the employee will experience multiple losses, such as friends, Social Security and medical benefits, or the permanent security of the facility program. One important role of the employment specialist is to function as an advocate at the job site (Moon, Goodall, Barcus, & Brooke, 1986), which includes modeling interactions for the employee and co-workers, training interpersonal skills, and serving as liaison for friendship development. In addition, employment offers the employee greater independence, increased wages, opportunities for community access, and improved perceptions by members of the community, opening up multiple avenues for interaction with nonhandicapped persons (Parent, Hill, & Wehman, in press). It is the responsibility of the employment specialist to assist the employee with identifying and accessing the social opportunities that are available.

Most concerns about loss of medical payments or benefits are related to losing eligibility rather than the actual subsidy itself. Social Security work incentives such as 1619 (a) and (b) allow an employee to earn money and still maintain eligibility for benefits or payments (Social Security Administration, 1987; Szymanski, 1988). A person's financial and insurance needs should be considered when making a decision regarding whether an employment situation is accepted. Threats to security can be lessened if the supported employment provider has incorporated provisions for job replacement after separation or job mobility into the initial service provision plan. The choice either to become employed in one job or to remain in a sheltered program does not greatly expand the choices for employment that are available to an individual.

FAMILY MEMBERS AND RESIDENTIAL STAFF. Parent support has been reported to be one of the critical factors associated with successful employment (Rehabilitation Research and Training Center Newsletter, 1985). Families operate as a system so that significant events do not affect one member in isolation but rather have an impact on the entire family unit. Therefore, efforts to secure family involvement in all of the supported employment planning and decision making needs to be a major priority.

The input provided by family members can be an important source of information for program development and improvement. In addition, linkage between satisfied parents who have chosen the supported employment program and those who are skeptical can be a persuasive technique for increasing the numbers of families in favor of supported employment options.

Family members often voice concern that their son or daughter will not be able to perform the job, that other people will tease or harm them, or that they will lose their job and not have an alternative program to which they may return. In addition to family members, residential staff may be hesitant to commit to a new program with varying hours and responsibilities that place new and probably increased demands on them. Both family members and residential staff should be provided with information describing supported employment through written materials, personal visits, workshops, and telephone conversations (Anderson, Beckett, Chitwood, & Hayden, 1985). An explanation of the employment specialist's role as trainer/advocate and provider of individualized, ongoing support services is reassurance that assistance will be available to the worker and the family. For example, the responsibilities of the employment specialist include making Social Security arrangements, providing transportation training, and teaching banking skills, if desired. Frequent contact by the employment specialist can establish trust and provide the opportunity for family members and residential staff to ask questions in order to alleviate their fears. The contacts made by the employment specialist are usually more frequent before placement and for several weeks or months afterward but will gradually be reduced as the parents or guardians become more comfortable with the new arrangements. In addition, once the benefits of the employee's job, such as financial contributions and reduced dependency, are felt at home, the concerns initially expressed often dissipate (Hill, Wehman, Kregel, Banks, & Metzler, 1987; Parent, Hill, & Wehman, in press).

Facility Manager, Board, and Staff. As managers and providers of supported employment services, a commitment by all facility personnel is required for successful service delivery. One characteristic of successful organizational change is commitment and active involvement by the facility director (Howes & Quinn, 1978; Lynn & Lynn, 1984). Facility managers play a critical role in the conversion process as demonstrated by their responsibilities in planning, implementing, and coordinating the change activities (McDaniel & Flippo, 1988). Evidence of the facility director's attitude that individuals with disabilities have a right to meaningful integrated work and the consequent allocation of resources necessary to deliver the appropriate support service displays a positive model for other facility personnel. The belief that persons with severe disabilities can and should participate in real work in the community is critical in order to shift staff attitudes from the need to train for employment to training at the job site after employment. Moving the training to the community offers the facility the advantage of utilizing staff skills and interests more effectively. In addition, the facility director, board members, and staff are excellent resources for the identification of potential job opportunities.

Often, staff are reluctant to assume the new responsibilities out of fear that they lack the required skills or that their job security is threatened. Others may be long-term employees with a personal investment in the "way things used to be" or viewers of supported employment as a passing trend with little chance of permanency. Another factor met with controversy is the work schedule of an employment specialist. While some individuals view the autonomy, flexibility, and diversity of the hours to be an attractive aspect of the job, others perceive these factors negatively. It is important that clearly written job descriptions be provided to staff, so that expected responsibilities are defined. A management-by-development system for evaluating performance gives the staff the opportunity to become actively involved in their own skill development. Written resources, job site observations, and staff development workshops will reduce the fears felt by staff about venturing into the unknown. Both monetary and verbal recognition of the work performed by the workshop staff and employment specialists who are out there "doing it" can reduce the costs resulting from high staff turnover and poor quality services.

The manager or board members may doubt the facility's ability to provide supported employment services, the permanency of the new service delivery approach, or the participant's willingness to support the facility's efforts to convert (Parent, Hill, & Wehman, in press). Frequent meetings with ongoing, two-way communication and regular status reports will keep the board informed about the facility's activities. Systematic comparison of services and outcomes with the facility's goals provides assurance that unsuccessful strategies will be identified so that modifications or alternative strategies can be implemented. Many arguments are made against conversion on the basis that the new services will not be readily accepted by the participants and community. However, two of the primary motivating factors behind the supported employment movement have been parent and consumer grassroots movements and positive business attitudes (Wehman, in press).

As defined by Campbell (1988), a stable organization is one that can withstand change and adapt to the state of the art as it evolves. The funding of twenty-seven states by the Office of Special Education and Rehabilitative Services to convert their service delivery system verifies the commitment of the federal government to the establishment of community-based employment services. The presentation of the facts and benefits associated with supported employment as well as site visits and communication with other conversion projects can be a persuasive technique for changing attitudes.

EMPLOYERS. The business community is also a consumer of supported employment services (Shafer, Parent, & Everson, 1988). If the employee receiving supported employment services is not performing the job to the company's standards, the long-term success of the employment situation is threatened. As most human service workers have not had extensive training in business and marketing, local businesses are a major resource for information on the economic factors of the labor market. By conducting a community analysis to identify the different types of jobs and task requirements, supported employment programs can identify the needs of the business community for use in marketing their services (Moon, Goodall, Barcus, & Brooke, 1986). The facility can utilize employer expertise by requesting the participation of several business representatives on the facility board or an advisory committee. In addition, employers are a valuable source of job leads with other businesses or other types of jobs that may be unfamiliar to the supported employment providers.

Labor market reports indicate that the business community is experiencing a shortage of workers primarily in the service positions, a shortage that is projected to increase through the 1990s (Shafer, Parent, & Everson, 1988). Although there is a documented need for workers, employers may be hesitant to hire employees who have a severe disability for fear that they will not be able to perform the job, that co-workers will act negatively, or that supervision will be a problem. The employment specialist's role is to develop a marketing approach that focuses on labor demands, factual information about workers with disabilities, and the benefits of supported employment (Parent & Everson, 1986; Shafer, Parent, & Everson, 1988). The key to effective marketing is to remember that employers have a need for qualified workers, and supported employment providers have a service to sell which meets that need. The employment specialist's commitment to provide job skill training, to ensure that the job is completed, to model supervisory strategies, and to provide ongoing support services as needed for as long as the worker is employed are positive selling points for most employers (Shafer, Hill, Seyfarth, & Wehman, 1987).

VOCATIONAL REHABILITATION COUNSELORS. The rehabilitation counselor plays a dual role in the delivery of supported employment services. One role is purchaser of services from a supported employment provider such as a rehabilitation facility (Hill, Hill, Wehman, Revell, Dickerson, & Noble, 1987). Functioning in this capacity, the rehabilitation counselor writes supported employment as the goal in the Individualized Written Rehabilitation Plan and then authorizes case service dollars to an approved vendor of services (Revell, Wehman, & Arnold, 1984; Hill, 1986). A second possible role for the rehabilitation counselor is direct service provider, either as the employment specialist or as the case manager and support services provider (Tooman, Revell, & Melia, 1988). The rehabilitation counselor is in the business of assisting persons with obtaining employment and as such is a financial and information resource in either of the above capacities.

Rehabilitation counselors often are hesitant to recommend supported employment services because they have been operating within the traditional model of time-limited services (Rubin & Rubin, 1988; Wehman & Moon, 1988). The recent passage of the Rehabilitation Act Amendments of 1986 has made supported employment an acceptable criterion for a Status 26 closure (closed, successfully rehabilitated). Accountability for rehabilitation counselors is determined by the number of successful case closures they receive. Supported employment offers the benefits of an alternative service option to assist with meeting the great demand for rehabilitative services, a mechanism for compliance with legislative mandates to serve persons with severe disabilities, and a proactive plan for providing ongoing job retention services—specifically, Status 24 (services interrupted) or Status 32 (postemployment services) (Bitter, 1979; Parent, Hill, & Wehman, in press).

MENTAL HEALTH/MENTAL RETARDATION OR DEVELOPMENTAL DISABILITY AGENCY. Supported employment requires an interagency approach in order to meet the legal mandates for ongoing services after the provision of time-limited services by the vocational rehabilitation agency (Hill, Hill et al., 1987). Because supported employment was originally developed for individuals with mental retardation, the mental health/mental retardation services or developmental disability agency is usually the primary long-term service provider. However, any agency that provides funds for day programming in a center-based facility can function as the provider of ongoing support services by redirecting the existing dollars (Hill, 1988). In addition to funding and providing support services, the agency representative can be a resource for the provision of case management services for supported employment recipients. For example, the case manager can assist the employee with housing, money management, crisis intervention, and medical referral services.

The development of an interagency agreement between the facility and the mental health/mental retardation or developmental disability agency will assist with defining the roles and responsibilities of both parties. It is important to include the criteria for transferring to follow-along service phase, the types of services that will be provided, and the provisions for referring a case back to vocational rehabilitation services for increased intervention. Workshops, local interagency meetings, and the exchange of needs assessment and outcome data will increase the support available to the facility from other social service agencies.

Determining Operational Procedures

Organizational decisions that affect the long-term operations of the facility must be determined by the management before the initial stages of program implementation. The issues frequently reported by other conversion programs include: coordination of service delivery, maintenance of the facility, and transportation (Bellamy, Rhodes, Mank, & Albin, 1988; Gardner, 1988; Parent, Hill, & Wehman, in press).

COORDINATION OF SERVICE DELIVERY. Facility managers face several challenges related to service provision. Three frequently asked questions are: (a) who is eligible to receive services? (b) how can placement numbers be estimated? and (c) what happens if an employee loses his or her job? Three variables are used to determine a supported employment placement: an available job opening, a potential employee whose abilities and availability match the job requirements, and an available employment specialist. Because of the individualized nature of the model, these variables are often difficult to predict in planning new employment placements. Demonstration projects have shown that one employment specialist performing all activities of the model can place between eight and twelve individuals per year (Rehabilitation Research & Training Center Newsletter, 1985). The number will vary according to the complexity of the jobs identified, the severity of clients' disabilities, the skills of the employment specialist, and the quality of job matches. Proficiency in the above skills tends to improve as the experience of the employment specialist increases.

The determination of a procedure for handling referrals for supported employment services is essential for smooth and ongoing service provision. A supported employment provider needs a pool of approximately fifteen to thirty referrals that have completed the consumer assessment process so that an identified job can be matched to the best candidate (Moon, Goodall, Barcus, & Brooke, 1986). A referral policy should clearly state the eligibility criteria, such as severity of disability, location of residence, current program status, acceptable referral sources, and facility affiliation. One strategy may be to place one person on the facility's waiting list for every two workers moved from the facility. In addition, the procedure for determining eligibility needs to be stated. Provisions for replacing those individuals who are separated from their job or who require a job change should be anticipated and the resources allocated upfront in the conversion process. Too often, workers are expected to keep one job, and if it is lost or no longer appropriate, the only alternative is to return to sheltered employment or be placed on a waiting list to receive services.

Facility managers play a key role as the coordinator of services and as such must undergo changes in their strategies and policies for supervising staff (Gardner et al., 1988; McDaniel & Flippo, 1988). In contrast to center-based services, supported employment necessitates a decentralized staffing arrangement, which means that the manager will not be able to observe the behavior of the employment specialist directly on a daily basis. Often, with a forty-hour per week placement, the manager and employment specialist may not have regular contact for several days or weeks. Communication can be maintained by telephone, on-site visits by the manager, after-hours staff meetings, or substitute coverage by another employment specialist.

MAINTENANCE OF THE FACILITY. During the conversion process, the facility manager is faced with the challenge of developing a supported employment program while maintaining facility operations. It is important to provide quality training of relevant work skills to those participants in the workshop while they are waiting to receive supported employment services. For example, training on such things as production rates, using a telephone, or taking a fifteen-minute break can reduce the amount of training time at the job site by the employment specialist. Encouraging workshop staff to visit the job site of an employee who is in a supported employment situation is one way of convincing in-house staff of the importance of providing functional skills training (Renzaglia & Hutchins, 1988; Snell, 1983).

The operational security of the facility is threatened by the loss of present contracts or the inability to complete those contracts to which the facility is already committed. In addition to contributing to the financial income supporting the facility, contracted work from local businesses is the primary activity for participants and the source of their wages. During the initial stages of the conversion process, the contract revenue can continue to maintain the operations of the facility for those individuals waiting for supported employment placements. As more people are placed into the community, the remaining workers will have additional work to complete, resulting in a higher income for those participants. The reduction in workshop staff required to supervise the decreased number of participants means that the contract revenue that is generated can be redirected to funding supported employment activities.

With increased placements, the number of persons working in the facility will decline, resulting in an excess of unused space. One strategy for utilizing the empty space in the facility is to rent it out to private businesses (Gardner et al., 1988). Hiring nonhandicapped workers to complete the existing or increased contract work is another option. The advantages of these methods are that the facility will continue to receive an income from the unused space, individuals remaining in the workshop will have opportunities for integration, and additional revenue is generated to fund supported employment services.

TRANSPORTATION. Lack of transportation is a problem frequently cited by supported employment programs. With the individual placement and cluster models, the workers are required to make travel arrangements rather than using the vans provided by the facility. One of the responsibilities of the employment specialist is to identify a method of transportation before placement and to provide travel training to and from the job site. Public transportation, such as the bus or specialized van service, is a valuable resource for those communities who have access to these options. Programs in rural areas or without public transportation services can consider carpooling, taxi services, driver contracting, or driving by a family member or friend. Another idea is to locate a job near an individual's home so that walking or riding a bike or moped present additional alternatives. it is important to include any transportation restrictions or limitations in the job matching process and to be creative in developing new options before ruling out a potential job.

Identifying Funding Sources

By definition, supported employment requires an interagency funding agreement in order to provide the ongoing support services that are characteristic of the model. Vocational rehabilitation dollars can be used to finance the initial time-limited services similar to the traditional rehabilitation approach (Hill, Hill et al., 1987). The 1986 Amendments to the Rehabilitation Act created Title VI-c formula grants and set aside $25 million to all state vocational rehabilitation agencies for supported employment. Of this total, 95 percent must be spent on direct service, with a 5 percent maximum allocated for administration. Once an individual is in a stable job—the ongoing support services may be/must be financed by another agency, such as mental health/mental retardation services or developmental disability agencies, which have been providing funding for the day activity programs and workshops (Hill, 1988). For example, in Virginia, stabilization is defined as the presence of the employment specialist at the job site during 20 percent or less of the employee's work hours for two consecutive weeks. As supported employment services are made available for persons with severe disabilities other than mental retardation, creative long-term funding options will have to be developed. One way is to have the individual purchase his or her own follow-along services using Social Security monies (Wood, 1988).

Funding issues present one of the greatest challenges to organizations interested in converting their services to supported employment. Existing contracts from a variety of sources create inertia and resistance to new, less predictable funding sources. Previous long-term commitments that the organization has struggled to establish must now be modified to allow funding to follow persons into the community without the requirement of filling the vacated "slot" with individuals from the waiting lists. Significant effort is required to explain to long-term funding agencies why, once funding follows an individual into the community, that position no longer exists in the in-house program. Additionally, established fee-for-service reimbursement fees may not cover costs due to lack of referral, a poor job market, or miscalculation in the estimated rate for supported employment. Many state vocational rehabilitation agencies allow a final billing from provider to ensure actual costs recovery. This method can be very helpful in reducing organizational financial insecurity.

Several options for accessing new funding sources or redirecting existing dollars to finance supported employment are available for rehabilitation facilities, including (a) fee-for-service arrangements, (b) expansion of facility service purchases, (c) reductions in facility operation costs, (d) new discretionary funding options, (e) private sector labor diversification, and (f) participant funding (Parent, Hill, & Wehman, in press).

The establishment of the facility as a vendor of supported employment services will allow for the trading of subsidized fees for actual cost fees. Organizations that have drawn the amounts required to provide a service from many sources both private and public in the past are now often approved by service purchasers at actual cost rates. This amounts to a net revenue increase for the organization.

There are many funding sources placing emphasis on supported employment that are looking for agencies able to provide the services. Often simple written proposals or informal negotiations can facilitate access to these funds. The following are potential discretionary funding sources into which providers might tap: (a) state developmental disabilities planning councils, (b) state special or vocational education programs, (c) state vocational rehabilitation, (d) Job Training Partnership Act Programs (JTPA), and their Private Industry Councils, and (e) state mental health/mental retardation/human resources (Parent, Hill, & Wehman, in press). Many states utilize Medicaid funds to finance supported employment through the Title XIX Home and Community Care Waiver funds. Organizations should contact their state mental health/mental retardation or developmental disability agency for information about the use of Title XIX for supported employment.

There are many new incentives for Job Training Partnership Act funds to be used for supported employment as a result of the Omnibus McKinney Homeless Assistance Act (R.L. 100-628). Within this act is the Jobs for Employable Dependent Individuals Act (JEDI), which provides bonuses to states that reduce welfare costs. Supplemental Security Income (SSI) recipients are identified as eligible within this new act. JTPA funds are an underutilized source for supported employment funding. Organizations should contact their state JTPA coordinator's office as well as the local Private Industry Council (PIC) that distributes the JTPA funds.

Taking the worker to the work opens many employment opportunities previously untapped, because the type of contracts procured do not have to be limited only to the type and number that can be completed in-house. Many clustered placements have been started by moving in-house contracts back to the originating company. For example, a mailing service contract completed in-house by thirty workshop participants can be relocated to the business so that six individuals are employed by the business in an integrated rather than segregated setting, and receive higher wages by performing the job under the supervision of an employment specialist.

Employees who receive supported employment services could purchase these services with their own Supplemental Security Income (SSI) and Social Security Disability Income (SSDI) (Wood, 1988). As reported by the Association for Persons in Supported Employment (APSE) in their recent newsletter, persons who meet the SSA regulatory criteria can deduct the costs for supported employment as Impairment Related Work Expenses available through SSI and SSDI from the monthly earnings that determine Substantial Gainful Activity (Social Security Administration, 1987) so that the amount paid is factored back into the determination of the SSI monthly payment (Wood, 1988, p. 5). (Refer to Chapter 15 for an overview of how this is determined.)

Developing Staff Competencies

One of the major problems reported by most supported employment programs is a lack of persons qualified to provide supported employment services (Kregel & Sale, 1988). These services are provided by professionals known as employment specialists or job coaches who are responsible for implementing all of the supported employment activities (Cohen, Patton, & Melia, 1986; Wehman & Melia, 1985). In the individual placement model, the employment specialist is responsible for conducting a consumer assessment, identifying a job in the community, completing the placement arrangements providing behavioral training of the job skills, systematically fading from the job site, and providing long-term follow-along support services (Wehman & Kregel, 1985). In some supported employment programs, the employment specialist's role is divided so that one individual is the job development specialist or the follow-along specialist while others assign one person for each placement. In the mobile crew or clustered placement models, one or two employment specialists are responsible for securing contracts, providing behavioral training at the job site for three to eight individuals, and providing supervision (Kregel & Sale, 1988; Mank, Rhodes, & Bellamy, 1986; Moon & Griffin, 1988; Rhodes & Valenta, 1985).

Additional competencies important for individuals functioning in the role of employment specialist include: knowledge of targeted jobs tax credit and social security procedures; techniques of systematic instruction; strategies of behavior management; principles of business operations, interpersonal communication skills, environmental modifications and adaptive equipment; and knowledge of other agency roles and functions (Parent, Hill, & Wehman, in press). A written job description will assist with clearly identifying the expected competencies of the facility's employment specialists and provide a tool for performance evaluation.

Facility staff function in two distinct capacities during conversion. One role is that of employment specialist who performs services outside the facility at businesses in the community. The second role is the workshop staff who provides systematic instruction of relevant job skills for those individuals waiting to receive supported employment services. Initially, a designated number of workshop staff may be allocated to provide supported employment services, or start-up funds may be utilized to hire additional staff members. As the numbers of workshop participants are reduced, the role of the in-house staff must be systematically redirected to community-based employment activities. Communication between the workshop staff and the employment specialists is important for staff morale and successful service delivery. Workshop staff can gain knowledge of the business community and the demands of real jobs to be incorporated into the simulated work training program. In addition, they can provide the employment specialist with consumer assessment information to assist with making a good job match. Emphasizing the importance and involvement of both staff positions during conversion will improve the quality of in-house services while facilitating staff investment in supported employment.

The employment specialists and workshop staff will be required to perform new and varied responsibilities (Gardner et al, 1988). An in service training model followed by technical assistance and apprenticeships has been found to be an effective method for training staff competencies (Barcus, Everson, & Hall, 1987; Barcus, Wehman, Moon, Brooke, Goodall, & Everson, 1987; Hill, 1986; Inge, Barcus, & Everson, 1988). Table 19.2 provides an example of an in-service training agenda including components and targeted participants. Regularly scheduled staff development workshops are useful for skill enhancement. Possible topic areas include Social Security regulations, other agency responsibilities, communication with parents, and problem-solving strategies. Another option for increasing staff knowledge and networking is the provision of funds and time off for attending professional conferences.

EVALUATING SUPPORTED EMPLOYMENT OUTCOMES

An important element essential for successful and cost-effective conversion is the evaluation of supported employment outcomes on the individual and organizational levels. Programs will often utilize a management information system for tracking the supported employment activities (Gardner et al., 1988). The collection and dissemination of outcome data by existing programs offers several benefits. These include: (a) the availability of information for other facilities interested in converting; (b) the development of strategies for improving conversion implementation procedures; (c) the establishment of a process for monitoring program service quality; (d) statistics for policy and funding decisions; and (e) evaluative feedback for the facility, participating agencies, employment specialists, parents, and employees.

Program evaluation measures and data collection procedures should reflect the values associated with supported employment. The consumer outcomes to be measured are: (a) wages, hours, benefits, and taxes paid; (b) integration, social relationships, and community access; (c) work performance and mobility; and (d) personal satisfaction (Parent, Hill, & Wehman, in press).

Suggested measures for monitoring facility goals and service quality include: (a) number of placements and retention rates; (b) consumer population served, (c) staff turnover rates, and (d) costs/expenditures (Parent, Hill, & Wehman, in press). These data should be collected on all participants regardless of employer for comparison of program effectiveness and quality across all sheltered and supported employment models.

Comparisons of factors affecting successful and unsuccessful rehabilitation/habilitation conversion programs is important for policy development and resource allocation. The emphasis on improving employment outcomes by increasing the number of supported employment programs has major implications for the rehabilitation service system. First, university rehabilitation counseling programs will need to modify their curricula to include supported employment in order to prepare graduates to provide or refer persons for supported employment services. Second, changes in the vocational evaluation and work adjustment components of the traditional rehabilitation services model are necessary because individuals receiving supported employment services are trained directly at the job site, eliminating the need for pre-employment preparation. Third, the criteria for program decision-making must shift from professional opinion to feedback from the local business community and persons with severe disabilities who are the consumers of supported employment services. Fourth, resources, such as funding, personnel, in-service training and technical assistance programs, and facility conversion implementation models need to be made available to all rehabilitation facilities so that informed decisions regarding conversion can be made. Fifth, provisions must be established in the rehabilitation guidelines to account for supported employment replacements for those employees who become separated from their jobs, who choose to move into another employment situation, or who demonstrate a need to advance to a more responsible position. As facility conversion projects create an increase in the availability of supported employment service options, the need to address these issues will become even more evident.

SUMMARY

This chapter has reviewed the issues and strategies involved with facility conversion from sheltered to supported employment services. Despite the challenges presented, multiple resources are available to motivate and assist facilities with implementing organizational change. The phases for successful change outlined in this chapter include planning for conversion, implementing the conversion process, and evaluating supported employment outcomes. Input and feedback by persons with severe disabilities, parents or guardians, employment specialists, facility staff, administrators, employers, rehabilitation counselors, and social service agency representatives are essential for the identification of implementation issues, strategies, and resources that will facilitate systems change from center-based to community-based employment services in the federal vocational rehabilitation program.

QUESTIONS (For answers see pp. 436-437)

1. Why were sheltered workshops and day activity programs developed?

2. What percentage of people leave sheltered workshops after two years for competitive employment?

Table 19.2 Inservice Training Modules

MODULE	COMPONENTS	TARGETED PARTICIPANTS
Values clarification	Values of supported employment Normalization Philosophical foundation Historical roots Supported employment models	Direct service staff Administrators Board members Parents/guardians
Organizational restructuring	Developing a mission Funding and budgeting Staffing Managing community-based service delivery Developing an organizational change plan and timeline Policy development Utilizing facility resources and completing contracts Community image	Administrators Board members
Interpersonal skills	Problem solving Decision making Cooperation and team work Communicating with consumers, parents, employers, and other agencies	Direct service staff Administrators Board members
Job development	Identifying local labor needs Conducting community analysis Contacting and interviewing employers Analyzing jobs	Direct service staff
Consumer assessment	Gathering assessment information Interpreting formal evaluations Completing a situational assessment	Direct service staff
Job placement	Job/consumer compatibility TJTC process Social Security regulations	Direct service staff
Job site training	Writing a task analysis Systematic instruction Co-worker involvement Advocacy Behavioral intervention strategies Data collection Job site modifications/rehabilitation engineering Fading	Direct service staff
Follow-along	Gathering supervisor evaluations Contacting consumers and families Interpreting employer and consumer problems Developing intervention strategies	Direct service staff Parents/guardians

Table 19.2 (cont.)

Interagency coordination	Interagency roles and responsibilities Vendorship requirements Cooperative agreements Communication Negotiation	Administrators Direct service staff
Evaluation	Consumer: Wages Hours Integration Quality of life Satisfaction Staff: Competencies Satisfaction Turnover Facility: #Placements %Retention Numbers reduction Cost-effectiveness Interagency agreements	Administrators Direct service staff Parents/guardians

3. Identify the major components involved in planning for conversion.

4. List at least three reasons why family support has been reported to be associated with successful employment.

5. Give three reasons why employers may be hesitant to hire workers with severe disabilities. How do the authors suggest these concerns be addressed?

6. Identify the dual role of the rehabilitation counselor in the delivery of supported employment services.

7. The number of clients one employment specialist can place in a year will vary depending on what factors?

8. By definition, does supported employment require an interagency funding agreement? If so, for what purpose?

9. List options described by the authors for accessing new funding sources or redirecting existing dollars to finance supported employment.

10. List at least five potential benefits of collection and dissemination of outcome data for agencies providing supported employment options.

11. What organizational decisions need to be made by the management before the initial stages of program implementation?

REFERENCES

Anderson, W., Beckett, C., Chitwood, S., & Hayden, D. (1985). *Next steps: Planning for employment.* Alexandria, VA: Parent Educational Advocacy Center.

Barcus, M., Everson, J. M., & Hall, S. (1987). Inservice training in human service agencies and organizations. In J. M. Everson, M. Barcus, M. S. Moon, & M. V. Morton (Eds.), *Achieving outcomes: A guide to interagency training in transition and supported employment.* Richmond: Virginia Commonwealth University, Project Transition Into Employment.

Barcus, J. M., Wehman, P., Moon, M. S., Brooke, V., Goodall, P., & Everson, J. M. (1988). Design and implementation of a short-term inservice training program for supported employment service providers. *Rehabilitation Education, 2,* 17–33.

Beckhard, R. & Harris, R. (1987). *Organizational transactions managing complex change* (2nd ed.). Reading, MA: Addison-Wesley.

Bellamy, G. T., Rhodes, L. E., Bourbeau, P. E., & Mank, D. M. (1986). Mental retardation services in sheltered workshops and day activity programs: Consumer benefits and policy alternatives. In F. R. Rusch (Ed.), *Competitive employment issue and strategies.* Baltimore: Paul H. Brookes.

Bellamy, G. T., Rhodes, L. E., Mank, D. M., & Albin, J. M. (1988). *Supported employment: A community implementation guide.* Baltimore: Paul H. Brookes.

Bitter, J. A. (1979). *Introduction to rehabilitation*. St. Louis: C. V. Mosby.

Brager, G. & Holloway, S. (1978). *Changing human service organizations' politics and practices*. New York: The Free Press.

Campbell, J. F. (1988). Rehabilitation facilities and community-based employment series. In P. Wehman & M. S. Moon (Eds.), *Vocational rehabilitation and supported employment*. Baltimore: Paul H. Brookes.

Chernish, W. A. & Beziat, R. (1988). Organizational analysis of values relative to supported work. In P. Wehman & M. S. Moon (Eds.), *Vocational rehabilitation and supported employment* (pp. 203–211). Baltimore: Paul H. Brookes.

Chernish, W. A., Britt, C., Nutter, S. O., & Sakry, L. A. (1987). *Components of a supported work model for private rehabilitation facilities*. Norfolk, VA: Louise W. Eggleston Center.

Cohen, D., Patton, S., & Melia, R. (1986). Staffing supported and transitional employment programs: Issue and recommendations. *American Rehabilitation, 12*(2), 20–24.

Federal Register. (May 27, 1987). Proposed Rules Vol. 52, No. 101, 19816.

Gardner, J. F., Chapman, M. S., Donaldson, G., & Jacobson, S. G. (1988). *Toward supported employment: A process guide for planned change*. Baltimore: Paul H. Brookes.

Hill, M. L. (1986). *Outline and support materials to assist in the preparation of proposals to provide time-limited and on-going services within a program of supported employment*. Richmond: Virginia Commonwealth University, Rehabilitation Research and Training Center.

Hill, M. L. (1988). Supported competitive employment: An interagency perspective. In P. Wehman & M. S. Moon (Eds.), *Vocational rehabilitation and supported employment* (pp. 31–49). Baltimore: Paul H. Brookes.

Hill, M. L., Banks, P. D., Handrick, R. R., Wehman, P., Hill, J. W., & Shafer, M. S. (1987). Benefit-cost analysis of supported competitive employment for persons with mental retardation. *Research on Developmental Disabilities, 8*, 71–89.

Hill, M., Hill, J. W., Wehman, P., Revell, G., Dickerson, A., & Noble, J. H. (1987). Supported employment: An interagency funding model for persons with severe disabilities. *Journal of Rehabilitation, 53*(2), 13–21.

Hill, M. L., Revell, G., Chernish, W., Morell, J. E., White, J., Metzler, H. M. D., & McCarthy, P. (1987). Planning for change: Interagency initiatives for supported employment. In P. Wehman, J. Kregel, M. S. Shafer, & M. L. Hill (Eds.), *Competitive employment for persons with mental retardation: From research to practice* (Volume II). Richmond: Virginia Commonwealth University, Rehabilitation Research and Training Center.

Hill, M. L., Wehman, P. H., Kregel, J., Banks, P. D., & Metzler, H. M. D. (1987). Employment outcomes for people with moderate and severe disabilities: An eight year longitudinal analysis of supported competitive employment. *The Journal of the Association for Persons with Severe Handicaps, 12*(3), 182–189.

Howes, N. J. R. & Quinn, R. E. (1978). Implementing change: From research to a prescriptive framework. *Group and Organizational Studies, 3*(1), 71–84.

Inge, K. J., Barcus, J. M., & Everson, J. M. (1988). Developing inservice training programs for supported employment personnel. In P. Wehman & M. S. Moon (Eds.), *Vocational rehabilitation and supported employment* (pp. 115–131). Baltimore: Paul H. Brookes.

Johnson, H. H. & Fredian, A. J. (1986, August). Simple rules for complex change. *Training and Development Journal*, 47–49.

Kettner, P., Daley, J. M. , & Nichols, A. W. (1985). *Initiating change in organizations and communities: A macropractice model*. Monterey, CA: Brookes/Cole.

Kiernan, W. E. & Stark, J. A. (Eds.). (1986). *Pathways to employment for adults with developmental disabilities*. Baltimore: Paul H. Brookes.

Kregel, J. & Sale, P. (1988). Preservice preparation of supported employment professionals. In P. Wehman & M. S. Moon (Eds.), *Vocational rehabilitation and supported employment* (pp. 129–143). Baltimore: Paul H. Brookes.

Lawrence, P. & Dyer, D. (1983). *Renewing American industry* (pp. 1–54). New York: The Free Press.

Lippitt, G. L., Langseth, P., & Mossop, J. (1985). *Implementing organizational change*. San Francisco: Jossey-Bass.

Louis Harris Poll. (1986, February). *A survey of the Unemployment of persons with disabilities.* Washington, D.C.: Author.

Lynn, G. & Lynn, J. B. (1984, November). Seven keys to successful change management. *Supervisory Management*, 30–37.

Mank, D. M., Rhodes, L. E., & Bellamy, G. T. (1986). Four supported employment alternatives. In W. Kiernan & J. Stark (Eds.), *Pathways to employment for developmentally disabled adults.* Baltimore: Paul H. Brookes.

McDaniel, R. & Flippo, K. (1988). Rehabilitation management and supported employment. In P. Wehman & M. S. Moon (Eds.), *Vocational rehabilitation and supported employment* (pp. 113–127). Baltimore: Paul H. Brookes.

Menz, F. (1987). An appraisal of trends in rehabilitation facilities: 1980 to 1984. *Vocational Evaluation and Work Adjustment Bulletin, 20*(2), 67–74.

Moon, M. S., Goodall, P., Barcus, M., & Brooke, V. (Eds.). (1986). *The supported work model of competitive employment for citizens with severe handicaps: A guide for job trainers* (rev. ed.). Richmond: Virginia Commonwealth University, Rehabilitation Research and Training Center.

Moon, M. S. & Griffin, S. L. (1988). Supported employment service delivery models. In P. Wehman & M. S. Moon (Eds.), *Vocational rehabilitation and supported employment* (pp. 17–30).

Parent, W. S. & Everson, J. M. (1986). Competencies of disabled workers in industry: A review of business literature. *Journal of Rehabilitation, 52*(4), 16–23.

Parent, W. S., Hill, M. L., & Wehman, P. (in press). From sheltered to supported employment outcomes: Challenges for rehabilitation facilities. *Journal of Rehabilitation.*

Rehabilitation Research and Training Center Newsletter. (1985). Richmond: Virginia Commonwealth University, Rehabilitation Research and Training Center, *3*(2).

Renzaglia, A. & Hutchins, M. (1988). A community-referenced approach to preparing persons with disabilities for employment. In P. Wehman & M. S. Moon (Eds.), *Vocational rehabilitation and supported employment* (pp. 91–110). Baltimore: Paul H. Brookes.

Revell, W. G., Wehman, P., & Arnold, S. (1984). Supported work model of competitive employment for persons with mental retardation: Implications for rehabilitation services. *Journal of Rehabilitation, 50*(4), 33–38.

Rhodes, L. & Valenta, L. (1985). Industry-based supported employment: An enclave approach. *Journal of the Association for Persons with Severe Handicaps, 10*(1), 12–20.

Rusch, F. R. (Ed.). (1986). *Competitive employment issues and strategies.* Baltimore: Paul H. Brookes.

Rubin, S. E. & Roessler, R. T. (1987). *Foundations of the vocational rehabilitation process* (3rd ed.). Austin, TX: Pro-Ed.

Rubin, S. E. & Rubin, N. M. (1988). *Contemporary challenges to the rehabilitation counseling profession.* Baltimore: Paul H. Brookes.

Shafer, M. S. (1988). Supported employment in perspective: traditions in the federal-state vocational rehabilitation system. In P. Wehman & M. S. Moon (Eds.), *Vocational rehabilitation and supported employment* (pp. 55–66). Baltimore: Paul H. Brookes.

Shafer, M., Hill, J., Seyfarth, J., & Wehman, P. (1987). Competitive employment and workers with mental retardation: Analysis of employers' perceptions and experiences. *American Journal of Mental Retardation, 92*(3), 304–311.

Shafer, M. S., Parent, W. S., & Everson, J. M. (1988). Responsive marketing by supported employment programs. In P. Wehman & M. S. Moon (Eds.), *Vocational rehabilitation and supported employment.* Baltimore: Paul H. Brookes.

Sither, G. (1988, December). From segregated to integrated employment: Alexandria, Virginia, targets 1991. *The Advance*, pp. 2–4.

Snell, M. E. (Ed.). (1983). *Systematic instruction of the moderately and severely handicapped* (2nd ed.). Columbus, OH: Charles E. Merrill.

Social Security Administration. (1987). *A summary guide to social security and supplemental income work incentives for the disabled and blind.* (SSA PUB NO 64-030). Baltimore: Social Security Administration, Office of Disabilities.

Szilagyi, A. & Wallace, M. (1983). *Organizational behavior and performance* (3rd ed.). Glenview, IL: Scott, Foresman.

Szymanski, E. M. (1988). Rehabilitation planning with social security work incentive: A sequential guide for the rehabilitation professional. *Journal of Rehabilitation, 54*(2), 28–32.

Tooman, M. L., Revell, W. G., & Melia, R. P. (1988). The role of the rehabilitation counselor in the provision of transition and supported employment programs. In S. E. Rubin & N. M. Rubin (Eds.), *Contemporary challenges to the rehabilitation counseling profession* (pp. 77–92). Baltimore: Paul H. Brookes.

United States Commission on Civil Rights. (1983). *Attitudes toward the handicapped*. Washington, DC: Author.

Wehman, P. (in press). Supported employment: Toward equal opportunity for persons with severe disabilities. *Mental Retardation*.

Wehman, P. & Kregel, J. (1985). A supported work approach to competitive employment of individuals with moderate and severe handicaps. *The Journal of the Association for Persons with Severe Handicaps, 10*(1), 3–11.

Wehman, P., Kregel, J., & Shafer, M. S. (1989). *Emerging trends in the national supported employment initiative: A preliminary analysis of 27 states*. Richmond: Virginia Commonwealth University, Rehabilitation Research and Training Center.

Wehman, P. & Melia, R. (1985). The job coach: Function in transitional and supported employment. *American Rehabilitation, 11*(2), 4–7.

Wehman, P. & Moon, M. S. (1988). *Vocational rehabilitation and supported employment*. Baltimore: Paul H. Brookes.

Wood, W. (1988, December). Social Security work incentives: Funding sources for SE services. *The Advance*, pp. 1, 5, 6.

CHAPTER

20

Employment Opportunities of the Future

Claude W. Whitehead
Employment Related Associates
Washington, DC

Employment opportunities and options today are significantly better than they were a decade ago, but the future promises even more improved and expanded opportunities for jobs in the integrated marketplace for persons with severe disabilities. A number of studies of the general employment opportunities for persons with disabilities have been conducted in recent years (Bowe, 1984; Carnes, 1984; Decker, 1984; Institute for Information Studies, 1982; Vachon, 1985), but most studies do not address the need for ongoing support, which is understandable because the special population with whom we are concerned generally has not been considered as candidates for competitive employment. The goal of this chapter is to provide a base of information on the labor market that will broaden the perspective of educators, trainers, and other service providers, as well as of persons with developmental disabilities, their parents and guardians, and others about the world of work—today and tomorrow.

We examine Department of Labor projections of labor market changes over the next decade and identify areas of growth. From this base we explore the potential for employing persons with severe disabilities within the parameters set by current demonstrations of supported employment and anticipated job developments. For example, one basic challenge lies in compensating for the lack of prior employment experience among most job candidates with disabilities (Whitehead & Marrone, 1986).

Employment opportunities in the integrated marketplace for persons with severe disabilities began opening up in 1985, and consequently any projection of employment in the future to some extent may be viewed as speculation. The concept of nonsheltered employment is being met with skepticism in some sectors of the human services system, even though the feasibility of integrated employment has been demonstrated in several locations nationwide (Kiernan & Stark, 1986; Rusch, 1986; Wehman & Hill, 1985). Also, a recent report on competitive employment placements of more than 82,000 persons with developmental disabilities (Elder, 1986) gives credence to the potential. As the level of penetration of the integrated market continues, the skepticism likely will vanish.

In recent years, a significant movement has been stimulated nationwide through a series of major initiatives. In 1985 an innovative, unprecedented interdepartmental agreement between the U.S. Department of Health and Human Services and the Department of

Education produced a demonstration project series designed to establish statewide networks of supported employment programs for persons with severe disabilities. As indicated in Chapter 1 and elsewhere in this text, ten states received grants in September 1985 and seventeen additional states received grants in 1986. This change follows a 1983 action by President Reagan to establish an Employment Initiative for Persons with Developmental Disabilities. Leadership in the move toward integrated employment opportunities was provided by two Federal agencies: the Administration on Developmental Disabilities (ADD), Office of Human Development Services, Department of Health and Human Services and the Office of Special Education and Rehabilitative Services (OSERS), Department of Education. The campaign was led by (then) ADD Commissioner Jean K. Elder and OSERS Assistant Secretary Madeleine C. Will, who promoted the new concepts of integration, independence, and productivity through numerous contacts with business leaders, conference presentations, and professional journal articles (e.g., Elder, 1984, Will, 1985).

Response to the new employment option for persons with developmental disabilities has far exceeded the expectations of many professionals. The Supported Employment Demonstration Projects generally have shown that persons in this group can obtain and retain employment in the competitive marketplace, but many of the initial demonstrations were restricted in the variety and complexity of jobs, thus suggesting that there is a need for a more creative and informed approach to developing employment opportunities in the integrated, competitive sector.

LABOR DEPARTMENT FORECASTS: WHERE THE JOB GROWTH WILL OCCUR

Projections of employment growth (U.S. Department of Labor, 1984) provide target areas for exploration of job opportunities for persons with severe disabilities. Total employment is projected to reach almost 123 million in 1995, a gain of almost 16 million jobs from 1984. Nine out of ten of these new jobs will be added in the services industry (transportation, communication, public utilities, trade, finance, insurance, real estate, miscellaneous services, and government). The remainder of these new jobs are projected in light industry (manufacturing, construction, mining, and agriculture).

Personick (1985) suggests that one component of the broadly defined service-producing sector, miscellaneous services (which includes business, personal, and medical services), will account for almost half of the 16 million new jobs. By 1995 this sector is expected to account for more than one out of every four jobs in the U.S. economy.

The business services industry is projected to have the most new jobs and the second-fastest rate of growth among 149 industries studied (U.S. Department of Labor, 1985). The continued shift toward contracting out some firm operations and increased growth in the demand for computer software and other modern business services are factors underlying this development.

Jobs in durable goods manufacturing industries are projected to rise by about 1.5 million, but this growth will be partly offset by a decline of 100,000 jobs in nondurable goods manufacturing. Employment in manufacturing is projected just to top 21 million by 1995, slightly below its 1979 peak.

Of the estimated 123.8 million employed for 1995, 8.9 million workers are expected to be nonagricultural, self-employed, and unpaid family workers. The number of persons who are self-employed has been rising in recent years, especially during the cyclical downswing. When new hiring is tight, some people go into business for themselves or supplement their salaried jobs with side business. Most self-employment jobs are concentrated in trade or service industries. Personick (1985) indicates that despite the shrinking importance of the cyclical factor, the projected continued shift to service sector employment will contribute to the growth of self-employment by, for example, increasing the demand for business and professional consultants.

The business sector growth is attributed to two major causes, both of which have implications for employment for persons with severe disabilities. First, many new types of services are integral parts of modern business operations; second, firms have found it more efficient to contract out many of these services rather than rely on in-house staff. An outside contractor can maintain a large specialized staff and enjoy economies of scale not possible for each individual firm. For permanent services, such as security or janitorial services, overhead and managerial expenses are reduced by contracting out, and for one-time, infrequent operations, it is often both quicker and cheaper to hire outside expertise (or labor) than to develop it in-house. Contracting out for the proliferation of new services required in today's economy has strongly spurred employment growth in the business services industry.

Employment in the data processing portion of the computer industry will also increase, but much less rapidly than jobs in programming and software services. Of interest to this study is the development of hardware that will allow more on-site data processing and of an increase in repetitive tasks that generally require less specialized skills than programming and software services. The developments in new hardware and software now permit a firm's own nontechnical personnel (or independent contractors) to perform routine processing, which presumably will bring jobs within reach of our target population.

The temporary help industry is another business service with potential for rapid growth. Firms have become more successful in using temporary help to meet peak loads and to weather business cycle swings without having to hire or fire regular employees. Also, more workers may be willing to work as temporaries in coming years because of the opportunities for flexible scheduling and for part-time employment. Between 1978 and 1983, employment in temporary help agencies grew a rapid 6.6 percent per year, and in 1984 alone the job level increased another third. The use of temporaries is expected to increase by 5 percent a year.

Trade industries also top the list of growth areas. Jobs in wholesale and retail trade and in eating and drinking establishments are expected to grow by 4 million, to more than 28 million by 1995. Of special interest is the projected shift in the type of eating establishments, from dominance by fast-food restaurants to more labor-intensive sit-down restaurants as the population ages and expresses its preference for a more relaxed meal. Other retail establishments showing projected large job gains include grocery and department stores, joined by miscellaneous shopping goods stores, such as those selling jewelry, books, cameras, and sporting goods. Declines are expected in the numbers of jobs in variety stores, general merchandise stores, fuel and ice dealers, household appliance stores, and furriers.

The health care industry is expected to sustain its major growth of the past decade, but the cost-containment measures recently initiated are expected to cause a shift from the general hospital to less intensive and less expensive nursing homes, extended care facilities, and home-based care. The needs of the expanding elderly population also will be a factor in the shift.

Employment in the insurance industry is not expected to show relative growth, but the industry is likely to become more automated, with functions once requiring skilled underwriters becoming feasible for clerical personnel.

The number of private household workers is expected to continue its long-term employment decline; however, the rate of the decline is expected to be considerably slower than it was during the past decade, according to Department of Labor projections (U.S. Department of Labor, 1985). This surprising projection is contrary to expectations of demand growth, in view of the steady current increase in the number of two-wage-earner families. Reports of recent expanding markets for crews of household cleaners employing workers with disabilities suggest that the market may actually be growing if the performance is assured, as it is in the case of the special crews.

Two factors that affect employment are worth noting: the expansion of detailed industries and the changing occupational structure of industries. For example, the growth of health-related occupations is closely tied to the growth of the health services industry, but the growth of the banking industry has little direct impact on the health occupations.

According to Personick (1985), the main causes of occupational structure changes within industries are: (a) technological changes, (b) changes in business practices and methods of operation, and (c) product demand change. Technological innovations may increase or reduce labor and/or skill requirements. In addition to technological innovations, changes in business practices and methods of operation affect the occupational structure of an industry. For example, the growing practice of businesses contracting building cleaning services will reduce the proportion of employment accounted for by janitors and cleaners in most industries. However, the negative effect on employment of janitors will be offset by significant gains in employment in the business cleaning services industry. As the development of work crews made up of persons with severe disabilities expands, this trend has special significance, as does the general trend toward hiring services on a contractual basis as described previously. Providing supported employment in the form of clustered placements and work crews seems to be a concept whose time has come, and equally important, the system is expected to experience continued growth in demand in the future.

IMPLICATIONS OF JOB PROJECTIONS

In order to assess the implications of the Department of Labor forecasts, it may be helpful to summarize the findings that seem to have significance for this analysis of future job opportunities.

High technology growth is good and bad news—technology will assist in overcoming physical limitations, reduce the impact of the decision-making requirement, and expand the range of feasible jobs. But the high technology job market is relatively small (although growing rapidly), and consequently the overall impact is likely to be limited.

The assumption that advanced technology requires higher skill levels has been challenged (National Academy Press, 1984). Sometimes a lesser skill is required; for example, advanced technology may reduce the level of skills needed through the use of new diagnostic tools.

Improved technology is having another impact on jobs, especially service occupations. As a result of medical and health technology expansion, the general population is living longer, thus changing the type and character of service needs (market for services). Implications for employment for the target population include more jobs in the food services industry as the demand shifts from fast-food to sit-down restaurants. Health care has shifted from hospital-based services to more nursing home and extended care services as a result of continued escalation of health services delivery costs and increased government efforts to control expenditures. As the needs of older people become more significant and patients require longer periods of care but are unable to afford hospital services, the shift away from hospital care will accelerate, which has potential in terms of job opportunities for aides, attendants, and assistants. Closely related to the extended care services growth is home health care, another area receiving attention in an effort to contain costs and create a more personal environment. The training of persons with developmental disabilities (as aides for homebound persons) has received very little attention, even though the market is already growing steadily.

Automation may eliminate some routine jobs traditionally filled by persons with disabilities, but it will also create new jobs. For example, modular construction techniques are enjoying increased popularity in equipment manufacturing because of ease of maintenance—the module (component) is simply replaced rather than repaired. One example is the computer industry: computer manufacturing is automated to the point that assembly and repair can be completed by assembling (or replacing) prefabricated modules and components, a task involving far less skill than was required by the previous equipment design.

Part-time and temporary jobs are expected to grow, expanding job opportunities for persons physically unable to sustain a forty-hour work week.

The practice of contracting for services is growing and expected to continue to expand as employers become more profit-conscious (U.S. News and World Report, 1985). This development would permit the current crew labor/work crew model, popular in supported employment, to expand to new fields of business and industry.

Companies are finding it advantageous to break manufacturing and production operations into smaller, autonomous units (Carnes,

1984), moving away from large industrial plants. This change also includes relocating jobs in the employee's home, a change made possible through the development of electronic terminals that can be linked to central computers. Both changes have implications for persons with severe disabilities: the shift to smaller components may increase attention to the continuing need for on-the-job support of employees, and the move to home-based employment may open the job market for persons with mobility and other transportation problems or needs. The advantages and disadvantages of these two trends need further consideration.

Small business enterprises operated by individuals with disabilities provide an untapped opportunity made more feasible with improvements in vocational education programs for students with disabilities. A variety of enterprises have been funded through various Federal resources (e.g., Small Business Handicapped Assistance Loan Program, Federal/ State Rehabilitation resources, and Developmental Disabilities grants), most often as demonstration projects. As experience is gained and technical assistance resources are developed, the self-employment option should expand considerably. It is important to note that the pathway to operating a business enterprise is most often through experience as an employee. Self-employment is not generally a beginner's option.

Labor turnover (hiring and firing/replacement) costs are expected to increase in the future. The turnover problem could represent another opportunity for job placement agencies that serve persons with disabilities to refer job-ready workers, assuming that there has been effective screening and that evaluation of the worker candidates is superior to the traditional services provided to other worker candidates by public and private employment agencies. In addition, the ability of the agency to provide follow-up and follow-along services of placed workers also will be an incentive for employers.

Fewer youths will be in competition for entry-level jobs as the population ages, opening the field for persons with disabilities and other disadvantaged groups.

JOB PROJECTIONS

Growth in selected occupations and declining employment in other areas need close state-by-state examination because of regional and geographic differences (e.g., Rustbelt versus Sunbelt), but for general purposes the projections of jobs (U.S. Department of Labor, 1985) can be summarized as follows:

SERVICES OCCUPATIONS. Services occupations are projected to have sustained growth. A variety of job clusters exists within the category, but the following seem to be the most realistic targets:

1. Health technologists and laboratory technicians;
2. Electronic technologists and technicians;
3. Administrative support occupations, including shipping and receiving clerks and teacher aides;
4. Other services occupations such as food and beverage preparation and service occupations, health (nursing aides, orderlies, and attendants), maintenance (for example, building custodians), and personal service (including cosmetologists);
5. Vehicle and mobile equipment mechanics and repairers, coin machine servicers and repairers, industrial machinery repairers, and office machine repairers.

It should be noted that the above listing is a tentative projection, based on Department of Labor categories. Considerable additional research will be necessary at both the national and state levels. Also, the occupation clusters listed above should be explored both as areas for skilled or semi-skilled placements and as areas in which unskilled workers might be placed as aides and helpers.

An abstract of the job outlook for the period from 1985 to 1995 developed by the U. S. Department of Labor (1984) is presented in Table 20.1 for specific jobs and job clusters that appear to have some employment potential for persons with developmental disabilities. It should be noted that although some positions may not be feasible—for example, for persons with mod-

Table 20.1 Sample of Potential Jobs for Persons with Special Needs

Cluster subgroup and occupation	Estimated employment (number) 1995	Percentage change in employment (percent) 1995	Numerical change in employment (number) 1995
Health Technologists and Technicians:			
Clinical laboratory technologists and technicians	209,000	66	83,000
Employment prospects: Employment expected to grow faster than average due to the importance of laboratory tests in medical diagnosis and treatment, the health care needs of a growing and aging population, and broad coverage of clinical laboratory services under public and private health insurance.			
Technologists and Technicians, Except Health:			
Electrical and electronics technicians	366,000	60	222,000
Employment prospects: Employment expected to increase much faster than the average due to increased demand for computers, communications equipment, military electronics, and electronic consumer goods. Opportunities will be best for graduates of post-secondary technical programs.			
Administrative Support Occupations, Including Clerical:			
Shipping and receiving clerks	365,000	18	[illegible]
Employment prospects: Employment expected to increase more slowly than average due to automation and the concentration of these clerks in slow-growing industries, principally manufacturing and wholesale trade. Nonetheless, many job opportunities are expected because the occupation is large.			
Health Service Occupations			
Dental assistants	153,000	42	64,000
Employment prospects: Employment expected to grow faster than average because of greater demand for dental care and dentists' desire to increase productivity by using assistants for routine tasks. If the abundant supply of dentists leads to lower patient loads, however, dentists may hire fewer assistants and employment will grow more slowly than currently anticipated.			
Nursing aides, orderlies, and attendants	1,218,000	35	423,000
Employment prospects: Employment expected to grow faster than average due to increasing demand for health care of a larger and longer-living population. Numerous job openings are expected, expecially in nursing homes and other long-term care facilities.			
Cleaning Service Occupations			
Building custodians	2,828,000	28	779,000
Employment prospects: Employment expected to grow about as fast as average as the number of office buildings, factories, hospitals, schools, apartment houses, and other buildings increases.			
Cosmetologists	519,000	20	103,000

Table 20.1 (cont.)

Employment prospects: Employment expected to grow about as fast as average as demand for beauty shop services rises. Opportunities for part-time work should be very good.

Mechanics and Repairers

Automotive body repairs	155,000	26	41,000

Employment prospects: Employment expected to increase as fast as average due to growing number of vehicles and traffic accidents.

Automotive mechanics	844,000	38	324,000

Employment prospects: Employment expected to grow faster than average due to the growing number of automobiles. Job opportunities will be plentiful for persons with formal training.

Other Mechanics and Repairers

Vending machine servicers and repairers	31,000	38	8,700

Employment prospects: Employment expected to grow about as fast as average due to the growing number of coin-operated machines in service. Excellent prospects are expected for persons with a background in electronics.

Industrial machinery repairers	330,000	29	95,000

Employment prospects: Employment expected to grow about as fast as average due to the need to maintain complex machinery used increasingly in manufacutring, coal mining, oil exploration, and other industries.

Office machine repairers	56,000	72	40,000

Employment prospects: Employment expected to grow much faster than average as the number of machines increases. Employment prospects will be good.

Construction Occupations:

Carpenters	863,000	29	247,000

Employment prospects: Employment expected to grow about as fast as average due to increasing construction of new structures and alteration and maintenance of old ones. Carpenters with all-around training will have the best prospects.

Cement masons and terrazzo workers	95,000	43	41,000

Employment prospects: Employment expected to increase faster than average due to growing construction activity and greater use of concrete as a building material.

Drywall applicators and tapers	76,000	41	31,000

Employment prospects: Employment expected to grow faster than average due to increasing commercial and residential construction.

Insulation workers	47,000	44	20,000

Table 20.1 (cont.)

Employment prospects: Employment expected to grow faster than average as emphasis is placed on energy efficiency of houses and other bulidings.

Painters	362,000	23	82,000

Employment prospects: Employment expected to grow about as fast as average as more workers are needed to paint new and existing buildings and industrial structures.

Employment prospects: Employment expected to increase faster than average due to use of air-conditioning and heating ducts and other sheet-metal products in new construction and high demand for more efficient air-conditioning and heating systems in existing buildings.

Production Occupations:

Blue-collar worker supervisors	1,200,000	27	320,000

Employment prospects: Employment expected to increase about as fast as average. Nonmanufacturing industries, especially trades and services, will account for a large part of the increase.

Bookbinders	30,000	20	6,100

Employment prospects: Employment expected to grow about as fast as average in response to growth in the printing industry. Opportunities for machine bookbinders are expected to be better than those for hand bookbinders.

Dental laboratory technicians	51,000	26	13,000

Employment prospects: Employment expected to grow about as fast as average due to rising incomes, growing popularity of orthodontia, and the increasing number of older persons who require dentures. Intensified competition among dentists could lead to more aggressive marketing of orthodontal and restorative dentistry, causing demand for dental laboratory services to rise even more. Excellent opportunities are expected for graduates of approved programs.

Furniture upholsterers	37,000	8	3,100

Employment prospects: Employment expected to increase more slowly than average as people buy new furniture instead of reupholstering the old.

Assemblers	1,313,000	25	332,000

Employment prospects: Employment expected to increase about as fast as average. Because most jobs are in durable goods industries, economic conditions and national defense spending will continue to affect job prospects.

Truck drivers	2,402,000	24	578,000

Employment prospects: Employment expected to grow about as fast as the average due to growth in the amount of freight being shipped. Keen competition is likely for jobs in this high-paying occupation.

Handlers, Equipment Cleaners, Helpers, and Laborers

Construction laborers and helpers	576,000	29	165,000

Employment prospects: Employment expected to grow about as fast as average. Job openings should be plentiful because turnover is high.

Source: *Occupational Outlook Quarterly*, U. S. Department of Labor, Bureau of Labor Statistics, Spring 1984.

erate or severe mental retardation—it is likely that there will be jobs such as helpers, material handlers, and other assisting jobs associated with those occupations. In other words, the growth in a specific job demand is expected to generate other jobs that complement that work.

In examining and evaluating the individual job listing, consideration should be given to the range of mental and physical functions represented in the developmental disability category as defined in Public Law 98-527 (amendments to the Developmental Disabilities Act). For example, a person could have good mental skills but be limited in physical function and therefore be a candidate for a job in which mental skills are more important. In addition to looking at potential jobs for the individual worker, reviewers should consider the capacity of work crews or similar group work (popular in supported employment models) to meet the job requirements, especially if the group includes persons with various functional skills and capacities.

This abstract of future job possibilities is intended to provide a catalog of possible jobs over the next several years and, as in most catalogs, the list can be expanded to similar areas. The important objective is to provide a base from which to plan training and related job development activities.

CAREER PATHS AND MOBILITY OPPORTUNITIES

The identification of new job opportunities has special significance. Too often the jobs secured have been entry-type, dead-end jobs with little or no opportunity for upward mobility or promotion, according to reports on the President's Employment Initiative (Elder, 1985) and several reports on the results of state-supported employment demonstration projects, for example, in Virginia, Maryland, Illinois, Montana, Oregon, and Pennsylvania. The creative job search may be expanded through broadening the information base.

Although career paths and upward mobility are becoming an increasing concern of persons with severe disabilities, the importance of getting the first job will continue to dominate placement efforts. Someone who cannot find a job and keep it cannot start an employment career. Instability of the first job should not be a major concern in placement. In the "regular" labor market, first jobs often offer low pay and scant advancement opportunity, but they provide the initial experience that every worker needs in order to advance. The point made by employers in a recent national seminar on the changing workplace (National Academy Press, 1984) was that "technology will change, business will change, the content of the job will change, and one's employer will change, but what will not change is the need to adapt to new opportunities" (p. 12). The major qualification required by employers is the *ability to learn and adapt to changes in the workplace*.

SUMMARY

The future is much more likely to hold promise for economic self-sufficiency for persons with developmental disabilities and others similarly disabled than was ever imagined by caregivers, advocates, parents, and educators. The demonstrated successes in the integrated job market are likely to open new doors of opportunity for members of this special group, who have had a history of discrimination in many areas of their lives. Equally important, we have not achieved the necessary systemic change that will ensure the provision of ongoing support for persons who need help in retaining their jobs, or in getting another job if they are not successful in the first one.

The future is promising, but the need for extensive cooperative community action is stronger than ever. The new worker will have potentially greater levels of support than was previously available but will require help and guidance in identifying career opportunities as well as accessing services. This help must originate in the school system before transition is attempted, and in the community system for adults who have no prior training or employment experience.

QUESTIONS (For answers see p. 437)

1. Ninety percent of the projected new jobs in the coming decade will be in what industry?

2. What business practice changes will result in more supported employment opportunities for persons with severe disabilities?

3. Improved health technology is resulting in the general population living longer. What implications does this have for the employment of individuals with disabilities?

4. Does the author suggest that each state base its plans for future supported employment on national labor projections? Why?

5. What types of jobs are usually available to individuals entering into supported employment?

6. What does the author suggest should dominate placement efforts?

7. In order to maximize the chances for supported employment to result in successful job placement for persons with severe disabilities, where must employment-related services originate?

REFERENCES

Bowe, F. (1984). *Employment trends: 1984 and beyond, where the jobs are.* Arkansas Rehabilitation Research and Training Center, University of Arkansas, Hot Springs, AR.

Carnes, P. (1984). *The future of work for people with disabilities: The view from Great Britain.* World Rehabilitation Fund Monograph, No. 28. New York: World Rehabilitation Fund.

Decker, R. (1984). *Enhancing the employability of handicapped individuals through the potential of small business.* A report of the eighth Mary E. Switzer Memorial Seminar. Alexandria, VA: National Rehabilitation Association.

Elder, J. (1986). *Accomplishments of 1985 under the Employment Initiative: A report on job placements of persons with developmental disabilities* (memorandum). Washington, DC: Office of Human Development Services, Department of Health and Human Services.

Elder, J. (1984). Job opportunities for developmentally disabled people. *American Rehabilitation. 10(2),* 26–27.

Institute for Information Studies (1982). *Small business enterprises for workers with disabilities.* Falls Church, VA: Author.

Karmin, M. W. (1985). Jobs of the future. *U. S. News and World Report, 99,* 40–49.

Kiernan, W. & Ciberowski, J. (1985). *Employment survey for adults with developmental disabilities.* (ADD grant no. 03DD135/12). Developmental Evaluation Clinic. Boston: Children's Hospital.

Kiernan, W. & Stark, J. (Eds.). (1986). *Pathways to employment for adults with developmental disabilities.* Baltimore: Paul H. Brookes.

National Academy Press (1984). *High schools and the changing workplace: The employers' view.* Report of the panel on secondary school education for the changing workplace. Washington, DC: Author.

Personick, V. (1985). A second look at industry output and employment trends to 1995. *Monthly Labor Review, 106 (11),* 24–36.

Rusch, F. (1986). Introduction. In F. Rusch (Ed.), *Competitive employment issues and strategies.* (pp. 3–6). Baltimore: Paul H. Brookes.

Shelp, R. K. (1983). Myths vs. reality—A service economy. *Journal of the Institute for Socioeconomic Studies. 8(3),* 26–38.

Silvertri, G., Lukasiewicz, J., & Fullerton H. (1983). Occupational employment projections through 1995. *Monthly Labor Review, 106 (11),* 39.

U.S. Department of Labor (1985). *Monthly Labor Review. 108(11).*

U.S. Department of Labor (1984, Spring). The job outlook in brief. *Occupational Outlook Quarterly, 28(1).*

Vachon, A. (1985). Inventing a future for work disabled individuals: Stategic thinking for American health and disability policy to the 21st century. National Institute of Handicapped Research, Washington DC (unpublished monograph).

Wehman, P. & Hill, J. (Eds.). (1985). *Competitive employment for persons with mental retardation: From research to practice.* Vol. I. Richmond: Rehabilitation Research and Training Center, Virginia Commonwealth University.

Whitehead, C. & Marrone, J. (1986). Time limited evaluation and training. In W. Kiernan & J. Stark (Eds.). *Pathways to employment for adults with developmental disabilities.* Baltimore: Paul H. Brookes.

Will, M. (1985). Bridges from school to working life: OSERS programming for the transition of youth with disabilities. *Rehabilitation World. 9(1).*

CHAPTER

21

Looking Toward the Future: Questions and Concerns of Supported Employment Service Providers

John R. Johnson
University of Illinios at Urbana-Champaign

The preceding chapters have focused on current issues, research, and practices in supported employment. While effective supported employment practices have been based on issues and research generated from the desire to achieve integrated employment, it is also important to identify the questions and concerns most frequently addressed by those who are directly involved in providing or receiving supported employment services. To some extent this will indicate the degree to which texts and publications such as this one are sensitive to the issues of most concern to service providers and consumers.

Staff of the Illinois Supported Employment Project (ISEP) housed at the University of Illinois at Urbana-Champaign undertook the task of identifying 100 of the most frequently asked questions of professionals engaged in developing, implementing, or promoting and/or regulating supported employment. The purpose of this exercise was not to answer the questions, although many of the respondents provided very specific and comprehensive answers. The purpose of this exercise was to identify the kinds of questions most frequently asked in order to identify issues that may require clarification, policy review and revision, or attention by researchers in the area of supported employment. In addition, implications might be drawn regarding some of the underlying assumptions predicating the questions and the impact of these assumptions on the development and implementation of effective supported employment services. This type of information may also be useful to supported employment service providers in assessing the commonality of the problems that must be dealt with on a day-to-day basis.

METHOD

In November, 1988 a letter was mailed to seventy-one individuals representing Supported Employment Projects from twenty-seven states and nine agencies with a specific interest in supported employment. Respondents were requested to submit at least ten of the most

TOM GRUBER

"Twelve ham please, cheese six, thank you," yells Tom Gruber as he works the grill area of a McDonald's Restaurant in Crest Hill, Illinois. Tom is one of 16 supported employment workers diagnosed with a chronic mental illness and is employed in the program through a local adult services facility.

Tom has worked at McDonald's since December 2, 1987, and loves his job. He began working in the lot and lobby area, but with hard work and determination he moved through a series of positions until he reached his goal: to be part of the grill team.

Once shy but hard-working, Tom is now assertive, confident, and independent. "Tom's skills (as a grill worker) are by the book," states the general manager of the Crest Hill McDonald's. "He works very hard and gets along great with the other workers." But these are not his only skills. Tom is an excellent utility person, working one of several stations whenever necessary and taking on more responsibility every day.

Tom has progressed in other ways as well. With SEP staff backing, Tom was referred in August, 1988, to a residential program. There he learned various independent living skills. Today Tom is sharing an apartment with a roommate in a supervised apartment program. Tom now does his own laundry, prepares meals, pays bills, manages a checking account, schedules appointments, and maintains medications. Tom states, "I've learned independence and discipline in the supported employment program. I've learned to set small goals and go after them; you just can't quit."

What is Tom's next goal? "I want to be a McDonald's Crew Trainer," he states proudly. "I enjoy training my co-workers on a job that I enjoy doing."

commonly asked questions about supported employment they had encountered and corresponding answers to those questions. Of the seventy-one individuals contacted, questions were submitted by twenty-seven agencies representing eighteen states implementing supported employment services and four federal agencies. A total of 568 questions were submitted with 338 (sixty percent) responses to the questions.*

Many of the questions submitted were clearly specific to state rules, regulations and/or programs and were not applicable to all states or supported employment programs. Also, many of the questions that were submitted were frequently encountered by only one of the respondents. Therefore, the primary goal was to summarize accurately all questions that might be of interest to any supported employment professional, parent/guardian, or supported employment consumer or employer and to identify those questions most frequently cited by respondents. Questions specific to state rules, regulations, or programs that may not be of interest to most supported employment programs were dropped from consideration. Questions that were submitted by only one respondent but could be applicable to any service provider or consumer of supported employment services were included to provide some indication of the scope of questions being addressed. This resulted in a total of 453 questions selected for review and summary.

There was one exception to the above procedures. As the results below indicate, virtually all of the respondents had encountered numerous questions about rules and regulations governing various entitlements and funding, most notably Title VI-C for supported employment services. Fortunately, a representative from the Office of Special Education and Rehabilitative Services provided a list of the nineteen questions most frequently encountered by their staff. After reviewing these questions and those provided by respondents regarding rules and regulations governing entitlements, ISEP staff felt that these questions reflected the majority of questions submitted by respondents on this topic; therefore, they were included in their entirety.

The final questions selected for review were grouped into forty categories representing the issues or topics that were most frequently addressed and that reflected each question. These were then summarized by topic into a second set of 122 questions including those developed by the Office of Special Education and Rehabilitative Services for the purpose of succinctly, accurately, and comprehensively representing the final 453 questions that were submitted by respondents. Results of a tabulation of final questions is provided below followed by a discussion of some implications that may be considered.

RESULTS

Table 21.1 is a list of topics representing the final questions by topic. The table clearly indicates that uppermost in service providers' minds were questions related to state and federal regulations governing supported employment services and the funding of supported employment services. Questions related to ongoing support, marketing/job development, and eligibility for supported employment were also frequently encountered by respondents.

Table 21.2 provides a list of ninety-three questions developed to summarize and condense the final 453 questions selected for review.

Table 21.3 is a list of questions related to federal regulations governing entitlements for supported employment and related services. As Table 21.1 indicates, the majority of respondents had submitted a large number of questions pertaining to federal rules, regulations, process, and policy. The questions included in Table 21.3 were considered to be most representative of the questions pertaining to this topic.

DISCUSSION

Clearly, the questions most encountered by supported employment professionals involved the development, acquisition, and maintenance of fiscal and human resources. This raises the basic question as to whether or not supported employment service providers and consumers have the resources necessary to effectively develop or implement many of the supported employment practices described throughout this text. It seems logical that, if funding is an ongoing concern for service providers, then the level of funding might currently be considered minimal or at a subsistence level. If this is the case, then implementing the best practices to achieve the best possible supported employment outcomes may be a logistical impossibility. Clearly, a major effort for the future must be to increase activities at the policy and legislative levels that result in significantly increased revenues for supported employment services.

Another issue that seemed to be frequently encountered was the inconsistency and lack of interpretability of federal entitlements. Clearly, many professionals are asking for clarification or revision in federal regulations governing entitlements that are consistent with integrated employment outcomes and the needs of supported employment consumers.

The questions that supported employment professionals encountered with funding and interpreting federal regulations may have the most significant impact on the implementation of ongoing support services. Initially, the definition of "support" clearly needs to be addressed as indicated in Chapter 8. The problem of ill-defined "support strategies" may seriously hamper the development and allocation of fiscal resources to implement these strategies.

Closely related to the questions about funding, regulations, and the provision of ongoing support are issues revolving around the training and retention of employment specialists. One area of research that has received little focus in supported employment is the impact of staff turnover among supported employment personnel upon supported employment consumers. Winking, Trach, Rusch, and Tines (in press) reported that the turnover rate for employment specialists employed during 1986 in the State of Illinois was forty-seven percent. The question is whether such a high turnover among employment specialists has any impact on the job retention of sup-

Table 21.1 Number of Final Questions Selected Included for Final Review and Number of Respondents Addressing Questions by Topic.

Topic	Number of Questions	Number of Respondent
1. Advantages and disadvantages of supported employment	3	3
2. Behavior	1	1
3. Assessment and evaluation	3	3
4. Case management	4	3
5. Conversion	8	4
6. Costs and benefits	10	5
7. Definitions	9	9
8. Disability related issues	17	7
9. Disincentives and incentives	2	1
10. Eligibility	24	14
11. Exploitation	7	4
12. Family	4	3
13. Federal rules, regulations, process, and policy	53	11
14. Friends	3	3
15. Funding	44	11
16. Information and data management	5	3
17. Integration and segregation	11	6
18. Interagency and intra-agency coordination	10	5
19. Job analysis and job match	10	3
20. Job coach/employment specialist issues	12	6
21. Job maintenance, retention, and separation	11	0
22. Job placement and training	22	10
23. Ongoing support or long-term follow-up	34	15
24. Marketing supported employment/job development	29	16
25. National issues	2	1
26. Program transfer, movement, or change	4	3
27. Supported employment program development, implementation, evaluation, and management	12	8
28. SSI, SSDI, Medicaid	18	13
29. Supported employment outcomes	5	3
30. Traditional v. contemporary employment programs	4	4
31. Transitional employment programs (TEP)	5	2
32. Transition from school to work	8	6
33. Transportation	10	9
34. Types of supported employment	7	5
35. Viability of supported employment	4	4
36. Viability of traditional adult day programs	10	7
37. Wages and benefits	9	7
38. Working hours	6	6
39. Other	13	8
Total Questions Selected for Review	**453**	

Table 21.2 Most Frequently Asked Questions about Supported Employment

Topic 1: Advantages and Disadvantages of Supported Employment

1) What are the benefits, limitations, advantages, and disadvantages of supported employment?

Topic 2: Behavior

2) What is the best means of providing supported employment services to persons with challenging behaviors?

Topic 3: Assessment & Evaluation

3) What types of assessment, evaluations, or indicators may assist the provision of supported employment services?

4) How should they be effectively used?

Topic 4: Case Management

5) Can on-the-job training or support be considered case management?

Topic 5: Conversion

6) What are the advantages, disadvantages, and costs of conversion?

Topic 6: Costs and Benefits

7) What are the "true" costs associated with supported employment including:

   a) the cost of establishing programs,

   b) the initial intensive training and support costs until worker stabilization;

   c) the ongoing, enduring costs following worker stabilization; and,

   d) conversion from facility-based to supported employment services?

Topic 7: Definitions

8) What is the definition of "severe disability"?

9) What is supported employment?

Topic 8: Disability-Related

10) What is the configuration of supported employment services for people experiencing chronic mental illness, physical disabilities, severe hearing impairments, etc.?

11) How should relapses or recidivism be managed for persons experiencing chronic mental illness?

Topic 9: Disincentives and Incentives

12) What incentives/disincentives continue to inhibit the integrated employment of people with disabilities?

13) What kinds of incentives and disincentives exist for rehabilitation facilities to convert to or provide supported employment services?

Table 21.2 (cont.)

Topic 10: Eligibility

14) Who is eligible for supported employment?

15) Who is best served by supported employment services?

16) How do you determine if someone is not "ready" for supported employment or experiences a disability that may be considered too severe for supported employment?

Topic 11: Exploitation

17) What types of procedures are in place for preventing and reporting cases of abuse, exploitation, and mistreatment (e.g., sexual, wage exploitation) on the job or going to/from work?

Topic 12: Family

18) How should client and parent interests, desires, and fears be addressed?

Topic 13: Federal Rules, Regulations, Process, and Policy*

Case closure

19) Following a case closure (successful or unsuccessful) can a case be reopened to provide supported employment services?

If so, under what conditions?

Conversion

20) What is the role of the state vocational rehabilitation and mental health and developmental disability agencies in promoting, managing, implementing and/or monitoring conversion to supported employment?

Retraining

21) What are the criteria for determining when VR will become involved with retraining a supported employee?

22) How is this process initiated?

*See also questions submitted by U. S. Department of Education, Office of Special Education and Rehabilitative Services, in Table 21.3

23) What are the regulations or conditions governing this process?

Services

24) What supported employment services do the state mental health and developmental disability agency provide and/or fund?

Time-Limited Services

25) At what point does the 18-month period of service begin?

26) What will be the criteria for determining when a supported employee has completed the time-limited rehabilitation services?

Vendorship

27) Do vendors that provide supported employment-only services need to be accredited?

Table 21.2 (cont.)

Topic 14: Friends

28) What social networks will replace the one which supported employees maintained in their previous adult service program?

29) Will and should supported employees lose their friends from the adult service program?

Topic 15: Funding

30) Who pays for ongoing support?

31) What are all the federal, state, and local funding sources that may be accessed and used for supported employment services, especially, ongoing support?

32) Under what conditions should selected funding sources be used for supported employment services?

33) How long will funding for ongoing support be available?

34) What types of supported employment services may be funded by Title I, Title XIX, and Title VI-C monies?

Topic 16: Information and Data Management

35) How long is an agency required to document supported employment activities and outcomes?

36) What types of information and data should be collected and with respect to what types of activities and outcomes?

Topic 17: Integration/Segregation

37) What criteria are reasonable for determining regular contact between supported employees and nondisabled persons?

38) Is regular contact limited to contact between supported employees and nondisabled co-workers and supervisors?

39) What is the rationale for limiting the supported employment of persons with disabilities to groups of no more than 8 persons?

Topic 18: Interagency/Intra-agency Coordination

40) Who will be responsible for approving commitments by agencies involving relationships with other agencies?

41) What is the best means of coordinating state and local agencies involved in the provision of supported employment and case management services?

Topic 19: Job Analysis/Job Match

42) What factors are essential in identifying jobs that address supported employee resources, skills, career aspirations, support needs, and personal, social, and vocational preferences?

Topic 20: Job Coach/Employment Specialist Issues

43) What are the skills an effective employment specialist should possess?

44) How does an employment specialist acquire the training necessary to possess these skills?

45) What is a fair salary for employment specialists?

Table 21.2 (cont.)

46) What is the turnover rate among employment specialists and how do we decrease this rate?

47) What are the effects of employment specialist turnover on supported employees?

Topic 21: Job Maintenance, Retention, and Separation

48) What options are available to supported employees who are separated from supported employment?

49) What are the criteria for determining "stabilization"?

Topic 22: Job Placement and Training

50) What are the most effective supported employment training strategies involving:

a) managing challenging behaviors;

b) withdrawing the employment specialist from the job site; and,

c) development of social skills.

51) What training strategies may be considered case management services (and vice-versa)?

52) How much initial training, supervision, and support is typically required until stabilization is achieved?

Topic 23: Ongoing Support or Long-term Follow-up

53) What are the sources for funding ongoing support?

54) Who is responsible for the provision of ongoing support?

55) Who determines what is considered ongoing support services and what are the criteria for this determination?

56) Does the "term of employment" refer to the specific job or to the supported employee's working life?

Topic 24: Marketing Supported Employment/Job Development

57) What are the most effective marketing and job development strategies:

a) in small towns, rural communities;

b) in economically depressed communities;

c) for developing unionized employment opportunities;

d) to expand the range of employment opportunities typically offered to supported employees;

e) for modifying, segmenting, adapting, or restructuring jobs; and,

f) for improving opportunities for advancement in wages, benefits, and job mobility?

58) Who is responsible for marketing and job development?

Topic 25: National Issues

59) What levels of impact and influence are the recent federal legislative changes likely to exert on future response and/or capcity change (e.g., Fair Labor Standards Act, SSA Work Incentives, Rehabilitation Act, Home and Community Care Amendments)?

Table 21.2 (cont.)

Topic 26: Program Transfer, Movement, and Change

60) Can supported employees work part-time and participate in traditional day programs at other times of the day?

61) Should supported employees be moved from crews and enclaves into individual placements when possible?

Topic 27: Supported Employment Program Development, Implementation, Evaluation, and Management

62) What standards and mechanisms for quality assurance are currently in place or are being developed?

63) What types of supported employment services and related options are available for individuals who do not live within reasonable proximity to organizations providing supported employment programs?

Topic 28: SSI, SSDI, Medicaid

64) What has been the impact of wages earned by supported employees on eligibility for, continuation of, and amount of federally subsidized benefits (e.g., SSI, SSDI, Medicaid, AFDC, etc.)?

65) What are the criteria for determining that a supported employee's benefits should be terminated and/or he or she is no longer eligible for benefits?

66) Are there federal regulations that disallow or discourage individuals with disabilities from residing in certain types of residential facilities and receiving supported employment services?

67) What types of supported employment services may be funded through SSA, AFDC, and other federally funded subsistence programs?

Topic 29: Supported Employment Outcomes

68) How successful is supported employment for people experiencing different disabilities?

Topic 30: Traditional vs. Contemporary Employment Programs

69) What distinguishes the contemporary model of supported employment from the traditional model of employment support and assistance provided to persons with disabilities?

70) Is supported employment compatible with traditional adult service programs?

71) What is the relationship between traditional adult service programs and supported employment?

Topic 31: Transitional Employment Programs (TEP)

72) How do transitional employment programs (TEP) fit into the supported employment program?

Topic 32: Transition from School to Employment

73) What is the role of the school in supported employment?

74) Does preplacement vocational training have a role in supported employment placements?

75) Should schools provide supported employment services, and if so, how is the provision of ongoing support managed?

Topic 33: Transportation

76) What options or arrangements are available to address transportation problems?

Table 21.2 (cont.)

77) Who is responsible for developing and implementing these options or arrangements?

Topic 34: Types of Supported Employment

78) What are the various models or types of supported employment and their distinguishing features?

79) What have been the outcomes (e.g., wages earned, hours worked, types of jobs, integration, disabilities experienced) associated with each of the models?

Topic 35: Viability of Supported Employment

80) Is the state-of-the-art in supported and other integrated employment sufficiently developed so as to ensure stability of program establishment?

81) What will be the impact of inflation, economic depression, and high unemployment on supported employment?

Topic 36: Viability of Traditional Adult Service Programs

82) Can/will supported employment replace sheltered employment as the exclusive employment option for persons with severe disabilities who require ongoing enduring support?

83) What will be the future role of traditional adult service programs for people with disabilities?

84) If facilities reduce the sheltered employment population, what are the implications in terms of continuing services to persons too severely disabled to engage in employment activities (too disabled to hold any job)?

Topic 37: Wages and Benefits

85) Is there a "minimum" subminimum wage that can/should be earned by supported employees?

86) Does a requirement that supported employees be paid at least $3.35 per hour represent a barrier to employment for some individuals with severe disabilities? If so, is this not a discriminatory practice if a goal of supported employment is to "serve all persons"?

87) Has the employment of supported employees affected the cost of insurance to employers?

Topic 38: Working Hours

88) Why does the definition require at least 20 hours of paid work per week?

89) Why can't supported employment services be funded for persons who may be unable to work a 20-hour week initially?

90) Are there conditions under which supported employment services may be funded for someone who may work less than 20 hours with the expectation that hours will increase to 20 or more per week?

Topic 39: Other

91) Will agencies be forced to provide supported employment?

92) How obligated are agencies to deal with students in transition?

93) What standards will apply to the evaluation or accountability of supported employment?

Table 21.3 Most frequently asked questions about supported employment submitted by the United States Department of Education, Office of the Assistant Secretary for Special Education and Rehabilitative Services, Rehabilitation Services Administration.*

1. The use of the term "traditionally time-limited post-employment services," as outlined in the State Supported Employment Regulations (34 CFR 363.7) appears to contradict the intent of the Title I basic vocational rehabilitation program concept of post-employment services. How can a case currently in active status, that is, receiving ongoing rehabilitation services, be in a post-employment status (32) when post-employment services are restricted to individuals already closed as successfully rehabilitated?

2. Is the process for supported employment clients any different or the same as the traditional process?

3. Can Title VI, Part C funds be used for supported employment if the employment opportunity is known to be or may be seasonal in nature?

4. Can the State VR unit pay for, or provide with agency staff, agency facilities, or other State unit resources, vocational rehabilitation services after the individual with an objective of supported employment has reached the 18-month maximum?

5. With regard to the 20 hours per week for each pay period requirement (34 CFR 363.7(a)(2)(i)), must a client *already be able* to maintain that level in order for Title VI, Part C funds to be expended, or demonstrate in the development of the IWRP *the potential to reach that level* at a time specified in the IWRP?

6. In some instances, long-term funding agencies in supported employment are approaching the VR agency about reinstituting VR funding for persons closed in status 26 in supported employment, when there is job loss, job destabilization or potential job upgrade. What are the federal requirements relating to VR reintervention post-26 closure?

7. Can Title VI, Part C resources be used once a case is moved into status 06 - Extended Evaluation?

8. If circumstances warrant, can services provided under the IWRP be concurrently or serially funded under both Title I and Title VI, Part C authority? Can long-term support services be funded under Title VII, Part A?

9. Does the time limit of "18 months before transition is made to extended services" (34 CFR 363.7(a)(2)(v)(c)) in the definition of traditionally time-limited post employment services apply to the lifetime of any individual client or to any period of time in which that client's case is opened or re-opened?

10. Is the use of on-the-job (OJT) training funds *and* a job coach under Title VI, Part C considered as paying twice for the same service, or is the OJT viewed strictly as a wage incentive for the employer's time to train either the job coach or the employee?

11. When an individual client is determined eligible for supported employment services, but at a time of development of the IWRP the ongoing support agency is not available, is VR responsible for developing and securing those resources?

12. Is a certificate of eligibility for services necessary for identifying supported employment directed clients?

13. What is included in the "required" supplemental evaluation as described in the law, Section 635(a)(1) and (2) and 635(b) and (c)?

14. What is meant by the notion that the Title VI, Part C program is "supplementary" to the Title I program? Operationally, does this mean there is a "program within a program" or a "program add-on" in the sense the social security related VR programs were years ago, thus allowing clients to transfer from program to program in light of funding availability or client changes regarding eligibility criteria?

Table 21.3 (cont.)

15. The regulations, 34 CFR Part 361, implementing the 1986 Amendments, authorized supported employment as an acceptable vocational outcome under the Title I program, and adopt most of the the key requirements of 34 CFR 363. What is the rationale for the separate discrete formula grant program authorized under Title VI, Part C of the Act?

16. Since the Title VI, Part C program is "supplementary" to the Title I program, are all of the Title I statutory authorities and requirements also applicable to Title VI, Part C program?

17. What are the conditions under which the VR agencies can use Title VI, Part C funds and Title I funds to support an individual in supported employment?

18. After an individual leaves a supported employment job, can VR open a new case even if it may have been less than a year since the individual's case was closed?

19. When an individual is targeted for supported employment and referred to VR, when does the "18-month period" begin? At the point of referral? When the placement planning begins? When actual job placement begins?

*Special thanks are extended to Mr. Fred Isbister and Ms. Judith Miller Tynes for their cooperation in this effort.

DOUG AND DON KRAMER

Doug and Don Kramer are twin sons of Paul and Jean Kramer of Watseka, Illinois. They were born February 5, 1966. The twins are the youngest in a family of five. They were not diagnosed as mentally retarded until the age of five. The local physician sent the family to the University of Illinois to be tested. From there the family was sent to a specialist at Michael Reese Hospital in Chicago. The parents were told the retardation was caused by their premature birth and possibly a lack of oxygen. The twins were diagnosed as having chronic brain dysfunction.

Doug and Don attended special education classes and graduated in 1985. Upon graduation, they remained in their parents' home, unable to find employment. Mr. Kramer contacted a counselor from the Department of Rehabilitation Services for the State of Illinois. The counselor contacted Inez Pedroza, an employment coordinator for a local SEP for the retarded. Doug and Don were given training on janitorial tasks at a supported employment worksite.

In March, 1986, Don started working twenty hours a week doing janitorial duties at Littelfuse, Inc., in Watseka, Illinois. Don did his work so well that he was given a forty-hour shift from 4:30 p.m. to 1:00 a.m. In 1988 Don was trained to operate one of the machines in the factory. He now works four hours operating a staking machine and four hours doing janitorial work each day at Littelfuse.

Doug started working at the Prairieview Lutheran Home in Danforth, Illinois, on June 30, 1986, doing janitorial duties for twenty hours a week. In March, 1987, he also started working at Hardee's in Watseka, Illinois, for twenty hours a week, performing janitorial duties. In January, 1988, he was given the opportunity to work on the food line, preparing sandwiches for approximately six hours weekly. Between the two job sites Doug works forty-six hours a week. The manager at Hardee's stated that Doug "has never called in sick or been late in over a year." Both men receive very good evaluations from their employers.

Doug and Don have shown that they are good additions to the daily work force and good citizens of Watseka, Illinois.

ported employment consumers or the provision of ongoing support to supported employment consumers. It may well be that preventing employment specialist turnover by improving employment specialist wages and benefits and professionalizing the employment specialist position might improve job retention. We suspect that it will almost certainly improve the possibilities for more consistency in the provision of support services to supported employees. However, this will only occur with increased revenues for supported employment programs and greater coordination among entitlement programs and regulations.

While many implications may be drawn from the nature of the questions, two in particular are worth noting. First, the questions seem to be directed more toward the development or implementation of effective supported employment services by professionals and less toward either ideological issues related to integration or supported employment. In short, the majority of questions seemed to be concerned with the means of achieving integrated employment outcomes. While this is certainly expected of supported employment professionals, it may also indicate signs of an ideological shift from concerns with the viability of supported employment to program implementation.

The second implication that might be drawn is that low-level funding, federal regulations governing entitlements, and lack of coordination among entitlement programs may have evolved into significant barriers to supported employment for people with disabilities. As a result, it may be that until a greater effort is placed on coordinating efforts on these levels with the goal of increasing revenues for supported employment programs, many of the strategies discussed in this and other texts may never be applied.

If these issues are not resolved, an ever-widening gap between research and practice in supported employment may develop as a result of the lack of resources to disseminate or acquire information, research, technology, expertise, or personnel. Clearly, these issues will remain an overriding concern of supported employment professionals, consumers, and parents for years to come.

NOTE

*A complete compilation of questions by state is available upon request from the first author.

REFERENCE

Winking, D. L., Trach, J. S., Rusch, F. R., & Tines, J. (in press). Profile of Illinois supported employment specialists: An analysis of educational background, experience, and related employment variables. *Journal of the Association for Persons with Severe Handicaps*.

PART

IV

Introduction: Special Section on School to Work Transition

Paul E. Bates
Southern Illinois University

One of the most significant results of PL 94-142 was the affirmation that school-age individuals with disabilities are entitled to the same educational opportunities as their nondisabled peers enjoy. For the most part, children with and without disabilities live at home, attend school with one another, receive educational services, and participate in a wide range of extracurricular activities. When parents of these children get together, they commonly share stories about their children's school experiences. These discussions usually confirm that the lifestyles of students with and without disabilities are similar during the school years.

Unfortunately, in the absence of effective transitions from school to work, lifestyles of school-age persons with disabilities and their nondisabled counterparts begin to diverge upon school exit. While young adults without disabilities get jobs and experience expanded opportunities for personal control of their lives, those with disabilities are unemployed and experience restricted opportunities for personal control or choice in their adult lifestyles.

Transition from school to work has emerged as a focal point for the diversity of issues that must be addressed to fulfill the promise and intention of PL 94-142. The federal priority on transition from school to work, formally acknowledged and funded in the mid-1980s (PL 98-199), has renewed the commitment to extend the entitlements of school-age persons to adults. Accordingly, transition should be viewed as a dynamic process involving a partnership of consumers, school services, and postschool services that allows people to attain maximum levels of employment, community living, integration, and participation. The pivotal role of employment must therefore be emphasized as a conduit for other significant changes in lifestyle. According to Will (1985), "... all youth with disabilities are capable of moving from school to employment with the provision of necessary support services tailored to the needs of those individuals," (p. 1). For the optimism of Will's statement to be realized, transition from school to work needs to comprise a variety of efforts, including individualized planning, community organization, and statewide interagency coordination.

The four chapters of Section IV provide information on each of these critical issues. In Chapter 22, Hutchins and Renzaglia present recommendations for the development and delivery of a longitudinal vocational training program. They advocate a significant shift in emphasis from prevocational preparation to extensive community work experience that culminates in employment prior to high school exit. This chapter focuses on the curriculum and training decisions that must be made to ensure successful transitions from school to work.

The specific information on program implementation provided in Chapter 22 is supported by Everson and Moon's presentation of a two-level community planning and service delivery model (Chapter 23). In Chapter 23, Everson and Moon discuss the importance of planned change in the development of vocational transition and supported employment programs to enhance the quality of life for persons with disabilities. They describe community planning teams as the primary vehicle to stimulate change in systems and meet the needs of persons with disabilities. At the individual level, they propose that service delivery teams address the issues of specific program implementation and coordination.

In this chapter, Everson and Moon offer insight into the complexity of issues that must be considered in fulfilling the goal of transition from school to work for all persons leaving school. As Ferguson and Ferguson (1988) observe, employment of adults with severe disabilities is more than a training issue; it is a social, economic, political, and historical issue. The emphasis in Chapter 23 on rational community planning through an interagency team approach provides an excellent framework from which to pursue community systems change to create a more receptive social, economic, and political climate for competitive employment opportunities.

The development of effective initiatives in the transition from school to work at the individual, community, and state levels has created new personnel preparation challenges. Renzaglia and Everson identify these challenges in Chapter 24 and propose specific guidelines for meeting a diversity of training needs related to the implementation of quality employment program indicators. The needs of contemporary transition models in the public schools will require personnel who can directly facilitate successful school-to-work transitions. The guidelines for personnel preparation and the delineation of competency areas described in Chapter 24 provide an excellent framework from which to address these needs. As described by Renzaglia and Everson, the competencies for training must be derived directly from the desired program or service outcome (e.g., community employment).

The final chapter of this section provides an excellent summary and comparative review of statewide transition planning efforts. Since federal priorities shift in emphasis over time, the degree to which various states have embedded transition planning and service delivery into their interagency systems may influence the long-term success of school-to-work initiatives. An awareness of activities in other states and the critical analysis provided by Snauwaert and DeStefano offer persons at the systems level guidance in structuring statewide efforts to enhance employment outcomes of persons completing special education. The authors discuss a variety of issues in this chapter and make recommendations regarding key variables such as multi-agency involvement, consensus, policy specificity, resource allocation, and local influences.

Transition is an outcome-oriented process that enhances the quality of life of persons with disabilities as they move from school to an adult lifestyle that includes community employment. The school to work transition needs to reflect a comprehensive concern for the individual with disabilities, the local community of opportunities and resources that support employment, and the statewide coordination of interagency policy. The four chapters of Section IV support this comprehensive approach and provide procedural detail for translating programmatic recommendations into practice. This section complements the previously covered material related to expanding employment opportunities and provides the programmatic precedent upon which adult service models of the future need to be based.

REFERENCES

Ferguson, D.L. & Ferguson, P.M. (1986). The new Victors: A progressive policy analysis for work reform for people with very severe handicaps. *Mental Retardation, 24*, 331–338.

Will, M. (1985). Transition: Linking disabled youth to a productive future. In *OSERS News in Print, 1*(1), 1.

CHAPTER

22

Developing A Longitudinal Vocational Training Program

Margaret P. Hutchins
Adelle M. Renzaglia
University of Illinois at Urbana-Champaign

During the past decade, an increased emphasis on providing appropriate vocational services to individuals with disabilities has produced a plethora of philosophies, implementation strategies, and methods for systems change related to facilitating community employment opportunities (e.g., Bellamy, Rhodes, Mank, & Albin, 1988; Kiernan & Stark, 1986; Rusch, 1986; Wehman, 1981). Historically, the professional perspective on employment has shifted away from merely demonstrating that individuals with disabilities can learn work tasks and maintain acceptable work production rates (e.g., Gold 1972; 1974; 1976; Hunter & Bellamy, 1976; Renzaglia, Wehman, Schutz, & Karan, 1978) to identifying vocational service delivery methods and strategies that ensure the targeted outcome of paid employment within integrated community businesses and industries (e.g., Connis, Sowers, & Thompson, 1978; Hutchins, Renzaglia, Stahlman, & Cullen, 1986). The 1980s witnessed a major shift in our vocational service delivery patterns. No longer supporting segregated sheltered employment, these patterns have encouraged objectives and activities that facilitate competitive and supported employment options for persons with disabilities. Strategies that are most often cited to accomplish employment objectives include developing and implementing plans for creative employment options (e.g., Bellamy et al., 1988; Wehman & Moon, 1988) and appropriate, community-relevant vocational programs (e.g., Rusch & Mithaug, 1980; Wehman, 1981).

A review of recommended practices for providing an appropriate vocational program for students before they depart high school reveals several key components, including (a) conducting a community assessment of potential employment opportunities; (b) identifying instructional objectives that are based on the requisite skills found in actual community businesses; (c) utilizing real materials and training sites to maximize skill generalization; and (d) initiating and maintaining interagency coordination to facilitate transition from school to work (e.g., Connis et al., 1978; Renzaglia & Hutchins, 1988). However, even close adherence to these suggested guidelines and the replication of many related and recommended activities cannot guarantee that an individual with disabilities will become successfully employed prior to the completion of his or her educational program, or even later in his or her adult life. In order to facilitate successful employment outcomes, education must integrate appropriate decision-making strategies with these suggested program components to produce an effective longitudinal vocational training program for its consumers.

A longitudinal vocational program can be conceptualized as one in which (a) specific potential employment opportunities are systematically selected and provided, through direct work experiences, to individual students, and (b) students' progress and employment needs are systematically evaluated in order to determine and secure the most appropriate job placement prior to the completion of their education. The intent of longitudinal vocational planning is to minimize the discrepancy between programmic intent and actual practices, ensuring successful employment outcomes as a result of education.

In past practice a "prevocational" training model has been used to prepare school-aged individuals with disabilities for future employment. Work skill acquisition was a generic focus, purporting to provide these individuals with opportunities to experience "work." However, "prevocational" training has been abandoned by special education and rehabilitation professionals because there is little documentation that training generic work skills actually facilitates employment, or that as a result of this type of training students exhibit generalized work behaviors across unrelated environments or tasks.

Current vocational training practices emphasize the use of natural community settings to teach requisite work skills (Rusch & Mithaug, 1980; Wehman, Hill, & Koehler, 1979). However, merely providing a diversity of community vocational experiences for students is not adequate. Many community work experience sites may not enhance specific vocational skill development, thus fostering outmoded practices that merely provide "experiences" with a generic focus on work behaviors. With a new emphasis on outcomes, we cannot assume generalization will occur from the classroom to the work setting (Bellamy, Rhodes, & Albin, 1986; Brown, Neitupski, & Hamre-Neitupski, 1976). Longitudinal vocational training must be implemented that utilizes strategies for systematically evaluating selected work experiences, employment goals, and the selection and placement of students into actual employment.

The purpose of this chapter is to focus on strategies and issues surrounding the development and implementation of a longitudinal vocational program for students. This program integrates key components of contemporary vocational training practices to produce a systematic plan for delivering an appropriate education. A discussion is provided, with examples, of (a) planning a longitudinal program to collect data that reflect the evaluation of community employment options and student needs, and (b) implementing vocational training practices that promote increasing and systematic student involvement in a well-defined and progressive employment program.

PLANNING A LONGITUDINAL VOCATIONAL PROGRAM

If the intended outcome of vocational training programs for students with disabilities is productive employment, then the training process must be initiated at a very early age. Certainly, by the age of thirteen students should be involved in structured vocational training activities. As students grow older the amount of time devoted to employment training should increase and the focus of training should become more specific. The desired vocational outcome should be actual employment before the student graduates from or leaves school programs.

A basic, necessary component in developing and implementing a longitudinal vocational program is the adoption of a systematic process for selecting work experiences and long-term job placements (Renzaglia & Hutchins, 1988). To effectively evaluate employment training and placement opportunities, two pools of information must be available. One set of relevant data can be obtained through systematic job assessment (refer to Chapter 6). The second source of needed information is gained through evaluation of student vocational needs (refer to Chapter 7). Together, these data sources provide a basis from

Figure 22.1 Developing Longitudinal Programs to Meet Individual Needs

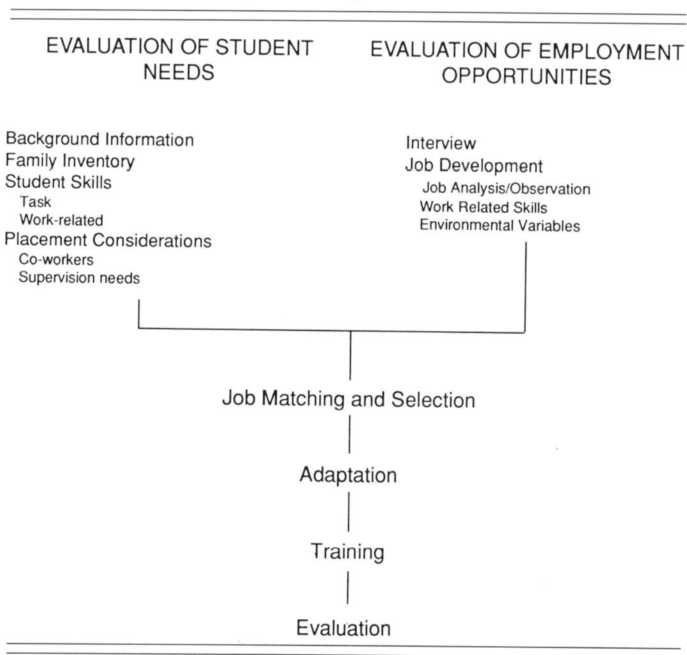

which decisions can be made about the direction and focus of an individualized vocational program and implementation strategies for facilitating employment. Figure 22.1 provides an outline of the process for developing programs designed to meet the longitudinal needs of individual students.

Evaluating Community Employment Opportunities

A number of professionals have supported the practice of developing and implementing procedures for conducting a community vocational assessment in job development (e.g., Brown et al., 1976; Hutchins et al., 1986; Martin, 1986; Rusch & Mithaug, 1980). Typically, job assessment procedures have included methods for investigating potential employment opportunities, requisite skills, and related factors that could affect successful job placements. Components of the job development process that are most often cited include employer interviews and job observations (Renzaglia & Hutchins, 1988). Within each of these components, specific information can contribute to subsequent selection of work experiences and job placements.

EMPLOYER INTERVIEWS. The obvious information that should be obtained in an employer interview includes relevant job types and corresponding descriptions of employee work responsibilities. However, additional information, about employer receptivity to on-site vocational training and/or placement, work schedules, wages, benefits, numbers of employees hired to fill specific job types, and turnover rates are invaluable in determining appropriate work experiences, curricula, and employment (Hutchins et al., 1987) (refer to Table 22.1). A variety of formats for conducting employer interviews have been developed and disseminated for use by vocational training specialists (e.g., Connis et al., 1976; Hutchins et al., 1986; Martin, 1986; Martin, Chapter 6 this volume; Rusch & Mithaug, 1980). The data collected from individual employers may contribute significantly to the pursuit of vocational opportunities that appear to best match the employment needs of a student, are most desirable with respect to wages, work hours, and benefits, and are

Table 22.1 Recommended Components of an Employer Interview

Demographics	Business Information	Experience	Receptivity
Business name	Job description	Previous experiences with persons with disabilities (personal and professional)	Work experience/training
Business type	Job responsibility		Job placement
Contact person and title	Number of employees	Previous contact with vocational service agencies	Adaptations to current employment structure/system
Interview date	Turnover rate		
	Work hours		Adaptations to current work tasks
	Wages		
	Benefits		

the most likely opportunities for future job placement.

JOB OBSERVATION AND ANALYSIS. Perhaps the most significant aspect of the job development process involves documenting the work tasks required of an employee, requisite work-related behaviors, and environmental variables (e.g., available supervision, potential hazards, co-worker presence) for each community business (e.g., Hutchins et al., 1986; Martin, 1986; Martin, Chapter 6 this volume; Rusch & Mithaug, 1980; Wehman, 1981). Information gained from assessing specific job types contributes to work experience and job placement selection as well as curriculum and training objectives.

Direct observation of work tasks in which the methods, the materials, and the frequency of task occurrence are recorded, permits an in-depth review of how a job is structured. Strategies for collecting work task data can vary from extensive note taking (i.e., writing out the sequence of tasks as performed by an employee) (Rusch & Mithaug, 1980) to developing and completing master observation checklists for specific job types (Hutchins et al., 1986). Figure 22.2 provides an example of a master checklist for the pots-and-pans-washer job type. This type of master checklist was developed by observing a number of employment sites that have employees in that job type and identifying the range of tasks, task sequencing, and materials that are required of employees performing the job. The master checklist was constructed, used, and revised to make future observations of employees in pots-and-pans positions easier and more efficient. Hutchins et al. (1986) has developed a number of master checklists for specific job types (e.g., laundry worker, hotel/motel housekeeper, fast-food worker). In communities with large numbers of employees in job types that are specific to those communities, master checklists can be developed and are of great assistance to the observers.

Work-related behaviors can be more subtle and most often are requisite competencies that are not directly related to performing the specified job tasks (e.g., social skills, taking breaks, communication, personal care) (Hutchins et al., 1986; Rusch, Schutz, Mithaug, Stewart, & Mar, 1982). An assessment of necessary work-related skills can be conducted through observation and/or an employer survey. Figure 22.3 provides an example of a format designed to assess work-related skill requirements for a specific job. The authors attempted to present the work-related skills as they may be necessary in the employment context rather than in isolation.

Environmental variables may also influence programmatic strategies and job selection. Curricular and placement decisions should incorporate an evaluation of supervision on the job, co-worker integration, accessibility of the work place, and work hazards to maximize a successful experience and to identify the need for

Figure 22.2 Sample format for master checklist for the pots and pans washer job type, used to conduct job analysis. (From Hutchins, M., Renzaglia, A., Stahlman, J., & Cullen, M. [1986] Developing a vocational curriculum for students with moderate and severe handicaps. Charlottesville, VA: University of Virginia; reprinted with permission.) (Project CO-OP, University of Virginia, Contract #300-82-0359) (V, H, Sp refer to need for vision, hearing, or speech to complete job task)

POTS & PANS WASHER OBSERVATION CHECKLIST

SITE ____________ Date ____________ Observer ____________

V	H	Sp	Skill	Required	Frequency*	Materials and Equipment	Comments
			I. PREPARATION FOR WASHING POTS AND PANS				
			A. Fills sink with soap and water for washg				
			B. Fills sink with water for rinsining				
			C. Retrieves dirty pots and pans to wash				
			takes cart to kitchen				
			loads cart with dirty pots and pans				
			pushes cart of dirty pots and pans to sink				
			D. Removes food from pots and pans				
			scrapes food directly into trash				
			scrapes food into bin to be dumped later into trash/ garbage disposal				
			scrapes food directly into garbage disposal				

*Frequency Code
1 - as needed
2 - 2-4 times a week
3 - one time a week
4 - 2 times a month
5 - one time a month
6 - less than one time a month

job adaptation or accommodation (Hutchins et al., 1986). Figure 22.4 presents a sample of an environmental variables survey developed by Hutchins et al. (1986).

The implementation of these procedures for obtaining specific business and job type information is a first step in designing an individualized longitudinal vocational program. Appropriate application of the information can promote a community-referenced program that can assist in the ongoing evaluation of targeted employment objectives.

Evaluation of Student Needs

The second kind of information that contributes to the development and implementation of a longitudinal vocational program pertains to the

Figure 22.3

WORK-RELATED SKILLS SURVEY

Name of Respondent: ______________________ Position Title: ______________________

Business Name: ______________________ Date: ______________________

PART A

Instructions: *Please select the response that reflects acceptable levels/methods of skill performance of an individual seeking employment in the position(s) marked above the response column. For items 1-5 read choices "a" and "b" and mark the appropriate response in the box(es) corresponding to the position(s) being considered. If "a" is selected, skip item "b" and go to the next category. If "b" is selected, mark all responses that apply.*

Response Column
Position Title

1. MOBILITY

1.a. a. Any method that an individual uses to move about the work setting is acceptable—no specific standards are mandatory.

b. Only the methods that are indicated below are acceptable in order for an individual to move about the work setting:

b.1. 1. being pushed in a wheelchair or by another person

b.2. 2. manipulating self in motorized or nonmotorized wheelchair

b.3. 3. walking with assistance (e.g., cane, crutches, walker)

b.4. 4. walking independently with no assistance

2. MODE OF EXPRESSIVE LANGUAGE

2.a. a. No specific mode of expressive language is mandatory for an individual in the work setting—any reliable method is acceptable

b. Only the methods that are indicated below are acceptable for an individual in the work setting:

b.1. 1. written/picture communication

b.2. 2. gestures/sign language

b.3. 3. oral communication

needs and abilities of the individual student. Students' skills can be evaluated with respect to specific job tasks and work-related skills that are relevant to actual employment opportunities identified through community assessment procedures (Menchetti & Flynn, Chapter 7 this volume; Menchetti & Rusch, 1988; Renzaglia & Hutchins, 1988). Task analyses and systematic informal assessment procedures should be used to identify a student's programmatic needs and capabilities with respect to job skills. Work-related skills (e.g., time-telling, social skills, functional academics) should reflect a vocational perspective and should be evaluated within an employment setting or context (e.g., taking breaks at appropriate times, greeting co-workers, signing a time card). In fact, the instruments used to assess work-related skills required in commu-

Figure 22.3 (Cont.)

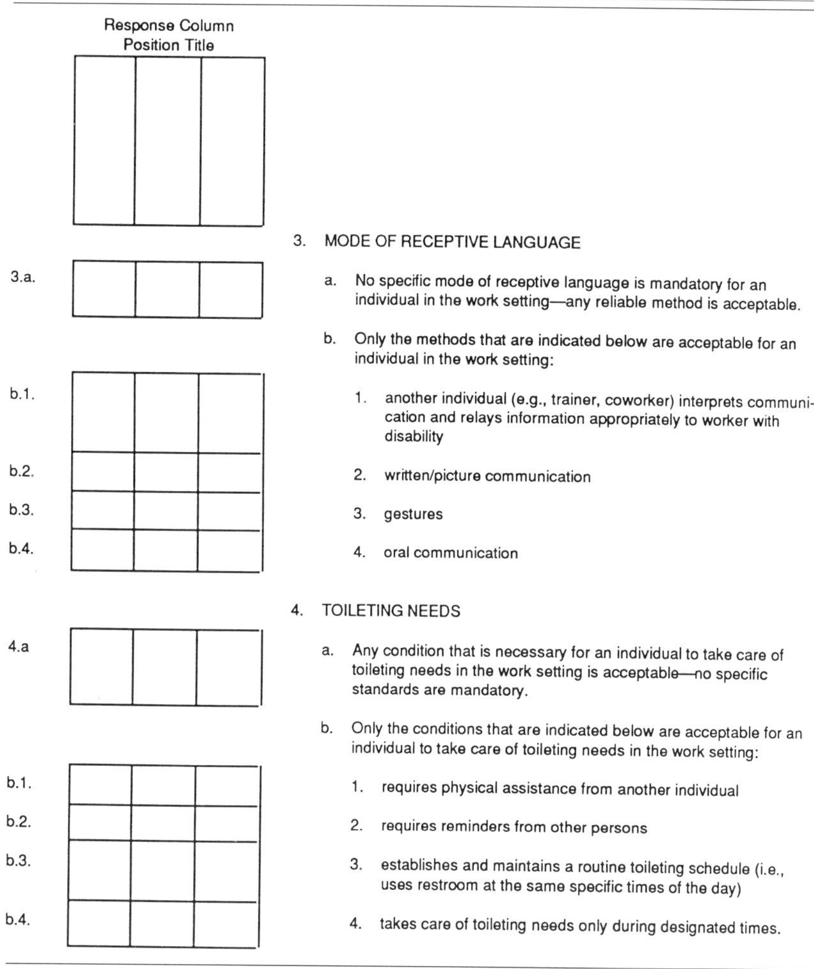

Response Column
Position Title

3. MODE OF RECEPTIVE LANGUAGE

3.a. a. No specific mode of receptive language is mandatory for an individual in the work setting—any reliable method is acceptable.

b. Only the methods that are indicated below are acceptable for an individual in the work setting:

b.1. 1. another individual (e.g., trainer, coworker) interprets communication and relays information appropriately to worker with disability

b.2. 2. written/picture communication

b.3. 3. gestures

b.4. 4. oral communication

4. TOILETING NEEDS

4.a a. Any condition that is necessary for an individual to take care of toileting needs in the work setting is acceptable—no specific standards are mandatory.

b. Only the conditions that are indicated below are acceptable for an individual to take care of toileting needs in the work setting:

b.1. 1. requires physical assistance from another individual

b.2. 2. requires reminders from other persons

b.3. 3. establishes and maintains a routine toileting schedule (i.e., uses restroom at the same specific times of the day)

b.4. 4. takes care of toileting needs only during designated times.

nity jobs can be modified to assess student skills as an initial step in student assessment followed by task analytic assessment on specific skills.

Parent interviews may assist in identifying a variety of family and individual concerns that can often interact with business variables when identifying appropriate work experiences and job placements. Family support has been identified as a crucial variable in successful job placements (Schutz, 1986). Factors that can be assessed with the student and/or family members include transportation, wages and benefits, desired work schedules, supervision, and job preferences.

An evaluation of student needs should include ongoing reviews of student skills and employment needs; evaluation should not occur only once. Ongoing evaluation will assist in documenting the learning progress and changing needs of students as they participate in the longitudinal vocational training program. It would be premature to make summative conclusions about an individual's vocational potential at a young age (i.e., less than sixteen years old) and ineffective to wait until a student is older (i.e., more than eighteen years old) before assessing vocational competence and needs. In a longitudinal vocational program a formative, ongoing evaluation is necessary for the purpose of revising a student's individualized vocational objectives.

1

ENVIRONMENTAL VARIABLES SURVEY

Site____________________ Job Type____________________

Respondent (if applicable)____________________ Observer________________ Date____________

Instructions: *Eight categories of environmental variables (Sections I-VIII) are represented on this instrument. For each item within a section check (√) one response. Items which have only one response may or may not be checked but should be considered. For sections I, if item 1 is checked disregard the other items in that section and proceed to the next section. For example: If item 1 in Section I is checked ("no equipment is used"), proceed to item 1 in Section II. Specific comments on the items and information on materials should be written in the Materials/Comments column.*

Variables	Materials/Comments
I. EQUIPMENT AND TOOL USE AND MAINTENANCE 1. ( ) No equipment is used on job (IF THIS ITEM IS CHECKED (√) PROCEED TO ITEM II)	
2. A. ( ) Unsophisticated equipment (e.g., mops) and/or tools (e.g., handtools) are used on the job	
B. (IF UNSOPHISTICATED EQUIPMENT AND TOOLS ARE USED) ( ) Designated person is contacted for any maintenance and repair that is required ( ) Employee is responsible for maintenance and repair beyond that associated with routine task performance	
3. A. ( ) Small equipment or machinery (e.g., push mowers, clippers, buffers, vacuum) is used on job	
B. (IF SMALL EQUIPMENT IS USED) ( ) Designated person is contacted for any maintenance and repair that is required ( ) Employee is responsible for maintenance and repair beyond that associated with routine task performance	
4. A. ( ) Major equipment and machinery (e.g., cars, trucks, buses, tractors) and/or tools (e.g., power saws) are used on job	
B. (IF MAJOR EQUIPMENT OR TOOLS ARE USED) ( ) Designated person is contacted for any maintenance and repair that is required ( ) Employee responsible for maintenance and repair beyond that associated with routine task performance	

IMPLEMENTING A LONGITUDINAL VOCATIONAL PROGRAM

A longitudinal vocational program should be designed to offer students increasing opportunities to participate in quality job skill instruction that results in acquiring a job. Components of a longitudinal vocational program that require careful decisions, design, and implementation by professionals include: (a) work experience and job placement "core skill," (b) curriculum planning, (c) training scheduling, and (d) instructional planning. Considerations concerning each of these components will change as the student acquires experiences and approaches the completion of his or her educational program. Evaluation and planning will result in the delivery of appropriate vocational services, in which each year of work experiences builds directly upon the skills acquired in previous years. Table 22.2 presents the interaction between age and the components of an effective vocational training program.

Selection of Work Experiences and Job Placements

Systematic identification of appropriate work experiences and placing of students on the job are critical to implementing an effective vocational training program. However, documented strategies for matching students with potential employment opportunities are few in number (Hutchins et al., 1986; Moon, Goodall, Barcus, & Brooke, 1985). Hutchins et al. (1986) described one method for work experience and job placement selection that focuses upon student age and a diversity of vocationally-related variables. Table 22.3 delineates considerations for selecting appropriate experiences and placements by student age.

Hutchins et al. (1986) suggested that for younger students, individual and training variables should be evaluated with respect to available community job types to identify all work experience possibilities. The focus of initial work experience selection procedures should be on an individual's physical and sensory abilities and the availability of training sites and materials. The desired outcome of the process for younger students is to encourage the review of all community-relevant vocational training options that maximize potential employment opportunities.

As a student grows older, the number of variables increases. As a student's on-the-job skills develop, individual needs (e.g., the need for supervision and long-term support) contribute directly to decisions about practical employment options. Ultimately, a review of student performance and needs will result in the identification of a potential job opportunity. In addition,

JENNIFER CORAL

Jennifer Coral is a 38-year-old woman who has been diagnosed with mild mental retardation. She lives with her parents in a western suburb of Chicago. Her brother and sister, each married, live nearby with their families.

Jennifer was enrolled in special education classes throughout most of her academic years. After finishing school, she did not participate in any day program services for thirteen years. In May, 1984, Jennifer was accepted at a local vocational training center and placed into the work adjustment training program. At that time, Jennifer demonstrated a lack of awareness of adult living and had no vocational goals. Jennifer gradually showed improvement, and on January 13, 1986, she was placed as a kitchen helper at Carmelite Carefree Village. She was hired at minimum wage and was eligible for medical benefits and a pension plan. At the beginning, Jennifer's job involved various tasks including making coffee, pouring milk, serving meals, cleaning the dining room, operating the dishwasher, and mopping the floors. Jennifer is currently carrying out the responsibilities of two different positions and is able to set tables, make sandwiches, fill and deliver room service trays, and vacuum rugs with a minimal amount of supervision. In the two years that she has been employed, Jennifer has received several pay increases and has earned two weeks of vacation time.

Before being employed, Jennifer participated in social activities offered by a local recreation group and attended various family gatherings. Since working at Carmelite Carefree Village, she has gone to the holiday parties for residents and staff and a dinner dance that was held for the employees. Jennifer talks on the telephone with some of her co-workers and often socializes with them outside the work setting.

Jennifer's employer describes her as a productive and valuable employee. She emphasizes that Jennifer has learned to respond cooperatively to the direction and authority of her supervisors and is able to work weekend shifts without supervision. Jennifer's parents report that she has become much more sociable, outgoing, and curious since working in the community. She shows self-confidence by becoming involved in things happening around her and not hesitating to ask questions as the opportunity arises. Jennifer feels accepted and needed by her co-workers and states that she hopes her job will continue for many years to come.

Table 22.2 Components of a Longitudinal Vocational Training Program

	Approximate Age Groups of Students		
	Under 16 years	16-18 years	19-21 years
JOB SELECTION	Sampling of a wider range of job experiences (1-6 job types)	Restricted sampling of job experiences (1-3 job types)	Selection of targeted employment site (1 position)
TIME	5-10 hours per week	10-20 hours per week	Number of hours defined by job position
CURRICULUM	Core skills	Core skills +	Skills required for employment by specific business
TRAINING	General case Frequent skills Sequential skills	General case Frequent skills Sequential skills	Mandatory skills for employment

student supervision requirements must be reevaluated with respect to targeted community businesses. Transportation needs, student/family preferences, and job-related variables (i.e., wages, benefits, work schedule) are reviewed and compared with student needs and desires. The outcome should produce a list of recommended long-term job placements that have been ranked in an objective manner.

The use of a systematic method for identifying priority training experiences and job placements is a crucial component of implementing a longitudinal vocational program. The benefit of early initiation of a job matching process is the development of a program that builds logically on previous experiences and considers both student and job variables so that rational decisions may be made about the eventual targeted employment for students with handicaps.

"Core-Skill" Curriculum Planning

"Core-skill" curriculum planning focuses on employment-related skills that are targeted for instruction. A community-referenced curriculum for students with handicaps should be based on the skills identified through community job surveys and the existence of community jobs sites that have been used for instruction. If students are systematically provided a range of work experiences across job types, an appropriate curriculum should feature skills required at each work experience site (Renzaglia & Hutchins, 1988).

Hutchins et al. (1986) developed a method for identifying "core skills" for community job types. "Core skills" are those tasks that have generic relevance to jobs representing one job type. By targeting representative "core skills" for job types in a longitudinal training program, generalization across jobs within a job type should be facilitated (see Chapter 9 this volume) and the skills acquired at young ages should contribute to future successful job placements. Table 22.4 presents a list of core skills for the pots-and-pans-washer job type. As mentioned above, these core skills were identified by observing numerous pots-and-pans-washers across at least 10 employment sites. General skills are those skills that at least 70 percent of the employers required of persons hired in this job type. Specific skills are components of the general skills and/or methods of completing general skills that were identified through job observations. The percentage represented with specific skills indicates the portion of employment sites that required that specific skill.

A "core skill" curriculum strategy should assist educators in targeting appropriate job and work-related skills for instruction with younger students (i.e., those students under the age of thirteen) The skills taught provide a foundation for further instruction in specific job types and making decisions related to placement. As students progress in their vocational training programs, additional objectives from the core skill list can be targeted in employment training. Once a stu-

Table 22.3 Considerations for Selecting Vocational Training Experiences or Job Placements

Students Under 16 Years Old (simulated job sampling)	Students 16-18 Years Old (community-based job sampling)	Students 19-21 Years Old (targeted employment)
types of available job opportunities	types of available job opportunities	businesses which include trained job types
training environments	training environments	employer receptivity to OJT and hiring
materials	materials	
physical capabilities	physical capabilities	physical capabilities
sensory capabilities	sensory capabilities	sensory capabilities
	previous training performance	previous training performance
	work-related skills	work-related skills
	environmental variables	environmental variables
		job desirability
		transportation

Source: From Hutchins, M., Renzaglia, A., Stahlman, J., & Cullen, M. (1986). *Developing a vocational cirriculum for students with moderate and severe handicaps*. Charlottesville, VA: University of Virginia; reprinted with modifications with permission.

dent has been placed in a site selected for long-term employment, core skills will no longer constitute the curriculum. Instead, the curriculum should reflect the skills specifically required by that business—those skills necessary to become a successfully integrated employee in the work force.

Issues related to the selection of relevant work experiences are (a) selecting the method used to determine the number of work experiences in which a student should participate, and (b) determining the evaluation process used to confirm continued training in any specific job type(s). Recommendations have been made suggesting that students should be involved in work experiences across job types for similar lengths of time in order to compare the acquired skill proficiencies of the student across those job types (Hutchins et al., 1986). However, specific strategies for determining the duration of an experience (e.g., three months, six months, one year) and the number of experiences to be targeted are not provided.

We recommend that at least two or three experiences in a school year be targeted for young students with an evaluation of student performance taking place after the year is completed. In some instances, the number of possible work experiences from which selections should be made may be limited because of individual considerations (e.g., physical or sensory impairments) or business variables (e.g., minimal employment opportunities due to low turnover, few employees, fewer job opportunities). These business variables should not result in eliminating training opportunities.

Vocational Training Schedule

Time spent in training and the schedule for accommodating multiple-work experiences constitute a third consideration in developing a longitudinal vocational program. The time that a student is involved in vocational training should increase as the student approaches completion of high school. The scheduling of work experiences is directly related to the number of experiences targeted for training and the age at which vocational training is initiated (Hutchins et al., 1986).

TIME. In the early years of school, vocational training should not be the major focus of in-

Table 22.4 Core Skill List for Businesses Hiring Employees in the Pots-and-Pans-Washer Job Type

Category	General Skill	Specific Skill	%
I. Preparation for washing pots and pans	Fills sink with soap and water for washing.	Scrapes food directly into trash.	
	Removes food from pots and pans.	Scrapes food into bin to be dumped later into trash/-garbage disposal.	20
			70
II. Washing pots and pans	Places dirty pots and pans into sink to soak.	Uses rinse sink.	80
	Scours pots and pans.	Uses hose in disposal area.	40
	Rinses pots and pans.	Dries items with towel.	11
		Stacks clean items to dry.	89
	Allows clean items to dry.		
	Drains sink.		
	Rinses sink.		
	Refills detergent bucket.		
III. Pots and pans storage	Takes clean pots and pans to storage area(s).	*Pots and Pans*	
		Stacks pots and pans on counters/shelves.	67
		Hangs pots and pans.	22
		Cooking Utensils	
		Places cooking utensils in appropriate drawers.	22
		Hangs cooking utensils.	56
IV. General duties	Cleans sinks.		
	Wipes surfaces in kitchen.		
	Sweeps floor.		
	Mops floor.		
	Disposes of trash to dumpster/garbage room.		

Source: From Hutchins, M., Renzaglia, A., Stahlman, J., & Cullen, M. (1986). *Developing a vocational curriculum for students with moderate and severe handicaps*. Charlottesville, VA: University of Virginia; reprinted with modifications by permission.

structional programs. Instead, the educational program should more appropriately emphasize domestic, leisure/recreational, and community skills. However, as a student grows older (perhaps older elementary age), structured vocational training periods should be scheduled. At these young ages, five to ten hours per week would seem adequate. As the student continues in the educational program, the emphasis on vocational training should be increased, so that by high school, one-half of the school day is spent in vocational training. Toward the end of high school, the student should spend increasing amounts of time in potential jobs. The amount of time to be spent on the job also may vary according to whether the student shares a job or is employed part-time. In either case, the longitudinal vocational program should provide the student with the opportunity for increasingly more relevant employment.

SCHEDULE. The scheduling of work experience training for a student is influenced by staffing, training needs, and number of job experiences targeted during the school year. Training in multiple job types or settings may be provided across consecutive periods of time within the school year (e.g., a laundry placement for 6 months and then a dishwasher placement for 6 months) or concurrently with job training on different job types rotated across the week (e.g., laundry experience on Monday, Wednesday, and Friday and dishwashing experience on Tuesday and Thursday). No empirical evidence is available to suggest whether a concurrent or consecutive training schedule is more effective. However, unless time periods in a consecutive schedule are relatively short (e.g., 3 months), there will be few opportunities for training multiple experiences and obtaining enough information to make decisions about student progress. On the other hand, skill maintenance may be an issue if training is provided for short periods of time. These issues must be carefully addressed when developing a training schedule for individual students. A longitudinal vocational program should systematically determine an appropriate training schedule that maximizes a method of providing job skill instruction resulting in meaningful learning.

Skill Training

The final component of a longitudinal vocational training program is the development of individualized training plans in which students learn the skills necessary for job success. The plan should result in the specification of a skill training program within a particular job type, and a curriculum should be identified that reflects demands and tasks relevant to that job type or business. Skills selected for instruction should include work tasks (e.g., mopping floors, washing dishes, making beds), work-related tasks (e.g., punching in/out on a time clock, requesting needed materials), and appropriate social behaviors (e.g., greeting co-workers, conversing at break time or lunch). In addition, the instructional period should be organized to provide students with opportunities to learn work routines that approximate the demands and conditions found at the site. Table 22.5 provides an example of a two-hour work routine for a bus person at a university dining hall. Use of this strategy will avoid the problems associated with training skills and parts of skills in isolation. Structuring the vocational training time to closely adhere to the realistic demands of the work site allows the student to participate in skill acquisition and/or maintenance for multiple objectives and to develop a sense of self-monitoring and job independence.

The selection of tasks for skill training during a work experience can be determined using a variety of approaches or rationales. One approach involves identifying and teaching a cluster of tasks in which employees for that job type are engaged for a majority of the work time (e.g., bussing tables for bus person; mopping and buffing floors for custodial workers; sorting clothes and loading washers and dryers for laundry workers) as opposed to tasks that have lesser significance and are completed on an infrequent schedule. A second approach may be to select a cluster of skills required on the job that have similar instructional needs or are similar in skill requirements but may not be completed in sequence in the job routine (e.g., wiping and dusting equipment and furniture; mopping, vacuuming, buffing large floor areas). A third approach emphasizes clustering skills together that result in a natural outcome or product (e.g., stripping and making beds for a housekeeper; removing clean dishes and utensils from the dishwashing machine, sorting, and storing them for a dishwasher) rather than selecting isolated skills that are unrelated and are not linked as part of a sequence of responsibilities.

The most important consideration in organizing the skill training program is to negotiate with the employer the tasks that would be most appropriate to target as objectives. Gaining insight into the perspective of the employer will result in the most effective and efficient approach to take. One purpose of the work experience is to permit a student to acquire valued and job-relevant work skills that demonstrate the student's proficiency in specific tasks within specific job types and to build the skills if the job type is selected for further training.

Students for whom job placement sites have been selected may benefit from the use of the previously-mentioned approaches to identifying appropriate skill clusters for instruction. However, prior to selecting an approach to targeting specific skill clusters for training, tasks to become the primary responsibility of the student employee must be validated with the employer. If alternative employment strategies (e.g., job restructuring, job sharing, part-time employment) are identified to meet the vocational needs of the student and are agreed upon by the employer, then it is imperative to specifically designate the range of tasks that constitute the "new" job description for the individual student. Skill instruction must occur on those tasks for which the student employee is respon-

Table 22.5 Sample Vocational Training Schedule for a Bus Person

Time	Instructional Program
8:30 - 8:35	Entering work site/reporting to Employee lockeroom
8:35 - 8:50	Uniform changing
8:50 - 9:00	Clock in
9:00 - 9:20	Bussing skill cluster
	a) wiping tables
	b) loading tray carts
	c) unloading carts onto the coveyor belt
9:20 - 9:40	Wiping skill cluster
	a) wiping tables
	b) wiping chairs
	c) wiping utensil station
	d) wiping drink dispenser station
9:40 - 9:50	Break time skill cluster
	a) use of timer to monitor break
	b) getting snack/drink
9:50 - 10:05	Bussing skill cluster
10:05 - 10:20	Wiping skill cluster
10:20 - 10:30	Clock out
10:30 - 10:45	Uniform changing
* Ongoing	Communication skill cluster
	a) greeting co-workers
	b) indicating needs (materials, assistance)
	c) responding to conversation
	d) initiating conversation

sible, and the number of tasks initially targeted can increase as proficiency is gained and the student spends more time at the work site.

The other factor related to skill instruction that must exist within a longitudinal vocational training program is the use of systematic instructional methodologies (Renzaglia & Hutchins, 1988). Skills must be directly taught and should not be expected to be acquired through mere exposure to work settings. Specific objectives should be identified that articulate conditions, measurable behaviors, and performance criteria in order to most adequately evaluate student performance. Training procedures should be delineated to provide consistent assistance and feedback to the student. Guidelines and examples for selecting and specifying procedural components are many (e.g., Bellamy, Horner, & Inman, 1979; Berg, Wacker, & Flynn, Chapter 9 this volume; Renzaglia, Bates, & Hutchins, 1981; Renzaglia & Hutchins, 1988; Rusch & Mithaug, 1980; Wacker & Berg, 1986; Wehman, Renzaglia, & Bates, 1985). At a minimum, instructional programs should include a description of the antecedent conditions (natural cues and prompts), a task analysis, consequences to be delivered (reinforcement and error correction), a method for withdrawing the additional assistance and supervision once skills have been acquired, and a method for evaluating performance across time and conditions. By specifying these procedures and those presented by Berg, Wacker, and Flynn (Chapter 9 this volume), teachers will be more consistent in their instructional interactions and expectations, thus promoting learning.

SUMMARY

In summary, if students are to achieve meaningful employment, a longitudinal approach is critical. Careful thought must be given to long-range goals and desired outcomes before designing any student's program. This is only possible if community opportunities have been systematically evaluated, and the skill requirements have been delineated and systematically selected based on individual student need. Then, carefully scheduled instruction is required. Through careful monitoring, documentation, and evaluation over time, placement in integrated employment settings prior to graduation from school programs can be a reality.

QUESTIONS (For answers see pp. 366-379)

1. What are the major features of a longitudinal vocational program?

2. What is the intent of longitudinal vocational planning?

3. What are the components of a longitudinal vocational program that require careful decisions, design, and implementation by professionals?

4. What are core skills?

5. In general terms, describe how much time a student should spend in vocational training throughout their school career?

6. At minimum, instructional programs should include what components?

REFERENCES

Bellamy, G. T., Horner, R., & Inman, D. (1979). *Vocational training of severely retarded adults.* Baltimore: University Park Press.

Bellamy, G. T., Rhodes, L., & Albin, J. M. (1986). Supported employment. In W. E. Kiernan & J. A. Stark (Eds.), *Pathways to employment for adults with developmental disabilities* (pp. 129–138). Baltimore: Paul H. Brookes.

Bellamy, G. T., Rhodes, L. E., Mank, D. M., & Albin, J. M. (1988). *Supported employment: A community implementation guide.* Baltimore: Paul H. Brookes.

Brown, L., Nietupski, J., & Hamre-Nietupski, S. (1976). Criterion of ultimate functioning. In M. Thomas (Ed.), *Hey don't forget about me!* (pp. 2–15). Reston, VA: Council for Exceptional Children.

Connis, R. T., Sowers, J., & Thompson, L. E. (1978). *Training the mentally handicapped for employment: A comprehensive manual.* New York: Human Sciences Press.

Gold, M. (1972). Stimulus factors in skill training of the retarded on a complex assembly task: Acquisition, transfer and retention. *American Journal of Mental Deficiency, 76,* 517–526.

Gold, M. (1974). Redundant cue removal in skill training of retarded adolescents on a complex assembly task: Acquisition, transfer, and retention. *Education and Training of the Mentally Retarded, 9,* 5–8.

Gold, M. (1976). Task analysis of a complex assembly task by the retarded blind. *Exceptional Children, 43,* 78–84.

Hunter, J. & Bellamy, T. (1976). Cable harness construction for severely retarded adults: A demonstration of training technique. *AAESPH Review, 1,* 2–13.

Hutchins, M. P., Renzaglia, A., Stahlman, J., & Cullen, M. E. (1986). *Developing a vocational curriculum for students with moderate and severe handicaps.* Charlottesville, VA: University of Virginia.

Kiernan, W. E. & Stark, J. A. (Eds.). (1986). *Pathways to employment for adults with developmental disabilities.* Baltimore: Paul H. Brookes.

Martin, J. E. (1986). Identifying potential jobs. In F. R. Rusch (Ed.) *Competive employment issues and strategies* (pp. 165-185). Baltmore: Paul H. Brooks.

Menchetti, B. M. & Rusch, F. R. (1988), Vocational evaluation and eligibility for rehabilitation service. In P. Wehman & M. S. Moon (Eds.), *Vocational rehabilitation and Supported employment* (pp. 79-90), Baltimore: Paul H. Brookes.

Moon, S., Goodall, P., Barcus, M., & Brooke, V. (1985). *The supported work model of competitive employment for citizens with severe handicaps: A guide for job trainers.* Richmond: Virginia Commonwealth University.

Renzaglia, A., Bates, P., & Hutchins, M. (1981). Vocational skills instruction for handicapped adolescents and adults. *Exceptional Education Quarterly, 2*, 61–73.

Renzaglia, A. & Hutchins, M. (1988). A community-referenced approach to preparing persons with disabilities for employment. In P. Wehman & M. S. Moon (Eds.), *Vocational rehabilitation and supported employment* (pp. 91-110). Baltimore: Paul H. Brookes.

Renzaglia, A., Wehman, P., Schutz, R., & Karan, O. (1978). Use of cue redundancy and positive reinforcement to accelerate production in two profoundly retarded workers. *British Journal of Social and Clinical Psychology, 17*, 183–187.

Rusch, F. R., (Ed.). (1986). *Competitive employment issues and strategies*. Baltimore: Paul H. Brookes.

Rusch, F. & Mithaug, D. (1980). *Vocational training for mentally retarded adults: A behavior analytic approach*. Champaign, IL: Research Press.

Rusch, F. R., Schutz, R. P., Mithaug, D. E., Stewart, J. E., & Mar, D. E. (1982). *Vocational assessment and curriculum guide*. Seattle: Exceptional Education.

Schutz, R. P. (1986). Establishing a parent-professional partnership to facilitate competitive employment. In F. R. Rusch (Ed.), *Competitive employment issues and strategies* (pp. 289-302). Baltimore: Paul H. Brookes.

Wacker, D. P. & Berg, W. K. (1986). Generalizing and maintaining work behavior. In F. R. Rusch (Ed.),*Competitive employment issues and strategies* (pp. 129–140). Baltimore: Paul H. Brookes.

Wehman, P. (1981). *Competitive employment: New horizons for severely disabled individuals*. Baltimore: Paul H. Brookes.

Wehman, P., Hill, J., & Koehler, F. (1979). Helping severely handicapped students to enter competitive employment. *Journal of the Association for Persons with Severe Handicaps, 4*, 274–290.

Wehman, P. & Moon, M. S. (Eds.). (1988). *Vocational rehabilitation and supported employment*. Baltimore: Paul H. Brookes.

Wehman, P., Renzaglia, A., & Bates, P., (1985). *Functional living skills for moderately and severely handicapped individuals*. Austin, TX: PRO-ED.

CHAPTER

23

Developing Community Program Planning and Service Delivery Teams

Jane M. Everson
Helen Keller National Center, Sands Point, New York
M. Sherril Moon
Children's Hospital Boston, Massachusetts

In a humorous fashion, Medard Gabel has defined planning as "an attempt to solve twenty-five-year regional or global problems with four-year local solutions staffed with two-year personnel funded with one-year allocations that have been budgeted by bureaucrats who cannot see more than six months in advance and who know next to nothing about the problems they are addressing." (Gabel, 1984, p. 21). Anyone who has ever been involved in a program planning effort, whether federally, state, or locally directed and funded, probably recognizes both the humor and the truth in this definition. Program development is a crucial task for community program personnel, yet very few professionals are aware of program development theory and practices and also have the skills to implement theory and practices within their local programs.

As vocational transition models and supported employment approaches become more widespread throughout the United States, community program personnel are being asked to assume new and different roles and responsibilities as community program planners. These new roles and responsibilities require skills commonly associated with the human services professions such as client assessment, skill training, case management, and client program development as well as skills commonly associated with the business professions such as economic development, marketing, and financial accountability. In addition, knowledge of exemplary vocational training and job placement practices and plain old-fashioned work experience have been described as desirable skills for supported employment program planners (Everson, 1989). It is the exceptional supported employment program planner, however, who is knowledgeable about program development theory and practices *and* has the desired skills described above.

One solution to this problem is personnel preparation, both at the preservice and inservice levels. Personnel preparation efforts in supported employment have been described in detail elsewhere (e.g., Buckley, Albin, & Mank, 1988; Kregel & Sale, 1988; as well as in chapter 24 in this book). Another solution (and one that should optimally be combined with personnel preparation efforts) is the development of community program planning and service delivery teams. Teams have been widely discussed in human services literature and, more recently, in vocational transition and supported employment literature (Bellamy, Rhodes, Mank, & Albin, 1988; Everson & Moon, 1987; Wehman, Moon, Everson, Wood, and Barcus 1988). The purpose of this chapter is to describe a rational and comprehensive approach (Brager & Hollowzy, 1978, Kettner, Daley, & Nichols, 1985; Mayer, 1985) to community program planning and development using interagency teams of local program personnel to plan, develop, and implement vocational transition and supported employment programs for individuals with disabilities. This comprehensive approach to community program planning requires the development of two levels of teams—community program planning teams and service delivery teams.

RATIONAL COMMUNITY PROGRAM PLANNING

Community program planning may be defined as a conscious and deliberate decision-making process engaged in by a formal team of individuals (Kettner et al., 1985; Mayer, 1985). "Rational" characterizes planning that uses reason "as opposed to impulse, prejudice, coercion, power, or arbitrary thinking in justifying an assertion or course of action" (Mayer, 1985, p. 9).

Rational community program planning may be further distinguished from unplanned change by four characteristics (Kettner et al., 1985). First, the planned change is guided by a team of community program personnel who agree to serve as change agents in their local community (Bellamy et al., 1988; Wehman et al., 1988). Second, the planned change is limited in scope, agreed upon by all team members, and formalized in a mission statement, program proposal, or interagency agreement (Bellamy et al., 1988; Wehman et al., 1988). Third, the planned change includes a role for all active consumers and potential consumers (Kettner et al., 1985). Fourth, the planned change is directed toward enhancing the quality of life of service recipients and is evaluated accordingly (Bellamy et al., 1988; Wehman et al., 1988). In summary, when vocational transition and supported employment programs are identified as a potential community need, a team of community program personnel must be willing to commit the time and resources to planning and developing programs that are defined by these characteristics. For the purpose of this chapter, the goal of a community program planning team is to rationally plan and develop vocational transition and supported employment programs. The goal of a service delivery team is to plan and provide program services to the target service recipients.

DEVELOPING COMMUNITY PROGRAM PLANNING TEAMS

The use of community program planning teams in vocational transition and supported employment programs has recently been described in professional literature (e.g., Bates, Suter, & Poelvoorde, 1986; Bellamy et al., 1988; Wehman et al., 1988). In addition, Virginia and Illinois state transition task forces have advocated their use, and Minnesota has formally mandated their use through state legislation (Everson, 1988). Indeed, state planning and service delivery teams have been federally mandated for infant and toddler pre-school handicapped programs by PL 99-457, the Education for all Handicapped Children Act Amendments of 1986. In each of these examples, the use of local planning and service delivery teams is based on two assumptions: (1) interagency planning and service delivery eliminates service gaps, avoids service duplication, and makes more efficient use of scarce resources; and (2) transdisciplinary planning and service delivery teams reduce professional territoriality and increase holistic planning and service delivery.

For the purpose of this chapter, a community program planning team may be defined as a team of key local professionals, parents, consumers of services, and other advocates who are committed to planning and facilitating local systems change. A team may be initiated and organized by any one or more potential team members or by external consultants.

Step 1: Initiating a Team

Alinsky (1971), Kettner et al. (1985) and Wehman et al. (1988) have advocated systems change initiation by local program managers and administrators, local program direct service personnel, parents, community advocates, and external consultants such as university faculty or program personnel from other programs or states. The individual or group of individuals who initiate the team's development are typically the first to identify a need or opportunity for change in the locality. This individual or core group of individuals typically have met informally to discuss the perceived problem or need. Eventually, the problem or need becomes more clearly defined and someone suggests the formation of a committee or task force to study the need. Unfortunately, this is where many committees begin and end (Tropman, Johnson, & Tropman, 1979).

Consider this example. A high school special education teacher has become increasingly frustrated with his job and the special education system. Over the past five years he has attended conferences and taken university courses that have emphasized the need for community-based vocational instruction, transition planning, and supported employment outcomes. Each year he has attempted to modify his curriculum and teaching practices to incorporate these concepts. Each year, however, he watches nearly every one of his students leave school with inadequate vocational training and poor employment prospects. Earlier this week he telephoned the local department of rehabilitation services and inquired about supported employment programs. The counselor he spoke with said she would be glad to refer clients to supported employment programs if they were locally available. Today in the teachers' lounge he expressed his frustration to another teacher who agreed with him. In many schools this is as far as this example would go. Increasingly, however, local school personnel are recognizing this frustration as an opportunity for local systems change efforts and are taking the next step—initiating the development of a task force or committee (Wehman et al., 1988).

Step 2: Defining the Community Need

A need may be defined as a lack of something useful or desired. In the example given earlier, the special education teacher and the vocational rehabilitation counselor recognized the need for improved high school vocational training, transition planning, and supported employment outcomes. Before a community program planning team is fully developed, the individual or group of individuals who have recognized the local need should spend some time defining the need more clearly. This is an important step to take *before* a community identifies a potential solution. Frequently, a need is recognized by both professionals and parents within a locality, but the need is never translated into a solution. In some cases a solution is identified without a careful analysis of the local need.

Once the need has been defined by one or more individuals, the next step is to answer the question: Is a community program planning team a potential solution to the local need? The concept of a community program planning team is flexible enough to address the needs of many communities where a lack of interagency coordination or service availability is the identified need. For example, if the community identifies the need as a lack of coordination between schools, vocational rehabilitation services, and case management services for young adults with disabilities or a lack of supported employment programs or even more broadly, a lack of community integration opportunities by young adults with disabilities, the development of a community program planning team may offer the locality a potential solution.

Step 3: Identifying Team Members

The next task that must be undertaken by this core individual or core group of individuals is the identification of additional key team members. Wehman et al. (1988) have noted that community program planning teams should include representatives from special education, vocational education, vocational rehabilitation, mental health/mental retardation, developmental disabilities agencies, parent groups, consumer self-advocates, universities or community colleges, Private Industry Councils (PICs), social security, rehabilitation associations, United Way and/or other community programs (p. 54). Figure 23.1 is a worksheet to assist local program personnel in identifying the key agencies or programs in their locality so that critical agencies and programs may be represented on the team.

Initially, the core individual or group of individuals should list *all* of the agencies and programs that they can think of under each category, being careful not to omit agencies and programs that they have not worked well with in the past. At this point, specific staff to represent the agency or program should not be identified.

Once the group has identified all of the agencies and programs they can think of, they should circle those that they feel are critical to addressing the identified local need. An umbrella group for each category could possibly represent the individual organizations or programs. For example, the local Association of Retarded Citizens (ARC) may be chosen to represent parents' concerns. The local association of rehabilitation facilities may be chosen in larger localities to represent each of the sheltered workshops. The pivotal agencies—education and rehabilitation services—will need strong representation from special educators, vocational educators, and rehabilitation counselors. Ideally, a team should be made up of between five and ten members (Wehman et al., 1988; Tropman et al., 1979).

Step 4: Holding an Initial Planning Meeting

Before the group identifies specific individuals to serve on the community program planning team, the individual or group of individuals assuming responsibility for the team's development must foster the participation of all the local organizations and agencies that have been identified as critical (Bertcher, 1979).

One way to accomplish this is to send a letter to the directors, superintendents, commissioners, or other leaders of the identified critical agencies and organizations. The purpose of the letter is to encourage each agency or organization to send a representative to an initial information sharing and planning meeting. The letter should include:

- A statement of the perceived community need.
- A rationale for the identification of a community program planning team as a potential solution.
- A statement of why the agency or organization's participation on the team is critical.
- A brief statement of the objectives and activities in which the community program planning team might participate.
- A meeting date, time, and place.
- A contact person for additional information.

The individual or group planning the development of the community program planning team should discuss and answer these questions:

- *Who* should send the letter?
- One or more agencies or programs?
- *Who* should sign it?
- Should it be written on letterhead?
- *Where* is the most appropriate location to hold the meeting?
- *What* is the best time for parents and professionals to attend?
- *How* should the letter be followed up?
- A telephone call?
- An enclosed response form to indicate participation?

Before the first meeting, the individual or group planning the team should establish an agenda that encourages information sharing among the identified agencies and organizations. The agenda should allow:

Figure 23.1

Other Local
Community Organizations

Parent, Consumer and
Civic Organizations

Educational Agencies
and Organizations

Your
Local Community

Business and
Industrial Organizations

Social Services
Agencies and Organizations

Rehabilitation Agencies

- Introductions, both formal and informal–*who* is attending and *whom* do they represent?
- A description of the perceived community need.
- Supporting community data to document the need.
- A restatement of the rationale for development of a community program planning team.
- A rationale for the inclusion of each of the agencies and organizations as a critical representative.
- Nomination of a temporary chairperson.
- A date, time, and location for a second meeting.

The objective of the initial meeting is to obtain the participation of key agencies and programs and to lay the groundwork for a commitment to rational community program planning. Over the next six to twelve months the newly-formed team should meet monthly or bimonthly to develop a proposal or action plan to meet the community's identified need (Bellamy et al., 1988; Wehman et al., 1988).

DEVELOPING A PROPOSAL OR ACTION PLAN

Step 5: Defining the Community Program Planning Team's Mission

The next step a newly-formed community program planning team must take toward developing a proposal or action plan for program change is to develop a shared value base and agree on a mission statement (Bellamy et al., 1988; Wehman et al., 1988). For example, a team that has identified a need for postsecondary employment programs for youth with disabilities must spend time exploring individual members' feelings about wages, integration, and support. A team that has identified a need for vocational transition planning must spend time exploring individual members' feelings about school personnel and adult service providers' roles and responsibilities as well as feelings about community-referenced curriculum.

One community program planning team in a rural Virginia school system found the activity in Figure 23.2 below helpful as they explored their feelings and values about community-based instruction and vocational transition planning. The next step for this team was to use the discussion from the activity to formulate a mission statement. An example of a mission statement for this team might be: "The mission of this community program planning team is to develop community-referenced curriculum and community-based instructional sites that reflect the opportunities available for adults in Hanover County. We are committed to developing functional and meaningful curriculum and integrated community-based instructional sites that offer opportunities for independence for our students."

Step 6: Assessing the Change Opportunity

The next step a newly-formed community program planning team should take is to assess the opportunity for change within the target agencies, organizations, and personnel. The purpose of this step is to gather needs assessment data that will assist the team in making decisions about the needed changes in local programs (Austin, Cox, Gottlieb, Hawkins, Kruzich, & Rauch, 1982). A decision-oriented needs assessment is one approach community program planning teams have found useful. A decision-oriented needs assessment assumes that local program evaluation is primarily useful because it enables key decision makers to answer questions about the future of the local program or programs (Austin et al., 1982).

Brooke & Jesiolowski (1987) identified the fifteen questions listed in Table 23.1 for use in a decision-oriented needs assessment of one local school system's special education program.

"CALIFORNIA DREAMING"

FIVE YEARS FROM NOW. . . . .

. . . . .how would you be spending a typical school day?

. . . . .how would your students be spending a typical school day?

. . . . .how would you be working with other agencies and programs?

. . . . .What would your students be doing as adults once they left your classroom?

Credit for the conceptualization of this activity should be given to Ms. Heather Kaney, Education Transition Center, Hayward, California.

Figure 23.2

Bellamy et al. (1988, pp. 53–56) and Wehman et al. (1988, pp. 56–57) have identified similar needs assessment questions for adult service agencies and programs.

The community program planning team should identify needs assessment questions and data collection techniques that enable the team to make decisions related to local program planning needs. With this purpose in mind, informal techniques such as community surveys, key informant interviews, community forums, and rates of consumer participation (Warheit, Bell, & Schwab, 1984) are as likely to yield valuable data as more formal evaluation procedures. Additionally, Austin et al. (1982) and Kimmel (1981) have noted that external evaluations may not be any less biased than evaluations conducted by the personnel responsible for the daily operations and program planning of local programs.

Step 7: Setting Objectives and Activities

Based upon the needs assessment data that have been collected, the next step for the community program planning team is to set objectives for program change. Setting objectives assists the team in moving from concern for past and present issues and politics to concern for future desirable services and outcomes (Kettner et al., 1985). This process assists the team in bridging the gap between the community's need and the team's mission statement.

Objectives assist the team in identifying short-term (typically one year or less) results (Daley, 1980). Objectives for community program planning teams should consist of four components (Kettner et al., 1985): (1) time frame, (2) target population, (3) result, and (4) criteria. During local program planning, teams should identify two types of objectives, process objectives and outcome objectives (Kettner et al., 1985). Outcome objectives refer to quality of life changes in a program's target consumer population. Process objectives refer to program management changes. For example, process objectives identify a team's efforts in service delivery, interagency cooperation, staff training, and parent participation. Outcome objectives identify a team's efforts in such areas as reducing unemployment rates, increasing consumers' wages, and increasing consumers' community independence.

Table 23.1 Sample Questions for a Decision-Oriented Needs Assessment

1. What is the school's overall philosophy of education for students with moderate and severe disabilities?
2. Does the school collect any follow-up data to determine what outcomes former students achieve and what services former students access? Are school personnel satisfied with former students' outcomes?
3. To what extent are students integrated into classes and activities with nondisabled peers?
4. How many students receive vocational services? How are curricula developed and delivered?
5. Do students receive community-based training? If yes, in what curricula domains?
6. Does classroom training target functional, age-appropriate activities?
7. Does the school systematically secure job placements for students prior to or immediately upon leaving school?
8. How do vocational training programs collect and utilize vocational assessment data?
9. Are students given the opportunity to participate in a variety of vocational training experiences?
10. Do students receive formal transition planning?
11. What professionals and agencies are involved in transition planning?
12. Are parents and students actively involved in transition planning and implementation?
13. Are parents and students provided information on locally available adult services?
14. Are release of information procedures in place to release students' records to adult service providers?
15. Are parent and peer support groups available during the transition years?

The involvement of all team members in the selection of objectives is critical to their comprehensive implementation. The team members must jointly discuss, write, revise, and agree with all proposed objectives. Each team's chairperson should assume responsibility for facilitating an objective-setting process that involves all team members and uses written procedures, telephone contacts, individual interviews, and team meetings to clarify and ensure agreement for the objectives (Kettner et al., 1985). Bertcher (1979) and Rothman, Erlich, & Teresa (1980) have outlined further procedures for ensuring participation from all members of community teams.

After setting objectives, team members should identify activities necessary to accomplish the objectives. The same procedures used to foster participation in objective setting should be used to ensure participation in and agreement with activities.

The combination of a mission statement, outcome objectives, process objectives, and activities form the proposal or action plan that the community program planning team will use to implement changes in the locality. A Gantt chart such as the one shown in Figure 23.3 is one way of visually organizing a team's planning and implementation efforts once activities have been specified.

Figure 23.3 illustrates part of an action plan developed by a community program planning team interested in developing a community-referenced vocational training and interagency transition planning program for high school students.

Step 8: Monitoring and Evaluating the Change Effort

Monitoring and evaluation are activities that community program planning teams must address during both the development and implementation of local action plans. Defining the community need, identifying team members, assessing the change opportunity, and setting objectives and activities are all steps that require careful monitoring and evaluation. However, the primary measure of the effectiveness of a community program change proposal is the extent to which targeted individuals achieve outcomes as specified by the local action plan and individual plans such as Individualized Transition Plans (ITPs) or Individualized Written Rehabilitation Plans (IWRPs). These efforts should be measured through an evaluation of both the outcome and process objectives. Therefore, it is imperative that the community program planning team determine methods for evaluating objectives and formally following-up students once the change process has been implemented. These evaluation procedures should be both formative and summative. Wehman et al. (1988) and Bates et al. (1986) for example, presented one way of comprehensively evaluating transition planning that is applicable both at the state and local levels. Their models include the development of state and local interagency agreements, student follow up surveys, individual service delivery teams, and a data sharing system between all three levels.

Table 23.2 is another monitoring instrument that local service delivery teams may use to monitor progress in vocational transition programs. Regardless of the evaluation approach selected and used, community program planning teams must ensure that their evaluation component is part of a comprehensive proposal or action plan that includes a mission statement, goals and objectives, timelines, staff responsibilities, and specific activities. Problems in the change process can emerge for numerous reasons—an inadequate data base, failure to involve the appropriate people, poor conceptualization of the need for change, poorly conceptualized goals and objectives, poor resource planning, poor communication, and so forth. (Kettner et al., 1985). Comprehensive monitoring and evaluation ensures that community program planning teams will be able to make both formative and summative decisions for change.

DEVELOPING SERVICE DELIVERY TEAMS

At the same time that the community program planning team is developing a proposal or action plan and is identifying a group of students or adults who need service changes, individual service delivery teams for each target recipient should be developed. The purpose of these teams is to plan and implement

Figure 23.3(a) Sample Gantt Chart

Sample Gantt Chart

Process objective: Within the next 10 months the community program planning team will work with two teachers of special needs classes who will establish community-based training sites with curricula across vocational, academic, leisure/recreation, and daily living areas.

Activity	Sept.	Oct.	Nov.	Dec.	Jan.	Feb.	Mar.	Apr.	May	June
1. Present proposal to schoolboard.										
2. Identify 2 teachers interested in implementing model classes.										
3. Hire consultant(s) to provide technical assistance to teachers and help with community inservice.										
4. Conduct teacher training.										
5. Conduct community site and school curriculum needs assessment.										
6. Target most appropriate sites for employment, housing, transportation, leisure opportunities, (according to needs assessment).										
7. Plan and schedule parent training.										
8. Plan and schedule training for school, community, and business personnel potentially involved with the 2 classes.										

individualized services for target recipients within the guidelines established by the community program planning team. These teams of professionals, volunteers, peers, or parents will include anyone directly responsible for training or delivery of support services to the target consumers (Everson & Moon, 1987). Effective ways to organize and implement the work of these teams have been described by Wehman, Moon, et al. (1988) and Wehman, Wood, Everson, Goodwyn, and Conley (1988) and includes the steps listed in Table 23.3. This process has been successfully used by transition teams for high school-aged youth in numerous localities. One way to help ensure appropriate outcomes for students with special needs is to have the service delivery teams write ITPs that include both process and outcome objectives. The objectives can be used to generate activities for which team members are individually responsible (Wehman, Moon, & McCarthy, 1986). An example of how outcome objectives and activities can be incorporated into an ITP is shown in Figure 23.4.

Similar to community program planning teams, service delivery teams must be able to work together by agreeing on common values

Figure 23.3(b)

Process objective: Within the next 10 months the community program planning team will pilot ITPs for ten students in their final three years of high school.

Activity	Sept.	Oct.	Nov.	Dec.	Jan.	Feb.	Mar.	Apr.	May	June
1. Develop a list of target students.										
2. Decide on format, general content areas of ITP and get approval from school district officials.										
3. Decide on procedures for selecting individual service delivery teams for each student and get approval from school district officials.										
4. Hold ITP meetings, write ITPs, collect individual student service delivery needs, and share data with community program planning team.										
5. Develop strategies for obtaining services started that were identified in Step 4 but do not currently exist or have lengthy waiting lists in community or school.										
6. Attend several ITP meetings to monitor and evaluate process. (Planning team member per meeting).										
7. Review process and revise and expand in upcoming year.										

and acceptable student outcomes (Everson & Moon, 1987). In addition, they must collect and share ITP data with the community program planning team in order to implement and evaluate service delivery changes (Wehman, et al., 1988).

SUMMARY

Rational community program planning is a conscious and deliberate decision-making process designed to bring about changes in local community programs, and ultimately in students' outcomes. As described in this chapter, it can be a lengthy and time-consuming process. However, comprehensive program planning has become a critical task for local program personnel to assume in the wake of changing services technologies, limited resources, and the push for accountability so evident in the 1980s. The eight-step process and examples included here are one approach to local community program change that community program teams in various localities have found useful in transition and supported employment program planning.

Table 23.2 Monitoring Checklist of a Comprehensive Secondary School-Adult Life Transition Program

---

Key

For each indicator please specify:

(+) the indicator is currently in place

(/) the indicator is in place but needs some adjustments

(−) the indicator is not currently in place

Phase 1: **Setting Policy and Gathering School and Student Information**

_______ State level interagency task force established

_______ Community program planning team

_______ Population of students specified for transition planning (i.e., age range, disability labels)

_______ District level coordinator designated

_______ School building level coordinator designated

_______ ITP format developed and approved

_______ Relationship between IEPs/ITPs specified

_______ Makeup of ITP teams specified

_______ Release of information forms between agencies developed and approved

_______ Comprehensive local needs assessment of school programs conducted

_______ Comprehensive local needs assessment of adult service programs conducted (i.e., vocational rehabilitation, mental health, mental retardation)

_______ Local formal interagency agreement for transition planning in place

_______ Transition planning procedures handbook developed

_______ Inservice training provided to school personnel

_______ Inservice training provided to adult service personnel

_______ Parent/guardian training/support program established

_______ Public awareness program established

_______ Listing of students compiled (i.e., name, date of birth, school, primary teacher)

_______ Other (Please describe) ____________________________________

____

____

_______ Other (Please describe) ____________________________________

____

____

Table 23.2 (cont.)

Phase 2:	**Planning and Implementing Transition Programs**
________	Parent/guardian questionnaire distributed
________	ITP meetings scheduled
________	ITP team members notified
________	Release of information forms signed
________	ITP meetings held
________	ITPs copied to non-attending members
________	ITP data compiled and forwarded to community program planning team
________	ITP evaluation procedures conducted
________	(As needed) Local Interagency agreement revised
________	(As needed) Inservice training conducted
________	(As needed) Transition planning procedures revised
________	Other (Please describe) ____
________	Other (Please describe) ____

Table 23.3 The Work of an Individual Transition or Service Delivery Teams

1. Identify and contact all students of the target age according to guidelines established by the community program planning team.
2. Identify and contact all team members for each target student to attend a scheduled ITP meeting.
3. Hold an initial team meeting to explain the purpose of and to write the ITP.
4. On the ITP form, write the responsibilities of each team member as defined by process and outcome objectives and timelines.
5. Have the team meet quarterly to assess progress and reassign team member responsibilities.
6. Assure that, as the student approaches the end of school services, there is an increased involvement by adult service providers.
7. Team members must formulate written activities and timelines to accomplish the objectives for which each has responsibility. These activities should be included in the ITP. Data should be channelled back to the community program planning team.
8. Hold an "exit" planning meeting to target specific outcomes and support services for the student and assign specific responsibilities for placement, training, and follow-along *before* graduation.
9. Assure that appropriate student objectives and support are officially carried over to adult service plans such as IWRPs at graduation.
10. Work within the community program planning team's guidelines to ensure follow-up of school graduates.

Figure 23.4

Process Outcomes and Objectives for Service Delivery Team.

Name: Susan Age: 18

EMPLOYMENT GOAL

To become employed part- or full-time in a competitive employment position by age 20.

SHORT TERM OBJECTIVES

Outcome objective	To participate in three varied real work experiencs in community work settings. Timeline: 1990-91 school year. Persons responsible: special education teacher and vocational education teacher.
Activities	(a) Student will participate in food service training in a community-based training site for a minimum of 2 hours/ day, 4 days/week. (1) bussing tables (Sept.-Nov. '90). (2) dish machine operator (Dec. '90-Feb. '91). (3) food preparation (Mar.-June '91). (b) Student will use public transportation to go to and from job training site.
Method	The supported work approach will be utilized for training on the job-training site and for the purpose of transportation training.
Process objective	To complete formal referral process for vocational rehabilitation services. Timeline: May 1990. Person responsible: rehabilitation counselor
Activities	(a) a financial eligibility application will be completed to determine eligibility for VR services. (b) A referral will be made for a vocational evaluation. (c) An IWRP will be written in conjunction with the ITP meeting.

QUESTIONS (For answers see pp. 437–438)

1. What skills do supported employment program planners need today?

2. Define community program planning.

3. Distinguish rational community planning from unplanned change.

4. Identify the goals of (a) a community program planning team, and (b) a service delivery team.

5. What assumptions support the use of local planning and service delivery teams?

6. List and describe the eight components of effective community program planning.

REFERENCES

Alinsky, S.D. (1971). *Rules for radicals. A primer for realistic radicals.* New York: Random House.

Austin, M. J., Cox, G., Gottlieb, N., Hawkins, J. D., Kruzick, J. M., & Rauch, R. (1982). *Evaluating your agency's programs.* Beverly Hills: Sage.

Bates, P., Suter, C., & Poelvoorde, M. (1986). *Illinois transition project.* Springfield, IL: Governor's Planning Council on Developmental Disabilities.

Bellamy, G. T., Rhodes, L. W., Mank, D. M., & Albin, J. M. (1988). *Supported employment. A community implementation guide.* Baltimore: Paul H. Brookes.

Bertcher, H. J. (1979). *Group participation. Techniques for leaders and members.* Beverly Hills, CA: Sage.

Brager, G. & Holloway, S. (1978). *Changing human service organizations: Politics and practice.* New York: Free Press.

Brooke, V. & Jesiolowski, C. (1987). *A needs assessment instrument for secondary special education vocational programs.* Unpublished manuscript. Richmond: Virginia Commonwealth University, Rehabilitation Research and Training Center.

Buckley, J., Albin, J. M., & Mank, D. (1988). Competency based staff training for supported employment. In G. T. Bellamy, L. E. Rhodes, D. M. Mank, & J. M. Albin (Eds.) *Supported employment: A community implementation guide.* (pp. 229-245). Baltimore: Paul H. Brookes.

Daley, J. M. (1980). Setting objectives in the human service agency. In K. Dea (Ed.), *Perspective for the future: social work practice in the 80's.* New York: National Association of Social Workers.

Everson, J. M. (1989). *A survey of personnel in supported employment programs in Rehabilitation Services Administration (RSA) Region III: A description of training needs, educational backgrounds, and previous employment experiences.* Unpublished dissertation. Richmond Virginia Commonwealth University.

Everson, J. M. (1988b). An analysis of federal and state policy on transition from school to adult life for youth with disabilities. In P. Wehman & M. S. Moon (Eds.), *Vocational rehabilitation and supported employment.* Baltimore: Paul H. Brookes.

Everson, J. M. & Moon, M. S. (1987). Transition services for young adults with severe disabilities: Defining professional roles and responsibilities. *Journal of the Association for Persons with Severe Handicaps, 12*(2), 87–95.

Gabel, M. (1984, October). Planning diseases. *The Futurist, 18*, 21–22.

Kettner, P., Daley, J. M., & Nichols, A. E. (1985). *Initiating change in organizations and communities.* Monterey, CA: Brooks/Cole.

Kimmel, W. (1981). *Putting program evaluation in perspective for state and local government.* Rockville, MD: Aspen Systems Corporation.

Kregel, J. & Sale, P. (1988). Preservice preparation of supported employment professionals. In P. Wehman & M. S. Moon (Eds.), *Vocational rehabilitation and supported employment.* Baltimore: Paul H. Brookes.

Mayer, R. (1985). *Policy and program development.* New York: Prentice-Hall.

Rothman, J., Erlich, J. L., & Teresa, J. G. (1980). Fostering participation. In F. M. Cox, J. L. Erlich, J. Rothman, & J. E. Tropman (Eds.), *Strategies of community organization* (pp. 385–397). Itaska, IL: Peacock.

Tropman, J. E., Johnson, H. R., & Tropman, E. J. (1979). *The essentials of committee management.* Chicago: Nelson-Hall.

Warheit, G. J., Bell, R. A., & Schwab, J. J. (1984). Selecting the needs assessment approach. In F. Cox, J. L. Erlich, J. Rothman, & J. E. Tropman (Eds.), *Tactics and techniques of community practice* (pp. 41–59. Itaska, IL: Peacock.

Wehman, P., Moon, M. S., Everson, J. M., Wood, W., & Barcus, J. M. (1988). *Transition from school to work. New challenges for youth with severe handicaps.* Baltimore: Paul H. Brookes.

Wehman, P., Moon, M., & McCarthy, P. (1986, January). Transition from school to adulthood for youth with severe handicaps. *Focus on Exceptional Children, 18*(5), 1–12.

Wehman, P., Wood, W., Everson, J. M., Goodwyn, R., & Conley, S. (1988). *Vocational education for multihandicapped youth with cerebral palsy.* Baltimore: Paul H. Brookes.

CHAPTER

24

Preparing Personnel to Meet the Challenges of Contemporary Employment Service Alternatives

Adelle M. Renzaglia
University of Illinois at Urbana-Champaign
Jane M. Everson
Virginia Commonwealth University

Throughout the 1980s secondary special education and adult service programs for individuals with disabilities have undergone drastic philosophical and service delivery changes. These changes have been the result of numerous successful employment demonstrations throughout the late 1970s and the 1980s (e.g., Kiernan & Stark, 1986; Rusch, 1986; Rusch & Mithaug, 1980; and Wehman, 1981). Changes have also been the result of recent legislation mandating rehabilitation services for Americans with severe handicaps (P.L. 93-112), special education services (P.L. 94-142), improved vocational education for youth with special needs (P.L. 98-524), and, most recently, supported employment services (P.L. 99-506).

As the number of youth and adults successfully employed through contemporary employment programs continues to increase (Wehman, Kregel, Shafer, & West, 1989), reduced unemployment rates for postsecondary special education youth, decreased reliance on sheltered settings, and decreased reliance on federal and state discretionary monies for demonstration programs would be expected. However, these expectations have not been met (Kregel, Shafer, Wehman, & West, 1989). The gap between our knowledge of quality employment program indicators and widespread practices in programs across the nation is disturbing. This discrepancy is due, at least in part, to the lack of adequately prepared personnel providing secondary special education and adult services (Harold Russell Associates, 1985; Rusch, Trach, Winking, Tines, & Johnson, 1989; Weissenstein, 1986).

EVIDENCE OF NEED

The need for trained personnel to provide management, direct service, technical assistance, client case management, and program evaluation services is great and continues to grow rapidly. In 1983, Menz stated that the predicted growth of employment programs for individuals with disabilities would require between 100,000 and 300,000 new personnel to staff rehabilitation facilities by 1990. This number does not include the number of personnel needed to staff the rapidly emerging non-facility-based supported employment programs or school-sponsored vocational training and employment programs. In an attempt to alert professionals to the potential need for supported employment providers, Hill argued that approximately 200 new professionals are needed in Virginia alone to serve individuals with developmental disabilities (M. Hill, personal communication, January 1989). Kregel & Sale (1988) have hypothesized that 4,000 supported employment direct service personnel are needed nationally to adequately serve individuals with developmental and other severe disabilities.

Currently, program managers in Virginia (L. Mays, personal communication, February 1989) and Nevada (G. Peterson, personal communication, November 1988) have expressed frustration at recruiting and hiring qualified supported employment staff. Rusch et al. (1989) hypothesized that low salaries and lack of systematic direct service skills may be responsible for high job turnover among job coaches in Illinois. In a 1988 study of eighty-five direct service personnel, forty-four personnel (52 percent) had master's or bachelor's degrees, yet the average salary reported was only $16,078 (Welsh, 1989).

Recently, the Rehabilitation, Research and Training Center (RRTC) on supported employment at Virginia Commonwealth University conducted a survey of 673 supported employment personnel (both program managers and direct service personnel) in the five-state and Washington, D.C. region encompassed by the Rehabilitation Services Administration (RSA) Region III. The purpose of this survey was to assess the self-reported training needs of supported employment personnel. The results indicated an overwhelming need for additional training for currently employed supported employment staff across thirty-nine supported employment competencies (Everson, 1989). Eighty-one percent of direct service personnel expressed interest in participating in one- to two-day supported employment workshops and in technical assistance programs. Seventy-four percent of program managers expressed interest in one- to two-day supported employment workshops and 81 percent expressed interest in technical assistance. Even more importantly, 57 percent of the surveyed direct service personnel indicated a willingness to participate in degree programs offering supported employment training if they were provided the opportunity to do so.

A recent national survey of rehabilitation counselors employed in federal-state rehabilitation agencies indicated that more than 50 percent of the 790 counselors surveyed identified training needs in the areas of the role and functions of rehabilitation counselors, selection of appropriate supported employment options, evaluation of service providers, evaluation of clients, and funding strategies (Shafer, in press).

In summary, because supported employment programs are just beginning to be fully implemented across the nation, it is difficult to accurately estimate the number of existing personnel that need additional training and the number of projected personnel that will need training. However, documented difficulties in filling existing personnel openings, documented need for training of currently employed personnel, and the predicted growth of vocational training and supported employment programs throughout the remainder of the century all point to a potentially massive need for personnel training and technical assistance.

TARGET PERSONNEL FOR TRAINING PROGRAMS

Everson and O'Neill (1988) have identified three levels of potential trainees: (1) systems level, defined as federal, state, and local funding agencies and policy makers; (2) provider level, defined as managerial and direct service staff such as teachers and job coach-

ALAN DAHL

Alan, our 23-year-old son, attended a special education school where his classification was developmentally disabled. He was graduated from school at the age of 21. He currently lives at home with his parents and his 18-year-old brother. Alan has a married brother and is the proud uncle of two nephews.

Socially, Alan enjoys bowling and basketball on a SOAR team, going out shopping with friends, and taking his parents out for dinner. A job he takes very seriously is his participation as a board member of a local developmental services support group. The group was established to give the supported employment workers an additional means of support, and it has allowed them opportunities to plan, interact, and recreate with other nondisabled and workers with disabilities. The events have included work-related activities such as an employer's speakers forum, as well as picnics, cookouts, and even a basketball game with the Chicago Bears. This is one of Alan's favorite projects.

In July, 1987, Alan started working as a housekeeper for a local motel chain. Alan was unable to maintain the standards of this position, and the program coordinator began talking to us about something called supported employment. It was a new concept to us, but her strong feelings led us to believe this was the right step for our son. And it was! On November 21, 1987, Alan started with a crew and a job coach at Burger King. He started on the broiler-steamer position and advanced to the specialty board. His latest and biggest achievement is his advancement to cashier. Alan was the first employee to be honored as "Employee of the Month," and in a press release, the manager indicated Alan was chosen for his spirit of cooperation and dependability as a model for all Burger King employees. The store presented Alan with a $50 check, and his name is on a plaque that hangs in the lobby where the community, his friends and family, and, most important, Alan himself can see it.

Alan also works a second job at the Bloomington-Normal Seating Company, a sister company of Diamond Star Motors, as a janitor for approximately 12 hours a week. He has received many compliments about the quality of his work and has recently been approached by the president of the company for a job within the corporation.

As Alan's parents, we have seen him grow in many areas, such as learning to use the transit system, increasing his assertiveness and self-confidence, taking pride in his uniform, and caring properly for it. Alan has always had a ready smile for everyone, but the job has enhanced his feeling of independence.

One person who is very important in Alan's development and has helped him in many ways is his job coach. He has always treated Alan as an equal, not a client, and has taught Alan through the job that he is important and can be independent.

---

es; and (3) consumer level, defined as individuals with disabilities, as well as family members and other users and purchasers of supported employment. Personnel and consumers within all of these levels should be considered needy recipients of employment services training.

Despite the diversity that now exists in job titles and roles and competencies among vocational training and supported employment programs across the United States, at least three major personnel types have recently emerged from the provider level of target trainees: (1) direct service personnel; (2) program managers; and (3) technical assistants. A fourth type of personnel cuts across the provider and consumer levels. This personnel type includes other state and local agency personnel, such as rehabilitation counselors whose job responsibilities include supported employment programmatic issues. Target personnel for preservice and inservice training programs include these four types of personnel who may be employed in public school and adult service agencies, including both professionals and paraprofessionals. The purpose of this chapter is to discuss personnel training models and strategies that may be used to provide training and technical assistance to these four types of personnel.

PERSONNEL TRAINING MODELS

Preservice Training

Personnel training models are typically described as either preservice or inservice in design. Preservice models are university-based baccalaureate or graduate programs that provide long-term and frequently disjointed training in a recognized discipline or specialization area (Bloom, 1987). They may range from one to five or more years in duration. Preservice programs in special education have traditionally emphasized curriculum and teaching strategies for elementary-age students with mild to moderate handicaps. Preservice programs in rehabilitation counseling, psychology, and sociology have traditionally emphasized theoretical foundations and research in broad disciplinary areas with opportunities for fieldwork. Core curriculum, faculty expertise, declining student enrollments, and funding constraints have made it difficult for colleges and universities to respond to the specific preservice needs of vocational training and supported employment personnel. Yet a recent survey of supported employment personnel indicated that 223 of 320 personnel (70 percent) surveyed had master's and/or bachelor's degrees. Of these, 130 bachelor's and 21 master's degrees were in education, psychology, social work, sociology, or rehabilitation counseling (Everson, 1989).

Karan and Knight (1986) have argued that preservice personnel programs must begin to respond proactively to emerging personnel needs by training personnel to work with adults as well as children in community-based settings instead of facilities, and with employers and the business community instead of just human service providers. The goal of preservice training for future vocational training and supported employment personnel should be to provide a strong theoretical base combined with the rudimentary practical skills necessary for competent vocational training (Haring, 1982; Kregel & Sale, 1988). Preservice programs are thus challenged with providing trainees with a broad theoretical foundation in a disciplinary area and predicting the future practical skill needs of the trainees.

Inservice Training

Many personnel employed in vocational training and supported employment programs will receive a theoretical foundation from a preservice baccalaureate or graduate program that will be supplemented by practical and specialized skills provided by inservice training and technical assistance.

Inservice training may be university-based, state or local agency-based, or in some cases, private program-based. Inservice training programs are traditionally geared toward professionals currently employed in specific professions or service programs. The goal of inservice training programs should be to provide a theoretical base combined with the specific practical skills necessary for competent vocational training (Inge, Barcus, & Everson, 1988). In addition, inservice programs are challenged with changing the attitudes of personnel currently providing services from segregated to integrated, from subsidized to independent, and from facility based to community based (Alper & Alper, 1980; Inge et al., 1988).

Unlike preservice training, inservice training is constrained by time, necessitating a training format that differs from most preservice training programs. Personnel trainers must work very closely with the school or adult service agency administrators and staff to establish a format compatible with the needs of the trainees being served. Furthermore, in many instances personnel development activities may require that the instructors (e.g., university professors) travel to the inservice participants rather than requiring the participants to convene on the instructor's territory.

Technical Assistance

A third model of personnel preparation is technical assistance. Ideally, technical assistance is provided as a follow-up component to either preservice or inservice training, but in reality this is seldom the case (Everson & O'Neill, 1988). Technical assistance is the provision of problem-solving and consultation to personnel who have specific, assessed, and immediate needs. Technical assistance may be provided by university faculty, state and local agency personnel, and other vocational training and supported employment providers. Technical assistance is limited in both duration and content and typically requires trainers to travel to the trainees' sites. An assumption is that technical assistants have the theoretical knowledge and practical skills necessary to guide recipients in addressing problems and concerns specific to their programs. The goal of technical assistance should be to provide participants with specific practical skills and problem-solving abilities needed for competent vocational training and employment services.

GUIDELINES FOR DEVELOPING PERSONNEL TRAINING PROGRAMS

Competency-Based Training

Most current personnel training programs providing preservice, inservice, or technical assistance are competency-based (e.g., Barcus, Wehman, Moon, Brooke, Goodall, & Everson, 1988; Buckley, Albin, & Mank, 1988; Cobb, Hasazi, Collins, & Salembier, 1988; Kregel & Sale, 1988). A 1988 review of thirteen personnel training programs funded by the U.S. Department of Education for transition preparation (Baker & Geiger, 1988) yielded fourteen curricular content areas which were used to organize 636 competencies. Kregel & Sale (1988) presented seven curricular competency areas that form the foundation of a master's level supported employment program, and Inge et al. (1988) identified seven goals of inservice training that dictate training objectives and content. Buckley et al. (1988) identified five supported employment program outcomes that they suggested should be used to develop specific staff knowledge and performance competencies. Table 24.1 summarizes the major competency areas that have been suggested by current literature for personnel providing vocational training and employment services to individuals with disabilities.

There is at present an abundance of both suggested training competencies and curricula for supported employment professionals. Generally, professionals agree on the major competencies needed by vocational training and employment personnel. However, the content needed and method for achieving these competencies are not agreed upon. Existing curricula and training materials have not been validated and are not replicable or comprehensive (Buckley et al., 1988; Everson & O'Neill, 1988). In addition, existing curricula and training materials frequently do not meet the needs of client populations with diverse employment and support needs, communities with diverse labor market needs, or supported employment programs with diverse programmatic needs (Everson & O'Neill, 1988). Buckley et al. (1988) have noted as well that the training competencies agreed upon in the literature are seldom translated into program outcomes and staff roles. Even with these criticisms, the majority of university faculty and other staff trainers agree that delineated competencies should form the foundation of effective preservice, inservice, or technical assistance personnel preparation programs.

Effective personnel trainers must define and evaluate the competencies suggested in Table 24.1 and develop a competency-based approach to training following a three-step process. First, trainees must be able to identify desired program or service outcomes for the individuals they serve. Suggested service outcomes for individuals with severe disabilities have included community presence, choice, competence, respect, and community participation (Wilcox & Bellamy, 1987). Buckley et al. (1988) identified five outcomes of establishing supported employment programs: (1) paid employment opportunities; (2) job analysis and trained employees; (3) coordination of individualized services; (4) integration; and (5) maintenance of the support organization. Barcus et al. (1988) developed a training outcome survey designed to assess the changes in service outcomes for individuals with severe disabilities. This survey evaluates changes in the number of jobs developed, job placements made, severity of the disability level of clients placed, and other variables affecting pre- and postservice training. Therefore, the effects of personnel training on the quality of services provided to persons with disabilities can be measured.

Table 24.1 Summary of Suggested Supported Employment Competency Areas from Current Literature

Competency Area	Selected Competency Components	Literature
1. Philosophy/historical considerations/legal policy issues	a. History of service provision b. Philosophical support for community employment c. Laws establishing guidelines for service d. Department of Labor regulations	Baker & Geiger, 1988; Bruyere, 1987; Buckley et al., 1988; Cobb et al., 1988; Everson & O'Neill, 1988; Inge et al., 1988; Kregel & Sale, 1988; Sharpton, 1988.
2. Interagency issues/systems change	a. Understanding of the roles of the disciplines and agencies providing services b. Funding sources and regulations for cooperative agencies c. Cooperative goal planning	Baker & Geiger, 1988; Bruyere, 1987; Buckley et al., 1988; Cobb et al., 1988; Everson & O'Neill, 1988; Harold Russell Associates, 1985; Kregel & Sale, 1988; Sharpton, 1988.
3. Program management/administration	a. Program regulations for establishing supported employment b. Funding sources and regulations c. Staff supervision d. Program evaluations	Baker & Geiger, 1988; Buckley et al., 1988; Everson & O'Neill, 1988; Harold Russell Associates, 1985; Kregel & Sale, 1988.
4. Individualized plan development/management	a. Establishing individual priorities b. Assessment of family concerns and priorities c. Assigning roles in implementing the individualized plan d. Case management	Baker & Geiger, 1988; Buckley et al., 1988; Cobb et al., 1988; Everson & O'Neill, 1988; Harold Russell Associates, 1985; Kregel & Sale, 1988; Sharpton, 1988.
5. Assessment of potential workers with disabilities	a. Evaluation of interests b. General skill assessment c. Specific performance assessment in work and work-related skills d. Developing longitudinal assessment procedures	Baker & Geiger, 1988; Bruyere, 1987; Buckley et al., 1988; Cobb et al., 1986; Danley & Mellen, 1987; Everson & O'Neill, 1988; Harold Russell Associates, 1985; Inge et al., 1988; Kregel & Sale, 1988; Sharpton, 1988.
6. Job development/job analysis/job placement	a. Job identification through community survey b. Assessment of employer receptivity c. Evaluation of job desirability d. Analysis of job skills e. Delineation of required work-related skills f. Evaluation of work environmental variables g. Selection of job training and placement sites that best meet an individual's needs based on student assessment information	Baker & Geiger, 1988; Bruyere, 1987; Buckley et al., 1988; Cobb et al., 1986; Danley & Mellen, 1987; Everson & O'Neill, 1988; Harold Russell Associates, 1985; Inge et al., 1988; Kregel & Sale, 1988; Sharpton, 1988.

Table 24.1 (cont.)

7. Job site training/support advocacy/job site modification	a. Developing and implementing systematic individual programs b. Withdrawing the trainer c. Identifying and implementing a plan for maintenance and follow-up support d. Facilitating co-worker relationships and advocacy e. Job restructuring, job adaptation and negotiations with employers for individualized approaches to employment	Baker & Geiger, 1988; Bruyere, 1987; Buckley et al., 1988; Cobb et al., 1986; Danley & Mellen, 1987; Everson & O'Neill, 1988; Harold Russell Associates, 1985; Inge et al., 1988; Kregel & Sale, 1988; Sharpton, 1988.

Second, effective personnel trainers must identify personnel roles and related responsibilities of those being trained to achieve these service program outcomes. For example, the personnel preparation program must design the program to train specific personnel such as lead employment specialists, job coaches, job developers, program managers, rehabilitation technologists, case managers, rehabilitation counselors, technical assistants, and so on. What roles and responsibilities do these personnel need to assume in order to achieve the designed service outcomes? Job descriptions and primary responsibilities of all target personnel should be developed or reviewed and matched to the suggested competencies or subcomponents of the competencies listed in Table 24.1.

Third, effective personnel trainers should use these competencies to develop an assessment instrument to evaluate target personnel's baseline knowledge and technical skills. Few training assessment instruments are currently available, resulting in a need for personnel trainers to develop valid and reliable instruments (Everson & O'Neill, 1988).

Knowledge-Based and Practical Skill-Based Training

Haring (1982), Inge et al. (1988), and Kregel & Sale (1988) have all emphasized that effective personnel preparation programs must include both a strong theoretical base and an opportunity to practice and refine practical skills. Many of the competencies described earlier require a knowledge base on which practical skills are built. Preservice programs, because of their duration, intensity, and disciplinary focus, generally provide a strong knowledge base. The following courses or content areas have been discussed by numerous personnel trainers and should be included in a training program to ensure a strong theoretical base:

1. Applied behavior analysis.
2. Systematic instruction.
3. Educational assessment and data-based programming.
4. Curriculum development for persons with handicaps.
5. Emergency medical procedures.
6. Physical aspects of persons with multiple handicaps.
7. Interagency coordination: working with professionals and families.
8. Vocational education and transition for persons with handicaps.
9. Legal issues and advocacy.

Inservice and technical assistance programs, because of their shorter duration, site-specific location, and specific skill focus, generally have the opportunity to provide a stronger practical skill base.

McDaniel, Flippo, and Lowery (1986) described four stages of adult learning for personnel trainers to consider when planning personnel training programs: awareness, knowledge, repatterning, and integration. Curricula and training strategies should incorporate knowledge-based and practical skills-based training in order to lead trainees through all four stages of learning. Knowles (1980) suggested that trainers classify training activities by their intended purpose. The following four questions about training objectives will assist personnel trainers in determining the purpose of training: (1) Is the objective to change attitudes? (2) Is the objective to develop knowledge? (3) Is the objective to teach a skill? or (4) Is the objective to encourage creativity? In response to these four questions, Everson, Barcus, Moon, and Morton (1987) and Inge et al. (1988) have delineated sample training techniques to use to meet each of these objectives. Table 24.2 applies their ideas to the four classifications suggested by Knowles (1980) and the stages of learning described by McDaniel et al. (1986).

The training activities presented in Table 24.2 should be matched to selected competencies for all three types of personnel training programs. In preservice training programs, the placement of students in fieldwork sites for practicum experiences complements knowledge-based classroom experiences. The provision of practicum experiences concurrent with coursework enables university faculty to assess technical skill competencies and to remediate knowledge and technical skills in classroom experiences.

Given the potential demands placed on personnel in vocational training and employment programs, preservice personnel training programs should require multiple practicum experiences with public school and adult service programs (Renzaglia, 1986); direct service and program management experiences (Kregel & Sale, 1988); and experience with individuals with a variety of disability labels (Everson & O'Neill, 1988).

In inservice training and technical assistance models, fieldwork experiences should also be provided to complement knowledge-based experiences. However, the shorter duration, site-specific location, and specific skill focus of inservice training and technical assistance necessitate a different format. Formats can range from knowledge and practical skill workshops in trainees' current employment settings to individual consultation that is provided at the trainee's vocational training or placement site. The optimal format combines a workshop and individualized technical assistance (Barcus et al., 1988;

Table 24.2 Classification of Training Activities by Intended Purposes

Purpose	Training Activities	Stage(s) of Learning
1. Change attitudes	Panels, site visits, slide shows, videotapes, teleconferences, group discussions, role-plays, games/activities, skits, case studies, field work	Awareness
2. Develop knowledge	Panels, site visits, slide shows, videotapes, teleconferences, lectures, reading materials, research papers, group discussions, role-plays, games/activities, skits, case studies, demonstrations, field work	Knowledge
3. Teach a skill	Teleconferences, videotapes, role-plays, games/activities, skits, case studies, field work	Knowledge, repatterning
4. Encourage creativity	Group discussions, role-plays, games/activities, skits, field work	Integration

Everson & O'Neill, 1988; McDaniel et al., 1986). Weissman-Frisch, Crowell, and Inman (1980) delineated four general guidelines for the provisions of effective inservice training: (1) use a variety of methods for evaluation; (2) include a small number of participants in group sessions; (3) incorporate lecture, discussion, modeling, direct application of intervention strategies, simulation, feedback, and reinforcement; and (4) use a competency-based model.

Program Evaluation

Given the relatively new emphasis on personnel preparation in vocational training and employment services, minimal evaluation research is currently available (e.g., Barcus et al., 1988; Bruyere, 1987). However, because personnel preparation programs are still in the developmental stages, they should be carefully and continuously evaluated (Everson & O'Neill, 1988; Mori, Rusch, & Fair, 1982). In addition, personnel training evaluation should be multifaceted and designed to assess all components and expected outcomes of the training (Barcus et al., 1988; Everson & O'Neill, 1988; Weissman-Frisch et al., 1980). Evaluation components should include trainee satisfaction, changes in trainee knowledge, changes in trainee technical skills, and changes in service delivery practices for individuals with disabilities. Another suggested component is employer satisfaction with trainer performance once training has been completed (Renzaglia, 1986). Table 24.3 suggests evaluation activities that are linked to training competencies, training activities, and desired outcomes.

The knowledge-based competencies included in a preservice training program will be met primarily through targeted coursework. In inservice training and technical assistance programs, they will be met primarily through workshops. Written exams and projects (e.g., literature reviews, position papers) provide one measure of a trainee's knowledge in preservice programs; pretest-posttest activities are often used in inservice training and technical assistance programs.

Evaluation activities designed to assess the effectiveness of preservice and inservice programs in providing trainees with the necessary technical skills should be conducted while the trainees are using the designated skills. This may occur in practicum sites during preservice training, or in "hands-on" activities during inservice and technical assistance training, such as those described in Table 24.2. Direct observation of trainee performance should be conducted repeatedly to assess trainee competence in delivering appropriate services to persons with developmental and other severe disabilities. Behavioral observations should be systematic with performance criteria clearly defined prior to observations. One way to accomplish this is by developing a performance checklist that a practicum supervisor or inservice trainer may use consistently across observations. Repeated observations will provide the trainer with data regarding a trainee's progress toward meeting competencies as well as a trainee's continued needs for training. Since inservice and technical assistance trainees are typically employed while participating in training activities, behavioral observations can be conducted whenever possible in their vocational training and employment sites.

The ultimate goal of personnel training is to increase the quality of vocational services provided to persons with severe and other developmental disabilities. Therefore, program evaluation should include an analysis of the effect of personnel training on student or client work performance (Everson & O'Neill, 1988; Thurman & Hare, 1979). Student and client performance data should be evaluated to determine if program trainees have, in fact, acquired the competencies necessary for successful vocational training. Unfortunately, minimal examples of valid and reliable instruments have been developed to assess this training effect (Barcus et al., 1988). Student and client performance data should also be collected repeatedly to monitor cumulative effects of service delivery as well as effects across time as the program trainees acquire more skills. These data can be used to assess the need for additional training and technical assistance.

A final component of program evaluation is an assessment of consumer satisfaction. Consumers,

Table 24.3 A Multifaceted Approach to Personnel Preparation Program Evaluation

Purpose of Evaluation	Training Activities	Evaluation Mechanism
To measure changes in trainee values and attitudes	Panels, site visits, slide shows, videotapes, teleconferences, group discussions, role-plays, games/activities, skits, case studies, field work	Pre-/post-values and attitude assessment scales
To measure change in trainee knowledge	Panels, site visits, slide shows, videotapes, teleconferences, lectures, reading materials, research papers, group discussions, games/activities, skits, case studies, demonstrations, field work	Examinations, individual/group presentations, activity checklists, observation checklists
To measure changes in trainee technical skills	Teleconferences, videotapes, role-plays, games/activities, skits, case studies, field work	Fieldwork checklists, observation checklists
To measure changes in student or client outcomes	Panels, site visits, slide shows, videotapes, teleconferences, lectures, reading materials, research papers, group discussions, role-plays, games/activities, skits, case studies, demonstrations, field work	Pre-/post-service delivery surveys, content analysis of service documents (e.g., IEPs, ITPs, IWRPs)
To measure trainee satisfaction with training		Posttraining evaluation scales and surveys
To measure employer satisfaction with trainee performance		Posttraining surveys

in this context, include both the program trainees and those persons employing program graduates. Trainee satisfaction data can be collected across a variety of settings and activities. Preservice course or inservice workshop evaluations should indicate trainees' satisfaction with the content and format of instruction. Practicum evaluations completed by trainees should indicate satisfaction with practicum sites, requirements, supervision, and the evaluation procedures used to assess trainee performance. Additional trainee satisfaction measures should be collected once a trainee is employed and has had the opportunity to use the skills acquired in the personnel preparation program. At this point, a trainee may be able to give critical feedback to the personnel preparation program based on the application of his or her skills in an actual employment situation. Assessing program trainees across a number of years or training sessions may also provide insightful information about the long-range effects of the training program.

Another component of evaluating consumer satisfaction is contacting employers of program graduates to determine their views of program graduates' competence. Employer satisfaction can be assessed by evaluating employers' perceptions of the competencies of the employees in performing their jobs. Additional questions might address employers' views of employees' strengths and weaknesses, and whether they would be willing to hire program graduates or trainees in the future. As with trainee satisfaction, assessment of employer satisfaction across years and training sessions would provide pertinent information on the durability and adaptability of trainee skills across time.

Although this multifaceted approach to evaluation may be costly and time-consuming (Weissman-Frisch et al., 1980), the information obtained will provide personnel trainers with valuable feedback. Furthermore, the multifaceted data that will be collected on the competencies required by effective vocational trainers and employment personnel and the personnel training strategies that prove effective should guide professionals in designing personnel preparation programs that result in highly trained program graduates, who ultimately will increase the quality and success of vocational training programs for persons with handicaps.

Adult Learning Principles

The use of adult learning principles has recently been discussed and applied to personnel preparation programs in the areas of vocational training and employment programs (e.g., Inge et al., 1988). The basic premise of adult learning principles is that adults learn differently from children and participate in personnel training programs for specific and unique reasons (Knowles, 1980; Robinson, 1979). Adults bring professional and life experiences to training programs and expect that their experiences will be valued by personnel trainers. Working under this expectation, adult trainees should be allowed and expected to participate in training programs and activities. Adult trainees should also be exposed to a variety of instructional and evaluation techniques.

The characteristics of personnel training programs discussed thus far—competency-based training, knowledge-based and practical skill-based training, and program evaluation—when guided by the use of adult learning principles will enhance trainees' learning, participation in training, and use of knowledge and skills after training. One way to ensure the use of adult learning principles is through the devel- opment of a training matrix that incorporates all of the characteristics of effective personnel preparation programs that have been discussed thus far. Table 24.4 is a sample training matrix that may be used for a preservice or inservice program.

SUMMARY

Research and literature in the areas of vocational training and competitive employment for persons with disabilities have demonstrated that individuals with severe and diverse disabilities are capable of being productive members of integrated work environments. As a result, there has been a recent emphasis on improving the quality of vocational training and employment programs. However, there remains a paucity of currently employed trained professionals and paraprofessionals who have the knowledge base and practical skills necessary for developing vocational training and employment programs. Additionally, the need for new professionals and paraprofessionals who are trained to provide community employment options is continuing to grow due to the growing numbers of persons with disabilities entering training programs. Therefore, personnel preparation programs must quickly begin to address these needs by developing, implementing, and evaluating training programs that produce competent professionals and paraprofessionals.

Although little research has been conducted to evaluate the necessary components of effective personnel preparation, a number of personnel trainers have suggested that training programs should be competency-based as well as field-based. Theoretical foundations should be rooted in behavioral technology and current best practices, and training curricula should be community referenced and grounded in adult learning theories. Given the lack of a database supporting these components, a continuous multifaceted evaluation plan should be designed and implemented.

Preservice needs, inservice needs, and technical assistance needs must be addressed by personnel training programs. The need for inservice and technical assistance has been emphasized here because of the vast number of service providers in public school and adult service programs who lack training, especially in the newly identified strategies for promoting community employment that result in students' and clients' obtaining meaningful, nonsheltered employment. Because of the varying types and degrees of disabilities experienced by vocational training program participants, trainees must be exposed to a wide range of practical skills. Special and vocational educators, vocational rehabilitation personnel, and other school and adult service

Table 24.4 Personnel Training Matrix

Competency	Knowledge-Based Activity	Practical Skill-Based Activity	Evaluation Mechanism
Ability to contact potential employers for supported employment placements and conduct job analyses	Lecture: guidelines for making employer contacts		
	Videotape: "Successful Job Contacts"	Role plays: employer contact situations	Trainer role play checklist
		Activity: marketing bloopers	
	Lecture: guidelines for job analyses		
	Videotape: "Successful Job Analysis"	Fieldwork: community application of employer contacts/job analysis	Trainer observation checklist
	Summary group discussion		

providers are among the target recipients of training if the needs of consumers of vocational training and employment services are to be met.

QUESTIONS (For answers see pp. 438–439)

1. Explain the discrepancy between our knowledge of quality employment program indicators and practices in programs across the nation.

2. As predicted in 1983, approximately how many new rehabilitation staff will be required by 1990 due to the growth of employment programs?

3. Identify the groups in need of employment services training.

4. Differentiate between preservice, inservice, and technical assistance models.

5. List and describe the seven competency areas for supported employment/vocational trainers suggested by the authors.

6. Identify some of the problems with the existing curricula for supported employment trainers.

7. Describe the components of the three-step competency-based approach to training.

8. Explain the necessity of including practicum experiences in personnel preparation programs.

9. Why should program evaluation be included as a component of all personnel preparation programs in the area of supported employment/vocational training?

10. What is the basic premise of adult learning principles and why should vocational training programs take these principles into account?

REFERENCES

Alper, S. & Alper, J. (1980). Issues in community-based vocational programming: Institutionalization of staff. In C. Hansen (Ed.), *Expanding opportunities: Vocational education for the handicapped* (pp. 121–143). Seattle: University of Washington, PDAS.

Baker, B. E. & Geiger, W. L. (1988). *Preparing transitional specialists: Competencies from thirteen programs.* Washington, DC: U.S. Department of Education, Office of Special Education Programs, Division of Personnel Preparation.

Barcus, J. M., Wehman, P., Moon, M. S., Brooke, V., Goodall, P., & Everson, J. M. (1988). Design and implementation of a short-term inservice training program for supported employment service providers. *Rehabilitation Education, 2,* 17–33.

Bloom, A. (1987). *The closing of the American mind. How higher education has failed democracy and impoverished the souls of today's students.* New York: Simon & Schuster.

Bruyere, S. M. (1987). *Supported employment training evaluation and training needs assessment.* Ithaca, NY: Cornell University.

Buckley, J., Albin, J. M., & Mank, D. M. (1988). Competency-based staff training for supported employment. In G. T. Bellamy, L. E. Rhodes, D. M. Mank, & J. M. Albin (Eds.), *Supported employment. A community implementation guide* (pp. 229–245). Baltimore: Paul H. Brookes.

Cobb, R. B., Hasazi, S. B., Collins, C. M., & Salembier, G. (1988). Preparing school-based employment specialists. *Teacher Education and Special Education, 11*(2), 64–71.

Danley, K. S. & Mellen, V. (1987). Training and personnel issues for supported employment programs which serve persons who are severely mentally ill. *Psychosocial Rehabilitation Journal, 11*(2), 87–102.

Everson, J. M. (1989). *A survey of personnel in supported employment programs in Rehabilitation Services Administration (RSA) Region III: A description of training needs, educational backgrounds, and previous employment experiences.* Unpublished doctoral dissertation. Richmond: Virginia Commonwealth University.

Everson, J. M., Barcus, M., Moon, M. S., & Morton, M. V. (Eds.). (1987). *Achieving outcomes: A guide to interagency training in transition and supported employment.* Richmond: Project Transition Into Employment (TIE), Virginia Commonwealth University.

Everson, J. & O'Neill, C. (1988). Technical assistance and staff development. In M. Barcus, S. Griffin, D. Mank, L. Rhodes, & S. Moon (Eds.), *Supported employment implementation issues.* Richmond: Rehabilitation Research and Training Center, Virginia Commonwealth University.

Haring, N. (1982). Review and analysis of professional preparation for the severely handicapped. In B. Wilcox & R. York (Eds.), *Quality education for the severely handicapped* (pp. 180–201). Falls Church, VA: Counterpoint Handcrafted Books.

Harold Russell Associates. (1985, January). *Development of staff roles for supported and transitional employment programs.* Technical Proposal PR1330C50080, Cambridge, MA.

Inge, K., Barcus, J. M., & Everson, J. M. (1988). Developing inservice programs for supported employment personnel. In P. Wehman & M. S. Moon (Eds.), *Vocational rehabilitation and supported employment* (pp. 145–161). Baltimore: Paul H. Brookes.

Karan, O. C. & Knight, C. B. (1986). Training demands of the future. In W. E. Kiernan & J. A. Stark (Eds.), *Pathways to employment for adults with developmental disabilities* (pp. 253–269). Baltimore: Paul H. Brookes.

Kiernan, W. E. & Stark, J. A. (Eds.). (1986). *Pathways to employment for adults with developmental disabilities.* Baltimore: Paul H. Brookes.

Kregel, J., Shafer, M. S., Wehman, P., & West, M. (1989). Policy and program development in supported employment: Current strategies to promote statewide systems change. In P. Wehman, J. Kregel, & M. S. Shafer (Eds.), *Emerging trends in the national supported employment initiative: A preliminary analysis of twenty-seven states* (pp. 15–45). Richmond: Rehabilitation Research and Training Center, Virginia Commonwealth University.

Kregel, J. & Sale, P. (1988). Preservice preparation of supported employment professionals. In P. Wehman & M. S. Moon (Eds.), *Vocational rehabilitation and supported employment* (pp. 129–144). Baltimore: Paul H. Brookes.

Knowles, M. (1980). *The modern practice of adult education: From pedagogy to andragogy.* Chicago: Follett Publishing.

McDaniel, R. H., Flippo, K., & Lowery, L. (1986). *Telesis: Supported employment resource manual.* San Francisco: University of San Francisco.

Menz, T. (1983). *Manpower needs in rehabilitation facilities: 1980–1990.* Menomonie: Research and Training Center, University of Wisconsin-Stout.

Mori, A., Rusch, F., & Fair, G. (1982). *Vocational education for the handicapped: Perspectives on special population/severely and moderately handicapped.* (Personnel Development Series: Document 1.) Champaign: Office of Career Development for Special Populations, University of Illinois.

Renzaglia, A. (1986). Preparing personnel to support and guide emerging contemporary service alternatives. In F. R. Rusch (Ed.), *Competitive employment issues and strategies* (pp. 303–316). Baltimore: Paul H. Brookes.

Robinson, R. (1979). *An introduction to helping adults learn and change.* Milwaukee: Omnibook.

Rusch, F. R. (Ed.). (1986). *Competitive employment issues and strategies.* Baltimore: Paul H. Brookes.

Rusch, F. & Mithaug, D. (1980). *Vocational training for mentally retarded adults: A behavior analytic approach.* Champaign, IL: Research Press.

Rusch, F. R., Trach, J., Winking, D., Tines, J., & Johnson, J. (1989). Job coach and implementation issues in industry. In W. E. Kiernan & R. L. Schalock (Eds.), *Economics, industry, and disability: A look ahead* (pp. 179–186). Baltimore: Paul H. Brookes.

Sharpton, W. (1988). *Competencies/activities/evaluation courses for graduate degree program of the University of New Orleans.* New Orleans: University of New Orleans.

Thurman, S. & Hare, B. (1979). Teaching training in special education: Some perspectives since 1980. *Education and Training of the Mentally Retarded, 14,* 292–295.

Wehman, P. (1981). *Competitive employment: New horizons for severely disabled individuals.* Baltimore: Paul H. Brookes.

Wehman, P., Kregel, J., Shafer, M., & West, M. (1989). Supported employment implementation I: Characteristics and outcomes of persons being served. In P. Wehman, J. Kregel, & M. S. Shafer (Eds.), *Emerging trends in the national supported employment initiative: A preliminary analysis of twenty-seven states* (pp. 46–74). Richmond: Rehabilitation Research and Training Center, Virginia Commonwealth University.

Welsh, J. (1989, Spring). Job satisfaction of supported employment specialists. *The Advance, 2* (1), 3.

Weissenstein, G. (1986). Preservice implications for secondary special education: Preparing teachers for the transition effort. *Interchange, 6* (3), 2–6.

Weissman-Frisch, N., Crowell, F., & Inman, D. (1980). Inservicing vocational trainees: A multiple perspective evaluation approach. *Journal of the Association for the Severely Handicapped, 5,* 158–172.

Wilcox, B. & Bellamy, G. T. (1987). *A comprehensive guide to the activities catalog. An alternative curriculum for youth and adults with severe disabilities.* Baltimore: Paul H. Brookes.

CHAPTER

25

A Comparative Analysis of State Transition Planning

Dale T. Snauwaert
Lizanne DeStefano
University of Illinois at Urbana-Champaign

As a part of the Education of the Handicapped Act Amendments of 1983 (PL 98-199) the 98th Congress enacted legislation authorizing grants for the purpose of strengthening and coordinating education, training, and related services to assist youth with handicaps in the transitional process, and to stimulate the improvement and development of programs of secondary special education (Section 626). The mechanism used to achieve this was the funding of research and more prominently the establishment of demonstration projects nationwide (DeStefano & Snauwaert, 1989).

The transition provisions enacted by the 98th Congress provided the foundation for a widespread employment initiative for individuals with handicaps enacted in the 99th Congress. This initiative included expanded provisions for transitional services, coupled with the removal of work disincentives in Social Security law, employer incentives in the form of job targeted tax credits, counseling services and vocational education programs for youths, supported employment, and removal of unfair wage practices under the Fair Labor Standards Act. Taken as a whole, the attainment of competitive employment for individuals with disabilities, including youths exiting public education, became a primary objective of federal disability policy (Destefano & Snauwaert, 1989).

In conjunction with the above Congressional action, the Office of Special Education and Rehabilitative Services (OSERS) developed and propagated a transition model that defined transition as an "outcome oriented process encompassing a broad array of services and experiences that lead to employment (Will, 1984, p. 3)." In effect, transition was conceived as a bridge between school and adult life, the bridge being composed of an array of services and experiences. Through the leadership of OSERS, states and localities were encouraged to begin planning for transition. Of special importance was the encouragement to form interagency links between educational agencies and adult service providers (Berkell & Gaylord-Ross, 1988).

This chapter examines the first phase of state-level implementation of transition policy. Implementation can be conceived as the linkage between policy and performance, a process composed of the decisions and actions of public officials that transform prior intentions into outcomes (Van Meter & Van Horn, 1975). Although there are a number of good analytic frameworks that conceptualize this process (e.g., Edwards, 1980; Mazmanian & Sabatier, 1983; Ripley & Franklin, 1982), Van Meter and Van Horn (1975) developed the model that most clearly captures the linkage between policy and performance.

The Van Meter and Van Horn model is composed of six clusters of variables: (a) standards and objectives; (b) resources; (c) interorganizational communication and enforcement activities; (d) the characteristics of the implementing agencies; (e) economic, social and political conditions; and (f) the disposition of implementors. Each cluster makes a relative contribution to the success or failure of the implementation process. Figure 25.1 illustrates this model.

From the perspective of the above model, state-level planning represents the broad intentions of congressional and executive policy, which are operationalized in terms of standards and objectives, the appropriation of resources (e.g., funding and human resources), and interorganizational communication and enforcement mechanisms. Planning on this level is no longer strategic but tactical. This is a crucial stage in implementation, for it specifies the direction to be taken, the resources needed, and the organizational structure necessary for the delivery of services. As the model indicates, these tactical specifications interact with the characteristics of implementing agencies and economic, social, and political conditions; this interaction determines the degree of performance. Consequently, tactical specifications must be sensitive to these conditions.

Our approach in this chapter is primarily descriptive rather than evaluative. Although some evaluation is possible, for example regarding comprehensiveness, a judgment concerning the quality of any particular state plan can only be made by taking into consideration the specific conditions within a given state, for each plan is context-specific. Consequently, due to the fact that our database does not include local conditions (i.e., characteristics of implementing agencies, economic, social and political conditions, and the disposition of implementors) nor outcomes, we are limited in this chapter primarily to describing what has been planned rather than what has been accomplished.

The central question of this chapter is: "What is the nature and extent of state transition plan

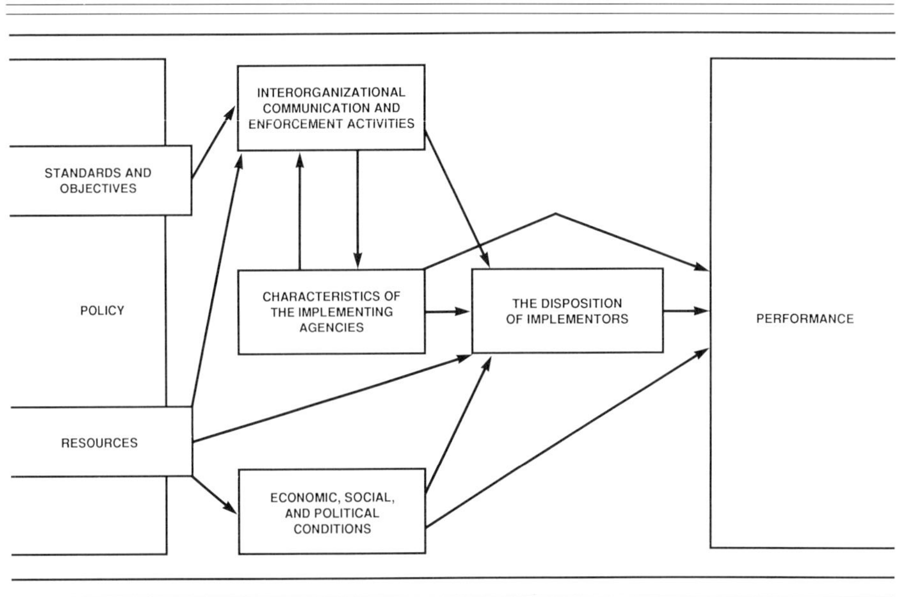

Figure 25.1 A Model of the Policy Implementation Process.

ning in a tactical sense?" Although data were collected regarding a number of variables relevant to this question (described below), in this chapter we present our findings concerning three fundamental variables that provide a portrait of the interorganizational communication and enforcement activities involved in state transition planning. These variables are: (1) identification of issuing, planning, and implementing agencies; (2) types of planning across states; and (3) the creation of new organizational units (agencies) designed to plan and/or coordinate the delivery of transition services.

ISSUING, PLANNING, AND IMPLEMENTING AGENCIES

Issuing agencies were judged to be those that distributed the policy document under their department letterhead or seal. Department officials had endorsed the document. The total number of issuing agencies was fifty-six (some states had multiple issuing agencies). Departments of education seemed to take the lead in transition policy development in most states, accounting for thirty-two of the fifty-six issuing agencies, followed by rehabilitation (ten), blind services (five), labor (four), and mental health (two).

Planning agencies were those that had been included in the development of transition policy statements. There were a total of sixty-six planning agencies identified from the forty-one states with plans. In this case, special education departments were the most prominent planning agency (thirty), followed by state departments of rehabilitation (sixteen). Given the increase in number from issuing agencies (n = 56) to planning agencies (n = 66) it appears that issuing agencies included other agencies in planning. These data indicate that the delivery of transition services is primarily contingent upon linkages within special education and vocational rehabilitation agencies.

One potential source of difficulty for successful implementation is the fact that the number of agencies involved as we move from planning (sixty-six) and issuing (fifty-six) to implementation increases (seventy-five). These data indicate that some agencies will be expected to implement plans which they have had no input in. Research strongly suggests that all implementors should play a role in the formulation of policy (Palumbo, 1987; Lester, Bowman, Goggin, & O'Toole, 1987). Their input in planning will increase the likelihood of successful implementation. Although the discrepancy between the number of planning and implementing agencies may appear small, in some states the separation of formulation and execution may be a barrier to successful implementation. Just as states vary in the agencies involved in planning and issuing state transition policy, the goals and types of policy developed varies from state to state. The next two sections describe goal statements and the various policy types.

GOALS

The specification of goals and objectives are a key part of the formation of public policy; they determine the course of action to be taken and define the standards according to which performance will be evaluated. Thirty-two states represented in this study have specified at least one goal for their transition plan. Ten states have articulated multiple goals. For descriptive purposes these goal statements have been categorized into eleven broad categories derived from the goal statements of the thirty-two states: (1) attainment of employment, (2) attainment of employment and independent living, (3) preparation for employment, (4) preparation for employment and independent living, (5) preparation for independent living, (6) development of a transition model, (7) development of an evaluation system, (8) staff training, (9) development of referral mechanisms from special education to vocational rehabilitation, (10) development and delivery of transition services, and (11) enhanced interagency coordination.

Table 25.1 illustrates the distribution of goal statements in terms of the above categories. Interestingly, the most common goal is the development and delivery of transition services (ten states), followed by the attainment of employ-

Table 25.1 Distribution of Goal Statements in Relation to Employment, Independent Living, Evaluation, Service Delivery Coordination, Staff Training, and Referral

Attainment of Employment	Attainment of Employment and Independent Living	Preparation for Employment and/or Independent Living	Evaluation
California	Hawaii	Arizona	California
District of Columbia	Kentucky	Connecticut	Hawaii
Maryland	Minnesota	Hawaii	Idaho
Maine	Missouri	New Mexico	Wisconsin
New York	North Dakota	Ohio	
Pennsylvania	Rhode Island	Wisconsin	
South Dakota			
Tennessee			
West Virginia			

Development and Service Delivery	Coordination	Staff Training	Referral
Alabama	California	California	Connecticut
California	Delaware	Wisconsin	New Mexico
Delaware	Hawaii	Kentucky	
Massachusetts	Idaho		
Maine	Minnesota		
Oregon	Nebraska		
Tennessee	Texas		
Texas	Wisconsin		
Virginia			
Wisconsin			

ment (nine states), enhanced interagency coordination (eight states), and the attainment of employment and independent living. However, if we combine the employment and employment and independent living categories, then the total number of states with the goal of employment and/or independent living climbs to twenty-two (due to multiple goals Hawaii was counted twice, reducing the total from twenty-three to twenty-two). From this distribution, it is clear that across a significant number of states the primary goal of transition programming is the attainment of employment and independent living. Not surprisingly, this focus is in keeping with federal intention.

Coupled with the above is a significant national focus on the development and delivery of transition services. Ten states have specified the delivery of transition services as a goal, combined with eight states where interagency coordination is a goal (California, Delaware, Texas, and Wisconsin have both as goals). Enhanced interagency coordination is clearly intended to facilitate service delivery. If we include the development of a transition model (two states), staff training (three states), and referral mechanisms (two states), all intended to facilitate the development and/or delivery of transition services, then the total number of states with development and/or delivery of services as a goal climbs to twenty-five.

PLAN TYPES

Seven plan types were identified among forty-one state plans: legislation, interagency agreements, demonstration projects, individual planning guides, position papers, state proclamations, and regulations. A number of states incorporated multiple plan types into their approach. What follows is a descriptive summary of each category; for those interested in more specific detail an appendix consisting of detailed summaries of representative states is provided at the end of this chapter.

States with Legislation

Table 25.2 lists twelve states that have enacted legislation regarding transition. In these twelve states legislation authorizes five general activities: (1) creates new agencies (e.g., California, Massachusetts, Kansas, Maine, Minnesota, and Texas); (2) mandates individual transition planning (e.g., Connecticut, Idaho, Indiana, Massachusetts); (3) establishes state level demonstration projects (e.g., California, Maine, New York); (4) establishes referral mechanisms between local education agencies and adult service providers (e.g., New York, Kansas, Oklahoma, and Texas); and (5) mandates the development of a state transition plan (Illinois).

In addition to legislation and its particular authorizations in a given state, eight of the twelve states have complementary activities. For example, New York, Idaho, and Texas have established demonstration projects and enacted interagency agreements. Minnesota has enacted a comprehensive interagency agreement in addition to state regulations, a state proclamation, and an individual transition planning guide. Connecticut, Massachusetts, and Oklahoma have enacted interagency agreements. In summary, of the twelve states with legislation seven have interagency agreements, five have demonstration projects, one has a planning guide, one has issued a position paper, one has enacted a state proclamation, and three have enacted state regulations.

States having Interagency Agreements without Legislation

Sixteen states that have not enacted legislation have interagency agreements (see Table 25.3). These agreements vary greatly in terms of length and specificity. In their most basic sense interagency agreements identify the agencies to be involved in transition service delivery, their respective roles, and a format for coordination. In general, these agreements exist between state agencies, most predominately between special education, vocational education, and vocational rehabilitation. Six states (New Mexico, Oregon, Alabama, North Carolina, Tennessee, and West Virginia) have cooperative agreements between state and local agencies.

In addition to enacting interagency agreements, six of the sixteen states have established complementary activities. For example, Maryland has produced an individual transition planning guide, a position paper, and a state proclamation. Hawaii has established demonstration projects along with issuing an individ-

Table 25.2 States with Transition Legislation

	Legislation	Interagency Agreements	Demonstration Projects	Planning Guides	Position Papers	State Proclamation	Regulations
New York	yes	yes	yes				yes
Idaho	yes	yes	yes				
Texas	yes	yes	yes				
Minnesota	yes	yes		yes		yes	yes
California	yes		yes				
Maine	yes		yes				
Connecticut	yes	yes					
Massachusetts	yes	yes					
Oklahoma	yes	yes					
Illinois	yes				yes		yes
Kansas	yes						
Louisiana	yes						
TOTAL	12	7	5	1	1	1	3

Table 25.3 States With Interagency Agreements in Transition Without Legislation

	Interagency Agreements	Demonstration Projects	Planning Guides	Position Papers	State Proclamation	Regulations
Maryland	yes		yes	yes	yes	
Washington	yes			yes	yes	
Hawaii	yes	yes	yes			
New Mexico	yes	yes			yes	
Oregon	yes					yes
South Dakota	yes					yes
Alabama	yes					
Arizona	yes					
Arkansas	yes					
Delaware	yes					
Michigan	yes					
North Carolina	yes					
Nebraska	yes					
Tennessee	yes					
West Virginia	yes					
Pennsylvania	yes					
TOTAL	16	2	2	2	3	2

ual transition planning guide. New Mexico has established state-level demonstration projects in addition to enacting a state proclamation. Both Oregon and South Dakota have enacted state regulations in addition to interagency agreements (see Appendix A).

States Having neither Legislation nor Interagency Agreements

Table 25.4 summarizes the remaining fourteen states that have neither legislation nor interagency agreements. Four of these states (Kentucky, Maryland, North Dakota, and Wyoming) have disseminated individual transition planning guides. Wyoming has both a planning guide and state regulations. Vermont and Wisconsin have issued position papers reviewing the transition problem and offering proposals for the delivery of transition services. The District of Columbia has established a demonstration project. Five states have miscellaneous activities; for example, Iowa has developed a transition model, and Ohio has developed a continuum of vocational training options.

States with Regulations, Planning Guides, and Demonstration Projects

Tables 25.5, 25.6, and 25.7 respectively summarize those states with regulations, planning guides, and demonstration projects. Eight states have enacted state regulations regarding transition (Table 25.5). Three of these states also have legislation, five have interagency agreements, and two have planning guides. New York has demonstration projects.

Seven states have developed individual planning guides to aid local agencies in planning transition for the individual student (Table 25.6). Three of the seven states (Minnesota, Maryland, and Hawaii) include planning guides as a part of an array of plan types. For a detailed summary of a planning guide, see Missouri in Appendix A.

Eight states have established state level demonstration projects (see Table 25.7). The existence of demonstration projects is often seen in states with comprehensive arrays of plan types. (See New York in Appendix A for a summary of a demonstration project.) States vary widely in the types and combinations of plan types associated with transition, creating a natural laboratory in which to observe and compare the effects of different types of planning on the growth and effectiveness of transition service delivery at the local level. Because the characteristics of implementing agencies and the economic, social, and political factors in a particular state will heavily influence implementation outcomes, it is likely that no one plan type will emerge as superior, but that

Table 25.4 States Without Legislation or Interagency Agreements in Transition

	Demonstration Projects	Planning Guides	Position Papers	State Proclamation	Regulations	Other
Kentucky		yes				
Maryland		yes				
NorthDakota		yes				
Wyoming		yes			yes	
Missouri		yes				
Virginia					yes	
Vermont			yes			
Wisconsin			yes			
Dist. of Columbia	yes					
Florida						yes
Iowa						yes
Ohio						yes
Rhode Island						yes
South Carolina						yes
TOTAL	1	5	2	0	2	5

different plan types will best suit the needs of different states. Local implementation will also be affected by the extent to which transition is planned for, coordinated, and budgeted at the state level. Several states have created agencies specifically for this purpose.

AGENCY CREATION

Successful transition is contingent on coordinated multi-agency service delivery. Pressman and Wildavsky (1984) found that the complexity of joint action is a major barrier to successful implementation. The creation of governmental units whose purpose is to plan and coordinate interagency service delivery may therefore be an important aspect of the transition initiative.

To this date twelve states have created agencies for planning, coordination, and/or advisement (see Table 25.8). Agencies in five states were created via legislation. Four states have created multiple agencies; California (two), Iowa (three), Massachushetts (two), and Minnesota (2). In all, seventeen new units have been formed.

In the true spirit of the transition initiative, ten states formed units comprised of representatives from multiple agencies. In other words, they are interagency units. For example, the California Interagency Policy Team is a planning body consisting of representatives from special education, vocational education, and vocational rehabilitation. Idaho has developed an Interagency Working Group on Transition comprised of representatives of special education, vocational education, rehabilitation, Department of the Blind, developmental disabilities, and the Department of Health. Kansas has established a State Transition Committee comprised of parents, consumer advocates, educators, community agencies, and representatives from the state Departments of Education, Rehabilitation and Health, and the Developmental Disabilities Council.

In five states singular units have been created. For example, California has created the Transition Programs and Services unit within the Department of Vocational Rehabilitation which is an interagency coordinating body. Minnesota has established the Interagency Office on Transition Services within the Department of Education to facilitate collaboration among state and local education agencies. Illinois has created a Transition Assistance Committee within the Governor's Planning Council on Developmental Disabilities. Massachusetts has established a Bureau of Transition Planning within the Executive Office of Human Services.

Given the multi-agency character of transition and the complexity of joint action, of primary importance is the function of each newly formed

Table 25.5 States with Regulations Concerning Transition.

	Legislation	Interagency Agreements	Demonstration Projects	Planning Guides	Position Papers	State Proclamation	Regulations
Illinois	yes				yes		yes
Oregon		yes					yes
South Dakota		yes					yes
Wyoming				yes			yes
Virginia							yes
Nebraska		yes					yes
New York	yes	yes	yes				yes
Minnesota	yes	yes		yes		yes	yes
TOTAL	3	5	1	2	1	1	8

Table 25.6 States with Planning Guides in Transition

	Legislation	Interagency Agreements	Demonstration Projects	Planning Guides	Position Papers	State Proclamation	Regulations
Minnesota	yes	yes		yes		yes	yes
Maryland		yes		yes	yes	yes	
Hawaii		yes	yes	yes			
Wyoming				yes			yes
Kentucky				yes			
Missouri				yes			
North Dakota				yes			
TOTAL	1	3	1	7	1	2	2

Table 25.7 States With Demonstration Projects in Transition

	Legislation	Interagency Agreements	Demonstration Projects	Planning Guides
New York	yes	yes	yes	
Idaho	yes	yes	yes	
Texas	yes	yes	yes	
California	yes		yes	
Maine	yes		yes	
Hawaii		yes	yes	yes
New Mexico		yes	yes	
District of Columbia			yes	
TOTAL	5	5	8	1

unit. There are three primary functions of these newly created agencies: planning, coordination, and advisement.

PLANNING. Agencies whose primary purpose is planning have been created in three states. Rhode Island has established a Transitional Planning Council on the state level comprised of representatives from the Department of Education, local education agencies, Vocational Rehabilitation, the Department of the Blind, and the Division of Retardation and Mental Health. The council's purpose is to identify the needs of youths, to develop referral procedures which would expedite the delivery of services, and to advise the Commissioner of Education on transition issues (it therefore also has an advisory function). In Iowa two agencies have been

Table 25.8 States Creating Agencies for Planning, Coordination, and/or Advisement

	Agency Created as a Result of Legislation	Single Unit	Multi-Units
California	Yes	Yes	Yes
Iowa	No	No	Yes
Idaho	No	No	Yes
Illinois	No	Yes	No
Kansas	Yes	No	Yes
Massachusetts	Yes	Yes	Yes
Maine	Yes	No	Yes
Minnesota	Yes	Yes	Yes
Nebraska	No	Yes	No
Pennsylvania	No	No	Yes
Rhode Island	No	No	Yes
Texas	Yes	No	Yes

created for planning. The Transition Planning Group is charged with the development of a transition model to be used statewide, and the Transition Oversight Committee is responsible for monitoring the ongoing development of the model. California has created an interagency policy team on both the state and local levels consisting of representatives from special education, vocational education, and vocational rehabilitation. These policy teams are primarily responsible for planning the interagency delivery of transition services. It is important to note here that the distinctions between planning, coordination, and advisement are not exact and contain some overlap. For example, coordination obviously involves planning, and the California interagency policy teams are an example of planning whose outcome is coordination.

COORDINATION. Four states have created units whose primary purpose is coordination. Idaho has created an Interagency Working Group on Transition which coordinates transition activities. The Group is composed of representatives from special education, vocational education, rehabilitation, services for the blind, developmental disabilities, and the Department of Health. Illinois' Transition Assistance Committee is charged with operationalizing and coordinating an ongoing commitment of interagency resources for the improvement of school and post-school transition services. Nebraska has established a State Transition Team to coordinate the implementation of the interagency agreement between special education and the department of rehabilitation. Pennsylvania created an Interagency Planning Committee to coordinate the implementation of an interagency agreement between the Bureau of Special Education and the Bureau of Support Services within the Department of Education and the Department of Labor.

PLANNING AND COORDINATION. Six states have created units whose primary function is both planning and coordination. California created the Transition Programs and Services Unit within the department of vocational rehabilitation. This unit is responsible for initiating a broad-based transition coordination effort to develop a comprehensive transition plan for the state, in collaboration with the community college system and the Departments of Education and Labor. This unit is also responsible for the development of assessment procedures to evaluate the rehabilitation potential of students referred to vocational rehabilitation. In addition, it is responsible for coordinating a grant program for community colleges to help establish technological resources to assist students with severe disabilities in the transition from high school to community colleges and four-year institutions.

Massachusetts established a Bureau of Transitional Planning which was designated as the central coordinator of transition service delivery. It has three primary functions: (1) to monitor the individual transition planning process, (2) to collect and analyze data on service needs, and (3) to develop a prospectus on statewide needs in funding and planning. In addition, it plays an important role in the individual transition planning process (ITP) process, reviewing and analyzing each ITP, assisting in identifying service gaps, describing the needs of underserved or inappropriately served clients, and indicating needed changes in programming structure and/or service delivery.

Minnesota created an Interagency Office on Transition Services within the State Department of Education. This unit is charged with assessing statewide needs, providing information and technical assistance, and planning for state and local agency collaboration. In addition, the State Transition Interagency Committee was created to facilitate working relationships among participating local and state agencies, and to provide leadership in the implementation of an interagency agreement.

Maine created an Interdepartmental Committee on Transition in order to plan and coordinate transition by establishing guidelines, monitoring grants, and evaluating the performance of demonstration projects. This unit was designed to serve as a decision-making body to resolve interagency coordination issues which could not be solved at the local level and as a clearinghouse to monitor the status of all statewide interagency efforts related to transition.

Texas established an Interagency Steering Committee as a unit to coordinate the implementation of the state transition plan. The committee was charged with developing appropriate mechanisms for advisory input from consumer organizations and local steering committees; coordinating three interagency subcommittees, training personnel, budget/planning, and auditing; ensuring the delivery of technical assistance; developing and recommending further legislation to the respective agencies; reviewing information available from each agency's existing data collection system related to transition services and recommending procedures or criteria for improving these systems; and evaluating annually the interagency efforts of the preceding year and plans for the following year.

Iowa created a Transition Team for the Visually Impaired and charged it with encouraging and facilitating timely cooperation and joint planning among rehabilitation personnel, educators, adult service providers, parents and employers, with a major thrust aimed at parental involvement.

ADVISEMENT. Kansas created a State Transition Committee whose primary function is to serve in an advisory capacity to the agency-based transition program. The purpose of the committee is to advise the Commissioner of Rehabilitation Services with respect to the development and maintenance of quality transition planning and vocational programs, and to ensure programs are consistent with the needs of the students and the community. Rhode Island's Transitional Planning Council is also charged with an advisory role, advising the Commissioner of Education on transition issues.

It is possible that states with agencies specifically created to plan, coordinate, and/or advise transition service delivery have gone further to ensure the future of transition in their states than those that have no specific agencies. Statements of this kind can only be substantiated as local implementation data are collected over time.

Evaluation

The public policy process is generally conceived of as consisting of three phases: formation, implementation, and evaluation. Evaluation primarily has two purposes: (1) to judge whether or not the goals of the policy have been achieved, and (2) to provide feedback in order to make adjustments that will improve service delivery. Consequently, the establishment of evaluation systems is vital to the ongoing development and success of transition programming.

As Table 25.9 illustrates, twenty-one states (out of forty-one) have planned to establish some type of an evaluation system. For example, Kansas proposed to establish a computerized data collection system to document characteristics of transitioning students, project the population count of such students, determine how many students are served and not served, identify the difference between services needed and services provided, and evaluate the results of transition planning. Illinois proposed evaluation studies that would investigate specific relationships between student characteristics, program

DAN BURRIS

Dan Burris is a 46-year-old man who was diagnosed as moderately mentally retarded, with a full-scale IQ of 53. He is the eldest of six children and has three sisters and two brothers. His current level of functioning is said to be related to extended institutionalization. Dan received little formal academic training. He entered programming with the a local adult services organization in 1979 and has progressed through work adjustment training, transitional employment, and regular work.

In May 1987, Dan entered a supported employment program as an attendant with the Villa Park Car Wash in Villa Park, Illinois. His duties included cleaning windows, scrubbing tires, and vacuuming cars. He continued to improve his speed and quality of work, as well as his interpersonal skills with customers. His employment continued uninterrupted until July 15, 1988, when he began a new position as butcher's assistant with Dominick's in Elmhurst, Illinois. His duties included sweeping; mopping; washing trays; disassembling, cleaning, and reassembling machines; and cleaning the walls and windows of the meat department.

As a result of Dan's steadily improved functioning, he has moved into a less-restrictive residential setting in a supported living arrangement where he has two roommates. They take turns cooking for themselves, shopping for groceries, and planning menus. Dan does his own laundry and banking. He now gets up in the morning on his own, dresses himself properly for work, and arrives punctually. Dan uses a three-wheel bike for transportation to and from work, which is about two miles from his residence.

He travels alone by train to Wisconsin to visit his family after arrangements are made for him. Dan also travels independently by train to see his girlfriend in Chicago.

His favorite hobby is his three-wheel bike. Dan purchased it with his own money, and when it breaks down, he takes it to the bike shop himself. He has equipped it with an electronic device that generates various sounds such as gunfire, bombs, buzzers, and alarms. On holidays, he appropriately decorates his bike.

Dan is so aware of his own progress that he recently requested the supported employment staff reduce the amount of time they spend with him. He has identified another worker who could benefit from supported employment.

components, and transition related outcomes. Idaho proposed to use a number of organizational rating scales in order to evaluate the frequency and effectiveness of linkages between agencies. Hawaii proposed to establish a computerized case management and tracking system to facilitate information exchange between high school and post-secondary service providers, and provide ongoing feedback to the state regarding implementation. In addition, survey methods (California, District of Columbia, North Dakota, and New York), longitudinal analyses (Maine), pre- and post-questionnaires (New Mexico), planning/evaluation forms (Kentucky), midpoint and final training evaluations (Wyoming), tracking systems (Maryland), monitoring and supervision systems (Minnesota), and interagency coordination evaluations were proposed (Delaware and Texas).

These proposals offer thoughtful planning regarding evaluation. However, the fact that approximately 50 percent of the states do not have provisions for evaluation may prove problematic. In the next section we identify issues to be addressed in future research and offer a set of hypotheses to guide these studies.

CONCLUSION

It is apparent that there is considerable variation among states in the three variables discussed in this chapter: (1) planning, issuing, and implementing agencies; (2) plan types; and (3) agency creation. According to the imple-

Table 25.9 States with Evaluation Plans

Alabama	Maine
California	Michigan
District of Columbia	Missouri
Hawaii	North Dakota
Iowa	New Mexico
Idaho	New York
Illinois	Pennsylvania
Kansas	Texas
Kentucky	Wyoming
Maryland	

mentation model used in this study (Van Meter & Van Horn, 1975) evaluation of effectiveness of each state's policy will necessitate examining it in the context of the characteristics of the various implementing agencies and the economic, social, and political conditions surrounding its implementation. The intensity of this level of analysis may necessitate that only a few states, selected because of their representative or unique policy characteristics or because of certain attributes of the states themselves, would be the focus of such a microanalysis.

In this analysis of state transition policy several issues or areas of variation among states have been identified. These variables may provide a framework for comparing the relative effectiveness of state planning. Five of these variables are discussed below.

MULTI-AGENCY INVOLVEMENT. Transition is a multi-agency phenomenon. Successful transition requires that all agencies involved with an individual work with a common purpose, clearly defined roles, and adequate resources. As you have seen, some states have stressed multi-agency involvement in state-level transition planning and others have not. Failing to include other agencies in developing state-level transition plans, yet relying on their services to make the transition happen at the local level, may be a serious flaw of some states' transition planning. On the other hand, the creation of multi-agency units at the state level, funded by a combination of state agency monies, reflects a high level of multi-agency involvement. We hypothesize that states with extensive multi-agency planning and coordination at the state level will have greater interagency coordination resulting in effective transition service delivery at the local level.

CONSENSUS. At present the various agencies involved in the delivery of transition have different policies regarding who is to be served, what those services should be, and how they should be delivered and paid for. In some cases states have made an effort to gain consensus in their transition planning, in other cases, single agencies issue their own transition policies. It is our hypothesis that state policy resulting from an effort to gain consensus among participating agencies will result in more extensive local implementation than policy where none is evident.

POLICY SPECIFICITY. The length and specificity of state policy varies widely. In some cases state transition policy refers to a single paragraph regarding transition embedded in the public school regulations. In other cases state transition policy may span several volumes detailing specific agency roles, timelines, and strategies for evaluating whether or not the system is working. Specificity enables local providers to know exactly who and what is involved in the delivery of transition services. Some may argue that specificity may stifle creativity at the local level, on the other hand specificity may encourage less creative localities to move forward more quickly than would naturally occur. A balance between state specificity and local creativity must be struck, however. We hypothesize that those states with the most specific state policy will have more extensive local implementation.

RESOURCE ALLOCATION. About one-half of the states fund transition from regular agency budgets, in some cases reallocating money for other programs to fund transition services. The remaining half have stipulated special budgets/ funds for transition, in some cases developing multi-agency funding mechanisms for transition. To be fully recognized as a routine special education or adult service option, transition should have its own funding mechanism. We hypothesize that those states who have allotted funds especially for transition will have greater success in implementation.

LOCAL INFLUENCES. Lastly, it became obvious as we looked at federal policy in transition that it would be necessary to examine state policy in order to get a clearer picture of what was actually happening in transition. About one-half of the states designate localities as the administrative focus of their transition plans. This means that direct service providers, local education agencies, and not-for-profit agencies have tremendous discretion in terms of how they implement transition services. While this discretion allows for pockets of excellence to develop, it also permits areas of substandard service to persist. While local transition teams may be best suited to plan for and coordinate transition services in their area, given their in-depth knowledge of the persons, resources, and employment context of the area, state-level coordination is necessary to ensure the overall quality of transition service delivery across the state.

SUMMARY

The next five years will be critical to the future of transition service delivery. Given the nature of federal transition legislation, the future of the transition initiative is in large part dependent on the status of state-level transition planning. Although a vast majority of the states have developed state-level policy concerning transition, little is known about the manner in which variations in state-level policy are interpreted at the local level. Local interpretation of state policy will determine the degree of institutionalization of transition service delivery. In turn, the extent to which transition is institutionalized at the state and local levels will impact the future of those students making the transition from school to work.

QUESTIONS (For answers see pp. p. 411–420)

1. Identify the three fundamental variables that provide a portrait of the interorganizational communication and enforcement activities involved in state transition planning.

2. What is the potential problem of having more implementation than planning or issuing agencies?

3. Identify the seven general plan types.

4. What is the function of legislation regarding transition in the twelve states that have enacted such legislation?

5. Is it likely that a single state transition plan will emerge as successful? Explain.

6. What are three primary functions of transition agencies?

7. What are the three phases of the public policy process?

8. Describe the authors' major conclusions in regard to their analysis of state transition policy.

REFERENCES

Berkell, D. & Gaylord-Ross, R. (1988). The concept of transition: Historical and current developments. In D. E. Berkell & J. M. Brown (Eds.) *Transition from school to work for persons with disabilities.* New York: Longman.

DeStefano, L. & Snauwaert, D. T. (1989). *A value-critical approach to transition policy analysis.* Champaign: Transition Institute, University of Illinois.

Edwards, G. C. III. (1980). *Implementing public policy.* Washington, DC: Congressional Quarterly Press.

Lester, J. P., Bowman, A. O., Goggin, M. L., & O'Toole, L. J. (1987). Future direction for research in implementation, *Policy Studies Review,* 7, 200–216.

Mazmanian, D. A. & Sabatier, P. A. (1983). *Implementation and public policy.* Glenview, IL: Scott, Foresman.

Palumbo, D. J. (1987). Introduction: Implementation: What have we learned and still need to know. *Policy Studies Review,* 7, 91–102.

Pressman, J. L. & Wildavsky, A. (1984). *Implementation* (third edition). Berkeley: University of California Press.

Ripley, R. B. & Franklin, G. A. (1982). *Bureaucracy and policy implementation.* Homewood, IL: The Dorsey Press.

Van Meter, D. S. & Van Horn, C. E. (1975). The policy implementation process: A conceptual framework. *Administration and Society,* 6(4), 445–488.

Will, M. (1984, June). Bridges from school to working life. *Interchange,* 2–6.

APPENDIX A

STATES WITH LEGISLATION

New York

Chapter 544 of the Laws of 1982, and Chapter 462 of the Laws of 1984 establish a mechanism for students with handicaps to be referred by their local school districts directly to appropriate adult service providers while they are still in school. These laws are primarily targeted at students with severe handicaps.

School districts initiate the process by referring each student to an appropriate adult service agency (e.g., vocational rehabilitation). There are five designated steps to be taken by the local educational agency: (1) identify students needing adult services, (2) send notice to parents, (3) obtain consent to release information, (4) make referral to adult agency(s), and (5) submit reports to the State Department of Education.

In addition to the above legislation, Cooperative Service Model Projects have been established that link special education, vocational education, and vocational rehabilitation within the State Department of Education. The purpose of the model projects is to (1) provide early vocational assessment to disabled students; (2) determine whether cooperative planning by rehabilitation counselors, special educators, and committees on special education will increase the job readiness of youth transitioning from the schools; and (3) determine if early referral to vocational rehabilitation will increase the number of youth with handicaps who can benefit from rehabilitation services.

The model consists of five main components: (1) determination of student eligibility for special education, (2) comprehensive planning for IEP implementation, (3) provision of vocational education assessment for special education students, (4) provision of comprehensive instructional programs, and (5) consistent placement/follow-up services. Ongoing vocational assessment is strongly emphasized. Services are provided by a team consisting of rehabilitation counselors, special educators, and vocational educators. Nine models have been piloted since 1984.

Minnesota

An Interagency Office on Transition Service within the Department of Education was established by legislation in 1985. It is responsible for assessing statewide transition needs, providing information and technical assistance, and planning for state and local agency coordination.

A state proclamation was issued in August, 1987 proclaiming the importance of interagency cooperation for transition. Based on this proclamation, an interagency agreement was developed between the community college system, the Parent Advocacy Coalition, the State Board of Vocational Education, the Department of Human Services, the Department of Education (special education, vocational education), the Department of Labor (rehabilitation services, visually impaired, and the job training office/JTPA), and the Governor's Planning Council on Developmental Disabilities.

Interagency agreements were established on three levels: (1) multidisciplinary interagency teams for individuals, (2) community transition interagency committees, and (3) interagency coordination between state agencies with transition-related responsibilities.

Interagency teams for individuals include members of transition-related agencies and are initiated by the LEA. The team develops transition goals and objectives as part of the IEP, designs and implements a coordinated, multidisciplinary assessment that identifies the abilities, interests, and needs of the individual, uses assessment information to determine the working and living environments in which the individual will function during secondary education and beyond, identifies the specific skills individuals will need to succeed in various environments, identifies the most effective strategies, resources, and least restrictive settings for skill training, develops written ITPs, and monitors the ITP.

Community transition interagency committees are designed to promote interagency coordination between agencies providing transition services at the local level. Community committees are composed of representatives of parent and consumer groups, businesses, community groups, and the agencies essential to transition. The responsibilities of the community committee are: (a) assure that involved agencies and services understand each other's functions and resources; (b) identify the anticipated service needs of individuals within the community to ensure availability of services and resources; (c) develop a local agreement to include mission statements, goals, objectives, and written implementation plans to ensure that transition needs are met; (d) design, fund, and implement new or revised service options; (e) assess the progress of transition services to assist the community and the state for planning purposes on a yearly basis; (f) provide leadership in raising community awareness and expectations of people with disabilities to live and work in local communities.

The primary responsibility of the state agencies is to promote local interagency coordination. State agencies will identify the needs of individuals and families statewide by collecting system data and information on an ongoing basis; develop policies and procedures to foster the development of local interagency planning; ensure that existing resources be used more efficiently and effectively through interagency service planning and coordination; update and disseminate the interagency agreement's implementation plan; propose monitoring, supervision, and evaluation systems for state and local agencies to ensure implementation of local interagency planning activities; recommend that licensure and other minimum professional standards for employing staff in education and human services include transition-related competencies; promote the expectations of people with disabilities to live and work in the community; and provide technical assistance to local committees and agencies.

Maine

The Interdepartmental Committee on Transition was established by statute in April, 1986. The COT was designated as the central planning body for transition programing. The purpose of COT is to establish guidelines, monitor grants, and evaluate the performance of programs developed through the grants.

The act also authorized expenditure of funds for local pilot projects designed to demonstrate the effective delivery of services by coordinating existing programs and establishing a mechanism for ongoing coordination of programs, such as LEAs, adult education, community health centers, regional mental retardation services, regional rehabilitation programs and other public and private agencies as appropriate. The act mandated that each pilot project also establish a method for the identification of unserved and underserved youth and develop services for these youth. It was also stipulated that governance of each local project had to be by a local coordinating committee, made up of representatives of state agencies, representatives of LEAs, parents, and other community members.

Connecticut

Connecticut enacted legislation (P.A. 87–324) in June, 1987 stipulating that commencing with the 1988–89 school year, and every year thereafter, an individual plan for the transition of a child from school to another program or community setting must be developed. Further, the plan must be developed no later than at the annual review of the prescribed educational program following the child's fifteenth birthday, and must be included as part of the prescribed educational program.

In response to this mandate, the Department of Education developed an interagency agreement between its divisions of curriculum and professional development, education support services, vocational, technical, and adult education, and rehabilitation services. The agreement specifies the roles and responsibilities of each agency.

These developments were originally based on a position paper entitled *Pathways to Employment* generated from three greater Hartford area conferences.

STATES WITH INTERAGENCY AGREEMENTS BUT WITH NO LEGISLATION

New Mexico

In January, 1984 the Department of Education finalized "A Plan for Cooperative Employment Preparation for Students with Disabilities." This plan was a collaborative effort between special education, vocational education, and vocational rehabilitation. The implementation of the plan was initiated with the development of five pilot projects with five school districts. The thrust of these efforts was to facilitate transition by strengthening the vocational components of special education curricula and developing appropriate referral mechanisms from secondary schools to vocational rehabilitation.

Evolving from these early transition efforts, vocational rehabilitation has maintained active cooperative agreements with several schools in an effort to expand and improve services to this population. Five of the cooperative agreements incorporate the Department of Labor's JTPA program. The goal for these projects is essentially the same as that of the original five pilot projects cited above; however, through JTPA they have been expanded to include increased work experience and on-the-job training opportunities.

Oregon

In order to facilitate transition, branch managers of vocational rehabilitation units will designate a liaison counselor for every secondary school within the jurisdiction of the office. Designated counselors will regularly contact secondary schools to which they have liaison assignments. The counselor will transfer clients who are in secondary schools, or have within the past six to twelve months left a secondary school to a counselor carrying a specialized school caseload when one is available in the area, providing this will not delay services. Unless physical or mental restoration services are required earlier, the counselor will focus efforts on students in their last year of school.

In addition to these regulations, many branches have local operating agreements with school districts. The purpose of these local agreements is to coordinate provision of vocational services in cooperation with LEAs. Branch managers will initiate the actions needed to develop operational plans in the branch's service delivery areas that are required by policy. The following steps are to be followed: (1) establish liaison roles and assignments; (2) determine the frequency and purpose of contacts; (3) agree to procedures for exchange and confidentiality of information; (4) define how the services of each agency will be delivered consistent with each organization's administrative policy and available resources; (5) describe staff training and orientation goals and responsibilities; (6) note the period of time covered by the local operational plan; (7) reference the local operational plan to the cooperative agreement or manual section that the plan will implement; (8) state how the plan will be reviewed and monitored, and the conditions of termination; and (9) receive the signatures of participants representing each agency group in an organized and efficient manner.

In addition, there has been recent emphasis on formal cooperative relationships with school districts. Local transition teams have been formed in which department of rehabilitation participation is a primary component. The State Department of Education is moving toward implementation of transition teams throughout the state.

Rehabilitation has sponsored training sessions for the school district staff in order to facilitate communication between the rehabilitation counselors and school personnel, as well as to clarify any questions about the rehabilitation process and eligibility criteria.

In April, 1986 the State Superintendent of Public Instruction appointed a special task force on transition. The task force had representatives from vocational education, special education, vocational rehabilitation, school personnel, a post-secondary institution, a community program, and the parents. In assembling the data, the task force became aware of the complexities in providing schooling, training, and agency services. The State Department of Education task force welcomed the passage of House Memorial 85 as a means of furthering articulation between the Department of Education and service providers. House Memorial 85 requests that the Legislative Educational Study Committee form an ad hoc task force to study transition. Vocational rehabilitation has continued to monitor the existing cooperative agreements with LEAs regarding transition with the intention of expanding this effort to other school districts where feasible and incorporating any necessary modification apparent from previous agreements. In addition, vocational rehabilitation is currently developing an agency transition policy.

STATES WITH NO LEGISLATION OR INTERAGENCY AGREEMENTS

Missouri

Missouri has developed a transition model to meet the needs of local education agencies (LEAs). The intent of the model is to develop a comprehensive conceptualization of transition that can be modified to fit the unique needs of each LEA. The model contains five phases: (1) career awareness (grades K to 6); (2) vocational exploration (grades 7 to 9); (3) vocational preparation (grades 9 to 10); (4) skill training and placement (grades 10 to 12); and (5) post-secondary transition (beyond 12th grade). In accordance with the OSERS model, three options of services—transition without special services, time-limited services, and ongoing services—comprise the fifth phase.

Planning for transition is stressed in the model. It is specified that a systematic means of planning the transition process is developed by all the potential participants in the process. This should include: (1) identifying the elements of a transition program currently in place in the LEA; (2) identifying the voids in a transition program needed to put an effective transition program into place for youths with handicaps; (3) coordinating the various agencies and institutions in the state and community that are involved in the transition process; (4) developing a plan to enhance existing transition elements and fill the voids in the transition process; and (5) developing an evaluation system to ensure that the transition process is comprehensive and fits the needs of youths with handicaps.

Ohio

Ohio has developed a continuum of vocational training options in order to facilitate transition. There are four vocation training options: (1) regular vocational education, (2) regular vocational education with an adjusted program, (3) regular vocational education with supplemental aids and/or specialized support personnel, and (4) specialized vocational education. A job training program designed for individuals with severe handicaps has been developed as a part of Option 4. It is the responsibility of the IEP team to select an appropriate option for each student.

Answers

CHAPTER 1

1. 1970 • *p. 5*
2. Late 1970s • *p. 5*
3. First, supported employment held that the issue is not whether or not people with mental retardation can perform real work, but rather what support systems are needed to achieve that goal. Second, it requires that the "place and pray" model be replaced with the "place-train-maintain" model. • *p. 6*
4. The "place and pray" model emphasized teaching job skills but did not provide the training and support systems necessary for successful integration once the person has been placed in competitive employment. The "place-train-maintain" approach emphasizes not only placement of the individual but continued support for that employee. • *pp. 6–7*
5. "Social validation ensures that intervention priorities regarding focus, procedures, and results are not arbitrarily or stipulatively prescribed, but are preferred and consensually agreed upon by community members" (White, 1986, p. 109). • *p. 7*
6. To actually implement the characteristics of supported employment. • *p. 11*
7. Because there is the need to change entire ecological systems. • *p. 11*
8. Integration, higher wages, and support. • *p. 11*
9. Integration. • *p. 11*

CHAPTER 2

1. 1978 • *p. 16*
2. 1984 • *p. 16*
3. (a) At the state level the Virginia Supported Employment Information System evaluates the effectiveness of community based employment programs and disseminates this information to federal funding agencies. It also provides an empirical basis for policy development and program management. •

   (b) At the local level this system allows program administrators to track their progress and compare their outcomes with that of other state programs. • *pp. 17–18*
4. About 200. • *p. 18*
5. Mental retardation. • *p. 19*
6. Mental illness and traumatic brain injury. • *p. 19*
7. Integration and fringe benefits. • *p. 21*
8. 48.5 percent • *p. 23*

CHAPTER 3

1. 1985 • *p. 32*
2. (a) Worker characteristics (demographics) •

   (b) Job coach/Co-worker Involvement—tracks number of hours and type of involvement, respectively. •

   (c) Benefit-Cost Analysis—tracks employees status, financial outcomes of employment, and additional programs or services the individual received. •

   (d) Job Separation—tracks reasons for job separation, average hours of job coach on-site assistance (per-week) prior to separation, etc. • *p. 33*
3. (a) community survey and analysis •

(b) job match •

(c) job placement •

(d) job maintenance •

(e) related services/interagency coordination • *p. 33–34*

4. Clustered placements—47 percent, individual placements—46 percent, and mobile crews—8 percent. • *pp. 34–35*

5. Light industry and janitorial/maintenance. • *p. 35*

6. Economic and social factors, job performance, other jobs, moving, etc. • *p. 38*

7. To study how the number of negative job separations can be reduced and to teach supported employees to gain more control over their jobs and enhance their interactions with co-workers. • *p. 38*

8. Yes. Persons with severe/profound mental retardation were far less likely to have been involved with co-workers than persons with mild or moderate mental retardation. • *p. 41*

CHAPTER 4

1. Yes, there is one source of funding, i.e., a single stream from the state level. • *p. 45*

2. Time-limited services include: work stations in industry, transitional employment programs, intensive on-the-job training for short periods, job clubs, expanded apprenticeships, and other short-term services. Time-enduring services are defined by supported employment options. • *p. 47*

3. Over a two-year period, almost four times as many jobs were developed as were actually utilized. • *p. 48*

4. No, there is a reduction over time. • *pp. 50–51*

5. Transportation, reductions in social security benefits, reduction of day program costs. • *p. 52*

6. Mental retardation and mental illness. • *p. 54*

7. Special education students. • *p. 54*

8. The need for flexible hours . . . • *p. 54*

9. Yes. Persons with mental retardation tend to require more support. In general, persons with severe handicaps tend to require more support than those with mild handicaps. • *p. 56*

10. Persons with physical disabilities. • *p. 56*

11. No. • *pp. 59–60*

12. (a) Conversion of segregated programs to community integrated programs; and (b) the conversion of existing funds to support community integrated activities. • *p. 60*

13. Employers have begun to assume supervision costs for supervisors in supported employment projects. • *pp. 60–61*

14. No. There is an organizational separation of data and research from actual program implementation. • *p. 61*

15. Huge waiting lists put pressure on agencies to serve the largest number of individuals possible. However, this approach does not guarantee that quality services are delivered for persons with severe handicaps. • *p. 61*

CHAPTER 5

1. Community (job) survey, job analysis, assessing clients current skill level, job match, follow-up, coordinating related services. • *pp. 66-68*

2. Wages, twenty hours of work per week, integration, and support. • *p. 76*

3. Integration, there are no accepted, reliable methods of assessing whether employment is truly integrated. • *p. 76*

CHAPTER 6

1. Work that matches interest increases motivation. • *p. 87*

2. (a) Establish a consumer-represented

board. (b) Determine job possibilities. (c) Develop community job match assessment sites. (d) Conduct job analyses. (e) Implement job match assessment process. (f) Construct consumer-directed employment plan. (g) Undertake job try-out. (h) Facilitate self-managed performance evaluation. (i) Redesign job (as needed). (j) Clarify public support financial details. • *pp. 88–93*

CHAPTER 7

1. (a) Services should be targeted for individuals who traditionally have not succeeded in competitive employment. •

   (b) Services should be provided in integrated community settings. •

   (c) Services should include the provision of long-term support from a variety of agencies and sources. • *p. 111*

2. Aptitude matching, work sampling, and behavior inventory approaches. • *p. 112–113*

3. Work samples approach. • *p. 112*

4. Work samples measure motor responses with apparatus rather than using paper and pencil tests. Work samples do not focus as much on intellectual and academic abilities. Work samples are designed to be used independently rather than as part of a larger battery. • *p. 113*

5. Social validation methodology is used to survey employers to determine entry-level skill requirements for different types of jobs available in a particular community. • *p. 113*

6. To select candidates and to plan programs for these individuals. • *p. 115*

7. On the grounds that supported employment has been conceptualized as a "zero-reject" program (Wehman, 1988). • *p. 115*

8. (a) There is insufficient empirical evidence to suggest that performance on standardized, norm-referenced instruments is related to the eventual employment success of an individual with a severe disability. •

   (b) Validation studies have failed to account for the influence of training and support on employment outcomes. •

   (c) Many widely used evaluation instruments were standardized using norm groups which have characteristics that are very different from those of persons seeking supported employment. • *p. 116*

9. No. Even if the IQ scale obtained is valid, one must also consider the effect of training, experience, and support on job success. • *pp. 116–117*

10. To identify vocational and social skills that should be improved in order to increase the number of job matches between the individual and his or her community. • *p. 118*

11. To improve the match or goodness-of-fit between an individual with a severe disability and his or her community. • *p. 119*

12. (a) Physical ecology. •

    (b) Social ecology. •

    (c) Organizational ecology. • *p. 121*

13. Coordinate community services; identify potential employers; assess reasons why employers wish to participate in supported employment; conduct behavioral analyses of local job sites; conduct ecological analyses of local job sites; identify areas for community education and intervention programs; assist in the development and management of training data systems and program evaluation. • *pp. 123–126*

CHAPTER 8

1. The individual, the job, the support agency. • *p. 132*

2. *Direct service*—occurs at or near the job site and directly involves the employee. *Indirect service*—job site activities that do not directly involve the target worker. *External strategies*—activities that usu-

ally take place away from the job site. • *p. 132*

3. By increasing the likelihood that persons perceived to have the most significant support needs will obtain access to integrated employment. • *p. 141*

CHAPTER 9

1. No, acquisition of specific work and social behaviors are necessary, but not sufficient goals. Long-term success in a community job requires an employee to respond to variations in the work setting that are encountered over an indefinite period of time. • *p. 145*
2. Generalization (or adaptability) is demonstrated when an employee adjusts his/her behavior to respond appropriately to novel stimuli encountered in the work environment. Maintenance refers to the continued performance of a specific behavior after acquisition of the response has occurred. • *pp. 145–146*
3. The demonstration of behavior under conditions that differ from the training conditions in which either no training has occurred, or substantially reduced amounts of training are required, for acceptable performance to occur. • *p. 146*
4. It could indicate the person did not successfully acquire the skill, or that she/he has not learned to generalize the response, to slightly different situations or to make minor changes in the behavior to fit slightly different tasks. • *p. 147*
5. When stimuli, which are external to the task, are introduced to limit the range of stimuli that guide the behavior of the individual. • *p. 150–151*
6. Programming Common Stimuli, Sufficient Exemplars, General Care, and Antecedent Cue Regulation. • *pp. 147–152*
7. The independent demonstration of the desired behaviors over time. • *p. 153*
8. Performance or motivation. • *p. 153*
9. Promoting maintenance of acquired behavior by adjusting the contingencies that maintain behavior. • *p. 153*
10. To ensure that naturally occurring reinforcers do not become (or remain) secondary to extraneous sources of reinforcement. • *pp. 153–154*

CHAPTER 10

1. Employees with and without disabilities are incorporated into and share equal membership in the same social network. • *p. 161*
2. Social skills are goal-oriented, socially acceptable, learned behaviors that are situation-specific and vary according to the social context. They also involve both observable and nonobservable cognition and affective elements that assist in eliciting positive responses and avoiding negative responses from others. • *p. 164*
3. Asking for assistance, responding to criticism, following directions, offering help to co-workers, providing information about the job, answering questions, greetings, conversing with others, using social amenities, giving positive comments. • *p. 166*
4. Workers exhibit both task and nontask-related social skills throughout the work day. The frequency of social behaviors varies depending upon the context of the interactions, and supervisors seem to be involved in fewer interactions than co-workers. • *p. 169*
5. Nonhandicapped co-workers seem less likely to interact with workers with disabilities. Workers with disabilities receive more commands and are less involved in teasing and joking interactions. • *p. 170*
6. To maximize the fit or congruence between the person and the environment. • *p. 170*
7. (a) A rationale as to why a given social behavior was desirable; •

   (b) An opportunity to observe examples of the behavior (modelling); •

(c) An opportunity to practice the behavior (usually role-play); and •

(d) Feedback regarding performance. • *p. 171*

8. Individuals are taught a generative process of social behavior rather than specific component behaviors. • *p. 173*

9. If service providers choose goals for workers and institute training programs for those goals, it is possible that training programs will be unsuccessful because the workers do not have a vested interest in the goals of training. • *p. 173*

CHAPTER 11

1. (a) Extending individual competence. •

   (b) Developing natural support in the workplace. •

   (c) Promoting social acceptance. • *p. 181*

2. The supported employee is seen as an active participant in his or her adjustment on the job. • *p. 181*

3. The job coach is seen as one who elicits existing support services for the employee in the working environment rather than imposing an external structure on the working environment. • *p. 182*

4. (a) Decision making. •

   (b) Performing independently. •

   (c) Self-evaluation. •

   (d) Adjusting future performance as a result of self-evaluation. • *p. 183*

5. Identify the natural support in the environment and match the support to the employees' identified needs. • *p. 184*

6. (a) Validating instructional strategies. •

   (b) Collecting subjective evaluations. •

   (c) Implementing training procedures. •

   (d) Collecting social comparison information. •

   (e) Maintaining work performance after skill acquisition. • *p. 186*

7. False. • *p. 187*

8. The process of identifying the supported employee's support needs and the support available in the worksite. • *p. 188*

9. Integration. • *p. 190*

10. (a) *Employment integration* refers to the participation of employees with and without disabilities as equal members within a workplace. •

    (b) *Integrated workplace* is formed when individual differences are accepted and individual competence is maximized by providing opportunities and support. • *p. 190*

11. (a) By utilizing social validation methodology. • *p. 190*

    (b) By managing social acceptance across time. • *p. 190*

12. A methodology that assesses the acceptability of an individual's performance by significant others. • *p. 190*

13. The employee's performance is evaluated by obtaining the opinions of significant others with whom the employee has contact. • *p. 190*

14. (a) Forms should be filled out by an employee who has responsibility for staff evaluations. •

    (b) Work performance evaluations should be conducted routinely. •

    (c) The work supervisor (*not* the employment specialist) should provide verbal feedback to the supported employee once the work performance evaluation has been completed. • *pp. 191–192*

CHAPTER 12

1. Changes in disability models, service delivery philosophies, service delivery strategies, and service delivery environments. • *p. 199*

2. Disability is currently seen from a sociopolitical perspective which views disability as a function of the interaction between the individual and his or her environment. • *p. 200*

3. Normalization, civil rights, and consumerism. • *p. 200*
4. It has been shown to be ineffective. • *p. 200*
5. Ecologically oriented approaches that take into consideration the environmental dimensions of behavior and intervention. • *pp. 200–201*
6. Special education has become "an outcome oriented process emcompassing a broad array of services and experiences" intended to lead to employment upon leaving school and to successful community living. • *p. 202*
7. Few states require evidence of special preparations to teach *secondary* special education. • *p. 202*
8: (a) Providing on-the-job training. •

   (b) Analyzing job tasks. •

   (c) Providing supervision. •

   (d) Managing behavior. •

   (e) Advocating for integrated relations. •

   (f) Fading assistance. •

   (g) Negotiating work-related issues. • *p. 202*
9. The characteristics include: (a) assessment and service delivery in natural environments, (b) sharing information across traditional disciplinary boundaries, and (c) indirect service delivery. • *p. 204*
10. (a) Individual attributes, (b) environmental attributes, (c) nature, quality, and sequence of interactions, and (d) perceptions of involved individuals. • *p. 204*
11. First, identify alternative goal possibilities and clarify the characteristics of each for all parties involved. Second, examine the discrepancies between the target employees' current skills and resources and those required by particular desired jobs in specific environments. • *p. 205*

CHAPTER 13

1. The coordination of programs, resources, and clientele in ways that: (1) minimize duplication and fragmentation; and (2) maximize cross component cooperation, efficiency and effectiveness. • *p. 215*
2. (a) A shift to integrated employment with ongoing support services.

   (b) Interfacing of agencies to accommodate the transition of people to move productive, independent, and community integrated environments.

   (c) An increased need for on-site evaluation and training to meet workplace demands.

   (d) An increased need for program reportability and accountability that focus on individual cost and outcome data. • *p. 215*
3. Changes in support services have included: (a) training employment staff in marketing principles; (b) developing job coach competencies; and (c) focusing on the program's capacity to provide long-term job-related support. • *p. 216*
4. (a) The individual with a severe disability. •

   (b) The employer. •

   (c) The family. •

   (d) The human service provider. • *p. 216*
5. (a) Creating job opportunities. •

   (b) Training and job placement. •

   (c) Maintaining job placement. • *p. 216*
6. Task group and matrix management approach (see Table 13.4) • *p. 218*
7. One evaluates a person's behavioral capabilities in light of the (work) environment's demands. Once identified, significant mismatches between the individual's capabilities and requirements of the (work) environment are then addressed through behavioral training techniques, prosthetic usage, and/or environmental modification. • *p. 219*
8. Recipient empowerment, cost containment, and outcome analysis. • *p. 223*

9. Measures documenting changes in levels of independence, productivity, and integration. The ultimate goal of supported employment is to improve the quality of life for workers with severe disabilities; as such, wages may not be the only measure of interest. • *p. 226*

CHAPTER 14

1. A good evaluation system is one that is well integrated into the program's daily operation and well suited to its information needs. • *p. 229*

2. (a) Compliance monitoring: assess the extent to which a program adheres to a set of standards. • *p. 230*

   (b) Process evaluation: requires the identification of critical components associated with supported employment and the development of criteria to detect their presence and absence in a specific supported employment program. • *p. 231*

   (c) Outcome evaluation: requires specification of objective, measurable, and relevant outcomes associated with supported employment. It may be desirable to set criterion levels for each outcome. • *p. 235*

   (d) Efficiency evaluation: describes the extent to which a program achieves its successes at reasonable cost. • *p. 240*

3. This instrument is designed to measure the extent to which program activities are carried out in a supported employment program. • *p. 231*

4. Individual, agency or employer, and community variables. • *p. 235*

5. Economic benefits derived from the job (e.g. job tenure, wages, hours worked, benefits) and integration derived from employment (including interaction oppportunities). • *pp. 235-236*

6. The Integration Index can be used for two purposes: (a) to evaluate the current status of employment integration for a specific employee, and (b) to assist direct service providers to assess opportunities for integration for prospective worksites. • *p. 236*

7. The Worker Performance Evaluation Form evaluates employer satisfaction. • *p. 240*

8. It allows continuous data entry and updating of evaluation information, thereby enhancing a project's capability to conduct ongoing formative evaluation as an aid to program management and decision making. • *p. 244*

9. Definitions, methods and timelines for data collection must be common to all participants. • *p. 245*

CHAPTER 15

1. The synergy of key actors (supported employees, parents/guardians/care givers, employment specialists, employers, the Social Security Administration, and social service agency personnel) operating in a beneficial environment to create a system that encourages rather than discourages integration into the workforce. • *p. 251*

2. An incentive is a stimulus that is perceived as being capable of satisfying a motive or drive. • *p. 251*

3. A disincentive is a stimulus that allows a person to act to avoid what is perceived as an otherwise punishing consequence. • *p. 252*

4. A preference curve is a graph representing the points at which a person is equally satisfied with the possible combinations of circumstances presented on the X and Y axes of the graph. • *p. 254*

5. Participation requires the individual to prove "diminished work capacity" which may encourage reduction of commitment to employment. • *p. 256*

6. Incentives: (a) increased wages and (b) opportunities for integration. Disincentives: (a) possible loss of benefits and seasonal work or (b) jobs with no opportunity for advancement. • *p. 257*

7. They are (a) more severely disabled, (b) less motivated to participate in VR, (c) more time consuming for VR counselors, (d) more expensive to serve, and (e) less likely to succeed than other persons referred for VR services. • *p. 258*

8. 1619(a) allows a worker to combine income from SSI and wages. SSI is reduced at a rate of $1 for each $2 earned up to a breakeven point (e.g. $793 in 1988). 1619(b) concerns the retention of Medicaid benefits. • *p. 261*

9. They are concerned that (a) the target employee may not succeed, and (b) cash and medical benefits will be forfeited in a failed attempt to work. • *p. 264*

10. Each person with a disability should have a single service plan that considers medical, vocational, and social well-being. There should be a single eligibility determination process based on functional capacity. • *p. 266*

CHAPTER 16

1. Such analyses can determine whether supported employment is worthwhile, whether it should be expanded or contracted, and whether it can be more effective and less costly. • *p. 272*

2. Because there is a dearth of information about the effectiveness of many of the current programs and there has been a failure to adequately compare outcomes and costs. • *p. 273*

3. (a) Specify tangible and intangible benefits from perspectives of employee, employer, government, and society.

   (b) Specify costs associated with provision of services from the four perspectives.

   (c) Identify factors other than employment services that affect outcomes.

   (d) Specify personal characteristics and functional limitation categories to carry out class-specific comparisons of costs and benefits.

   (e) Specify variations in service provision. • *p. 273*

4. To identify the effectiveness of programs in reducing the negative consequences of disabling conditions. • *p. 273*

5. It calculates the level of benefits per dollar of costs. • *p. 274*

6. Savings in costs that would be incurred if clients were placed in alternative (i.e., nonsupported employment) programs. • *p. 278*

7. Supported employment programs may be shown to have substantial economic benefits when compared to alternative programs which tend to result in lower earnings for consumers and higher costs of services. • *p. 279*

8. When *marginal benefits* associated with the expansion are greater than the marginal costs of the expansion, regardless of the overall relationship of benefits to costs. • *p. 280*

9. Fixed costs, such as rent, electricity, and insurance will probably remain constant. • *p. 282*

10. Earnings should rise as employees gain experience and seniority on their jobs or become more productive in their work. Also, staff should become more adept in placement as they gain experience and have access to an increased number and variety of jobs. Costs should fall because of the decreased level of support for employees required as they become accustomed to their jobs, fewer start-up costs, and the increase in efficiency of supported employment programs that will come with experience. • *p. 284*

CHAPTER 17

1. To shift services from a variety of segregated day programs to integrated employment by redirecting resources already available in the system. • *p. 289*

2. (a) Access is expanding but severely limited. •

   (b) Persons with mild and moderate retardation have greatest access. •

   (c) Facility programs are involved in implementing supported employment. •

   (d) Access to vocational resources is expanding. •

   (e) Costs are variable. •

   (f) Federal funds have provided incentives, but state resources are providing the greater share of funding. •

   (g) Implementation strategies include some variety. • *pp. 290–291*

3. Because program costs are variable, a fixed rate may discourage flexibility and innovation. • *p. 291*

4. In 1985, via incentive money to states in the form of Title III demonstration grants. The monies were contingent upon assurances of interagency coordination and proposals to change basic day service systems. • *p. 291*

5. (a) Many early requests focused on building consensus and providing basic information. •

   (b) Early requests included a focus on demonstrating features of state change. •

   (c) Recent requests include a focus on expansion to other disabilities. •

   (d) Recent requests seek to refine and expand features of systems change following successful demonstrations. •

   (e) Overall, the changes suggest a fundamental shift from efforts to begin an initiative to broad systems change. • *p. 292–293*

6. (a) Improve quality in implementation, (b) increase access and (c) provide stability for integrated employment over time. • *p. 293*

7. (a) Expand conversion of existing long-term resources. •

   (b) Seek new resources. •

   (c) Encourage employer leadership and full participation. •

   (d) Continue transition projects. • *pp. 296–297*

CHAPTER 18

1. To provide integrated employment opportunities for individuals who have never been employed. • *p. 302*

2. Social incompetence. • *p. 302*

3. Psychiatric and mild mental retardation. • *p. 303*

4. Forty-four percent occur within the first three months. • *p. 303*

5. Job responsibility, task-production competence, social-vocational competence, economy, health, change in job status. • *pp. 304–305*

6. Lack of job responsibility. • *p. 305*

7. People indicated they no longer wanted to work. • *pp. 305–306*

8. The majority of job separations were due to the economic situation of the employer. • *p. 307*

9. The majority of job separations were due to production-related reasons. • *p. 307*

10. (a) Individual level: parents may not place a great deal of value on employment, thus affecting the perceptions and attitudes their son or daughter may have towards the world of work. •

    (b) Small group level: low pay, part-time hours, and the absence of benefits. •

    (c) Organizational level: ignoring the impact of community employment on existing friendships and social networks; lack of input into where the individual will ultimately be employed. •

(d) Community/societal level: disincentives of entitlement programs, e.g., SSDI and Medicaid. • *p. 309*

11. (a) Supported employment programs must identify potential support systems available in community settings and develop strategies to enable active participation in those networks by employees with disabilities. •

    (b) Agency personnel must develop strategies to enable consumers to more actively participate in the job selection process. •

    (c) More attention should be paid to evaluation of wages, work characteristics, and the culture of the workplace prior to placement in order to ensure better job match and job satisfaction. • *p. 310*

12. (a) Length of time that the company has been in operation. •

    (b) Employment record. •

    (c) Identification of company personnel currently performing targeted tasks. •

    (d) Seasonal nature of work. • *p. 311*

13. (a) Failure to promote consumer independence; lack of on-the-job descriptions by employment specialists indicates a lack of priority at the organization/agency level. •

    (b) Inadequate job analysis results in a less-than-optimal job match. •

    (c) Lack of rehabilitation engineering at the job site. •

    (d) Lowered expectations by employment specialists and/or co-workers. • *p. 311*

CHAPTER 19

1. To provide long-term evaluation, job skill training, and work adjustment for the purpose of preparing individuals for competitive employment. • *pp. 317–319*

2. Three percent. • *p. 318*

3. Present state of facility is assessed, future state is defined, and strategies for reaching the future state are identified. • *p. 318*

4. (a) Families operate as a system, so significant events do not affect one member in isolation but rather have an impact on the entire family unit. •

   (b) Input provided by family members can be an important source of information for program development and improvement. •

   (c) Linkage between satisfied parents who have chosen the supported employment program and those who are skeptical can be a persuasive technique for increasing the numbers of families in favor of supported employment. • *pp. 323–324*

5. (a) Employers may be afraid disabled workers will not be able to perform the job. •

   (b) Employers may be afraid co-workers will react negatively. •

   (c) Employers may be afraid that supervision will be a problem. The employment specialists should provide factual information about workers with disabilities and the benefits of supported employment to the employer and co-workers. • *p. 325*

6. Purchases services from a supported employment provider and is a direct service provider. • *pp. 325–326*

7. The complexity of the jobs identified, the severity of clients' disabilities, skills of the employment specialist, and the quality of job matches. • *p. 327*

8. Yes, to provide ongoing support services. • *p. 328*

9. (a) Fee for service arrangements. •

   (b) Expansion of facility service purchases. •

   (c) Reduction in facility operation costs.

   (d) New discretionary funding options. •

   (e) Private sector labor diversification. •

   (f) Participant funding. • *p. 329*

10. (a) Availability of information for other facilities interested in conversion. •

    (b) Development of strategies for improving conversion implementation procedures. •

(c) Establishment of a process for monitoring program service quality. •

(d) Statistics for policy and funding decisions. •

(e) Evaluative feedback for the facility, participating agencies, employment specialists, parents, and employees. • *pp. 330–331*

11. Coordinating service delivery, maintaining the facility, and transportation. • *pp. 326-338*

CHAPTER 20

1. The service industry. • *p. 338*
2. Businesses are contracting out more services which will spur the development of work crews and enclaves. • *p. 340*
3. There will be an increased demand for personnel in sit-down restaurants and as aides for the homebound elderly. • *p. 340*
4. No. State-by-state examination is required due to regional and geographic differences in economic trends. • *p. 341*
5. They are usually entry level, dead-end jobs with little or no opportunity for upward mobility or promotion. • *p. 345*
6. Getting a first job. • *p. 345*
7. This help must originate in the school system before the transition from school to adult life is attempted. • *p. 345*

CHAPTER 22

1. Specific potential employment opportunities are systematically selected and provided through direct work experiences provided to individual students. Student progress and employment needs are systematically evaluated in order to determine and secure the most appropriate job placement prior to the completion of their education. • *p. 366*
2. To ensure successful employment outcomes by minimizing the discrepancies between programmatic intent and actual practices. • *p. 366*
3. Work and job placements, curriculum planning, training, scheduling, and instructional planning. • *pp. 372–379*
4. Tasks that have generic relevance to jobs representing one job type. • *p. 374*
5. In general, the time a student spends in vocational training should increase as they grow older. For example, five to ten hours per week during late elementary years and up to one-half day or more in the last year or two of high school. • *p. 376*
6. (a) A description of antecedent conditions (natural cues and prompts).

   (b) A task analysis.

   (c) Consequences to be delivered (both reinforcement and error correction).

   (d) A method for withdrawing assistance and supervision once skills have been acquired.

   (e) A method for evaluating performance across time and conditions. • *p. 378*

CHAPTER 23

1. Skills commonly associated with the human services profession such as client assessment, skill training, case management, and client program development as well as skills commonly associated with the business professions such as economic development, marketing, and financial accountability. • *p. 381*
2. A conscious and deliberate decision-making process engaged in by a formal team of individuals. • *p. 382*
3. Planned change is guided by a team who agree to serve as change agents in their local community. The change is limited in scope, agreed upon by the team, and formalized in a mission statement. The change includes a role for all active consumers and potential consumers. It

is directed toward evaluating the quality of life of its recipients and is evaluated accordingly. • *p. 382*

4. (a) A community program planning team rationally plans and develops vocational transition and supported employment programs.
(b) A service delivery team plans and provides program services to the target service recipients. • *p. 382*

5. Interagency service delivery eliminates service gaps, avoids service duplication, and makes more efficient use of scarce resources. Transdisciplinary service delivery teams reduce professional territoriality and increase holistic planning and service delivery. • *p. 382*

6. (a) Initiating a team.
(b) Defining community need.
(c) Identifying team members.
(d) Holding an initial planning meeting.
(e) Defining the community program planning team's mission.
(f) Assessing the change opportunity.
(g) Setting objectives and activities.
(h) Monitoring and evaluating the change effort. • *pp. 383–388*

CHAPTER 24

1. The discrepancy is due, in part, to the lack of adequately prepared personnel providing secondary special education and adult services. • *p. 395*

2. Between 100,000 and 300,000 new personnel. • *p. 396*

3. Funding agencies and policy makers, direct service staff, individuals with disabilities and their families. • *pp. 396–397*

4. (a) Preservice models are university-based baccalaureate or graduate programs that provide long-term and frequently disjointed training in a recognized discipline or specialization area. The goal of preservice training for future vocational training and supported employment personnel should be to provide a strong theoretical base combined with the inclimentary practical skills necessary for competent vocational training.
(b) Inservice training may be university-based, state or local agency-based, or in some cases, private program-based. Inservice training programs are traditionally geared toward professionals currently employed in specific professions or service programs. The goal of inservice training programs should also be to provide a theoretical base combined with the specific practical skills necessary for competent vocational training. In addition, inservice programs are challenged with changing attitudes of personnel currently providing services from segregated to integrated, from subsidized to independent, and from facility-based to community-based. •
(c) Technical assistance is the provision of problem-solving and consultation to personnel who have specific, assessed, and immediate needs. Technical assistance may be provided by university faculty, state and local agency personnel, and other vocational training and supported employment providers. Technical assistance is limited both in duration and content and typically requires trainers to travel to the trainees' sites. An assumption is that technical assistants have the theoretical knowledge and practical skills necessary to guide recipients in addressing problems and concerns specific to their programs. The goal of technical assistance should be to provide participants with specific practical skills and problem solving abilities needed for competent vocational training and employment services. • *pp. 398–399*

5. (a) Philosophy/historical considerations/legal policy issues.
(b) Interagency issues/systems change.
(c) Program management/administration.
(d) Individualized plan development/management.

(e) Assessment of potential workers with disabilities.
(f) Job development/job analysis/job placement.
(g) Job site training/support/advocacy/job site modification. • *pp. 400–401*

6. Curricula do not meet the needs of client populations with diverse employment and support needs, communities with diverse labor market needs, or supported employment programs with diverse programmatic needs. • *p. 399*

7. (a) Trainers must be able to identify desired program or service outcomes for the individuals they serve.
(b) Personnel trainers must be able to identify personnel roles and related responsibilities of those being trained to achieve these service program outcomes.
(c) Personnel trainers should use these competencies to develop an assessment instrument to evaluate target personnel's baseline knowledge and technical skills. • *p. 401*

8. Given the potential demands placed on personnel in vocational training and employment programs, preservice personnel training programs should require multiple practicum experiences with public school and adult service programs, direct service and program management experiences, and with individuals with a variety of disability labels. • *p. 402*

9. The ultimate goal of personnel training is to increase the quality of vocational services provided to persons with severe and other developmental disabilities. Therefore, program evaluation should include an analysis of the effect of personnel training on student or client work performance. Student and client performance data should be evaluated to determine if program trainees have, in fact, acquired the competencies necessary for successful vocational training. • *p. 403*

10. The basic premise is that adults learn differently than children and that they participate in personnel training programs for specific and unique reasons. Adult trainees should therefore be allowed to participate in training programs and activities. • *p. 405*

CHAPTER 25

1. These variables are: (1) identification of issuing, planning, and implementing agencies; (2) types of planning across states; (3) the creation of new organizational units designed to plan and/or coordinate the delivery of transition services. • *p. 411*

2. Implementation agencies will be expected to implement plans into which they had no input. • *p. 411*

3. Legislation, interagency agreements, demonstration projects, individual planning guides, position papers, state proclamations, and regulations. • *pp. 413–414*

4. It creates new agencies, mandates individual transition planning, establishes state-level demonstration projects, establishes referral mechanisms between local education agencies and adult service providers, and mandates the development of a state transition plan. • *p. 413*

5. No, the characteristics of implementing agencies and the economic, social, and political factors within given states varies widely. • *p. 415*

6. Planning, coordination, and advisement. • *pp. 416–417*

7. Formation, implementation, and evaluation. • *pp. 418–420*

8. (a) States with extensive multi-agency planning and coordination at the state level will have greater interagency coordination resulting in effective transition service delivery at the local level.
(b) State policy resulting from an effort to

gain consensus among participating agencies will result in more extensive local implementation than policy where none is evident.
(c) States with the most specific state policy will have more extensive local implementation.
(d) States that have allocated funds especially for transition will have greater success in implementation.
(e) The extent to which transition is institutionalized at the state and local levels will impact the future of those students making the transition from school to work. • *pp. 420–421*

Index

About the Editor

Frank R. Rusch

Dr. Frank R. Rusch is a Professor of Special Education at the University of Illinois at Urbana-Champaign. His primary areas of research include self-management strategies to persons with moderate and severe handicaps, co-worker-related interactions among persons with and without disabilities, development of high school curricula that promote the transition of youth into the work force, and design and development of supported employment models for persons with severe disabilities. He is the author of over 100 chapters and articles and five books. These books include *Vocational Training for Mentally Retarded Adults: A Behavior Analytic Approach* (with Dennis E. Mithaug), *Competitive Employment Issues and Strategies, Introduction to Behavior Analysis in Special Education* (with Charles R. Greenwood and Terry Rose), *Why Special Education Graduates Fail/How to Teach Them to Succeed* (with Dennis E. Mithaug, James E. Martin, and Martin Agran), and *When Will Persons in Supported Employment Need Less Support?* (with Dennis E. Mithaug, James E. Martin, James V. Husch, and Martin Agran). The text titled *Introduction to Behavior Analysis in Special Education* is the only text of its kind that contains illustrations of behavior analysis in integrated settings only.

Professor Rusch has also given over 100 workshops and presentations throughout the United States and abroad. He has worked with the Indian National Institute for the Mentally Handicapped in the development of supported employment alternatives. He has also conducted several television series on social integration and employment. His presentations include over thirty keynote addresses.

Professor Rusch was a classroom teacher for third and fourth grade students with behavior disorders after completing his Bachelor and Master's degrees at the University of Oregon. In 1975 he was responsible for the development of an employment training program, the first of its kind in the United States that focused on competitive employment for persons with moderate and severe mental retardation at the Child Development and Mental Retardation Center at the University of Washington. After completing his doctoral studies at the University of Washington in 1977, he became an Assistant Professor with the Department of Special Education at the University of Illinois. Currently he is the Principal Investigator and Director of the Secondary/Transition Intervention-Effectiveness Institute, a federally funded institute focusing on transition-related problems among students and young adults with disabilities. He is also the Principal Investigator and Director of the Illinois Supported Employment Project, which is tri-funded by the Illinois Department of Mental Health and Developmental Disabilities, Department of Rehabilitation Services, and the Governor's Planning Council.

Professor Rusch has served on several editorial boards since 1975. He is currently an Associate Editor for *Research in Developmental Disabilities*. He has been a guest Associate Editor for the *Journal of Applied Behavior Analysis* and is currently on the editorial boards of *The Journal of the Association for Persons With Severe Handicaps*, *Applied Research in Mental Retardation*, and *Journal of Applied Behavior Analysis*. He has also served on the editorial boards of *Education and Training in Mental Retardation*, *American Journal of Community Psychology*, *American Journal on Mental Retardation*, *Analysis and Intervention in Developmental Disabilities*, *The Journal of Applied Rehabilitation Counseling*, *Education and Training of the Mentally Retarded*, *Behavior Therapies in Experimental Psychology*, *Behavior Research of Developmental Disabilities*, *Exceptional Education Quarterly*, *Education and Training of Children*, *Journal of Industrial Teacher Education*, and *Mental Retardation*.

Born and raised in Oregon, Professor Rusch has resided in Illinois since 1977 with Janis Chadsey-Rusch and his two daughters, Alexia and Emily. Dr. Janis Chadsey-Rusch is a Professor in the Department of Special Education at the University of Illinois.